The NATURE of LEADERSHIP

To Kingman Brewster—17th President of
Yale University—for his moral leadership in times of crises

The NATURE of LEADERSHIP

EDITORS

JOHN ANTONAKIS
UNIVERSITY OF LAUSANNE

ANNA T. CIANCIOLO
YALE UNIVERSITY

ROBERT J. STERNBERG
YALE UNIVERSITY

SAGE Publications
International Educational and Professional Publisher
Thousand Oaks ▪ London ▪ New Delhi

For information:

Sage Publications, Inc.
2455 Teller Road
Thousand Oaks, California 91320
E-mail: order@sagepub.com

Sage Publications Ltd.
1 Oliver's Yard
55 City Road
London EC1Y 1SP
United Kingdom

Sage Publications India Pvt. Ltd.
B-42, Panchsheel Enclave
Post Box 4109
New Delhi 110 017 India

Printed in the United States of America

Library of Congress Cataloging-in-Publication Data

The nature of leadership/edited by John Antonakis, Anna T. Cianciolo, Robert J. Sternberg.
    p. cm.
Includes bibliographical references and index.
ISBN 0-7619-2714-X (Cloth) — ISBN 0-7619-2715-8 (Paper)
    1. Leadership. I. Antonakis, John. II. Cianciolo, Anna T.
III. Sternberg, Robert J.
HD57.7.N377 2004
658.4′092—dc22   2003017250

This book is printed on acid-free paper.

04   05   06   07   08   10   9   8   7   6   5   4   3   2   1

Acquisitions Editor:	Al Bruckner
Editorial Assistant:	MaryAnn Vail
Production Editor:	Diane S. Foster
Copy Editors:	A. J. Sobczak, Kate Peterson
Typesetter:	C&M Digitals (P) Ltd.
Indexer:	Molly Hall
Cover Designer:	Janet Foulger

Contents

Preface

Why "The Nature of Leadership?"

This 14-chapter edited book is the first to provide a sufficiently broad, yet concise and integrated, cutting-edge review of leadership that will appeal to academicians and practitioners. This book was conceived as a result of closely following the development of leadership as a domain of knowledge, in which we found the following:

1. There have been many great scientific advances in understanding the nature of leadership; however, the leadership literature is voluminous, seemingly disparate, and inaccessible to many.

2. There is a great interest in the phenomenon of leadership by both academicians and practitioners; however, we find the scientific backing questionable for many claims regarding "new" or "undiscovered" characteristics, traits, competencies, or behaviors of effective leaders.

In relation to the above two points, our objective was, therefore, to present high-impact and comprehensively researched perspectives of leadership to separate the wheat from the chaff and science from myth.

To accomplish this objective, we reviewed the literature to determine the most important areas of leadership research that should be incorporated in a complete yet concise handbook. In addition to providing an introductory chapter in Part I and a concluding chapter in Part VI, we focused on four major themes corresponding to the four central sections of the book. The book is thus divided into the following parts:

1. Part I: Introduction (Chapter 1)

2. Part II: The Complexity, Science, and Assessment of Leadership (Chapters 2–4)

3. Part III: The Major Schools of Leadership (Chapters 5–8)

4. Part IV: Leadership Success and Its Development (Chapters 9–10)

5. Part V: Emerging Issues in Leadership—Culture, Gender, and Ethics (Chapters 11–13)

6. Part VI: Conclusions (Chapter 14)

Then, we worked with 26 subject-matter experts—ranging from the eminent to the up-and-coming—in each area of leadership to provide readers with a state-of-the-art review of these themes. In this way, we produced a book whose chapters, when seen together, are complementary and cohesive. As a concise volume, *The Nature of Leadership* is unique—unmatched in breadth and depth—and fills an important gap in the leadership literature.

Ideally, this book will serve the following audiences:

1. *Scholars,* for whom the book will be a useful reference of current leadership theory

2. *Instructors,* who will find the book suitable for a one-semester leadership course

3. *Students,* who can retrieve information quickly from an accessible and complete source

4. *Consultants and HR specialists,* who can update their knowledge on the validity of various leadership approaches (and how these approaches might be implicated in selection and leader development)

5. *Managers,* who will be able to critically evaluate popular-press or consultants' claims about leadership, and thus become discerning consumers of leader-ship products

We hope that our volume will create interest in leadership, which is arguably one of the most important functions of society. As John Gardner (1965), leadership scholar and politician, stated:

Leaders have a significant role in creating the state of mind that is the society. They can serve as symbols of the moral unity of the society. They can express the values that hold the society together. Most important, they can conceive and articulate goals that lift people out of their petty preoccupations, carry them above the conflicts that tear a society apart, and unite them in the pursuit of objectives worthy of their best efforts. (p. 12)

Gardner's ideas are still valid, and possibly even more applicable, today. As Warren Bennis eloquently elaborates in the book's conclusion, in our time, we witness scandals, bankruptcies, war, misery, and suffering, mostly because of corrupt and immoral leadership. Between here and Bennis's concluding chapter, readers will learn to bring to light the many facets of "the nature of leadership."

—JA, ATC, and RJS

Acknowledgments

First, we extend our gratitude to our chapter authors for their superb work and cooperation. Next, we thank Al Bruckner, our acquisitions editor at Sage, for his patience and guidance. We also thank the production staff and the copy editors at Sage Publications for their professional assistance. John Antonakis acknowledges the diligent help of Camilla Watz Johannessen and the advice and support of Cathy Ramus and Suzanne de Treville. He is most indebted to Artemis, Athena, and Saskia for their encouragement and understanding throughout this project. Finally, we gratefully acknowledge the countless leaders who generously have given their time to leadership research. Without them, this book could not have been written.

—JA, ATC, and RJS

PART I

Introduction

CHAPTER 1

Leadership

Past, Present, and Future

John Antonakis

Anna T. Cianciolo

Robert J. Sternberg

> *"The study of leadership rivals in age the emergence of civilization, which shaped its leaders as much as it was shaped by them. From its infancy, the study of history has been the study of leaders—what they did and why they did it."*
>
> (Bass, 1990, p. 3)

Leadership is a complex and diverse field of knowledge, and trying to make sense of leadership research can become an intimidating endeavor. After about a century of scientific study, the theoretical foundations of leadership research on which we currently stand are firmly supported. How did we get to this point? What are the major theoretical paradigms of leadership? Where is leadership research heading?

To answer these questions and to better understand the focus of our book and the chapters that constitute it, it is essential that readers have some knowledge of the history of leadership research, the various theoretical streams of which it is composed, and emerging issues that are currently pushing the boundaries of the domain forward.

Complicating our task, however, is the fact that 100 years of leadership research has led to several paradigm shifts and a voluminous body of knowledge. Furthermore, on several occasions, scholars of leadership became quite frustrated by the large amount of false starts, incremental theoretical advances, and contradictory findings. As stated more than four decades ago by Bennis (1959), "Of all the hazy and confounding areas in social psychology, leadership theory undoubtedly contends for top nomination. And, ironically, probably more has been written and less is known about leadership than about any other topic in the behavioral sciences" (pp. 259-301).

For those who are not aware of the crises leadership researchers faced, imagine the following task: Take bits and pieces of several sets of jigsaw puzzles, mix them, and then ask a friend to put the pieces together into one cohesive picture. Analogously, leadership researchers have struggled for most of the last century to put together an integrated, theoretically cohesive view of the nature of leadership, invariably leading to disappointment in those who studied it. At times, there was much dissatisfaction and pessimism (e.g., Greene, 1977; McCall & Lombardo, 1978; Schriesheim & Kerr, 1977) and even calls for a moratorium on leadership research (e.g., Miner, 1975).

Today, though, a clearer picture is beginning to emerge. Leadership scholars are more optimistic than ever before, and research efforts have been revitalized in areas previously shut down for apparent lack of consistency in findings. Nowadays, our accumulated knowledge allows us to explain, with some degree of confidence, the nature of leadership, its antecedents, and its consequences. This accumulated knowledge is reflected in the present volume, which will provide readers with a thorough overview of leadership and its complexities, the methods employed to study it, and how it is assessed (see Part II). We include four major theoretical perspectives for studying leadership: traits, information-processing, situational-contingency, and transformational (see Part III). We also focus on the factors affecting the success and development of leadership (see Part IV). Furthermore, we present emerging issues relating to leadership, including national culture, gender, and ethics (Part V).

To provide readers with the background necessary to understand the chapters that follow—and their summaries appearing at the end of this chapter—we first acquaint readers with the concept of leadership and why leadership is necessary. Then, we briefly trace the history of leadership research and examine its major schools, most of which are reviewed in this book. Our historical overview is also necessary as an organizing framework because chapter authors frequently refer to elements of the history of leadership research. Next, we discuss emerging issues in leadership research and how findings are being consolidated. Finally, we provide an overview of the book and a summary of each chapter.

The Concept of Leadership

Leadership is one of social science's most examined phenomena. The scrutiny afforded to leadership is not surprising—leadership is a universal activity evident in humankind and in animal species (Bass, 1990). Indeed, reference to leadership is evident throughout classical Western and Eastern writings (Bass, 1990), with a common belief that leadership is vital for effective organizational and societal functioning.

Leadership is easy to identify in situ; however, it is difficult to define precisely. Given the complex nature of leadership, a specific and widely accepted definition of leadership does not exist and might never be found. Fiedler (1971a), for example, noted: "There are almost as many definitions of leadership as there are leadership theories—and there are almost as many theories of leadership as there are psychologists working in the field" (p. 1). Even in this absence of universal agreement, a broad definition of leadership is necessary before introducing leadership as a domain of scholarly inquiry.

Most leadership scholars probably would agree, in principle, that leadership can be defined as the nature of the influencing process—and its resultant outcomes—that occurs between a leader and followers and how this influencing process is explained by the leader's dispositional characteristics and behaviors, follower perceptions and attributions of the leader, and the context in which the influencing process occurs. For us, a necessary condition for effective and authentic leadership is the creation of empowered followers in pursuit of a moral purpose, leading to moral outcomes that are guided by moral means.

A definition of leadership also requires that we differentiate it conceptually from power and management, because these concepts are often confused with leadership. *Power* refers to the means leaders have to potentially influence others; for example, referent power (i.e., followers' identification with the leader), expertise, the ability to reward or punish performance, and so forth (Bass, 1990; see also Etzioni, 1964; French & Raven, 1968). Thus, the ability to lead others requires that one has power.

As regards its differentiation from management, *leadership*—as seen from the "new" perspective (i.e., transformational and charismatic leadership theories; see Bryman, 1992)—is purpose driven, resulting in change based on values, ideals, vision, symbols, and emotional exchanges. *Management* is objectives driven, resulting in stability based on rationality, bureaucratic means, and the fulfillment of contractual obligations. Although some view leaders and managers as different sorts of individuals (see Zaleznik, 1989), others argue that successful leadership requires successful management, that leadership and management are complementary, that leadership goes beyond management, and that leadership is necessary for outcomes that exceed expectations (see Bass, 1985, 1998).

Leadership is necessary for a variety of reasons. On a supervisory level, leadership is required to complement organizational systems (Katz & Kahn, 1978) and to enhance subordinate motivation, effectiveness, and satisfaction (Bass, 1990). At the strategic level, leadership is necessary to ensure the coordinated functioning of the organization as it interacts with a dynamic external environment (Katz & Kahn, 1978). Thus, leadership is required to direct and guide organizational and human resources toward the strategic objectives of the organization and ensure that organizational functions are aligned with the external environment (see Zaccaro, 2001).

The Study of Leadership

In this section, we first discuss how the study of leadership evolved. Our description is cursory, because many of the details relating to the various theoretical perspectives of leadership are discussed in the chapters that follow. Our intention here, therefore, is to provide readers with an understanding of how leadership theory evolved into the major paradigms presented in this book. We then discuss emerging issues, which are included throughout the book, relating leadership to context and ethics, among other concepts. Finally, we discuss how leadership findings are being integrated into cohesive frameworks (i.e., hybrid approaches).

A Brief History of Leadership Research

We have divided leadership research into eight major schools (see Figure 1.1) and classified the schools on two dimensions: temporal (i.e., the time period in which the school emerged) and productivity (i.e., the indicative degree to which the school attracted research interest in a *specific* period of time). The derivation of the schools and the research productivity of the schools are based on our professional judgment; however, we have also been guided by a recent review in *Leadership Quarterly* of the literature that appeared in the last decade (Lowe & Gardner, 2000). We also have relied on historical reviews by Bass (1990), House and Aditya (1997), and Van Seters and Field (1990), to which readers should refer for more complete accounts of the history and development of leadership research.

Trait School of Leadership

The scientific study of leadership began at the turn of the 20th century with the "great man" perspective, which saw history as being shaped by exceptional individuals (Bass, 1990). The "great man" school of thought suggested that certain dispositional characteristics (i.e., stable characteristics or traits) differentiated leaders from nonleaders. Thus, leadership researchers focused on identifying individual differences (i.e., traits) associated with leadership. In two influential reviews (see Mann, 1959; Stogdill, 1948), certain traits (e.g., intelligence, dominance) associated with leadership *were* identified. (A common belief that we wish to help dispel is that traits are not consistently associated with leadership emergence/effectiveness.) However, trait research, for most intents and purposes, was shut down following the rather pessimistic interpretations of these findings by many leadership scholars.

This was the first major crisis that leadership research faced. It took almost 30 years for this line of research to reemerge, following Lord, De Vader, and Alliger's (1986) reanalysis of Mann's data, which found intelligence to be strongly correlated with leadership. Studies by Kenny and Zaccaro (1983) and Zaccaro, Foti, and Kenny (1991) also were instrumental in kick-starting research that linked stable leader characteristics to leader emergence. McClelland (1975, 1976), in the meantime, led another independent line of inquiry linking leaders' implicit

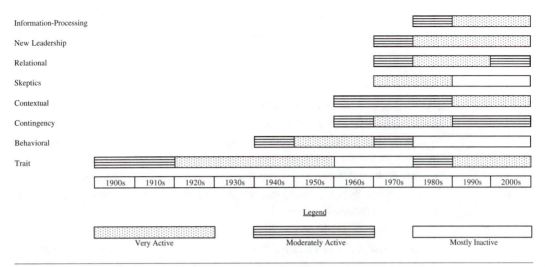

Figure 1.1   A Brief History of Major Schools of Leadership

motives (i.e., subconscious drives or desires) to leader effectiveness (see also House, Spangler, & Woycke, 1991). Currently, the trait perspective appears to be enjoying a resurgence of interest (see Lowe & Gardner, 2000).

Behavioral School of Leadership

Given pessimistic reviews of the trait literature, the trait movement gave way to the behavioral styles of leadership in the 1950s. Similar to Lewin and Lippitt's (1938) exposition of democratic versus autocratic leaders, this line of research focused on the behaviors that leaders enacted and how they treated followers. The well-known University of Michigan (see Katz, Maccoby, Gurin, & Floor, 1951) and Ohio State (Stogdill & Coons, 1957) studies identified two dimensions of leadership generally referred to as consideration (i.e., employee-oriented leadership) and initiating structure (i.e., production-oriented leadership). Others extended this research (e.g., see Blake & Mouton, 1964). Leadership research was again in crisis, however, because of contradictory findings relating to the behavioral approaches. It then became apparent that success of the style of leader behavior enacted was contingent on the situation. As a result, leadership theory in the 1960s began to focus on leadership contingencies. Interest in behavioral theories per se is currently very low (Lowe & Gardner, 2000); however, many of the ideas of the behavioral movement have been incorporated into other perspectives of leadership (e.g., contingency theories, transformational leadership theories).

Contingency School of Leadership

The contingency theory movement of leadership is credited to Fiedler (1967, 1971a), who stated that leader-member relations, the task structure, and the position power of the leader would determine the effectiveness of the type of leadership exercised. Another well-known contingency approach was that of House (1971), who focused on the leader's role in clarifying the paths that would lead to followers' goals. Kerr and Jermier (1978) extended this line of research into the "substitutes-for-leadership" theory by focusing on the conditions under which leadership is unnecessary as a result of follower capabilities, clear organizational systems and procedures, and other factors. Other lines of research that presented theories of leader decision-making style and various contingencies include the work of Vroom and associates (e.g., Vroom & Jago, 1988; Vroom & Yetton, 1973). Work on contingency theories continues (see Fiedler, 1993; House, 1996), although interest appears to have tapered off somewhat (Lowe & Gardner, 2000; Schriesheim & Neider, 1996), possibly because parts of this literature have led to contextual approaches (discussed below).

Relational School of Leadership

A little after the contingency movement became popular, another line of research, labeled the relational theory perspective of leadership, generated substantial research. This movement was based on what was termed vertical dyad linkage theory (Dansereau, Graen, & Haga, 1975) and has evolved into what is now termed leader-member exchange (LMX) theory (Graen & Uhl-Bien, 1995; Uhl-Bien, Graen, & Scandura, 2000). LMX theory describes the nature of the relations between leaders and their followers. High-quality relations between a leader and his or her followers are based on trust and mutual respect (i.e., the in-group) whereas low-quality relations between a leader and his or her followers (i.e., the out-group) are based on the satisfaction of contractual obligations. LMX theory predicts that high-quality relations generate more positive leader outcomes than do lower-quality relations. This line of research has been productive, and interest in this area appears to be moderate (Lowe & Gardner, 2000).

Skeptics of Leadership School

Leadership research faced other series of crises in the 1970s and 1980s. The validity of questionnaire ratings of leadership were severely challenged by those arguing that ratings may be tainted by the implicit leadership theories of those providing the ratings (e.g., Eden & Leviatan, 1975; Rush, Thomas, & Lord, 1977). This position would suggest that what leaders do is largely irrelevant and that leader ratings may reflect simply the implicit leadership theories that individuals carry "in their heads" (Eden & Leviatan, 1975, p. 740).

In a related field of research, it was argued that leader evaluations merely reflected attributions that followers make in their quest to understand and assign causes to organizational outcomes (Calder, 1977; Meindl & Ehrlich, 1987). These researchers suggested that what leaders do might not matter and that leader outcomes (i.e., the performance of the leader's group) affect how leaders are rated (see Lord, Binning, Rush, & Thomas, 1978). Finally, another line of research questioned whether leadership existed or was needed, and whether it actually made any difference to organizational performance (Meindl & Ehrlich, 1987; Pfeffer, 1977).

Many of the above arguments have been tempered or countered by scholars of leadership who could be classed as "realists" (e.g., Antonakis & Cacciatore, 2003; Bass, 1990; Day & Lord, 1988; House, Spangler, et al., 1991; Shamir, 1995; J. E. Smith, Carson, & Alexander, 1984; Waldman & Yammarino, 1999; R. Weber, Camerer, Rottenstreich, & Knez, 2001; Weiss & Adler, 1981). Interest in the "skeptics" perspective, at least as judged by the work of Meindl and associates, appears to be waning (see Lowe & Gardner, 2000). Although there are still unanswered questions posed by the skeptics of leadership, the study of leadership has benefited from this school by (a) using more rigorous methodologies, (b) differentiating top-level leadership from supervisory leadership, and (c) focusing on followers and how they perceive reality. The study of followership and the resultant information-processing perspective of leadership have generated many theoretical advances from which leadership research has benefited immensely.

Information-Processing School of Leadership

The major impetus for the information-processing perspective is based on the work of Lord, Foti, and De Vader (1984). The focus of the work has been primarily on understanding why a leader is legitimized by virtue of the fact that his or her characteristics match the prototypical expectation that followers have of the leader.

The information-processing perspective also has been extended to better understand how cognition is related to the enactment of various behaviors (e.g., see Wofford, Goodwin, & Whittington, 1998). Also notable are the links that have been made to other areas of leadership—for example, prototypes and their relation to various contextual factors (see D. J. Brown & Lord, 2001; Lord & Emrich, 2000; Lord, Brown, Harvey, & Hall, 2001). Information-processing perspectives of leadership have recently generated much interest (Lowe & Gardner, 2000) and should continue to provide us with novel understandings of leadership.

The New Leadership (Neocharismatic/ Transformational/Visionary) School

At a time when leadership research was beginning to appear dull and ready to face another crisis, the work of Bass (1985) and his associates (Avolio, Waldman, & Yammarino, 1991; Bass, 1998; Bass & Avolio, 1994; Hater & Bass, 1988) and others, promoting visionary or charismatic leadership theories (e.g., Bennis & Nanus, 1985; Conger & Kanungo, 1988; Sashkin, 1988a), reignited interest in leadership research in general (Bryman, 1992; J. G. Hunt, 1999) and in related schools of leadership (e.g., trait school).

Bass (1985) built on the work of House (1977), Burns (1978), and others to argue that previous paradigms of leadership were transactionally oriented: that is, focused on the mutual satisfaction of transactional obligations. He believed that a different form of leadership was required to account for follower outcomes centered on a sense of purpose and an idealized mission. He referred to this type of leadership as transformational leadership, in which idealized (i.e., charismatic), visionary, and inspiring leader behaviors induced followers to transcend their interests for that of the greater good. Interest in this school of leadership has been intense. Indeed, over the last decade more than one third of articles published in the *Leadership Quarterly* emanated from the new school of leadership (Lowe & Gardner, 2000).

Emerging Issues

We currently have a good understanding of leadership, but there are still many areas that require further research. We will briefly discuss some of these areas, which include context, ethics, and alternative dispositional predictors (i.e., traits) of leadership. We also discuss how future leadership research could be consolidated.

Related to the contingency movement is the contextual school of leadership (see Shamir & Howell, 1999; Zaccaro & Klimoski, 2001). From this perspective, contextual factors are seen to give rise to or inhibit certain leadership behaviors or their dispositional antecedents. These contextual factors can include leader hierarchical level, national culture, leader-follower gender, organizational characteristics, among others (Antonakis, Avolio, & Sivasubramaniam, 2003). This perspective, first looking at the role of national culture, goes back several decades (e.g., Hofstede, 1980; Meade, 1967). We believe that it is crucial to understand the contextual factors in which leadership is embedded before we can obtain a more general understanding of leadership.

Ethics is another important emerging topic in leadership research. Ethics, however, has not been the mainstay of leadership researchers. Indeed, Bass (1985)— one of the most prominent figures in the field of leadership research—did not make the distinction between authentic (i.e., ethical) transformational and inauthentic (i.e., unethical) transformational leaders until more than a decade after he published his theory (see Bass, 1998; Bass & Steidlmeier, 1999). Nowadays, the ethics of leadership and leaders' degree of moral development are increasingly becoming essential elements of leadership research. Future leadership models should consider the ethics of leader means and outcomes (e.g., Bass & Steidlmeier, 1999; J. M. Howell, 1988) and ways in which leader moral orientation can be improved.

Another emerging issue relates to leader traits. Although much progress has been made in linking leader traits to leader outcomes, that progress has been slowed by the way in which dispositions have been conceived (Hedlund et al., 2003) and by the conditions under which traits are considered important (see Fiedler, 1993). For example, cognitive ability typically is seen as a unitary construct, mostly relating to academic ability, that may not account for an individual's creativity or ability to solve practical problems (Sternberg, 1988, 1997). Interest in understanding practical problem-solving abilities of leaders is growing (e.g., Marshall-Mies et al., 2000; Mumford, Zaccaro, Harding, Jacobs, & Fleishman, 2000), as is interest in linking tacit knowledge (i.e., implicit knowledge derived from experience that requires practical problem-solving ability) (see Sternberg, 1988, 1997) to leader effectiveness (Hedlund et al., 2003). We anticipate that future research efforts will uncover alternative conceptualizations of intelligence that can be linked to leadership emergence or effectiveness and its development (e.g., see

Cianciolo, Antonakis, & Sternberg, in press) and also determine configurations of traits (e.g., intelligence, dominance, self-efficacy; see J. A. Smith & Foti, 1998) that predict leadership emergence/effectiveness.

Finally, given how much is currently known about the nature of leadership, we believe that researchers are now in a position to integrate overlapping and complementary conceptualizations of leadership. Van Seters and Field (1990) argued that the new era of leadership research will be one of converging evidence and integration. It appears that our accumulated knowledge is such that we can begin to construct hybrid theories of leadership (i.e., integrating diverse perspectives such as cognitive and situational) (see Bass, 1990) or even hybrid-integrative perspectives. An example of an integrative perspective is the work of House and Shamir (1993), who integrated various "new" leadership theories. Zaccaro's (2001) hybrid framework of executive leadership links cognitive, behavioral, strategic, and visionary leadership theory perspectives. Zaccaro's work also is a good example of a hybrid-integrative perspective, given that he also integrated overlapping perspectives of leadership. Finally, another example of a hybrid-integrative framework is that of Bass (1985), who integrated transformational and transactional-type theories, as well as discussing possible individual-difference correlates and contextual factors affecting leader emergence.

There are many other ways in which hybrid approaches could be developed. One example is LMX theory, which we introduced in the section on the relational school of leadership. LMX theory has been criticized for not specifying behavioral antecedents of high- or low-quality relations (see House & Aditya, 1997). LMX theory potentially could be integrated with the transformational-transactional leadership theory, because the style of leadership employed is related to the type of leader-follower relations and exchanges (see Deluga, 1990; Gerstner & Day, 1997; J. M. Howell & Hall-Merenda, 1999).

It is only through efforts to consolidate findings that leadership research will go to the next level—where we may finally be able to construct and test a general theory of leadership. Previous research has laid the foundations for such a theory. Now, leadership researchers need to begin to conceptualize ways in which many of the diverse findings can be united, examples of which are evident in the chapters of this book.

Organization and Summary of the Book

We have introduced readers to the major paradigms and current issues relating to leadership. In the remainder of this chapter, we provide a summary of the chapters constituting *The Nature of Leadership*.

Part II: The Complexity, Science, and Assessment of Leadership

Chapter 2. Hunt demonstrates that leadership is immersed in a complex, dynamic, and interactive web, which he refers to as a "historical-contextual superstructure."

He asserts that conceptions of leadership are integrally linked to various factors, including among others the nature of reality and ontological issues, stakeholder perspectives, and levels-of-analysis issues. Thus, how leadership is defined and studied will depend on one's conception of leadership. Hunt provides various examples of conceptions of leadership (e.g., leadership as cognition, leadership and culture, leadership development), which provide insightful perspectives and an organizational framework to be related to the remaining chapters of the book.

Chapter 3. Antonakis, Schriesheim, Donovan, Gopalakrishna-Pillai, Pellegrini, and Rossomme, show that knowledge of leadership must be derived from the results of scientific research. The chapter covers important methodological points that are often overlooked, an oversight that could threaten the validity of research findings. Examples of the application of methods are interspersed throughout the chapter and demonstrate typical problems faced by leadership scholars (e.g., ensuring equivalence when conducting cross-cultural comparisons, testing for moderators). Various issues relating to methodology are discussed ranging from the basic (e.g., types of research, study design) to the advanced (e.g., structural-equation modeling, levels of analysis), with a special emphasis on contextual perspectives.

Chapter 4. Kroeck, Lowe, and K. W. Brown argue that to understand and develop leadership we must be able to assess the constructs constituting the theoretical framework and must link the constructs to outcomes that are useful. As realists, they argue that leadership is required and does make a difference to organizational effectiveness. Linking to other leadership paradigms presented in the book, they discuss what is assessed in terms of independent dimensions (e.g., leader traits, behaviors), the methods employed to make these assessments, and units that are surveyed to provide leader ratings. To give readers an idea of the range of instruments that are available to study leadership, Kroeck and his coauthors have compiled a detailed, selective summary list of some of the often-used leadership measures.

Part III: The Major Schools of Leadership

Chapter 5. In this chapter, Zaccaro, Kemp, and Bader provide a review of trait theory. They point out the mistakes and misunderstandings of the past and show why trait theories can provide a very useful understanding of leadership. A variety of trait perspectives are covered (including alternative dispositional predictors), and the authors differentiate them into distal or proximal predictors of leader processes. This chapter also serves as an example of integrating and hybridizing leadership research. For example, Zaccaro and colleagues argue that configurations of traits should be linked to leader processes (e.g., behaviors) and the contexts in which they emerge, and by this means be used to predict leadership.

Chapter 6. D. J. Brown, Scott, and Lewis review an area of leadership research that is quite young but that has had a substantial impact on the leadership field. The information-processing perspective of leadership, rooted in social and cognitive psychology, takes a person-perception approach in attempting to answer how leaders and followers construct their reality and make decisions based on this reality. Perceptions of leaders by followers and of followers by leaders are the focus of this approach, as are the factors that affect how those perceptions are generated. The authors also show how perceptions and implicit theories are rooted in the context in which leadership is observed. Finally, they discuss how information-processing perspectives can be extended by making links to theories based on self-concept so that follower perceptions of leaders can be explained and linked to follower actions and behaviors.

Chapter 7. Ayman reviews situational and contingency theories of leadership, demonstrating that relations between leader characteristics (e.g., traits, behaviors) and leader outcomes depend on the situation in which the influencing processes occur. She shows that the success of leadership is a function of contingencies, which moderate the relations of leader characteristics to leader outcomes. Ayman also clarifies a common misunderstanding—one in which contingency theorists (i.e., those following the Fiedler tradition) supposedly believe that a leader's style is fixed. She argues that leaders are capable of environmental monitoring and of adjusting their style to fit a particular context.

Chapter 8. Sashkin reviews the literature on transformational, charismatic, and visionary theories of leadership—the line of research that currently dominates the leadership field—and focuses on top-level leadership. Sashkin synthesizes various "new" theories of leadership into a set of conceptually overlapping behaviors and also links the emergence and effectiveness of leadership to dispositional antecedents (e.g., cognitive capacity). This chapter therefore is another example of a hybrid-integrative theory. Finally, Sashkin incorporates context into his model and focuses on the roles of leaders as creators and shapers of organizational contexts.

Part IV: Leadership Success and Its Development

Chapter 9. McCauley presents perspectives used for judging whether leadership is successful or unsuccessful and the conditions that are likely to lead to successful or unsuccessful leadership. She shows that leader success can be operationalized in terms of a leader's current effectiveness—judged by various constituents and using a variety of criteria—by a leader's advancement in the organization and by a leader's ability to transform followers and organizations. McCauley links her discussions to many themes covered in this book, including the assessment of leadership, theories of leadership, and leadership development. Finally, organization-level issues relating to leader assessment, selection, and development are linked to successful and unsuccessful leadership.

Chapter 10. London and Maurer extend the previous chapter by focusing on the development of leadership. They use a dynamic model linking organizational and individual factors to the leader (i.e., individual leader competencies) and to leadership (i.e., organizational-level competencies) development. They cover important elements linked to leader and leadership development, including theories of leadership, learning, and training interventions. London and Maurer use their model to show how needs, processes, and outcomes can be assessed so that interventions are conducted in an appropriate and valid manner. Key to their argument is that congruency must exist between individual and organizational-level developmental goals. They consolidate relevant scientific research and provide guidelines for practitioners, consultants, and researchers.

Part V: Emerging Issues in Leadership—Culture, Gender, and Ethics

Chapter 11. Taking a contextual approach, Den Hartog and Dickson review research regarding the relationship between leadership and the national culture. They draw on literature from cultural anthropology and cross-cultural psychology to show that national culture equips individuals with common ways of perceiving and acting, which systemically affect what followers expect from leaders and how leaders enact their behaviors. They show that certain leader traits and behaviors may be context specific and that others may be universal but differentially enacted according to context.

Chapter 12. Eagly and Carli focus on another contextual perspective: gender-based expectations of leaders and how they constrain the type of leadership that is enacted. They discuss the validity of arguments related to male-female differences from various perspectives, including societal, evolutionary, and prejudicial. Eagly and Carli review literature demonstrating that women may not have the same opportunities to lead and that women are more constrained than are men in the behaviors they can display. Even though female leaders are disadvantaged by stereotypes and restricted role expectations, they are as effective as male leaders, and women actually display certain prototypically effective leader styles more often than do men.

Chapter 13. Ciulla's chapter is focused on another emerging issue: ethics and leader effectiveness. Her chapter is thought provoking, at least for traditional leadership scholars, because she writes from the unique perspective of a philosopher. Ciulla underlines the limitations of traditional leadership theorists' attempts to weave ethics into their theories by simply exhorting that ethical leadership is important. Although inroads have been made by some leadership scholars, Ciulla shows how philosophy can be used to highlight ethical dilemmas of leadership, how to judge the ethics of leader outcomes, and the implications for leader-follower relations. She sees leader ethics and leader outcomes as inextricably intertwined and correctly makes the argument that leaders cannot be considered to be effective unless they are ethical.

Part VI: Conclusions

Chapter 14. The final chapter was written by an omnipresent figure in leadership: Warren Bennis. Using an engaging writing style, Bennis's essay takes the reader into an odyssey of leadership. He provides practical examples, subtly integrating and applying many of the book's themes, and brings to light the nature of authentic leadership. He touches on numerous issues and how they relate to leader emergence and effectiveness, focusing on leader traits and alternative conceptions of intelligence (e.g., "adaptive capacity" or creativity), experiential learning, coalition building, contexts and contingencies, national culture, among other topics. He relates these issues to current events and to the interplay of factors that "make" leaders. These are the "crucibles" of leadership, conditions in which leaders face great tests and crises, from which they emerge molded with a vision and with values to inspire others to do what is morally correct.

Conclusion

This book introduces readers to what we feel is a fascinating body of literature. We hope the complexity and mystique surrounding leadership will slowly yield to understanding as you read the 13 chapters that follow.

In the past century, the often-misunderstood phenomenon of leadership has been tossed and battered while social scientists have tried to make some sense of something they knew existed, but which seemed beyond the reach of scientific inquiry. Remarking about the difficulties leadership researchers have faced, Bennis (1959) noted: "Always, it seems, the concept of leadership eludes us or turns up in another form to taunt us again with its slipperiness and complexity" (p. 260).

Today, the concept is still complex, but it is better understood and much less slippery. We still have much to learn about leadership. We are guided, though, by a spirit of optimism emanating from the findings of those researchers who, before us, went through their own "crucibles." Pummeled but unbowed, they continued to study leadership and to inspire succeeding generations of scientists to continue their exploration. All the while, leaders influenced followers, and they will continue to do so regardless of the nadirs and zeniths of leadership research.

PART II

The Complexity, Science, and Assessment of Leadership

CHAPTER 2

What Is Leadership?

James G. (Jerry) Hunt

Chief executive officer (CEO) Greg Warren was concerned about the ability of his management team and the employees of his firm to function and cooperate under pressure. Several months ago, he had chosen to form a number of his fast-track people into a cross-functional team, including himself, to participate in a simulated exercise that would help team members to work on their interpersonal skills, enhance decision making, and form a more cohesive group. The simulation would be an exercise that would require the combination of the talents and expertise of all the team members to solve a complex problem of extreme urgency, and it would last a maximum of 72 hours. The problem was to be centered on the potential loss of the firm's largest client to a major competitor. The team would have to combine resources to come up with a contract that would offer the client superior service, at reduced costs, from the one that the competitor was offering.

With the current instability in the information technology (IT) market, the exercise scenario was one that was of the utmost importance to maintaining

---

Author's Note: I thank John N. Davis for brainstorming with me on different ideas of "what is leadership" used in this chapter and for comments on the manuscript. I also thank Naomi Boyd for her manuscript preparation activities and for preparing a revision of an earlier version of the chapter's opening scenario, originally written by George E. Dodge, who along with Robert Hooijberg also provided some insights on its interpretation, as did Glen Brown on the current version. Finally, I thank Donna Hunt and Justin Brisco for manuscript preparation activities and Kimberly Boal and Larry Jauch for manuscript comments.

market share, or even survival, for the company, should it be faced with a similar situation. The small firm already was struggling to maintain its current position as a result of larger IT firms' abilities to generate economies of scale and scope that the small firm simply could not produce. The board of directors was going to evaluate the outcome of the exercise to make decisions on whether the current management team was proficient enough to weather the current, extremely adverse, market conditions.

Deep into Day 2 of the simulation, Warren was receiving the update on the status of the group from the team leader. The finance, marketing, software design, and technical engineering team members seemed to be working well together on the problem, despite the fact that the functional structure of the organization had kept the managers separated into their own areas in the past. This was the first time that they had been brought together as a team, and it seemed to be working well thus far.

The briefing was interrupted by one of the firm's junior managers, who had received a call from Braxton Financial Group requesting immediate technical assistance with the transaction processing system (TPS) the IT firm had installed for Braxton last month. The financial services firm used the system to provide real-time pricing for its mutual fund shares, so the temporary downtime of the system had the potential to cost Braxton a large amount of money should the price of the shares change dramatically and be sold at the previous prevailing price.

The CEO heard enough of the conversation to understand that the client was frantic about the crash of the system and that her request had come directly to this junior manager rather than being correctly routed through to the technical support department. The junior manager, wanting to solidify his chances for promotion, in the near future, had already dispatched a service team to travel to Braxton's main headquarters to fix the glitch in the system. The CEO praised the manager for his prompt response to the service request but suggested that he reroute the assignment down through the technical support department. He told one of his key team leaders to make sure that one of the sales managers who was not involved in the simulation be sent over to Braxton to ensure that things were smoothed over with the firm. He also asked that the team leader remind him to call Braxton's CEO later in the day to see if she needed any other assistance with getting the TPS back online. He had the team leader phone the head receptionist, to inform her of the misdirected call, and the support department, to apologize for the hasty, off-site dispatch.

Warren then noticed that the data feed from the firm's in-house enterprise resource planning system (ERP) had stopped transferring information to the team involved in the simulated exercise. Upon discussing with the team leader the malfunctioning of the software, Warren learned that the firm had outsourced the installation of the software and that the technical engineers were having difficulty integrating the new software into their existing system. He found out further that the headquarters of the outsourcing firm was in Ireland. He asked the team leader for the current time in Ireland, then initiated a call to the vice president of operations of the firm responsible for the installation of the software to request a software system to be used in conjunction with the newly installed ERP software that would alleviate some of the current problems. By happy coincidence, Warren had gone to graduate school with the vice president of that firm before being hired on to head up the IT firm.

In the above scenario, the CEO is embedded in a complex, fast-changing simulated setting requiring vision, prudent unconventionality, farsightedness, and the ability to see the big picture—all parts of a broad-ranging view of leadership. In addition, the CEO demonstrates a broad-gauged conception of leadership through his understanding of the handling of the TPS, thinking through his dealings with subordinates and their interactions with their subordinates, and his handling of the extra software system with his former graduate school buddy, now the vice president of operations of the installation firm. Finally, based partly on understanding gained from his extensive view of leadership, he demonstrates a complex range of leader behaviors directed toward the cross-functional team operations, Braxton's CEO, the in-house enterprise planning system, Warren's subordinates, and the vice president of operations of the software installing firm. All the while, competition swirls around him and he is threatened with the crash of a critical transaction processing system installed by his firm. It is these kinds of challenging aspects in this dynamic scenario that form the basis for this chapter, examining the question of "What is leadership?"

The scenario is consistent with arguments that numerous leaders' jobs, in a wide range of organizations, have broadened to cover, among many other things, services to subordinates, forming cross-functional teams, shaping organizational and subunit strategy, and helping clients in the field (see Kanter, 1989). Here, managerial leaders, "have to learn to [lead] in situations where [they] don't have command authority, where [they] are neither controlled or controlling" (Drucker, 1993, p. 115). They also need to lead upward and laterally, in addition to leading downward (Conger, 1993; J. G. Hunt, 2000; Osborn, Hunt, & Jauch, 1980; Sayles, 1993).

As pointed out above, this scenario illustrates a very expansive view of leadership. Indeed, that view is broader than is typically considered, even with the newer conceptions of leadership increasingly emphasized today (see Zaccaro & Klimoski, 2001). It provides a concrete lead-in to the perspective of leadership developed in this chapter. This development is explicated in Figure 2.1—a framework that focuses on a number of contextual antecedents that have a bearing on one's conception of "What is leadership?"

The framework is a modified version of the "Historical-Contextual Superstructure" model developed earlier for a different purpose (see Hunt & Dodge, 2000). This framework serves as a key organizing motif for the remainder of this chapter. Note that each of five superstructure antecedents and components surrounds and is interconnected with nine selected examples representing conceptions of what leadership is ("What is leadership?" sets, explained in depth later in this chapter). These examples were chosen from a review of the literature, my judgment concerning movements in the leadership field, and leadership topics covered in this book. Finally, the selection also was reinforced by a recent book by Zaccaro and Klimoski (2001).

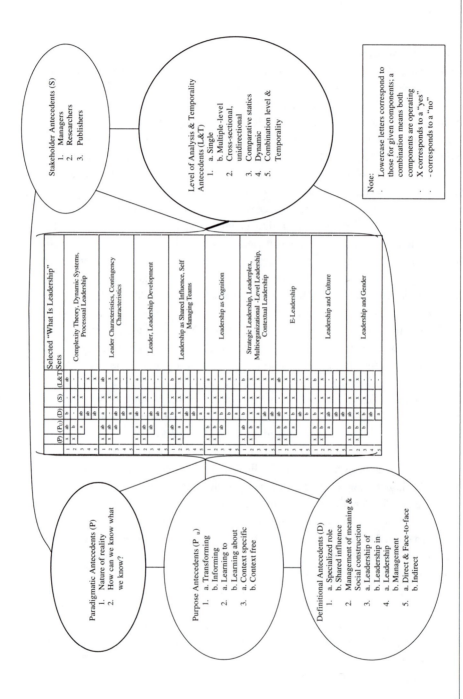

Figure 2.1 A Contextual Antecedent Superstructure Applied to Example Sets of "What Is Leadership?"

Overview of the Modified
Historical-Contextual Superstructure Model

Paradigmatic Antecedents

Whereas one can start with different aspects of the superstructure model and there is some overlap across antecedents, many would argue that the paradigmatic antecedents are the most basic of all starting points (see Figure 2.1). Here, consistent with those such as S. D. Hunt (1991), we use the term "paradigm" to reflect the commonly held perspectives of leadership academicians and practitioners concerning their ontological, epistemological, and methodological beliefs. The numerous experiences accrued across time give distinct form to the leadership conceptions. These experiences inform worldviews, which become the moral, philosophical, and other bases for involvement in the leadership field. These paradigmatic antecedents are concerned with the ontology and epistemology of leadership. In other words, what is the nature of reality and how can we know what we know?

For many, an unquestioned and indeed often unrealized assumption is that leadership is "real"; it can be measured in a relatively objective manner and has generalizable and law-like relationships waiting to be discovered. In sharp contrast, there are others who question such presuppositions when applied to concepts like leadership. They argue that subjective assumptions of the observer will determine what is found and how it is to be interpreted (Boal, Hunt, & Jaros, 2003). The first of these positions is sometimes called a scientific realist one, and the latter is often termed interpretivist, social constructionist, or some similar term, of which there are many. These contrasting positions reflect substantially different assumptions about the social world and the way in which it is appropriate to investigate it.

In paradigmatic antecedent terms, each differs in terms of *ontology*—assumptions about the essence of the phenomenon under investigation. Is the "reality" to be investigated external to the individual—imposing itself on individual consciousness from outside—or the product of individual consciousness? Is reality objective or the product of one's mind? Put succinctly, we return to the "nature of reality" question.

Related to the ontological assumptions just mentioned are those involving *epistemology.* How might we begin to understand the world and communicate this knowledge to others? As an example, do we identify and transmit knowledge in hard and real forms? Or, instead, is "knowledge" softer, more subjective, or even spiritual or transcendental, based on insights of a unique and essentially personal nature (see Burrell & Morgan, 1979)? Again, as mentioned earlier, the question is raised: "How can we know what we know?"

Here, it is useful to extend the previous discussion in terms of a six-position scientific realism/social constructionist philosophy of science continuum (see Boal et al., 2003; J. G. Hunt, 1991). On the extreme left is leadership reality as a concrete, static structure position with a machine metaphor and a quest for predictable deterministic underlying laws to explain and predict an orderly world. On the extreme right is the most radical social constructionist position, viewing reality as a projection of human imagination, with a transcendental metaphor. In that position, there is a phenomenological world, and leadership reality is a projection of individual consciousness and may be accessible only through phenomenological modes of insight (see Morgan & Smircich, 1980). The "transcendental" metaphor is described in the following way:

> Knowledge here rests within the subjective experience. The appreciation of world phenomena is seen as being dependent on the ability to understand the way in which human beings shape the world from inside themselves. . . . In each case [Husserl's, 1965, phenomenological tradition, studying experiential learning phenomenologically, and drawing on non-Western modes of philosophy], the grounds for knowledge demand that human beings transcend conventional scientific modes of understanding and begin to appreciate the world in revelatory, but as yet largely uncharted, ways. (Morgan & Smircich, 1980, p. 497)

As continuum anchors, each of the previous positions is an extreme one and provides a dramatically different perspective on the question of "What is leadership?" The machine metaphor position more nearly reflects traditional conceptions of leadership, although people such as McKelvey (1997) have argued that this linear, deterministic Newtonian mechanics perspective puts us into Daft and Lewin's (1990) "normal science straitjacket" and is really an outmoded version of Newtonian mechanics. More moderate scientific realist views move us toward the middle of the continuum, represented by the "reality as a contextual field of information" position with metaphors of a hologram, cybernetics, or the human brain. This ontological position calls for epistemologies based on the cybernetic metaphor, emphasizing the importance of understanding contexts in a holistic fashion (Morgan & Smircich, 1980, p. 436). There is an emphasis on how organizations and environments evolve together. Causality is not a concern because it is impossible to find a point at which causal forces begin. Relationships change together and cannot be reduced to a set of determinate laws and propositions—the whole is stored in all the parts (F. G. Hunt, 1991, pp. 46–47; Morgan & Smircich, 1980, pp. 495–496).

Purpose Antecedents

The superstructure figure next emphasizes the purpose antecedents, or the reasons why one chooses to focus on leadership. Some very different purposes are to identify leaders, to select leaders, to discover what leaders do, to discover why leaders are effective, and to determine whether they are necessary or not (Yukl, 2002). A few other purposes are prediction, finding retrospective explanations to justify past actions, and using the reasoning as an action lever to change aspects of organizations (J. P. Campbell, 1977; Peterson & Smith, 1988). To these one can add Blair and Hunt's (1986) context-specific versus context-free purpose, where context is used to refer to organizational type. The former focuses on phenomena embedded within a specific organizational type (e.g., health care, public sector). The latter emphasizes phenomena free of the specific organizational type in which the phenomena are encountered. Those with a context-free purpose tend to focus on relatively few variables across many organizations, whereas those emphasizing context-specific aspects focus on many variables in one kind of organization.

A number of these differing purpose ideas are captured in the simplified "informing" and "transforming" (changing the nature of leadership and/or the organization) and "learning to" and "learning about" leadership labels in Figure 2.1. The purposes mentioned for the antecedents are clearly very different and can have a substantial impact on other superstructure antecedents, especially the definitional antecedents, which are discussed in the next section. Finally, although it seems as if purpose would be obvious to consider, it typically is not, at least explicitly. This lack of attention is despite arguments for the importance of purpose by those such as J. P. Campbell (1977), J. G. Hunt (1991), Karmel (1978), and Yukl (2002).

Definitional Antecedents

Closely accompanying purpose is the definition of leadership, which of course is implied by the title of this chapter. To start, it is important to realize that there are many definitions of leadership—not just one—and, of course, a leadership scholar or practitioner's purpose will have a strong impact on the definition selected. As one example, Yukl (2002) lists nine different definitions, and Bass's *Handbook of Leadership* (1990) lists a dozen. Whereas the specifics of these definitions differ, two notions underlying most of them are *process* and *influence*. It also is important to note that although it is common to talk about individual leaders, the previously mentioned definitions emphasize *leadership* (the process of leading) as opposed to *leaders*.

Specialized Role or Shared Influence

The person designated to perform the specialized leadership role is considered to be "the leader." Others are considered to be "followers" even though they themselves may help the leader in performing leadership functions. Furthermore, it is possible for a person to be a leader and a follower at the same time (e.g., subordinate managers in an organization) (see Yukl, 2002).

In contrast, an increasingly popular view is to treat leadership as a shared influence process in which leadership is seen as a process that any member of a group or social system may carry out at any time. Various functions are enacted by different people as the occasion demands. In other words, "one takes leadership where one finds it"—and it does not have to be restricted to a given group but instead can cut across informal groups or formal work units; hence the use of "social system" above (see J. G. Hunt & Ropo, 1997).

Management of Meaning and Social Construction

A definition of leadership different from many, and consistent with positions past the middle on the previously mentioned scientific realism/social construction-ist continuum, is the management of meaning. This is the process whereby one or more individuals succeeds in attempting to frame and define the reality of others (Smircich & Morgan, 1982, p. 258) and is itself a part of the social construction of reality, in which it is assumed that there is no reality outside that constructed by one or more people. This definition not only is particularly germane as a defini-tional antecedent but also harks back to the paradigmatic antecedent in terms of underlying assumptions.

Leadership of and in Organizations

A key notion here, very strongly related to purpose but intertwined with definition, is *leadership of* versus *leadership in* organizations (see Dubin, 1977). Leadership *of* organizations connotes leadership at or near the top of a hier-archical organization (i.e., strategic leadership), whereas leadership *in* organi-zations reflects lower-level leadership; of course, leadership *in* may be involved in leadership *of* as well, in terms of leading direct subordinates. This notion is an important first cut because the *of* and *in* aspects have influence both on more specific definitions and on what will or will not be included as part of "leadership." As an example, "leadership *of*" studies include strategy, organiza-tional design, culture, and a variety of other aspects not typically included in traditional "leadership *in*" studies, which have tended to involve lower-level, face-to-face emphases. The preponderance of relevant literature typically emphasizes these latter kinds of works, but there is an increasing emphasis on leadership *of*, or strategic leadership studies (see Sashkin, Chapter 8, this volume; Zaccaro & Klimoski, 2001).

Leadership Versus Management

Related to the just-mentioned purpose thrust is that of leadership versus man-agement. Whereas the military has tended to differentiate between leadership and managerial roles for some time, this differentiated notion has now been more gen-erally recognized by Zaleznik (1977). A few other authors also consider leadership as broader than management (e.g., Hersey & Blanchard, 1988, p. 5). More typically, a role perspective has been taken, and leadership is seen as one of the many roles of a manager (e.g., Mintzberg, 1973/1980), even though Mintzberg argued that lead-ership is needed in dealing with nine other managerial roles. In addition to Zaleznik (1977), Bennis and Nanus (1985), B. Schneider (1989), and Kotter (1990), there are others who sharply differentiate between leaders and managers or leadership versus management.

W. L. Gardner and Schermerhorn (1992) pull together these general notions in a three-part conceptualization:

1. leadership equals management;

2. leadership does not equal management (they are entirely separate concepts); and

3. leadership and management are complementary.

The previous discussion cries out for a specific definition of the two concepts when they are being compared. Typically, the essential function of *leadership* is seen as producing adaptive or useful change, and *management* is seen as being used essentially to make the organization operate smoothly (see Kotter, 1990). For Kotter, planning is a managerial process very different from what he terms the *direction setting* aspect of leadership. Direction setting is a process that produces vision and strategies, as opposed to planning. Kotter emphasized a key aspect of leadership as *alignment*—getting people to understand, accept, and line up in the direction chosen. He differentiated this from the managerial function of *organizing*. He also emphasized motivation and inspiration as key aspects of leadership and argued that leadership functions may require more than one person (one of the points mentioned in the shared influence treatment, above). Finally, he pointed out the inadequacies of traditional managerial hierarchies and stressed the need for supplementation with "thick networks of relationships."

It is important to note that, at least for Kotter, both management and leadership are important, but they are complementary and do not have to be done by the same person. Thus, Gardner and Schermerhorn's third definition appears to capture this conception. Indeed, whereas it probably is useful to recognize differences in the two concepts, it is hard, at least in formal leadership in organizations, to differentiate them as sharply as the definitions or descriptions would suggest. As an example, following the broad conception of management mentioned earlier, it seems clear that at least for the leadership *of*, by top officials, many activities such as organizational design, environmental monitoring, and strategy formulation and implementation would extend beyond typical leadership activities, but there would be an oscillation back and forth between leadership and management.

In addition, in considering this antecedent, it should be noted that each of these conceptions would frame what would and would not be included in a given leadership study, application, or discussion. As an example, those using the "leadership equals management" conceptualization probably would include aspects that would not be included in either of the W. L. Gardner and Schermerhorn conceptualizations. Also, as pointed out above, much the same would be likely to happen in the leadership *of* and *in* perspectives, where, for some, the broader organizational notions of the conceptualizations probably would shade over into management.

Direct and Face-to-Face Versus Indirect Leadership

Most leadership work traditionally has assumed leadership to have a direct impact on a criterion variable or, in its more sophisticated guise, assumes that the criterion variable has a direct impact on leadership or perhaps that there is reciprocal impact. Direct impact is all part of the "Lone Ranger white hat syndrome" permeating much traditional leadership research. Indeed, there are many instances where leadership can accurately be defined or described as having a direct impact for good or ill. Usually, in addition to face-to-face contact, such leadership could be by telephone or other direct, synchronous or asynchronous means of communication.

However, for multiple-level leadership, strategic leadership, and leadership *of* approaches, in general, there are many situations in which leadership at higher levels has indirect effects cascading down the organizational hierarchy (see J. G. Hunt, 1991). Such effects often accompany more direct leader-follower effects higher in the organization. These indirect effects operate through other variables. Effects such as these are a part of the strategic leadership; Leaderplex; multi-organization-level; and complexity/dynamic systems/processual, contextual leadership approaches discussed later, in the leadership examples, as part of the superstructure model and summarized in Figure 2.1.

Level of Analysis and Temporality Antecedents

Level-of-analysis antecedents, in terms of theory building, measurement, and observation implications, have now become so important that there is an annual book series devoted to the topic, not to mention a recent special issue of a journal and a two-volume book set (see Dansereau & Yammarino, 1995, 1998). In leadership, level of analysis began being treated seriously with the advent of statistical means for analyzing leadership effects simultaneously at multiple levels while separating leadership effects on individual subordinates within a level of analysis framework (Dansereau, Alutto, & Yammarino, 1984). Related work has now been refined and is spreading beyond a small group of scholars (see Dansereau, Graen, & Haga, 1975). That work is treated in Dansereau and Yammarino (1998) and further discussed in Antonakis et al. (Chapter 3, this volume).

Consistent with the above theme, Waldman and Yammarino (1999), among numerous others, argued that it is important to specify the level of analysis at which constructs occur in a theoretical model. Constructs such as leadership typically are associated with the behavior of a single person or the individual (leader) level of analysis, and the manifestation and effects of leadership can be seen at the dyadic or small group level of analysis. Criteria such as performance can be considered at the level of individuals, groups, and organizations.

Klein, Dansereau and Hall (1994) conceptualized a number of multiple-level models useful to consider. Initially, following Rousseau (1985), they treated cross-level models, where relationships are formed between independent and dependent variables at different levels (Waldman & Yammarino, 1999). For instance, a top manager's leadership could influence organizational performance. Next, Klein and associates deal with mixed-effects models, where a single construct may have effects at multiple levels of an organization. For example, CEO leadership influences individual-level worker performance, as well as both group and organizational performance. Third, these authors treat mixed determinants models where predictors at various levels influence a given criterion; for example, CEO leadership and individual worker effort influence overall organizational performance. Finally, Klein et al. (1994) deal with multilevel models—sometimes termed "cross-level models"—where relationship patterns are replicated across levels of analysis. Here, CEO effort and performance, individual effort and performance, and group effort and performance may all be related in organizations.

To utilize such level-of-analysis notions, one needs explicit hypotheses concerning the role of leadership in a given situation. Also, once again, the other antecedents are important. For instance, J. G. Hunt and Ropo (1998) contrasted grounded theory with mainstream leadership approaches. Each of these differs in terms of paradigmatic assumptions and other superstructure antecedents.

The terms *levels of management* and *hierarchical levels* are often used in leadership and are discussed in more detail under the multi-organizational-level leadership section later in this chapter and in Figure 2.1). For now, it is important to recognize that levels of analysis are distinct from hierarchical levels. Here, there is a linkage with the leadership *of* and *in* distinctions mentioned earlier and in Figure 2.1. Leadership *of* is leadership at the highest managerial level, whereas leadership *in* considers leadership conceptualized at one or more levels of analysis (Waldman & Yammarino, 1999). Thus, whereas they are distinct, there is consideration of each in terms of levels of analysis.

Moving now to temporality, one again sees an increasingly important and rapidly evolving antecedent area emphasized in recent special issues and features in the *Academy of Management Journal* (see Barkema, Baum, & Mannix, 2002) and the *Academy of Management Review* (see Goodman, Ancona, Lawrence, & Tushman, 2001). Traditionally, most leadership theories have failed to describe the treatment of time and temporal conditions as aspects of a theory (McGrath & Kelly, 1986). At best, these conditions are implied. Typically, time is dealt with as cross-sectional or single discrete sections of a linear and unidirectional flow (i.e., clock or calendar time). Even longer-term studies tend to stress comparative statics, a series of linear "snapshots" over a given time period. Hinings (1997) and Melcher (1976) are two of many who have criticized leadership or related research as static or at best emphasizing comparative statics.

An increasing number of scholars are now emphasizing more comprehensive treatments of temporality, conceptually and empirically (e.g., Barkema et al., 2002, Goodman et al., 2001). Particularly interesting and important is consideration of process, where the path—or *how* one moves from one period's observations to those of the next—is emphasized (e.g., Ropo, Eriksson, & Hunt, 1999), and by Hinings (1997) and Pettigrew (1997), who discuss details of processual analysis and the importance of such analysis. These join those, such as Melcher (1976, 1977), J. G. Hunt (1991), Ropo and Hunt (1999), and C. Jacobsen and House (2001), who emphasize leadership applications of temporality.

Currently, there is a combining of level-of-analysis thrusts and temporality (e.g., Dansereau, Yammarino, & Kohles, 1999; Morgeson & Hofman, 1999). These authors showed a priori ways in which specific levels of analyses can change across time periods. Such examples suggest that the combination of level of analysis and temporality is likely to become increasingly important (see Figure 2.1).

Stakeholder Antecedents

Joining the above antecedents in importance is that of stakeholders, as shown in Figure 2.1. Here, there is a focus on those who are concerned with or benefit from (cui bono) specific aspects of leadership knowledge. Stakeholders include such people or entities as publishers or publication outlets, research support agencies, students, research colleagues, various kinds of managers, consultants, those with research sites, and even social movement groups (see Peterson & Smith, 1988). Readers may think of still more stakeholders of special interest to them.

Each of these stakeholders is likely to be quite different in terms of such factors as interests, orientations, background, and knowledge bases. More to the point, each of these stakeholders can emphasize quite different paradigmatic antecedents as well as different purposes, definitions, and levels of analysis/temporality aspects. Particularly important are differences in concerns between managers and researchers, who along with editors and publishers, are focused on in Figure 2.1. Shirvastava and Mitroff (1984) and McGuire (1986) are among those who discuss these manager and researcher differences in some detail.

Selected Leadership Example Sets

The leadership examples first mentioned as a part of the Figure 2.1 antecedents framework are summarized in the middle portion of the figure as "What is leadership?" example sets. In considering each one of the examples, one should systematically move through each contextual antecedent and its components in terms of how well it facilitates an understanding of the research and practical implications for each example set. I have designated antecedents by capital letters and each antecedent component by a number or sometimes a number and a lowercase letter in Figure 2.1. The figure also indicates the importance of each in terms of my understanding of literature I used in compiling this chapter. Thus, for example, the current literature for the complexity theory, dynamic systems, and processual theory set is assessed as emphasizing the shared influence component of the definitional antecedents. The remainder of the components here and in all the other antecedent and component sets are assessed in the same manner.

The results of this assessment, shown in Figure 2.1, are helpful in making the connection between the antecedents and components in the current literature. To go further, in using this framework, it is useful for readers to systematically go through each of these antecedents and components in terms of the specific "What is leadership?" example in which they are interested (or even other possible examples of interest that are not treated here). In that way, they can make a comprehensive evaluation of the nature of what should be considered for their leadership question of interest. This approach will clearly highlight the differences and similarities involved in each of the "What is leadership?" examples.

Complexity Theory, Dynamic Systems, and Processual Leadership

In terms of the earlier-mentioned scientific realist/social constructionist continuum, as part of the paradigmatic antecedent (Figure 2.1), the point was made that traditional conceptions of leadership tended to reflect the deterministic, machine metaphor position on the continuum. As counters to this rigid view were a number of social constructionist leadership perspectives. I argued that a more moderate scientific realist perspective was reflected in the "reality as a contextual field of information" position, toward the middle of the continuum. This position is operationalized through complexity theory and closely related dynamic systems perspectives, which are receiving increasing attention in the leadership literature (see J. G. Hunt & Ropo, in press; Marion & Uhl-Bien, 2001).

This position is consistent with McKelvey's (1997, 1999) "stochastic idiosyncrasy," scientific realist notion, which he argued deals with such social constructionist positions as multiple causality, nonlinearity, self-organization, and adaptive learning, while using such scientific realist notions as objective measurement, replication, falsifiability, and self correction—all traditional scientific hallmarks (e.g., Nicholas & Prigogine, 1989).

One can set the stage for a summary of the essence of complexity theory by means of the following quotation from S. Levy (1992):

> A complex system is one whose component parts interact with sufficient intricacy that they cannot be predicted by standard linear equations; so many variables are at work in the system that its over-all behavior can only be understood as an emergent consequence of the holistic sum of the myriad behaviors embedded within.
>
> Reductionism does not work with complex systems, and it is now clear that a purely reductionist approach cannot be applied; . . . In living systems the whole is more than the sum of its parts. This is the result of . . . complexity which allows certain behaviors and characteristics to emerge unbidden. (pp. 7–8)

Organizations operate as complex dynamic systems composed of a diversity of agents who interact with one another and thus promote novel behavior for the entire system that influences the system's environment (Marion, 1999; Osborn, Hunt, & Jauch, 2002). Here, there are basic "laws" illustrated by decision rules of scripted relationships between organizational members in an institutional arrangement. Each time an agent interacts with another, the agent is free to follow, ignore, or slightly alter the institutional arrangement. Actions and interactions have consequences in the form of feedback loops. Where the organization faces a dynamic and unpredictable environment, the feedback is nonlinear. Small changes could have very large consequences. Agents in such a system must move around the nonlinear feedback loops if order is to be maintained (e.g., Osborn, Hunt, & Jauch, 2002; Sanders, 1998).

Depending on the extent of change in the roles and scripts, there is a range of more or less stable outcomes. Here, when such feedback operates in a state poised at instability, behavior is simultaneously both stable and unstable. In the long term it is unstable and unpredictable; in the short term it is the opposite in terms of its qualitative structure or pattern, thus allowing short-term predictability. Behavior near stability, termed "the edge of chaos," thus follows a random unpredictable path over time but does so within limits. However, the bounds may change, and a new order could emerge around a new set of "attractors"—the end state toward which a dynamic system moves (Osborn, Hunt, & Jauch, 2002). Some attractors (i.e., "strange attractors") may never settle into a steady state. These attractors hold an inherently chaotic, nonlinear organizational system together and give it shape; the attractors never repeat over time.

Organizations at "the edge of chaos" are stable enough to maintain information about themselves and their environment while being sufficiently vibrant to process that information (Marion, 1999). They map their environment and interact with and become a part of that environment (Marion, 1999). Different actors within a system resonate (affect their own individual behaviors) with each other and may augment the capabilities of the broader organization, thus influencing an organization's "self-organizing" capabilities. Traditional views of complexity theory such as the one expressed by Kauffman (1993) thus argue that "order is free," because it comes from the bottom up, with no overriding central command. Here, the role of the leader shifts from a position of top-down command to one of attempting to facilitate such bottom-up interactions (Marion & Uhl-Bien, 2001). The relational and collectivist group notions discussed later also become important here, because the bottom-up interactions are largely distributive or collectivist in nature (see a discussion by McKelvey, 2000; Marion & Uhl-Bien, 2001).

Of course, these characteristics are in sharp contrast to those of classical science, which seeks order and stability as opposed to recognizing dynamism, nonlinearity, and unpredictability (see Prigogine, 1997). Thus, examining leadership at the edge of chaos moves the analysis from studying the combined impact of context and leadership on performance to examining the co-evolutionary dynamics among the environment of the firm, its viability in the setting, and its collective leadership. It is important to stress the reverberating changes from firm to environment as well as from environment to firm.

The underlying tenets of complexity theory also are operative in dynamic systems perspectives. Such systems approaches tend to use computer-assisted computational modeling. Leadership examples using variations of dynamic systems have tended to model various aspects of traditional leadership approaches such as charismatic leadership (e.g., Davis, 2002; Jacobsen & House, 2001) or Quinn's competing values framework (J. A. Black, King, & Howell, 2000), which will be discussed shortly but using dynamic systems approaches. Processual leadership perspectives tend to incorporate many of the dynamism notions of complexity theory and dynamic systems; however, they use such methodologies as grounded theory or related approaches (see J. G. Hunt & Ropo, in press, for an elaboration).

All the leadership examples in this section emphasize dynamism, embeddedness, nonlinearity, temporal interconnections, and holism. In this way, Figure 2.1 suggests that they differ substantially from most of the other leadership examples, discussed below, across many of the antecedents. We also should note that, here and wherever else there are combined example sets (e.g., strategic leadership, Leaderplex, multi-level leadership, and contextual leadership), the assessments in Figure 2.1 go across the combined example set. There sometimes could be differences within the set.

Leader Characteristics and Contingency Characteristics

These leader characteristics and leadership contingency examples of leadership are the most traditional of the various illustrations. Leader characteristics hark back to "great man" and leadership trait approaches, according to which those with "the right stuff" either were seen as leaders or were argued to have superior outcomes as compared to nonleaders or those with "different stuff" (see Bass, 1990). Thus, there were numerous studies to isolate leader/nonleader or effective/less-effective traits. For a number of reasons, these approaches fell into disrepute, but now, with the advent of increasing knowledge, traits are making a comeback. Listed below is a selected subset of characteristics with respectable empirical and conceptual support, which conveys the flavor of the approaches focusing on leader traits (see House & Aditya, 1997; S. A. Kirkpatrick & Locke, 1991; Yukl, 1998).

1. Emotional maturity: Well adjusted, does not suffer from severe psychological disorders.

2. Integrity: Behavior consistent with espoused values; honest, ethical, and trustworthy.

3. Cognitive ability, intelligence, and social intelligence: Ability to gather, integrate, and interpret information; intelligence; and understanding of social setting.

4. Task-relevant knowledge: Knowledge about the organization, industry, and technical aspects.

Aside from their use in and of themselves, traits such as these often are used in combination with behaviors or leadership contingencies, discussed below, as components in current leadership models or theories (e.g., House, 1977). Zaccaro, Kemp, and Bader (Chapter 5, this volume) devote their chapter to leader characteristics such as those just summarized.

More typically considered leader characteristics involve leader or leadership behaviors. Behaviors were first systematically recognized in the Ohio State and University of Michigan studies of the early 1950s as a response to the earlier lack of success with trait characteristics (see Bass, 1990). They have evolved across time, and there are now comprehensive taxonomies (see Yukl, 2002). One especially interesting illustration, encompassing aspects related to numerous other taxonomies, including Mintzberg's, mentioned earlier, is the competing values framework (CVF) of Quinn and his associates (Quinn, Faerman, Thompson, & McGrath, 2003). The CVF utilizes eight roles, arranged as in Figure 2.2.

Here the roles with horizontal arrows are seen as fitting in the same flexibility/ control or internal/external quadrant describing organizational characteristics (e.g., innovator/broker). In contrast, those with vertical arrows are envisioned as fitting in opposite quadrants (e.g., innovator/coordinator or to be contradictory or competing). Each role also has three more specific competencies embedded within it. The model reflects well a wide range of behaviors and competencies (including those that for some might be classified as management rather than leadership). A unique feature is the CVF's competing values emphasis, where it is argued that effective leaders must be able to engage in both similar (e.g., innovator/broker) and competing or contradictory (e.g., producer/facilitator) roles. In other words, an effective leader must be able to handle paradoxical roles. Furthermore, all the roles are critical, and where a leader is incapable of enacting them all, then one or more other people on the "leadership team" would be expected to supplement the leader's role enactment.

Although comprehensive, the CVF does not deal explicitly with the currently popular charismatic or transformational leadership, though one can infer such behaviors from the various competencies embedded in the roles (e.g., vision is mentioned as one of the competencies in one of the roles, and managing change is involved with another). The mention of charismatic and transformational leadership reminds one that about one-third of recently conducted leadership research emphasizes these or closely related notions in one way or another (see J. G. Hunt & Conger, 1999). Most such studies have used either a variation of House and associates' work (e.g., House & Aditya, 1997) or Bass and associates' work (e.g., Bass, 1998). Bass emphasized transformational leadership behavior, of which charisma is one key component, and contrasted it with the transactional, or traditional exchange-based, leadership. In contrast, House's work has a much heavier emphasis on charisma per se. Space precludes more detailed discussion, but see House and Aditya (1997), Bass (1998), or Yukl (2002).

Leadership Contingency Characteristics

Leader characteristics examples concentrate on a leader as if leader characteristics are the sole predictor of who will become a leader or which designated leader will be more effective. However, there is a body of literature that also considers specific characteristics of the situation, as well as leader characteristics (e.g., Fiedler, 1967). People subscribing to this view think of leadership as being moderated by various "contingencies" that change the various outcomes. Here one assumes that different characteristics will be effective in different situations and that the same characteristic is not optimal in all situations (Yukl, 2002). A number of traditional

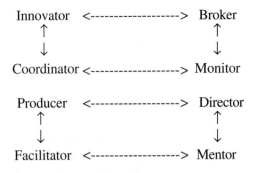

Figure 2.2   Competing Values Framework

SOURCE: Adapted from Quinn, Faerman, Thompson, and McGrath (2003).

leadership contingency approaches are being discussed in the literature. A few such contingency characteristics are unit size, leader position power and authority, task structure and complexity, task interdependence, follower characteristics, and sometimes environmental aspects (see Yukl, 2002, and Ayman, Chapter 7, this volume, for comprehensive treatments of contingency characteristics).

Leader and Leadership Development

Some people, when considering leaders or leadership, think in terms of developmental aspects. For them, the emphasis is on the development of leaders or managers. Here, the earlier mentioned "leadership versus management" antecedent category comes to mind, where there is some overlap but the two are separated as in Figure 2.1.

Management development is seen as primarily including managerial education and training (Latham & Seijts, 1999; Mailick, Stumpf, Grant, Kfir, & Watson, 1998), along with the acquisition of specific types of knowledge, skills, and abilities to enhance task performance in various managerial roles (e.g., Baldwin & Padgett, 1993). Management development typically has a heavy training orientation (Day, 2000). In contrast, leadership development emphasizes the collective capacity of organizational members to engage in leadership roles and processes (Hooijberg, Bullis, & Hunt, 1999; McCauley, Moxley, & Van Velsor, 1998). Such processes enable groups or teams to work together, regardless of position, whereas management development is tied closely to organizations and positions (Keys & Wolfe, 1988).

Finally, some researchers such as Day (2000) recently have contrasted leader development with both of the above notions. Here, a sharp distinction is drawn between leaders and followers. Thus, development is emphasized through training individual leader skills and abilities, with an interpersonal orientation (Lepack & Snell, 1999). Readers are invited to compare and contrast the brief treatment above with detailed discussion of developmental aspects by London and Maurer (Chapter 10, this volume) and of course to check Figure 2.1 for antecedent example linkages.

Leadership as Shared Influence, and Self-Managing Teams

A key definitional issue is whether to consider leadership as a specialized role or as a shared influence process. In a specialized-role interpretation, there is an individual emphasis on the leader, typically in a hierarchical relationship to one or more followers. This is a traditional definition of leadership, and we have discussed it at several places in this chapter. Similarly, we have treated leadership as shared influence. The shared influence perspective takes many forms, with specialized labels, all of which might be encompassed under the term *relational leadership* and are combined in the leadership example set in Figure 2.1. Leadership of self-managing teams also is discussed in this section.

Social Network Analysis

Social network analysis is now receiving substantial attention and has origins that go back more than 50 years to early sociometric work (see Jennings, 1947). That work, and its current, intricate social network metamorphosis, essentially tracks social influence patterns or networks and utilizes various sophisticated indices to answer a wide range of influence questions (e.g., Burt, 1992).

Network studies of social capital have become increasingly important (Zaccaro & Klimoski, 2001). These focus on relationships between and among individuals or groups and the accompanying access to information, resources, opportunities, and control. Patterns of interactions emerge, and social networks form. Strong (connecting to central others) and weak (connecting with others who are not connected) ties are emphasized, along with their leadership implications. Various situational contingencies also are considered (see Brass & Krackhardt, 1999; Burt, 1992).

Extensions of Leader/Member Exchange

Traditional exchange conceptions have emphasized leader-follower exchange relationships. Here, the followers provide the leader with extra status, esteem, and the like in exchange for the leader's unique goal contribution (Hollander, 1978; Jacobs, 1970). These approaches are much more explicit than the more implicit exchanges of many leadership approaches (e.g., House, 1971).

Graen and his associates have gone the furthest with explicit exchange notions about such exchanges, as exemplified in the well-known leader-member exchange theory (LMX). In earlier versions of the theory, leaders classified followers into in-group or out-group members and treated the former more favorably. In turn, in-group members engaged in various activities to enhance the leader's role.

Graen and Uhl-Bien (1995) recently have broadened LMX theory to include others outside the traditional leader-follower exchange dyad, and LMX has become much more a broad-ranging relational theory. Cogliser and Schriesheim (1994) also have integrated LMX into social network approaches.

Lateral and Distributive Approaches

Sayles (1964, 1979, 1993; Sayles & Chandler, 1971; Sayles & Stewart, 1993), over the years, has emphasized a wide range of relationships emphasizing contacts or relations with others outside a leader's hierarchical line of authority. Osborn, Hunt, and Jauch (1980) combined these ideas with the external relations literature (see Melcher, 1976) in what they termed "lateral leadership." A specialized case of this notion, called "representational leadership," has been used by Baliga and Hunt (1988) and by Ropo and Hunt (1999) to link various aspects of leadership.

House and Aditya (1997) discussed "distributed leadership" to cover such notions as division of roles and peer leadership, where several people enact the same roles contemporaneously. Here, in a manner different from traditional hierarchical superior subordinate relations, Osborn, Hunt, and Skaret (1977) used a similar notion focused on dual leaders.

Related Social Influence Process Notions

Some Europeans (e.g., Dachler, 1988; Hosking & Morley, 1988) have been especially likely to emphasize shared influence process approaches—sometimes labeling these as "collective" or "distributive," not unlike some of the usages above but with a heavy social constructionist perspective. The term *systems leadership*, as used in this section, emphasizes relationships—the many separate and individual and organizational elements in a system, however defined, across time—that are important. Traditional leader-follower interactions are but one small part of this. It is key relationships of the system as a whole that exert leadership and are influenced in a manner not unlike traditional specialized role leadership (see Acar, 2002, and J. G. Hunt & Ropo, 1997, for a more detailed description).

Self-Managing Teams

Increasingly emphasized in the literature are self-managing teams. Like the leadership examples above, these too illustrate leadership as a social influence process. Interestingly, given their attention in the literature, it is difficult to find explicit and systematic treatments of the leadership of such teams (but see Zaccaro, Rittman, & Marks, 2001). What the literature does suggest is that leadership needs to be considered both inside and outside teams of this kind.

Most self-managing teams have highly interdependent activities and are responsible for producing a distinct product or service. Usually, the members have similar functional backgrounds, and they often take turns performing the various tasks for which the team is responsible (Yukl, 2002). The parent organization usually determines the mission, the scope of operations, and the budget for these teams. The amount of authority for other types of decisions varies greatly across organizations. Typically, the teams can set work schedules, deal directly with external customers, set performance targets, conduct training, and the like (Yukl, 2002).

The internal leadership role involves management responsibilities assigned to the teams and shared by group members. Often, the leader is elected by members and the position is rotated. Most important responsibilities, however, are shared by group members. Sometimes difficult supervisory functions are performed collectively. The external leadership role involves managerial responsibilities not delegated to the team. The external role typically emphasizes coaching, facilitating, and consulting to the team, and usually the person filling the external role will serve as coach and facilitator for several teams (Yukl, 2002).

Leadership as Cognition

In the earlier-mentioned scientific realism/social constructionist continuum, several of the positions emphasized various aspects of management of meaning and social construction of reality. There, indeed, the core of these notions was ontological and epistemological assumptions about reality (see Figure 2.1), and these assumptions implied measurement methods very different from those typically used by scientific realists. In the present "leadership as cognition" illustrative focus, leadership is seen as socially constructed via cognition, but the measurement methods are hard-core scientific realist ones. This difference helps clarify the use of "social construction" in this section.

The emphasis on leadership cognition has increased rapidly since the middle 1970s, when Eden and Leviatan (1975) argued that "leadership factors are in the mind of the respondent. It remains to be established whether or not they are more than that" (p. 741; cited in Lord & Emrich, 2000, p. 551). I review a few basic notions here and refer readers to the Lord and Emrich article for more detailed treatment.

The first key focus is on follower attributions of leadership (follower use of information about leader actions, changes in performance of a group or organization, and external conditions to reach conclusions about leader success or failure) (Yukl, 2002). Second, I focus on what have been termed implicit leadership theories (ILTs; beliefs and assumptions about the characteristics of effective leadership) (Yukl, 2002). As a part of this focus, a cognitive *schema* is defined as a cognitive structure that represents organized knowledge about a given concept or type of stimulus. It contains not only the attributes of the concept but also the relationships among the attributes. Schemas reflect the active construction of reality, in which individuals create meaning and add onto it the raw data of the objective world (S. T. Fiske & Taylor, 1984). Schemas are triggered primarily as a way of dealing with information overload and often are automatically called forth to help interpret new situations (J. G. Hunt, 1991).

In terms of attributions about leadership, one important attributional factor is the clarity of performance and its increasing or decreasing trend for the leader's unit or organization (see Yukl, 2002). If performance is clearly good and improving, there is a tendency to attribute competency to the leader (see Lord & Maher, 1991b). Leader actions also are considered—for example, when highly visible leader actions seen as relevant are taken, employees will tend to attribute competence to the leader, especially when there is a crisis with which the leader successfully deals (see J. G. Hunt, Boal, & Dodge, 1999). Similarly, good or poor external conditions affect attributions, as do leader constraints and perceived intentions. Where there is solid information on the above, attributions tend to be more accurate (see Antonakis & Atwater, 2002). However, followers make attributions anyway.

In terms of ILTs, it is useful to expand the schema notion in terms of "prototypes." These refer to an abstract set of features commonly associated with members of a category who exhibit similar perceived features. There are different levels of categories, varying in specificity (e.g., good vs. poor leaders, political vs. industrial leaders, or bank leaders vs. army leaders). Each of these category levels would have a set of perceived characteristics (e.g., decisive, trustworthy) that would be invoked as people observed a person in a leadership role. If there was a good fit between the person in a leadership role behavior and the prototype for a "good" leader of some type, then the person in the leadership role would be seen as a good leader and there would be positive responses from those viewing the person in that manner (see J. G. Hunt, Boal, & Sorenson, 1990; Lord, Foti, & De Vader, 1984). As with the attributional approach, classification of a good leader is in the eye of the beholder.

Yukl (2002) discussed these general notions in somewhat greater detail, and Lord and Emrich (2000) provided a detailed literature review extending and refining them, with particular emphasis on collective cognition. Also, especially relevant here, these authors examine the oft-mentioned specialized role versus social system question as a function of the leadership cognition literature going back to 1990. Finally, Brown, Scott, and Lewis (Chapter 6, this volume) provide a very informative chapter treating ILTs and related concepts in some detail.

Social Contagion

Returning now to the notion of charisma, I note that it is often considered an attribution on the part of a follower to a set of selected leader behaviors. However, Meindl (1990) argued that it also may be a social contagion effect whereby followers influence each other in terms of attributing charisma to a leader whom they have never even met (e.g., in a political faction, new religion, or social movement). Social contagion involves a group of people, whose inhibitions or latent behavioral tendencies are released by observing someone else openly display the behavior. Many people have an inhibited heroic social identity; however, they are waiting for a leader and a cause to activate this identity. Activation is more likely to occur in a social crisis that threatens the self-esteem, or even the survival, of people. The particular leader is less important than the process just described (see Yukl, 2002, for a discussion).

Strategic Leadership, Leaderplex, Multiorganizational-Level Leadership, and Contextual Leadership

The leadership example set here, like a number of the other examples, actually consists of several related, but different, examples that are more specific. All are bound together by the earlier-mentioned leadership *of* and *in* definition (Figure 2.1), and all involve consideration of a very wide range of vertically focused and horizontally focused organizational variables as well as consideration of organizational and external environment relationships. We first touch on various aspects of strategic leadership, then move to the other related examples.

Strategic Leadership

Perhaps because of the recency of systematic study (only from about the middle 1980s) (Finkelstein & Hambrick, 1996) and its depth, the strategic leadership area has a less-developed research tradition than do many other leadership areas. A small body of theoretical literature focusing on the role of leaders and top management teams, as well as on the process of strategic formulation and implementation, has slowly emerged (House & Aditya, 1997). Here I summarize both the processes by which strategic managers make strategic decisions, with some emphasis on the behavior of such managers as organizational leaders, and the composition and functioning of top management teams (see Edmonson, Roberto, & Watkins, 2003; Jackson & Ruderman, 1995). Finkelstein and Hambrick (1996) provided a conceptual framework and comprehensive literature review of strategic leadership. The key aspects include:

1. The decision-making discretion of strategic leaders (there are many factors restricting or enhancing such discretion) (see Finkelstein & Hambrick, 1996; J. G. Hunt & Osborn, 1982)

2. Whether strategic leaders matter in terms of organizational performance (they do, but as with their discretion, there are many constraints) (see House & Aditya, 1997, and their short review of a number of recent empirical works)

3. The effects of leadership succession on organizational performance (House and Singh, 1987, showed that more often than not, such succession makes a substantial difference in organizational effectiveness. However, once again, there are many constraints, so the results are not entirely consistent.)

Recently, the strategic leadership literature has been criticized for emphasizing demographic variables in place of underlying explanatory variables in its important thrust regarding management teams (see Boal & Hooijberg, 2001; Cannella & Moore, 1997; Priem, Lyon, & Dess, 1999), and there appears to be some movement toward tapping the underlying explanatory factors, as difficult as such tapping may be for high-level managerial leaders (see Edmonson et al., 2003).

It also has been argued that newer thrusts should be considered. The first thrust is the argument that the essence of strategic leadership is the creation and maintenance of absorptive capacity, coupled with adaptive capacity and managerial wisdom. *Absorptive capacity* focuses on the ability to learn. It involves the capacity to recognize new information, assimilate it, and apply it toward new ends. *Adaptive capacity* refers to the ability to change. It is argued that in the new competitive landscape—characterized by increasing discontinuities and disequilibrium conditions, hyper-competitive markets, and increasing emphasis on innovation and continuous learning—organizational effectiveness is influenced heavily by strategic flexibility or the ability to change (Boal & Hooijberg, 2001; Hitt, Keats, & DeMarie, 1998).

Finally, Boal and Hooijberg (2001) argued for *managerial wisdom.* Such wisdom combines properties of discernment and Kairos time (Bartunek & Necochea, 2000). Discernment involves the ability to perceive variation in the environment (see Osborn, Hunt, & Jauch, 1980), along with an understanding of the social actors and their relationships (e.g., social intelligence, including social awareness and social skills) (C. D. McCauley, 2000). As regards the use of Kairos, or time, it reflects the capacity to take the right action at a critical moment (Boal & Hooijberg, 2001).

Leaderplex

To the newer thrusts summarized above, it is useful to add some emergent leadership approaches in terms of their potential contributions to the capacity to learn, the capacity to change, and managerial wisdom. For this, I focus on the ideas of the competing values framework (CVF), discussed in the earlier leader characteristics example; behavioral complexity; cognitive capacity; and social intelligence.

These components constitute the Leaderplex model of leadership (see Hooijberg, Hunt, & Dodge, 1997). In this model, behavioral complexity is represented by the eight roles in the CVF. Cognitive complexity or capacity assumes that cognitively complex individuals process information differently from, and perform selected tasks better than do, cognitively less complex people because they use more categories to discriminate among stimuli and see more commonalities among these categories (for reviews, see J. G. Hunt, 1991; Stish, 1997; and Streufert, 1997). Cognitive complexity is seen as underlying absorptive capacity. Relatedly, Elliott Jaques (Jacobs & Jaques, 1987a; Jaques, 1989; Jaques & Cason, 1994; Jaques & Clement, 1991) has developed the concept of cognitive capacity or cognitive power, which connotes those mental processes that tap the scale and complexity of the world one is able to pattern and construe. It is the raw mental power enabling one to sustain increasingly complex mental processes.

Social intelligence is another leader characteristic that was touched on earlier. It is the ability to notice and make distinctions among other individuals—in particular among their moods, temperaments, motivations, and intentions (H. Gardner, 1985, p. 239). Beyond the ability to understand is the ability to *act* on one's understanding of others. It is this latter point that ties the general social intelligence to managerial wisdom. Boal and Hooijberg (2001) thus integrated the Leaderplex model (Hooijberg, Hunt, et al., 1997) with the three earlier-mentioned notions of absorption, change, and wisdom. To these, they added charismatic/transformational and vision leadership aspects, which were touched upon earlier. Their combined model clearly cuts across much leadership *of* and *in* literature and remains to be tested.

Multiorganizational-Level Leadership

The cognitive capacity/power concept of Jaques and colleagues, discussed above, also is a key component of multiorganizational-level leadership. Here, Jaques focused on conceptualizing hierarchical organization levels, as treated earlier, in terms of the amount of cognitive capacity/power required at each of these levels, or groupings of levels, into domains (i.e., systems leadership, the very highest organizational levels; organizational leadership, middle to upper middle levels; and production leadership, lower levels).

Jaques's essential notion is a simple one—at increasing hierarchical levels or domains, the time span of decision making increases until, for the systems domain, these time spans can be 10-20 years or even more. As the time span requirements increase, a higher level of cognitive capacity/power is called for. Leadership is considered more effective the closer the match between time spans required and the leader's cognitive capacity to deal with the time span requirements. This general model has been extended by J. G. Hunt (1991) and R. L. Phillips and Hunt (1992) and includes many of the other leadership notions discussed in this chapter. More current treatments are provided by Jacobs and McGee (2001) and Sashkin (Chapter 8, this volume).

Contextual Leadership

The above kinds of notions, as well as what were generally categorized as macro leadership models in the 1970s and early 1980s, form the basis for the recently developed Osborn, Hunt, and Jauch (2002) contextual theory of leadership. Before summarizing that theory, it is important to consider briefly what is meant generally by the term *contextual.* It is increasingly being emphasized in the literature and has been used frequently in this chapter, not always in the same way.

A recent issue of the *Journal of Organizational Behavior* focused on the different connotations of context. These span the gamut from the meaning of constructs to characteristics of workers, work units, and the larger setting (Rousseau & Fried, 2001). The latter comes closest to the Osborn, Hunt, and Jauch (2002) meaning. More specifically, that usage includes organizational, external environment, worker-job, and time factors, all of which are represented in one way or another in the work of Osborn and associates.

The genesis for the contextual theory of leadership came from the macro models of those such as Khandwalla (1977), Osborn, Hunt, and Jauch (1980), and Melcher (1976, 1977). Essentially, those researchers recognized in one way or another that leadership was embedded within the environment, structure, and technology of organizations. The "context" was defined bureaucratically, following the work of those such as Pugh, Hickson, Hinings, and Turner (1969) and Thompson (1967). The underlying logic was consistent with that of the leadership situational contingency models of the time, models that were mentioned earlier in this chapter (e.g., Fiedler, 1967). Like trait theory, this earlier impetus for contextual models waned but is now being reincarnated, as in the previously mentioned contextual theory.

Contextual leadership theory conceptualizes the interplay of leadership with the four contexts of stability, crisis, dynamic equilibrium, and edge of chaos; the latter is operationalized through a complexity theory/dynamic systems perspective (which is treated here separately as a leadership example in its own right) (see Figure 2.1). Each context and type of leadership is discussed, in terms of "network leadership" and a dimension termed "patterning of attention." The contexts encourage those studying leadership to reconsider temporality, causal relations, units of analysis, and dependent variables consistent with the social construction of human agency within the given context.

E-Leadership

The newest, and what many would consider least traditional, example of "What is leadership?" is e-leadership. It is defined as a social influence process mediated by advanced information systems to produce a change in attitudes, feelings, thinking, behavior, and/or performance with individuals, groups, and/or organizations. It can occur at any hierarchical level and can involve both one-to-one and one-to-many interactions within and across large units and organizations. E-leadership may be associated with one individual or shared by many as its locus changes across time (Avolio, Kahai, & Dodge, 2001).

E-leadership is seen as operating within the new context of advanced information technology (AIT). The focus is on how AIT interacts with leadership and how leadership, in turn, influences AIT's adoption and its effects on organizations. Advanced information systems are defined as tools, techniques, and knowledge that enable multiparty participation in organizational and interorganizational activities through sophisticated collection, processing, management, retrieval, transmission, and display of data and knowledge (DeSanctis & Poole, 1994). It includes, among other things, e-mail systems, message boards, groupware, group support systems, knowledge management systems, executive information systems, and collaborative customer relationship management and supply-chain management systems. Such technologies can help leaders scan, plan, decide, disseminate, and control information (Avolio, Kahai, & Dodge, 2001). As with some of the other leadership examples (e.g., contextual leadership), context again looms large. Thus, for e-leadership, the context is a part of the construct being studied.

Avolio, Kahai, and Dodge (2001) proposed studying e-leadership and its context through adaptive structuration theory (AST) (DeSanctis & Poole, 1994). In AST, human action is guided by structures, which are defined as rules and resources that serve as templates for planning and accomplishing tasks (DeSanctis & Poole, 1994). Structures are provided by an advanced information technology system and a work group's internal system, task, and environment. Structures also emerge when a work group acts on structures and produces new information, both of which serve to shape subsequent interaction. These various sources of structure define the context or attributes of the physical and social systems in which a work group exists (Nord & Fox, 1996).

Leadership and Culture

Up to this point, we have focused on "What is leadership?" example sets without explicitly recognizing that important leadership work takes place other than in, and is different outside, North America (e.g., J. G. Hunt, Sekaran, & Schriesheim, 1982; Peterson & Hunt, 1997). Thus, the definitional antecedent looms increasingly large as we focus on comparative leadership across various societal and organizational cultures (see Figure 2.1). Culture has been shown to be a primary differentiator when we consider "What is leadership?" The GLOBE (Global Leadership and Organizational Behavior Effectiveness) project, based on differences and similarities in 61 countries throughout the world, is by far the most ambitious and comprehensive work revealing similar and different styles of leadership (Den Hartog, House, Hanges, Ruiz-Quintanilla, & Dorfman, 1999).

Some highpoints revealed by a preliminary version of the Den Hartog et al. (1999) GLOBE manuscript convey the project's flavor and reinforce the similar and different findings. A central question in this research was the extent to which specific leadership attributes and behaviors are endorsed universally versus being functions of societal culture.

The authors set out to examine the following specific objectives in their study. First, to what extent are leader behaviors, attributes, and organizational practices universally accepted and effective across cultures versus being accepted and effective in only some cultures? Second, how do attributes of both societal and organizational cultures affect leadership and organizational practices that are accepted and effective? Third, what happens if one violates cultural leadership and organizational practice norms? Fourth, what is the relative standing of each culture on core dimensions of culture identified by the researchers? Finally, can the GLOBE authors develop underlying theory that explains universal and culture-specific aspects of leadership and organizational practices?

The above objectives convey the essence of this broad and in-depth work. Space precludes the listing of the large number of specific findings with regard to the above; however, Den Hartog and Dickson's chapter on culture (Chapter 11, this volume), captures much of this essence as well as including other related work. It is quite clear from such content that both societal and organizational culture loom large in terms of thinking about "What is leadership?"

Leadership and Gender

We conclude the "What is leadership?" example set (Figure 2.1) by considering leadership and gender, a topic that is developed at some length by Eagly and Carli (Chapter 12, this volume). This topic has continued to elicit increasing emphasis as the role of female leaders has become more important in the United States and a number of other developed cultures. Especially salient in terms of understanding "What is leadership?" is the question of women's entry into leadership positions (see Vecchio, 2002). The proportion of women in leadership roles tripled in the last three decades of 2000, the number of female business owners is increasing, and worldwide participation of women in the labor force and in managerial positions has increased (Vecchio, 2002).

Statistics such as these have been accompanied by a considerable number of research studies seeking to find answers to such questions as whether males and females differ in the forms of leader behavior exhibited. Does their effectiveness in managerial positions differ? Do the two groups differ in terms of being followers? Underlying all of the above is the question of whether or not there is a leadership gender advantage. Vecchio (2002) addressed these issues, among others, and concluded that results are inconclusive, largely because of a large number of poor research designs in the field. Unfortunately, one cannot tell from this treatment whether or not leadership truly differs as a function of gender.

A less optimistic picture of women's rise in leadership roles is presented by Eagly and Carli (Chapter 12, this volume). They focused on a number of questions related to what they term "women's underrepresentations in leadership roles." This topic is quite similar to Vecchio's "women's entry into leadership positions," but the questions relating to the topics are quite different. Eagly and Carli report that gender differences exist, but the differences are not large. They argue that gender differences and related issues are more complex than first meet the eye, and both they and Vecchio appear to agree that research designs must be more sophisticated than those that typically have been utilized.

Still another aspect of the focus on gender is epitomizing feminist organizational values (see Calás & Smircich, 1996). A whole feminist literature is based on this view. The argument essentially is that by using feminist theories (e.g., liberal, radical, psychoanalytic, Marxist, socialist, poststructurist/third world postmodern, [post]colonial) as conceptual lenses, a more inclusive study of organizations (and presumably leadership) can be created, one that brings in the concerns of others, not just women, who are directly affected by organizational processes (Calás & Smircich, 1996).

Summary and Conclusions

I started this chapter with a fast-moving description of a small information technology organization's computer-driven simulation, which was intended to enhance interpersonal relations, decision making, and cohesion in a top management cross-functional team. The firm was headed by Greg Warren as its CEO and key member of the cross-functional managerial leadership team involved with the simulation. We followed him as he exerted leadership in many ways and in various places, across time and continents, and contemplated leadership in a complex and realistic simulation emphasizing vision, innovativeness, farsightedness, and the ability to see the big picture. All the while, the CEO was called upon to demonstrate broad-gauged conceptions of leadership through his handling of problems such as the crashing of a system provided by his firm, in-house enterprise resource planning system difficulties, his dealings with subordinates and their interactions with their subordinates and other units and organizations, and his dealings with an international vice president. All these activities were in addition to those called for by the complex, dynamic simulation.

A variation of J. G. Hunt and Dodge's (2000) historical-contextual superstructure perspective was then used to shape readers' thoughts concerning "What is leadership?" It was argued that to decide what leadership is, a superstructure of leadership antecedents and their components is important in influencing one's conceptions of leadership. Thus, the superstructure focused on paradigmatic antecedents, purpose antecedents, definitional antecedents, level-of-analysis and temporal antecedents, and stakeholder antecedents. Then we loosely coupled (Weick, 1976) various aspects of the antecedents to a wide range of illustrative "What is leadership?" example sets drawn from current and earlier literatures.

The argument here is that what connotes leadership to those involved with leadership concerns really is an important function of the various antecedents. These antecedents provide direct linkages to the "What is leadership?" example sets in helping to understand and interpret which aspects of Greg Warren's scenario would be looked at, attended to, and focused on for purposes of research and application. Paradigmatic antecedents would set the stage to be followed by purpose, definitional, level-of-analysis and temporality, and stakeholder antecedents, and the specific leadership aspects would be a function of these. Thus, one could focus on direct, face-to-face, leader-subordinate aspects at one point in time or at one level in the organization, or at an individual level of analysis. In strong contrast, one could consider antecedents and leadership sets that recognized dynamism, shared influence processes, and context—defined in various ways—and involving the embedding of leadership within context in numerous ways. Of course, a wide range of variations between these two extremes could be considered.

Clearly, the treatment of leadership in this chapter and in this book as a whole allows one to answer the "What is leadership?" question in a variety of ways. However, the scenario and my own perspective argue that leadership is contextual, broad-ranging, dynamic, and exciting. Just as Ashby's (1952) law of requisite variety made the point, many years ago, that an organization must be designed to be just complex enough to deal with the complexity of its environment, so too must the treatment of "What is leadership?" example sets be complex enough to deal with the complexity and dynamism of the field as it is reflected today.

Put more precisely, my perspective in focusing on the antecedents and leadership example sets considers the following kinds of emphases to be increasingly important in understanding, researching, and applying leadership concepts:

- One's leadership purpose and definition should be considered explicitly.
- Leadership *of* organizations (e.g., strategic leadership) should be conceptualized differently from leadership *in* organizations (e.g., lower-level, direct leadership).
- The question of whether management should be conceptualized differently from leadership should be considered.
- The history preceding a given leadership issue in question should be recognized: Leadership issues do not spring forth from a vacuum, and history matters.

- The broad organizational and environmental context, within which leadership is embedded, should be emphasized.
- A focus on relational and networking aspects of leadership should be emphasized wherever they are likely to be important; leadership as a shared influence process should be considered, and leadership should not necessarily be restricted to a specialized role definition.
- A dynamic or processual approach should be used, wherever feasible.
- Level of analysis and temporality should be emphasized and recognized as a function of each other.

CHAPTER 3

Methods for Studying Leadership

John Antonakis

Chester A. Schriesheim

Jacqueline A. Donovan

Kishore Gopalakrishna-Pillai

Ekin K. Pellegrini

Jeanne L. Rossomme

U nderstanding and conducting leadership research requires knowledge of research methodology. In this chapter, we provide an overview of important elements relating to the use of research methods and procedures for studying and making inferences about leadership. We anticipate that our chapter will provide readers with useful pointers for conducting and for assessing the quality of leadership research. Apart from a basic review, we also cover some advanced topics (e.g., use of levels of analysis, structural-equation modeling) that should be interesting to researchers and graduate students. Where possible, we have attempted to write the chapter using mostly nontechnical and nonstatistical terminology so that its contents are accessible to a comparatively large audience.

In the sections that follow, first we define science and differentiate it from intuition. Then we discuss the nature of theory and how it is tested and developed. Next, we discuss methods of research, differentiating between quantitative and qualitative modes of inquiry. We also discuss the major categories of research, including experimental and non-experimental methods. Finally, we discuss potential boundary conditions of theories and how boundaries can be detected.

Our Knowledge of the World: Science Versus Intuition

As readers have ascertained from the first two chapters of this book, leadership is a complex concept; however, its complexity does not render it immune from scientific study. To appreciate or conduct research in the field of leadership, one must first understand some fundamentals about science, scientific theories, and the way in which theories are tested.

Science differs from common knowledge in that it is systematic and controlled (Kerlinger & Lee, 2000). Scientists first build theories, then conduct research in a systematic fashion that subjects their theories to controlled empirical testing. Lay or nonscientific persons tend to use theory loosely and to accept theories or explanations that have not been subjected to rigorous testing. Scientists also use controls in an effort to isolate relationships between variables so as to uncover causality and ensure that other presumed causes, as well as chance, have been ruled out. In contrast, lay people tend to accept causal explanations that may be based merely on associations—whether putative, spurious, or actual—between variables. Scientists also discard untestable explanations of phenomena, whereas nonscientists may accept such explanations (Kerlinger & Lee, 2000).

In our day-to-day lives, we are all "commonsense" or "intuitive" psychologists in the sense that, by using data from personal observations or secondary sources, we try to figure out the world and people around us (L. Ross, 1977). In our interactions with the world, we try to make sense of events or causes of outcomes and often use explanations that are intuitively appealing. We all have "theories" about how the world works and "test" these theories daily through our observations. Sometimes our theories are confirmed, either because our theories are correct, because we have created a self-fulfilling prophecy, or perhaps even as a result of chance; other times, we process information consistent with our theories (see S. T. Fiske, 1995; Merton, 1948b). As intuitive psychologists, however, we often are wrong (L. Ross, 1977; Tversky & Kahneman, 1974). We probably are more likely than others to fall prey to our false beliefs in trying to understand the phenomenon of leadership because many of us, as followers or leaders, have experienced leadership first hand. Thus, it is important that we establish our knowledge of the world using the scientific method.

Readers of this book probably would not trust a "witch doctor"—offering a concoction of crushed rhinoceros nose, bat claws, and frog eyes, mixed in python blood—to cure a deadly disease, no matter how much experience or how many satisfied clients the witch doctor may have or claims to have. Readers would rightly expect that a medical treatment has been subjected to rigorous scientific tests to determine whether the treatment is safe and efficacious in fighting a particular illness.

Similarly, one would expect that readers, as users of leadership theory or as consumers of leadership training programs, self-help guides, books, and the like, would select models and methods whose validity has been established. Unfortunately, consumers of leadership products cannot turn to an authority—akin, for example, to the Food and Drug Administration—to determine whether a particular product is "safe for consumption" (i.e., valid). Whether intentionally or unintentionally, producers of leadership products may cut a few corners here or there knowing that there is no administrative body that keeps a watchful eye on what they peddle to unsuspecting consumers. Thus, we believe that the need to understand the methods and procedures used in leadership research is imperative not only for those who study leadership, but for those who consume its products as well.

The Scientific Method

Slife and Williams (1995) stated that the goal of science is to "establish with some authority the causes of events, and provide an understanding of phenomena that is objective and uncontaminated by traditions and subjective speculations" (p. 173). The scientific approach involves four steps (Kerlinger & Lee, 2000). The first is the expression of a problem, obstacle, or idea (e.g., why do some leaders motivate followers better than do other leaders?). In this step, the idea is not refined; it may be vague or based on unscientific "hunches." The second step is the development of conjectural statements about the relationship between two or more phenomena (e.g., behavioral leadership style is associated with motivation for reason X). The next step is the reasoning or deduction step. During this step, the consequences of the conjectural statements are developed. Specifically, the types and results of hypothesized relationships between variables are speculated (e.g., democratic leadership is positively associated to motivation, whereas autocratic leadership is negatively associated with motivation, under conditions Y). The last step includes observation, testing, and experimentation to put the scientist's reasoning to empirical test to determine if the hypothesized relation (or difference) between the variables is statistically probable and not merely attributable to chance (i.e., the scientist measures the leadership styles of the leader and the corresponding degree of motivation in followers to determine if there is a statistically significant relation between leader style and motivation).

Rigorous scientific research adheres to a specific set of standards and guidelines at every step in the process (Filley, House, & Kerr, 1976). The process must be rigorous in order for drawn inferences to be valid. Rigor is defined as "methodology and argument that is systematic, sound, and relatively error free" (Daft, 1984, p. 10). Rigor deals with the process and not the outcome, whereas quality deals with the outcome of the process, which includes the overall contribution of the work and the degree to which findings mirror the real world (Kerlinger & Lee, 2000). There may be a trade-off between the rigor of the process, on one hand, and the real-world contribution and generalizability of the study, on the other. This trade-off occurs because there are many interactions among phenomena in real-world settings, and studying specific, isolated relationships in scientific research may yield findings that do not mirror the relationships that occur in their natural settings. Because adherence to the scientific process creates these types of generalizability issues, this trade-off must be considered when any type of scientific research is planned or evaluated. We revisit this issue later.

What Is Theory?

The creation of theoretical frameworks that can explain a practical phenomenon is the ultimate aim of science (Kerlinger, 1986). Unfortunately, nonscientists may not necessarily have a positive perspective of theory. One often hears definitions of theory that include such phrases as "something that is not testable," "something unproven," "something hypothetical," and "an ideal." These definitions of theory are incorrect. Lewin (1945) once stated, "Nothing is as practical as a good theory" (p. 129). A theory must, therefore, reflect reality and be applicable to practice. If it does not reflect reality, it cannot be applicable to practice; hence, it is not a good theory.

Theories advance our knowledge of social life by "proposing particular concepts (or constructs) that classify and describe [a] phenomenon: then they offer a set of interrelated statements using these concepts" (Pettigrew, 1996, p. 21). Theories are not absolute laws; they are always tentative and are based on probabilities of events occurring (Pettigrew, 1996; see also Popper, K. R. (1965)). According to J. P. Campbell (1990), the functions of theory are to (a) differentiate between important and less important facts, (b) give old data new understanding, (c) identify new and innovative directions, (d) provide for ways to interpret new data, (e) lend an understanding to applied problems, (f) provide a resource for evaluating solutions to applied problems, and (g) provide solutions to previously unsolvable problems.

A theory is a collection of assertions that identify which elements are important in understanding a phenomenon, for what reasons they are important, how they are interrelated, and *under what conditions* (i.e., boundary conditions) the elements should or should not be related (Dubin, 1976). Specifically, Kerlinger (1986) defined theory as being "a set of interrelated constructs (concepts), definitions, and propositions that present a systematic view of phenomena by specifying relations among the variables, with the purpose of explaining and predicting the phenomena" (p. 9). At this point, we should clarify the distinction made between the terms *construct* and *variable* (Bacharach, 1989). A construct cannot be observed directly, whereas a variable can be observed and measured. Based on this distinction, relationships among constructs are set forth by propositions, and relationships among variables are described by hypotheses. A theory thus includes propositions regarding constructs and their hypothesized relations. The consequence of the hypothesized relation, in the form of measured variables and their interrelations (or differences), is what researchers directly test (Kerlinger, 1986). The types of statistical methods to test for relations and differences are briefly introduced later.

Following Filley et al. (1976), we make two distinctions concerning theory: (a) the method of theory development and its implications for testing and (b) the purpose of the theory. Theories may be inductive or deductive (Dubin, 1976). Inductive theories flow from data to abstraction. Here, the emphasis is on theory building, whereby a researcher uses observations, data, or the conclusions and results of other studies to derive testable theoretical propositions. The flow of development is from specific observations to more general theory. Deductive theory focuses on theory testing by beginning with a strong theory base. Deductive theory building flows from abstraction to specific observation; it places the emphasis on testing hypotheses derived from propositions and thus attempts to confirm hypotheses derived from theory.

The second distinction is the purpose of the theory, which may be descriptive or prescriptive. Descriptive theories concern actual states—they describe what "is" or "was." For example, the full-range leadership theory is purported to include nine leadership dimensions, ranging from the passive-avoidant leader to the inspiring and idealized leader, and each of the dimensions is hypothesized to predict certain leader outcomes (see Avolio, 1999; Bass, 1998). In contrast, prescriptive theories are normative and describe what "should occur." For example, Vroom and associates (Vroom & Jago, 1988; Vroom & Yetton, 1973) have developed a normative decision-making model of leadership that suggests which leadership style should be used in certain environmental contingencies. Of course, a descriptive theory also can be prescriptive, and prescriptive theory must be built on a description of sorts. For example, based on empirical studies and theoretical reasoning, Bass (1998) and Avolio (1999) stated that passive-avoidant leadership should be used least often, because it is associated with negative follower outcomes, whereas active and idealized leadership should be used most often.

Filley et al. (1976) developed five evaluative criteria for judging the acceptability of theory. First, a good theory should have internal consistency. That is, it should be free of contradictions. Second, it should be externally consistent. That is, it should be consistent with observations and measures found in the real world (i.e., data). Third, the theory must be testable. The theory must permit evaluation of its components and major predictions. Fourth, the theory must have generality. That is, it must be applicable to a range of similar situations and not just a narrow set of unique circumstances. Finally, a good theory must be parsimonious. A simple explanation of a phenomenon is preferred over a more complex one.

Hypotheses

Once a theory and its propositions have been developed, it needs to be tested for external consistency. To do this, constructs need to be associated with measured variables (i.e., empirical indicators), and propositions must be converted into testable hypotheses. A hypothesis is a conjectural statement about one or more variables that can be tested empirically. Variables are defined as observable elements that are capable of assuming two or more values (Schwab, 1980). Whereas variables, as manifest indicators, are observable, constructs are not directly observable (Maruyama, 1998). Hypotheses are the working instruments of theory because they help the scientist disconfirm (or fail to disconfirm) a theory by not supporting (or supporting) predictions that are drawn from it.

Good hypotheses must contain variables that are measurable (i.e., that can assume certain values on a categorical or continuous scale) and must be testable (Kerlinger & Lee, 2000). Hypotheses should not be in the form of a question. For example, "Does leader supportiveness have an effect on group performance?" is not testable and therefore is not a hypothesis but instead a research question, which may be valuable for guiding research per se. An acceptable hypothesis would be that "Leader supportiveness is positively associated with group performance." Furthermore, hypotheses should not contain value statements such as "should," "must," "ought to," and "better than." Finally, hypotheses should not be too general or too specific. If they are too vague and general, they cannot be tested. If they are too specific, research findings may not be generalizable and therefore may make less important substantive contributions to knowledge.

Theory Development

The process of developing a good theory involves four steps (Dubin, 1976). The first step is the selection of elements whose relationships are of interest (e.g., the relation between leader style and follower motivation). All relevant elements should be included in the theory, but those that may be viewed as extraneous should be left out.

Once the above elements are chosen, the second step is to specify how the elements are related. In particular, what impact do the elements have on one another? In this step, specific relationships must be articulated (e.g., democratic leadership is positively associated with motivation).

The third step specifies the assumptions of the theory. These include justifications for the theory's elements and the relationships among them. The step also involves the specification of boundary conditions within which the elements interact and are constrained (Dubin, 1969). The boundary conditions set forth the circumstances to which the theory may be generalized and are necessary because no theory is without boundaries. Bacharach (1989) noted that theories are bounded by the implicit values of the theorist, as well as by space and time boundaries. Boundaries refer to the limits of the theory; that is, the conditions under which the predictions of the theory hold (Dubin, 1976). The more general a theory is, the less bounded it is (Bacharach, 1989).

To revisit our democratic-autocratic example, a potential boundary could be national culture or risk conditions. That is, in some cultural contexts, autocratic leadership may be more prevalent because of large power differentials between those who have power (e.g., leaders) and those who do not (e.g., followers). Thus, in that context (i.e., boundary), the nature of the relation between a leader's style and follower motivation changes, and we may find that autocratic leadership is positively related to motivation. Thus, cultural context can be referred to as a moderator of leadership effectiveness but also as a contextual factor affecting the type of leadership that may emerge, as we will discuss later.

In the fourth step, there must be specification of the system states in which the theory operates. A system state is "a condition of the system being modeled in which the units of that system take on characteristic values that have a persistence through time, regardless of the length of time interval" (Dubin, 1976, p. 24). In other words, the system states refer to the values that are exhibited by units constituting the theoretical system and the implications associated with those values.

Methods of Research

Qualitative and Quantitative Distinctions

According to F. Williams (1992), there are two major methodological research traditions: qualitative and quantitative methods. Quantitative methods should be utilized when the phenomenon under study needs to be measured, when hypotheses need to be tested, when generalizations are required to be made of the measures, and when generalizations need to be made that are beyond chance occurrences. As noted by Williams, "if measures are not apparent or if researchers cannot develop them with confidence, then quantitative methods are not appropriate to the problem" (p. 6). Thus, choice of which approach to use will depend on a number of factors.

Leadership researchers typically have used quantitative approaches; however, to better understand complex, embedded phenomena, qualitative approaches to studying leadership are also necessary (see Alvesson, 1996; Bryman, Stephens, & Campo, 1996; Conger, 1998). However, "qualitative studies remain relatively rare . . . [and should be] the methodology of choice for topics as contextually rich as leadership" (Conger, 1998, p. 107). Given the contextual and complex nature of leadership, it is important that qualitative methods—as a theory-generating approach—complement quantitative methods, whose strengths are in theory testing. The reasons for using qualitative methods to study contextually rich and holistically embedded phenomena are discussed below.

Quantitative approaches to scientific inquiry generally rely on testing theoretical propositions, as previously discussed, in regard to the scientific method. Contrarily, qualitative approaches focus on "building a complex, holistic picture, formed with words, reporting detailed views of informants, and conducted in a natural setting" (Creswell, 1994, p. 2). A qualitative study focuses on meanings as they relate in context. Lincoln and Guba (1985), referred to the qualitative approach as a post-positivist [i.e., postquantitative] *naturalistic inquiry* method of inquiry. Unlike the positivist, the naturalist "imposes no a priori units on the outcome" (Lincoln & Guba, 1985, p. 8).

Lincoln and Guba (1985) also argued that positivism constrains the manner in which science is conceptualized, is limited in terms of theory building, relies too much on operationalizing, ignores meanings and contexts, and attempts to reduce phenomena to universal principles. Lincoln and Guba stated that the weakness of the positivist approach includes the assumption that phenomena can be broken down and studied independently, while ignoring the whole. Moreover, the distancing of the researcher from what is being researched, the assumption that sampling observations in different temporal and spatial dimensions can be invariant, and the assumption that the method is value free further limit this approach. Lastly, Lincoln and Guba stated that instead of internal and external validity, reliability, and objectivity, naturalists strive for credibility, transferability, dependability, and confirmability of results.

Qualitative research has often been criticized for being biased. Because qualitative analysis is constructive in nature, the data can be used to construct the reality that the researcher wishes to see—thus creating a type of self-fulfilling prophecy stemming from expectancy-based information processing. The result, therefore, may be in "the eye of the beholder," in a manner of speaking. That is, the observer may see evidence when he or she is looking for it, even though contrary evidence also is present (see S. T. Fiske, 1995). Thus, special controls—or triangulation— must be used to ensure that results converge from different types or sources of evidence (Maxwell, 1996; Stake, 1995; Yin, 1994).

As can be seen from the above discussion, qualitative and quantitative paradigms of research differ on a number of assumptions, and the selection of qualitative over quantitative approaches will depend entirely on the purpose and nature of the inquiry (Creswell, 1994). Similar to quantitative methods, qualitative methods employ a variety of techniques to acquire knowledge and may include (Creswell, 1994): (a) ethnographies, in which a cultural group is studied over a period of time; (b) grounded theory, where data are continually used, categorized, and refined to inform a theory; (c) case studies, in which a single bounded case or multiple cases are explored using a variety of data-gathering techniques; and (d) phenomenological studies, which examine human experiences and their meanings. Qualitative research also can include the active participation of the researcher in an intervention, a practice normally labeled as participatory action research (Greenwood & Levin, 1998; W. F. Whyte, 1991).

For some specific examples relating qualitative and quantitative research-gathering methods for leadership research, refer to Kroeck, Lowe, and Brown (Chapter 4, this volume). Because the vast majority of research that is conducted in the leadership domain is quantitative in nature and because theory can be tested appropriately only with quantitative methods, we will focus the rest of the chapter on the quantitative paradigm and its associated methods.

Categories of Research

Kerlinger (1986) stated that although a large part of research using the scientific method was generally experimental in nature, much research nowadays in the behavioral sciences involves non-experimental research. Because there are many possible causes for behavior, Kerlinger argued that the most dangerous fallacy in science is the *"post hoc, ergo propter hoc* [fallacy]: after this, therefore caused by this" (p. 347). This fallacy is most likely to occur in non-experimental conditions; that is, conditions in which the scientist does not have control over the independent variables "because their manifestations have already occurred or because they are inherently not manipulable. Inferences about relations among variables are made, without direct intervention, from concomitant variation of independent and dependent variables" (p. 348). Based on the above distinction between experimental and non-experimental research Kerlinger (1986) classified research into four major categories or types, namely (a) laboratory experiments, (b) field experiments, (c) field studies, and (d) survey research.

Laboratory Experiments

According to Kerlinger (1986), laboratory experiments are useful for manipulating independent measures in an isolated situation, thus yielding precise and accurate measures. Variables are studied in pure and uncontaminated conditions, because participants are assigned randomly to groups to ensure that the resultant variance in dependent outcomes is accounted for by the independent measures. Laboratory experiments are useful for testing predictions and for refining theories and hypotheses. Kerlinger, however, noted that some disadvantages exist in laboratory experiments; namely that the effect of the independent measures may be weak because they do not exist in real-life conditions or have been artificially created. Thus, the results of a laboratory experiment may not be generalizable to real-life situations and may lack external validity even though they have high internal validity.

Binning, Zaba, and Whattam (1986), for example, experimentally manipulated group performance cues (i.e., indicators of effectiveness) to determine whether they influenced ratings of the group's leader. Binning et al. exposed subjects to a video of a problem-solving group and then obtained ratings of the leader's behavior and effectiveness under either good or bad group performance cues. They found that leader behavior and global effectiveness ratings were susceptible to performance cues, especially leader behavior that was not richly described (i.e., for which raters did not have sufficient information to construct an accurate schema). Thus, important here is the identification of the conditions (i.e., low information conditions) under which ratings are susceptible to performance-cue effects.

A second example is a study by J. M. Howell and Frost (1989), who experimentally manipulated three leadership styles using trained confederate leaders (i.e., individuals working for the researcher) and who exposed participants to either a high or low productivity group, also including confederates. Their results showed that participants working under a charismatic leader generally had better work outcomes and were more satisfied than were participants under a considerate or structuring leader. Furthermore, followers under charismatic leaders were equally influenced irrespective of group productivity standards. An important element of this study is that leader charisma was manipulated in a laboratory setting.

Laboratory studies thus can provide valuable insights about leader processes and perceptions and are particularly useful for studying research from many perspectives (e.g., information processing, trait, behavioral, contingency). Indeed, laboratory studies of leadership have been conduced as far back as the 1930s (e.g., Lewin & Lippitt, 1938) to assess the impact of leadership behavioral style (e.g., democratic, autocratic). However, according to D. J. Brown and Lord (1999), leadership researchers, especially from the "new leadership" paradigm, have not yet made full use of experimental methods. They argued that nonconscious information-processing functions—integral to how leaders are legitimized and how followers perceive leaders—can be studied only in controlled laboratory settings. Furthermore, Brown and Lord stated that laboratory research is useful for studying unique interactions of independent variables and for untangling the unique effects of highly correlated leader dimensions that are not easily distinguishable in the field because of their co-occurrence.

Field Experiments

Kerlinger (1986) defined a field experiment as a study that occurs in a real setting in which both the independent variables and group assignment are under the control of the researcher. The degree of control that the researcher has in comparison to laboratory conditions is less, suggesting that other independent variables that are not under the control of the researcher may have a bearing on the dependent measures. Like laboratory experiments, field experiments are useful for testing theory and are applicable to studying leadership from many points of view; however, because field experiments occur in real settings, they are also useful for finding answers to practical problems. Similar to laboratory studies, field experiments unfortunately are not very common in leadership domain. We discuss two examples below, focusing on the effects of leadership training interventions.

In a field experiment, Barling, Weber, and Kelloway (1996) demonstrated that training interventions can change managers' leadership styles (including their charisma), resulting in increased organizational commitment of subordinates (i.e., a subjective dependent measure) and improved organizational financial outcomes (i.e., an objective dependent measure). In another example, using a military sample, Dvir, Eden, Avolio, and Shamir (2002) tested the efficacy of a leadership training intervention on leaders' direct and indirect followers. They found that transformational leadership training had a more positive effect on direct follower development and on indirect follower performance than did eclectic leadership training. A major implication of these studies is that leadership can be taught through interventions by making leaders aware of their leadership style as they and others perceive it and by facilitating a learning and goal-setting process conducive to the development of a more effective leadership style.

Field Studies

According to Kerlinger (1986), field studies are non-experimental, occur in real-life situations, and attempt to discover important variables and their inter-relationship by studying "the relations among the attitudes, values, perceptions, and behaviors of individuals and groups in the situation" (p. 372). The major weakness of field studies is that the researcher has no control over the independent variables and, hence, the variance that is exhibited in the outcome measures. As with laboratory and field experiments, many types of research questions can be answered using this type of research.

For example, Atwater, Dionne, Avolio, Camobreco, and Lau (1999) linked individual characteristics of military cadets to their leadership effectiveness/emergence both cross-sectionally (i.e., at one point in time) and longitudinally (i.e., where subjects were tracked over a period of time—another rarity in leadership research). As regards to the longitudinal results, they found that measures of physical fitness and prior leadership experience (measured at Year 1) were significantly associated with leader effectiveness and emergence (measured at Year 4). These results suggest that the potential to lead can be predicted using individual-difference measures.

Bass, Avolio, Jung, and Berson (2003) studied the relations between the leadership style (i.e., transformational or transactional leadership, or nonleadership) of military commanders and the simulated performance of their units. Leadership style of platoon lieutenants and sergeants was measured several weeks before their units participated in a training simulation. Bass et al. found that the leadership styles of the lieutenants and the sergeants were significantly associated with platoon performance in the field and that the impact of the leadership styles was partially mediated by the potency and cohesion of the platoon.

Survey Research

Researchers use survey research to determine the characteristics of a population so that inferences about populations can be made. Surveys generally focus on "the vital facts of people, and their beliefs, opinions, attitudes, motivations, and behavior" (Kerlinger, 1986, p. 378) and generally are cross-sectional in nature. Data for surveys can be gathered in a number of ways, including in-person interviews, mail questionnaires, telephone surveys, and the Internet. Survey research is practical to use because it is cheap and relatively easy to conduct. Although this type of research is limited by the questionnaire or interview format used, it can be quite useful if properly designed. Survey methods have been used to answer many types of research questions emanating from all leadership perspectives. Indeed, the leadership field is replete with survey research; thus, in the interest of saving space, we do not list any studies here (refer to Kroeck et al., Chapter 4, this volume, for examples of survey instruments).

In conclusion, the type of research used will depend on the type of research questions to be answered. For example, if a researcher wishes to determine whether there is cross-situational consistency in individuals' leadership styles and whether certain traits are predictive of leadership in different situations, then that researcher would be advised to use rotation designs, similar to those used by Kenny and Zaccaro (1983) and Zaccaro, Foti, and Kenny (1991), in which leaders' situational conditions (e.g., group composition and task demands) vary (refer to Zaccaro, Kemp, & Bader, Chapter 5, this volume, for further discussion of these studies). The remaining chapters in this book—especially those in Part III—provide interesting examples of the different types of research methods used.

Research Design and Validity Issues

The design of a study is integrally linked to the type of research used. There are three important facets of design (see Kerlinger, 1986). First, the design should ensure that the research question is answered. Second, the design should control for extraneous variables, which are independent variables not intended to be measured by the study that may have an effect on the dependent variables. This is referred to as internal validity. Third, the study should be able to generalize its results to a certain extent to other subjects in other conditions; that is, it should have some bearing on theory. This may also be referred to as external validity. Thus, Kerlinger stated that congruence must exist between the research problem and the design, what is to be measured, the analysis, and the inferences to be drawn from the results (refer also to Cook, Campbell, & Peracchio, 1990, for issues relating to validity). By adequately taking the above points into account in the planning stages of research, the researcher increases the likelihood of drawing accurate inferences and conclusions about the nature of the problem investigated. This is because the design dictates what is to be observed, how it is to be observed, and how the data must be analyzed.

As suggested previously, external validity may be an issue with experiments; however, according to C. A. Anderson, Lindsay, and Bushman (1999), the external validity threats of experiments are exaggerated, given that findings in laboratory and field settings generally converge. To avoid problems associated with external validity, researchers should draw from a sampling frame that is representative of the population and control as well as possible the level of artificiality, recognizing that some artificiality may be inherent in laboratory experiments. Furthermore, the researcher must ensure that the experimental manipulation has had the required effect (i.e., the manipulation was perceived as intended). A manipulation check usually is used to address this issue.

As for non-experimental research, causation is an important caveat. One of the dicta of scientific research is that correlation does not imply causation. Furthermore, typical of survey methods is the assessment of two variables that are intended to represent different constructs, with the data gathered using the same method from the same source (e.g., a self-report questionnaire) (see Avolio, Yammarino, & Bass, 1991). The observed relationship between the variables may be attributable to a true relationship between the constructs or to bias resulting from the use of a common source and a common data collection method. This issue has long been of concern to psychologists (D. T. Campbell & Fiske, 1959; D. W. Fiske, 1982), particularly with respect to self-report measures (Sackett & Larson, 1990).

Finally, there are other ways in which to go about doing research, which cannot be described by the four categories of research discussed above but which can shed interesting perspectives on the study of leadership. As an example, the analysis of historical data, which is not traditionally used in applied psychological settings and which is usually associated with the qualitative research paradigm (e.g., case studies) (see Yin, 1994), cannot be placed in the above classification scheme. Refer to Simonton (2003) for a discussion on the quantitative and qualitative analyses of historical data, and to House, Spangler, and Woycke (1991) for an example in leadership research.

Methods of Statistical Analysis

Analytical techniques (e.g., regression analysis) are nothing more than tools by which the researcher is able to test and refine research hypotheses and, subsequently, theories. The hypotheses and characteristics of the data should drive the types of analysis conducted, not vice versa. Readers who have not had a thorough introduction to statistics and psychometrics should consult one of the many available books (see, e.g., Nunnally & Bernstein, 1994; Sharma, 1996; Tabachnik & Fidell, 2001). Briefly, there are three major classes of methods: (a) *dependence methods* of analysis, which are used in order to test the presence and strength of an effect; (b) *interdependence methods*, which are used to determine relationships between variables and the information they contain; and (c) *structural-equation models*, which are the newest generation of analytical techniques useful for testing complex models of both presumed cause and effect that include latent/unobserved variables and the effects of measurement error. Structural-equation modeling (SEM) is based on, and simultaneously uses principles of, path analysis, regression analysis, and factor analysis. It is thus a very powerful and flexible statistical methodology for testing theoretical frameworks (see Bollen, 1989; Kline, 1998; Maruyama, 1998). Applications of SEM in leadership are discussed below.

Context and the Boundary
Conditions of Leadership Theories

The context in which leadership is enacted has not received much attention, leading House and Aditya (1997) to state that "it is almost as though leadership scholars . . . have believed that leader-follower relationships exist in a vacuum" (p. 445). Further calls have been made to integrate context into the study of leadership (Lowe & Gardner, 2000) and organizational behavior (Johns, 2001; Rousseau & Fried, 2001). Context constrains the variability that potentially can be measured (Rousseau & Fried, 2001), is linked to the type of leadership that is considered as being prototypically effective (Lord, Brown, Harvey, & Hall, 2001), and determines the dispositional antecedents of effective leadership (Zaccaro, 2001).

Zaccaro and Klimoski (2001) argued that "unlike the situation as a moderator [as in contingency theories of leadership], we view situation or context as boundary conditions for theory building and model specification" (p. 13). According to R. M. Baron and Kenny (1986), a moderator is a categorical or continuous "variable that affects the direction and/or strength of the relation between an independent or predictor variable and a dependent or criterion variable" (p. 1174). Thus, in addition to finding moderators that alter the strength or the direction of a relationship between an independent (e.g., leader behavior) and dependent (e.g., leader outcomes) variable, situations also could be conceived as range restrictors of the types of independent variables that emerge. In other words, context should be considered in attempts to understand how phenomena like leadership emerge, and not only the extent to which or how context may affect the strength of relations between independent (e.g., leadership) and dependent (e.g., organizational effectiveness) variables (see Shamir & Howell, 1999).

In striving to generalize phenomena, leadership researchers often overlook context and draw incorrect conclusions about how a phenomenon is modeled (Antonakis, Avolio, & Sivasubramaniam, 2003). For example, a leadership model (e.g., the transformational, transactional, and laissez-faire models) may be universal in the sense that the constructs of which it is composed can be measured across different contexts; however, if the phenomenon is by nature contextually sensitive (i.e., leader prototypes and expected behaviors vary by context), the phenomenon may "work" in a similar manner only when sampling units are homogeneous and not when sampling units are heterogeneous (Antonakis, Avolio, et al., 2003). In other words, the emergence and enactment of a behavior may vary by context, which includes the following, among others:

1. National culture—some leader behaviors and their enactment may be universal or may vary systemically as a function of national culture (e.g., refer to Den Hartog & Dickson, Chapter 11, this volume; see also Brodbeck et al., 2000; Hofstede, 1980; Koopman et al., 1999; Meade, 1967).

2. Hierarchical leader level—leadership differs qualitatively depending on whether leadership is exercised at a high (e.g., strategic) or low (e.g., supervisory) hierarchical level (e.g., refer to Sashkin, Chapter 8, this volume; see also Antonakis & Atwater, 2002; D. J. Brown & Lord, 2001; J. G. Hunt, 1991; House & Aditya, 1997; Lord, Brown, Harvey, et al., 2001; Lowe, Kroeck, & Sivasubramaniam, 1996; Sashkin, 1988a; Waldman & Yammarino, 1999; Zaccaro, 2001; Zaccaro & Klimoski, 2001).

3. Organizational characteristics—organizational stability, organizational structure (e.g., bureaucratic vs. organic environments), and so forth affect the type of leadership that may be necessary (refer to Brown, Scott, & Lewis, Chapter 6, this volume; see also Antonakis & House, 2002; Avolio, 1999; Bass, 1998; Lord & Emrich, 2000).

4. Leader and/or follower gender—leader behaviors may vary systematically as a function of leader gender or follower gender because of gender-role expectations and other factors (refer to Eagly & Carli, Chapter 12, this volume; see also Eagly & Johnson, 1990; Lord, Brown, Harvey, et al., 2001).

5. Leadership mediated by electronic means (i.e., e-leadership; see Avolio, Kahai, & Dodge, 2001; Avolio, Kahai, Dumdum, & Sivasubramaniam, 2001; see also Antonakis & Atwater, 2002; Shamir, 1999; Shamir & Ben-Ari, 1999)—the nature of the influence process may vary in conditions where leaders and followers are not face-to-face.

Types of leader behaviors that are enacted may vary as a function of context; however, so may the dispositional (i.e., leader characteristics) antecedents linked to those behaviors. For example, cognitive requirements differ as a function of leader hierarchical level (Zaccaro, 2001; see also Zaccaro et al., Chapter 5, this volume, and Sashkin, Chapter 8, this volume). Finally, the level of analysis at which a leadership phenomenon may hold will also vary by context (Antonakis & Atwater, 2002; Waldman & Yammarino, 1999). That is, the level at which leadership operates may vary from individual to group, or organizational level, depending on the context (e.g., CEO-level vs. supervisory-level leadership) in which it is enacted.

It thus becomes evident that researchers need to consider contextual factors and levels of analysis in theory development and measurement (see Antonakis, Avolio, et al., 2003; Dansereau, Alutto, & Yammarino, 1984; Schriesheim, Castro, Zhou, & Yammarino, 2001; Zaccaro & Klimoski, 2001) and then use the appropriate methods to gauge these factors and levels (i.e., boundaries). This perspective should complement traditional notions of context, in which context is seen as a moderator of the relation between leader characteristics (e.g., traits, behaviors) and leader outcomes.

The Detection of Boundary Conditions of Theories

How are boundary conditions of theories detected? In this section, we discuss four quantitative approaches that are useful in detecting moderators or contextual factors, which can be considered as boundary conditions of theories (see James, Mulaik, & Brett, 1982). For each of the four methods discussed below (i.e., levels of analysis, structural-equation modeling, moderated regression, and meta-analysis), we provide relevant examples from the leadership literature to which readers may refer. We do not cover interaction effects—as in traditional factorial ANOVA designs, which are useful for the detection of moderation (see R. M. Baron & Kenny, 1986), especially in experimental designs—because we assume that most readers are familiar with the technique. In our discussions below, we focus extensively on levels-of-analysis issues, because many, if not most, researchers in psychology and management generally ignore levels-of-analysis concerns. We also extensively discuss structural-equation modeling, a very powerful but underutilized statistical method in leadership research.

Levels of Analysis

In recent years, level of analysis has emerged as an important issue in organizational research (e.g., Klein, Dansereau, & Hall, 1994; Rousseau, 1985). Organizations are inherently multilevel, because individuals work in dyads and groups. Furthermore, several groups or departments make up an organization, organizations make up an industry, and so on. Few, if any, constructs are inherently restricted to one level of analysis. Typically, constructs may operate at one or more levels, such as individuals, dyads, groups, departments, organizations, and industries (Rousseau, 1985).

Thus, it is now increasingly recognized that good theory should also specify the level of analysis at which its phenomena operate (see Dansereau, Alutto, et al., 1984), because level of analysis can be conceived as a boundary condition of a theory (Dubin, 1976). Levels of analysis might even be considered as a sixth criterion that should be assessed when one considers a theory's adequacy (in addition to Filley et al.'s, 1976, original five criteria discussed previously).

Levels of analysis make studying leadership in organizations very complex because leadership phenomena may operate on any or all levels. Consider, for example, performance. This variable can be examined on an individual, dyadic, group, departmental, organizational, or industry level. The specification and testing of the levels at which constructs of a theory operate is therefore important because research conclusions may differ as a function of the level of analysis that is employed (Dansereau, Alutto, et al., 1984; Klein et al., 1994).

The correlates or causes of individual performance may be very different from the correlates or causes of group or organizational performance. Because obtained results may vary depending on the level at which the data are analyzed, erroneous conclusions can be drawn if the level tested is incongruent with the level specified by a theory (Dansereau, Alutto, et al., 1984; W. H. Glick, 1985). These erroneous conclusions include, among others, ecological fallacies (i.e., using aggregated data to make inferences about individuals) or individualistic fallacies (i.e., using individual-level data to make inferences about groups; see Pedhazur, 1997, for examples) and other types of misspecifications (Rousseau, 1985).

A recent special issue of *Leadership Quarterly* (2002, Vol. 13, No. 1) highlighted problems of failing to take levels into account. For example, a data set purposefully analyzed at the individual level of analysis using regression techniques failed to detect a moderation effect of leadership climate on task significance of followers, because the moderation effect did not operate at the individual level of analysis (Bliese, Halverson, & Schriesheim, 2002). However, when using various methods designed to test for multilevel effects, evidence of a moderator (i.e., leadership climate) was evident (see Bliese & Halverson, 2002; Gavin & Hofmann, 2002; Markham & Halverson, 2002) and leadership climate exhibited group-level affects that were ignored by other methods.

Thus, if theory, analysis, and measurement level are not correctly specified and aligned, "we may wind up erecting theoretical skyscrapers on foundations of empirical jello" (Schriesheim, Castro, Zhou, et al., 2001, p. 516). For example, if a leader's behavior—as perceived by followers—is not homogeneously viewed by followers, then the leader's behavior operates at the individual level of analysis. Therefore, any inferences that are made should be based on the individual and use individual-level data, because individual responses are independent. However, if the leader's behavior is viewed homogeneously, then it is justifiable to aggregate the individual data to the group level and make inferences at the group level of analysis, because individual responses are dependent on group membership.

There are several examples of leadership research incorporating levels-of-analysis perspectives. However, in leadership research only a small group of researchers have used methods developed to test levels-of-analysis effects. We cite three examples below of levels-of-analysis perspectives regarding leadership theories and show that consideration of the boundary condition of levels leads to better theories that are more applicable to practice. Although there is now a broader range of researchers testing theories using multilevel methods, we stress that there is *still insufficient attention paid to levels-of-analysis* issues by mainstream leadership, organizational behavior, and management researchers.

In the first example, Yammarino (1990) demonstrated that correlations between leader behavior and outcome variables may exhibit differential levels-of-analysis effects. For instance, the correlation between a leader's group-directed initiating-structure behavior and role ambiguity perceptions of followers may be valid at the individual level of analysis; however, the correlation between a leader's group-directed consideration behavior and role ambiguity perceptions of followers may be valid at the group level of analysis. The practical implications of such results suggest that leaders enact their initiating-structure behaviors in an individualized manner with respect to follower role ambiguity (because individual perceptions of these behaviors are not homogeneously held by followers). In contrast, when follower perceptions with an outcome (e.g., role ambiguity) are homogeneous, then the leader can enact group-wide behaviors. Yammarino (1990) also demonstrated that raw (i.e., total) correlations may be ambiguous because correlations of similar magnitudes may have different levels of analysis effects. Finally, Yammarino's study is notable for showing that wording questions in a way that uses the group as a referent does not ensure that the group will be the resulting level of analysis. This finding has implications for question or item design.

In the second example, Schriesheim, Castro, Zhou, et al. (2001) argued that although leader-member exchange (LMX) theory was originally conceived of as being a dyadic theory (i.e., that the level of analysis is the leader-follower dyad), current conceptualizations of the theory basically ignore the theory's dyadic roots and generally analyze LMX data either from the leaders' or followers' perspectives. Unfortunately, the theory is still not well understood, because level-of-analysis effects associated with the theory have hardly been tested (Schriesheim, Castro, & Cogliser, 1999; Schriesheim, Castro, Zhou, et al., 2001). After testing the levels-of-analysis effects of the theory, Schriesheim, Castro, Zhou, et al. (2001) found relatively strong support for the dyadic nature of the theory, a finding with important implications for data gathering and analysis practices. That is, matching data (i.e., using both followers and corresponding leaders) should be collected, and levels-of-analysis effects should be examined on the dyadic relation (while ruling out competing levels). Until we have more research that tests the level of analysis at which the theory is valid, "all the extant [LMX] research is fundamentally uninformative" (Schriesheim, Castro, Zhou, et al., 2001, p. 525).

In the third example, Yammarino and Dubinsky (1994) showed that even though the literature explicitly or implicitly asserted that transformational leadership would be evident at a higher level of analysis than the individual level, empirical data suggest that most of the effects are evident at the individual level of analysis. That is, "what one individual perceives differs from what others perceive" (Yammarino & Dubinsky, 1994, p. 805), even though these individuals may be perceiving the same social object (i.e., their leader). These results have been demonstrated repeatedly (e.g., Yammarino & Bass, 1990; Yammarino, Spangler, & Dubinsky, 1998), suggesting that transformational (and transactional) leaders have differential effects on followers and that they do not cause similar outcomes in groups of followers (refer to Antonakis & Atwater, 2002, for theoretical arguments concerning when level of analysis may be expected to change).

Multilevel Analysis Methods. There are many ways in which one can test for levels effects, from whether it is appropriate to aggregate data to a higher level of analysis (e.g., aggregating a group of followers' ratings of a leader) to partitioning variance in outcome measures (i.e., determining the extent to which outcomes are accounted for by various independent variables). We briefly discuss four statistical procedures that are useful for conducting research at multiple levels of analysis. For more technical discussions regarding the strengths and weaknesses of the procedures, refer to Castro, (2002), George and James (1993), Schriesheim (1995), Yammarino (1998), and Yammarino and Markham (1992).

The r_{wg} coefficient (James, Demaree, & Wolf, 1984) was developed primarily as an index of interrater agreement within a single group (Castro, 2002). As such, it is useful to determine whether responses of group members can be aggregated to the group level; however, it is less useful for making comparisons between groups (i.e., to determine whether variability exists between groups) because it was not designed to perform such a function (see Castro, 2002; Yammarino & Markham, 1992). Thus, it may be more lenient than the other aggregation-testing methods discussed below.

Intraclass correlation coefficients (ICCs) are useful for determining the extent to which variance of individual responses is attributed to group membership and whether means of groups are reliably differentiated (see Bliese, Halverson, et al., 2002; Castro, 2002). Thus, by design, ICCs may be more generally useful than is r_{wg}, especially if between-group variability is theoretically important and requires detailed examination.

Within and between analysis (WABA) assess the extent to which variables—and their covariation—exhibit variation within or between groups by testing the within- and between-group variation for statistical and practical significance (Dansereau, Alutto, et al., 1984). WABA should be used when the assumption for aggregating to a higher level requires testing, especially if between-group variation is theoretically important (see Yammarino, Dubinsky, Comer, & Jolson, 1997). WABA also can be used to test certain types of cross-level effects (Castro, 2002; Yammarino, 1998).

WABA has been criticized for being too conservative, especially in situations where range restrictions may exist between groups. For example, in many of the studies cited previously that used WABA (e.g., Yammarino & Bass, 1990; Yammarino & Dubinsky, 1994; Yammarino, Spangler, et al., 1998) and found individual-level effects for leadership, sampling units were restricted to the same or similar contexts. Thus, it is possible that because of similar between-group contextual conditions and the resulting range restriction that occurs, higher levels of analysis effects were attenuated and thus not detected by WABA (see George & James, 1993; Schriesheim, 1995). Therefore, one must very carefully choose heterogeneous sampling units if one is looking for between-group differences (Yammarino & Markham, 1992). Practically speaking, though, as an omnibus test, WABA is particularly useful for determining the extent of within-group homogeneity, whether higher-level relations are evident, and whether higher-level entities are useful as predictors of outcome variables (Schriesheim, 1995; Yammarino, 1998).

Hierarchical linear modeling (HLM) is a regression-based procedure useful for testing relationships that exists at different levels of analysis (i.e., cross-level hierarchical relationships) (Hofmann, 1997). Specifically, HLM can estimate different sources of variance in dependent variables attributable to independent variables at the same or higher level of analysis and can be used for detecting cross-level moderators (Castro, 2002; Gavin & Hofmann, 2002). HLM does not test whether it is appropriate to aggregate data at a higher level of analysis (Castro, 2002; Hofmann, 1997; Yammarino, Dubinsky, et al., 1997). Thus, HLM should be complemented by other procedures designed to test whether aggregation is appropriate (Castro, 2002). For extensions of HLM-type procedures using structural-equation modeling (i.e., MLM or multilevel modeling), refer to Heck and Thomas (2000).

Structural-Equation Modeling

Multiple-groups structural-equation modeling (SEM) can be useful for the detection of moderators (R. M. Baron & Kenny, 1986; James, Mulaik, et al., 1982; Kline, 1998). Although this is a potentially powerful and useful procedure, unfortunately, it is "not used all that frequently . . . in social science literature" (Maruyama, 1998, p. 257) and in leadership research in particular. Indeed, we found it difficult to locate a good example (see Dorfman, Howell, Hibino, Lee, Tate & Bautista, 1997) of the procedure in the leadership literature.

Essentially, the question asked in this type of analysis is "Does group membership moderate the relations specified in the model[?]" (Kline, 1998, p. 181). In this type of analysis, one is thus interested in testing whether structural parameters are equivalent across groups. For example, one can test whether the relation between an independent variable (e.g., leader behavior) and an outcome factor (e.g., follower motivation) is the same across groups. In this case, the grouping variable is the moderator. If the constraint of equivalence in the parameter does not result in a significant decrement in model fit, then one can conclude that group membership does not moderate the relation between the independent and dependent variable (Kline, 1998). If, however, the fit of the constrained model is significantly worse, then one can conclude that the grouping variable moderates the particular structural relation (Kline, 1998).

Using the procedures discussed above, Dorfman, Howell, Hibino, et al. (1997) found that the relations between leader behaviors and leader outcomes varied when using several national cultures as moderator groups (for further discussion of their results, refer to Den Hartog & Dickson, Chapter 11, this volume). Note that in this example, the moderator variable was a grouping factor (i.e., a categorical variable).

However, interaction effects using continuous moderator variables also can be specified in SEM (see Kenny & Judd, 1984).

On a more basic level, SEM also is useful for determining whether constructs are equivalent across theoretically distinct groups (e.g., based on national culture). There are various degrees of equivalence or invariance. For example, one can determine whether the same indicators for a factor are associated in the same way across groups (i.e., factor pattern loadings are the same). This condition is referred to as configural invariance (Vandenberg & Lance, 2000). Establishing configural invariance is absolutely critical so that further tests between groups can be conducted, because if the factors are not associated with the same indicators, then the "respondent groups were [not] employing the same conceptual frame of reference" with respect to how the factor is perceived (Vandenberg & Lance, 2000, p. 37). Once configural invariance is established, further intergroup restrictions can be placed to determine if the model fit becomes significantly worse based on the chi-squared difference test (i.e., likelihood ratio test between the configural condition and the more restrictive condition). An example of a study in which a configural invariance condition was tested is that of Gillespie (2002), who found that a 360-degree leadership feedback survey did not satisfy the criteria for configural invariance across four cultures. This result suggests that the raters in the various countries conceptualized the factors in different ways, indicating that further cross-country comparisons on the factors would be unwarranted.

A more stringent condition of equivalence is metric invariance, which, if found, suggests that a unit change in the factor can affect the indicators in the same way across different groups (Vandenberg & Lance, 2000). If metric invariance is found, one is confident that the loadings of the respective indicators of the factor are equivalent between groups (e.g., see Dorfman, Howell, Hibino, et al., 1997). Finally, scalar invariance tests whether the intercepts of the indicators are equivalent across groups, a result that has implications regarding systematic bias in responses (Steenkamp & Baumgartner, 1998; Vandenberg & Lance, 2000). If a model has configural, metric, and scalar invariance, or at least partial configural, metric, and scalar invariance, then further substantive tests (e.g., latent mean difference tests, see Byrne, Shavelson, & Muthén, 1989; Steenkamp & Baumgartner, 1998) can be performed (e.g., Antonakis, Avolio, et al., 2003, conducted a latent mean difference test on a range of leadership dimensions using leader-follower gender as a grouping factor).

Unfortunately, however, Cheung and Rensvold (2000) noted that oftentimes researchers take what they called a naive approach, especially when conducting cross-cultural research, by simply comparing scales (i.e., item composites) across groups using a *t* test or an ANOVA-type procedure, without having verified whether what is being compared is equivalent (see X. Zhou, Schriesheim, & Beck, 2001, for an illustration of how invariance may be tested). Thus, the "observed difference, if there is one, may be due to a [grouping] difference; however, it may also be due to one or more invariance failures in the measurement model" (p. 188). As an example, Kakar, Kets de Vries, Kakar, and Vrignaud (2002) compared Indian and U.S. managers on a range of leadership factors and found significant mean differences between the groups using a *t* test. Thus, because they did not establish model equivalence before they made comparisons, their results should be viewed as highly suspect.

Moderated Regression

As noted by Schriesheim, Cogliser, and Neider (1995), testing for moderation using regression was (and often still is) conducted by using a median split in the moderator variable and then running separate regressions for the groups to determine whether parameter estimates differed. A more powerful procedure, moderated multiple regression (see Cohen & Cohen, 1983), treats the moderator variable as a continuous variable, thus retaining more information on the interaction effect (Schriesheim, Cogliser, et al., 1995). Moderated multiple regression uses a hierarchical regression procedure in which the independent variable is added first to the regression model, followed by the moderator variable. In the final step, the interaction (i.e., the cross-product) is added and assessed to determine the unique variance that is predicted by the interaction term (see also Schriesheim, 1995).

As demonstrated by Schriesheim, Cogliser, et al. (1995), who reanalyzed the data of a study conducted by Schriesheim and Murphy (1976), major discrepancies can arise between the split-group and moderated regression procedures. For example, although Schriesheim and Murphy originally found that role clarity did not moderate the relation between leader behaviors and outcomes (e.g., follower performance and satisfaction), Schriesheim, Cogliser, et al. (1995) actually found moderation effects. Specifically, initiating structure was positively associated with performance under high role clarity conditions but negatively associated with performance under low role clarity conditions. However, initiating structure (and consideration) was negatively associated with satisfaction under high role clarity conditions but positively associated with performance under low role clarity conditions. The results relating to performance were opposite to what was hypothesized, as based on the prevailing literature. Given that previous studies testing for moderation have used the weaker procedure, Schriesheim, Cogliser, et al. (1995) concluded "we do not believe that sound conclusions can be drawn from much of the existing leadership literature—at least not without making heroic (and quite probably unfounded) assumptions about the equivalency of analytic procedures and, of course, the results they produce" (p. 135). For further information about moderated regression analysis and how to improve the likelihood of finding moderators in leadership research, refer to Villa, Howell, Dorfman, and Daniel (2003).

Meta-Analysis

Glass (1976) differentiated three levels of analysis in research: *primary analysis*, in which researchers analyze the results of data they have gathered; *secondary analysis*, which refers to the reanalysis of primary data to better answer the original research question or to answer new questions; and *meta-analysis*, which is the analysis and synthesis of analyses of independent studies. This technique is useful where a domain needs to be synthesized, by integrating the results of various studies and reconciling their diverse or conflicting findings (for various meta-analytic techniques, refer to Hedges & Olkin, 1985; Hunter & Schmidt, 1990; Rosenthal, 1991). Essentially, with meta-analysis, the researcher can determine the population correlation coefficient— or other indicators of effect—between independent and dependent measures by controlling for measurement and statistical artifacts (i.e., errors). Meta-analysis also is useful for detecting moderator effects (see Sagie & Koslowsky, 1993).

Lord, De Vader, and Alliger (1986) reanalyzed Mann's (1959) data and found that intelligence showed a mean corrected correlation of .52 with leadership emergence (whereas Mann had declared that intelligence was not strongly associated with leadership). As mentioned by Antonakis, Cianciolo, and Sternberg (Chapter 1, this volume) and Zaccaro et al. (Chapter 5, this volume), the Lord et al. study was instrumental in refocusing efforts on individual-difference predictors of leadership, and the main the reasons why Lord et al. were able to show strong links between intelligence and leadership was that they used a more sophisticated and applicable method to synthesize research findings.

An example of a meta-analysis in which moderators were detected is the study of Lowe, Kroeck, et al. (1996), who analyzed the results of studies using the Multifactor Leadership Questionnaire (MLQ). They found that the type of organization (i.e., public or private) in which leadership measures were gathered and the type of criterion used (i.e., subjective or objective) moderated the relations between leadership measures and outcome variables. For example, Lowe et al. reported that the mean corrected correlation between charisma and effectiveness was .74 and .59 in public and private organizations, respectively, and that the difference between the correlations was significant. Many other interesting examples of meta-analytic studies have been conducted in the leadership field (e.g., DeGroot, Kiker, & Cross, 2000; Eagly & Johnson, 1990; Judge, Bono, Ilies, & Gerhardt, 2002; Schriesheim, Tepper, & Tetrault, 1994), to which readers are encouraged to refer.

Conclusion

In conclusion, we have presented a summary of key research-method subdomains and other important research-related issues that are likely to have value for persons interested in reading about or conducting leadership research. Because competency in research methods requires extensive knowledge, we could only brush the surface in many of the areas that we have discussed. We therefore would like to encourage readers to pursue further knowledge in the different areas by consulting and reading the reference citations that appear throughout this chapter and in the other chapters that have discussed research findings. By doing so, they are likely to improve the quality of future leadership research, as consumers demand higher-quality research and producers take the necessary precautions to ensure the validity of their findings.

Prior to concluding this chapter, we would like to address one final issue—that of judging the quality of the "concluding" or "discussion" section of a paper, article, or chapter. The discussion section of any of these addresses the implications of the results for future theory and, perhaps, leadership practice. Discussion sections sometimes get speculative, with implications and conclusions being drawn that go well beyond what the data actually support. Readers therefore need to evaluate such discussions carefully and in the light of the actual study findings or the findings of other research in the same domain. Discussion sections oftentimes talk about needed new directions for future research and comment on limitations of the reported research, such as a study's use of convenience sampling, which can be helpful in highlighting concerns that others can address in future research. The practice of acknowledging study shortcomings is also congruent with the philosophy of science position that all research is flawed in one way or another and that knowledge can be built only through multiple investigations of the same phenomena, using different samples, methods, analytic practices, and so forth. The analogy that we sometimes use is that doing research is like fishing with a net that has one or more holes (shortcomings). Using multiple nets, each with holes in different places, enables us to catch and hold that which we seek (knowledge), whereas the use of a single net is much less likely to do so.

To conclude, we will ask a question that probably crossed the minds of many readers. How is it possible that we need to make exhortations about raising the quality of research? Do journals not ensure that the research they publish is of a high quality? Indeed, most research published in top-quality journals is well done; however, from time to time, even top journals have holes in their review nets. Furthermore, there are journals and then there are *journals*! In other words, journal quality is variable, and not all journals publish high-quality scientific work. Thus, research that is not published in high-quality journals or that does not meet the necessary standards of scientific research must be looked at skeptically, especially if this research is published in popular books that address fashionable topics (e.g., traits that have not been tested scientifically and that have not demonstrated incremental predictive validity over and above established psychological traits) (see Antonakis, in press; Zeidner, Matthews, & Roberts, in press).

We trust that we have made the point that to generate scientific knowledge that is useful for society is not an easy task and requires extensive methodological expertise. If one chooses to drink the elixirs of witch doctors, one does so at one's own peril!

CHAPTER 4

The Assessment of Leadership

K. Galen Kroeck

Kevin B. Lowe

Kevin W. Brown

I n this chapter, we consider the different ways that leadership traditionally has been measured. In our review of the literature, we were struck by the lack of any formal analysis or direct comparisons of the different methods of assessment. It is our intention to describe and compare some of the different assessment techniques, supplementing this discussion with current research in the field; our review is representative rather than exhaustive. The idea of leadership has been constructed in such a vast variety of ways that the occasional forays into integration of the concept are thwarted upon first attempts to ascertain even a working definition. Thus, a discussion of leadership assessment is possible only by invoking reference to some of the divergent notions of leadership itself.

How a leader creates change or influences others has been a matter of substantial speculation over the decades. Actual evidentiary analyses pale in comparison to the array of philosophical theses found in the leadership literature. It may well be that there are as many theories of what good leaders are and do as there are practicing managers and proletariat academics. Judging by the popular press, nearly every successful chief executive officer (CEO) and a host of professional and collegiate coaches stand willing to readily divulge their secrets to leadership success.

Whether leaders use their personality traits (Judge, Bono, Ilies, & Gerhardt, 2002), their commitment to values (Avolio & Locke, 2002), their cognitive abilities (Zaccaro, Mumford, Connelly, Marks, & Gilbert, 2000), their leadership skills (Shipper & Davy, 2002) and competencies (Bennis, 1989), or whether they simply engage in specific actions and behaviors at the right time to fulfill the role of leader (see Pullig, Maxham, & Hair, 2002), is the matter of considerable debate. Some have even suggested that it is what leaders *don't* do at the right time and in the right situations that may contribute to their role effectiveness (see Kerr & Jermier, 1978; Mintzberg, 2001; Simpson, French, & Harvey, 2002).

To understand leadership as a phenomenon, we must be able to measure its components to determine whether they are meaningfully related to outcome measures. This undertaking becomes complex because the literature is amorphous and cuts across virtually every realm of human endeavor; hence, each practical and each theoretical field has its own parochial forum for all those who adopt the notion of leadership as their own. In this regard, Schruijer and Vansina (2002) implore the field to look at leadership from the perspectives of history, psycho-dynamic theory, organizational development, sociology, and so forth, to gain a deeper understanding of the phenomenon. It is our position, however, that the understanding of leadership, at this time, can best be served by redefinition of the construct. This redefinition would reassemble the notion into a set of categories that would allow us to discuss leadership in a specific regard by identifying not so much what a particular aspect encompasses but, more important, what it excludes. The recent thrust to disentangle references to "leadership" from being synonymous with "management" (see Drucker, 1974; Kotter, 2001) is one example of this approach of definition by exclusion.

The Multidimensional Nature of Leadership

The field of leadership inquiry is a conundrum of theories, definitions, measurements, descriptions, prescriptions, and philosophies. Few other topics in applied behavioral research have been granted as much attention, but the myriad theories and conceptualizations may be more diversion than asset. The literature is dense and widespread, and the true grit and meat of leadership research is neither easily found nor readily discernable. Whereas leadership researchers certainly have benefited from the popularity of the topic—due no doubt to its inherent value—the quality of the research may suffer from this diversity, a point that has been declared by authors within the field for more than a decade (e.g., Yukl, 1989a). This is not to say that progress has not been made: The sheer number of competing frameworks and theoretical conceptualizations have most certainly narrowed over the last 20 years. However, the fundamental variants among these theories continue to keep the field well divided. As a result, leadership research has taken on several, often competing, directions, yielding a literature that appears more haphazard in nature than deliberate. For instance, findings of various studies are often contradictory (Yukl, 1989a), and even research claiming to share a common framework tends to lack a unifying understanding of the construct. Therefore, the leadership literature has clearly advanced, but its progress is lagging. As Yukl (1989a) stated, the acquired "knowledge is much less than would be expected from the immense literature on leadership" (p. 279).

The current literature is dominated by a handful of theoretical frameworks, including transformational theory (Bass, 1985), contingency theory (Fiedler, 1967), situational theory (Hersey & Blanchard, 1982a), grid theory (Blake & Mouton, 1964), path-goal theory (House & Mitchell, 1974), and vertical-dyad linkage theory (Dansereau, Graen, & Haga, 1975; Graen & Uhl-Bien, 1995). Each of these conceptual schools of thought have fairly extensive literatures, seemingly separate but not quite (see Ashour, 1982; Ashour & Johns, 1983; Blake & Mouton, 1982; House, 1996). That is, they all claim to study the single construct of leadership, though each conceptualizes it in quite disparate ways and often at different levels of analysis. As such, each utilizes different methodologies and instruments when conducting leadership research. Herein lies the dilemma: This diversity may handicap our ability to make conclusive judgments regarding the relationship between leadership and any number of important outcomes. For this reason, much of the research to date has notable limitations for practical application to organizational settings.

Some streams of literature are more developed and unified than others. For instance, the literature on transformational leadership exhibits some unity of measurement and practice through the consistent use of the Multifactor Leadership Questionnaire (MLQ), a widely used and well-supported instrument. In contrast, situational theory and grid theory suffer from the use of a broad range of instruments that evolved from the Leader Behavior Descriptive Questionnaire (LBDQ), at one time the predominant instrument in behavior-based leadership research (Gioia & Sims, 1985). Inconsistency of measurement, at least in this instance, may have contributed to the decline in focus on description of leader behavior and situational theories during the previous decade.

Although the clarity of leadership as a construct arguably suffers from the sheer breadth of the field, the solution may not be as simple as narrowing the scope of leadership research or, for that matter, adopting a single framework or grand theory to which all contributors adhere. Instead, there may be a need to revise the leadership construct itself. That is, perhaps there *can* be more than one kind of leadership. This is echoed in Alvesson's (1996) critique of the leadership literature wherein he suggested that "aspirations to develop a grand theory . . . about leadership [should be] forgotten or, at least, downplayed and that the researcher [should] take seriously the ambiguity of that which may be interpreted as 'leadership'" (p. 464). For instance, intuitively, leadership at the CEO level is different from leadership at the level of a line manager, or even different levels of middle management. The measures of success are very different, and the traits/behaviors/competencies required for good leadership at one level may not necessarily translate to good leadership at another level. Therefore, this chapter does not set out to advocate one theory as correct—or even more correct—than any other. Indeed, consistent with London and Maurer's (Chapter 10, this volume) discussion of leadership development, we argue that the theory in use should in large part explain the choice of assessment tools and techniques. Nor do we set out to debunk any theories that may not reflect our personal opinions regarding the nature and structure of leadership. The focus of this chapter is limited to the measurement of leadership. Theory will be discussed to the extent that it affects assessment.

Thus, in this chapter, we will strive to answer four primary questions: (a) Why should we measure leadership? (b) What do we measure when we assess leadership? (c) How do we measure leadership? and (d) How valid are measures of leadership in predicting important organizational outcomes, such as performance, change, and profit? In addition, we will also discuss important methodological and analytical issues that have emerged in the leadership literature, as well as look forward to trends and directions in which leadership research *will*, or in some cases *should*, progress in the coming decade as they relate to assessment.

Rationale for Assessment

It was once fashionable to argue that the *real* impact of leadership was minimal. Structural constraints such as prior technology investments, environmental trends, and industry-specific factors were posited as *the* determinants of organizational effectiveness (Lieberson & O'Connor, 1977; Pfeffer, 1977, 1993, 1994; Salancik & Pfeffer, 1977). Others suggested that organizational design factors could substitute for many aspects of leadership (J. P. Howell, 1997; Kerr & Jermier, 1978). Yet other scholars suggested that leadership was little more than a form of organizational mythology, a social construction used to attribute complex system outcomes and the vagaries of chance to individuals (Meindl & Ehrlich, 1987; Meindl, Ehrlich, & Dukerich, 1985). Consequently, the incremental impact of leadership was judged to be small at best. More recently, the pendulum of scholarly and popular opinion has swung dramatically back to a wide acceptance of leadership as important to organizational effectiveness. Hogan (1994) stated that leadership *is* organizational effectiveness, and Day (2001) wrote, "Put simply, leadership, like personality, matters in the real world" (p. 385).

Interest in leadership, and thereby assessing leadership, is near an all-time high. To develop and gain organizational support for a leadership assessment effort, two questions must be answered: (a) What is the purpose of the assessment? and (b) Does the assessment of leadership produce a positive economic value? We address these questions in the following sections.

Purpose of Assessment

If you were to ask a group of senior human resource or organizational development executives why leadership assessment is important, you would invariably get different answers. In this section we consider the impact of two variables:

Table 4.1   Assessment Time Horizon and Purpose

Time Horizon	Assessment Level—Individual	Assessment Level—Organization
Past term—assessment for feedback	Provide leadership performance feedback	Create a leadership balance sheet, identify incompetent managers
Near term—assessment for development	Identify opportunities for improvement, enhance awareness and use of strengths	Identify common leadership training and develop needs across the organization; identify emphasis for recruitment and selection needs (short-term focus)
Long term—assessment for career management	Involve employee in career planning, increase awareness of a systematic approach to building competence, improve individual understanding of the development focus in each position	Succession planning, career paths based on competencies and skills, developmental assignments based on potentialities and weaknesses, recruitment and selection needs (long-term focus)

1. Assessment purpose (e.g., past performance, near-term and long-term horizon), which is associated with the rationale for assessment (e.g., feedback, development, career management)

2. Level of assessment use (e.g., individual or organizational)

Table 4.1 shows the relation of assessment time horizon and assessment purpose to the rationale for assessment.

Two common themes pervading the organizational literature are that near-term performance is required to maintain legitimacy, and capacity must be built to maintain long-term survival. Similarly, the assessment of leadership should include both a short-term performance dimension and a long-term capacity (i.e., development) dimension. We now briefly review the implications of this dynamic interplay between assessment and development needs. For a more extensive review of the development process, see London and Maurer (Chapter 10, this volume).

Assessment for Feedback (Past Leadership Performance)

Similar to the manner in which an income statement records financial performance over time, assessment for feedback captures the performance of a leader over a prior period. Overall performance appraisal ratings or embedded unidimensional ratings of "leadership" are insufficient proxies for the data required for accurate assessment and feedback because they fail to disentangle leadership competencies from performance ratings that are dominated by concerns for managerial performance. If organizations are to develop and improve leadership, they must assess leaders and leadership as qualitatively different people and behaviors (Day, 2000; Kotter, 1990; Zaleznik, 1977).

At the individual level, assessing past leadership has a number of functional outcomes, including closure on leadership development opportunities leveraged or missed as well as the implications of these outcomes for future development challenges. At the organizational level, this process pressures the organization to increase clarity and communicate shared understanding of what is it is to be a leader and to display leadership. The words "leader" and "leadership" gain increased clarity through an explicit linkage between specific past behaviors and performance feedback to the leader. Idiosyncratic and ambiguous definitions of leadership may be increasingly extinguished through concrete discussions of what was and was not leadership, improving shared understanding across the organization. Assessment for feedback also can be used to create a leadership balance sheet, assessing the organization's stock of leadership competencies and deficiencies such as the abilities to manage change, build a team, and communicate a vision. This leadership balance sheet could also identify leader incompetence, estimated to have a base rate of 50%-75%, to prevent prior mistakes of assigning employees to positions where their technical and managerial competencies exceed their leadership competencies (DeVries, 1992; Hogan, Raskin, & Fazzini, 1990).

Specific leadership assessment data can improve the conversation quality and utility with an employee who is a valuable individual contributor or team member but whose leadership performance has resulted in a reassignment. Improved communication and feedback regarding the reassignment enhances perceptions of fairness, thereby reducing the likelihood of turnover of competent and valued employees. Pinpointing the assignment failure as one of leadership rather than technical or managerial competence might enhance individual willingness to correct the deficiency via training, mentoring, or a host of other interventions. Thus, past performance assessment, focused specifically on leadership competencies, provides significant input for identifying near-term leadership development plans, a topic we turn to next.

Assessment for Development (Near-Term Performance)

In an organization characterized by stability in its strategy, structure, and work flow, the assessment of past leadership performance might completely identify future developmental needs. These factors are seldom constant; therefore, myriad variables may differentiate the applicability of assessment for feedback (what was) from assessment for development (what is about to be). Lateral transfers, promotions, reorganization, reengineering, and downsizing all affect developmental prospects. The leader might remain in the existing job (e.g., manager-R&D) and within the existing structure (e.g., product groups), but the strategic focus of the organization could change (e.g., technological leadership to cost focus), resulting in a different set of assessment criteria (e.g., innovation to efficiency) and a different lens on the leadership capacity needed for future organization success. When macro variables are constant, changes in work group composition, such as loss of highly experienced members to retirement or the marketplace, will affect team dynamics, and thus the assessment focus might shift from improving team performance to rebuilding the team and maintaining team performance.

At the organizational level, accurately matching assessment for development with the opportunities for development in jobs will identify common leadership training and development needs across the organization. For example, identifying that 30 individuals need enhanced visioning skills or the ability to articulate a teachable point of view supports the economic case for dedicating resources to a program. As a result, near-term performance should be enhanced and organizational capacity built for the long term. Conversely, identifying a wide range of development needs and developmental opportunities with few matches between the two, perhaps because of an overly short-term focus on getting results or poorly structured jobs, would signal a need to better align near-term assignments with long-term leadership development needs.

Another benefit of effective assessment for development is the information provided to inform recruitment and selection efforts. Effective assessment for development might identify a leadership surplus (e.g., increasing leadership equity in the balance sheet analogy), a leadership deficit (e.g., negative leadership equity), or surpluses/deficits within certain skill groups (e.g., a leadership surplus in manufacturing and a deficit in information systems). Insights into the organization's near-term leadership needs would perhaps elevate the assessment of leadership skills in the organization's frame of reference for recruitment and selection, reducing overreliance on other criteria such as the much-maligned overemphasis on technical competence in the United States.

Assessment for Career Management (Long-Term Performance)

Assessment for career management, while certainly complemented by assessment for development, is differentiated by the long-term nature of the assessment. Assessment for career management focuses more on potential than on demonstrated competence (i.e., feedback) or immediate opportunities (i.e., development). For example, the organization may be projecting investments in information technology that will result in increased usage of geographically dispersed and virtual teams in 7–10 years. The current level of technology investment, however, may preclude both the demonstration and the opportunity to display these competencies. Many organizations have long had processes devoted to identifying high potentials. It is not clear, however, to what extent these processes weight or accurately assess leadership capacity, are the most effective mechanisms for leadership development, or are simply self-fulfilling prophecies. What is clear is the need to view the assessment of high potentials for leadership as an exercise in identifying (a) current, demonstrated capacity; (b) developmental capacity relating to the near- and medium-term job assignments; and (c) potentiality (i.e., future capacities needed but not demonstrable under current organizational structure and system constraints).

At the organization level, feedback for career management enables more systematic succession with respect to leadership skills and expands that assessment beyond an elite group of people with high potential. Recent work suggests that organizations that create systemic and distributed leadership capacity are likely to be more successful (Day, 2000; Gronn, 1999). Assessment for career management would be expected to positively influence long-term recruitment and selection. With the knowledge of current leadership capacity obtained through assessment for development and a projection of the leadership potentiality of current constituents, recruitment and selection could be focused on a thoughtful trade-off between short-term and long-term leadership needs. For example, the organization might determine that the capacity to effectively energize a team was sufficient in the short term and would be overly abundant in the longer term. Consequently, that leadership capacity might be underemphasized in the next recruiting cycle, with a greater weight given to an identified deficiency. Whereas our examples have tended to focus on recruitment and selection under conditions of expansion or growth, a parallel argument could be made for downsizing and other workforce reduction programs.

The Economic Rationale for Leadership Assessment

The field of leadership is in need of studies identifying the value of assessing leadership and demonstrating this value in traditional return on investment language (Moretti, 1994). Empirical investigations of leadership assessment efforts are scarce but supportive (see Barrick, Day, Lord, & Alexander, 1991). For example, Cascio (1994) demonstrated the economic value of an assessment center with utility analysis. He reported on an assessment center that selected 1,116 first-level managers who subsequently averaged 4.4 years in the job. The estimated value of the performance improvement from assessment with a predictive validity of .388, compared to random selection, was $21.8 million against the assessment center cost of $2.4 million. Compared with an organization's existing interview procedure with a predictive validity of .13, the payoff (net of the $2.4 million assessment center cost) was $13.1 million, for a return on investment in excess of 500%. Whereas there are legitimate concerns that the assessments used in such centers lack construct validity and their predictive validity is lower than some other selection techniques (see Sackett & Tuzinski, 2001; F. L. Schmidt & Hunter, 1998), the central thesis of the utility of improved assessment is inviolate. Other authors have provided rough empirical evidence and others anecdotal qualitative evidence of the economic impact of leadership assessment (see Howard & Bray, 1990; Ritchie, 1994).

To summarize, leadership assessment is a valuable tool for enhancing organizational effectiveness. The purposes of assessment should drive the types of questions asked and the selection of raters. If multiple leadership assessment needs are identified, it will be necessary to utilize different raters completing different instruments with different criterion variables to avoid using sources of assessment without the proper perspective. In cases where some raters are positioned to evaluate a leader from multiple development perspectives, different instruments with different criterion variables may need to be administered over time to avoid rater fatigue.

What Is It That We Assess?

Leadership is conceived in numerous ways, such that the degree of specificity with which it is described and measured defines the approach. Research conceptualizations of the construct range from very specific to very general levels of analysis, including *behavioral* descriptors, leadership *styles*, *trait-based* models, *skill* and *competency* formulations, *values* orientations, and *themes* of effectiveness.

At the *behavioral* level of analysis, instruments such as the Leader Behavior Description Questionnaire (LBDQ), Leadership Opinion Questionnaire (LOQ), Leader Member Exchange Measure (LMX), and others have been the primary sources of assessment in the literature. Such analyses invoke the theoretical underpinnings of expectancy theory, vertical dyad linkage theory, and path-goal theory, to name a few. It is quite difficult to separate the behavioral level from the leadership style level of analysis because most research links a set of behaviors into a *leader style* in order to provide meaning to a range of similar actions and behaviors, such as consideration and initiating structure using the LBDQ, type of role behavior using LMX, or supportiveness, achievement-orientation, direction, and participativeness with the sundry measures of path-goal concepts. This is not to say that all behavioral descriptions of leader effectiveness drift to a style description, merely that integration of a set of similar behaviors tends to impart meaning to those behaviors (Fleishman, 1953; Pfeffer & Salancik, 1975; Podsakoff & Tudor, 1985). Indeed, specific behavior that can be shown to be related to effectiveness outcomes may provide as much or more meaning than description of behavior as a *style*. For example, both Wayne, Shore, Bommer, and Tetrick (2002) and De Cremer and van Knippenberg (2002) found that use of procedural justice in administering contingent rewards affected perceived support and cooperation. Use of delegation, empowerment, and participation has been found to affect effectiveness outcomes for many years (see Lewin, Lippitt, & White, 1939; Schriesheim, Neider, & Scandura, 1998; Vroom & Jago, 1978). Clearly, use of specific leader behavior does affect organizational outcomes. More recently, Sweetman (2001), for example, found that leaders admitting to the need for help under conditions of uncertainty improved subordinate intentions to perform. Day, Schleicher, Unckless, and Hiller (2002) found self-monitoring behavior to be associated with leader emergence. Such findings may provide a greater practical value in leader development than other units of analysis. Findings such as these and their own research served as grounds for McKenna, Shelton, and Darling (2002) to conclude that *behavioral style* assessment techniques are superior to *trait-based* assessments in the prediction of specific criterion outcomes.

Trait-based analyses of leadership commonly resort to theories of personality or other individual differences to identify those traits that are associated with success in the leader role. The rise and fall of trait theories is discussed in-depth by Zaccaro, Kemp, and Bader (Chapter 5, this volume). This resurgence of interest in trait-based theories has also spawned new models of leadership that have advanced the literature considerably. Most notably, transformational leadership theory (Bass, 1985) posits that transformational leaders are defined by four primary qualities:

charisma, inspiration, intellectual stimulation, and individualized consideration. Of course, transformational leadership theory, though arguably derived from historical trait models (see Burns, 1978), incorporates both contextual and behavioral factors that contribute to leadership. Sternberg (Sternberg & Vroom, 2002) has also introduced yet another refined trait-based model, wherein he poses that leadership requires three primary traits: wisdom, intelligence, and creativity (*synthesized*) (WICS model). Again, this model builds on the strengths of historical trait-based theory while incorporating relevant roles for learning and development. These new advances in trait-based leadership theory have returned trait theories to prominence, and, with the accumulation of continued empirical support, they will likely help to drive and direct leadership research well into the future.

Leadership as a set of *skills* or *competencies* is an idea that has been advanced for more than half a century. A *competency* has been defined as an underlying characteristic that leads to superior or effective performance (Boyatzis, 1982). In this view, leadership is wholly a learned skill. That is, leadership is developed in the same way that any other skill or competency is developed. The most prominent "competency-based" framework is perhaps the Vroom and Yetton (1973) normative model, which suggests that the most appropriate "style" of leadership is very much contingent on the context of the decision. However, a basic assumption is that individuals have the capacity to learn how to engage in various "styles," thus implying that leadership is not merely behavioral, as mentioned above, but that it may also be learned, much like any other competency. This illustrates an important note—the boundaries of these classifications are quite amorphous, and "true" versions or reflections are quite rare. However, competency-based models continue to gain ground. Recently, Alldredge and Nilan (2000) demonstrated the practical application of a leadership competency model for 3M, advancing competency leadership models from research to practice. Shipper and Davy (2002) identified six specific *skills* necessary for leader effectiveness: participation, facilitating, recognition, planning, time emphasis, and control of details.

Leadership as a *value orientation* has gained momentum in the literature. Turner, Barling, Epitropaki, Butcher, and Milner (2002) described and reviewed some of the literature suggesting that transformational leadership is accentuated, if not driven, by a moral value system. Avolio (1999, p. 34) postulated that transformational leadership is fundamentally morally uplifting.

Closely allied with the values orientation concept of leadership is the "themes of effectiveness" viewpoint in which, typically "best practices" lists are grouped to identify common themes for leader success (see Kets de Vries & Florent-Treacy, 2002). Both the *values* orientation and the *themes of effectiveness* conceptualization tend to falter in the empirical domain, but measurement instruments currently are in a nascent state of development.

In summary, it is important to reiterate that few theories are "pure" versions of any of the above. Most are interactionist models that discuss leadership in the context of multiple domains, including trait, behavior, context, and competency. For instance, Fiedler's (1967) contingency model clearly demonstrates how combinations of these (trait, behavior, situation, etc.) contribute to successful leadership and perceptions of leader effectiveness. Efforts to categorize the most prominent theories, therefore, is made difficult by the fact that they may very well reflect elements of more than one base.

The State of Leadership Assessment: A Review of Procedures

How is leadership measured? More important, perhaps, how *should* leadership be measured? These questions are best answered with a resounding, "it depends." That is, the answer depends on whom you ask, what theoretical framework you espouse, and what resources are available to you, among many other things. It is very difficult to say that one method of measurement is good and another is bad, though we can infer that some methods may be superior to others in some settings. However, judgments of quality are better made at the level of the instrument, and selection of a measure should take into consideration one's needs as well as the limitations and constraints of the situation. For example, computer-based simulation may offer valuable tools in capturing elusive elements of the construct, but the cost and equipment requirements may not make it a realistic option for many companies. Instead, a well-developed paper-and-pencil test may present a more realistic alternative. There are any number of variants in the measurement of leadership, each with unique strengths and weaknesses that must be evaluated in the context of the user, environment, intended purpose, and population of interest, regardless of theory or measurement format.

A representative sampling of the variety of instruments and techniques for assessing leadership is shown in Appendix 4.1, page 94. This appendix illustrates many methodological and procedural variants within the measurement of leadership that will be touched on at various points throughout this chapter. This section will focus specifically on methodological variants, including the qualitative versus quantitative debate, format issues, and assessor variations.

Qualitative Versus Quantitative Assessment

The quantitative versus qualitative distinction was introduced by Antonakis, Schriesheim, Donovan, Gopalakrishna-Pillai, Pellegrini, and Rossomme (see Chapter 3, this volume). In this section, we link this distinction to assessment issues.

Leadership research traditionally has been dominated by a positivist, quantitative epistemological orientation that places the emphasis on "ideals" such as objectivity, neutrality, procedure, technique, quantification, replicability, generalization, and discovery of laws (see Alvesson, 1996). Consequently, researchers have attempted to use qualitative methods to better understand leadership. Despite the potential validity of their claims, proponents of qualitative methods have presented few studies, or at least few published studies, that illustrate the strength and feasibility of using qualitative methods in conducting research on leadership. That is, most of the debate has been purely methodological up until now, with only limited empirical backing.

Quantitative methodologies, though clearly flawed, have an advantage in that they are theory driven and focus on yielding interpretable outcomes with some degree of objectivity. Although the critics perceive theory and the pursuit of objectivity as the primary weakness of quantitative methods, the inherent ease of interpretation and theory is desirable, particularly with the leadership construct's relevance to business. In other words, leadership is not merely an academic interest; practical research arguably should offer insights into application and development of leadership within real-world settings, something qualitative methodologies have yet to demonstrate.

Of course, qualitative methods do contribute some very important tools that have long been components of leadership research, such as observation and interviews. However, the incorporation of these tools has been accomplished in such a way that they typically adhere to procedures that attempt to establish rules and standards for their interpretation and evaluation, ultimately yielding quasi-quantified data for empirical analysis. Nonetheless, a thorough review of leadership measurement must include an exposition of both qualitative and quantitative methods of data collection, as well as their respective strengths and weaknesses. The ultimate decision of which method to use falls to the researcher and clearly will depend on by the needs and uses of the resulting information.

The remainder of this section will review the predominant methods used in the measurement of leadership. For the purpose of organization, we will first review qualitative methods, then follow with a review of quantitative methods. Table 4.2 provides a more detailed review of test format and related variants in leadership assessment.

Qualitative Methods

Interview. The interview is a popular technique used in gathering information and data pertaining to leadership, particularly in the organizational setting. Its ease and convenience relative to the amount of information gathered make it an attractive alternative. Of course, the extent to which an interview adheres to a strictly qualitative paradigm varies dramatically. That is, according to most proponents, the most beneficial uses of the interview are with open-ended and unstructured forms (Alvesson, 1996). From this perspective, interviews should be loosely structured, and interviewers should feel inclined, if not encouraged, to pursue lines of questioning that will yield the most important information, without concern for standardization.

The interview, while providing a wealth of unfettered information, has some serious shortcomings. As both Silverman (1989) and Alvesson (1996) have cautioned, interviews themselves are social situations, and it can be difficult to determine the extent to which interview statements reflect the subjective reality of the leader-member relationship on the job as opposed to situational cues within the

Table 4.2   Methodological Variants in the Measurement of Leadership

	Methodological Variants
Method	Qualitative, quantitative
Format	Interview; ethnography; content analysis; text production; observation; diary; paper-and-pencil questionnaire; simulation; Web-based/computer-based questionnaire
Assessor	Self, supervisor, peer, subordinate, client/customer, other
Scale	Behavioral index, trait-based, competency assessment
Theoretical underpinnings	LMX, transformational, situational, path-goal theory, contingency theory, other
Purpose or intended use	Prescriptive, descriptive
Direction of assessment	Positive leadership, negative leadership

interview. In plain language, unstructured interviews pose two major problems: (a) the extent to which the interviewee distorts the leader-member relationship is unknown, and (b) even if the accuracy of interview statements could be verified, how should a researcher interpret those statements?

Addressing the weaknesses of the interview, many researchers have developed methodologies that yield more structured, objective, and interpretable data (see Brtek & Motowidlo, 2002). To this end, the use of structured interviews, frequently with a limited response set, provides for the collection of more "quantifiable" data. Of course, proponents of qualitative methods view this less as an interview and more as a "talking questionnaire" (Potter & Wetherell, 1987). Nonetheless, these additions can and do enhance use of the interview as a tool in empirical studies of research.

Ethnography. Ethnography is a data collection method that typically utilizes a number of methods, with a strong reliance on interviews and prolonged observation (Alvesson, 1996; Atkinson & Hammersley, 1994; Kunda, 1992; Rosen, 1991; Schwartzman, 1993; Van Maanen, 1979). This method provides a plethora of qualitative information, focusing expressly on the specific situation or context. The heavy reliance on observation helps to reduce the distortions of individual responses that is common in methods that rely solely on interviews for information. Ethnography, however, has its own set of shortcomings. To begin, it is very time-consuming and, therefore, very expensive—two considerations of great importance when dealing with organizations. Furthermore, there is a risk that the researcher may "go native" (Alvesson, 1996), in that the researcher loses his or her ability to look beyond the immediate context in order to apply his or her findings to other external settings.

Content Analysis. Content analysis describes a family of procedures used in analyzing written text, such as letters, memoranda, reports, speeches, interviews, or article abstracts (Insch, Moore, & Murphy, 1997). It is a tool that is seldom used in organizational research, but recent work has begun to demonstrate how it may be useful in such research. A handful of leadership studies have used content analysis as the basis of the research (Barley, Meyer, & Gash, 1988; Bettman & Weitz, 1983; D'Aveni & McMillan, 1990; Gibson, Fiedler, & Barrett, 1993; House, Spangler, & Woycke, 1991; J. M. Howell & Higgins, 1990; Isenberg, 1986; Meindl et al., 1985; Sims & Manz, 1984). Content analysis, as envisioned by Insch and colleagues (1997), blends together the depth of information gathered using qualitative methods and the empirical rigor of quantitative methods. In this sense, Insch et al. (1997) argued that content analysis is more a "middle-ground" methodology than purely qualitative. The basis of content analysis lies in the development of a coding scheme; that is, developing a means of classifying communication into meaningful categories of behavior, motives, values, and so forth. However, this form of analysis is prone to rater bias—the development of categories and the classification of communication is certainly not value-free (Insch et al., 1997). Furthermore, proponents of qualitative methods argue that if only data that are considered "meaningful" to the particular rater are coded, much data are lost as the process "extracts sparse data from the richness of context" (Insch et al., 1997, p. 20). For a more complete review of content analysis and procedure, refer to Insch et al. (1997).

Observation. Observation is a fundamental element of science, regardless of discipline. As a qualitative method of data collection, it has remained an important factor in all quantitative empirical work. It is arguably the core of most theory development (Conger, 1998), and it most certainly is a key foundation of most questionnaires or surveys that dominate the empirical literature. However, the uses and methods of observation vary dramatically within the literature. From a qualitative perspective, observation provides for an unobstructed view of the social reality that exists within the situational context. Of course, as the Hawthorne studies clearly demonstrated, observers are not merely "flies on the wall"; they are actors within the environment and therefore alter and become part of the social context. Furthermore, some authors have suggested that the incorporation of observational methods in assessment has been overly simplistic in the past (Conger, 1998; Yukl, 1994). According to Conger (1998), "Effective participant observation would include the interviewing of respondents and informants, observation and direct participation, document analysis, and introspection" (p. 112) in order to ensure "between-method triangulation." This is critical in addressing the difficult challenge of discerning "operational data" (i.e., genuine, spontaneous data) from "presentational data" (i.e., contrived behavior to maintain a desired public image), as leadership research is especially prone to respondent distortions and effects of social desirability (Van Maanen, 1979). Conger (1998) argued that engaging in observation at multiple levels with various methods provides the researcher with better insight into making those difficult distinctions.

As with interviews, researchers have developed several strategies to improve the usefulness and interpretation of observational research. To this end, they may use multiple raters, behavioral coding strategies, behavioral counts, or other similar methods to yield more objective, quantifiable data for empirical analysis. Furthermore, technological devices such as video cameras have provided new tools to make observation less intrusive and minimize observer effects. With such changes, observation as a data collection technique has improved over the past few decades.

Quantitative Methods

Paper-and-Pencil Questionnaire. Paper-and-pencil questionnaires have been the dominant means of measurement of leadership for most of, if not all, the construct's development throughout the 20th century and into the present. They offer perhaps the greatest ease and convenience in assessing leadership and yield data that lends themselves well to empirical analysis. However, the paper-and-pencil questionnaire has many limitations. First, there is the issue of operationalization of the leadership construct, where questionnaires are limited in tapping the full breadth of its domain (Conger, 1998). Questionnaires tend to focus on a single level of analysis, particularly behavioral dimensions, which neglect the role of many contextual factors (Conger, 1998; Yukl, 1994). Some critics have suggested that paper-and-pencil questionnaires "more often measure attitudes about behavior rather than actual observed behavior and are influenced by social desirability concerns of respondents" (Conger, 1998, p. 109).

Another criticism waged against questionnaires is that they limit the range of responses to just a few choices and that these responses are "usually remotely distanced from actions, events, feelings, relations, articulations of opinions . . . emerging in every day life situations" (Alvesson, 1996; p. 461). As a result, much information is virtually forfeited by pigeonholing participants' responses into but a few possible response alternatives. In doing so, it is argued that we "trade off" the how and why questions of leadership for "abstracted concepts and descriptions which allow us only to generalize across a range of contexts at relatively superficial levels" (Conger, 1998, p. 109).

Despite the shortcomings of the questionnaire, its prominence in the measurement of leadership is not likely to diminish in the foreseeable future. Its ease of application and interpretation make it an attractive tool in the arsenal of leadership researchers. Few, if any, would argue that the instruments are perfect, but questionnaires have long demonstrated their usefulness, validity, and reliability in the measurement of leadership, a point that will be discussed in detail later in this chapter. Furthermore, advances in knowledge and technology offer continued prospects for improving questionnaires and mitigating some of the shortcomings while maximizing the value and utility of survey use.

Computer-Based Questionnaire. Building off the long history of paper-and-pencil questionnaires, Web-based or computer-based survey instruments are becoming more and more popular in the measurement of leadership. They offer many advantages over traditional paper-and-pencil questionnaires, helping to address some of the major criticisms of most survey research. Perhaps the most important element that computer-based testing (CBT) has brought to survey construction is the use of multimedia approaches. The addition of aural, visual, and video content arguably expands the domain that can be captured using a questionnaire. These new tools allow for the development of questionnaires that act more like simulations than paper-and-pencil surveys. What's more, the ease of use, automatic and immediate scoring, and relative convenience make CBT an attractive alternative for organizations when selecting a leadership instrument. Of course, research on CBT in leadership measurement is still in the infant stage; however, the overabundance of CBT instruments that have flooded the market clearly illustrates the direction of the field and suggests that computer-based questionnaires will become an integral part of leadership research over the next decade.

Simulation/Assessment Center. Thousands of organizations currently use assessment centers for selection and promotion of management (Thornton & Byham, 1982). Assessment centers typically consist of multiple instruments and/or simulations, increasing fidelity by utilizing reality-based work samples. Generally, assessment centers have been well supported in their prediction of leader performance (Gaugler, Rosenthal, Thornton, & Bentson, 1987; Schmitt, Gooding, Noe, & Kirsch, 1984). However, the extent to which they exhibit cost-effective incremental improvements in prediction over other, less expensive alternatives is still very much the center of debate (McEvoy & Beatty, 1989). McEvoy and Beatty (1989) have identified several primary weaknesses of the assessment center in the assessment of leadership. First, there is concern over the construct validity of assessment center ratings; that is, there is much debate over how assessment center ratings are determined and exactly what they reflect (Russell, 1987; Sackett, 1982). Second, given that it is not well understood why assessment centers work in most situations, there is even less known as to why they do not work in other situations. This reiterates concerns over the construct validity of assessment centers. Finally, there is a significant threat of criterion contamination in assessor ratings of managers (Turnage & Muchinsky, 1984). For instance, criterion contamination may occur when the criterion and the predictor are not independent; that is, contamination may occur when the assessor is knowledgeable about the individual's performance on the predictor variable.

Aside from psychometric concerns, assessment centers require other practical considerations before they should be adopted. Put simply, assessment centers are expensive, are time-intensive on both the development and administration sides, and require a substantial commitment by the organization for successful implementation. Evidence does suggest, however, that assessment centers exhibit good empirical prediction; of course, as mentioned above, the extent to which they provide incremental prediction over paper-and-pencil questionnaires is still in debate. Despite these criticisms, the role of assessment centers in leader assessment is a strong and viable alternative for researchers and practitioners alike.

The Dilemma of "Who": The Role of the Rater in Leadership Assessment

When selecting methods for assessment and research, the role of the rater in leadership measurement must be considered. That is, the determination of *who* will be used as a source of ratings is paramount. Traditionally, performance appraisal and measurement have relied most heavily on supervisor ratings (Facteau, Facteau, Schoel, Russell, & Poteet, 1998). However, over the previous decade or longer, researchers and organizations have begun to embrace the use of other sources as well, frequently in combination with one another. The prospect of evaluating leadership with ratings from subordinates, peers, supervisors, self, and customers has intuitive appeal, and research has shown that the use of these other sources is associated with several positive outcomes, including improved performance information (Mohrman, Reswick-West, & Lawler, 1989), improved reliability (Wholers & London, 1989), and improved leader performance following the delivery of feedback (Atwater, Roush, & Fischtal, 1995; Daw & Gage, 1967; Smither, London, Vasilopoulos, et al., 1995). Given these findings, the interest in using alternative sources for leader evaluation is growing, and the use of 360-degree feedback by practitioners is far ahead of the research findings (Facteau et al., 1998; Testa, 2002; Waldman, Atwater, & Antonioni, 1998). Although its use in practice has outpaced the advance of empirical research, some studies have provided evidence for "moderate" convergent, discriminant, and predictive validity for the alternative sources (Harris & Schaubroeck, 1988; London & Wholers, 1991; McEvoy & Beatty, 1989; Tsui & Ohlott, 1988; Wholers & London, 1989). According to Romano (1994), companies spent $152 million in developing and implementing 360-degree feedback programs in 1992 alone. It is safe to say that the figure is much higher today.

Despite the apparent value of using alternative sources in the assessment of leadership, the selection of sources must also take into consideration theoretical and analytical constraints. That is, one must ensure that the data are collected and analyzed at the appropriate levels of analysis, as discussed by Antonakis et al. (Chapter 3, this volume).

Leader Level and Criteria

Leaders play different roles in the organization (Mintzberg, 1973), and the manners in which these roles are conducted vary considerably across jobs (Stewart, 1967). Even assessing what a candidate needs for a particular job can be very difficult. For example, Reginald Jones retired at the "early" age of 62 to make way for Jack Welch, in part because he knew the CEO role in his organization, General Electric, now required a different kind of leadership (H. Levinson, 1994; H. Levinson & Rosenthal, 1983). In this section, we discuss why the level of the leader must be considered in choosing leadership assessment criteria.

Kotter (2001) distinguished leadership and management as complementary systems of action: Managers cope with complexity, whereas leaders cope with change. It is clear that leaders at different levels in the organization are distinct and that the behaviors or competencies that spell success at lower levels may become less relevant at higher levels in the organization (Dalton, 1989). A middle manager's competencies are insufficient or inappropriate at the executive level. Hence, the criteria used to establish the predictive usefulness of some assessment device must be appropriate to the level of leader being assessed. Otherwise, we are left with an empirical literature characterized by a set of findings subject to the vagaries of readily available data. Unfortunately, a considerable amount of research has found differential correlational strength between leader behaviors and outcome variables, depending on the nature of the effectiveness criteria used. For example, using meta-analysis, Lowe, Kroeck, and Sivasubramaniam (1996) showed a differential pattern of prediction of MLQ scores for hard (i.e., objective or organizational) and soft (i.e., subjective perceptions) criteria of effectiveness.

Figure 4.1 shows a conceptualization of leadership criteria based on the idea that the focus of leaders varies at different organizational levels. The figure distinguishes those criteria relevant to measuring management effectiveness from those measuring leadership effectiveness. The model heeds the call for a change in how assessment devices are related to criteria at different hierarchical levels (Gavin & Hoffman, 2002), different units of analysis (Gronn, 2002), and the use of multilevel analyses (refer to Antonakis et al., Chapter 3, this volume, for further discussion on multilevel issues). In expressing their belief in how the field can best advance, Schriesheim, Castro, Zhou, and Yammarino (2001), in their treatise on the folly of theorizing "A" while testing for "B," exhorted theorists and empiricists to specify the level of analysis for which their concepts of leadership apply.

Whereas it is beyond the scope of this chapter to provide a painstaking review of all the studies that have manifested the problems identified above, we can offer some analysis of why many studies have questionable or limited validity in assessment of leader effectiveness. The problems that we have noted in various studies include (a) choice of an inappropriate criterion for the leader's level in the organization, (b) improperly aggregating data on leaders functioning at different organizational levels, (c) choice of an assessment device or instrument that is inappropriate for the leader's function or level, (d) aggregation of scores that should not be aggregated (e.g., average LMX score across a set of subordinates), (e) misspecification of tests of the theory (hypothesizing A while testing for B), (f) not identifying contaminating factors likely to affect leadership scores (e.g., varying subordinate preferences for leadership, cognitive biases, implicit theories), (g) misspecification of the assessment device or instrument with regard to important criteria, (h) fluctuations in importance of different criteria of effectiveness, (i) failure to take into account effects over time or the longitudinal impact of some behavior on criteria of effectiveness and failure to consider recency effects, and (j) lack of systematic evaluation of methodological issues associated with the psychometric properties of instruments (including using scales with weak factor structure, extracting scales on a piecemeal basis, lack of reliability, failure to recognize effects of skewed instrument and/or criterion data, and failure to recognize method variance effects). Refer

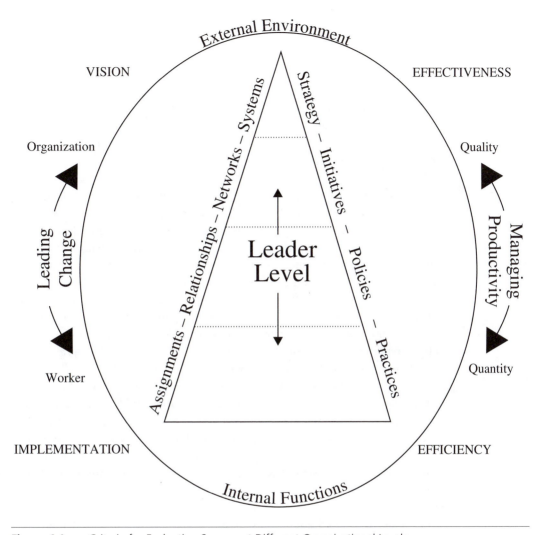

Figure 4.1   Criteria for Evaluating Success at Different Organizational Levels

to Brown, Scott, and Lewis (Chapter 6, this volume) for further discussion on methods variance effects.

Taking these factors into account in the design of empirical research should improve our understanding of how leadership affects those criteria that are appropriate for the leader's level, focus, and level of development. The following sections further describe how these empirical issues and the level of the leader (Figure 4.1) are pertinent to the study and understanding of leadership phenomena.

Leader Level and Assessment Requirements

Common to many models of leadership development is the notion that leaders go through sequential developmental stages characterized by increasing scope, task ambiguity, and accountability for change management (see Charan, Drotter, & Noel, 2000; Ployhart, Holtz, & Bliese, 2002; Sloan, 1994). Whereas a discussion of these stage models is beyond the scope of this review (refer to London and Maurer, Chapter 10, this volume), relevant to our discussion of assessment is that leadership requirements and their attendant competencies change as leaders advance. As can be inferred from Figure 4.1, the leadership competencies associated with success are linked to the hierarchical level in the organization and to the attendant scope of responsibilities associated with that level. (Refer to Zaccaro et al., Chapter 5, this volume, for further discussion regarding traits associated with leader level.) If what leaders do to be successful changes, it logically follows that what should be assessed changes. Sloan (1994) noted that there is little theorizing regarding the specific skills, knowledge, and attributes required for success at different organizational levels of management, and there is even less research than theory. It would be overly pessimistic, however, to suggest that we know little about what matters and what should be assessed at different organizational levels. The literature provides some guidance within an organizational level about the competencies required for leadership effectiveness. Thus, depending on the frame of reference (i.e., assessment for feedback, development, or career management), there is some direction regarding required competencies. For example, Ritchie (1994) reported on data from the AT&T Advanced Management Program, which was designed to identify middle managers (concerned with relationships, policies, workers, and quantity in Figure 4.1) with senior management potential (concerned with networks, initiatives, organization, and quality). Middle managers participated in 3.5 days of exercises at an assessment center, completed IQ tests along with objective and projective personality inventories, and were interviewed by a clinical psychologist. Assessors rated 24 different senior management characteristics derived from analyses of successful AT&T managers, a literature review, psychologist interviews, and input from managers in major corporations outside the industry. The 24 characteristics were grouped into six categories labeled Work Motivation, Communication Skills, Interpersonal Skills, Management Problem Solving, Development Potential, and Coping with Change (e.g., behavior flexibility, risk taking, creativity, coping with stress, tolerance of uncertainty). The raters first assessed upward mobility potential (i.e., assessment for career management) and then formulated development issues (i.e., assessment for development).

The lack of theory and research is more pronounced at the strategic leadership level (Day, 2000; Finkelstein & Hambrick, 1996), where, as Figure 4.1 depicts, leaders have responsibility for aligning systems and strategy with the external environment (refer also to Sashkin, Chapter 8, this volume). The lack of theoretical development may be due in part to criteria being less valid at higher organizational levels (H. Levinson, 1994), to small sample sizes precluding statistical validation (Day, 2001), and to criteria for assessment incorporating both internal and external targets (Day & Lord, 1988). Industry factors may also place considerably different leadership requirements on upper-echelon leaders (Hambrick & Mason, 1984; H. Levinson, 1994), but assessment norms for validated instruments seldom differentiate performance requirements by industry group.

Some guidance also is available for assessment with top-level leaders. Whereas reports on top-level leaders are uniform in describing these leaders as highly intelligent (McCall & Lombardo, 1983; Van Velsor & Leslie, 1995), what may separate effective from ineffective leaders at top levels is a form of intelligence related to making sense from complexity (Day, 2001). Weick (1988) suggested that under conditions of complexity, leaders will increasingly rely on habits and familiar environmental cues. Day (2001) argued that it may be the ability to accurately perceive and engage complexity that separates effective from ineffective top-level leaders. To the extent that this assertion is true, there remains the issue of how to measure this form of intelligence with predictive validity for organizational work. Figure 4.1 suggests that a model to measure this form of intelligence would need to include an organizational vision aligned with the external environment through the appropriate strategy and systems (e.g., acceptable performance at lowest cost or differentiated product attributes).

Criteria Over Time

Earlier, we alluded to the idea that our instruments may not be predictive or reliable to the extent that the organization's direction or strategic focus may shift over time. The criteria used to measure leader effectiveness will be useful only if they are contemporaneously appropriate. We also discussed the developmental nature of leadership as a process by which leadership activity may change over time, such that attempts to compare leaders at different developmental stages may result in misleading findings regarding what is effectiveness (see Boyatzis, McKee, & Goleman, 2002). We would be remiss if we did not also discuss some of the longitudinal effects of leadership and the criteria used to measure that success. Hawkins and Tolzin (2002), for example, discussed how long-term relationships between supervisors and subordinates may mitigate the impact and application of traditional leadership theories such as LMX. Other longitudinal effects of leadership behavior are coming to light in the empirical literature, such as how it affects group performance (Lester, Meglino, & Korsgaard, 2002; Sivasubramaniam, Murry, Avolio, & Jung, 2002), leader emergence (Wolff, Pescosolido, & Druskat, 2002), and trickle-down effects of CEO behavior on supervisory practices (Zohar, 2002). The relevance of these studies is unmistakable: We are better at predicting when we take into account the time factor in evaluating leadership effectiveness.

Cross-Cultural Issues in the Assessment of Leadership

Arguments presented earlier discussed the fact that different types of behaviors may be associated with leader emergence or effectiveness as a function of leader level. So too must one consider the impact of national culture context on leader assessment. Den Hartog and Dickson (Chapter 11, this volume) provide ample examples of the universality as well as the cultural specificity of leadership practice. On a methodological note, when conducting cross-cultural studies, the issue of measurement invariance must be taken seriously before comparisons of assessments can be made (see Antonakis et al., Chapter 3, this volume).

Focus on Leadership Competence of Individual Leaders

Leadership competence, as conceived among the array of theories and measures of it, comprises a broad variety of skills, values, characteristics, actions, and relationships. Whereas some conceptualizations emphasize measures of planning and vision, others focus on the leader's task structuring, delegation, negotiating, influencing, concern for people, or conduct in interpersonal relationships. Some theories and measures concentrate on dissemination of visionary strategy as the primary function of leadership. Other theories recognize this component of leadership as clearly necessary for effectiveness, but they focus instead on the complementary sound management practices required to see that the vision is implemented. Still other theories spotlight the leader's interpersonal relationships, using individuals directly reporting to the leaders to describe the leader's effectiveness and competence. Certainly, the foci of these various conceptualizations of leadership will be evident in how leaders are differentially evaluated by subordinates, peers, or superiors (or in self-ratings) as different emphases of the leadership construct lend themselves better to certain viewpoints than to others.

The point is that the leadership construct is an amorphous one and is measured by a relatively large variety of dimensions or emphases, depending upon how it is conceived. More important, the various theories upon which the construct is based probably correctly identify one or more dimensions that might be captured and described under the vague, general rubric of "leader competence." It is difficult to imagine a single individual manifesting all the skills, values, characteristics, actions, and relationships evaluated by the measures used in different theoretical approaches. If we assume that all these various dimensions of leadership are necessary for effectiveness, it becomes even more difficult to imagine that leadership, when measured by a single instrument with a narrow focus on only some of the demands for leader effectiveness, would correlate very highly with measures of success, particularly when success is measured by objective criteria (see Lowe, Kroeck, et al., 1996). That we do find significant correlation with success is a tribute to the construct validity of our instruments, even when those relationships explain a relatively small amount of variance in group or organizational performance.

We often hear the question "Why are there so few great leaders?" The answer to this may reside in the fact that our expectations of leadership may exceed that which but a few can demonstrate. Indeed, the requirements for what most of us think of as leadership competence are many and diverse, as well as perhaps, realistically, quite uncommon. In fact, leaders often surround themselves with a team of people to complement their shortcomings and do so necessarily. The people-oriented leader often has a taskmaster as his or her "second." Structuring and visionary leaders often need a team of managers capable of buffering and implementing the tough policies set forth. Unfortunately, most of our current empirical data are populated with assessments of various dimensions of leadership by a single individual leader and how those dimensions correlate with different performance criteria. That we currently conceptualize and measure *leadership* as something exhibited by single individuals may be the flaw in our attempts to find strong relationships with meaningful criteria of success. Perhaps we would be better served to measure the leadership offered by the entire leadership team. We might best move the field forward by developing theories around a paradigm of leadership not fully invested in the "single individual" concept of the leadership phenomenon. A shift to measurement of leadership competence as demonstrated by the full management team would serve the purposes of both prediction and understanding.

Conclusion

To summarize, the level of the leader in the organizational hierarchy and other contextual factors have clear implications for the assessment of leadership. As the leader's job scope increases, the requirements for effective leadership change in substantial ways. If, for example, we adopt Kotter's (1990) assertion that leadership is about adaptive and constructive change, the competencies required to effect that change will be substantially different for a front-line team leader than for the CEO of a multinational corporation. Organizational type and cultural differences also will reflect these criteria of effectiveness and, concomitantly, the instruments most useful for assessing different types and levels and contexts of leaders. Roles and emphases change over time, and often the effects of leadership take time to be revealed. Consequently, assessment tools used to identify the potential to be successful in these roles versus the assessment tools required to provide feedback regarding in-role leadership performance will be different, and they will be accurate to the extent that they take these factors into account. The various instruments for assessing leadership reviewed in this chapter provide a starting place for matching technique and instrumentation to assessment needs. However, this matching process will also identify a number of significant gaps between the tools available and assessment needs. The need to focus on a more comprehensive view of leadership, perhaps as a team phenomenon rather than the skills, values, characteristics, actions, and relationships of a single individual, has been pointed out as one limitation of current thinking. Nevertheless, despite all the challenges identified here, we agree with Dionne, Yammarino, Atwater, and James (2002), who, after failing to identify any moderators as alternative substitutes for leadership, concluded, "Leadership does matter."

Appendix 4.1 Summary and Review of Published Leadership Measures

Instrument	Acronym	Creator and Approximate Date of Creation	Publisher	Purpose	Raters	Scales	Format	Theoretical Bases
16-Personality Factors (5th edition)–Human Resources Development Report	16-PF	Dee-Burnett, Johns, Russell, and Mead (1997, 2002)	Institute for Personality and Ability Testing	Assessment, placement, and training/development	Self-report for managers	Leadership Style; Interacting with Others; Decision Making; Initiative; Personal Adjustment	Paper and pencil	Cattell's 16-Factor Personality Theory
Hogan Leadership Forecast		Hogan (2001)	Hogan Assessment Systems	Assessment, placement, and training/development	Self-report for managers	Potential; Challenge; Values	Paper and pencil	Competency Model
Kirkpatrick Management and Supervisory Skills Series	LMDMI	Kirkpatrick (1995)	Kirkpatrick	Assessment of managerial skills and practices; selection and development	Self-report for managers or management candidates	Communication Inventory; Human Relations Inventory; Managing Change Inventory; Management Roles Inventory; Coaching and Performance Appraisal Inventory; Time Management Inventory; Leadership, Motivation, and Decision-Making Inventory	Paper and pencil	NA
Leadership Effectiveness and Attitude Description (LEAD) Questionnaire	LEAD	Hersey and Blanchard (1974)	NA	Assessment of leadership style	Self-report for managers	Leader Consideration; Initiating Structure	Paper and pencil	Grid Theory
Leader Behavior Description Questionnaire	LBDQ	Stogdill and Coons (1957)	NA	Assessment of leadership	Self-report for managers and subordinates	Leader Consideration; Initiating Structure	Paper and pencil	Grid Theory
Leader Behavior Questionnaire, Revised	LBQ	Sashkin (1988–1996)	HRD Press	Assessment of leader behavior	Self-report for managers and raters	Visionary Leadership Behavior Scale; Visionary Leadership Characteristics Scale; Visionary Culture Building Scale	Paper and pencil	Transformational Leadership Theory
Leader Member Exchange Measure	LMX-7	Graen and Uhl-Bien (1995); Scandura and Graen (1984)	NA	Assessment of LMX quality	Self-report for managers and subordinates	Subordinate LMX; Supervisor LMX	Paper and pencil	LMX Theory

Instrument	Acronym	Creator and Approximate Date of Creation	Publisher	Purpose	Raters	Scales	Format	Theoretical Bases
Leadership Practices Inventory	LPI	Kouzes and Posner (1990–1992)	Pfeiffer & Company International Publishers	Assessment of leadership	360-degree feedback	Challenging the Process; Inspiring a Shared Vision; Enabling Others to Act; Modeling the Way; Encouraging the Heart	Paper and pencil	Competency Model
Leadership Opinion Questionnaire	LOQ	Fleishman (1960)	Science Research Associates, Inc.	Assessment of leadership	Self-report for managers	Consideration; Structure	Paper and pencil	Grid Theory
Leadership Practices Inventory-Delta	LPI-Delta	Kouzes and Posner (1988–1992)	Jossey-Bass Pfeiffer	Assessment and training/ development	Self-report for managers or management candidates	Challenging the Process; Inspiring a Shared Vision; Enabling Others to Act; Modeling the Way; Encouraging the Heart	Paper and pencil	Competency Model
Leadership Profiles Inventory-Individual Contributor	LPI-IC	Kouzes and Posner (1990–1997)	Jossey-Bass Pfeiffer	Assessment and training/ development of nonmanagerial leaders	Self-report for nonmanagerial leaders or observers	Challenging the Process; Inspiring a Shared Vision; Enabling Others to Act; Modeling the Way; Encouraging the Heart	Paper and pencil	Competency Model
Least Preferred Co-worker Scale	LPC	Fiedler (1973)	NA	Assessment of leadership	Self-report for managers	LPC Score	Paper and pencil	Fiedler's Contingency Theory
LMX-6	LMX-6	Schriesheim, Neider, Scandura, and Tepper (1992)	NA	Assessment of LMX quality	Self-report for managers and subordinates	LMX	Paper and pencil	LMX Theory
LMX-MDM	LMX-MDM	Liden and Maslyn (1998)	NA	Assessment of LMX quality	Self-report for managers and subordinates	LMX	Paper and pencil	Vertical-Dyad Linkage Theory
Management Inventory on Modern Management	MIMM	Kirkpatrick (1984)	NA	Assessment	Self-report for managers	Leadership Styles; Selecting and Training; Communicating; Motivating; Managing Change; Delegating; Managing Time; Managing Change; Total Score	Paper and pencil	None
Management Style Questionnaire	MSQ	McBer and Company (1974–1980)	McBer and Company	Diagnosis and self-assessment	Self-report for managers and subordinates	Coercive; Authoritative; Affiliative; Democratic; Pacesetting; Coaching	Paper and pencil	McClelland's Need Theory

(Continued)

Appendix 4.1 (Continued)

Instrument	Acronym	Creator and Approximate Date of Creation	Publisher	Purpose	Raters	Scales	Format	Theoretical Bases
Management Styles Inventory		Hall, Harvey, and Williams (1964–1990)	Teleometrics International	Assessment of leadership style under different conditions	Self-report for managers	Philosophy; Planning and Goal Setting; Implementation; Performance and Evaluation; Total	Paper and pencil	Grid Theory
Management Styles Questionnaire	MSQ	Michalak (1974–1983)	Michalak Training Associates, Inc.	Assessment and training/development	Self-report for managers and subordinates	Task Orientation; People Orientation	Paper and pencil	Grid Theory
Manager Style Appraisal		Hall, Harvey, and Williams (1967–1990)	Teleometrics International	Assessment of managerial style	Self-report for managers	Philosophy; Planning and Goal Setting; Implementation; Performance and Evaluation; Total	Paper and pencil	Grid Theory
Managerial Competence Index	MCI	Hall (1980–1989)	Teleometrics International	Assessment and training/development	Self-report for managers or management candidates}	Team Management; Middle-of-the-Road Management; Task Management; Country Club Management; Impoverished Management	Paper and pencil	Grid Theory
Managerial Competence Review	MCR	Hall (1980–1989)	Teleometrics International	Assessment and training/development	Subordinates	Team Management; Middle-of-the-Road Management; Task Management; Country Club Management; Impoverished Management	Paper and Pencil	Grid Theory
Multifactor Leadership Questionnaire for Research	MLQ	Bass and Avolio (1985–1995)	Mind Garden, Inc.	Assessment, selection, and training/development	Self-report for managers and raters	Idealized Influence (Self); Idealized Influence (Behavior); Inspirational Motivation; Intellectual Stimulation; Individualized Consideration; Contingent Reward; Management by Exception (Active); Management by Exception (Passive); Laissez-Faire; Extra Effort; Effectiveness; Satisfaction	Paper and pencil	Transformational Leadership Theory

Instrument	Acronym	Creator and Approximate Date of Creation	Publisher	Purpose	Raters	Scales	Format	Theoretical Bases
Performance Skills Leader	PS Leader	Human Technologies, Inc. (1996)	HRD Press	Assessment and training/development	360-degree feedback	Strategic Focus; Business Focus; Work Force Focus; Interpersonal Focus; Personal Focus	Computer-based	Competency Model
Profile Aptitude for Leadership	PAL	Training House, Inc. (1991)	Training House, Inc.	Assessment of leadership style	Self-report for managers	Manager; Supervisor; Entrepreneur; Technician	Paper and pencil	NA
Project LMX	PLMX	Uhl-Bien and Graen (1992)	NA	Assessment of LMX quality	Self-report for managers and subordinates	Project LMX	Paper and pencil	LMX Theory
Superior Vertical Measurement		Wakabayashi and Graen (1984)	INA	Assessment of LMX quality	Self-report for managers and subordinates	LMX	Paper and pencil	LMX Theory
Team Leadership Practices Inventory	TEAM-LPI	Kouzes and Posner (1992)	Pheiffer & Company International Publishers	Assessment of team leadership	Self-report for team members	Challenging the Process; Inspiring a Shared Vision; Enabling Others to Act; Modeling the Way; Encouraging the Heart	Paper and pencil	Competency Model
Team Member Exchange	TMX	Seers and Graen (1984)	NA	Assessment of LMX quality	Self-report for managers and subordinates	Team LMX	Paper and pencil	LMX Theory
Vertical Exchange		Wakabayashi, Minami, Hashimoto, Sano, Graen, and Novac (1981)	NA	Assessment of LMX quality	Self-report for managers and subordinates	LMX	Paper and pencil	LMX Theory
Vroom and Yetton		Vroom and Yetton (1973)	NA	Prescription of leadership behavior	Self-report for managers	Leadership Style	Paper and pencil	Normative Leadership Decision Model

PART III

The Major Schools
of Leadership

CHAPTER 5

Leader Traits and Attributes

Stephen J. Zaccaro

Cary Kemp

Paige Bader

The concept of leader traits and attributes is indeed an old one, predating the scientific study of leadership and reaching back into antiquity, across several early civilizations (Bass, 1990; Zaccaro, in press). For example, in Chinese literature from the 6th century B.C., Lao-tzu described the qualities of effective leaders (Hieder, 1985). The wise leader, according to Lao-tzu, was to be selfless, hardworking, honest, able to time the appropriateness of actions, fair in handling conflict, and able to "empower" others (to use a more current vernacular). Early and medieval mythology (e.g., Homer's *Iliad* and *Odyssey*; Alfred, Lord Tennyson's *Idylls of the King*) focused on the attributes of heroes, whereas biblical writing emphasized wisdom and service to others as leadership qualities. Plato's *Republic* (1960) emphasized that in the ideal nation-state, effective leaders used reasoning capacities and wisdom to lead others. He offered a lifelong "assessment plan" to help select such leaders (the first leader selection program?). His student Aristotle argued in *Politics* (1900) that leaders were to help others seek virtue; they would do so by themselves being virtuous. He offered a plan for educating future governors (the first leader development program?). Niccolò Machiavelli, in *The Prince*

(1513/1954), defined power and the ability of leaders to understand social situations and to manipulate them in the practice of leadership as key leader attributes. Contrary to Aristotle, Machiavelli suggested slyness as a leader attribute, prescribing that leaders use less than virtuous means of gaining power and social legitimacy if more virtuous means were inadequate. Bass (1990) noted in his review that notions about leader qualities could be found in early Egyptian, Babylonian, Asian, and Icelandic sagas. Wondering about and identifying the qualities of the effective leader, the great hero, or the wise monarch, then, preoccupied the earliest thinkers and storytellers.

The scientific modeling of this question perhaps began with Galton (1869), who examined the correlated status of leaders and geniuses across generations. He defined extraordinary intelligence as a key leader attribute and argued that such leader qualities were inherited, not developed. He also proposed eugenics, which relied on selective mating to produce individuals with the best combination of leadership qualities. Terman (1904) produced the first empirical study of leadership, examining the qualities that differentiated leaders from nonleaders in schoolchildren. He reported such attributes as verbal fluency, intelligence, low emotionality, daring, congeniality, goodness, and liveliness as characterizing youthful leaders. Similar studies burgeoned after Terman's (see Stogdill, 1948, for a review), forming the initial empirical backdrop for trait research.

These early writings from antiquity to the first part of the 20th century attest to the enduring and compelling notions that leaders have particular qualities distinguishing them from nonleaders, and that these qualities can be identified and assessed. However, beginning with Stogdill (1948), who stated in an oft-cited quotation, "A person does not become a leader by virtue of the possession of some combination of traits" (p. 64), researchers began to perceive leader trait models as having low utility for explaining leadership emergence and effectiveness. A survey of textbooks in industrial/organizational and social psychology that appeared after Stogdill's work points to the demise of trait-based leadership theories. Witness the following quotations:

> If there is a general trait of leadership that plays a part in all situations it is relatively unimportant in determining an individual's success as a leader. To a considerable extent the manifestation of leadership is determined by the social situation. Under one set of circumstances an individual will be a good leader and under others he will be a poor one. (Ghiselli & Brown, 1955, p. 471)

> [The trait method] does not provide the psychologist with much insight into the basic dynamics of the leadership process. (Blum & Naylor, 1956, p. 420)

> Like much early research in the behavioral sciences, the initial approach to leadership was to compare individuals, in this case to explore how leaders differ from nonleaders. This tactic is generally acknowledged to have been premature. Few stable differences were found. (Secord & Backman, 1974, p. 343)

[There is] little or no connection between personality traits and leader effectiveness. (Muchinsky, 1983, p. 403)

The conclusion . . . that leaders do not differ from followers in clear and easily recognized ways, remains valid. (Baron & Byrne, 1987, p. 405)

More recently, the trait, or individual difference, approach to leadership has regained some prominence. Some of the problems and shortcomings that plagued its earlier ascendant period, however, still exist to limit the potential reach of such models. This chapter will examine the recent research on leader attributes and will provide a set of propositions and conceptual prescriptions to guide future research. We begin by defining the notion of "trait" as it applies to the leadership domain, and we provide a somewhat brief history of the trait model, detailing milestones and the reasons for its initial demise and its recent resurgence. We then summarize recent empirical findings and conclude with some propositions and prescriptions.

The Meaning of "Trait"

The term *trait* has been the source of considerable ambiguity and confusion in the literature, referring sometimes and variously to personality, temperaments, dispositions, and abilities, as well as to any enduring qualities of the individual, including physical and demographic attributes. Furthermore, its utility for explaining behavioral variance has been severely challenged by Mischel (1968), although this view has been eclipsed by more recent arguments (Kenrick & Funder, 1988). Indeed, the rise, fall, and resurgence of leader trait perspectives roughly parallel the popularity (or lack thereof) of individual difference research in general psychology, as well as in industrial and organizational psychology (see Hough & Schneider, 1996). During this cycle, the notion of traits, as well as their relationships to behavior and performance, has evolved to reflect greater conceptual sophistication.

Allport (1961) defined a trait as a "neuropsychic structure having the capacity to render many stimuli functionally equivalent, and to initiate and guide equivalent (meaningfully consistent) forms of adaptive and expressive behavior." (p. 347)

This perspective highlights the notion that traits refer to stable or consistent patterns of behavior that are relatively immune to situational contingencies— individuals with certain traits denoting particular behavioral predispositions would react in similar ways across a variety of situations having functionally diverse behavioral requirements. Indeed, it was this cross-situational consistency that was challenged by Mischel (1968). Kenrick and Funder (1988), while supporting the utility of trait concepts, noted that the influence of situations, as well as of person-by-situation interactions, "must be explicitly dealt with before we can predict from trait measures" (p. 31).

For the purposes of this chapter, we define *leader traits* as relatively stable and coherent integrations of personal characteristics that foster a consistent pattern of leadership performance across a variety of group and organizational situations. These characteristics reflect a range of stable individual differences, including personality, temperament, motives, cognitive abilities, skills, and expertise.

As we assert later in this chapter, effective and successful leaders do have qualities and attributes that are not generally possessed by nonleaders. This is not to argue that the situation has no bearing on leader behavior—we will strongly suggest otherwise. Likewise, some individuals can be successful as leaders in some situations but not in others. We would argue, however, that such success is a function of narrowly prescriptive leadership contexts that respond to a specific set of leader competencies, such as lower-level or direct line supervision (Jacobs & Jaques, 1987b; Zaccaro, 2001). As leadership situations become more complex and varied, we suspect that personal attributes play a more substantial role in predicting success.

The Rise, Fall, and Rise of Leader Trait Research

The roots of leader trait research were planted in the functionalism that characterized early American psychology, in the applied focus of some early American psychologists, and especially in the mental testing movement. Functionalism reflected an emphasis on the "typical operations of consciousness under actual conditions" (Angell, 1907, p. 61), in which the focus was on discerning the purposive nature of behavior. This focus was fertile ground for the emergence of applied psychology and yielded the first textbook in industrial/organizational psychology (Munsterberg, 1913). This book had several sections on personnel selection and identifying the qualities of best workers in various work domains, but it contained nothing on the processes and characteristics of effective leaders.

Functionalism also facilitated a growing interest in mental testing (Cattell, 1890) to identify individual differences that contribute to performance variability. The early focus in mental testing was on the identification of differences in intelligence, following from the work of Goddard (1911) and Terman (1916). The first association of this testing movement with questions of leadership came in the development of mental ability tests for the U.S. Army in World War I. Robert Yerkes, who was one of several early psychologists in charge of this effort, wrote in a letter to the army surgeon general that one of the purposes of the mental ability exams was "to assist in selecting the most competent men for special training and responsible positions" (Hothersall, 1984, p. 323, citing Yerkes, 1921, p. 19). Thus, by the second decade of the 20th century, psychologists had begun to associate certain individual differences, in particular intelligence and mental ability, with high work performance in positions of authority.

The next three decades saw a burgeoning of research focusing on identifying those qualities that distinguish leaders from nonleaders. Bird (1940), Jenkins (1947), and Stogdill (1948) published early reviews of this research. The studies summarized in these reviews reflected the use of six primary approaches methods (Stogdill, 1948, pp. 36–38): (a) observation of behavior in group situations that afforded leader emergence, (b) sociometric choices by peers, (c) nominations by qualified observers and raters, (d) selection of individuals into leadership positions, (e) analysis of biographical data and case histories of leaders and nonleaders, and (f) interviews with business executives and professionals to specify leader characteristics. The studies cited in these reviews were conducted across a range of age groups, from preschool to adulthood, and across many types of organizations.

Several observations emerge from an examination of the various early reviews of individual differences that were associated with leadership. First, early researchers investigated a wide range of individual difference. Bird (1940) listed 79 leader qualities! Bass (1990) placed Stogdill's 32 attributes into six categories: physical characteristics, social background, intelligence and ability, personality, task-related characteristics, and social characteristics. This diversity of attributes indicates that leadership researchers in this early period focused more on descriptive research, and less on conceptual models that defined leadership and hypothesized associations between leadership concepts and particular leader attributes. The result was an atheoretical miasma of attribute–leadership associations that could not be sustained consistently across different leadership situations.

Also problematic was the fact that the methods by which data were observed or collected were limited and confounded by possible errors and biases such as halo effects, variable misspecification, leniency, measure unreliability, and social desirability (Gibb, 1954). Finally, the leadership situations and methods of leader identification were so diverse as to overwhelm the likelihood of observing consistent attributes across studies (Gibb, 1954). Samples ranged from children in nursery school to business executives and well-known historical figures. The specification of leadership ranged from popularity ratings to the attainment of leadership positions. This variety of research settings, together with a lack of theory linking leadership and leadership situations to prescribed leader characteristics, decreased the likelihood of finding consistent differences between leaders and nonleaders.

This lack of consistency was reflected in several reviews published in the 1940s and 1950s. Gibb (1947) argued, "Leadership, then, is always relative to the situation . . . in the sense that the particular set of social circumstances existing at the moment determines which attributes of personality will confer leadership status" (p. 270). Jenkins (1947), in his review of military leadership, observed that "no single trait or group of characteristics has been isolated which sets off the leader from the members of the group" (pp. 74-75). Stogdill (1948) concluded that "persons who are leaders in one situation may not necessarily be leaders in other situations" (p. 65). Gibb (1954) noted that "numerous studies of the personalities of leaders have failed to find any consistent pattern of traits which characterize leaders" (p. 889). As a final example, Mann's (1959) empirical review of correlations among a variety of attributes and leader status indicated that few, if any, associations were of sufficient magnitude to warrant unambiguous conclusions.

As a group, these studies sounded the demise of leader trait models. However, close readings of these articles, in particular Stogdill (1948) and Mann (1959) (perhaps the two most influential of the early reviews), shows an overly harsh interpretation of their conclusions about leader traits. The following excerpts suggest a significant role to be attributed to individual differences between leaders and nonleaders.

> [Evidence from 15 or more studies indicates that] the average person who occupies a position of leadership exceeds the average member of his group in the following respects: (1) intelligence, (2) scholarship, (3) dependability in exercising responsibility, (4) activity and social participation, and (5) socioeconomic status. [Evidence from 10 or more studies indicates that] the average person who occupies a position of leadership exceeds the average member of his group in the following respects: (i) sociability, (ii) initiative, (iii) persistence, (iv) knowing how to get things done, (v) self-confidence, (vi) alertness to, and insight into, situations, (vii) cooperativeness, (viii) popularity, (ix) adaptability, and (x) verbal facility. (Stogdill, 1948, p. 63)

> A number of relationships between an individual's personality and his leadership status in groups appear to be well established. The positive relationships of intelligence, adjustment, and extroversion to leadership are highly significant. In addition, dominance, masculinity, and interpersonal sensitivity are found to be positively related to leadership, while conservatism is found to be negatively related to leadership. (Mann, 1959, p. 252)

Thus, whereas the claims of these researchers, and others, about the importance of group situations in determining leadership had significant validity, the conclusions drawn from their findings by subsequent leadership researchers about the low utility of leader traits were perhaps unwarranted.

The demise of leader trait models in the 1940s and 1950s was facilitated by "rotation design" (see Kenny & Zaccaro, 1983, in which the term was coined) research paradigms that varied group situations to test the hypothesis that leader status was stable. Such designs varied (a) group membership such that each member was in a group with each other member only once, (b) group tasks such that each group completed several different tasks, or (c) both. Two studies that varied group composition (Bell & French, 1950; Borgatta, Bales, & Couch, 1954) found that leadership rankings of a member in one group were highly correlated with rankings of the same member in different groups. Such findings were problematic, however, because similar tasks were used across different groups—leader status could still be attributed to situational demands.

Two other studies (Carter & Nixon, 1949; Gibb, 1949) varied the task while keeping group composition constant. Each of these studies reported that leader status remained stable across group tasks that required different leadership contributions. These conclusions also were problematic, however, because leader status established on the first task could well have influenced team processes and member rankings on subsequently ordered tasks.

Work by Barnlund (1962) represents the single study at that time that varied both task and composition. Barnlund reported a statistically nonsignificant correlation of .64 between leader emergence in one situation and similar status in group situations of differing tasks and members, and he concluded that his results lent "credibility to the idea that leadership grows out of the special problems of coordination facing a given group and the available talent of the participants" (p. 51).

The conclusions from the leader trait reviews and the rotation design studies provided impetus for the emergence of "leader situationism" models. These models perhaps started with A. J. Murphy (1941), who argued, "Leadership does not reside in the person. It is a function of the whole situation" (p. 674). The models continued with the work of Jenkins (1947), Sherif and Sherif (1948), Hemphill (1949), and Gibb (1947, 1954, 1958). The situationism perspective emphasized that certain group situations would call for specific leader qualities, and the individual who possessed those qualities would be effective as a leader in that situation; however, under a different group situation, another person could be more appropriate or effective in the leadership role.

Fiedler (1964, 1971b) provided perhaps the most conceptually sophisticated framework of leader situationism with his contingency model. He articulated the features of group situations that produced favorable circumstances for certain stable patterns of leadership exhibited by an individual. Leaders were likely to be effective when their leadership patterns matched situational contingencies. Hersey and Blanchard (1969b), House (1971), Vroom and Yetton (1973), and Kerr and Jermier (1978) offered similar situation-matching models. Unlike Fielder's contingency theory, however, each of these models specified that leaders could vary their individual responses to changes in situational contingencies. Thus, presumably, the same individual could lead effectively across different situations. Nonetheless, these situational approaches dominated the zeitgeist in leadership in the 1960s and 1970s.

Although the trait approach to leadership was generally in decline in this period, psychologists in applied settings who were interested in leader and executive selection still utilized individual difference models. The research by Miner (1965, 1978) and that by Bray, Campbell, and Grant (1974; see also Bray, 1982; Howard & Bray, 1988, 1990) were two well-known examples. Miner examined the associations between several patterns of managerial motives and subsequent advancement. He found that need for power, need for achievement, and a positive orientation toward authority were significantly correlated with promotion to higher leadership positions in organizations. Bray et al. (1974) collected assessments of many attributes in organizational managers during a 3-day assessment center session, and followed that initial assessment with subsequent assessments 8 and 20 years later. They also conducted interviews with the bosses and supervisors of the original participants during the years between assessments. They found that attributes reflecting advancement motivation, interpersonal skills, intellectual ability, and administrative skills predicted attained managerial level 20 years after initial assessments. McClelland (1965), Boyatzis (1982), Moses (1985), Sparks (1990), and Bentz (1967, 1990) conducted similar trait-based studies of managerial performance and promotion.

The general resurgence of leader trait perspectives came in the 1980s and can be attributed to several research lines. The first was a statistical reexamination of both the early leader trait reviews and the rotation design studies. Lord, De Vader, and

Alliger (1986) used validity generalization techniques to correct the correlations reported by Mann (1959) for several sources of artifactual variance (i.e., sampling error, predictor unreliability, and differential range restriction across studies) and to calculate a population effect size. They also added leader attribute studies published after Mann's study to their analysis. Using only Mann's data, they reported corrected correlations of .52 for intelligence, .34 for masculinity, .21 for adjustment, .17 for dominance, .15 for extraversion, and .22 for conservatism. Adding the newer studies produced corrected correlations of .50 for intelligence, .24 for adjustment, .13 for dominance, and .26 for extraversion. They concluded that "personality traits are associated with leadership perceptions to a higher degree and more consistently than the popular literature indicates" (p. 407). A similar meta-analytic review by Keeney and Marchioro (1998) reported comparable findings.

Kenny and Zaccaro (1983) reexamined the findings of rotation design studies, particularly that of Barnlund (1962). They decomposed the correlations reported by Barnlund into the variance in leader ratings that could be attributed in part to the rater, to the interaction of rater and ratee, and to the characteristics of the person being rated (i.e., the potential leader). They estimated the association between ratee effects found across Barnlund's groups situations and found that between 49% and 82% of the variance in leadership ratings could be attributed to stable characteristics of the emergent leader. Zaccaro, Foti, and Kenny (1991) completed a similar rotation design, in which both task and group composition were varied, and reported a significant amount of trait-based variance in leader ratings (.59) and leader rankings (.43). In another similar study, Ferentinos (1996) reported an estimate of 56% for trait-based leadership variance. Taken together, these studies provide solid evidence that leaders who emerged in one group situation also were seen as leaders in different groups with different members, and across different situations, requiring different leadership responses.

Studies of charismatic leadership represent another line of research that energized leader trait perspectives in the 1980s. House (1977) put forth the first of such theories, followed shortly by Burns (1978), Bass (1985), Tichy and Devanna (1986), Conger and Kanungo (1987), and Sashkin (1988a). Whereas these models differed on many important concepts and parameters (see House and Shamir, 1993, for a summary of their differences), they all highlighted the special qualities of the leader that compelled strong followership. Several of these models postulated specific leader qualities that were linked to displayed charismatic influence. After reviewing these models and corresponding empirical research, Zaccaro (2001) specified the following as key leader attributes predicting charismatic influence: cognitive ability, self-confidence, socialized power motives, risk propensity, social skills, and nurturance.

In the late 1980s and the 1990s, the charismatic leadership models produced a deluge of empirical research across a variety of samples and using a variety of measures and methods (Conger, 1999). Whereas a substantial part of this research specified the contextual aspects of charismatic influence (e.g., Shamir & Howell, 1999), another consistent trend has been increasing study of the attributes of the charismatically influential leader (House, 1988; House & Howell, 1992; Zaccaro,

2001). The charismatic leadership research paradigm, together with the recent meta-analytic reviews, new rotation design studies, and longitudinal studies of managerial advancement, have contributed to a revitalization of the leader trait model. Indeed, Bass's (1990) comprehensive book summarizing the leadership literature devoted nine chapters (or 163 pages) to the personal attributes of leaders.

An Empirical Summary
of Leader Trait Research, 1990–2003

Bass (1990) provided a comprehensive review of the leader trait literature up to the late 1980s, building in turn on reviews by Stogdill (1948, 1974). In this section, we review studies of leader attributes that were published between 1990 and 2003. We consider these recent studies within the context of leader attribute categories offered by Mumford, Zaccaro, Harding, Fleishman, and Reiter-Palmon (1993) and by Mumford, Zaccaro, Harding, Jacobs, and Fleishman (2000). They specified five categories of leader attributes: (a) cognitive abilities, (b) personality, (c) motivation, (d) social appraisal and interpersonal skills, and (e) leader expertise and tacit knowledge.

Cognitive Abilities

General cognitive ability has been one of the most frequently studied leader attributes. The conceptual and empirical reviews by Bird (1940), Stogdill (1948), Mann (1959), Lord, De Vader, et al. (1986), and Keeney and Marchioro (1998) all pointed to its ubiquity. This popularity has continued in the time period of the present review. Recent studies also have examined other cognitive abilities, such as creative reasoning abilities and complex problem-solving skills, as determinants of leadership.

Several common themes are apparent across these studies. First, general intelligence continues to exhibit a strong connection to various indices of leadership and leader effectiveness, and this association has been observed under a variety of research settings. For example, Morrow and Stern (1990) examined scores on a variety of mental ability tests among a sample of more than 2,200 participants in IBM's assessment center program and associated these scores with rated predictions of managerial success by observers. Mental ability test scores were significantly and positively associated with rated probability of managerial success. Spreitzer, McCall, and Mahony (1997) also reported a significant association between analytical ability and ratings of executive potential as well as current managerial performance. Zaccaro, White, et al. (1997) indicated significant associations between general intelligence and both attained organizational level and ratings of executive potential in a sample of 543 army civilian managers. Using an undergraduate student sample, Ferentinos (1996) found that general intelligence was significantly correlated with leader emergence scores in a laboratory-based rotation design study. J. A. Smith and Foti (1998) also found significant correlations between intelligence and performance in laboratory teams, although they did not use a rotation design. LePine, Hollenbeck, Ilgen, and Hedlund (1997) found in laboratory decision-making teams that leader cognitive ability was significantly associated with team decision accuracy, although the effects were moderated by the degree of cognitive ability possessed by team staff members. Other studies have reported significant associations between leader intelligence and subordinate ratings (Atwater & Yammarino, 1993) and leader emergence (Atwater, Dionne, Avolio, Camobreco, & Lau, 1999; Kellett, Humphrey, & Sleeth, 2002; Roberts, 1995; Taggar, Hackett, & Saha, 1999). Taken together, these studies continue to support the consistent finding that leaders generally possess higher intelligence than do nonleaders.

These studies depart from earlier research, however, by their reliance on multivariate methodologies. A long-standing complaint in the leader trait literature has been the tendency to examine individual characteristics in isolation from other attributes, even when the researcher had assessed multiple attributes—such researchers often will report only the bivariate correlation of a particular attribute with an index of leadership. Most of the studies reviewed above, however, considered the influence of general intelligence in conjunction with at least one other variable, and they found (a) unique contributions of cognitive abilities to at least one index of leadership beyond the contributions of other attributes (e.g., Ferentinos, 1996; Roberts, 1995; Spreitzer et al., 1997; Taggar et al., 1999; Zaccaro, White, et al., 1997) or (b) joint contributions of general intelligence and other leader attributes to the prediction of leadership (e.g., LePine et al., 1997; Morrow & Stern, 1990; J. A. Smith & Foti, 1998). These studies, then, extend understanding about both the magnitude of intelligence as a leader attribute and its connection with other central leader traits.

Recent studies have proposed creative or divergent thinking as an important leader trait, particularly in organizational contexts requiring complex problem solving (Mumford & Connelly, 1991; Mumford, Marks, Connelly, Zaccaro, & Reiter-Palmon, 2000; Mumford, Scott, Gaddis, & Strange, 2002). In support of this proposition, Baehr (1992) found that in a sample of 1,358 managers in companies from four different industries, attained organizational level was associated with creative thinking—executives displayed higher creative potential scores than middle or lower-level managers. Using a case study approach, Bolin (1997) reported that exemplary entrepreneurial leaders shared creative thinking skills as a key attribute. Mouly and Sankaran (1999) indicated that leader creative capacity was associated with leader performance, whereas Tierney, Farmer, and Graen (1999) found that leader creative skills were related to the creativity displayed by group members. Connelly et al. (2000) found in a multivariate analysis of more than 700 army officers that, of 16 leader attributes, creative thinking and creative writing skills were among the strongest predictors of leader achievement. In a similar multivariate study, Zaccaro, White, et al. (1997) found a link between creative problem-solving skills and two indices of leadership—supervisory ratings of leader performance, and ratings of senior leader potential. The last two studies are particularly noteworthy because they considered the influence on leadership of creative thinking capacities along with other cognitive and personality variables, and they each found support for unique contributions.

Recent studies also have considered the influence of cognitive complexity and metacognitive skills on indices of leadership processes and performance (Bader, Zaccaro, & Kemp, 2003; Banks, Bader, Fleming, Zaccaro, & Barber, 2001; Hendrick, 1990; Offermann, Schroyer, & Green, 1998; Wofford & Goodwin, 1994). These studies report evidence for linking these attributes to leadership criteria. Zaccaro (2001) also reviewed a number of studies linking cognitive complexity to executive leadership and performance in complex domains.

Personality

Perhaps the largest set of leader trait studies published in the last decade has focused on leader personality. These studies have examined primarily (a) leadership and the Big Five model and (b) leadership and dimensions of the Myers-Briggs Type Indicator (MBTI). A number of other studies have examined other attributes, such as locus of control, adaptability, optimism, and destructive personality characteristics.

Research in personality has coalesced around the premise that personality traits can be broadly organized into five major headings: neuroticism (or emotional stability), extroversion, openness to experience, agreeableness, and conscientiousness (Digman, 1990; McCrae & Costa, 1987, 1991). Barrick and Mount (1991) applied this categorization to job performance. During the period of the current review, a number of researchers also have applied this model, or linked at least one of the five factors, to leadership. Salgado (1997) found that emotional stability, conscientiousness, extroversion, and agreeableness, but not openness, were valid predictors of managerial job performance in the European community. Connelly et al. (2000) also did not find any effects of openness on career achievement in a sample of military officers. Zaccaro, White, et al. (1997), however, did find that openness was associated with attained organizational level among army civilian managers. Neither study included any of the other Big Five factors. Brooks (1998) reported significant findings for agreeableness, conscientiousness, and openness in predicting job performance of managers across three retail organizations, although the effects of openness disappeared after controlling for organization. Stevens and Ash (2001) found that conscientiousness and extroversion were positively correlated with preferences for managerial work and job performance. They also found that agreeableness and openness were associated with greater preferences for participative management styles. Crant and Bateman (2000) reported that of the Big Five factors, only extroversion was related to perceptions of charismatic leadership.

Judge, Bono, Ilies, and Gerhardt (2002) used meta-analysis to examine 78 studies that linked one or more of the Big Five factors to leadership. They reported that extroversion exhibited the strongest relationship to leadership, followed by conscientiousness, neuroticism, and openness. Agreeableness demonstrated the weakest relationship to leadership. Judge et al. also differentiated between leader emergence and leader effectiveness, finding that all factors but agreeableness were associated with emergence; all five factors, though, were significantly associated with effectiveness. Ployhart, Holtz, and Bliese (2002) reported some stronger evidence for agreeableness, however, finding in a longitudinal study of leadership growth and development that agreeableness was associated with increased displays of adaptability.

Taken together, these studies find robust associations between most of, if not all, the Big Five personality factors and leadership. Indeed Judge et al. (2002) reported a multiple correlation of .48 with leadership.

Another substantial body of leadership research has examined the associations between dimensions of the MBTI and leadership indices. The MBTI measures four types of preferences regarding information, experiences, and making decisions (M. H. McCauley, 1990). The first measure, extroversion versus introversion, indicates a preference for social engagement versus a preference for introspection and ideas. The sensing versus intuition measure indicates a preference for sense data and facts (what can be experienced) versus a preference for possibilities and theoretical patterns. The measure of thinking versus feeling indicates a preference for using logic and rational analysis in making decisions versus a preference for making decisions using personal values and emotional reactions. Finally, the judging and perceiving measure reflects a preference for planning and organizing versus spontaneity and flexibility.

Barber (1990) compared the types (as measured by the MBTI) of senior military officers with those of the general population and found that military executives were more likely to reflect sensing, thinking, and judging preferences. M. H. McCauley (1990) examined several comprehensive MBTI databases containing scores from more than 92,000 subjects, ranging from college students, to managers in many different industries from all organizational levels and from many different countries, to leaders in government and public institutions. In summarizing the findings regarding which types and preferences most likely predicted advancement to top executive ranks, M. H. McCauley (1990) noted:

> Though any type can reach the top, executives most likely to do so are somewhat more likely to prefer extraversion and intuition, and are highly likely to prefer thinking and judgment. Leaders who inspire by communicating a vision of a better future may come from intuitives, especially the intuitives with feeling. (p. 411)

Jacobs and Jaques (1990) noted that because executives often face tasks of developing conceptual frameworks of their complex operating environments, they ought to possess a temperament reflecting a desire to engage in reflective thinking and to build mental models. Labeling this temperament "proclivity," they argued that it reflected the degree to which individuals felt rewarded by the cognitive activity of organizing complex experiences. They also argued that this temperament might be operationalized as the intuition-thinking (NT) profile from the MBTI. To assess this hypothesis, Zaccaro (2001) used the tables from M. H. McCauley (1990) to compare successful executives with a sample of middle- and lower-level managers and unsuccessful executives. He found that a greater proportion of NTs (40%) were represented in the successful executive sample than in the sample of lower-level managers or less-effective executives (21%).

Several other recent studies have found links between dimensions of the MBTI and leadership. B. Schneider, Ehrhart, and Ehrhart (2002) reported preferences for extroversion and judging to be associated with teacher and peer ratings of leadership in a sample of high school students. Connelly et al. (2000) found that preferences for intuition predicted army officer career achievement. Ludgate (2001) reported higher preferences for extroversion, intuition, perceiving, and sensing in a sample of managers from a cross-section of U.S. corporations.

These studies, together with those of M. H. McCauley (1990) and Zaccaro (2001), suggest that leaders differ somewhat from nonleaders in their preferences for extroversion, intuition, thinking, and judging, although some contradictory findings have been reported for sensing and perceiving. We hasten to add McCauley's cautionary note that "there is evidence that all 16 MBTI types assume leadership positions" (p. 414). Knowlton and McGee (1994) argued that top-level leadership requires the development and display of preferred and secondary information acquisition and decision-making styles.

Other recent leader personality research has examined such attributes as optimism (Bader, Zaccaro, et al., 2003; Pritzker, 2002), proactivity (Crant & Batemen, 2000; Deluga, 1998, 2001), adaptability (Ployhart et al., 2002), locus of control (J. M. Howell & Avolio, 1993), and nurturance (S. M. Ross & Offermann, 1991). These studies typically investigated targeted leader attributes within a multivariate framework and found support for unique contributions of particular leader traits. House, Hanges, et al. (1999) investigated a number of leader attributes in a large multinational, multimethod, and multiphase study, titled Project GLOBE (see also Abdalla & Al-Homoud, 2001). This effort has found that (a) the influences of some leader attributes on key leadership criteria extend across cultures and that (b) the influences of other attributes present culture-specific effects.

Finally, some researchers have focused on destructive personal attributes that contribute to harmful or negative leadership influences (Costanza, 1996; Hogan, Raskin, & Fazzini, 1990; Mumford, Gessner, Connelly, O'Connor, & Clifton, 1993; Sarris, 1995; Van Velsor & Leslie, 1995). Although this line of research is in its early stages and has yielded somewhat inconsistent findings, it has begun to provide a counterperspective to the overwhelming body of research that has pointed to the personality attributes that facilitate leadership.

Motivation

Leadership researchers have examined primarily the following motive-states as influences on leadership: need for power or need for dominance, need for achievement, need for affiliation, and need for responsibility. The latter is similar to another motive-state that has emerged recently in the leadership literature—motivation to lead (Chan & Drasgow, 2001).

House, Spangler, and Woycke (1991) completed an archival-based analysis of U.S. presidents and investigated the association between needs for power, achievement, and affiliation, respectively, and five indices of presidential performance. They found that need for power was related positively to four of the five indices (but negatively related to economic performance), whereas needs for achievement and affiliation were negatively related to three performance criteria. Using other indices of presidential greatness, Deluga (1998) also reported significant positive effects for power needs but no effects for achievement and affiliation. Thomas, Dickson, and Bliese (2001) examined the degree to which the effects of power and affiliation needs on leadership ratings for ROTC cadets were mediated by extroversion. This study is valuable because it provides a process model linking personality and motives to leadership. They found that whereas both motive-states were associated with extroversion, the latter fully mediated the effects of affiliation on leadership; that is, need for power had both direct and mediated effects on leadership effects.

J. A. Smith and Foti (1998) found that need for dominance motives were positively associated, in conjunction with intelligence and general self-efficacy, to leader emergence scores. Connelly et al. (2001) indicated that dominance and achievement needs were not associated with leader career achievement and rated solution quality to leadership problems. Zaccaro, White, et al. (1997), however, reported that achievement and dominance motives did predict attained organizational level, career achievement indices, and ratings of senior leadership potential among army civilian managers. These effects held even after controlling for cognitive, personality, and problem-solving skills in a multivariate analysis.

Taken together, these studies provide fairly strong and consistent evidence that need for power is significantly associated with multiple indices of leader effectiveness. The results for achievement are more mixed, whereas no recent study supports a significant association between affiliation needs and leadership.

A focus on individual differences in a person's "motivation to lead" is a recent addition to the empirical literature investigating leader motives (Chan & Drasgow, 2001). Chan and Drasgow argued that this individual difference construct "affects a leader's or leader-to-be's decision to assume leadership training, roles, and responsibilities and that affects his or her intensity of effort at leading and persistence as a leader" (p. 482). They also argued that this motive construct will mediate the influences of general cognitive ability, Big Five personality factors, sociocultural values, leadership efficacy, and past leadership experience values on other leadership criteria. They found some support for their assertions across three samples (Singaporean military recruits, Singaporean college students, and U.S. college students). Motivation to lead was positively associated with leadership potential ratings from a military assessment center and from surveys distributed at the end of basic military training (for the military subjects only). These effects held even after controlling for all other predictors in a multivariate analysis. Leader experience, leader efficacy, and several of the personality and value attributes predicted variance in motivation to lead, suggesting support for at least a partially mediated model.

The results of Chan and Drasgow (2001) are promising and deserve further inquiry. Several prior studies have linked leadership with motive-states related to motivation to lead. Miner (1978; Berman & Miner, 1985) found that managerial motivation was associated with advancement and promotion. Connelly et al. (2000) found that need for responsibility, a related construct, was associated with career achievement among military officers. Indeed, the extensive reviews by Stogdill (1974) and Bass (1990) cite responsibility motives as key leader attributes. Chan and Drasgow (2001) took this research a step further by decomposing the construct of motivation to lead, embedding it into a conceptual model, and examining its influences in a multivariate context.

Social Appraisal Skills

Zaccaro and his colleagues (Zaccaro, 1999, 2001, 2002; Zaccaro, Foti, et al., 1991; Zaccaro, Gilbert, Thor, & Mumford, 1991) have argued that social appraisal skills, or social intelligence, reside at the heart of effective leadership. Social intelligence refers to "the ability to understand the feelings, thoughts, and behaviors of persons, including oneself, in interpersonal situations and to act appropriately upon that understanding" (Marlowe, 1986, p. 52). Zaccaro (2002) defined social intelligence as reflecting the following social capacities—social awareness, social acumen, response selection, and response enactment. These capacities refer to a leader's understanding of the feelings, thoughts, and behaviors of others in a social domain and his or her selection of the responses that best fit the contingencies and dynamics of that domain.

Several studies have supported the importance of such skills-for-leadership criteria. Zaccaro, Foti, et al. (1991) associated scores on a measure of self-monitoring skills with leader emergence rankings and ratings taken within the context of a rotation design. Self-monitoring reflects skill in monitoring social cues and controlling one's own expressive behavior. Zaccaro, Foti, et al. found that self-monitoring was associated with leader rankings and with perceived behavioral responsiveness to situational contingencies. A recent meta-analysis of 23 samples by Day, Schleicher, Unckless, and Hiller (2002) found that self-monitoring displayed a robust relationship with leadership.

Other studies have explored the association between measures of social intelligence and behavioral flexibility, respectively, and leadership. Ferentinos (1996) found in a rotation design that social intelligence predicted leader emergence, even when controlling for general intelligence. Zaccaro, Zazanis, Diana, and Gilbert (1994) found a significant linkage between social intelligence and leadership rankings in military training groups. Gilbert and Zaccaro (1995) reported that social intelligence scores were associated with career achievement and attained organizational level of military officers. Ritchie (1994) reported that behavioral flexibility scores predicted advancement 7 years after assessment. Kobe, Reiter-Palmon, and Rickers (2001) found that social intelligence was associated with leadership experience, even when controlling for emotional intelligence (see below). Hooijberg (1996) reported that indices of behavioral flexibility were linked to leader effectiveness ratings in a sample of business managers. Taken together, these studies demonstrate strong evidence, across different samples and methods, supporting the importance of social intelligence skills for leadership.

A related leader attribute, emotional intelligence, has received considerable recent scrutiny in the leadership literature. Such intelligence refers to "the ability to perceive emotions, to access and generate emotions to assist thought, to understand emotions and emotional knowledge, and to regulate emotions reflectively to promote emotional and intellectual growth" (Caruso, Mayer, & Salovey, 2002, p. 56). Because emotions are essential self-information, their accurate appraisal is crucial for effective self-regulation in the context of leadership. Note that emotional intelligence has at its core the awareness of self and others—their needs, motives, desires, emotions, and requirements.

Salovey, Mayer, and Caruso (Caruso, Mayer, et al., 2002; Caruso & Wolfe, in press; Mayer & Salovey, 1997; Salovey & Mayer, 1990) have defined four distinct emotional intelligence skills. These are (Caruso, Mayer, et al., p. 59) the following:

- *Emotion identification:* This refers to skills in identifying and appraising one's own feelings, as well as the emotional expression of others. It also reflects skills in expressing emotions and distinguishing real from phony emotional expression.
- *Emotion use:* This refers to skill in using emotions to direction attention to important events and environmental cues. It also reflects skills in using emotions in decision making and problem solving.
- *Emotion understanding:* This refers to skill in understanding emotions within a larger network of causes and meaning, to understand how different emotions in oneself and others are connected.
- *Emotion management:* This refers to an ability to stay aware of emotions and particularly "the ability to solve emotion-laden problems without necessarily suppressing negative emotions."

Recent studies have begun to link emotional intelligence to leadership (Caruso, Mayer, et al., 2002; Caruso & Wolfe, in press; Goleman, Boyatzis, & McKee, 2002; Sosik & Megerian, 1999). Wong and Law (2002) examined the effects of emotion management skills on job performance, job satisfaction, organizational commitment, and turnover intentions. They also examined the "emotional labor" of the job as a moderator of these predicted influences. Emotional labor refers to the extent to which the job frequently or infrequently requires incumbents to display particular emotions and to manage and regulate their emotional expressions, particularly in response to the emotion expressions of others. Wong and Law hypothesized that emotion management skills would be more strongly related to performance in highly emotionally laborious jobs than in those involving less emotional labor.

They found that emotional intelligence was related to job performance and job satisfaction. Furthermore, the emotional labor of the job indeed moderated the effects of emotional management skills, such that these skills were more strongly related to job performance, organizational commitment, and turnover intentions when jobs demanded high emotional regulation.

These findings reflect the influence of a leader's emotional intelligence on his or her own job outcomes. Wong and Law (2002) also investigated the effects of leader emotion management skills on subordinate work outcomes. They found that leader skills predicted follower job satisfaction and extra-role behaviors, even after controlling for subordinate emotion management skills, job perceptions, educational level, and tenure with the company. This is one of very few empirical studies in the leadership literature to link leader emotion management skills to subordinate outcomes.

Interest in emotional intelligence and leadership is relatively new, although it is the subject of several popular books written primarily for business managers (e.g., Cherniss & Goleman, 2001; Goleman, 1995; Goleman et al., 2002). Taken together, the aforementioned empirical studies provide support for this linkage; however, additional research is necessary to identify the unique contributions of emotional intelligence beyond other conceptually similar constructs. For example, Kobe et al. (2001) found that emotional intelligence did not predict leadership criteria after controlling for social intelligence; however, social intelligence retained its ability to explain variance in leadership after controlling for emotional intelligence. These constructs are closely related conceptually, and their independent contributions to leadership will need to be pursued further.

Leader Problem-Solving Skills, Expertise, and Tacit Knowledge

Mumford, Zaccaro, et al. (2000) argued that leadership represented a form of social problem solving and that, accordingly, social problem-solving skills were important proximal leader attributes predicting leader performance. In support, Connelly et al. (2000) found that skills in problem construction and solution generation predicted leader career achievement, even after controlling for the influences of general intelligence, creative thinking capacities, personality, and motives. Zaccaro, White, et al. (1997) found that such skills were associated with attained organizational level in army civilian managers, also after controlling for cognitive, personality, and motivation attributes.

The application of problem solving and appraisal skills to experience drives the acquisition of tacit knowledge. Tacit knowledge can be defined as "what one needs to know to succeed in a given environment, and is knowledge that is typically not explicitly taught and often not even verbalized" (Sternberg, 2002, p. 11). Sternberg (2002; see also Sternberg et al., 2000) argued that tacit knowledge and its corresponding attribute of practical intelligence are strongly related to leader adaptability. Research reported by Sternberg and colleagues indicates that measures of tacit knowledge were significantly associated with indices of leader effectiveness given to military officers at different organizational ranks.

Knowledge emerges when individuals acquire new experiences and have the cognitive appraisal skills that allow them to draw the lessons from these experiences. Banks, Zaccaro, and Bader (2003; see also Bader, Fleming, Zaccaro, & Barber, 2002; Banks et al., 2001) provided evidence for this assertion by demonstrating that developmental work experiences were associated with higher tacit knowledge when army officers possessed higher levels of metacognitive skills; such experiences were not so efficacious for officers having low metacognitive skills. Spreitzer et al. (1997) also pointed to the ability to learn from experience as an important leader quality.

Summary

This summary of leader attributes indicates a burgeoning number of studies published over the last 10–14 years that support the importance of leader attributes for a variety of leadership outcomes. Table 5.1 summarizes the leader attributes, by categories, that have received substantial empirical support in the period since the publication of Bass's (1990) *Handbook of Leadership.*

Table 5.1   Key Leader Attributes, 1990–2003

1. Cognitive capacities
   General intelligence
   Creative thinking capacities

2. Personality
   Extroversion
   Conscientiousness
   Emotional stability
   Openness
   Agreeableness
   MBTI preferences for extroversion, intuition, thinking, and judging

3. Motives and needs
   Need for power
   Need for achievement
   Motivation to lead

4. Social capacities
   Self-monitoring
   Social intelligence
   Emotional intelligence

5. Problem-solving skills
   Problem construction
   Solution generation
   Metacognition

6. Tacit knowledge

Despite the support for leader attributes suggested by past reviews, recent conceptual models, and the empirical review described in this chapter, considerable questions remain in textbooks and reviews concerning the utility of such perspectives. We agree that leader trait research does present a number of concerns that have mitigated the extent of its contributions. These concerns have been described elsewhere (Bass, 1990; Gibb, 1954; Stogdill, 1974). In the next section, we offer some summary propositions that we hope will guide future research on leader traits and attributes.

Leader Traits and Attributes: Some Propositions

The research reviewed in this chapter and studies reviewed in Bass (1990), Hogan, Curphy, and Hogan (1994), and S. A. Kirkpatrick and Locke (1991) point to the strong conclusion that leaders do differ from nonleaders on a number of attributes, and that these differences contribute significantly to leader effectiveness. The rotation design research by Kenny and Zaccaro (1983), Zaccaro, Foti, et al., (1991), and Ferentinos (1996) indicates that approximately 55%-60% of the variance in leader emergence ratings across different groups and different tasks was attributable to characteristics of the ratee (i.e., the emergent leader). House, Spangler, et al. (1991) reported that charisma, leader personality, and leader age, together with the presence of a crisis, predicted from 24% to 66% of the variance across several presidential effectiveness indicators. One situational variable (crisis) was included in these variance estimates, and the contributions of leader personality and charisma explained the bulk of leadership variance. Judge et al. (2002) reported from their meta-analysis a multiple correlation of .48 between the Big Five personality factors and leadership. The promotion and advancement studies of Howard and Bray (1988) indicate that leader attributes predict managerial advancement years after their assessment. Studies by Hitt and Tyler (1991), Koene, Vogelaar, and Soeters (2002), and Russell (2001) linked the personal characteristics of top executives to such outcomes as corporation acquisition decisions, company costs, and estimated company profitability, respectively; Hitt and Tyler (1991) demonstrated the influence of leader traits, even after controlling for industry and environmental characteristics. This body of work, extending from laboratory settings to corporative environments, indicates that personal attributes of the leader matter greatly in leadership.

Thus, we propose the following: *Leader traits contribute significantly to the prediction of leader effectiveness, leader emergence, and leader advancement.*

The research on leader attributes has suffered greatly from univariate examinations of particular leader traits (Bass, 1990; Keeney & Marchioro, 1998; Kenny & Zaccaro, 1983). Such research strategies appear to be based on the premise that a single attribute can be largely responsible for significant variance in leadership. Even studies that examine a few leader characteristics still take an inadequate approach to the question of explained variance in leadership. Such an approach will lead invariably to the finding that a particular trait, or a small set of traits, will have a small, albeit statistically significant, association with leadership, and that this relationship will not exhibit a high degree of consistency—exactly the kind of criticism that has been leveled at leader trait research since Stogdill (1948) and Mann (1959). Leadership represents a complex and a multifaceted performance domain and, like any complex behavior pattern, will be predicted by a constellation of attributes.

We argue that leadership is multiply determined by sets of attributes that contain cognitive capacities, personality dispositions, motives, values, and an array of skills and competencies related to particular leadership situations. Table 5.1 presents characteristics suggested by our empirical review of the recent literature. Some characteristics will carry more weight than will others in certain contexts (Zaccaro & Klimoski, 2001). For example, several researchers have argued that certain leadership qualities become more potent as leaders ascend an organizational hierarchy (J. G. Hunt, 1991; Jacobs & Jaques, 1987b; Katz & Kahn, 1978; Zaccaro, 2001). We acknowledge that situationally driven performance requirements will highlight the value of certain skills and competencies; however, we would also argue that certain fundamental abilities and dispositions contribute to leader success across multiple domains. These attributes are not few in number, and the amount of variance they might explain in leadership may shift from situation to situation, but, taken together, they will have a large influence on leadership. Indeed, a number of recent studies have taken a multivariate approach to leader traits and have explained significant amounts of variance (e.g., Connelly et al., 2000; Hammerschmidt & Jennings, 1992; Howard & Bray, 1988; Judge et al., 2002; Zaccaro, White, et al., 1997).

Thus, we propose the following: *Leadership is best predicted by an amalgamation of attributes reflecting cognitive capacities, personality orientation, motives and values, social appraisal skills, problem-solving competencies, and general and domain-specific expertise.*

Leader traits convey the premise of behavioral invariance—that persons possessing certain attributes will behave the same way across different situations. An individual's ability to respond effectively to a variety of different behavioral demands, however, represents a fundamental requirement for leader effectiveness in most organizations. Kenny and Zaccaro (1983) argued, "Persons who are consistently cast in the leadership role possess the ability to perceive and predict variations in group situations and pattern their approaches accordingly" (p. 683). The rotation design studies by Zaccaro, Foti, et al. (1991) and Ferentinos (1996) demonstrated that leadership status was stable across separate situations, but such status was significantly associated with attributes specifically reflecting skill in being able to respond effectively to different situations. These studies also provided evidence that leaders changed their responses in accordance with task demands. Over the last 12 years, there has been substantial interest in social intelligence (Zaccaro, 1999, 2002; Zaccaro, Gilbert, et al., 1991), emotional intelligence (Caruso et al., 2002; Goleman, 1995; Goleman et al., 2002; Mayer & Salovey, 1997; Salovey & Mayer, 1990), and behavioral complexity (Hooijberg, 1996; Hooijberg, Hunt, & Dodge, 1997; Hooijberg & Schneider, 2001). All these attributes specifically promote leader adaptability and flexibility.

Thus, we propose the following: *The constellation of critical leader attributes includes traits that promote a leader's ability to respond effectively and appropriately across situations affording qualitatively different performance requirements.*

Recently, individual difference theorists have begun to distinguish between traits that are more distal to behavior performance and those that are more proximal to outcomes (Ackerman & Humphreys, 1990; Hough & Schneider, 1996; Kanfer, 1990, 1992). Chen, Gully, Whiteman, and Kilcullen (2000) define these as "trait-like" individual differences and "state-like" individual differences, respectively. Trait-like individual differences are not situationally bound and thus are relatively stable across time and contexts. State-like individual differences are more specific to certain situations, and they reflect skills, competences, expertise, belief systems, and attitudes that exert influence largely in response to situational parameters. A basic premise of this perspective argues that trait-like individual differences are more distal in their influence on performance, manifesting such influences through their effects on state-like individual differences (Ford, Smith, Weissbein, Gully, & Salas, 1998).

There have been few attempts to articulate a multistage model of leader characteristics and performance. Mumford, Zaccaro, et al. (1993) offered a model that was later revised by Mumford, Zaccaro, et al. (2000). This model defined general cognitive abilities, crystallized cognitive abilities, motivation, and personality as distal attributes. It defined problem-solving skills, social appraisal and interaction skills, and knowledge as proximal skills predicted by distal attributes. The proximal attributes also predicted the quality of leader problem-solving activities, which in turn predicted leader performance. Connelly et al. (2000) provided support for this model by demonstrating that problem-solving skills and leader knowledge partially mediated the effects of cognitive capacities, personality, and motives on leader achievement indices.

Figure 5.1 presents a model of leader attributes that is similar to the ones offered by Mumford and colleagues (Mumford, Zaccaro, et al., 1993; Mumford, Zaccaro, 2000). It, too, articulates cognitive, personality, and motives as distal predictors of leader social appraisal skills, problem-solving skills, expertise, and tacit knowledge. The model specifies the latter sets of skills as predicting leader problem-solving processes, which in turn predict leader performance. The model proposes that situational influences, identified as the leader's "operating environment," determine (a) the quality and appropriateness of displayed skill and knowledge and (b) the appropriateness of particular leadership processes. Such influences also moderate the effects of proximal skills and knowledge on processes as well as the effects of processes on leader emergence, effectiveness, and advancement.

Thus, reflecting this model, we propose the following: *Cognitive abilities, personality, and motives will influence leadership processes and outcomes through their effects on social appraisal skills, problem-solving competencies, expertise, and tacit knowledge.*

Situational or contextual influences will be manifested mostly in the nature and quality of appropriate skills, in knowledge, and by defining the leadership processes and behaviors required for success.

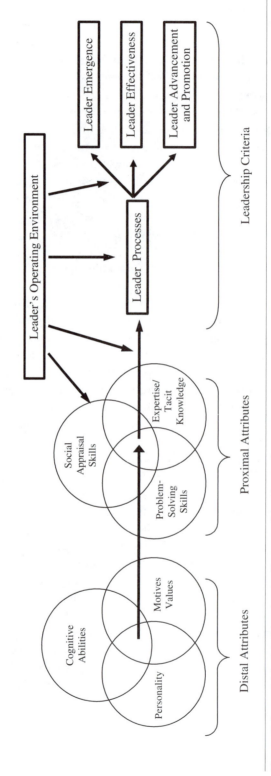

Figure 5.1 A Model of Leader Attributes and Leader Performance

The model in Figure 5.1 indicates the three sets of distal predictors and the three sets of proximal predictors as overlapping circles. This represents the premise that each set of predictors operates jointly with other predictors to influence particular outcomes; that is, each set is defined as being necessary but not sufficient for the prediction of targeted criteria. Thus, skills and expertise derive from the joint influence of cognitive capacities, personality orientations, and motives. For example, organizational executives often are required to use conceptual capacities to interpret the meaning of complex events occurring in their operating environment. The successful growth and use of such capacities likely depends on their having a personality orientation that reflects openness to experience and tolerance of ambiguity. Furthermore, certain motive-states, such as motivation to lead or high need for power, are necessary to motivate the effort required to engage in complex thinking. Thus, the influence of each set of attributes on leadership is conditioned on the other two attribute sets (see Zaccaro, 1999, 2001).

Leadership processes, in turn, reflect the combined influence of social appraisal, problem-solving skills, and expertise. Successful problem solving requires an accurate appraisal of social system requirements and dynamics (Zaccaro, Gilbert, et al., 1991). In turn, social appraisal depends heavily on social expertise that can be applied to interpret social events (Cantor & Kihlstrom, 1987; Zaccaro, Gilbert, et al., 1991). Likewise, problem construction (a key problem-solving skill) requires appropriate knowledge stores that can be used to interpret events in a problem space (Mumford, Zaccaro, et al., 2000). The development of successful solutions contributes to subsequent growth in leader expertise. Thus, at the level of proximal leader attributes, each set of attributes depends on, and contributes to, each other set in its effect on leadership. Understanding leader traits and attributes will require a deeper conceptualization of how such traits, both distal and proximal, operate jointly to influence different leadership outcomes.

Thus, we propose the following: *A leader's cognitive capacities, personality, motives, and values are necessary but not sufficient in isolation to influence growth and utilization of proximal skills and expertise; the influence of these distal traits derives from their joint application.*

A leader's social appraisal skills, problem-solving competencies, expertise, and tacit knowledge are necessary but not sufficient in isolation to influence the display and quality of particular leadership processes; the influence of these proximal traits derives from their joint application.

Conclusion

The question of how leaders differ from nonleaders is one of the oldest in psychology, yet it remains a source of disagreement and controversy in the leadership domain. A consensus remains elusive regarding the magnitude of leader trait effects on leadership, and, if a large magnitude is conceded, what specific and critical attributes contribute to such effects. In this chapter, we have sought to contribute to the building of a consensus about leader traits by summarizing the applicable literature, both empirical and conceptual, and offering a series of propositions to guide further thinking and research. Knowing the history of these questions, we suspect that such a consensus will remain elusive until researchers undertake the challenge of conducting more conceptually and methodologically sophisticated research. We note, though, that the current resurrection of leader trait research rested on studies that exhibited more conceptual breadth, methodological soundness, and statistical sophistication than its predecessors. We anticipate that such progress will continue.

CHAPTER 6

Information Processing and Leadership

Douglas J. Brown

Kristyn A. Scott

Hayden Lewis

I n this chapter, we take stock of how the investigation of information processing has illuminated contemporary understanding of leadership. Whereas many other approaches to leadership focus on external and observable outcomes, such as a leader's behaviors, in this chapter we shift the empirical spotlight into the heads of the principal participants: leaders and followers. In contemplating the gains that can be made by approaching leadership from this perspective, consider for a moment the following questions: How does a subordinate decide whether his or her supervisor is a leader? Why does an organizational supervisor punish one subordinate for poor performance but not another? Why does a supervisor utilize a particular behavioral style? In the end, as the research reviewed throughout this chapter will suggest, the answer to each of these questions lies in the minds of leaders and subordinates.

As a starting point, we conceptualize leadership as a social process, one involving both a leader and a follower (Graen & Scandura, 1987; Hollander & Offermann, 1990; Lord & Maher, 1991b). Leadership is the investigation of how one individual, labeled a leader, influences a second individual, or group of individuals, labeled followers (Yukl & Van Fleet, 1992). Fundamentally, the social scientific examination of leadership focuses on understanding how the behavior or actions of one individual

Authors' Note: The authors would like to thank Lisa Keeping and the editors for their helpful feedback on previous versions of this chapter.

changes the behavior or actions of a second individual. As Dwight D. Eisenhower has been credited with saying: "Leadership is the art of getting someone else to do something you want done because he wants to do it." Although this statement captures behavior, which is the essence of leadership, it neglects the underlying processes that cause behavior. Behavior, whether it is a leader's or a subordinate's, does not simply occur; instead behavior is proximally determined by intermediary cognitive processes. Researchers using information-processing approaches focus on these processes, attempting to discern how individuals acquire, store, retrieve, and use information in order to better understand how those individuals (i.e., leaders and followers) function and adapt to the current context (Lord & Maher, 1991a). Thus, whereas information-processing theories still define leadership as influence, they do so by examining the cognitive mechanisms that mediate the influence process, rather than focusing on overt behavioral displays (e.g., transformational behavior).

Understanding the content, creation, and deployment of knowledge is central to the information-processing viewpoint. Thus, it is important that we set forth certain basic ideas regarding knowledge, ideas that will recur throughout our review. First, we consider the basic building blocks of knowledge to be the symbols or categories that are stored in long-term memory. These symbols form interconnected sets known as *schemas* or *schemata* (see S. T. Fiske, 1995; S. T. Fiske & Taylor, 1991). Although many different forms of schemata have been discussed in the cognitive and social cognitive literatures (e.g., script, person schema, relational schema, self-schema, prototype), functionally they are quite similar. Schemata assist us in interpreting and making sense of our surroundings (Weick, 1995) and in generating adaptive responses (Johnson-Laird, 1989; Newell, Rosenbloom, & Laird, 1989). As an example, imagine trying to understand a lecture or behave appropriately during it if you do not already possess well-developed schemata for professor, student, lecture, and test. In all likelihood, without these schemata, a lecture would make little sense, leaving you utterly confused. Similarly, leaders and followers have schemata that guide their perceptions and actions. Leaders, for instance, might symbolically represent a subordinate as a "good worker" or as a "poor worker," whereas subordinates might categorize their supervisor as a "prototypical leader" or "nonprototypical leader" (Lord & Maher, 1991a). Many of the studies and theories discussed throughout this chapter concern the key issue of how the content and structure of leaders' and subordinates' knowledge configurations affect leadership processes.

Schema content is important, but equally relevant is schema activation. An important determinant of whether or not knowledge is used is its relative accessibility (Stapel & Koomen, 2001). Given the large number of schemata that exist in long-term memory and the limitations of working memory, only a small subset of all available schemata can be activated at any given moment. Regardless of the cognitive architecture that is presumed to underlie human cognition, knowledge must be retrieved, activated, or re-created to influence actions and perceptions. In this regard, many symbolic models of human cognition have suggested that our memories, knowledge, and schema are content addressable (e.g., J. R. Anderson, 1987), being activated by relevant external (e.g., subordinates) and internal (e.g., current goals) stimuli and cues. As a result, a second recurring theme throughout this chapter is how particular knowledge structures become activated and the factors that influence activation.

Information Processing From the Leader's Perspective

Relative to subordinate focused research, scant attention has been devoted historically to understanding a leader's information processing. We begin by discussing research and theories that are relevant for understanding the nature and structure of a leader's schemata. Next, we consider relevant environmental factors that can activate different schemata.

Knowledge Structure and Content

More so than any other approach, the investigation of behavioral styles has dominated the leadership field. Behavioral approaches are among the most salient exemplars within the discipline's history (e.g., Ohio State Leadership Studies) and can be largely credited with the current revitalization that is underway in the field (e.g., Bass, 1985). Although numerous behavioral taxonomies of effective leader behavior have been suggested (Yukl, 2002), these approaches have focused exclusively on overt behavioral displays rather than on the underlying knowledge structures that produce these behaviors. Recently, however, some scholars have begun to examine whether we might learn something about a leader's behavioral style by analyzing the memory structures he or she holds in long-term memory (Mumford, Zaccaro, Harding, Jacobs, & Fleishman, 2000; Wofford & Goodwin, 1994).

Exemplary of this approach is the work conducted by Wofford and his colleagues (Goodwin, Wofford, & Boyd, 2000; Wofford & Goodwin, 1994; Wofford, Goodwin, & Whittington, 1998). Theoretically, Wofford and Goodwin have speculated that the underlying reason that transformational and transactional leaders display different behavioral patterns lies in the schemata that the two types of leaders possess for behavior (i.e., scripts), subordinates (i.e., person-schema), and themselves (i.e., self-schema). For instance, Wofford and Goodwin (1994) suggest that whereas transformational leaders' schemata contain expectations that subordinates are self-reliant and innovative, transactional leaders' schemata contain expectations that subordinates are motivated by rewards and require role clarity. As a result of these differing schemata, individuals comprehend, perceive, and ultimately behave in a distinctively transformational or transactional manner.

To investigate this issue, Wofford and his colleagues (Wofford, Goodwin, et al., 1998) recruited 96 managers and 157 of their immediate subordinates. To evaluate managerial schemata and scripts, a series of open-ended questions was administered to the managers in their sample (e.g., "My way of getting the most from people is to . . ."), which were later content analyzed for transformational and transactional statements. Actual transformational and transactional leadership behavior was assessed independently through subordinates' Multifactor Leadership Questionnaire-5x (MLQ) (Bass & Avolio, 1988) ratings. Results indicated that the greater the degree to which managers' schemata had been coded as transformational, the more highly they were rated by their subordinates as having displayed transformational leadership behaviors. Conversely, the greater the degree to which managers' schemata had been coded as transactional, the more highly they were rated by subordinates as having displayed transactional leadership behaviors. Thus, consistent with earlier predictions, these data suggest that the schemata stored in memory may be a pivotal precursor to a leader's behavior. Although Wofford's work has focused exclusively on transformational and transactional schemata, we see little reason to doubt that subsequent work can extend his findings to other behavioral styles, although this remains an empirical question.

An immediate implication of Wofford's model is that the likelihood that a leader will utilize a particular behavioral style is contingent on that leader first establishing appropriate schema in memory. Sensibly, individuals cannot act in a transformational manner unless they possess the appropriate schemata and scripts, nor can they regulate their behavior around a transformational identity unless they fully understand what it means to be transformational (see W. Gardner & Avolio, 1998). Despite limited direct evidence for this position, indirect verification can be surmised by carefully considering leadership training protocols (e.g., Barling, Weber, & Kelloway, 1996). The hub of many training interventions appears to be schema creation (e.g., scripts). For instance, a key component of the transformational leadership training program discussed by Barling et al. involved extensive discussions of what transformational leadership behavior is and how to enact this behavior (e.g., scripts). Similarly, the Pygmalion leadership training program described by Eden (Eden, Geller, et al., 2000), focuses partially on changing supervisory beliefs about subordinates (i.e., person schemata) and establishing new behaviors (i.e., scripts). In addition, scholars in the leadership development (i.e., London, 2002) and coaching literatures (Smither & Reilly, 2001) have noted that direct interventions designed to improve leadership work in part because they create new schemata (e.g., self-schemata). Thus, whereas direct assessments of schema creation do not exist, the application of this perspective seems reasonable and practically important.

Logically, if schemata and knowledge are the proximal determinants of a leader's behavior (Wofford & Goodwin, 1994), we might anticipate that variation in leader effectiveness should be a function of the schemata held in memory. Leaders with better and more broadly developed schemata and knowledge should perform more effectively than those leaders with poorly developed leader knowledge bases (Hooijberg & Schneider, 2001). Indeed, research has demonstrated that leadership emergence is contingent on an individual's ability to flexibly adjust his or her behavior to the current context (Zaccaro, Foti, & Kenny, 1991). From an information-processing standpoint, one might suggest that expertise (Chi, Glaser, & Farr, 1988) will be associated with a leader's effectiveness. In fact, studies comparing experts and novices across a multitude of domains indicate that the quality of the solutions generated by experts far exceeds that of solutions generated by novices

(Lord & Maher, 1991a; VanLehn, 1989). Why do these discrepancies emerge? It is in part because experts have developed richer, more sophisticated schemata. As a result, they can encode and retrieve information more efficiently, require fewer attentional resources, process information in terms of principles rather than surface features, and can match the current context to solutions held in long-term memory.

To test whether effective leadership is dependent on possessing complex and highly organized schemata (i.e., expert knowledge), Connelly and her colleagues (Connelly et al., 2000) conducted a large-scale study of army officer performance. Utilizing a sample of 1,807 army officers, Connelly et al. assessed the extent to which expert leader knowledge was associated with the quality of the solutions generated on structured leadership problems and with actual military achievement. According to Connelly et al, expert knowledge should be positively associated with these outcomes because knowledge is the basis of problem representation, information encoding, solution evaluation, and understanding situational constraints. To assess leader expertise, army officers completed a leadership task sort, a procedure commonly employed in the expertise literature. For this task, each participant sorted 78 leader task statements into self-generated categories. Following this task, judges assessed the coherence, number, and organization of the categories as well as the degree to which the categories were principle based. Relative to novices, experts possess a greater number of categories, and these categories should be more coherent, organized, and principle based (i.e., rather than surface based). Analyses revealed that expert leader knowledge was positively associated with both military achievement and the quality of the solutions generated for subsequent leadership problems. Moreover, expertise remained a significant predictor of these outcomes even after general cognitive ability and personality were controlled.

A key issue presented by Connelly et al.'s (2000) findings lies in how leaders develop expert knowledge. As noted by some authors, expertise can take upwards of 10,000 hours to establish (Ericsson & Charness, 1994), suggesting that the development of an expert leader knowledge base will be a slow and progressive process—leaders are not born; rather, they are created. To assess this possibility, Mumford, Marks, Connelly, Zaccaro, and Reiter-Palmon (2000) cross-sectionally contrasted junior, mid-level, and senior level army officers in terms of their leadership expertise. As was the case in the Connelly et al. (2000) investigation, expertise was assessed by having participants sort leadership tasks into categories, which were in turn evaluated on the basis of overall organization, number, coherence, and whether or not they were principle based. Not surprisingly, given prior expertise literature (e.g., Ericsson & Charness, 1994), significant differences emerged between officer knowledge structures and experience. With increasing experience, the knowledge structures of the officers transformed, becoming increasingly more organized, coherent, and principle based. Furthermore, subsequent analyses suggested that these properties were significantly related to performance differences.

Given the highly restricted samples employed in the previous two studies (i.e., army officers), one might question whether expertise is important in other settings. In another investigation, Day and Lord (1992) compared the manner in which chief executive officers (CEOs) (experts) and MBA students (novices) categorized problems. As might be expected based on the discussion above, whereas the CEOs tended to categorize problems in terms of the underlying principles represented, the MBA students organized problems in accordance with superficial surface-level structures. One advantage afforded by the principle-based under-standing exhibited by the CEOs was their ability to arrive at solutions more quickly than did the students.

Although the previous studies indicate that "expert" knowledge structures are essential precursors to effective leadership performance, this literature has done little to inform us of the underlying cognitive skills that lead to knowledge structure development. One promising approach that could shed light onto this issue has been advanced by Robert Sternberg and his colleagues (Cianciolo, Antonakis, & Sternberg, in press; Sternberg, 2002). According to Sternberg, skillful leadership is dependent upon an individual's practical intelligence, or his or her ability to learn from experience and apply experiential knowledge (also known as tacit knowl-edge). From a cognitive standpoint, Sternberg's model suggests that tacit knowledge is dependent on an individual's ability to selectively encode, combine, and compare available information. Despite its nascent state, initial indications suggest that the integration of practical intelligence into the leadership domain will be promising not only for the selection of leaders but also for their development.

So far, our review has uncovered the following: (a) Knowledge structures are proximal determinants of a leader's behavior (e.g., Goodwin et al., 2000; Wofford, Goodwin, et al., 1998); (b) leader schemata are potentially the result of training and experience (e.g., Barling et al., 1996) or practical intelligence (Cianciolo et al., in press; Sternberg, 2002); and (c) the extent and organization of this knowledge may determine success in a leadership position (Connelly et al., 2000; Mumford, Marks, et al., 2000). Before proceeding, it is worth mentioning that some scholars have begun the task of cataloging the role of social knowledge in leadership (e.g., Hooijberg, Hunt, & Dodge, 1997). These authors have suggested that as individuals ascend the organizational hierarchy, social intelligence becomes an increasingly rel-evant determinant of who will and will not be successful (e.g., Zaccaro, 2002). Those readers interested in this burgeoning field can refer to the recently published book edited by Ronald Riggio and his colleagues (Riggio, Murphy, & Pirozzolo, 2002).

Schema/Knowledge Activation

The content of a leader's knowledge is only one component of the information-processing puzzle, albeit an important one. Leadership behavior is not simply the result of possessing knowledge; instead, situations must be perceived, and these situational perceptions must be related to knowledge structures. Given this inter-pretation, the next logical question is, What are the relevant situational cues that influence a leader's knowledge activation? Some hint to this question may be ascer-tained from contemporary descriptions of leadership functions (House & Aditya, 1997; Mumford, Marks, et al., 2000), which suggest that leaders must be oriented toward two elements of the world. At the supervisory level, leadership is focused on regulating the "day-to-day activities of work unit members" (House & Aditya, 1997, p. 444), such as providing guidance and corrective feedback to subordinates. In contrast, at the strategic level, leadership is focused on giving "purpose, meaning, and guidance to organizations" (House & Aditya, 1997, p. 444). Coinciding with this duality, in the next several sections we discuss how leaders make sense of their subordinates and the external environment. In addition, we point out how this categorization influences subsequent responses and schema activation.

Categorization of Subordinates

From a leader's perspective, some of the most important categorizations that can occur are those that are formed regarding subordinates. Over the last quarter century, a substantial quantity of empirical data have demonstrated that a leader's categorization of subordinates may have important implications for organizationally relevant outcomes, such as subordinates' performance. In fact, a leader's expectations of a subordinate may become a self-fulfilling prophecy (SFP). As initially proposed by Merton (1948a) in this context, SFPs refer to a three-stage process that begins with a perceiver's belief or expectation (false at the time that it is held) that an event will occur in the future. The second stage produces or leads to a new behavior that is based on the expectation, and, in the third stage, the expected event occurs and the prophecy is fulfilled. Thus, simply put, an SFP is the process through which the expectation that an event will occur increases the likelihood of the event's occurrence (Eden, 1992). Over the last 20 years, Dov Eden and his colleagues (e.g., Eden & Shani, 1982; Davidson & Eden, 2000) have integrated SFP research, initially conducted in educational settings, with leadership processes, introducing the Pygmalion effect.

Eden's Pygmalion experiments are among the most carefully developed field experiments conducted by leadership scholars (Eden, 1992). In nine separate field experiments, Eden and his colleagues have shown that interventions focused on shifting supervisory cognitions of subordinates, which may take as little as 5 minutes to induce experimentally, can dramatically affect a subordinate's subsequent performance. To better comprehend the subtlety of the Pygmalion effect, consider for a moment Eden's first investigation, conducted with four highly experienced instructors and 105 trainee soldiers in the Israel Defense Forces. In this experiment, Eden and Shani (1982) manipulated the beliefs that instructors held of each of their trainees. In this regard, instructors were informed that trainees had completed a battery of tests designed to assess command potential (CP) and that, based on testing, each trainee had been categorized as possessing high, regular, or unknown CP. In reality, trainee assignment to each of the three CP conditions was completely random. Results indicated that instructors' beliefs about a trainee's CP dramatically influenced trainee performance at the end of basic training, as assessed both by neutral observers who were blind to the experimental treatment and objective tests (e.g., grades from four courses).

Eden's work provides only indirect verification, although it is consistent with the perspective outlined previously, that a leader's perceptions of his or her subordinates activates different behavioral schemata. Wofford and his colleagues (Goodwin et al., 2000; Wofford, Joplin, & Comforth, 1996), however, have directly assessed whether leader schema activation shifts with differing perceptions of subordinates. In one such study (Wofford, Joplin, et al., 1996), 76 business students were recruited to participate in an experiment in four-person groups. Upon arrival at the lab, each participant was ushered into a separate room and informed that he or she had been selected at random to lead the other three participants and that all subsequent communication between the leader and group would be written. Leaders were assigned at random to one of six group performance and group member ability conditions (3 group performance × 2 group member ability). First, each leader was informed that the group was performing either very poorly, poorly, or quite well. Second, each leader was informed that his or her group members either had high ability and motivation to complete the task, or low ability and motivation to complete the task. Following the feedback, each leader completed a series of behavioral intention items, designed to assess whether he or she planned to utilize a directive style in subsequent interactions with the group. Overall, the results indicated that group performance information and group member ability interacted such that leaders shifted toward more directive leadership scripts when informed that the group was having difficulty with the task, particularly when group members were believed to be low in ability and motivation.

Goodwin et al. (2000) extended the above findings by more directly assessing whether different schemata are activated under alternative subordinate categorization conditions. In their study, Goodwin et al. had 72 human resource students assume the role of the supervisor for a production manager, Frank, and had them read a scenario that described the company and Frank's performance within it over the last 6 months. It is important to note that half of the participants were informed that Frank was a poor performer, whereas the other half of the participants were informed that Frank was a good performer. Subsequent to the familiarization period, all participants completed 13 open-ended questions regarding Frank and themselves, which served as the dependent variable. For instance, participants were asked to describe Frank, their own leadership style, and how they would encourage Frank. Following previous coding schemes (Wofford, Goodwin, et al., 1998), responses to these 13 items were coded for the occurrence of transformational and transactional schemata. Participants assigned to the condition of poorly performing employee spontaneously reported a greater number of transactional thoughts relative to those in the condition of the employee performing well. The opposite pattern of schema activation emerged for transformational leadership. Thus, the subordinates' performance, as effective and ineffective, activated different cognitive schemata.

In summary, given the extant literature (i.e., Eden, 1992; Goodwin et al., 2000; Wofford, Goodwin, et al., 1998) it seems reasonable to conclude that leader categorizations of subordinates constrain the behavioral schemata that are most accessible. These findings should come as little surprise to readers who are familiar with contingency models of leadership (see Ayman, Chapter 7, this volume), which suggest that effective leadership depends on the ability to behave flexibly across different situational constraints (see Chemers, 1997). Thus, whereas the ability to respond flexibly to different targets may be quite advantageous (Hooijberg & Schneider, 2001), what is less clear is how leaders make sense of a subordinate's actions. We turn to this issue next, reviewing perhaps the most well-established area of leader information-processing inquiry: leader attributions.

Categorization of Subordinates: Attributions

During the course of a single day, a manager will interact numerous times with his or her subordinates, providing them with encouragement when they behave exceptionally or correcting them when they behave inappropriately. Logically, by distributing rewards and punishments, leaders attempt to regulate the performance of their subordinates and work groups. A more complicated question is, What dictates a leader's response? One intriguing, and extensively researched, possibility is that a leader's responses are mediated through the causal attributions that he or she forms of a subordinate's behavior (Green & Mitchell, 1979; Mitchell, Green, & Wood, 1981).

Imagine that a subordinate, George, fails at a task that he has been assigned to complete. Should George's supervisor infer that George's failure is due to some limitation within George (e.g., George's effort or ability) or that it was contextually determined (e.g., task difficulty or bad luck)? Drawing upon Kelley's (1967) attributional framework, Green and Mitchell (1979) suggested that the attribution drawn by George's supervisor would depend on three informational cues. First, is the same behavior exhibited in similar situations at different times (i.e., consistency)? Second, do others behave similarly (i.e., consensus)? Third, does the individual behave similarly in other situations (i.e., distinctiveness)? According to this framework, when distinctiveness and consensus are high, but consistency is low, supervisors should make external attributions for a subordinate's behavior. In contrast, when distinctiveness and consensus are low, but consistency is high, supervisors should form internal attributions. Which of these two attributions is formed may have important ramifications for supervisory responses. For instance, it makes little sense to punish or sanction a subordinate for an event that is not of his or her own doing.

In an initial test of this model, Mitchell and Wood (1980) examined the attributions and responses of nursing supervisors following the presentation of a poor performance episode by a nurse. In a repeated-measures design, 23 nursing supervisors were presented with six vignettes that fully crossed three levels of attributional cues with two outcome severity levels (serious vs. not serious). Along the attributional variable, each vignette varied in terms of whether it provided (a) information consistent with an internal attribution, (b) information consistent with an external attribution, or (c) no attributional information. Results indicated that the presentation of cues that were indicative of an internal attribution, coupled with a severe outcome, led nursing supervisors to draw internal attributions to a greater extent than that of supervisors in the other conditions. Furthermore, the attribution that was formed influenced how the nursing supervisors responded to the event. When internal attributions were drawn, the nursing supervisors were more likely to direct their response at the nurse in question (i.e., reprimand, monitor future performance, terminate, counsel). Subsequent studies, using alternative stimulus materials and populations, have reinforced the basic tenets of the framework (e.g., Ashkanasy, 1995; Mitchell & Kalb, 1981), suggesting that attributions are a critical mediating cognitive process between supervisory perceptions of subordinates and supervisory responses.

In addition to confirming the model, ensuing studies have extended the attributional framework, investigating potential moderators and mediators. In one line of research, Dobbins and Russell (1986a) examined supervisory liking, predicting that leaders would attribute poor performance to internal factors and respond more punitively toward a disliked, versus a liked, subordinate. A laboratory and a field study largely confirmed these hypotheses. In a second extension, Dobbins and Russell (1986b) found that, because of self-serving biases, leaders were more inclined to draw internal attributions for subordinate behavior (i.e., because doing this deflects blame from the leader). Interestingly, other data indicate that one way to mitigate this bias is to provide supervisors with direct experience in a task domain (e.g., Mitchell & Kalb, 1982). That is, the more experience a supervisor has, the more likely he or she is to consider situational/environmental factors when formulating an attribution, and the less likely he or she is to recommend changes to the task (e.g., simpler materials).

One limitation of the data reviewed previously is that they were collected from single interactions with subordinates and thus did not examine whether a leader's attributions influence his or her subsequent interactions with subordinates. To address this issue, Offermann, Schroyer, and Green (1998) assigned participants at random to leader or subordinate roles on a two-trial experimental task (building abstract designs). Following the initial trial, leaders were provided with bogus feedback regarding subordinate performance (either good or poor) and whether this performance could be attributed to ability, effort, or luck. Offermann et al. anticipated that the behaviors of the leaders would depend on the type of attribution that they made for the group's performance. For instance, whereas poor performance that was attributed to effort (an internal and unstable cause) might motivate leaders to intervene actively, similarly poor performance that was attributed to luck (an external and unstable cause) might not motivate any response. Indeed, results demonstrated that the attributions made regarding group performance significantly affected a leader's subsequent interactions and behavior toward a group. For example, when a group's poor performance on Trial 1 was attributed to effort, group leaders became significantly more talkative during Trial 2. Interestingly, when a group's good performance on trial 1 was attributed to luck, group leaders also became significantly more talkative on Trial 2. Similar findings were found for the evaluative nature of the leader's comments and his or her recommendations to punish the group. Overall, these findings suggest that the attributions formed by leaders are important antecedents to their subsequent behavior.

Monitoring the External Environment

Although researchers traditionally have concentrated on understanding how lower-level leaders influence subordinates, recently a shift has occurred as scholars have become interested in understanding strategic-level executive leadership (Yukl, 2002, p. 341). Interest in strategic-level leadership is not surprising given the impact that senior level executives have on organizational performance (e.g., Day & Lord, 1988; A. B. Thomas, 1988). One of the essential functions performed by strategic-level leaders, relevant to the information-processing perspective taken in this chapter, is environmental monitoring and scanning. Unlike supervisory leaders, who monitor, categorize, and react to their subordinates (e.g., Green & Mitchell, 1979), leaders at strategic and upper levels must direct their attention beyond the internal milieu of the work group to the external environment within which the organization exists (Kraut, Pedigo, McKenna, & Dunnette, 1989). Because organizations are open systems (Katz & Kahn, 1966), the external environment must be understood so that organizational fit can be ascertained and appropriate responses generated (Lawrence & Lorsch, 1967). Thus, as was the case with supervisory leadership, categorizations of the environment serve to regulate and direct subsequent action.

External environments can be assessed and perceived along several dimensions, such as certainty (Milliken, 1987). Here, however, we restrict our discussion to perhaps the most widely investigated environmental categorization, that of threats versus opportunities (Dutton & Jackson, 1987; Jackson & Dutton, 1988). Utilizing categorization theory, Dutton and Jackson have conceptualized threats and opportunities as two perceptual schemata, suggesting that the degree of overlap between current environmental cues and each schema (i.e., prototype match) dictates whether the external environment is labeled a threat or an opportunity. In an initial investigation, Jackson and Dutton (1988; Study 1) outlined the structure of each of these schemata by asking 78 executives to rate the extent to which 56 environmental conditions were characteristic of an opportunity or a threat. Interestingly, their results suggested that distinctive environmental cues characterized threats versus opportunities. Specifically, environmental cues that were negative, were uncontrollable, and could lead to a loss were considered as threats, whereas environmental characteristics that were positive, were controllable, and could lead to a potential were considered to be opportunities.

Although the initial experiment outlined the content of the threat and opportunity schemata, it left unanswered the question of whether schema-consistent cues actually would lead perceivers to categorize environments as threats or as opportunities. To examine this question, Jackson and Dutton (1988; Study 2) recruited 83 MBA graduates and had them evaluate four types of scenarios, which varied in terms of the threat/opportunity information provided. In this study, scenarios contained either (a) distinctive threat cues, (b) distinctive opportunity cues, (c) ambiguous cues (cues judged to be both a threat and an opportunity), or (d) neutral cues (cues judged to be neither a threat nor an opportunity). Following each scenario, participants evaluated the situation in terms of the degree to which it represented a threat or an opportunity. As expected, the distinctive threat cue scenario and the distinctive opportunity cue scenario were categorized by perceivers as a threat and an opportunity, respectively. Interestingly, the ambiguous cue condition was categorized as threatening, leading Jackson and Dutton to conclude that strategic leaders may be biased toward categorizing environmental conditions as threatening.

One unresolved issue is whether threat and opportunity categorizations have any implications for how strategic-level leaders respond. Given our earlier discussion of supervisory leaders (e.g., Offermann, Schroyer, et al., 1998), it should come as no surprise that environmental categorizations are considered to be proximal causes of subsequent organizational responses (Chattopadhyay, Glick, & Huber, 2001; Dutton & Jackson, 1987; J. B. Thomas, Clark, & Gioia, 1993). Supporting this notion, Chattopadhyay and his colleagues examined the degree to which perceptions of threats and opportunities were associated with internal or external organizational responses. Following prospect theory (Kahneman & Tversky, 1979), they hypothesized that organizations would be risk seeking when faced with likely losses (i.e., threat), seeking external solutions affecting the external environment; whereas they would be risk averse when confronted with likely gains (i.e., opportunity), seeking internal solutions affecting the internal organizational structure. The results partially supported these hypotheses, demonstrating that the initial categorization of the environment as a threat led to a greater likelihood of responding with a riskier external solution. Chattopadhyay et al.'s work is promising, but given the dearth of studies that have directly investigated this topic, additional work is needed before firm conclusions can be drawn regarding how strategic leaders' categorizations affect organizational responses.

A final consideration is whether or not aspects of the individual perceiver or situation will predispose strategic leaders to rely on an opportunity or a threat schema. Given the number of potential schemata available, activation is determined jointly by chronic individual differences and situational factors. Within the strategic leadership literature, some theoretic models indicate that the personal characteristics of strategic leaders, such as experience and values, can color environmental perceptions (e.g., Hambrick & Mason, 1984). Coinciding with this perspective, research has shown that a perceiver's self-efficacy is positively associated with the likelihood that a situation will be categorized as an opportunity (Mohammed & Billings, 2002). Similarly, research also has indicated that the time frame of an event can influence the use of threat and opportunity schemata (Highhouse, Mohammed, & Hoffman, 2002). Thus, although the categorization of the environment as a threat or an opportunity has important implications, to date insufficient attention has been directed toward understanding the individual-difference and contextual variables that moderate usage of these schemata.

Future Directions

Our review has highlighted many of the advances that have been made in terms of understanding leader information processing. Despite these gains, many challenging questions remain. For instance, to date, only a narrow slice of the environment has been considered by scholars, but it is abundantly clear that leadership is contextually embedded and that leaders must simultaneously react to, and make sense of, an enormous number of environmental cues (Lord, Brown, & Harvey, 2001; Zaccaro, Mumford, Connelly, Marks, & Gilbert, 2000). How can such an enormous array of features be simultaneously modeled? Although promising frameworks have been suggested (e.g., Lord, Brown, & Harvey, 2001; Lord, Brown, Harvey, & Hall, 2001), future research is needed to examine their usefulness. Relatedly, a greater amount of attention must be paid to how executive leaders solve the ill-defined problems that typically characterize much of their work (Mumford, Zaccaro, et al., 2000). Finally, more attention should be devoted to better integrating the information-processing perspective with other approaches, many of which are outlined throughout this book. It seems likely that such efforts would illuminate why many of our most popular leadership constructs are important. For example, whereas strong evidence supports an association between an individual's personality and leadership outcomes (e.g., Judge, Bono, Ilies, & Gerhardt, 2002), personality-based work has not highlighted clearly why such associations exist. One possibility is that personality affects outcomes through schema creation (C. D. McCauley, 2001), serving to influence both an individual's openness and the motivation to learn (Ericsson & Charness, 1994).

Information Processing From the Subordinate's Perspective

To this point, we have concentrated on the information processing of leaders; in the remainder of the chapter, we shift our focus to the minds of subordinates. Given that leadership is a social process that unfolds between at least two social agents, a leader and a follower, the effectiveness of leadership depends on how leaders affect subordinates. That leads to the question, What is it about a leader that enables him or her to influence a subordinate? A cursory examination of the leadership literature suggests that scholars have sought the answer through investigating the behaviors or behavioral styles exhibited by leaders (Brown & Lord, 2001). However, just as our previous review suggested that leaders do not directly react to environmental stimuli, neither do subordinates. Instead, the effects of a leader's actions depend on the symbolic structures that subordinates utilize to represent these actions (Lord & Maher, 1991b). Below, we concentrate on these internal symbolic knowledge structures, discussing their origin, their structure, and the processes that lead to their application. Practically speaking, knowledge about subordinate sense-making and about categorization processes is pivotal for understanding effective leadership, as it is these mental processes that mediate the impact of a leader's behaviors on relevant outcomes (Hollander & Julian, 1969; Lord & Maher, 1991b).

Content and Structure of Leader Schemata

Before continuing, take a moment and contemplate how you might respond if you were asked to distinguish a leader from a nonleader. Following some meditation on this topic, it is probable that many readers would reply to our inquiry by articulating a long list of features that characterize leaders. Readers might, for instance, suggest that leaders are intelligent, dedicated, self-sacrificial, goal-oriented, and decisive people, to name but a few possibilities. As this simple exercise highlights, each of us holds within his or her long-term memory a large and well-elaborated belief system regarding those features that we each believe distinguish leaders (Lord, Foti, & Phillips, 1982), often referred to as an implicit leadership theory (Lord, Foti, & De Vader, 1984). In fact, our knowledge of social categories, such as "leader," are an essential means by which we navigate our world, allowing us to direct our limited attention to relevant aspects of the environment and fill in information that is not readily apparent. For instance, research into implicit leadership theories has documented their pivotal role in subordinates' perceptions and attributions of leaders, as well as the ways in which subordinates respond to behavioral questionnaires (e.g., Eden & Leviatan, 1975; Lord, Foti, & De Vader, 1984). In contrast to the limited attention devoted to studying a leader's schemata, considerably greater strides have been made over the last 25 years to better understand perceivers' schemata of leaders.

According to Lord and his colleagues (Lord, Foti, & De Vader, 1984), the decision to label an individual as a leader depends on the extent to which the features of a target overlap with the features that distinguish the leader category or prototype. Following the probabilistic view of concept organization (Rosch, 1978), Lord et al. have suggested that the leader category that individuals hold in memory is fuzzy and ill-defined. Simply put, although each of the features of the category may be typical for category members, no single feature defines the category. Thus, as a result, the absence of any single feature in a target does not eliminate the possibility that the target belongs to a particular category; instead, it simply implies that the target is less prototypical of the category. For instance, although "birds" typically fly, the fact that a particular animal does not fly (e.g., a chicken) does not preclude it from membership in this category; it simply suggests that the target may be less prototypical than other exemplars (e.g., a robin).

The prior paragraph suggests that the leader category is composed of a fuzzy set of features whose presence or absence dictates the degree of fit with the category, but what are these fuzzy features? Following Cantor and Mischel (1979), Lord has suggested that the leader category is structured around the traits that distinguish leaders. The centrality of traits for social categories, such as that of leader, should come as no surprise to readers who are familiar with contemporary social-cognitive research. Social-cognitive research has shown that perceivers spontaneously and automatically encode behavior in terms of the underlying trait constructs that are implied by a behavior (e.g., Uleman, Newman, & Moskowitz, 1996). Coinciding with these basic person perception processes, Lord, De Vader, and Alliger (1986) found, in a meta-analytic investigation, that many personality traits are highly associated with leadership perceptions (e.g., dominance and intelligence). Although this work indicates that the content of perceivers' implicit leadership theories (ILT) may be largely trait-based, it does not precisely clarify the content of these categories.

In perhaps the most comprehensive analysis of the content of ILTs, Offermann and her colleagues (Offermann, Kennedy, & Wirtz, 1994) conducted a five-stage investigation. During the first phase of their work, Offermann et al. had 115 undergraduate students generate lists of up to 25 trait terms that described a leader, resulting in 160 unique traits. In the second phase, the researchers presented 686 undergraduates with these 160 traits and had them rate, on a 10-point scale, the degree to which each of the traits was characteristic of a leader. These item ratings, in turn, were subjected to a principal components factor analysis, resulting in 57 items representing eight distinctive leader category dimensions: sensitivity, dedication, tyranny, charisma, attractiveness, masculinity, intelligence, and strength. As further verification, the dimensionality of perceivers' implicit theories was assessed by having a new group of 44 participants categorize the 57 items identified during the previous phase into the eight factors. During this phase, items that were not correctly sorted by at least 70% of participants were eliminated, resulting in a final set of 41 items. During the final two phases of the project, the dimensional structure of the instrument was compared between males and females and examined in a sample of 260 working adults. These last two stages revealed that the eight-factor structure was robust across these groups, suggesting that there is a culturally shared, multidimensional knowledge structure regarding what it means to be a leader. However, is there simply one leader category held in long-term memory? Are our beliefs about leaders the same, regardless of whether they are, for example, political, academic, or religious leaders? To address this issue, we turn our attention back to Rosch's seminal work on category structure (Rosch, 1978) and Lord's extension of this work to leadership (e.g., Lord, Foti, & De Vader, 1984).

Rather than individuals possessing a single category, Rosch (1978) suggested that their mental categories can be hierarchically arrayed into three levels: superordinate, basic, and subordinate. At the highest, most inclusive level, referred to as superordinate, are the broadest and most abstract representations of the prototype (e.g., animal). Immediately below this level are the basic-level representations of the category (e.g., bird), and embedded below this are the subordinate representations of the category (e.g., robin). The most important and useful level of representations are the prototypes located at the basic level, because they provide the greatest level of differentiation among stimuli (because the basic level is the least inclusive). Extending Rosch's viewpoint, Lord and colleagues (Lord, Foti, & De Vader, 1984; Lord, Foti, & Phillips, 1982) have posited that just as natural objects can be differentiated into three hierarchical levels, so too can our cognitive representations of leaders. At the superordinate level is the most general distinction between a leader and a nonleader. At the basic level, perceivers take into account contextual information and differentiate between leaders from different contexts. For instance, Lord, Foti, and De Vader (1984) suggest, on the basis of a content analysis of media outlets, that 11 different basic-level leaders can be differentiated: business, finance, minority, education, religion, sports, national politics, world politics, labor, media, and military. Finally, at the lowest level, leaders are differentiated within each of the contexts, providing a contextually defined leadership prototype (e.g., female military leader vs. male military leader).

As the previous literature suggests, perceivers possess large, multidimensional, contextually sensitive schemata for leadership, but do all perceivers share precisely the same schema? Given that leader prototypes are social constructs, formed on the basis of interactions within a given group, plausibly we might predict the emergence of distinct prototypes among groups. Motivated by increasing globalization and diversity and by the possibility that expatriate managers fail because their definition of leadership does not coincide with that of subordinates in the host country (J. B. Shaw, 1990), some researchers have investigated whether leader prototypes exhibit cross-cultural variability (e.g., Den Hartog, House, Hanges, Ruiz-Quintanilla, & Dorfman, 1999; Gerstner & Day, 1994). To assess the plausibility of this idea, Gerstner and Day (1994) had 142 graduate students from eight countries ($n = 10$ to $n = 22$) evaluate the prototypicality of 59 attributes that had been identified in prior work (Lord, Foti, & De Vader, 1984). Coinciding with their hypotheses, discernible differences emerged in the leader prototypes as a function of culture. Although it is encouraging, one clear limitation with the Gerstner and Day investigation lies in our ability to draw conclusions on the basis of such a limited and restricted sample. In part to circumvent this limitation, others have investigated leader prototypes across a broader spectrum of societies (Den Hartog, House, et al., 1999).

In their investigation, Den Hartog et al. (1999; see also Den Hartog & Dickson, Chapter 11, this volume) examined the extent to which leader attributes were universally shared. To test this idea, they had 15,022 middle managers, from 60 different societies (average per society of 250) rate the degree to which 112 leadership items (composing six second-order factors) impede or facilitate effective leadership. Three of these second-order factors emerged as characteristic of outstanding leadership across all or most of the 60 societies investigated (charismatic, team-oriented, and participative), one was universally endorsed as inhibiting leadership (self-protective), and the last two were culturally contingent (humane orientation and autonomous). Similarly mixed results were found at the item level. Although many items were universally endorsed (e.g., just, honest), a relatively large number of attributes exhibited substantial cross-cultural variability (e.g., self-sacrificial, enthusiastic, individualistic). Together, the available data (e.g., Den Hartog, House, et al., 1999; Gerstner & Day, 1994) indicate that although universal attributes of leadership exist, there is substantial variability in our definitions of leadership, seemingly arising from our personal experiences. Inconsistencies in the prototypes across cultures suggest that leaders may have difficulty transitioning across cultures.

Beyond cultural influences, are other experiences pivotal in shaping the content of the leader category? One possibility, investigated by Keller (1999), is that influential role models from our past shape the content of our leader categories. Following the logic of social learning theory, Keller hypothesized that individual endorsement of prototypical leader elements is conditional on parental characteristics. Using the prototypical elements isolated by Offermann, Kennedy, et al. (1994), Keller had participants rate the extent to which each characteristic was descriptive of their mother, their father, and an ideal leader. Several interesting relationships emerged, and the findings suggested that participants' perceptions of their parents colored their image of the ideal leader. For instance, father tyranny (e.g., manipulative and power-hungry) was negatively associated with the degree to which participants endorsed sensitivity as a characteristic of an ideal leader, but father tyranny was positively associated with participants' beliefs that tyranny was an ideal characteristic of a leader. Similarly, father dedication was positively related with participants' beliefs that dedication was descriptive of an ideal leader. Beyond Keller's examination, little effort has been directed toward understanding leader prototype formation; however, given that leader influence depends on leadership perceptions, developing a better understanding of prototype development warrants additional attention.

Our review suggests that the leader category is a large, multidimensional, hierarchically arranged, contextually sensitive structure whose content is determined in part by a social agent's experiences (e.g., culture, paternal behavior). What is the developmental trajectory of the leader category? Based on prior developmental theory, Matthews, Lord, and Walker (1990) argued that as people age, their leadership perceptions and judgments shift from being based on specific exemplars and observable characteristics to being based on abstract prototypes. To test this idea they recruited 159 participants from the 1st, 3rd, 6th, 9th, and 12th grades and had them complete a series of open-ended questions regarding what it means to be a leader. Coinciding with the researchers' expectations, significant differences emerged in terms of how children of different ages conceptualized leadership. Relative to older children (i.e., those in the 6th, 9th, and 12th grades), younger children (i.e., those in the 1st and 3rd grades) held leadership judgments that were based more on specific actions, outcomes, and exemplars (e.g., parents). Older children based their judgments more on a highly elaborated leader prototype. These data suggest that with repeated exposure and experience, children generate an underlying leader prototype, which comes to serve as the standard against which they form their leadership judgments.

How Do We Label Leaders?

How do we decide that someone is a leader? Information-processing research has highlighted two possible pathways (Lord, 1985). First, the label "leader" may be ascribed on the basis of a perceiver's recognition that the actions, traits, and behaviors of a target are consistent with the information contained in the perceiver's leader schema. Second, a "leader" label can be inferred by perceivers, based on any outcomes that are associated with the target individual or the current context. We begin by discussing evidence for the recognition-based pathway, then follow up by reviewing evidence for the inference-based processes.

Recognition-Based Processes

In their categorization theory of leadership perceptions, Lord and his colleagues suggested that the assignment of the "leader" label is contingent on the degree to which a given target's features overlap with a perceiver's leadership category (Lord, Foti, & De Vader, 1984). That is, the greater the overlap that exists between a target's features and the prototype that is held in a perceiver's long-term memory, the more strongly the category label of "leader" will be applied to the target. In one of the original investigations to test this notion, Lord, Foti, and De Vader (1984; Study 3) examined the degree to which individuals' leadership ratings and causal ascriptions to a leader target were contingent on a target's fit to the leader prototype. In this investigation, the researchers randomly assigned 95 participants to read one of three vignettes, which varied in terms of whether the target, John Perry, displayed prototypical, neutral, or antiprototypical leadership behaviors. After reading these descriptions, participants were asked to rate John Perry's leadership; the likelihood that he would engage in prototypical, antiprototypical, and neutral behaviors; and his accountability and responsibility for the success of a new product. Overall, the results indicated that the leader manipulation accounted for significant variance in all three relevant outcomes ($\eta^2 = .31$ to 59), thereby providing strong support for the categorization perspective. Perhaps most interesting, however, was the fact that once a target was categorized, perceivers formed expectations for the target's future behavior, hinting at the possibility that perceiver categorization may initiate a self-fulfilling prophecy (see Eden, 1992), although this possibility requires empirical examination.

Since the initial investigations, subsequent studies have replicated and extended categorization theory, providing further refinement and understanding of how categorization processes function. For instance, research has documented that leader categorization (a) mediates the relationship between observable target behaviors and leadership ratings (Fraser & Lord, 1988), (b) does not depend on the availability of cognitive resources (Maurer & Lord, 1991), (c) explains ratings of real-world leaders (Fielding & Hogg, 1997; Foti, Fraser, & Lord, 1982), and (d) biases information retrieval (Rush & Russell, 1988). In addition, researchers have extended the categorization framework by assessing possible boundary conditions. In perhaps some of the most intriguing and interesting work in that area, Hogg and his colleagues (see Hogg, 2001) have integrated the categorization model with social identity theory.

Based on contemporary social psychological work on social identity theory, Hogg proposed a social identity theory of leadership (Hogg, 2001). Hogg developed the theory to explain relationships between groups, but social identity theorists have more recently extended this framework to understand intragroup phenomena. Unlike Lord's categorization theory, which focuses strictly on how the normative leader prototype will dictate leadership perceptions, the social identity perspective suggests that leadership perceptions will depend on a target's fit with a group's prototype. As is the leader prototype, the group prototype is fuzzy, representing the prototypical values, attitudes, and norms of a group. As a result, whereas no single individual precisely fits the group prototype, individuals do vary along a group prototypicality gradient. A key tenet of this perspective is that the stronger the degree to which a perceiver identifies with a group, the greater the extent to which a target's fit to the group prototype will guide leadership perceptions.

To test the core propositions of the theory, Hains, Hogg, and Duck (1997) recruited 184 undergraduate students to participate, ostensibly, in a group exercise. At the outset of the experiment, the researchers manipulated participants' identification with the group (high identification vs. low identification) and varied two pieces of information about a leader. In terms of information about the group leader, both his or her fit with the group prototype (high vs. low) and his or her fit with the leader prototype (high vs. low) were varied. Following the manipulation of this information, participants completed a series of measures intended to assess their endorsement of the leader. As predicted by the social identity perspective, when participants' group salience was higher, they were more likely to endorse the leader if the leader was prototypical of the group. Interestingly, fit with the leader prototype remained an important predictor of participants' leadership judgments ($\eta^2 = .22$). Thus, overall, these results suggest that the leader prototype is important in forming leadership perceptions, and fit to the group prototype may also be important, particularly when an individual's group identification is salient. Finally, it is worth noting that these effects are not isolated; they have been replicated both in the field (Fielding & Hogg, 1997) and with alternative experimental paradigms (Hogg, Hains, & Mason, 1998).

One potential implication of Hogg's work for the theory of leader categorization is that the leader category may be a much more fluid and adjustable knowledge structure than previously indicated. Is it possible that those individuals who possess high group identification activate leader prototypes very different from those of individuals who are low in identification? If so, what are the relevant factors that influence the leader category, and how are different pieces of information integrated? To address these questions, Lord and his colleagues (Hanges, Lord, & Dickson, 2000; Lord, Brown, & Harvey, 2001; Lord, Brown, Harvey, et al., 2001) have suggested that rather than being fixed memory structures that are retrieved from long-term memory, perceivers' leader categories are dynamically created on the fly. Utilizing connectionist models of human information processing, Lord has argued that perceivers simultaneously integrate a multitude of internal (e.g., identification with group) and external (e.g., societal culture) sources of information, thereby generating a contextually appropriate leader prototype. Consistent with this line of thinking, prior research has shown that the leader prototype that is generated by a perceiver depends on such factors as the hierarchical level of the leader in the organization, his or her gender, national culture of the leader and of the perceiver, and task type (see Lord, Brown, Harvey, & Hall, 2001). Thus, although more research is needed, it seems quite plausible that findings such as Hogg's can be integrated parsimoniously into newer leader prototype generation models.

One final matter that deserves consideration is whether any situational triggers enhance the likelihood that perceivers will utilize the leader category when forming target perceptions. As many readers already may suspect, innumerable categories are available to subordinates (e.g., gender, race, leader) and, as a result, it is necessary not only to understand the structure of the leader prototype, but also to comprehend those aspects of the context that increase the accessibility of the leader category. Given that a critical leader function is to provide direction during times of uncertainty, it seems plausible that situational factors that induce uncertainty in perceivers will increase the usage of leader prototypes. In line with these expectations, several studies have shown that crisis contexts enhance perceivers' attributions of leadership to targets (Hunt, Boal, & Dodge, 1999; Meindl, Ehrlich, & Dukerich, 1985; Pillai, 1996) and that crises may unconsciously activate the leader category (Emrich, 1999). Whether there are additional contextual features (e.g., culture), beyond crises, that accentuate leader category accessibility remains an underinvestigated but intriguing area of inquiry.

Inference-Based Processes

Imagine an organization that surpasses all performance goals, earning well beyond what was expected for the quarter or year; this is a thriving, flourishing company that consistently meets or exceeds all targets. Without giving it much thought, who should be credited for the organization's success? Many readers will assign credit to the leader at the helm of the organization—the CEO or president. Seemingly, our implicit theories suggest that leaders "do or should have the ability to control and influence the fates of the organizations in their charge" (Meindl, Ehrlich, et al., 1985, p. 96). Effective leaders are expected to produce positive outcomes. When they fail, we fire or replace them; when they succeed, we credit and reward them. Logically, if our notions of leadership are intertwined with group outcomes, the valence of these outcomes should color the inferences that we draw regarding a leader. Is this the case? Numerous studies, extending back over the past 20 years, have utilized the performance-cue paradigm to investigate this very issue (e.g., Binning & Lord, 1980; Larson, 1982; Larson, Lingle, & Scerbo, 1984; Lord, Binning, Rush, & Thomas, 1978; J. S. Phillips & Lord, 1982).

In a characteristic performance-cue experiment, participants are brought into the lab and asked to view a videotaped group, ostensibly because the researcher is investigating perceptions of group interaction. Subsequent to viewing the tape, participants are asked to rate the group's leader on a behavioral scale that contains prototypical and nonprototypical leader behaviors. Prior to providing these behavioral ratings, however, participants randomly receive either positive performance-cue information (i.e., the group performed well) or negative performance-cue information (i.e., the group performed poorly). The central issue of interest within this paradigm is whether or not perceivers' behavioral ratings will be colored by the performance cue, as they should if outcome information is part of our implicit leadership theories.

Resoundingly, the extant literature suggests that performance cues have a dramatic impact on our perceptions of leadership (e.g., Binning & Lord, 1980; Larson, 1982; Larson, Lingle, et al., 1984; Lord, Binning, et al., 1978; J. S. Phillips & Lord, 1982). The available data also suggest that the effect is quite robust, as it (a) is equally potent regardless of whether it is delivered before or after viewing the leader (Larson, 1982), although the cognitive mechanism may differ (Larson, Lingle, et al., 1984); (b) influences ratings even when the perceiver has interacted with the group (Binning & Lord, 1980); (c) affects global ratings of leadership (e.g., initiating structure) more than ratings of specific behavior (Binning, Zaba, & Whattam, 1986; Gioia & Sims, 1985); and (d) functions in an additive fashion with categorization processes (Lord, Binning, et al., 1978). Despite its generally robust nature, it is noteworthy that the performance-cue effect may be bound by the observer's processing goals (M. R. Murphy & Jones, 1993) and by the social distance (the degree of leader-follower intimacy and social contact) between a follower and a leader, which accentuates the attributions that followers might make (Shamir, 1995). For instance, whereas distant followers may use overall organizational performance, close followers may rely on actual leader performance (for recent extensions of these ideas, see Antonakis and Atwater, 2002). Given the dearth of available research, more work is needed to better understand the boundary conditions of performance-cue effects.

One question raised by our previous discussion is whether there is anything leaders can do to mitigate the potentially deleterious impact of negative performance cues. One intriguing possibility lies in perceivers' shared understanding of emotions. According to appraisal theories, the emotions displayed by a target act as cues that communicate the appropriateness of different interpretations (C. A. Smith & Ellsworth, 1985). For instance, whereas unfavorable outcomes, when they co-occur with sadness, are perceived to be internally caused, the same negative events—when they co-occur with anger—are perceived to be externally caused (Tiedens, 2000). As a result of such processes, emotional expressions may be able to shift the attributions that are formed by perceivers for a negative event. In line with this thinking, Tiedens (2001) examined whether perceivers' impressions of a target depended on the emotions exhibited. To test this idea, she had participants view one of two video clips of President Bill Clinton's testimony to the grand jury regarding the Monica Lewinsky scandal. In the first condition, participants viewed an angry Clinton, whereas in the second condition, participants viewed a sad Clinton. Regardless of their political affiliation, participants in the angry condition rated Clinton much more favorably than did those assigned to the sad condition. Although speculative, these findings suggest that emotional expressions may lessen the impact of negative performance cues.

More generally, the message conveyed by Tiedens's (2000) work is that emotional expressions, as is the case with performance cues, are important cues that perceivers use to infer status and leadership. In this regard, Tiedens and her colleagues have examined the interrelationship between emotional expressions and status conferral. For example, in one series of laboratory studies, participants who viewed an angry target rated the target as being of higher status, more powerful, and more competent than did participants who viewed a sad target (Tiedens, 2001). Similarly, participants given no information about status assumed an angry individual was an executive and that a sad individual was his assistant (Tiedens, Ellsworth, & Mesquita, 2000). Although indirect, Tiedens's investigations lend credence to the possibility that emotions are an additional inferential route to leadership perceptions.

Beyond Perception

Up to this point, we have focused on individuals' perceptions. To understand leadership fully, however, we cannot limit ourselves simply to perceptions.

Ultimately, leadership is an influence process in which one individual (a leader), through his or her actions, changes the way that a second individual (a subordinate) behaves, thinks, or feels. The question we have been exploring is how this occurs. However, another interesting perspective recently outlined by scholars is that a leader's actions transform the manner in which subordinates conceptualize themselves (e.g., Lord, Brown, & Freiberg, 1999; Shamir, House, & Arthur, 1993). Contemporary research suggests that the self is a dynamic, multifaceted memory structure, one that contains far more schemata than can be activated at any given moment. As a result, only a limited and contextually activated number of schemata are salient, a portion typically referred to as the working self concept (WSC) (Markus & Wurf, 1987). Once activated, it is this WSC that guides our behavior (Banaji & Prentice, 1994). Extending this thinking, Lord and Brown (2001, in press; Lord, Brown, & Freiberg, 1999) have proposed that leaders exert their influence over subordinates and, by extension, affect organizational outcomes by activating different portions of a subordinate's WSC. In essence, leaders change the way in which we envision ourselves.

Generally speaking, Lord and Brown (in press; Lord, Brown, & Freiberg, 1999) proposed that the self-concept can be divided into three basic levels: individual self, relational self, or collective self. In addition, they suggested that different leader activities (e.g., behaviors, decision making, perception formation) map onto each of these broadly defined dimensions of the self-concept. For instance, in their model they proposed that the effect of charismatic, transformational, and self-sacrificial behavioral styles operate through the activation of the collective self-concept. Thus, as a result of engaging in transformational leadership behavior, leaders are able to get group members to redefine themselves in terms of group-level characteristics (e.g., group prototype). Coinciding with this prediction, Paul, Costley, Howell, Dorfman, and Trafimow (2001) tested the extent to which alternative leadership styles activate aspects of a perceiver's self-concept. They randomly assigned 353 participants to read one of three written vignettes describing a leader as charismatic, as individually considerate, or as a combination of the two. After reading about the leader, participants completed a measure of collective self-concept activation. Interestingly, participants exposed to a charismatic leader had significantly higher scores on the collective self-concept measure than did those exposed to an individually considerate leader. Given the nascent nature of this approach, more work will be needed before firm conclusions can be drawn regarding what relationship, if any, leader behaviors have with subordinates' self-concepts.

Future Directions

Over the past 30 years, researchers have made substantial strides in terms of what we know about how perceivers form leadership impressions. Recent trends suggest, however, that there are many exciting new opportunities and challenges for scholars in this realm. For instance, technology has dramatically transformed the manner in which people communicate with one another in organizations. Technological advances have lessened the need for direct face-to-face interactions between supervisors and subordinates (Avolio, Kahai, Dumdum, & Sivasubramaniam, 2001). For the most part, our models and our research on leadership perceptions have been based on face-to-face interactions; how perceptions are formed in a "virtual" environment remains unknown. Similarly, the demographic composition of the workforce has shifted in recent years. Today, visible minorities are the fastest growing component of the labor market, resulting in a greater number of demographically dissimilar supervisor-subordinate dyads. The manner in which leadership perceptions form in such dyads has not been considered, but should become increasingly important as the workplace diversifies. Finally, greater attention must be paid to understanding how perceptions of leadership translate into actions of subordinates. Work in this area has begun (e.g., Lord & Brown, in press; Lord, Brown, & Freiberg, 1999; Shamir, House, et al., 1993), but more is required if we are to fully understand the mechanism behind a leader's influence.

Conclusion

On the basis of material reviewed in this chapter, we suggest that the study of leadership can benefit from understanding the information processing of leaders and subordinates. Although our review should not be taken to be exhaustive, it has, we think, highlighted the dominant themes. We see in the material indications that the content of the schemata held by leaders and subordinates is essential for understanding leadership processes. For leaders, schemata are the source of one's own behaviors (e.g., Wofford & Goodwin, 1994), whereas for subordinates, they are the standards against which these behaviors are compared (e.g., Lord, Foti, & De Vader, 1984). In addition, prior research has highlighted that schemata are contextually organized and cued. The behavioral schemata activated by leaders depend on how they perceive subordinates (e.g., Mitchell & Wood, 1980) or the environment (Chattopadhyay et al., 2001; Dutton & Jackson, 1987). Similarly, perceivers possess multidimensional schemata, and different portions of these schemata may be activated (e.g., Lord, Foti, & De Vader, 1984) or re-created (e.g., Lord, Brown, Harvey, et al., 2001). Despite these advances, it is also evident that the attention devoted to examining information processing has been limited, relative to the attention paid to other areas of leadership research. We hope, therefore, that this chapter will motivate others to examine the role of information processing in leadership.

CHAPTER 7

Situational and Contingency Approaches to Leadership

Roya Ayman

S ince antiquity, scholars around the world have held a pervading fascination with identifying one or more universal characteristics of leaders. Historically, in various societies around the world, scholars and philosophers have advised the leaders of their era on how to be effective (Ayman, 1993, 2000). For example, Mencius guided the Chinese leaders of the 4th century B.C.; in the 12th century, Unsuru'1-Ma'ali advised the leaders of Persia; and in 16th-century Florence, Italy, Machiavelli addressed the magnificent Lorenzo di Piero de Medici in his work *The Prince* (Ayman, 1993; see also Machiavelli, 1513/1954). In all these ancient writings, the focus was on the leader.

In Europe, two schools of thought emerged that influenced modern research on leadership in the United States: Carlyle's (1907) "great man theory" and Karl Marx's (1906) "zeitgeist" approach. The great man theory guided leadership research in the first part of the 20th century, focusing researchers' attention on the characteristics of leaders through the trait and behavioral approaches. The zeitgeist school of thought purported that leadership does not reside in a person but instead is a result of temporal and spatial forces. Empirical studies of the mid-20th century reflecting the latter school of thought focused on the situational characteristics of leadership.

By the second half of the 20th century, these two schools of thought had merged into the contingency approaches to leadership.

I begin this chapter with a brief overview of the leader- and situation-oriented approaches to studying leadership, then move into the contingency approaches. Next, I review the classic contingency/situational theories of leadership. Following that is a close examination of the concept of contingency and the leadership situation. In addition to the well-known conceptualizations of leadership situation, such as the contingency model of leadership effectiveness and substitutes for leadership theory, I also explore other potential contingencies such as the leader's gender or ethnicity. Next, I discuss the nature of the interaction between the leader and contingencies by introducing moderators and mediators. Finally, I examine the leader-situation interaction. When this interface is at its best, it can optimize the performance of the leader and the group.

Focus on the Leader

The dominant line of research on leadership seems to have adhered to Carlyle's (1907) "great man theory." This focus has manifested in two main approaches: the trait approach and the behavior approach. As I demonstrate below, the situation plays an important role in determining the effectiveness of leadership, regardless of the leadership paradigm used.

For example, a recent addition to leadership theory has been the information-processing (i.e., cognitive) approach. Research in this approach has demonstrated that contingencies affect the individual's expectations, schemata, or prototypes (i.e., implicit leadership theory) of a leader, thus implying how leaders should behave in different contexts (Lord, Brown, Harvey, & Hall, 2001; Lord & Emrich, 2000; see also Brown, Scott, & Lewis, Chapter 6, this volume). Ayman (1993), among others, has mentioned that leader behavior research depends primarily on perceptual processes, which are inseparable from implicit leadership theory. This perspective makes it evident that contingencies affect both the observers' and the leader's expectations, which in turn can affect evaluations of behaviors or their effectiveness. Therefore, implicit leadership theory has implications for all leadership theories that are dependent on leader behaviors. Whether one looks at leadership from a trait, behavioral, or information-processing perspective, any path of investigation of universal predictors eventually faces the same challenge: the presence of moderators or contingencies.

Trait Approach

The trait approach to studying leadership has experienced hills and valleys in popularity (refer to Zaccaro, Kemp, and Bader, Chapter 5, this volume, for further discussion). Traits do account for variance in leader emergence and effectiveness; however, traits still should be considered along with contextual factors in predicting leader emergence and effectiveness, as acknowledged by Zaccaro, Kemp, et al. (Chapter 5, this volume).[1] The debate about the relative importance of context persists. From my point of view, Stogdill's (1974) summary of the trait approach, wherein he acknowledged potential moderators, is still valid today:

> A person does not become a leader by virtue of the possession of some combination of traits, but the pattern of personal characteristics of the leader must bear some relevant relationship to the characteristics, activities, and goals of the followers. . . . The evidence suggests that leadership is a relation that exists between persons in a social situation, and that persons who are leaders in one situation may not necessarily be leaders in other situations. (pp. 63–64)

Recent work on traits and leaders has also recognized potential intraperson moderators. For example, a recent meta-analysis on self-monitoring and work behavior (Day, Schleicher, Unckless, & Hiller, 2002) found that self-monitoring strongly predicted the emergence of leaders; but the individual's gender was noted as a moderator. Additionally, Barrick and Mount (1993) demonstrated that autonomy moderated the relationship between the "Big Five" personality characteristics and organizational effectiveness. Furthermore, the relationship between a trait and leadership not only can be moderated by the situation but also can vary across different people.

When, in the middle of the 20th century, researchers abandoned traits—because of inconsistencies in how traits predicted leadership—in favor of behavioral measures, it may have been an oversight. Even though they are proponents of leader trait models, House, Shane, and Herold (1996) acknowledged that the manifestation of traits in leaders or leadership behavior can depend on a slew of variables, including the proximity of the trait, behavioral, and situational measures. Finally, in reviewing the role of the Big Five factors in industrial/organizational psychology, R. J. Schneider and Hough (1995) provided a model of potential moderators affecting the relationship between personality and job performance. They categorized these moderators as personal, situational, and criterion. These will be the contingencies discussed later in this chapter.

Leader Behavior

House and Aditya (1997) described the evolution of the leader behavior approach as being the consequence of researchers' disenchantment over the inconsistency of results with traits and leadership. Starting with Lewin, Lippitt, and White (1939) and Lippitt and White (1943), who conducted experiments with Boy Scout troops, the search began for the universal effective leader behavior. Their study recognized that authoritative, democratic, and laissez-faire leader behaviors have differing effects on a team. Their findings showed support for a durable effect when the leader was democratic. They also found support, however, that the group was productive under an autocratic leader when the leader was present in the room.

Subsequent to this research, three groups of researchers launched investigations on leader behavior; at Harvard (Bales, 1954), at The Ohio State University (Stogdill & Coons, 1957), and at the University of Michigan (Kahn & Katz, 1953; Likert, 1961). Whereas some used laboratory settings to examine leaders in small groups, with observers describing leader behaviors (Bales, 1954), others went into work settings and had subordinates of leaders describe their leaders' behaviors. In either case, the three groups of researchers categorized leader behavior into one of two main categories: people oriented/considerate behaviors or task oriented/initiating structure behaviors. This leadership paradigm dominated the field of leadership research until the 1980s. These studies were beneficial in training leaders (e.g., Blake & Mouton,1985, as cited in Bass, 1990); nevertheless, as further studies were compiled, there seemed to be inconsistency in the results. Korman (1966) presented the argument that there are situations in which one behavior may be more effective than another.

Yet, the search for universals still persisted. Influenced by the work of Burns (1978), Bass (1985) introduced a paradigm shift in the leader-behavior research. In this new paradigm, a leader's behavior was seen as more than a transaction between the leader and the follower; it was seen as transformational. Once again, there was a search for universal leader behavior. For the purpose of discussion here, I present below the recent findings on this model as it relates to moderators.

Ten years into the research on the transformational-transactional leadership paradigm, Lowe, Kroeck, and Sivasubramaniam (1996) conducted a meta-analysis including more than 35 studies—and excluding self-reports data of leaders—on the various dimensions of transformational-transactional leadership and effectiveness. They hypothesized several moderators (i.e., organizational level, type of organization, and effectiveness criteria) that may affect the relationship between transformational leadership and effectiveness. Although the overall result supported the predictions of the model, they reported differential correlations of leader behaviors to outcome measures depending on the measure of effectiveness used and whether outcomes were subjective (e.g., subordinate perceptions) or objective (i.e., organizationally determined) measures of performance. They also found that leaders in the public sector exhibited more transformational leadership behaviors and were more effective than were leaders in the private sector. Although we now have a better understanding of this theory, Yukl (1999) mentioned that the discovery of additional moderators was needed to better understand its workings.

In addition to contextual or situational factors, meta-analyses examining the relationship between gender and leader behavior show slight gender differences (Eagly, Johannesen-Schmidt, & van Engen, in press; Eagly & Johnson, 1990). Compared with men, women are more participative and transformational and also are engaged in more contingent reward behaviors. Using studies on status characteristic theory and social role theory, Carli and Eagly (1999) concluded that, as compared with men, women who engaged in assertive and self-confident behaviors received less favorable evaluations. In other words, the behaviors that contributed to men's emergence as leaders may not have had the same effect for women. Furthermore, the context of the interaction complicated the prediction. For example, in business environments (as compared with educational settings), where there is a tradition of masculine management style, women's task-oriented behaviors were not endorsed as highly as those of men (Becker, Ayman, & Korabik, 2002). Thus, there is evidence that gender moderates the relationship between certain leader behaviors and outcomes (refer to Eagly and Carli, Chapter 12, this volume for further discussion on gender effects). In summary, all universal quests have ended in one point: Whether it is a leader's trait or a behavior under consideration, its contribution to success depends on particular contingencies.

Situational Focus

Simultaneous with the work on leaders' characteristics mentioned above, some social psychologists were examining the contribution of the situation in leadership. One might say that those focused on the role of the situation represented the zeitgeist school of thought. This approach considers the social context of leadership, in contrast to the trait or behavior approaches that focus primarily on the leader as the key factor. Chemers (1997) summarized this line of research using three main topics. One category of studies focused on the impact of group communication patterns on leadership emergence. Another series of studies concentrated on the relationship between spatial (seating) arrangements and leadership. Finally, the third series looked at the effect of support and feedback on leader emergence.

Studying group communication patterns resulted in identifying different levels of information accessibility. Leavitt (1951) compared four different types of communication patterns such as a chain, a wheel, a Y, and a circle. He reported that the person in the central position of the wheel or the Y was more often identified as a leader. However, in communication patterns that allowed the team members more chances to communicate with each other (e.g., in a circle), there was easy access to information across team members, and therefore each member had an equal chance of being identified as a leader. It was not the characteristics or behavior of the individual, then, but his or her position in the flow of information that led to emergence as a leader.

Another aspect of the situation that seems to affect leadership is space and seating arrangements. Researchers have studied team members' seating in relation to who was designated as the leader. The results demonstrated that, most often, people who sat at the head of the table were leaders of the team (Howells & Becker, 1962). The main rationale for this finding appears to be that the more eye contact a person has with others and the more control he or she has of the situation, the more likely it is that he or she will be identified as the leader (Chemers, 1997; M. E. Shaw, 1981). These could be the reasons why leaders tend to choose visible seating locations—because these locations offer better access to all team members. The use of space at the table is also a way that team members communicate dominance and control. For example, Sommer (1967), among others, has reported that people of high status occupied the most favored positions, reinforcing their status accordingly.

Another set of studies demonstrated that situations that convey confidence to an individual can bestow that individual with leadership status. The trait literature has identified confidence as an individual characteristic that separate leaders from nonleaders. From a situational perspective, chances are that an individual who feels support from team members and is endorsed by them will contribute more. Moreover, an individual who contributes positively to a group's goal may be recognized as the leader. To demonstrate this dynamic, Gruenfeld, Rance, and Weissenberg (1969) examined leaderless groups. In their experiment, a red and green light was placed in front of each member. If the person said something of value to the group, they received a green light; if their contribution was not considered of value, the red light would shine. The experimenters manipulated the color of the lights, randomly choosing who would see a green versus a red light. Those who received more green lights spoke more often and eventually had more chance of being chosen as a leader. Rather than the individual's own characteristics, it was the situation that determined the leader by conveying to the individual the group's confidence.

Finally, Shartle (1951) demonstrated the importance of workplace norms for how leaders behave. He found that the best predictor of a leader's behavior in organizations is the behavior of his or her boss, not the leader's personality. Thus, the organizational culture and the types of leader behaviors exhibited in a work setting can be strong contributors to a leader's future behavior in that setting.

In summary, the situation, independent of the individual, can influence leader emergence and behavior. It was in this period of the history of leadership research that some researchers started examining contingency concepts. In the 1960s, researchers developed contingency models to examine the interplay of the situation and the leader. Contingencies in leadership can be categorized into leader-situation interactions, intraleader factors, and methodological factors that moderate the relationship between a leader's characteristics and leader effectiveness. Before discussing these categories of contingencies, I will briefly review five classic and frequently cited leadership contingency models.

Contingency Models

From the late 1960s through the 1970s, several models and theories of leadership were developed that demonstrated that leadership effectiveness is a result of the interaction between the leader's characteristics and the situation. Some models focused on the leader's internal state and traits, such as the contingency model of leadership effectiveness and cognitive resource theory (Fiedler, 1978; Fiedler & Garcia, 1987). Others focused on the leader's perceived behaviors, such as the normative decision-making model (Vroom & Jago, 1978; Vroom & Yetton, 1973), path goal theory (House, 1971; House & Mitchell, 1974), and situational leadership theory (Hersey & Blanchard, 1969a). In the following sections, I briefly describe each of these models. I present the models in a matrix (Table 7.1) to compare them based on their approach to assessing the leader, the situation, and leadership effectiveness (outcome).

Table 7.1   Comparisons of Contingency Models' Treatment of the Leader, the Situation, and Outcomes

	Contingency Model of Leadership Effectiveness	Cognitive Resource Theory	Normative Model of Leadership Decision Making	Path-Goal Theory	Situational Leadership
The Leader					
Source	Leader	Leader	Mostly the leader, some from the subordinates	Subordinates	Subordinates
Characteristic	Trait (LPC scale): task and interpersonal orientation	Intelligence and experience	Decision strategies (five styles): Autocratic I and II, consultative I and II, and group II	Supervisory behavior: Participative, consultative, achievement oriented, and production oriented	Supervisory behavior (LEAD):[a] Selling, telling, participating, and delegating
The Situation					
Source	The leader and the experimenter	The leader	The leader and the experimenter	The subordinate	The leader or the experimenter
The Variables	Leader-member relationship Task structure Position power	Stress with the boss Stress with coworkers Stress with the task	Availability of information Team support and cohesion Time available (These are a simplified representation of 11 conditions)	Subordinates' need, values and ability Subordinates' task structure and difficulty	The subordinates' willingness and ability (follower maturity index
Outcomes					
Group	Performance Satisfaction (with leader and subordinates)	Performance	Performance Satisfaction	Satisfaction Job stress (mixed empirical results)	Satisfaction
Team Members	Stress (leader's)				

a. Leadership Effectiveness and Adaptability Description.

Leader's Trait Contingency Models

Contingency Model of Leadership Effectiveness

Fiedler (1964) was the first scholar to formulate a trait contingency model of leadership derived from empirical evidence. In this model, Fiedler (1978) predicted the leader's or group's success from the interaction of the leader's Least Preferred Coworker score (LPC) with the leader's situation. A detailed review of this model and its strength and weaknesses is presented elsewhere (Ayman, 2002; Ayman, Chemers, & Fiedler, 1998).

The contingency model of leadership effectiveness, also known as the leader-match concept, predicts that leaders who are more relationship oriented will be more effective than task-focused leaders in moderate situational control, whereas leaders who are more focused on task than on interpersonal relationships will be more effective in both high- and low-control situations. When leaders are in the situation where the model predicts their greatest effectiveness, they are considered "in match." When they are in situations where the model predicts they will be less effective, they are referred to as being "out of match."

Based on this model, Fiedler and Chemers (1984) designed a leadership-training model that received a favorable evaluation in a meta-analysis by Burke and Day (1986). Furthermore, researchers have tested the validity of the model's predictions in three separate meta-analyses (Peters, Hartke, & Pohlmann, 1985; Schriesheim, Tepper, & Tetrault, 1994; Strube & Garcia, 1981). Overall, these reports supported the general prediction of the model and called for further development and extension (Ayman, 2002). To further explain this model, I briefly present each component.

A leader's orientation, sometimes referred to as style, is assessed with the Least Preferred Coworker (LPC) scale, a bipolar-adjective, quasi-projective test. The leader's orientation, measured by the LPC scale, assesses the leader's internal state, not behavior. Thus, this orientation is fairly stable as compared with other personality traits or with intelligence. This construct has been the subject of many debates, and its psychometric properties have been highly scrutinized (see Ayman, 2002, for a detailed review). Through the years, several versions of this scale have been developed. The most frequently used LPC scale has 18 items (Ayman & Romano, 1998). Overall, the internal validity of the instrument is sound, with an alpha of about .90. The LPC's test-retest reliability also is acceptable (Ayman, 2002; Fiedler, 1978; Rice, 1978b).

Some scholars have voiced concerns regarding the LPC scale's face validity. More recently, new evidence has reconfirmed Fiedler's (1978) initial interpretation; low scores (below 64) on the LPC scale indicate a person being more intrinsically motivated, focusing primarily on the task. Individuals with high LPC scores (above 72) are more extrinsically motivated and focus primarily on relationships (Chemers & Ayman 1985; Rice, Marwick, Chemers, & Bentley, 1982). Several construct validity studies have tried to match the LPC score with other trait measures that assess a similar concept, such as cognitive complexity, intelligence, intolerance for ambiguity, authoritarianism, social desirability, locus of control, Protestant work ethic, need for achievement, and gender role. The results have shown that the LPC score does not correlate with other self-reported trait measures (e.g., Kennedy, Houston, Korsgaard, & Gallo, 1987; Rice, 1978a). In addition, LPC scores are not directly related to leader behavior or effectiveness but, for the most part, interact with the leader's situational control in predicting effectiveness.

The leader's situational control in this model is based on three aspects of the situation: the team's climate, the leader's task structure, and the leader's position power. The situation defines the leader's ability to influence the accomplishment of the group's task. The team's climate, better known as the leader-member relationship, assesses the cohesion of team members and their support toward the leader. The task structure includes two aspects of the leader's task: the dimensions of task structure and the leader's background (i.e., the leader's experience and training). The final task-structure score is determined by comparing the task's structure with the level of the leader's experience and training. Position power reflects the leader's legitimacy, as well as the authority for punishing and rewarding the team members (Ayman, 2002; Fiedler, 1978).

Initially, in laboratory studies, the experimenter designed these aspects of the situation (Fiedler, 1978). In most field studies, however, the leader provides the information using structured measures (Ayman & Romano, 1998). In the laboratory studies, the situation was categorized into eight possible octants, which varied based on the level of structure and favorability of the three situational aspects.

Recent research on the contingency model has not used the eight categories reflected in laboratory studies (e.g., Ayman & Chemers, 1991; Chemers, Hays, Rhodewalt, & Wysocki, 1985). As meta-analyses have shown (e.g., Strube & Garcia, 1981), some conditions were not easily replicated. Therefore, instead of using the eight octants based on possible combinations of the three situational aspects, situational control is defined as high control in Octants 1 and 2, moderate control in Octants 3 through 6, and low control in Octants 7 and 8.

The order of importance of the situational aspects is based on their contribution to the leader's sense of control and their usefulness in prediction in a situation. For Fiedler (1978), leader-member relationship is twice as important as task structure. Task structure is twice as important as position power (Ayman, 2002; Ayman, Chemers, & Fiedler, 1995, 1998). Interestingly, although the relative level of importance of the situational aspects was determined by empirical means, it resembled the relative importance of French and Raven's (1959) sources of power (Ayman, 2002). Independent of Fiedler's determination about the situational aspects' relative importance, Podsakoff and Schriesheim (1985) found that referent power and expert power were the most effective sources of power, thus lending more credence to Fiedler's assigned order of importance for the situational aspects.

Finally, the leader effectiveness criterion in this model most often has been defined as group performance (Fiedler, 1978). In response to some criticisms, Rice (1981) suggested that the model can also predict team satisfaction, a suggestion subsequently supported empirically (Ayman & Chemers, 1991). In addition, Chemers, Hays, et al. (1985) found that if the leaders were out of match, they experienced high levels of stress and reported extreme clinical symptoms of illness that neared the point of requiring hospitalization.

The model has been validated mostly at the group level of analysis (Ayman, Chemers, et al., 1995, 1998). However, Ayman, Chemers, et al. noted that the design of the model allows for it to function at other levels, such as the individual and the dyadic levels of analysis. For example, in the work by Chemers et al. (1985), the level of analysis was the individual leader. Results of two other studies, one laboratory (Chemers, Goza, & Plumer, 1978) and one field (Tobey-Garcia, Ayman, & Chemers, 2000), tentatively supported a dyadic level of analysis. These studies showed that in moderate-condition situations, relationship-oriented leaders with task-oriented subordinates yielded the highest satisfaction and performance. In addition, task-orientation leaders having a key task-oriented subordinate seemed to do the worst.

Overall, the model is expanding and evolving as new studies are conducted. For example, Ayman and Chemers (1991) introduced a self-monitoring trait. Other additions have included the model's capacity to assess and predict leadership effectiveness at multiple levels of analysis.

Cognitive Resource Theory (CRT)

CRT is the second contingency model that includes leader traits. According to Fiedler and Garcia (1987), leaders' effectiveness can be predicted based on the interaction of two individual internal characteristics—intelligence and experience—and the situation. Intelligence has been one of the most frequently studied characteristics of leaders (Stogdill, 1974); however, the findings regarding its predictive validity have been somewhat inconsistent. Furthermore, although Lord, De Vader, and Alliger (1986) found intelligence to be strongly predictive of leadership, it must be noted that their outcome variable was leadership emergence and not effectiveness.

CRT proposes that the situation will affect whether leader intelligence experience is predictive of leadership effectiveness. Fiedler (2002) incorporated Sternberg's (1995) explanations of intelligence referring to "fluid" intelligence versus experience being akin to "crystallized" intelligence. The first refers to cognitive ability to deal with novelty, and the second refers to automatization of responses that is reflective of experiences and mastery. The situation in this theory is defined by the leader's level of stress. A leader can experience job stress in various ways, such as role conflict and overload, and from various sources, such as coworkers, the task, or the leader's superior (Fiedler, 1993). Empirical studies using this theory have used stress with the boss superior as the situational constraint.

Fiedler (1993, 1995) summarized the findings of several studies in both the laboratory (e.g., S. E. Murphy, Blyth, & Fiedler, 1992) and the field (Potter & Fiedler, 1981) in which, under stress, the leader's performance was positively related to their experience and negatively related to their intelligence. In low-stress situations, however, the leader's intelligence was positively related to performance, and experience had less of an effect. Fiedler (2002) further concluded, "People can be experienced and bright or experienced and stupid. But the performance of a particular job requires the leader to give priority either to experience or to analytical or creative analysis in solving the particular problem" (p. 102).

A combination of the contingency model of leadership effectiveness with CRT could demonstrate that leaders who are out of match are stressed. These leaders then may need to rely more on their experience than on their intelligence in order to perform well. Zaccaro (1995) considered CRT a promising starting point and encouraged theorists to consider the roles of multiple traits such as ego resilience and social intelligence.

Leader Behavioral Contingency Models

Normative Model of Leadership Decision Making

In a democratic society, we expected leaders to use participative decision-making techniques. Evidence revealed to date, however, shows that, like leadership traits, the effectiveness of decision-making strategies depends on the situation (Locke & Schweiger, 1979).

Vroom and Yetton (1973) and later Vroom and Jago (1988) proposed a contingency model of normative leadership decision making. Vroom (Sternberg & Vroom, 2002) was quite particular that his model not be included in the same category as Fiedler's theory. Vroom acknowledged that the normative model is more focused on situations and how leaders respond than on leader characteristics and how they interact with the situation. Although Vroom and subsequent authors have not used the term "contingency" as part of the name of this model, it nevertheless proposes that a leader's choice of decision style or strategy is situationally bounded.

Overall, the normative model focuses on the interaction between a leader's choice of decision-making strategies and the decision situation, an interaction that predicts the quality of the decision and subordinate commitment to the decision. This model is narrower in focus than other leadership contingency approaches (Vroom & Jago, 1998). It is a prescriptive model of leaders' decision-making processes (hence the use of the term "normative"). The model has multiple names, including the participative leadership model, Vroom and Yetton's normative model, and the Vroom-Jago model.

Vroom and Jago (1998) identified five leadership strategies for decision-making, which are to be chosen based on 11 heuristics. The five strategies are on a continuum from autocratic (Autocratic I and II) to consultative (Consultative I and II) to full group participation (Group II). They represent, respectively, solo decision making by the leader, the inclusion of the subordinates at some level, and full involvement of the subordinates in the decision.

The decision heuristics describe the situation based on four criteria: improve the quality of the decision, improve subordinate involvement, reduce the time spent, and develop the subordinates (Vroom & Jago, 1998). These criteria are also the basis for measuring the effectiveness of the decision. The leader is presented with a decision-making tree with yes/no questions reflecting the heuristics. The full representation of this decision-process flowchart is in other sources (e.g., Vroom & Jago, 1998).

If decision quality is critical, the leader has to assess his or her knowledge level, the degree of problem structure, subordinates' agreeableness, and subordinates' knowledge about the issue. The less the leader knows and the more knowledgeable are subordinates, the more group involvement is advised.

If time is of concern, the involvement of the group becomes infeasible. Past research on group versus individual decision making has demonstrated that the quality and accuracy of the decision increases with team involvement. It also is known that the greater the number of individuals involved in decision making, the more time it takes to make a decision. However, a balance can be achieved between the number of people involved, the characteristics of the individuals, the quality of the team process, and the final result. Therefore, in time-pressured situations, it seems that most leaders avoid excessive group involvement and move toward more autocratic decision-making strategies.

If the acceptance and commitment of the employees are critical for the decision to be implemented, then more employee involvement improves the final product. Therefore, the leader needs to consider the role of subordinates not only in providing quality decisions but also in being motivated to treat the decision as their own. In such situations, the leader may have to pay the cost of time and perhaps sacrifice the quality of the decision to ensure team support and cohesion. Thus, the leader must achieve a balance between quality, time spent, and support.

Based on the normative model, one can assess the leader's decision-style tendencies by having the leader choose the appropriate behavior across 30 situational conditions. The model, however, is mostly prescriptive, helping leaders learn how to respond to particular situations. In descriptive studies, it has appeared that the situation is three times as strong as the leader's style in affecting outcomes (Vroom & Jago, 1998). This finding further justifies the notion that the model is accepting of the leader's flexibility in choice of style. Research results have shown more variability in choosing a style as a result of the situation than variability within a given preferred style in response to a given situation. As the authors of the model have stated, the situation drives the model more than do the leader's characteristics.

Additional Contingencies: Additional contingencies implicated in the normative model include choice of criteria, the ability of the leader to be able to use all five strategies, the leader's gender and cultural context, and the role of information source. For instance, research has shown that subordinate involvement is critical in gaining subordinates' satisfaction. However, if the criterion is quality or efficiency rather than subordinates' satisfaction, then subordinates' involvement in the decision-making process may not be consistently appropriate, especially when the subordinates do not have the necessary information. Thus, the styles that will be recommended to the leader will vary according to the criteria chosen for leadership effectiveness.

One concern that has been voiced using some of the variations of the model is the extent to which the leader can comply with the prescriptive style (Jago & Vroom,

1980). Leaders with less skill in facilitation may need training in group problem solving and team facilitation. With such training, the leader will be more likely to choose the appropriate decision-making strategy and know the best method of implementing that strategy.

The gender of the leader is another contingency. Reports by Jago and Vroom (1983) and by Heilman, Hornstein, Cage, and Herschlag (1984) have stated that participative style was favored by both genders. However, Jago and Vroom (1983) also found that whereas male leaders who were perceived as autocratic were evaluated as modestly positive, female leaders perceived as autocratic were rated negatively. Thus, there seems to be a potential gender contingency in the relationship between decision-making styles and outcomes.

Cross-cultural studies testing the model showed that the cultural values of the social environment also affected leaders' decision-making strategies. The data from one study (Jago, Maczynski, & Reber, 1996) show a trend for more participative practices from the time before the fall of communism in Poland to afterward. As compared with Austrian and U.S. managers, Polish managers had a harder time agreeing with the normative model's prescriptions. As the importance of the problem increased, they used a more autocratic style (Maczynski, Jago, Reber, & Boehnisch, 1994).

Researchers investigating the effect of role and the perception of decision-making effectiveness (Field & House, 1990; Heilman, Hornstein, et al., 1984) have demonstrated that the description of the leader's decision-making style and the favorableness of the strategy varied depending on the role the perceivers had (i.e., being a leader or a subordinate). For example, those assuming a leader role are more inclined to favor autocratic styles of decision making (Heilman, Hornstein, et al., 1984). Field and House (1990) concluded that the model was supported when the data were collected from the leader but not when they were collected from the subordinates. These results indicate that perceiver role is a contingency factor.

In conclusion, the participative leadership model or normative model of leadership decision making has received sufficient empirical support for its predictions. Based on the evidence, the model does demonstrate that the level of participation in decision making needs to be gauged based on the situation and the criteria used for judging effectiveness. Other contingencies also appear to moderate the effectiveness of the leader's choice of decision-making style.

Path Goal Theory

House (1971) proposed a path goal theory of leader effectiveness (see also House, 1996), taking inspiration from Evans (1970), who further expanded the work of Georgopoulus, Mahoney, and Jones (1957). The genesis of this theory was in the Ohio State leader-behavior approach (Stogdill & Coons, 1957) and the expectancy theory of motivation (Vroom, 1964). In response to Korman (1966), House (1971) and House and Mitchell (1974) developed propositions to try and reconcile some of the inconsistent results emanating from the behavioral studies. House (1971) identified four leadership behaviors as independent variables of the theory: directive, achievement oriented, supportive, and participative. It should be noted that the first two are more task focused (e.g., assigning tasks, scheduling, and emphasizing deadlines) and the latter two are more considerate (e.g., making people feel at ease, being open to suggestions, and encouraging team members). Additionally, according to Evans (1996), the majority of the studies on the theory have included measures of instrumental/directive and supportive/considerate leadership styles. Schriesheim and Neider (1996) stated, "The need for such leadership [behavior] is moderated by characteristics of the environment as well as by characteristics of the subordinates" (p. 317).

Schriesheim and Neider (1996) cited two meta-analyses that were conducted to validate path goal theory (Indvik, 1986; Wofford & Liska, 1993). Wofford and Liska (1993), who included 120 studies covering the span of two and a half decades, concluded that "of 16 moderator tests that could be conducted, 7 met the criteria as moderators; however, the effect of one moderator was in the opposite direction to the hypothesized. The analysis indicated that much of the research testing path goal theories has been flawed" (p. 857).

The most frequently studied work-environment moderator in this paradigm has been subordinates' task structure (Evans, 1996). Wofford and Liska (1993) did not find support for the moderating effect of task structure on the relationship between leader's initiating structure and subordinates' satisfaction, performance, and role clarity. In addition, across studies, the moderating effect of task structure on the relationship between considerate leader behavior and satisfaction was not supported (Indvik, 1986; Wofford & Liska, 1993). However, subordinates' task structure was found to have a positive effect on the relationship between considerate leader behavior and performance. When the task was unstructured as opposed to structured, a stronger relationship was found between considerate leader behavior and effectiveness.

Few studies have examined the personal characteristics of the subordinates as moderators (e.g., ability and locus of control). Schriesheim and Schriesheim (1980) demonstrated that the subordinates' need for affiliation, their authoritarianism, and their ability and experience moderated the relationship between leader behaviors and outcomes. A study by Algattan (1985) showed that subordinates with an external locus of control were more satisfied with participative than with directive leaders, and they were more productive with these leaders. However, subordinates with an internal locus of control were more productive and were happier when the leader's behavior was task oriented.

Overall, the Wofford and Liska (1993) meta-analysis demonstrated that ability was the only subordinate characteristic that moderated the relationship between the leaders' behavior and the outcomes. Subordinates with low ability, as compared with those with high ability, preferred leaders who engaged in structuring and task-related behaviors.

Various authors have highlighted several limitations of the path goal theory. One issue is related to the instrument(s) used to measure leader behavior (Fisher & Edwards, 1988; Schriesheim & Von Glinow, 1977). Another concern has been the broad conceptualizations of leader behaviors (Yukl, 1989b). Because most studies have examined either task or subordinate characteristics, Stinson and Johnson (1975) as well as Wofford and Liska (1993) recommended testing a multiple-moderator model. Finally, Wofford and Liska (1993) also expressed concern that the majority of the studies testing the theory suffered from same-source bias (i.e., common-methods variance). Evans (1996) concluded, "In light of the absence of studies testing the critical motivational hypothesis of the theory, it is hard to argue that the theory has undergone reasonable testing. It has not" (p. 307).

On a positive note, path goal theory can be seen as encouraging the evolution of leadership conceptualizations. It was the basis for the development of theories of charismatic leadership and substitutes for leadership (House, 1996) and potentially had an impetus for the development of a vertical dyad linkage model (Dansereau, Graen, & Haga, 1975).

Situational Leadership Theory

Hersey and Blanchard (1969a) proposed that the effectiveness of four leadership behaviors—telling, selling, participating, and delegating—depends on whether they complement the subordinates' task maturity (e.g., ability, education, and experience) and psychological maturity (e.g., willingness, self-esteem, and motivation). Although the theory does have a measure to assess the leader's style—the Leadership Effectiveness and Adaptability Description (LEAD)—many of the empirical studies on this model seem to use the Leader Behavior Description Questionnaire (LBDQ) in measuring the leader's behaviors (e.g., Case, 1987; Vecchio, 1987; Vecchio & Boatwright, 2002).

According to the major tenets of the theory, the leader should "delegate" (i.e., exhibit both low consideration and structuring behaviors) in conditions where subordinates are able and willing. When subordinates are willing and unable, the appropriate leader behavior is "selling" (i.e., engaging in both high consideration and structuring behavior). In situations where the subordinates are unwilling but able, the leader should engage in "participative decision making" (i.e., show both high consideration but low structuring behavior). When the subordinates are unwilling and unable, the leader needs to "tell" them what to do (i.e., demonstrate both low consideration but high structuring behavior). Although situational leadership theory has intuitive appeal, it has undergone only limited empirical examination. Reviews and empirical tests have been mostly critical of the model and have not found much support for it (e.g., Fernandez & Vecchio, 1997; Graeff, 1997; Vecchio, 1997; Vecchio & Boatwright, 2002; York, 1996).

Both path goal theory and situational leadership theory focus on the subordinates' perspective. The attentiveness of these theories to the needs of the situation and their incorporation of the subordinates in the leader's choice of action give them strong face validity and public appeal.

In summary, comparing the leadership contingency models and theories presented in this section shows that whereas all are models of leadership effectiveness that acknowledge the role of the situation, they are distinctly different. The path goal theory and situational leadership theory are different from the normative model of leadership decision making; they differ regarding the scope of the leader's behavior. In the normative model, the focus is on the leader's decision strategy, whereas in the path goal and situational leadership theories, the leader's supervisory behaviors are key. The difference between the contingency model of leadership effectiveness and the path goal theory concerns how the leader is assessed and how the situation is approached, among other factors. In the path goal theory, the perceived leader behavior is the focus, whereas in the contingency model of leadership effectiveness, the leader's trait or internal state is the focus. In the path goal theory, the situation is assessed according to subordinates' perceptions; however, in the contingency model of leadership effectiveness, the situation is described from the leader's point of view. Finally, Evans (1996) differentiated the theories according to how they were derived. He noted that Fiedler's model was empirically driven and, regarding path goal theory, that House "was led to the contingency aspects of his theory by both inconsistent empirical findings and theoretical insight" (p. 307).

Contingencies

The studies I have reviewed to this point demonstrate that the relationship between a leader's characteristics and effectiveness is moderated or influenced by other factors, referred to in general as contingencies. As I discuss below, contingencies can be viewed from two perspectives: (a) what they are; that is, their nature, such as the situation or the leader's characteristics; or (b) the pattern of interaction between the contingency and the primary leader characteristics.

The Nature of Contingencies

Most of the theories and models in the contingency approach consider the situation as the contingent factor that interacts with the leader's characteristics, be they traits or behaviors. Vroom wrote (Sternberg & Vroom, 2002), "We need a taxonomy of the situation, or at least dimensions on which the situations vary. Fiedler is one of the few psychologists to offer a language for describing both context and individual difference" (p. 317). Although Fiedler very eloquently presented a taxonomy of the leader's situation (Ayman, 2002; Sternberg & Vroom, 2002), more discussion is needed to understand the various types of contingencies. Many authors in the contingency approaches to leadership have focused on the situation. My discussion below starts with an overview of a classic conceptualization of the situation, called substitute for leadership theory, which emerged from path goal theory. I then present the multiple linkage model, which is not as well researched. Finally, I impart other conceptualizations of the role of context or situation in predicting the person and situation interaction.

Substitutes for Leadership Theory

Jermier and Kerr (1997) have provided a reflective overview of the development of substitutes for leadership theory (see Kerr & Jermier, 1978). Jermier and Kerr stated that the focus of this theory was on the main factors that affect employee attitudes and behaviors. From their perspective, the leader's behavior accounts for less variance in predicting outcome variables than do situational factors (i.e., substitutes for leadership).

Kerr and Jermier (1978) proposed a taxonomy of 14 situational contingencies, which were divided into three classes: characteristics of the subordinates, the nature of the subordinates' tasks, and organizational characteristics. Kerr and Jermier also provided a measure (a questionnaire) of substitutes for leadership and leader behavior; they had subordinates complete this measure.

Many studies have been conducted to test their propositions. Podsakoff, Mackenzie, and Bommer (1996) concluded, in a meta-analysis, that

> the findings showed that the combination of the substitutes variables and leader behaviors account for a majority of the variance in employee attitudes and role perceptions and a substantial proportion of the variance in in-role and extra-role performance; on average, the substitutes for leadership uniquely accounted for more of the variance in the criterion variables than did leader behaviors. (p. 380)

The key point to remember in Kerr and Jermier's (1978) theory is that the contingencies were conceived as substitutes for or neutralizers of the leader's behaviors. Subsequently, others expanded these notions by including enhancers and supplements of leader behaviors (J. P. Howell, Dorfman, & Kerr, 1986). To further clarify these concepts, Schriesheim (1997) described these types of situational factors as they relate to leadership and outcome variables. He described *substitutes* as factors that were directly related to the employee's outcome and that block the effect of leader behavior. *Neutralizers* were those factors that inhibit the leader's behavioral influence on the outcome. The distinction between the two factors is based on the relationship that the situational factor has with the leader's behavior. In the substitute condition, the situational factor and the outcome variable are correlated regardless of the leader's behavior. Neutralizers, however, are correlated with neither the leader's behavior nor the outcome, but they nullify the effect of the leader's behavior on the outcome. *Enhancers* are factors that augment the relationship between the leader's behaviors and the outcome. *Supplement* factors are those that are related to outcome variables but neither augment nor cancel the effects of the leader's behaviors (Bass, 1990).

As Podsakoff and Mackenzie (1997) have mentioned, research on the theory supports the notion that leader behavior does not have a universal effect on outcomes. Recent work on the theory has gone beyond the interactional model to theories of self-management (Manz & Sims, 1980). Bass (1990) considered the theory a paradox wherein it is very difficult to separate some of these substitute factors from leadership roles. For example, an assignment that is well structured and has clear criteria is most often designed by a manager or a leader. Although empirical testing of the substitutes for leadership theory has yielded equivocal results (see Dionne, Yammarino, Atwater, & James, 2002), the theory has been useful in the development of a detailed taxonomy of situations.

Multiple Linkage Model

Yukl (1971; as cited in Yukl, 1994) proposed that contingencies intervene between leader behaviors and outcome criteria. Although his model has not been tested empirically, it does provide a valuable taxonomy for better understanding contingencies. Yukl—inspired by Likert (1967), who initially suggested the presence of intervening variables to explain delayed effects of leader behavior—identified six intervening variables that are quite similar to the substitutes variables. Yukl's intervening variables include the subordinate's ability and effort, the work setting and task organization, and the presence of support and resources.

Furthermore, Yukl (1994) stated that there are also situational variables that enhance or reduce the magnitude of the intervening variables. For example, recruitment and selection systems can create situations that increase the presence of highly qualified individuals in the work unit. This in turn will affect the need for considerate instead of more directive leadership behavior. Other situational factors that can affect the appropriateness of leader behavior include the type of technology, the geographical dispersion of the work unit, the nature of work flow, the size of the team, and team member characteristics that may affect work-group cohesion (Yukl, 1994). Finally, the presence of resources and of an organizational flowchart that determines how resources and interdepartmental relationships are maintained both can influence the suitability of a particular leadership style. Similar to the substitutes of leadership theory, the multiple linkage model has added to understanding of the value of situational contingencies; however, its empirical support is still limited. In addition, concerns similar to those that Bass (1990) had posed for the substitutes for leadership model also apply to this model.

As previously noted, by the 1970s leadership researchers had become quite involved with the person-situation interaction paradigm. At this time, other social scientists also investigated the critical role that the situation played in the individual's behavioral expressions (E. T. Hall, 1976; Mischel, 1977; Pelto, 1968). Mischel (1977) stated that strong settings, as compared with weak settings, have norms and demands that can control the individual's behavior. For example, in the military, the latitude for self-expression is less than in civilian organizations; therefore, military organizations are considered stronger work settings. Similarly, Pelto (1968) defined cultures as being tight or loose. The more explicit the cultural norms, the tighter the culture and the less chance there is for the expression of individual differences in responses and behaviors. Finally, E. T. Hall (1976) referred to high-context versus low-context cultures, where high-context cultures encourage social conformity and sociocultural stratification, whereas low-context cultures allow individuals' expressions and are less class conscious. In high-context cultures, interlocutors choose specific communication patterns that vary depending on the setting (i.e., the topic, the persons with whom they are talking, and the location). For example, in Japan, a high-context culture, women are expected to use very specific words and phrases when communicating. In the Middle East, another high-context culture, the choices of words and expressions vary depending on the status of the parties in an interaction. In contrast, in low-context cultures such as the United States, the communicator's values and personality often guide the pattern of communication and the choice of words (refer to Den Hartog and Dickson, Chapter 11, this volume, for further discussion on national culture and leader behavior).

Thus, it appears that the situation as a contingency or an intervening factor plays an important role. For example, it is possible that, in some cultures, leaders do not have the flexibility to express their personal values and beliefs because situational demands dictate their behavior. Situations provide restrictive norms that may not allow for a full representation of an individual's (i.e., a leader's) behavioral choices. The significance of this is that leadership needs to be considered within a context because the context influences how individuals (e.g., leaders) can behave (Rousseau & Fried, 2001).

Other Contingencies

So far, I have focused on situational factors that affect the relationship between leader characteristics and outcomes. However, as R. J. Schneider and Hough (1995) suggested, personal contingencies also influence the relationship between a person's traits and that person's own outcome. Personal contingencies can refer to the interplay of a leader's characteristics (e.g., values and traits) with each other, such as the effect of self-monitoring on the relationship between attitudes and behaviors (Gangestad & Snyder, 2000). Self-monitoring is a trait that differentiates those whose behaviors are more directed by situational cues (i.e., high self-monitors) from those whose behaviors are more directed by their internal values and beliefs (i.e., low self-monitors). Research has shown that for high self-monitors the relationship between values and attitudes and the person's behavior is likely to be weak. Another example is the interaction of the leader's traits and the leader's surface characteristics (e.g., gender and color) in relation to perceived leadership behaviors and outcomes. For example, many studies have demonstrated slight gender differences in leader behaviors (Eagly, Johannesen-Schmidt, et al., 2003; Eagly & Johnson, 1990). More specifically, there is some indication that women leaders who engage in agentic behaviors are evaluated less favorably than are men who behave in that manner (Carli & Eagly, 1999). As mentioned earlier, studies have demonstrated that gender moderates the effect of autocratic decision-making style on a leader's effectiveness (e.g., Jago & Vroom, 1983). These studies supported the notion that female leaders who were perceived as behaving autocratically were rated as less effective than their male counterparts (refer also to Eagly and Carli, Chapter 12, this volume).

Most leadership studies that have examined multiple traits have tested the main effects of the traits on the leaders' outcomes. Some studies, such as that of Ayman and Chemers (1991), demonstrated that self-monitoring interacted with the leader's match—based on Fiedler's contingency theory—in predicting subordinates' satisfaction with work. In that study, leaders who were out of match benefited by being high in self-monitoring and had more satisfied subordinates than their low self-monitoring counterparts. Future studies are needed to examine multiple aspects of the leader and the interrelationships of how the leader's traits influence the leader's behavior or effectiveness.

Another set of contingencies that R. J. Schneider and Hough (1995) identified included outcome criteria. The characteristics that they highlighted about the criteria were reliability, prototypicality, and time of measurement. They described prototypicality as the extent to which a behavior or outcome is central and highly expected within a given situation. The more relevant the measure of the behavior is to the trait being measured, the higher the chances are that the result will support a relationship. Time of measurement refers to the extent to which there is a lapse of time between the measurement of the trait and the behavior or outcome. R. J. Schneider and Hough argued that when the task is simple, a short time is sufficient to yield the related outcome; however, if the task is complicated, then criterion measures may not be immediately predictable. Being a relational phenomenon, the impact of leadership requires time to be manifested in outcomes. Thus, length of time or tenure in the leadership position may be an important contingency.

Concerns about sources of data seem to play a role in the relationship between trait and behavior or between behavior and outcome. As already mentioned, Field and House (1990) examined Vroom and Jago's model and found that two sources of data, the self-descriptions of the leader's decision strategy and the subordinates' description of the leader's decision strategy, yielded different results.

In summary, contingencies in leadership research have been focused primarily on situational characteristics—either the level of the leader's situational control and power, or the subordinates' needs and abilities. Other contingencies, including personal and criterion characteristics, also need more attention within leadership theory development and validation.

Our attention will now move from the nature of the contingency to the pattern of relationships. The pattern of relationship that the contingencies assume affects the potential ways that the contingencies can influence the relationship between the leader's characteristics and the outcomes. In most contingency models, the *situation* has been referred to as a moderator of the leader's characteristics and the outcome relationship; however, the contingencies sometimes can mediate relationship between the leader's *characteristics* and the outcomes.

Moderators and Mediators

Most of the discussion so far has referred to contingencies only as moderators. The work of R. M. Baron and Kenny (1986) has shed light on the fact that some of the relationships of a third variable—with such variables indiscriminately referred to as moderators—may actually be mediating relationships. We need to be particular about the distinction between moderators and mediators so that we can further understand the dynamic of the interplay among variables. Baron and Kenny argued that "in some areas disagreement about mediators can be resolved by treating certain variables as moderators" (p. 1173). Also, certain variables considered as moderators may function more effectively as mediators. It is important to notice that, depending on the type of relationships hypothesized (i.e., moderator or mediator), the analysis conducted to test the hypothesis would vary.

Moderators

Moderators are variables that may not be related to either the independent or the dependent variable, but whose presence changes the nature of the relationship between the independent variable (i.e., the leader's characteristics) and dependent variable (i.e., the outcomes). Analysis of variance and hierarchical moderator regression are two methods recommended to test the effect of the moderator on the relationship between the independent and outcome variables (refer to Antonakis et al., Chapter 3, this volume, for further discussion on moderation).

Mediators

Mediators are variables that are intermediaries between independent (e.g., the leader's characteristics) and dependent (e.g., leader outcomes) variables; that is, they must be correlated with both the leader and the outcome variables. Testing for mediators is accomplished by using path analysis, regression analysis, or structural-equation modeling (SEM) (e.g., LISREL). The SEM method has the capacity to test not only the mediation relationship but also the reciprocal nature of the relationship (R. M. Baron & Kenny, 1986).

Dionne et al. (2002) have distinguished between moderators and mediators among the various situational contingencies that could have interfered between the leader behavior and the outcome decision strategy. In addition to differentiating between the moderator and mediator relationships, these authors also tested for same-source bias. Their results indicated that many of the previous findings concerning moderation effects in substitutes for leadership theory could be due to inflated same-source (i.e., common-methods) bias. When they used two or three sources to collect data, the results could not support the moderating or mediating effects of situational factors. Thus, this study further demonstrated that study design and methodology are important considerations when building models of leadership effectiveness and validating leadership theories.

Conclusion

In this chapter, I have reviewed classic contingency theories of leadership. I classified the theories into two types: (a) those that were based on the relationship between the leader's traits and the outcomes (i.e., contingency model of leadership effectiveness and cognitive resource theory), and (b) those that related the leader's behavior to the outcome (i.e., the normative decision-making model, situational leadership theory, path goal theory, and the multiple linkage theory). The conceptualizations of the contingencies that have been theorized primarily concern the situation of leadership. I also proposed other contingencies, such as leader gender and self-monitoring. I further elaborated on these factors by introducing the distinction between moderators and mediators as well as the role of the source of the data as potential contingencies in studies of leadership effectiveness. Thus, I highlighted not only that universal approaches to leadership are an oversimplification, but also that understanding the role of contingencies can become very complex.

When thinking of contingency approaches to leadership, it is key to remember that this approach is based on a person-situation fit concept. The models in this approach have demonstrated that effective leaders respond to the situation by changing their behaviors, by being perceived as behaving differently, or by choosing and managing their situation. This position is similar to Sternberg's (1988) definition of intelligent functioning, which refers to the individual's "purposive adaptation to, selection of, and shaping of real-world environments relevant to one's life and abilities" (p. 65).

Finding an optimal match is what Chemers (1997) referred to as "mettle." For Chemers, "Mettle captures the sense of a confident and optimistic leader whose perceptions, thoughts and mood provide a reservoir of enthusiasm and energy for meeting the challenges presented by the leadership task" (p. 166). This state is somewhat similar to Csikszentmihalyi's (1990) concept of "flow," which refers to situations when an individual's skill and knowledge are neither more nor less than needed. In this state, leaders manifest the height of their potential, expressing optimism and feeling efficacious (Chemers, 2002). Fiedler (1978) referred to this state as a leader being in match. When the situation is congenial to the leader's characteristics, the leader functions with ease.

Overall, the contingency approach has alluded to the fact that leaders consciously or unconsciously try to reach their optimal level of performance by being aware of their situation and responding accordingly. With that in mind, training programs such as leader match (Fiedler & Chemers, 1984) and situational leadership (Hersey & Blanchard, 1982b) prepare leaders to be sensitive, responsive, and flexible. Attainment of these training outcomes can be measured either by the leaders' behavior adjustment as described by the subordinates, or by the leaders' descriptions of how they managed the situation. Managing the situation most often depends on the leader's actions.

Although at first glance there seems to be an inconsistency between leaders managing the situation and being flexible, in essence there is no difference between the two. In either case, the leader's persona does not change. For example, a high self-monitoring leader does not become a low self-monitor, nor does a high-LPC leader become a low-LPC leader. Instead, leaders engage in behaviors and strategies that bring them closer to being in match with the situation and experiencing "flow." More specifically, a low-LPC leader in a moderate-control situation (out of match) may realize that he or she needs to include other team members in the decision-making process; he or she may then use a nominal group technique to create a structured method of managing the situation. The leader may use a consultative style rather than a group decision-making strategy, though, so that he or she maintains some of the control over the outcome. A simple matter of accepting drop-ins versus meeting only by appointment may seem small, for example, but it may have implications in the situational match of a leader. Therefore, when we talk about flexibility, it is in reference to behavior and to managing the situation, not to changing one's traits and personality.

It is possible that the use of the term "style" has caused confusion about how a leader could have a fixed trait such as LPC score and still have varying responses to a situation. Fiedler initially referred to the LPC score of the leader as the leader's style. Other leadership researchers have referred to behaviors (i.e., considerate, transformational, autocratic, and consultative) as leaders' styles. In the latter case, the leader's "style" refers to a person being perceived by subordinates as engaging in a certain set of behaviors (e.g., transformational leadership behavior). The fact that the same word—"style"—was used by both sets of scholars may have given the reader a sense that the leader's persona or identity is changing. The researcher in the behavior approach knows only that the leader has been perceived by some subordinates as behaving in a certain way. When a researcher endeavors to measure a leader's intelligence or other traits, though, the situation is different. In that case, an aspect of the leader's persona is being measured, and thus the researcher can refer to an intelligent or an extroverted leader, with those traits persisting across situations.

It appears, given the considerations above, that the style of writing common to the field of leadership may have contributed to the confusion, implying that a leader can have the ability to change his or her behavior while maintaining a fixed orientation toward tasks or people. As a matter of fact, one trait that has received strong support in leadership research is flexibility. This is the ability (i.e., an internal state of a person) to adjust to situations/contingencies. The trait is a fixed trait or ability (i.e., being able to respond), but the behaviors vary, by definition, from one situation to another.

Is there a universal leadership characteristic? Based on contingency and situational approaches, the answer must be "It depends." A combination of skills plus competencies of sensitivity, responsiveness, and flexibility may help a leader reach "mettle." These competencies can be manifested in various ways through particular traits, skills, or behaviors, depending on the person, the method of assessment, and the leadership situation. Therefore, contingencies in leadership cannot not be ignored.

Note

1.   Editors' note: These authors distinguished between distal (i.e., context-free) and proximal (i.e., context-specific) traits.

CHAPTER 8

Transformational Leadership Approaches

A Review and Synthesis

Marshall Sashkin

I n this chapter, I examine leadership approaches that combine two or more of the elements of the leadership theories presented in the preceding chapters of Part III of this book, "Major Schools of Leadership." That is, I will review leadership approaches that center on some combination of leadership traits, behavioral skills, and the situational context of leadership. The approaches I will review also share an important perspective. They all focus on what Bryman (1992) and others have called the "new paradigm" of leadership; that is, transformational or charismatic leadership.[1]

At least two other efforts have been made to integrate various transformational, charismatic, and visionary leadership approaches. House and Shamir (1993) included five of the eight approaches I will deal with here, focusing on traits and behaviors but omitting the situational context along with three of the approaches I will cover. Antonakis and House (2002) made another attempt, within the framework of Bass's (1985) theory or, more accurately, the latest development of that

---

Author's Note: This chapter draws on materials originally prepared with the assistance of Margaret Gorman, Charles Higgins, Chris Johnson, and David Schwandt, all of the Center for the Study of Learning, George Washington University. Their contributions are gratefully acknowledged. Some portions are based on material in Sashkin and Sashkin (2003).

theory, which is now called the "full range leadership theory." Again, this effort omits some of the approaches I see as important as well as limiting the key variables of concern to traits and behaviors.[2]

My aim in this chapter is to offer a synthesis of current research-based knowledge about top-level leadership. I will include in my review most of the major approaches to transformational leadership. My integration of these varied approaches will, perhaps understandably, center on my own approach. This approach, "visionary leadership theory," which I now more often refer to as "leadership that matters" (Sashkin & Sashkin, 2003), is itself a synthesis of research and theory by those within as well as distant from the field of leadership research.

As Bennis and Nanus (1985) observed in their book *Leaders,* "Multiple interpretations of leadership exist, each providing a sliver of insight but each remaining an incomplete and wholly inadequate explanation" (p. 4). Indeed, most scholars and researchers in this field seem to hold their own "slivers" of truth tightly to their respective breasts while loudly proclaiming they (each) have the whole answer. My aim in this overview is to describe briefly the content of each of the major slivers and then bring them together, to form what I believe to be a meaningful whole picture of leadership.

Hybrid Theories: Beginnings of the Study of Transformational Leadership

As readers will have gathered from reading through Chapters 1–7, leadership research has gone through various paradigm shifts, the most important of which arguably were the trait, behavioral, and contingency perspectives. Leadership research concentrating on these approaches has by no means ended. What has changed is that various new approaches have incorporated more than just one of the classic triad of trait, behavior, and situational variables. Moreover, most of these "hybrid" approaches go beyond the notion of exchange. That concept is most evident in such explicitly transactional approaches to leadership as those initiated by Hollander (1958, 1980) and by Graen and his associates (Graen & Cashman, 1975; Graen & Uhl-Bien, 1995). The exchange notion, however, underlies all the other leadership approaches discussed previously in this book.

These new approaches look at what some call "charismatic" and others refer to as "transformational" leadership. To some degree, all these approaches are grounded in the work of one scholar, the political scientist and social historian James McGregor Burns (Burns, 1978). It is these various theories and approaches, which I choose to refer to as transformational leadership, on which I will concentrate this chapter.

Burns (1978) has been one of the most influential scholars in transformational leadership theory and research, and his impact has been felt in particular over the past decade. Burns's work served to reacquaint scholars with a critical distinction first raised by German sociologist Max Weber (1924/1947): the difference between economic and noneconomic sources of authority. Burns amplified and focused this important definition, using leadership illustrations (e.g., Mohandas Gandhi and Franklin D. Roosevelt) that made the distinction between leaders and managers so striking that it could not be ignored.

In fact, when I look back historically to the research base for the traditional approaches to studying leadership, I see that all these approaches dealt with *supervision*, not *leadership*. Supervisory management—while certainly of great organizational importance—is quite different from leadership. Burns (1978) observed that management and supervision are based on a *contractual* relationship between employee and boss. That is, the employee agrees to carry out certain activities and duties; in exchange, he or she receives from the organization and through the boss certain rewards (e.g., pay, job security). In other words, the parties engage in a contractual *transaction*. In highlighting the limitations of that leadership approach, Burns argued that *transformational leadership* is more complex and more powerful. A transformational leader "looks for potential motives in followers, seeks to satisfy higher needs, and engages the full person of the follower. The result . . . is a relationship of mutual stimulation and elevation that converts followers into leaders and may convert leaders into moral agents. (Burns, 1978, p. 4)

Burns (1978) was not the only one or the first to apply some of Weber's (1924/ 1947) concepts to better understand leadership. Downton (1973), for example, was the first to use a typology of transactional, charismatic, and inspirational leadership. Shortly thereafter, Berlew (1974) wrote of "custodial," "managerial," and "charismatic" leaders. Not long after that, House (1977) first presented his theory of charismatic leadership. Nonetheless, it was Burns who, more than anyone else, seems to have inspired leadership researchers to explore this new paradigm.

Burns's (1978) work has led to the development of several new approaches to the study of what many now refer to as transformational leadership. That term is used to contrast this new leadership with the older, *transactional* leadership—or management—approach. The transactional approach is based on economic or quasi-economic transactions between a leader and followers. In contrast, the new transformational approaches all incorporate the idea that leadership involves what Weber (1924/1947) called noneconomic sources of authority. Another feature of these new approaches is that all incorporate more than just one of the three classic categories of research variables: traits, behaviors, and situational contingencies.

In the following review, I first briefly sketch out the best known of these approaches. I then look for commonalities among the approaches, with a focus on the specific variables examined within each of the three categories. Finally, I show how these underlying commonalities are reflected in my own synthesis approach.

Some Limitations. Although I will review eight approaches to transformational leadership that I judge to be central to theory, research, and practice, I recognize that I have omitted others that have direct or indirect relevance. I have avoided approaches like that of Tichy and Devanna (1986), which used a subjective metaphor (in their case, actors in a play on a stage) to help one understand what transformational leadership is about. I do not deny the possible utility of such work, especially for those interested in developing a deeper personal understanding of what they do as leaders, but I find little in it that can be translated into concepts that are organized around the observable activities of leaders.

I also omit reference to works grounded primarily in the sociology of leadership (e.g., Trice & Beyer, 1986) and involving case analyses (e.g., Trice and Beyer examined how charisma was "routinized" in two social movement organizations). I believe that organizational-level structures and processes must be included to understand transformational leadership. That will be obvious not only from my own biases but also on the basis of aspects common among many of the approaches I will review. However, I do not see structures and processes at the organizational and social system level as being the central focus for such an understanding. For similar reasons, I omit reference to the work of Boal and Bryson (1988), which takes a structural approach centered on the way that crises create opportunities for charismatic leadership.

Finally, I have not included in this review the important theoretical work of Kuhnert and Lewis (1987) on the stages of development of transformational leadership. I left out this work because it is similar to the developmental model incorporated in the motivational theory and research of McClelland (1975, 1987), which serves as the focus for the leadership work of House and his associates (e.g., House & Shamir, 1993; Shamir, House, & Arthur, 1993), reviewed here in some detail.

In sum, I am well aware that this review is neither complete nor comprehensive; however, my selection of what to include and what to leave out was made not simply on the basis of my own theoretical and empirical biases but in the light of what I judged to be the approaches central to a research-based understanding of transformational leadership.

Transformational Leadership Approaches

James McGregor Burns: Defining a New Paradigm

I already have reviewed the central essence of Burns's (1978) views, presented in rich detail in his classic book *Leadership*. One of the first modifications made in his approach was the result of research by Bass (1985), who demonstrated that transactional and transformational leadership were not opposite ends of a bipolar dimension. They are, instead, independent aspects of leadership, much as task orientation and relationship orientation are independent behavior dimensions.

Burns (1978) was clear as to the concept of and the moral basis for transformational leadership. He did not, however, attempt to explain what types of action or general strategies transformational leaders use. Furthermore, he focused on neither specific traits of leaders nor the specific aspects of the social-organizational context that leaders attempt to "transform." Formal exploration of these factors was left to the various researchers who were engaged by Burns's new paradigm of leadership.

Bernard Bass: Leadership and Performance Beyond Expectations

Bass (1985) was the first to initiate major research around Burns's ideas. He did so by developing an assessment tool, the Multifactor Leadership Questionnaire (MLQ), which has gone through many revisions. Bass suspected and, through data obtained with the MLQ, demonstrated that transactional and transformational leadership are separate and independent dimensions. From its inception, Bass's approach has incorporated both the earlier behavioral approach, grounded in what many now called transactional leadership, and the new transformational approach, making it the first of what might be called hybrid approaches.

The MLQ measures both transactional and transformational leadership, but its focus is on the latter. Transformational leadership is broken down into the following scales: idealized influence (formerly labeled "charisma"), individualized consideration, intellectual stimulation, and inspirational motivation (formerly called "inspirational leadership"). The MLQ also measures several dimensions of transactional leadership, assesses the dimension of laissez-faire leadership (i.e., the absence of leadership), and contains a section on perceived outcomes (i.e., effort, effectiveness, and satisfaction).

Bass (1985) argued that by engaging in transformational leadership behaviors, leaders transform followers. That is, followers are changed from being self-centered individuals to being committed members of a group. They are, then, able to perform at levels far beyond what normally might have been expected. Bass has, on several occasions, revised the MLQ, which has been used in many research studies.

There is some argument about the true relative importance of the four dimensions assessed by the MLQ. Early research data showed that 60% of the total variance is due to the charisma (now idealized influence) scale. The other three transformational scales accounted for only very small amounts of the total variance. Moreover, an examination of the items on this scale suggested that it measured respondents' attributions (feelings toward leaders) rather than leaders' behaviors. The current version of the MLQ addresses these issues by splitting this scale into two subscales, attributions and behaviors (Avolio, Bass, & Jung, 1995; Bass & Avolio, 1995). Still, the question remains of the extent to which this dimension is actually captured by behaviorally specific items.

For present purposes—examining common concepts, scales, and dimensions across various transformational leadership approaches—it is the transformational dimensions that are of particular interest. Following is a description of the factors from the latest version of the MLQ (Form 5X; refer to Bass & Avolio, 1995):

1. *Idealized influence* (attributions): How followers view the leader's power and confidence, and whether the leader has a moral purpose

2. *Idealized influence* (behaviors): Behaviors centered on values, beliefs, and a sense of purpose

3. *Individualized consideration*: Developing and demonstrating concern for followers

4. *Intellectual stimulation*: Encouraging followers to look at problems from different perspectives and seek new solutions

5. *Inspirational motivation*: Articulating a vision and displaying optimism and confidence that vision will be achieved

Bass's approach has guided extensive research, with evidence supporting the model (see Antonakis, Avolio, & Sivasubramaniam, 2003). There also is strong evidence that leaders who score higher on Bass's MLQ achieve better performance outcomes. In many studies, the measure of performance was the subjective report of those who rated the leader, resulting in possible same-source data bias that could produce a spurious positive association between transformational leadership and performance. There have been, however, a number of research reports that have used stronger performance measures (e.g., see the meta-analyses of Dumdum, Lowe, & Avolio, 2002, and Lowe, Kroeck, & Sivasubramaniam 1996). In sum, the work of Bass and his associates provides a sound initial groundwork for the scientific study of transformational leadership.

Key Concepts. The most central or key concepts in Bass's approach can be categorized as *behaviors* and *characteristics*. The four behavior dimensions are actions that produce feelings of charisma (toward the leader) in followers, behavior that inspires by communicating a vision, actions that express consideration and caring toward followers, and behaviors that engage and challenge followers to think and act for themselves. Bass's approach also is based on the concept of a trait or characteristic of charisma, although Bass has argued explicitly that charisma is necessary but not sufficient for transformational leadership.

Warren Bennis: Behavior Strategies of Exceptional Chief Executives

In the early 1980s, Bennis conducted an extensive study, interviewing at length and in depth 90 CEOs of private and public organizations of all sorts. These individuals were all nominated as exceptional leaders. The interviews lasted from 2 hours to 2 days. Bennis (1984) reviewed notes and records of the interviews to come to some conclusions about common threads that linked most of or all these exceptional leaders. He identified several patterns of action, which he called "strategies," "competencies," "skills," and other similar labels, in various reports. The best known is the book *Leaders*, coauthored with Bert Nanus (Bennis & Nanus, 1985). In that book, they identified four "strategies" characteristic of these outstanding leaders:

1. Attention through vision involves the ability to focus people's attention on an exciting vision, through the use of dramatic metaphors and exciting presentations.

2. Meaning through communication involves not only the ability to communicate clearly on a one-to-one basis but also the activity of creating meaning with others.

3. Trust through positioning involves the ability to inspire trust in one's self on the part of followers through exhibiting consistency in action, particularly action that implements the vision.

4. Deployment of self means knowing and nurturing one's strengths and making sure they fit with the organization's needs, concentrating on achieving success with others, rather than focusing on avoiding failure.

The fourth strategy, deployment of self, involves positive self-regard or self-confidence and willingness to risk success as opposed to fearing failure. Bennis and Nanus (1985) pointed out that empowerment is the central focus and aim of transformational leadership. That is, transformational leaders empower followers to realize the organization's vision. All of this is worked out as leaders design and construct what Bennis and Nanus called *social architecture* and others commonly refer to as *culture*.

Although Bennis and Nanus (1985) clearly defined certain behaviors as important for effective leadership, they went beyond a strictly behavioral approach. They devoted a large portion of their treatment of leadership to the leader's role as "organizational architect." That is, they argued that the purpose of the behaviors they identified is not simply to motivate followers to perform at higher levels. Rather, they suggested that leaders act in the ways described in order to construct organizational systems or, as E. H. Schein (1990) called it, organizational culture. Thus, Bennis and Nanus brought an explicitly situational aspect to their concept of leadership.

Key Concepts. Bennis and Nanus's approach included behaviors and characteristics and also considered the organizational context. Three central behaviors are communication, developing a climate of trust, and creating empowering opportunities. The traits most important in Bennis and Nanus's conceptualization are self-confidence, orientation toward empowerment, and vision. The contextual variable is social architecture or culture.

James Kouzes and Barry Posner: Best Leadership Behaviors

Kouzes and Posner (1987) asked managers to write detailed memoirs of their own greatest, most positive leadership experience. These "personal best" cases, some of which were 10 pages or longer, were analyzed to identify specific characteristics of each case. Using those results, the researchers constructed questions about leadership behavior. They developed a long list of questions, then asked hundreds of managers to answer these questions, describing exceptional leaders they had known personally. Finally, they examined the results using factor analysis. They identified five clear factors, all describable in terms of concrete behaviors. Ultimately, Kouzes and Posner constructed a questionnaire to measure transformational leadership: the *Leadership Practices Inventory (LPI)*. The LPI has five scales, one for each of the five leadership behavior factors. Each factor consists of two specific leader behaviors. Following are brief descriptions of the factors and behaviors.

1. "Challenging the process" means *searching for opportunities* and experimenting, even *taking sensible risks*, to improve the organization.

2. "Inspiring a shared vision" sounds a lot like Bass's category "inspirational motivation," but it is focused less on inspiration per se and more on what leaders actually do to *construct a future vision* and *build follower support* for that vision.

3. "Enabling others to act" concerns what leaders do to make it possible for followers to take action. That is, leaders *foster collaboration*, as opposed to competition, and *support followers in their personal development*.

4. "Modeling the way" refers to how leaders *set examples* through their own behaviors. They also help followers focus on *step-by-step accomplishment* of large-scale goals, making those goals seem more realistic and attainable through a process of many "small wins."

5. "Encouraging the heart" means that leaders *recognize followers' contributions* and find ways to *celebrate their achievements*.

The 5 practices and 10 behaviors of exemplary leadership identified by Kouzes and Posner (1987) are much more specific and behaviorally focused than the transformational leadership dimensions developed by Bass or the behavioral strategies identified by Bennis and Nanus (1985). Unlike most of the approaches reviewed here, however, that of Kouzes and Posner focuses almost entirely on behavior, ignoring situational context and leadership traits. Nonetheless, the focus on "vision" suggests, implicitly, that Kouzes and Posner's approach recognizes that leadership involves some sort of personal characteristic or trait relating to vision.

Kouzes and Posner (1987) developed their approach out of empirical case data provided by leaders, and its great strength stems from its concrete basis of evidence. A weakness of their approach, however, is that although it incorporates clear behavioral detail, there is no equally clear theory base. That is, it appears that "The Leadership Challenge," as presented by Kouzes and Posner (1987), offers no theoretical framework within which one can understand transformational leadership.

There has been some research on Kouzes and Posner's (1987) approach using their assessment questionnaire. Results seem mixed, though at least somewhat supportive of the conclusion that use of the five practices is associated with better performance outcomes.

Key Concepts. Kouzes and Posner discussed so many behaviors that it is difficult to focus on those they considered most important. These probably include searching for opportunities, taking sensible risks, communicating the vision, empowering followers, developing followers, modeling desirable behavior, and recognizing followers' accomplishments. The single leadership characteristic that comes across clearly is vision.

Elliott Jaques: How Leaders Develop Requisite Organizational Structures

"Stratified systems theory" (SST) grew out of Jaques's (1986) research on individuals' *cognitive power*. This term refers to an individual's ability to think over a certain span of time; that is, to think through cause-and-effect relations so as to understand what must be done to achieve one's goals. Individuals differ in this ability; some can think over only relatively short time spans, such as a few days, weeks, or months. Others can think through more complex and interactive sequences of cause and effect, over periods of a year or so, whereas those with more cognitive power think over time spans of a few years, 5 to 10 years, or even a generation. Jaques argued that different and increasingly higher levels of cognitive power are required at higher and higher levels of the organizational hierarchy. Individuals at the top levels of cognitive power are required at the CEO level because only such persons have the cognitive power to design and control large, complex social systems.

Although the SST approach stresses the overwhelming importance of the leadership trait of cognitive power, it does take note of various behavioral skills of effective leaders (Jaques & Clement, 1991). Jaques (1986), however, considered emotion and affect irrelevant for leaders. The key to effective leadership, in his approach, is the match between a person's cognitive power and the requirements of the job, based primarily on the scope of systems thinking required by the job.

Unlike others working within the transformational leadership paradigm, Jaques did not refer explicitly to transformation or reference Burns (1978). Nonetheless, Jaques was quite clear in arguing that top-level leaders, especially CEOs, have as their central task the construction of organizational systems and structures. In this respect, his ideas are similar to those of Bennis and Nanus (1985) and E. H. Schein (1992) and are consistent with Burns's ideas and the notion of transformational leadership.

The work of Jaques and his colleagues (Jacques, 1986; Jaques & Cason, 1994; Jaques & Clement, 1991) has two prominent characteristics. First, the theory is highly systems focused. Second, it explicitly asserts that the only variable needed to understand leadership, in particular, and human behavior in organizations, in general, is cognitive power.[3] Jaques's model is based on extensive organizational research. Substantial data obtained in British government organizations support his approach (Jaques, 1961, 1976).

Key Concepts. Jaques and his colleagues considered various basic managerial skills as relevant behaviors, but it is clear that their approach centers on two key variables. The first is the characteristic or trait of vision, expressed as cognitive capability. The second is the contextual factor of organizational system design, in terms of structure.

David McClelland/Robert J. House:
Leadership and Power Motivation

House and his associates (e.g., Spangler & House, 1991; House, Spangler, & Woycke, 1991) have extended and developed an approach to leadership first defined by McClelland (1975) in his studies of human motives and needs. Whereas McClelland initially expected effective leadership to be based on the need to achieve, he discovered that the actual driving force was the *need for power* (McClelland, 1975; McClelland & Burnham, 1976). Moreover, he found that this need could be directed positively or negatively. In the former case, leaders are able to postpone immediate gratification; they have high impulse control or, to put it the other way, low impulsivity. McClelland and Boyatzis (1982) called this the leadership motive pattern: high need for power (with high impulse control) and low need for affiliation.[4] McClelland did not develop his work into a full-blown leadership approach; his focus was always on power.

House (1977), however, and later his associate Shamir (1991), did develop a formal theory of leadership centered on motives (House & Shamir, 1993; Shamir, House, et al., 1993). House and his colleagues concentrated on how effective leaders use their need for power—that is, by means of exciting speech and actions, they motivate followers by arousing appropriate motives. For example, when action is needed to confront and battle a competitor, effective leaders arouse followers' need for power; however, when followers must exert exceptional efforts to attain difficult goals, the leader would, instead, try to arouse followers' need for achievement. House also took note of these leaders' high self-confidence and ability to develop a vision. Later, Shamir formally added the idea of self-efficacy to the theory.

House (1977, 1995b) did identify some specific behaviors used by transformational leaders. These include the leader's striking communication of a vision. Transformational leaders model self-sacrifice aimed at attaining the vision. They express clear, specific, and high expectations of followers. At the same time, they show confidence in followers' ability to achieve those goals, empowering followers to do so. Overall, transformational leaders are careful to model behavior that is consistent with their vision.

McClelland's (1975) work actually predated that of Burns (1978), as did House's (1977) initial work on his new approach to leadership. Although House and his associates (House, Woycke, & Fodor, 1988) incorporated some of Burns's concepts, they are indebted to McClelland to a far greater degree. Still, although the work of House and his colleagues is built on the foundations laid by McClelland and his associates, these concepts of leadership are quite consistent with Burns's notion of transformation, of speaking to the moral motivation of followers.

It is interesting that just as Jaques (1986) asserted that the only variable important for understanding leadership is a cognitive variable, House and his associates (e.g., House, Spangler, et al., 1991) have insisted that the only important factor is motivation and that cognition is unimportant in comparison. Although the central variable in the McClelland/House approach, need for power, is a personality characteristic, later extensions included behavior (Shamir, House, et al., 1993). Most recently, even cognition and tacit knowledge have been considered as variables within this approach (Antonakis & House, 2002).

More than a quarter-century ago, McClelland (1975) presented strong research evidence to show that the leadership motive pattern is associated with high performance. The research of House and his associates is equally well designed but involves many more measures. The results are generally supportive but complex.

Key Concepts. Two behaviors seem central to this approach. The first is, most generally, communication behavior, which is focused on arousing in followers the specific motive need relevant to the leader's vision and the situational context. The second important behavior is creation of empowering opportunities for followers, which has become a more important aspect of the theory as it has developed over the past quarter-century. Two traits are basic to the approach. The first is, of course, the power need, crucial for anyone wishing to lead as well as necessary for a leader who aims to create empowering opportunities. The second, self-efficacy—the belief that one can control one's world and attain one's desired outcomes—has become an important part of the theory as developed by Shamir and his associates (House & Shamir, 1993; Shamir, House, et al., 1993).

John Kotter and James Heskett: How Leaders Build Culture

Basing their thoughts on a series of qualitative studies in more than 200 organizations, Kotter and Heskett (1992) concluded that leadership effectiveness stems from leaders' influence over culture and their ability to change organizational culture. Leaders who can do this have certain characteristics or attributes and engage in certain leadership behaviors. With respect to characteristics, Kotter and Heskett spoke of a record of effective leadership, which is more of a personal history than anything that can be translated into action. However, two other characteristics they list are somewhat more action-oriented: a broad *outsider's perspective* and specific *insider knowledge* of the organization. In addition, they defined four more specific action strategies used by effective leaders:

1. *Creation of the need for change* refers not only to making followers aware of the need for change through what Bennis and Nanus (1985) called "management of attention" but also to establishing a sense of crisis that energizes followers by arousing their concern.

2. *Development of a direction-setting vision* means challenging the status quo and involving others in that challenge by ensuring that the vision developed by the leader actually incorporates followers' needs.

3. *Broad-based communication of the vision* is what Bennis and Nanus call "management of attention" and "management of communication." This strategy includes encouraging open discussion, using challenges to build motivation and support for the vision, and displaying the values that underlie the vision though the leader's own behavior.

4. *Encouraging subordinate managers to take leadership action to implement the vision* means empowering followers but goes even further, to encourage followers to act like—and become—leaders. Not only does this mean creating opportunities for others to "buy in" to the vision, as Kouzes and Posner as well as Bennis and Nanus described; it also means helping others understand the many actions needed to implement change.

Kotter and Heskett (1992) used an extensive database to identify the strategies and link them to organizational culture. However, they conducted no further research to test their model.

Key Concepts. Kotter and Heskett defined a set of leadership actions, some of which are behaviors and others of which seem to be more like traits or characteristics of leaders. Six important behaviors are energizing followers with a need for change, including followers' needs in the vision, challenging the status quo, communicating the vision, modeling the vision, and empowering followers to act. Three leader characteristics they identified are vision, an organizational outsider's perspective, and an insider's knowledge.

Jay Conger and Rabindra Kanungo: Charismatic Leadership Behavior

Conger and Kanungo (1988, 1994, 1998) proposed that there is little fundamental difference between charismatic and transformational leadership. The distinguishing characteristic lies, they argued, in the perspective from which leadership is seen. That is, charismatic theories and research have measured leadership from the standpoint of followers' *perceptions* of leaders' behavior. In contrast, transformational theories have concerned themselves primarily with follower *outcomes*. Thus, Conger and Kanungo concluded that charismatic leadership is best examined by measuring the leadership *behaviors* that produce the *outcomes*. They conducted studies resulting in the development of a questionnaire that assesses the following six specific, stable dimensions of leader behavior, as seen by others:

1. *Environmental sensitivity* means, in part, recognizing opportunities and constraints.

2. *Sensitivity to followers' needs* is expressed by personal concern and through liking and respect.

3. *Going against the status quo* is breaking with normal or accepted courses of action.

4. *Articulation of a vision* involves generating new ideas and goals and inspiring followers to carry out those ideas and reach those goals.

5. *Unconventional behavior* is using nontraditional means of action that may even surprise others.

6. *Personal risk* means being willing to incur risk and, if necessary, endure self-sacrifice for the good of the organization.

Conger and Kanungo (1994) developed an instrument, the C-K questionnaire, to measure these behaviors. The results, however, showed that the dimensions are not easily defined by cohesive groupings of questions. What is more, personal characteristics of leaders seem to be mixed with leadership behaviors. Still, the C-K questionnaire is relatively well developed in terms of reliability and internal consistency. Little research, however, has tested whether the leadership behaviors predict performance outcomes in a manner consistent with the theory. In Conger and Kanungo's (1998) most comprehensive recent treatment of their approach, not a single empirical research study testing the model is reported, other than the earlier psychometric analyses conducted in developing the C-K questionnaire.

Key Concepts. Five behaviors are clearly identified by Conger and Kanungo. These are articulation of a vision (communication), going against the status quo, taking risks, unconventional behavior, and sensitivity to followers' needs (caring). Two leadership characteristics defined are sensitivity to factors in the environment and willingness to take risks and make personal sacrifices.

Marshall and Molly Sashkin: The Visionary Leader—Leadership That Matters

At about the same time that Bass (1985) and Kouzes and Posner (1987) were working on their models of transformational leadership, Marshall Sashkin was constructing the first draft of his Leader Behavior Questionnaire/The Visionary Leader (LBQ) (see Sashkin, 1984). This first version of the LBQ was based on the work of Bennis and Nanus (1985), described above. Sashkin (1984) used Bennis's (1984) original five behavior categories to develop a questionnaire. In the current version of this assessment, called The Leadership Profile (TLP), these have been reduced to the four behavioral dimensions discussed below.

Communication Leadership

This scale measures Bennis and Nanus's (1985) "management of attention," which involves focusing the attention of others on key ideas, the most important aspects of the leader's vision. In practice, this means, for example, coming up with metaphors and analogies that make clear and vivid what might otherwise remain abstract ideas. It also involves good basic communication skills, such as active listening and giving and receiving feedback effectively.

Credible Leadership

To measure, behaviorally, the "management of trust," Sashkin (1984) observed that leaders establish trust by taking actions that are consistent both over time and with what the leader says. Trust, of course, exists in the minds and hearts of followers and is not an obvious aspect of leader behavior, but consistency over time and between words and actions produces trust in followers by establishing the leader's credibility.

Caring Leadership

What Bennis and Nanus (1985) called "management of respect" involves demonstrating respect and concern for people. Psychologist Carl Rogers (1951) called this behavior "unconditional positive regard." By this he meant caring about and respecting another person regardless of one's feelings or judgments about that person's actions. Caring is shown not just by "big" actions, such as ensuring job security, but also by many everyday actions, such as remembering people's birthdays or even something as basic as learning and using their names.

Creative Leadership

Bennis and Nanus (1985) associated this behavior with risk taking and unwillingness to focus primarily on risk avoidance. The underlying issue, however, is more complicated. Transformational leaders empower followers by allowing them to accept challenges, taking on and "owning" a new project, for example. But transformational leaders also are careful to plan ahead and not to ask more of followers than the followers are capable of doing. Followers might honestly feel a sense of risk in accepting a challenge, but a transformational leader does all that is possible to ensure that any risk is relatively low, that with the right resources and (if necessary) help the follower can and will be successful. This leadership behavior dimension is called "creative" because it refers to the extent to which leaders create opportunities for followers to be empowered and succeed in achieving goals for which they have been empowered to strive.

Sashkin (1984) used the categories identified by Bennis and Nanus (1985) to create a questionnaire with a scale for each category and five questions on each scale. Then, like Kouzes and Posner (1987), he collected data and used factor analysis to show that the dimensions are replicated in people's real experience. Kouzes and Posner, however, started inductively by capturing significant experiences and, from those experiences, generated questions that identified their five practices. Sashkin, in contrast, came from the opposite direction, developing behavioral measures deductively on the basis of Bennis's concepts and then validating his measure by analyzing leaders' and followers' reports of their experiences, as assessed by the LBQ and, later, the TLP. The fact that these two independent research efforts, coming from different directions, wound up in essentially the same place gives us confidence that we are on to something, that the behaviors identified are real and important.

Although he began his work on the foundation established by Bennis (1984) and Bennis and Nanus (1985), Sashkin (1988a) soon concluded that there had to be more to transformational leadership than just the a set of behaviors. Kurt Lewin (1935) had long ago asserted that behavior is a function of personality and situational context. More recently, Hilgard (1980) had argued that a full understanding of the human mind, of human psychology, must incorporate explicit attention to each of three basic elements: conation (action), affect, and cognition. Where, then, do these concepts fit in a psychological understanding of leadership?

Sashkin (1988a) identified three specific *personal characteristics* that mark the differences among exceptional transformational leaders, average leaders, transactional leaders (i.e., managers), and nonleaders. These three characteristics address the three aspects of the human mind defined by Hilgard (1980). None of these characteristics must be viewed as a trait, in the traditional sense, because all of them are subject to change and development.

Sashkin (1988b) then constructed additional questionnaire scales to assess the extent to which leaders act on the basis of each of these three characteristics. The three scales were then added to the LBQ and maintained in revisions, including the TLP. The three personal characteristics identified by Sashkin are *self-confidence,* the *need for power,* and *vision.* Two of these are drawn directly from leadership approaches of others, specifically those of McClelland/House (House, 1977; McClelland & Boyatzis, 1982) and of Jaques (1986). I will describe briefly the nature of each of these three personal characteristics.

Confident Leadership

The first and perhaps most basic characteristic of transformational leaders is self-confidence. Psychologists call this "self-efficacy" or "internal control." It is, in essence, the belief that one controls one's own fate. The extensive research of Bandura (1982, 1986, 1997) and his associates is a primary source of this construct, which also relates to the social psychological research of Merton (1968) on the "self-fulfilling prophecy." Sashkin (1988a) also drew on (a) the classical animal research of Seligman and his associates (Maier & Seligman, 1976; Seligman, 1993; Seligman & Beagley, 1975), (b) the groundbreaking work of Rosenthal (1964, 1976; Rosenthal & Jacobson, 1968) on how the expectations of experimenters (and teachers) affect the outcomes of their studies (and teaching activities), and (c) the extension of Rosenthal's research to the context of management and organizations by Eden (1990).

The leader characteristic of confidence is important, in one sense, as a necessary but not sufficient prerequisite for transformational leadership. That is, why would a person who lacks self-confidence bother to attempt to transform people and organizations? More important, a primary means by which confident leaders transform followers into more self-directed leaders themselves is by creating empowering situations in which followers' successes build their self-confidence. In other words, transformational leaders need self-confidence not only to engage in such leadership to begin with, but also in order to transform followers into self-confident leaders.

Follower-Centered Leadership

I noted above the work by House and associates on power (House & Shamir, 1993; Shamir, House, et al., 1993), based on the foundations developed by McClelland (1975). Sashkin's (1988a) second personal characteristic incorporates these works as crucial for understanding the nature of leadership. The rationale is simple; getting things done in organizations depends on power and influence. Of course, the need for power is only one part of this issue; of equal importance, as shown by McClelland and Burnham (1976), is the way that need is manifested.

People who use power to manipulate others to serve their own self-centered ends are often seen as charismatic. Sashkin and Sashkin (2003) observed that this is how such leaders dupe others into doing as they, the leaders, wish. This helps explain why one must be careful about measures of charisma, such as that contained in Bass's MLQ, and about theories, like that of House and his associates, that may appear to glorify charismatic leadership.

In the United States, people tend to associate charisma with admirable leaders such as Franklin Roosevelt and John Kennedy, but in Europe, charisma often is identified with tyrants such as Napoleon Bonaparte and Adolf Hitler. Roosevelt and Kennedy certainly were seen as charismatic, but they did not use charisma to control others, promising followers they could become powerful like the leader, if followers would obey the leader's every command. Instead, these and other great leaders who might be cited as positive models, people such as Mohandas Gandhi or Winston Churchill, appealed to what Abraham Lincoln called "the better angels of our nature." These are simply the basic values about what is right, what is good, what should be done, and what should be avoided that guide people toward positive long-run goals.

Visionary Leadership

This third personal characteristic is taken from the work of Elliott Jaques (1961, 1976, 1986). Exceptional leaders have vision or, as Jaques called it, "cognitive power." Jaques (1986) believed that cognitive power is a fixed, unchangeable trait. Sashkin (1988a, 1990), however, disagreed with Jaques, arguing that cause-effect thinking can be both improved and increased over time, in terms of both complexity and the span of time covered.

In Sashkin's (1988a) approach, vision is not an aspect of charisma or inspiration or some trait such as creativity. Vision instead is based on the ability to construct the future first mentally and then behaviorally. Leaders do this by thinking through what is happening, to determine causes, and by identifying how complicated chains of cause and effect actually work. Only after this mental processing can a person figure out how to bring about desired outcomes. Visionary leaders do not simply think up a vision and sell it to followers. If it is more than just a slick sales pitch, the long-term ideal that a leader comes up with will derive from as well as incorporate the needs and ideas of followers.

In the approach detailed by Sashkin and Sashkin (2003), the personal characteristics of effective leaders are somewhat from those addressed by traditional "trait" theories of leadership. That is, none of the three personal characteristics is simply something people are born with. Each of these characteristics can, at least to a degree, be developed. This has been shown empirically in research reported by Axelrod and Sashkin (2000). Development can be planned and carried out over one's life and career. Indeed, transformational leaders teach followers to develop these characteristics for themselves, rather than simply using their own capabilities to do things for followers (Dvir, Eden, Avolio, & Shamir, 2002). Thus, my position is similar to that of Sternberg (1998a), who viewed abilities as forms of developing expertise.

To incorporate the three personal characteristics into visionary leadership theory, the LBQ was modified to include a total of 10 scales (Sashkin, 1988b). These included the five original scales developed to assess certain types of leader behavior, along with new scales designed to examine how specific characteristics important for transformational leadership show up in leaders' actions. In this final approach, there is still more to the transformational leadership equation. We have examined the person and behavior. What about that context? Sashkin and Sashkin (2003) addressed this issue by looking at organizational *culture* as the situational or contextual focus of transformational leadership.

Leadership and Culture

E. H. Schein (1992) observed that the only really important thing leaders may do is construct culture. Bennis and Nanus (1985) made a similar point. What differentiates this view from the traditional situational leadership approaches is that rather than adapting one's leadership style or behavior to the situation, transformational leaders engage in constructing or transforming situations. This seems to me to be a crucial yet commonly ignored aspect of transformational leadership.

Burns (1978) observed that transformational leadership does more than affect followers; it also transforms the *social system* within which leaders and followers are embedded. Such systemic or organizational transformation comes about through leaders' efforts to construct or change culture—the pattern of norms, values, beliefs, and assumptions commonly held by the members of an organization or social system. Transactional leaders—managers—look to the situation to determine what leadership style to use. In contrast, transformational leaders determine what the situational context—the culture—should be and go about creating it.

The elements of organizational culture are not determined by random chance. They deal with the most important and fundamental issues faced by people in organizations. These were defined in the classical sociological theory of Parsons (1956a, 1956b, 1960). Parsons argued that all social systems must deal effectively with four issues: *adaptation,* or how people deal with external forces and the need to change; *goal attainment,* or the nature of organizational goals, how they are defined, and their importance; *coordination,* or how people work together to get the job done; and *shared values and beliefs,* or the degree to which people in the organization generally agree that certain values and beliefs are important and should guide their actions.

Sashkin (1988b) added two final scales to the LBQ. One assessed the extent to which a leader's actions facilitate successful operation of the four organizational functions. The other measured the degree to which a leader is effective in inculcating values and beliefs that work in a positive way to support the operation of the four functions.

When the LBQ was revised to create the TLP, the two culture-centered scales were merged into a single measure, called "principled leadership." At the same time, the two communication-related scales based on Bennis's (1984) original five behavior dimensions were combined into a single measure (as noted above).

Finally, two new scales were added to assess transactional leadership (i.e., effective management). The first is a general measure, labeled "capable management." The other, "reward equity," is focused on the extent to which a managerial leader is effective in distributing rewards.

A number of research studies have established strong and significant relationships between transformational leadership, measured by TLP self-assessments and assessments of the leader by others, as well as by independent measures of performance. Research that demonstrated such strong positive relationships has, for example, been conducted in banks (Sashkin, Rosenbach, & Mueller, 1994), retail stores (Colyer, 1997), for-profit health care-related firms (Harter & Sashkin, 2002), engineering development teams (Silver, 1999), schools (Major, 1988), and hospitals (Dixon, 1998).

Key Concepts. Four behaviors, three leadership characteristics, and a contextual factor have been described in detail. The behaviors are communication, trust building, caring, and creating empowering opportunities. The characteristics are self-confidence, empowerment, and vision. The contextual factor is culture.

Varied Views of Leadership

It has become commonplace to recognize that there are literally hundreds of definitions of leadership, with a puzzling lack of agreement not only among leaders themselves but also among scholars who study them. This review has covered what might appear to be a dizzyingly dissimilar array of elements, behaviors, dimensions, characteristics, and so on. Not one pair of the approaches reviewed is completely consistent. Thus, it is not surprising that, taken all together, the varieties of concepts and categories may seem confounding. There are, however, some consistent commonalities. These similarities take two basic forms, described as follows.

Three Basic Aspects of Transformational Leadership. All the theories, approaches, and applications I have described cover some combination of the three basic aspects of leadership: leaders' personal characteristics (traits), leader behavior, and the situational context of leadership. Even those that concentrate on one factor, such as that of House (1988), whose central focus was the leader's need for power, usually include a second. In House's case this would be the actions (behaviors) used by leaders to direct the power need. Jaques (1986), too, concentrated on just one personal characteristic, cognitive power. Nonetheless, Jaques incorporated in his approach both the organizational context, in terms of leaders' structural design of organizational systems, and basic behavioral skills of managers. I believe it is useful to look across the various approaches reviewed so far to see how different theorists and researchers focus on one or another of these three basic aspects of leadership.

Consistencies Across Approaches. Despite the many different variables and the many different ways of referring to the same factors, I find there to be extensive, real consistencies across the varied approaches. I have often pointed out or alluded to commonalities between or among approaches as I reviewed them. I now concentrate specifically on those common consistencies, grouped first according to personal competencies, next by behavioral competencies, and, finally, in terms of contextual commonalities. First, however, I will make clear what I mean by this term I have just introduced, "competencies."

The Search for Competencies: A Competent Approach to Competency Research

There are two serious flaws in the approaches typically used to study competencies, whether in leadership or in any other area. Mayer, Salovey, and Caruso (2000) pointed this out in their critical analysis of research on emotional intelligence. That is, competency approaches have often failed to distinguish among the skills, the knowledge, and the personal characteristics or traits that permit one to engage in specific competent actions. This is a critical flaw, for skills and knowledge can, for the most part, be learned, sometimes with relatively little effort. In contrast, characteristics may or may not be modifiable. Traits, in contrast, typically are thought of as relatively fixed aspects of individuals' personality structures. Mixing all these together and labeling them as a single thing, whether that label is "emotional intelligence" or "leadership," only confounds and confuses our understanding.

Second, there has often been a severe problem with respect to the "validation" of competencies. What generally takes place is the identification of high and of low performers in a specific job position (e.g., midlevel managers). This identification is often accomplished by methods that are questionable if not obviously flawed. For example, performance ratings might be used to identify individuals in each group (i.e., exceptionally good and especially poor performers). Performance ratings, however, are notoriously inaccurate as measures of actual performance achievement. An often-used alternative approach is to have superiors nominate exceptional performers. Again, such a process inherently is fraught with bias. One reason is that superiors may simply attribute good performance to individuals they like and poor performance to those they dislike. What also often happens is even worse: Superiors are interviewed and asked to identify the characteristics of the high performers that separate them from average or poor performers. This, of course, simply compounds the potential for bias, bringing in the superiors' own "implicit" theories of leadership and performance, which may have little or nothing to do with real performance (e.g., see Eden & Leviatan, 1975).

The first flaw can be avoided by understanding the differences between, and by carefully separating, skill competencies from competencies that are actually personal characteristics, perhaps even traits. To use the competency concept in a meaningful and valid way, it is crucial to distinguish between skills and personal capabilities. The second problem, validity, can be addressed by ensuring that competencies are identified and validated on the basis of sound research using well-defined quantitative measures of performance. Both of these requirements, separating behavioral skills from personal characteristics and using well-designed quantitative research as the basis for selection and validation of competencies, must be part of a sound approach to understanding leadership.

Aspects of Leadership Common Across Varied Approaches

Aside from the seminal work of Burns (1978), I have reviewed a total of eight approaches to transformational leadership or something very much like it. Whereas some are derived from or are related to others, they are, for the most part, relatively independent. Yet except for Bennis and Nanus (1985) and Sashkin (1988a, 1990; Sashkin & Sashkin, 2003), each insists that the whole of leadership is contained within the individual theorist's own special "sliver" of the truth. Thus, I will look at those aspects of leadership common to most of or all these approaches, to identify those that appear to be central to transformational leadership. I shall adopt a simple and, to a degree, arbitrary criterion: Aspects of leadership common to more than one-third (three) of the eight approaches reviewed will be considered as central to an understanding of transformational leadership.

First, I will examine the behavioral competencies common to three or more of the approaches I briefly reviewed. Next, I will look at personal competencies. Finally, I will turn to those aspects of the situation or context considered especially important in the various approaches reviewed here, in order to get a complete picture of leadership and its expression in organizational contexts.

Common Competencies

Common Behavioral Competencies

As Table 8.1 demonstrates, four behavioral aspects of leadership are shared by three or more of the approaches outlined in this chapter. These are (a) communicating a vision (seen in seven approaches), (b) creating empowering opportunities (common to seven approaches), and (c) caring, that is, showing respect for followers (common across five approaches). I will look at how each of these behavioral competencies is expressed by the various approaches.

Communicating a Vision. Conger and Kanungo (1998) labeled this "vision articulation," Bennis and Nanus (1985) called it "management of attention," and Kotter and Heskett (1992) simply spoke of "communicating a vision." Kouzes and Posner (1987) described "enlisting others" as getting the vision across to them. Finally, Sashkin (1984, 1988b) referred to "clarity" of focus and "communication leadership." House and his associates (e.g., House & Shamir, 1993; Shamir, House, et al., 1993) were concerned with the leader's arousal of the power need in others. This clearly implies that leaders communicate as a means of motivating followers to act. In all these

Table 8.1   The Behaviors, Traits, and Contexts of Transformational Leaders

Dimension	Corresponding Theory							
	1	*2*	*3*	*4*	*5*	*6*	*7*	*8*
Behaviors								
Communication (of a vision)	x	x	x		x	x	x	x
Management skills				x				
Communicating the need for change						x		
Trust		x						x
Caring (consideration)	x	x	x				x	x
Modeling			x		x			
Recognizing accomplishments			x					
Challenging the status quo							x	
Developing followers			x					
Unconventional behavior							x	
Charisma-producing actions	x							
Creating empowering opportunities ("risk")	x	x	x		x	x	x	x
Traits								
Charisma	x							
Environmental sensitivity							x	
Outsider perspective						x		
Insider knowledge						x		
Willingness to risk and sacrifice							x	
Self-confidence		x			x			x
Empowerment orientation	x	x			x			x
Vision (cognitive capability)	x	x	x	x		x		x
Contexts								
Organizational context (structure)				x				
Organizational context (culture)		x						x

NOTE: An "x" under a numbered column represents a dimension that is included in that particular theory. The numbers in column headings correspond to the theories of 1 = Bass, 2 = Bennis and Nanus, 3 = Kouzes and Posner, 4 = Jaques, 5 = McClelland/House, 6 = Kotter and Heskett, 7 = Conger and Kanungo, 8 = Sashkin and Sashkin.

approaches, the essential behavior or skill is communicating; what is communicated generally is seen as having to do with a vision of the organization's future.

Creating Empowering Opportunities. Bennis and Nanus (1985) spoke of risk or, more specifically, of not focusing one's energies on avoiding risk. The inverse of this is really the more appropriate focus; that is, the creation of opportunities for followers to "buy in" to a vision, to "own" a piece of that vision and seize the opportunity to make it real. This is clearly the way Sashkin (1988a; Sashkin & Sashkin, 2003) saw risk; that is, as creating opportunities. Kotter and Heskett's (1992) empowerment behavior on the part of leaders involves encouraging others to take actions; that is, to actively create opportunities for others. Finally, Kouzes and Posner (1987) identified as leadership behaviors the "search for opportunity" and taking risks.

Showing Caring and Respect for Followers. Respect can be expressed directly, as both Bennis and Nanus (1985) and Sashkin and Sashkin (2003) indicated. Caring also may be shown indirectly, through Bass's (1985) "individualized consideration" or Conger and Kanungo's (1998) "sensitivity to employee needs." Actions that implicitly express care and respect were identified by Kouzes and Posner (1987) as "recognizing contributions" and "celebrating accomplishments."

Several behavioral aspects of leadership are found in just one or two approaches. Kouzes and Posner (1987) as well as Kotter and Heskett (1992) referred to the leader's modeling of behaviors; that is, displaying behaviors the leader sees as important to followers as a means of showing that the leader is "practicing what he or she preaches." Sashkin and Sashkin (2003) along with Bennis and Nanus (1985) included development of trust between leaders and followers as an important behavior.

Finally, I see some uncommon or unique behaviors described as essential by certain of the approaches. Conger and Kanungo (1998) pointed to "anti–status quo" behavior. Kotter and Heskett (1992) observed that leaders may actually create crises in order to instill acute awareness of the need for change. Although these are not exactly the same, neither are they totally different. However, only Kouzes and Posner (1987) included developing followers as a crucial behavior. Only Bass (1985) cited charisma-producing actions. Only Conger and Kanungo (1998) listed unconventional behavior. Only Jaques (1986) included a general managerial skills element.

The Crucial Role of Behavioral Competencies

Developing a vision obviously requires that one believes that one's vision can make a difference. Similarly, one would not bother to construct a vision unless one were motivated to achieve that vision; through power and influence used to empower members of an organization. Most obviously, developing a vision requires a high level of cognitive power; that is the basis of the ability to construct a vision and is, therefore, the basis for visionary leadership. However, in the absence of behavioral competencies in the leader, the leader's vision will remain nothing more than a dream, for it is with and through people, by empowering them to act in concert toward a common aim, that visions are made real.

Common Personal Competencies

One can see from Table 8.1 that only three personal competencies are common to three or more of the approaches reviewed. These are *vision, the power need and its expression,* and *self-confidence.*

Vision. Six of the eight approaches identified a personal leadership factor associated with or identical to the leader's ability to construct a vision of what the organization might be. Bass (1985) referred to "inspirational motivation," providing a vision of what lies ahead. Jaques (1986) called this "cognitive power." Kouzes and Posner (1987) referred to it as "envisioning the future." Conger and Kanungo (1998) combined it with a behavioral focus, referring to "vision articulation." Both Kotter and Heskett (1992) and Sashkin and Sashkin (2003) used the simple term "vision." All are clearly speaking of some cognitive ability on the part of leaders that enables them to develop long-term plans of action that, in effect, create the future. Some, like Sashkin and Sashkin, as well as Kouzes and Posner, believe that leaders can develop this ability. Others, like Jaques, have argued that this ability is really a fixed trait. Kotter and Heskett were silent on this issue. Nonetheless, all the approaches reviewed cite the importance of vision; this is clearly the single most-agreed-upon personal aspect of these varied approaches to leadership.

Power. Four of the eight leadership approaches referred to power, although often using very different terms. Bennis and Nanus (1985) spoke explicitly of the importance of the leader's orientation toward empowerment of followers. For McClelland (1975), as for House and his associates (e.g., House & Shamir, 1993; Shamir, House, et al., 1993), the need for power and its expression is at the core of leadership—little else is relevant. Bass (1985) spoke of "idealized influence," a term he came to use in place of the former "charisma," which is one approach to power and influence (Kelman, 1958). Finally, Sashkin and Sashkin (2003) adopted McClelland's view of power as their own.

Self-Confidence. This final shared characteristic is found in just three of the eight approaches (no other characteristic is specified by more than one of the eight). Leadership confidence was identified explicitly by Bennis and Nanus (1985). It was part of the expansion and extension of the McClelland/House approach made explicit by Shamir, House, et al. (1993). Finally, it was most clearly defined and presented as a crucial personal characteristic by Sashkin and Sashkin (2003).

The Context of Leadership

Three of the eight leadership approaches reviewed here include a concern for the context of leadership; that is, the organizational environment or *culture* within which leaders exercise leadership and which is, itself, a prime focus of leaders' actions. Indeed, E. H. Schein (1992) has observed that it may be that the *only* important thing leaders really do is construct cultures. According to Schein, organizational cultures are composed of values, beliefs, and assumptions that are shared by most of or all the members of an organization.

Bennis and Nanus (1985) spoke of the leader as an "organizational architect." They saw concern for the context as a crucial aspect of leadership, in much the same way as E. H. Schein (1992). Although the contextual aspect seen as important for leaders is more limited in Jaques's (1986) approach, it is still a central feature of that leadership theory. Most directly, Sashkin (1988a; Sashkin & Sashkin, 2003) pointed to the critical importance of leaders' understanding of how certain values support and sustain the four basic system functions defined by Parsons (1956a, 1956b, 1960) as adapting, attaining goals, coordinating efforts, and maintaining a strong culture.

Although the situational context is not an explicit element of the other approaches, it is relevant to several of them. For example, many of the behaviors identified by Kouzes and Posner (1987), such as fostering collaboration, center on inculcating certain specific values (e.g., the value of cooperation). Kotter and Heskett (1992) emphasized the importance of "resource knowledge," an in-depth understanding of the organization and its culture. A similar construct, "environmental sensitivity," was defined by Conger and Kanungo (1998).

Transformational leaders construct cultures that foster effective management of change. They do this by defining and inculcating in organization members the belief that they can affect, if not control, their environment, including government regulation, market competition, and technological change. These leaders also build cultures that enable the organization to achieve its goals effectively by instilling values regarding the importance of achievement and of meeting customers' needs. Effective transformational leaders design cultures that help individuals, teams, departments, and divisions work together effectively by sharing the value of cooperation. Finally, successful transformational leaders create cultures that are self-sustaining as a consequence of the strength of widely shared values.

Summary: An Uncommon Understanding of Transformational Leadership

I have in this review aimed at first describing the theories and approaches that form the basis of our current understanding of transformational leadership. My aim was not to present these approaches in complete detail. Rather, I have tried to provide only as much information about each as was needed to look across these varied approaches to identify commonalities and similarities among some or all of them.

The greatest area of agreement across the approaches I have reviewed is with regard to certain personal characteristics. Almost every theory or approach incorporates the concept of "vision"; the majority also include some aspect of the leader's need for and use of power. Self-confidence is common to three of the eight approaches. No other personal characteristic or trait appears to cut across the eight approaches or even to be shared by two of them. Overall, then, I find strong general agreement on a very small number of variables that represent specific personal characteristics seen as crucial for transformational leadership.

For the behavioral variables, there is greatest agreement on the importance of behavior that expresses the leader's vision. Almost all the approaches incorporate some behavioral factor dealing with the expression, articulation, or communication of vision. It is interesting that behaviors dealing with the expression of power rank as the second most common among the eight approaches. Thus, the first two common behaviors—communication and empowerment—parallel the first two most commonly seen leadership characteristics of vision and power. Perhaps surprising, however, is the appearance of expression of respect, concern for others, and consideration and caring for followers as equally important. This behavior has no direct analogue among personal characteristics, yet is clearly seen to be of general significance. Finally, the only additional behavior dealt with by any number of approaches is action that models values and sets an example on the part of the leader. Although I find several other behavioral variables described among the approaches reviewed, none is shared by more than two of the approaches, and most are identified only by one.

With respect to contextual factors, I find that some approaches (e.g., Bass, 1985; House, 1977) simply do not deal with the organizational context of leadership. Others (e.g., Bennis & Nanus, 1985; Jaques, 1986) do so in unique or idiosyncratic ways. Several, however, do attend to the organizational context by focusing on values that define and support culture (e.g., Kouzes & Posner, 1987). Other commonalities are the identification of internal operations or functions and the external environment as important contextual factors, as seen in the approaches of Conger and Kanungo (1998), Kotter and Heskett (1992), and Sashkin (1988a). The agreement on context among several of the approaches reviewed is in large part reflected in and, perhaps, derived from the seminal work of Parsons (1956a, 1956b, 1960), expressed in his theory of action and "action framework." Whereas E. H. Schein (1992) and Sashkin and Sashkin (2003) provided the most specific detail here, the cultural/contextual focus initially developed by Parsons also can be seen, indirectly, in the ideas presented by Kotter and Heskett and by Kouzes and Posner.

Conclusion

My focus here has been on the extent of agreement among approaches I view as most important for a sound understanding of transformational leadership. However, agreement does not imply truth or accuracy. Only research can determine which variables are, in fact, crucial for transformational leadership. Furthermore, only longitudinal research can answer questions regarding the development of leadership characteristics, skills, or the understanding of organizational culture that is needed to make use of those characteristics and skills.

This review offers a starting point for deeper investigation of those aspects of transformational leadership generally seen as important. Fortunately, most of the approaches reviewed are research based. A closer look at those approaches is in order, to begin to examine with a more critical eye the areas of agreement identified and to accept or reject them on the basis of the research evidence.

Notes

1.   Charismatic and transformational approaches are related but not the same; they are, however, often treated as though they are essentially similar (e.g., Yukl, 2002) or identical (e.g., Conger & Kanungo, 1998). In this chapter, I shall make it clear just how and why I believe it is important to differentiate clearly between the two.

2.   Antonakis and House (2002) did include context in their model; however, they viewed the type of leadership emerging (transactional or transformational) as a function of context. In my view, it is context that is constructed by transformational leaders, as the creators and shapers of culture.

3.   Over the course of a long and productive career, Jaques used a variety of terms to refer to his single and key variable. These included "time span," "cognitive complexity," "span of discretion," and "cognitive power." In his later work (Jaques & Cason, 1994) he used the term "human capability."

4.   Following the results of McClelland and Boyatzis (1982), who did not find a high need for achievement to be characteristic of top-level leaders, House and others have argued that in addition to the motives specified in the leadership motive pattern, a low to moderate need for achievement is useful for effective leadership, especially at top levels of the hierarchy. I think, however, that the range might instead be moderate to high. Examination of the four-stage model of power need development presented by McClelland (1975, 1987) suggests to me that as an individual becomes involved in leadership, whether transactional or transformational, independent power (Stage 2), which seems to me to be in essence the need for achievement, is transformed into interdependent power (Stage 3). Thus, one might find that a late Stage 3 individual has a low to moderate achievement need while an early Stage 3 leader has a moderate to high need for achievement. McClelland, as best I can determine, was never explicit on this matter. For further discussion on this point, see Sashkin, Rosenbach, and Sashkin (1995).

PART IV

Leadership Success and Its Development

CHAPTER 9

Successful and Unsuccessful Leadership

Cynthia D. McCauley

How do groups, organizations, or communities judge when their leadership has been successful and when it has not been successful? They likely (a) note the degree of positive collective outcomes; for example, whether goals are accomplished, high levels of achievement are reached, and stakeholders are satisfied; and (b) assess the degree to which individuals with leadership responsibility contributed to these positive outcomes. These are complex judgments, fraught with subjectivity and attributional biases. Nevertheless, these judgments are constantly being made in groups, organizations, and communities. They form the bases of many decisions: Are new leaders needed? To be more successful, do the leaders need to develop different competencies? How much should the organization be investing in leadership development? How effective are leadership processes in the organization? Should changes be made to these leadership processes?

In the field of leadership, scholars and practitioners have also worked to better understand what differentiates successful from unsuccessful leadership. A wide variety of approaches have been taken, resulting in many different conceptualizations, frameworks, and models. In this chapter, it is my goal to integrate the various approaches and results and also to provide a roadmap so that readers can orient themselves and more easily access and compare the work most relevant to their own needs. I examine the various ways scholars and practitioners have tried to understand successful and unsuccessful leadership, the themes that have emanated from this work, and how organizations are making use of the emerging knowledge and expertise.

Strategies for Studying Successful and Unsuccessful Leadership

Perhaps the most frequently examined question in leadership research takes the form "What are the _____ of successful leaders?" Based on this question, one can assume that leaders—individuals with responsibility for the collective outcomes of groups, organizations, and communities—vary in the degree to which they are successful or effective in these roles (i.e., one assumes that some leaders are more successful than others are). The question is usually asked about formal leaders although it can be directed toward individuals who more informally take on leadership roles for the collective. One also assumes that there are factors that can explain the variability in leader success. The "blank" in the question can be filled with a wide range of constructs: characteristics, skills, behaviors, thoughts, actions, competencies, backgrounds, experiences, and so forth. The question can be asked over and over (without becoming repetitive) because (a) how success is defined can vary, (b) numerous constructs might be considered important for understanding successful leadership, and (c) there are many settings in which leadership can be examined.

Defining Successful Leadership

How successful leadership is operationalized varies widely across studies. Frequently, researchers use the views of people who work closely with a leader to determine his or her degree of effectiveness. In other words, a successful leader is one who is assessed as effective in his or her role by subordinates, peers, and/or the boss. Leader competency models are often validated by correlating ratings on the competencies with overall ratings of effectiveness by the boss or by coworkers (Leslie & Fleenor, 1998). Leadership theories that focus on the leadership roles played by managers in relation to their direct subordinates (e.g., leader-member exchange theory) tend to equate more successful leadership with high performance ratings from subordinates or high subordinate satisfaction and commitment.

Another definition of success focuses on employees' movement up the management hierarchy in an organization. In this view, a successful leader is one to whom the organization is willing to give increasingly broader leadership responsibility. Longitudinal research conducted at AT&T by a team of researchers (Bray, Campbell, & Grant, 1974; Howard & Bray, 1988) is one of the best examples of studies in this category. These researchers examined how well traits and skills assessed early in a manager's career predicted advancement in the organization. Cross-sectional research has also used organizational level as an indicator of higher leadership capacity. For example, studies showing that managers at higher organizational levels score higher on measures of conceptual capacity are used as evidence of the importance of conceptual complexity for executive-level leadership (Zaccaro, 2001). It is important to note, however, that studies using management progression as a criterion often frame their research questions around issues of *managerial success* (rather than *leadership success*), although leadership is usually considered an important aspect of managerial work.

Aspects of the first two definitions of successful leadership can be combined; that is, successful leaders are those who have been effective in their leadership roles to date and are expected to continue to be successful as they are promoted higher in the organization. In their study of the career experiences of successful executives, McCall, Lombardo, and Morrison (1988) worked closely with senior human resource managers and the top executives in each of six organizations to generate samples of people who had been successful to date and who were judged to have the best shot at the top jobs in each company. An interesting variation on this approach has been used to study executive derailment (McCall & Lombardo, 1983; Van Velsor & Leslie, 1995). In these studies, successful executives are defined as those who were identified early in their careers as having high potential for executive-level positions and who lived up to that potential. Unsuccessful, or derailed, executives are those who were also identified as having high potential for executive-level positions but did not succeed at those levels (i.e., plateaued at lower levels or were demoted or fired from executive-level jobs).

A self-referenced approach to defining success is less frequently used yet yields another perspective. This approach assumes that an individual is at some times more successful at leadership and at other times less successful. Kouzes and Posner (1987) developed a self-referenced methodology for their research on what people did when they were at their "personal best" in leading others. Participants in the research used the personal-best leadership experience survey to identify and describe a project or experience when they were most successful as a leader. Kouzes and Posner assumed that they could find predictors of success by asking ordinary people to describe extraordinary experiences.

Researchers have also defined success in terms of the outcomes achieved by the group or organization. A successful leader is one whose group or organization is successful. The well-known Michigan Leadership Studies (Likert, 1961, 1967) used objective measures of group productivity to classify group leaders as relatively successful and unsuccessful. The success of a team leader is often assessed by how well the team performs. And the effectiveness of top-level leaders is likewise equated with their organization's performance. Organizational performance can be assessed in a myriad of ways, including financial performance, effectiveness in achieving operational goals, efficiency, and positive image and reputation (Day, 2001).

Organizational effectiveness has also been used as an indicator of successful leadership throughout the organization (i.e., not just as an indicator of the success of the top leaders). For example, Denison (1997) looked at how supervisory leadership behaviors in an organization predicted its financial performance over 5 years. Similarly, a Gallup Organization study found that companies in which employees rate their relationship with their immediate boss as positive are more likely to have productive employees and be able to retain employees (Zipkin, 2000).

A final way that successful leadership has been defined is based on the degree to which the leader or a group of leaders is able to bring about change. For example, Collins (2002) found a particular approach to leadership ("Level 5 Leadership") differentiated the top leaders in organizations that had been transformed from solid performing companies to top-performing when compared to the leaders of companies in which a leap in performance had not occurred. This bringing-about-change perspective of success has also been utilized in studies of how leaders influence the culture of an organization (e.g., Schein, 1992), how leaders "take charge" (e.g., Bennis & Nanus, 1985), how top-level leaders craft and implement large-scale change in organizations (e.g., Beer, 1988), and how leaders create conditions favorable for learning and innovation in organizations (e.g., Senge, 1990).

There is not one best way to determine the degree to which leadership in a team, organization, or community has been successful or unsuccessful. Some criteria may be more important for looking at certain aspects of leadership or at leaders in particular settings. For example, team outcomes might be the most important criteria if one is trying to understand successful and unsuccessful team leadership. Or movement up the management hierarchy might be the best criterion if one is concerned with selecting individuals early in their careers and grooming them for high-level positions of leadership.

One clear trend is that most leadership studies have focused on distinguishing various degrees of success or effectiveness. Only the studies of executive derailment attempted to specifically explain the dynamics of leadership failures. Perhaps scholars assume that failure is the same as "low success," and thus understanding the factors that contribute to successful leadership is the same as understanding the factors that contribute to unsuccessful leadership. And leadership development practitioners are likely to frame their work as increasing the occurrence of successful leadership rather than preventing failed or unsuccessful leadership.

It is important to pay attention to how a particular research study or theory defines success. One reason that choice of criteria is important is because using different criteria for determining success can yield different findings. Luthans, Hodgetts, and Rosenkrantz (1987) found that the activity profiles differed for managers who had been rapidly promoted in their organizations compared to managers who had subordinates with relatively high satisfaction and commitment and who were judged to have effective organizational units. Managers who had moved up more rapidly engaged relatively more in networking activities, and managers who had more satisfied subordinates and effective units engaged relatively more in communicating and human resource development activities.

Long-term programs of research that test and expand particular models of leadership often use multiple criteria to assess leadership effectiveness. For example, although Bass's (1985) theory of transactional and transformational leadership has been most often tested using various subordinate ratings of effectiveness, a number of studies have used objective measures of organizational outcomes to assess success (Lowe, Kroeck, & Sivasubramaniam, 1996). Similarly, leader-member exchange theory (Graen & Uhl-Bien, 1995) has produced a substantial body of research using a variety of outcome measures: subordinate satisfaction and commitment, subjective and objective measures of subordinate performance, and organizational citizenship behavior.

Identifying Factors for Predicting Successful Leadership

Leadership scholars have also examined a wide variety of predictors of successful leadership. Most of these predictors represent some characteristic of individuals that different leaders possess to different degrees; that is, they represent individual difference variables. How aspects of followers or the context influence successful leadership has also been examined.

Individual Difference Variables

Predictors of success in this category include competencies, deficiencies, behaviors, styles, expertise, experiences, and maturity level.

A *competency* is broadly defined as an underlying characteristic of a person that results in effective or superior performance (Klemp, 1980). A competency is a general characteristic—a trait, skill, motive, or body of knowledge—that can manifest itself in many forms of behavior or a wide variety of actions (Boyatzis, 1982). For example, a creativity competency would be associated with the actions such as generating new product ideas, developing a novel strategy for solving a problem, or articulating connections between disparate ideas. In the past decade, many organizations have worked to develop leadership competency models that describe effective leadership in their organization (Dalton, 1997).

A *deficiency*—sometimes referred to as a flaw—might be thought of as the opposite of a competency; that is, as an underlying characteristic of a person that results in ineffective or inferior performance. For example, an interpersonal deficiency would manifest itself in various ways that demonstrate an inability to relate to people in productive ways (e.g., being insensitive, dictatorial, arrogant, or manipulative). Not surprisingly, deficiencies have most often been studied as predictors of unsuccessful leadership (Hogan & Hogan, 2001; Van Velsor & Leslie, 1995).

Behaviors focus on what leaders actually do, their observable actions. A great deal of psychology-based research on leadership has examined how effective leaders differ in behavior from ineffective leaders. A wide variety of methodologies have been used, including observations, diaries, interviews, behavior description questionnaires, laboratory and field experiments, and critical incidents. A major problem in this research has been the identification of behavior categories that are relevant and meaningful for all leaders (Yukl, 2002). Yukl noted, "The past four decades have witnessed the appearance of a bewildering variety of behavior concepts pertaining to managers and leaders" (p. 61). He attributed this variety among leadership behavior taxonomies to differing levels of behavior specificity across studies, different purposes for the taxonomies, and different methodologies used to create the taxonomies.

A leadership *style* is a particular approach to leadership. For example, the leader may tend to use a participative style, involving subordinates more directly in the leadership process, or a more autocratic style, choosing to make many decisions without input from others. Some leaders are more focused on task-oriented functions such as setting goals for the group, planning and organizing, coordinating activities among group members, and obtaining resources. Others are more focused on relationship-oriented functions such as showing appreciation for group members, helping them with problems, showing trust and confidence, and developing subordinates. Styles are usually defined by a cluster of behaviors. However, research on leadership styles differs from other behavior-based approaches in that a style denotes a preference for a particular way of carrying out leadership. Different leadership styles are often portrayed as each being a legitimate approach, but with each having strengths and limitations. Different styles are also often seen as being more or less effective given the situation; that is, some styles are more effective in one situation whereas a different style is more effective in a second situational context (e.g., Vroom & Yetton, 1973).

The knowledge or *expertise* that leaders possess is another potential differentiator in successful and unsuccessful leadership. This includes expertise about leading and expertise about the leader's particular context (e.g., his or her organization, business, and industry). One operationalization of expertise—the concept of "tacit knowledge"—has been applied to leadership effectiveness. Tacit knowledge is practical, action-oriented knowledge acquired through experience (Sternberg, Wagner, Williams, & Horvath, 1995). Sternberg et al. summarized research that demonstrates how managers at different organizational levels have specialized tacit knowledge that is differentially related to success. For example, knowledge about influencing and controlling others differentiated "outstanding" and "underperforming" managers at all levels, but was a particularly strong differentiator for upper-level executives.

Amount and type of *experience* has also been used as predictors of leadership success. For example, McCall et al. (1988) examined the types of career experiences executives reported as key to their success. In cognitive resources theory, leader experience is hypothesized as a predictor of group performance, particularly in high-stress situations (Fiedler, 1986). An assumption of these approaches is that leaders learn needed competencies, behaviors, and expertise as a result of their experiences and that knowing what individual capabilities differentiate effective from ineffective leaders is not enough— knowing where individuals develop these capabilities is equally, if not more, important. Models of leader development (C. D. McCauley, Moxley, & Van Velsor, 1998; Mumford, Marks, Connelly, Zaccaro, & Reiter-Palmon, 2000) draw heavily on an understanding of developmental experiences.

Finally, leaders' *maturity levels* have been examined in relation to leadership success. Drawing from theories of adult development, leadership scholars have hypothesized that for leaders to be successful (particularly at higher organizational levels where leadership work becomes more complex), they need more complex ways of understanding themselves and their environment (Drath, 2001;

Jacobs & McGee, 2001). Increasingly complex ways of understanding are applied to leadership work as the leader develops through stages that represent qualitatively different frames of reference. This interest in the developmental maturity of leaders shares with the experience-based approach an emphasis on how the leader learns and grows over time.

Contextual Variables

In predicting leadership success, contextual variables are most often viewed as moderator variables—variables that influence the degree to which particular individual difference variables are related to leadership success. Contextual variables include (a) the type of work that the group or organization is engaged in (e.g., extent to which there are standard operating procedures to accomplish tasks, objective indicators of how well the task is being performed, dimensions of the work that are stressful or dangerous, and interdependencies among work groups), (b) characteristics of the followers (e.g., their experience or maturity, personal commitment to the work, trust and cooperation with each other, and expectations of the leader), and (c) and the resources available to the leader (e.g., position power, resources needed by the group to accomplish their work, interpersonal networks in the organization).

The path goal theory of leadership (House, 1971; see also House, 1996) illustrates the most common way that contextual variables are used to predict leadership success. In this theory, four types of leader behavior are delineated:

1. Supportive: Expressing concern for the needs and welfare of subordinates and creating a positive work climate

2. Directive: Providing subordinates with clear expectations, guidance, rules, and procedures; and scheduling and coordinating work

3. Participative: Involving subordinates in decisions and taking their views and suggestions into account

4. Achievement oriented: Setting challenging goals and performance standards and showing confidence that subordinates will attain them

These behaviors are hypothesized to be more or less effective for successful leadership depending on characteristics of the task and of subordinates. For example, directive behaviors are more effective when subordinates are inexperienced, supportive behaviors are more effective when the task is stressful or tedious, participative behaviors are more effective with subordinates who have a high need for achievement and autonomy, and achievement-oriented behaviors are more effective when the task is unstructured. Thus, the path goal leadership theory uses an individual difference variable (leader behavior) and contextual variables (task characteristics and subordinate characteristics) to predict leadership success.

The multiple-linkage model (Yukl, 2002) illustrates how contextual variables can be used in more complex ways to contribute to the understanding of successful leadership. The model describes the interaction effects of leader behavior and contextual variables on intervening variables that determine the performance of a work group. Yukl's model identifies six intervening variables important in determining work group performance: subordinate effort, role clarity and task skills, organization of work, cohesiveness and cooperation, resources and support, and external coordination. Some situational variables are called "neutralizers." They represent conditions that produce high levels of an intervening variable without any action from the leader. For example, interesting and challenging work can yield high levels of subordinate effort without intervention from the leader. Other situational variables make the intervening variable particularly important. For example, when task roles in the work group are highly interdependent, cohesiveness and cooperation within the group become more important. Thus, in situations where an intervening variable is important and neutralizers for that variable are low, leader behaviors become particularly important for group performance.

Choosing the Leadership Setting

The final factor contributing to the breadth of leadership studies is setting: successful and unsuccessful leadership has been studied in a wide variety of settings. A major dimension of leadership setting is *what is being led:* individual followers, teams or groups, entire organizations, or larger communities. Successful leadership has thus been investigated in leader-follower dyads, in work units, in all types of teams (which are generally distinguished from work units based on the interdependency of their tasks to carry out a focused objective), in organizations, and in more loosely organized communities—in almost any setting where individuals have to work together to produce collective outcomes.

Closely related is the dimension of *organizational level.* Leader effectiveness has been studied at every organizational level from first-line supervisory and project team leaders to chief executive officers (CEOs) and governing boards. It is often assumed that the demands and work requirements of leadership varies by organizational level (Zaccaro & Klimoski, 2001). For example, leaders at higher levels have more influence on organizational choices, have to integrate work across multiple groups and functions, and tend to create rather than carry out organizational strategies. Thus, the dynamics of successful leadership likely varies across organizational levels.

Leadership studies also vary in terms of assumptions about the *source of leadership.* Most leadership research occurs in settings where there is a formal leader role and assumes that the person in that role is the primary source of leadership. Other studies have examined the dynamics of shared leadership across multiple roles (Pearce, Perry, & Sims, 2001). And others make distinctions among formal and informal leaders. For example, Heifetz (1994) described how leaders in positions of authority have access to different resources and use different influence strategies than those who take on leadership work without being in positions of authority. Thus, successful leadership might be understood quite differently in settings where leadership is shaped by formal leaders and where it is shaped by informal leaders.

Successful and Unsuccessful Leadership: Key Themes

A great deal of knowledge has been generated about what contributes to successful (and unsuccessful) leadership. Yet, because of the variety of approaches that have been taken to better understand this phenomenon, it is difficult to integrate findings across the many streams of research. However, several approaches in the literature do stand out as having been particularly fruitful. Each of these approaches reflects a unique combination of definition of success, type of predictors of success, and/or setting for studying leadership. Each is best represented by a key question:

1. *What do groups need from their formal leaders to be effective?* This approach tends to focus on how managers' behaviors are related to subordinate or coworker ratings of leadership effectiveness. It has yielded useful taxonomies of effective managerial behavior that are widely used for assessing, selecting, and developing managers.

2. *What competencies enable individuals to be successful in a variety of leadership roles?* This approach focuses on the role of intrapersonal and interpersonal competencies in leadership success. It has highlighted the role of emotional intelligence in successful leadership.

3. *How do leaders create commitment to collective work and organizational change?* This approach emphasizes subordinate satisfaction and high-performing groups as the markers of successful leadership and delineates the behaviors of transformational leaders—one of the most generative leadership frameworks in the field.

4. *What characterizes leaders who are more successful at higher organizational levels?* This approach focuses on executive-level leadership and the competencies and expertise needed to be successful at that level. It has highlighted the complexity of executive-level work and the cognitive and social development needed to be effective in these roles.

5. *Why do some leaders fail at higher organizational levels?* This approach focuses on what causes managers who were successful earlier in their careers to fail when they reach higher levels of leadership responsibility. It points to specific flaws—flaws that might not have mattered as much at lower levels—as the source of failure.

6. *What kinds of experiences contribute to developing effective leaders?* Unlike the other approaches, this approach looks at the developmental experiences of leaders rather than at specific behaviors, competencies, or abilities that leaders display. It provides useful insights into how successful leaders expand the capabilities over time.

The streams of research related to each of these questions rarely overlap or draw significantly from one another. They each represent a particular lens for better understanding some aspect of successful leadership. Below, the primary theme related to each question is summarized. These themes are further illustrated in Table 9.1. The descriptors in the table are examples of what each theme suggests one would see in a leader who was deemed successful or unsuccessful.

To contribute to the success of their groups, formal leaders balance concern for task efficiency, human relations, and adaptive change. Managing each of these concerns requires a different set of behaviors from leaders (Yukl, 2002). Task efficiency requires behaviors directed toward accomplishing tasks, using people and resources efficiently, and maintaining orderly and reliable operations. Human relations require behaviors directed toward building relationships and helping people, increasing cooperation and teamwork, and increasing employee satisfaction and commitment. Adaptive change requires behaviors directed toward adapting to change in the environment, increasing flexibility and innovation, and making changes to processes and products.

Many taxonomies of leader behavior can be organized along these three dimensions. See Table 9.2 for three examples. The content in the table illustrates that although there are some unique aspects in each taxonomy, each covers behavioral categories that address the three concerns of task efficiency, human relations, and adaptive change. Taxonomies such as these are used frequently in the assessment, selection, and development of individuals in managerial roles in organizations.

Individuals with high intrapersonal and interpersonal competence are more successful in leadership roles. If relationships are the primary vehicle through which leadership responsibilities are carried out, then people's intrapersonal and interpersonal competencies are central to their effectiveness in leadership roles because these competencies affect the quality of their relationships. Intrapersonal and interpersonal competencies have appeared in many models of leadership (Boyatzis, 1982; Kouzes & Posner, 1987; McCall et al., 1988; C. D. McCauley et al., 1998; Yukl, 2002). More recently, Goleman (1995, 1998) has labeled these competencies as "emotional competencies" and has associated them with "emotional intelligence"—an affective capacity distinct from IQ. Although there are several distinct models of emotional intelligence (see Bar-On, 2000; Gardner, 1983; Salovey & Mayer, 1990), at its most general level, emotional intelligence refers to the ability to take in and understand affective information. Goleman's model suggests four major domains of intrapersonal and interpersonal competencies: self-awareness, self-management, social awareness, and relationship management.

Self-awareness is the ability to recognize one's own emotions and how they affect performance. It allows people to know their strengths and weaknesses, seek out feedback, and know where they need to improve. Self-confidence is also a component of self-awareness. Self-management is the ability to control one's emotions and act in reliable and adaptable ways. It consists of several components: remaining calm and unfazed in stressful situations, acting in ways consistent with one's values and principles, being self-disciplined in carrying out one's responsibilities, being comfortable with adapting to new situations, being optimistic about one's ability to improve, and being proactive to avoid problems before they happen.

Table 9.1   Example Descriptors of Successful and Unsuccessful Leadership in Each Research Stream

Successful Leadership	*Unsuccessful Leadership*
Theme: Balance concern for task efficiency, human relations, and adaptive change.	
When making decisions, takes into account the needs of the organization and needs of employees.	Hires people with good technical skills but poor ability to work with others.
Gets things done without creating adversarial relationships.	In implementing a change, does not take the time to explain the rationale or listen to concerns.
Coaches employees in how to meet expectations.	Is unable to deal firmly with loyal but incompetent employees.
Theme: Develop intrapersonal and interpersonal competence.	
When working with another group, gets things done by finding common ground.	Is not adaptable to many different types of people.
Does an honest self-assessment.	Is emotionally volatile and unpredictable.
Quickly gains trust and respect from customers.	Overestimates own abilities.
Theme: Engage in transformational and charismatic behaviors.	
Is a visionary able to excite other people to work hard.	Does not help individuals understand how their work fits into the goals of the organization.
Rewards hard work and dedication to excellence.	Orders people around rather than working to get them on board.
Gains commitment of others before implementing changes.	Fails to encourage and involve team members.
Theme: Think and act in more complex ways.	
Once the more glaring problems in an assignment are solved, can see the underlying problems and patterns that were obscured before.	Is overwhelmed by complex tasks. Cannot make the transition from technical manager to general manager.
Understands higher management values and how they see things.	Prefers to work on day-to-day problems rather than long-range strategies.
Recognizes that every decision has conflicting interests and constituencies.	
Theme: Overcome deficiencies that limit success.	
Does not become hostile when things are not going his or her way.	Does not use feedback to make necessary changes in behavior.
Does not blame others or situations for own mistakes.	Selects people for a team who do not work well together.
Does not become paralyzed or overwhelmed when facing action.	Is self-promoting without the results to support it.
Theme: Seek a wide variety of leadership experiences.	
Is prepared to seize opportunities when they arise.	Resists learning from bad decisions or mistakes.
Is willing to make a lateral move to gain valuable experience.	Chooses an overly narrow career path.
Accepts change as positive.	Feels uncomfortable in situations that call for untested skills.

Table 9.2   Leader Behavior Taxonomies

Yukl (1989)	Guest, Gratzinger, and Warren (1998)	Center for Creative Leadership (2000)
Task efficiency		
Planning and organizing	Informing	Problem solving
Problem solving	Using resources efficiently	Taking organizational
Clarifying roles and	Planning	action
objectives	Problem solving	Business skills and
Informing	Providing performance	knowledge
Monitoring operations	feedback	
	Taking responsibility	
Human relations		
Supporting	Creating relationship	Acting with integrity
Developing and mentoring	Developing staff	Communicating
Recognizing	Motivating teams	Building and maintaining
Team building	Networking	relationships
Networking		Developing people
		Valuing diversity
Adaptive change		
Motivating and inspiring	Influencing	Demonstrating a sense of
Consulting	Creating a vision	purpose
Delegating	Improving quality	Supporting innovation and
	Promoting innovation	creativity
	Empowering	Learning and adapting

Social awareness is the ability to read people and groups accurately. People with high social awareness are astutely aware of others' emotions, concerns, and needs, and show that they care about these concerns and needs. They are also able to read the currents of emotions and political realities of groups. Relationship management is a broad set of competencies that increases the likelihood that one will induce desirable responses in others. It includes the abilities to communicate clearly and convincingly, to persuade others, to disarm conflict, to build strong personal bonds, to develop others, to inspire others to work toward common goals, and to enlist others in the pursuit of new initiatives.

Goleman's popularization of the construct has stimulated further research on emotional intelligence as a capacity that enables various leadership competencies, including perspective taking, pattern recognition, developing others, coordinating group tasks, motivating and inspiring others, understanding followers' needs, providing feedback, and rewarding performance (Barling, Slater, & Kelloway, 2000; Palmer, Walls, Burgess, & Stough, 2001; Wolff, Pescosolido, & Druskat, 2002). It has also stimulated the development of interventions to improve emotional competencies. These efforts are broadly directed toward better understanding and improving emotional competence in all facets of human endeavors, but there continues to be a specific interest in the role of intrapersonal and interpersonal competence in effective leadership (Fernández-Aráoz, 2001; Goleman, Boyatzis, & McKee, 2002).

Successful leaders motivate others and generate commitment to collective goals through transformational and charismatic behaviors. Theories of transformational and charismatic leadership have been particularly prominent in the past 20 years of leadership research (see Bass, 1985, 1995; Conger, 1989; Conger & Kanungo, 1998; House & Shamir, 1993). These theories focus on the leader as a change agent and as a catalyst for motivating others to do more than they intended or expected. This perspective emphasizes the role of leadership in organizational change and transformation.

Conger (1999) identified nine components shared across the dominant transformational and charismatic leadership theories:

1. *Vision:* Successful leaders articulate some idealized goal of what the organization can achieve in the future. The process of crafting a vision involves actively examining shortcomings in the status quo and seeking to understand what followers hope for and desire to accomplish. Leaders may not be the original source of the vision, but they are active in crafting and articulating it for the collective.

2. *Inspiration:* Successful leaders display enthusiasm and optimism for shared goals, heightening followers' awareness of the importance and value of these goals. They arouse team spirit and encourage followers to support each other in the achievement of goals.

3. *Role modeling:* Successful leaders are consistent in their behavior, demonstrating high standards of ethical and moral conduct. Followers identify with these leaders and want to emulate them.

4. *Intellectual stimulation:* Successful leaders encourage followers to question assumptions, reframe problems, and look for new approaches. Followers are included in efforts to address and solve group and organizational problems, and creativity is encouraged.

5. *Meaning-making:* Successful leaders engage followers in interpreting the meaning of organizational events and situations. They help followers make sense of new challenges and complex problems.

6. *Appeals to higher-order needs:* Successful leaders focus on the intrinsic rewards of work, de-emphasizing the extrinsic side. They emphasize the heroic, moral, and meaningful aspects of work. They pay special attention to each individual's needs for achievement and growth and create a supportive climate for learning.

7. *Empowerment:* Successful leaders see their relationship with followers as one of mutual influence. Rather than using control strategies to manage followers, these leaders develop followers' capability and confidence in taking actions and making decisions that are in alignment with and support collective goals.

8. *Setting of high expectations:* Successful leaders challenge followers to meet high performance expectations and to strive for idealized goals. They demonstrate

their own dedication to these high expectations and their confidence in the ability of individuals and groups to meet these expectations.

9. *Fostering of collective identity:* Successful leaders encourage followers to abandon their individual self-interests for collective undertakings. They tie the self-concepts of followers to the goals and vision of the collective, making organizational work inseparable from individual achievements.

At higher organizational levels, leadership work becomes more complex; thus, leaders at these levels need to think and act in more complex ways. Numerous distinctions have been made among the leadership demands at lower, middle, and upper levels of organizations. For example, Katz and Kahn (1978) distinguished how organizational structure is used at different levels: Upper-level managers create structure, middle-level managers interpret structure, and lower-level managers use structure. In a review of literature on executive leadership, Zaccaro (2001) noted two consistent themes in conceptual models distinguishing executive leadership from leadership at lower levels of the organization: (a) Executive leadership involves the coordination and maintenance of the organization as a whole system, and (b) executive leadership establishes organizational purpose. Organizational systems are complex, consisting of multiple, interconnected elements—elements that are sometimes in conflict with one another and are in dynamic interaction with the environment. Establishing purpose can also be complex at the organizational level because the needs of multiple constituency groups have to be integrated.

To deal effectively with these complex demands, organizational leaders need to develop complex cognitive and social capabilities. Although developing increasing complexity is central to much of the research in this arena, different researchers have relied on different theoretical underpinnings and have taken different approaches to understanding these capabilities. Three approaches are highlighted below.

Jacobs and Jaques (1990) focused on the leader's frame of reference—a conceptual map of the relationships among the various elements and events that comprise the leader's operational environment. To be successful at the executive or systems level, these conceptual maps become increasingly complex with numerous elements and many cause-and-effect relationships. They are more abstract than the maps of lower-level managers, and they include consequences over a longer span of time. These more complex frames of reference allow executives to consider multiple options and multiple strategies, to deal with more complex forms of organization and a wider variety of influential constituent groups.

Building on Jaques (1976) earlier work, Jacobs and McGee (2001) proposed that the development of more complex frames of reference is a function of an individual's conceptual capacity. Conceptual capacity is associated with reflective processing of experience, openness to new ideas, the capacity to form and integrate multiple perspectives about one's environment and experience, and a tendency to organize information in a networked or spatial—rather than a linear—fashion.

Mumford, Zaccaro, Harding, Jacobs, and Fleishman (2000) highlighted three problem-solving capabilities needed by organizational leaders that enable them to successfully engage in the complex issues they face: creative problem solving, social judgment skills, and organizational knowledge. *Creative* problem solving is needed because the dynamic systems environment in which executives operate yields novel and ill-defined problems. Creative problem solving involves the selection and screening of information during problem definition, the generation of new understandings of the problem and alternative solutions, evaluation of solutions, and the generation of idea implementation strategies. *Social* judgment skills are needed because executives must develop and implement solutions in a social context. Social judgment skills include the understanding of social dynamics within a problem situation, the ability to take on the perspectives of others' in the situation, awareness of the fit of the problem solution to the social dynamics of the situation, and understanding of unintended consequences of problem solutions. *Organizational* knowledge is important because solutions need to be tailored to the organization. Organizational knowledge includes knowledge about business drivers, the requirements of key constituents and internal operations, and the people who will be implementing solutions.

Finally, Drath and Van Velsor (in press) have applied Kegan's (1994) adult development framework to understand the capabilities needed by executives at higher organizational levels. Higher-level leaders face demands, such as balancing the perspectives of diverse constituency groups and making choices between actions that will have equally positive (and equally negative) consequences, that call for a qualitatively different way of understanding oneself in relation to the world. Drath and Van Velsor label this perspective "self-authoring." Individuals with a self-authoring perspective assume that who a person is is determined by his or her own self-creating processes (i.e., one's identity is independent from the responses and judgments of others and independent of external ideas and values). This is a more complex framework than what Drath and Van Velsor label "self-reading." Individuals with a self-reading perspective assume that a person's identity is determined by what important people and ideas in his or her life reflect back to the person about who he or she is. Individuals who have developed a self-authoring perspective are better able to deal with the demands faced by executive-level leaders.

Certain deficiencies in leaders will limit their success. Examining the causes of unsuccessful leadership provides an additional lens for understanding the dynamics of leadership success. Those who take this approach assume that failure is more related to having undesirable characteristics rather than to lacking desirable ones (Hogan & Hogan, 2001). For example, having the characteristic of "unfriendliness" is assumed to be qualitatively different from being "low on friendliness." Or "avoiding risk" is assumed to be qualitatively different from being "low on risk-seeking."

In a review of research on why managers derail, Van Velsor and Leslie (1995) identified four categories of deficiencies that consistently predict derailment: problems with interpersonal relationships, failure to build and lead a team, inability to change or adapt during a transition, and failure to meet business objectives.

Managers who derailed due to problems with interpersonal relationships tended to be described in one of four ways: (1) as insensitive and manipulative toward others, (2) as overly critical of others, (3) as using others to further their own ambitions, or (4) as solitary and aloof. These managers were likely successful earlier in their careers because they could get things done through their intellect, independence, drive, and ambition, but, in higher-level jobs, they had to develop relationships with more people—and with people who are less likely to tolerate their interpersonal deficiencies.

Failure to build a team also becomes more noticeable and less tolerated as an individual moves from doing the work oneself to hiring and leading those who do the work. This failure is often described as an inability to transition from doing the work oneself to facilitating the people and processes for getting the work done. Managers with this deficiency are described as avoiding conflict, failing to motivate others, not sharing credit, and unwilling to delegate (Chappelow & Leslie, 2001).

Inability to adapt or change becomes increasingly problematic as an individual moves up in an organization and takes on broader leadership responsibility. These broader responsibilities often require new capabilities and approaches to leadership work. However, the very fact that an individual has been given broader responsibilities signals that he or she is successful and thus may be reluctant to change a "winning formula." Managers with this deficiency are described as avoiding risk, closed to feedback, unable to handle pressure, and not strategic in their thinking (Chappelow & Leslie, 2001).

Finally, derailment because of failure to meet business objectives was typically associated with one of two deficiencies: lack of follow-through or being overly ambitious (i.e., spending more time politically positioning oneself for the next promotion than paying attention to the needs of the current job). This latter characteristic—high ambition—likely propels derailers up the management hierarchy earlier in their careers. But as they reach higher-level jobs that are more complex and critical to the organization, failure to give the business the attention it needs will more quickly lead to noticeable business problems.

Hogan and Hogan (2001) have examined the aspects of personality that underlie deficiencies that derail managers. They identified 11 personality dimensions that correlate with observers' (bosses, spouses, and coaches) descriptions of derailing behavior (e.g., yells at people when they make mistakes, is self-promoting, is indecisive). These dimensions are described in Table 9.3.

Successful leaders have a wide variety of leadership experiences. The range of capabilities that contribute to effectiveness in leadership roles is large. To hone such a well-rounded set of capabilities in individuals requires time and a variety of learning experiences. When asked about their key learning experiences, successful executives highlight the breadth of experiences that they have had across their careers (McCall et al., 1988; Morrison, White, & Van Velsor, 1992). These experiences are of four major types: job assignments, relationships, hardships, and formal learning events. Successful executives report learning from a variety of experiences within each type. This variety is illustrated below for one type of experience: job assignments. For a more in-depth review of each of type of experience, see C. D. McCauley et al. (1998).

Job assignments provide direct leadership experience, and different types of assignments pose different leadership challenges (C. D. McCauley, Ruderman,

Table 9.3   Personality Dimensions Underlying Management Derailment

Dimension	Description
Excitable	Moody and hard to please; intense but short-lived enthusiasm for people, projects, or things.
Skeptical	Cynical, distrustful, and doubting others' true intentions.
Cautious	Reluctant to take risks for fear of being rejected or negatively evaluated.
Reserved	Aloof, detached, and uncommunicative; lacking interest in or awareness of the feelings of others.
Leisurely	Independent; ignoring people's requests and becoming irritated or argumentative if they persist.
Bold	Unusually self-confident; feelings of grandiosity and entitlement; overevaluation of one's capabilities.
Mischievous	Enjoying risk taking and testing the limits; needing excitement; manipulative, deceitful, cunning, and exploitative.
Colorful	Expressive, animated, and dramatic; wanting to be noticed and needing to be the center of attention.
Imaginative	Acting and thinking in creative and sometimes odd or unusual ways.
Diligent	Meticulous, precise, and perfectionistic; inflexible about rules and procedures; critical of others' performance.
Dutiful	Eager to please and reliant on others for support and guidance; reluctant to take independent action or go against popular opinion.

SOURCE: Hogan and Hogan (2001). Copyright © by Blackwell Publishers. Used with permission.

Ohlott, & Morrow, 1994). One stream of research (C. D. McCauley, Ohlott, & Ruderman, 1999) identified five basic categories of leadership challenges:

1. *Creating change:* A leader with a mandate to create change may be responsible for taking an organization in new directions, carrying out a reorganization, fixing problems created by a predecessor, or dealing with problematic employees. These jobs require the leader to take numerous actions and decisions in the face of uncertainty and ambiguity.

2. *Managing at high levels of responsibility:* Assignments with high levels of responsibility have greater breadth, visibility, and complexity. Leaders in these jobs have to deal with broader and more complex problems, and their decisions often have a bigger impact on the organization.

3. *Managing boundaries:* Some assignments make higher demands on a leader to work across internal and external organizational boundaries. Leaders in these jobs face the challenge of working with people over whom they have no direct authority and whose perspectives and priorities might be quite different from their own.

4. *Dealing with diversity:* Some assignments require working with a more demographically diverse group of subordinates. These jobs require leaders to

work with individuals who are not like them—people with different values, with different backgrounds and experiences, and with different workplace needs. They also require the leader to build alignment and commitment among subordinates who may not understand each other well or have high trust.

5. *Experiencing a job transition:* A transition is a change in work roles or responsibilities, such as a change in job content, status, or location. Transitions often require building new relationships and managing unfamiliar work.

From these different types of job assignments, leaders learn to deal with different leadership situations and develop the different capabilities called on by these situations (C. D. McCauley et al., 1999). For example, managers are more likely to report improvement in their ability to deal with problem subordinates when having to create change. They are more likely to report improved adaptability in assignments high in transition challenges or when dealing with diversity. They are more likely to report learning how to better deal with conflict when in assignments requiring managing boundaries. Thus, as these examples illustrate, the wider the variety of assignments a leader experiences, the higher likelihood of developing a broader repertoire of competencies and skills.

Conclusions. A wide variety of individual characteristics have been studied as predictors of successful leadership. Each of the themes above emphasizes a particular subset of characteristics. These differing areas of emphasis exist because the leadership role being examined differs: managing groups, developing influential relationships, leading change, leading organizational systems, and moving up a management hierarchy. Despite differences in what is emphasized in each theme, there is overlap and congruence when looking at the themes as a whole. Relationship-building capabilities are perhaps the most consistently emphasized across streams of research. Creating a sense of direction is also emphasized, although the primary means for achieving a sense of direction varies across themes (e.g., goals, vision, a collective purpose). Developing knowledge, expertise, and broader perspectives over time is also emphasized in several themes.

It is important to note that many of the characteristics identified as predictive of successful leadership are not specific to leadership. Characteristics such as self-awareness, social awareness, relationship-building skills, ability to build teams, adaptability, and complex frames of reference, and a broad base of experience are useful in many human endeavors. Many of the capabilities are more accurately thought of as *human* capabilities applied to leadership roles and responsibilities rather than as *leadership* capabilities. From this perspective, leadership development and personal development are difficult to separate and share many of the same dynamics (C. D. McCauley et al., 1998).

Summaries of the predictors of successful leadership can give the impression that effective leaders have all the characteristics that predict success. In reality, every successful leader possesses some of the characteristics to a great degree and is average or even below average on others. When leaders are assessed on a set of competencies (or behaviors or skills), there are clusters of competencies that tend to correlate highly with one another, but these clusters tend not to be highly correlated with other clusters, indicating that the same leaders are not high on all dimensions being assessed. A behavioral taxonomy or competency model is a set of "ideal" characteristics against which individual leaders can assess the strengths and weaknesses that they bring to their leadership roles and responsibilities.

Organizational Practices for Successful Leadership

Many organizations tend to see themselves as not having enough leadership talent. In 1997, about half of the respondents to a Conference Board survey rated their company's leadership capacity as excellent or good. In 2001, the proportion who rated their leadership capacity as excellent or good had dropped to one third (Conference Board, 2002). This sense of a gap in leadership capacity is at least a partial explanation for the continuing growth in the investment organizations are making for leadership development and executive education (Vicere & Fulmer, 1997).

To increase their leadership capacity, organizations are thus seeking ways to put into practice the growing knowledge base about successful and unsuccessful leadership. One of the most widespread applications is the articulation of leader competency models; that is, clear specification of the capabilities needed for successful leadership in the organization. Once a competency model is articulated, ways of assessing individuals in relation to the model are often designed. These models and their assessment tools then serve as the foundation of leader selection and promotion processes and of leadership development initiatives.

Competency Models

A leader competency model describes the characteristics that an organization desires in its leaders or some designated subset of its leaders. These characteristics are usually described as behaviors, or more broadly as competencies (as noted earlier, a competency is a underlying trait, skill, motive, or expertise). Organizations typically invest a great deal in developing these models (Dalton, 1997). They might begin with a more general model developed from research in the field (e.g., Goleman's emotional competency model or Bass's transformational leadership model) and adapt it to their context and needs, or they might develop a model "from scratch"; that is, from examining what has predicted successful leadership in their organization or exploring what is expected to predict successful leadership in the future. There are three issues to consider in developing these models:

1. What leadership roles is the competency model appropriate for? Some organizations want to develop a more generic model that applies to leadership roles throughout the organization. Others develop models specific to each management level or to certain functions or business units. Others try to combine the two

approaches, articulating a general framework of competencies with different levels or aspects of the competency needed for different jobs.

2. Should the competency model be focused more on success in the current organization or on what is anticipated as needed for success in the future? There are well-developed methodologies for identifying the most-needed competencies in the current organizational context. Yet, based on their strategic planning work, organizations often have a sense of how the leadership context will be different in the future. Developing connections between competencies and leadership success in some future context is more problematic. In these cases, organizations often look for knowledge bases outside of their organization. For example, if the organization expects in 3 years to be operating in a global rather than a domestic context, it can draw on existing knowledge about leadership success in a global context from organizations that have already made this transition.

3. How will organizational acceptance of the model be obtained? In developing competency models, organizational members are more likely to accept and act on conclusions that are reached through their own efforts or those of people they trust (Dalton & Hollenbeck, 1996). Thus, the more employee involvement in the generation and interpretation of the data used to build the competency model, the more likely the resulting model will be accepted and used. Also, buy-in is increased the more the model is built into organizational systems and processes, and use of the model is demonstrated throughout the organization.

Assessment of Leader Behaviors and Competencies

Once a competency model has been developed, organizations typically want to assess their leaders and potential leaders against the model. Various methodologies have been employed to assess competencies. Most frequently used are multirater (360-degree) surveys, simulations, interviews, and personality inventories. Multirater surveys contain a number of items describing a particular behavior or competency. Coworkers who are familiar with the person being assessed rate the degree to which he or she demonstrates the competency. In simulations, individuals are observed in simulated leadership situations, and professional observers evaluate the degree to which various competencies are demonstrated. Interviews can be with the person being assessed or with coworkers. In the former case, the interviews are typically designed to elicit examples of how competencies have been demonstrated in past leadership situations or to assess depth of knowledge or expertise. When interviewing coworkers, the approach is similar to that used with 360-degree surveys, although specific examples of when competencies have been demonstrated can be elicited. Finally, personality inventories—once out of favor as an assessment method in organizations—are returning, particularly as a method to assess potential derailing characteristics or motivation to take on leadership roles.

Organizations typically develop a range of assessment methodologies with different methodologies used for different purposes. Interviews are more frequently used when assessing candidates for a particular leadership position. Simulations are often used to identify a pool of individuals with high potential for taking on higher levels of leadership responsibility. Multirater surveys are used primarily as part of leadership development initiatives. When multirater surveys are used for administrative purposes, such as making selection or promotion decisions, they are typically designed for this specific purpose (i.e., even though the same methodology is used, separate tools are designed for use in administrative decision making and in leadership development).

Leader Selection

Organizations fill most leadership roles with internal candidates (Howard, 2001). When these leadership roles are at lower levels of the organization, they are prone to two common errors. First, high-performing individual contributors are often placed in first-level supervisory or team leadership roles without assessing their capabilities for the leadership role. There is likely some overlap in the competencies needed to be a successful individual contributor and to be a successful leader of other individual contributors, but many competencies needed for the leadership role may be missing or underdeveloped in the high-performing individual contributor.

Second, individuals who excel in their first leadership positions are often moved too quickly up the organizational hierarchy, not giving them the time in any one position to experience the consequences of their actions or to develop the competencies and knowledge to master the challenges of that position. They end up at higher organizational levels without the broader perspective a variety of assignments can provide and without the insights gained from living with the consequences of their actions. Incorporating what has been learned about successful and unsuccessful leadership into their lower-level leader selection processes could help decrease the frequency of these errors.

More careful attention is generally given to leader selection decisions at higher organizational levels. An effective selection process at these levels does the following (Sessa & Taylor, 2000):

- Uses a selection committee to make the selection decision. The committee is made up of variety of individuals who will work with the new leader.
- Assesses the organizational context and job requirements, and articulates the competencies needed to be successful given the context and requirements. All of this is completed before the search process begins.
- Recruits a qualified pool of candidates.
- Takes a disciplined approach to gathering and integrating information about each candidate's fit with needed competencies and job requirements.
- After the selection is made, prepares the individual for the position and prepares the organization for the new leader.

Leadership Development

Developing individuals for leadership roles is an ongoing and multifaceted activity in most organizations. Organizations typically employ different leadership development strategies for the different types of leadership roles in an organization. For example, for specific leadership roles at lower levels (e.g., first-level supervisors, project managers, or team leaders), the organization might design a development program for all individuals who are new to those positions. The organization might identify middle-level managers with high potential for moving into executive-level roles and give them special developmental attention, such as making sure they have a mentor in the organization, sending them to off-site educational programs, and putting them in key developmental assignments. For executives with a particular deficiency or developmental need, the organization might use coaches for customized one-on-one development work. Any number of specific leadership roles might be identified and a development initiative designed for it (e.g., global roles, leading cross-functional teams, business turn-around roles). At the same time, ongoing leadership development throughout the organization can be embedded in general human resource practices, such as performance development, succession planning, and career planning.

Reviews of leadership development practices (Conference Board, 2002; Conger & Benjamin, 1999; Fulmer & Wagner, 1999; Moxley & Wilson, 1998; Vicere & Fulmer, 1998) are consistent in highlighting factors associated with successful initiatives to increase an organization's leadership capacity:

1. The initiatives are closely linked to the organization's goals and strategies, business issues, and challenges.

2. The initiatives use multiple learning and development methods (i.e., formal learning experiences, job assignments, and developmental relationships).

3. The initiatives are linked across organizational levels in an effort to develop consistent leadership at all levels.

4. The initiatives are constantly evaluated and adapted to meet changing needs.

5. Other organizational systems and practices support the objectives and outcomes of the leadership development initiatives.

Emerging Perspectives and Practices

In this chapter, successful leadership is viewed as arising primarily from effective leaders. This is the dominant view in the leadership field. However, scholars and practitioners have begun to look at the issue of increasing leadership capacity in organizations from a broader perspective. While continuing to acknowledge that the capabilities of individuals in leadership roles is a key aspect of successful leadership in organizations, they point to other sources that contribute to successful leadership and that should be considered targets of leadership development.

Day (2000) proposed that the development of social capital is as important as the development of human capital for successful leadership in organizations. By developing social capital he meant, "building networked relationships among individuals that enhance cooperation and resource exchange in creating organizational value" (p. 585). Thus, successful leadership relies not just on human capabilities but on strong relationships among organizational members—relationships that enhance mutual obligation and reciprocal trust.

Drath (2001) suggested that the tasks of leadership are carried out more effectively in organizations when organizational members hold shared principles of leadership or implicit theories about how leadership is carried out. Cognitive leadership research has been building evidence that collective leadership schemas—socially constructed ways of understanding leadership derived from exchanges and interactions among multiple individuals in an organization—are used by organizational members to generate leadership behavior and perceptions (Lord & Emrich, 2000). Thus, in addition to human capabilities and strong relationships among organizational members, successful leadership requires shared implicit theories of leadership.

Finally, there is an emerging recognition that practices that are typically labeled "organizational development" or "team development" are targeted to affect the same outcomes as "leadership development" (Beer, 2001; Drath, 1998; Hughes, 2002): a sense of direction and purpose among organizational members, collective commitment to the work necessary to move in that direction, and an alignment of these efforts. Certainly, there is promise in efforts to integrate the more macro perspectives of organizational and team effectiveness with the more micro perspective of individual leader effectiveness that has traditionally dominated the leadership field.

Conclusion

A wide variety of approaches have been taken in examining the question of what differentiates successful and unsuccessful leadership. These approaches differ in how they define successful and unsuccessful leadership, the kind of predictors they choose to focus on, and the settings in which they examine leadership. Several approaches stand out as having been particularly generative: taxonomies of effective managerial behavior, the role of interpersonal and intrapersonal competencies in leader success, transformational leadership models, the development of executive-level capabilities, management derailment, and the developmental experiences of leaders. Knowledge developed from these approaches is useful for assessing, selecting, promoting, and developing leaders in organizations.

CHAPTER 10

Leadership Development

A Diagnostic Model for Continuous Learning in Dynamic Organizations

Manuel London

Todd J. Maurer

This chapter presents a model of organizational and individual linkages that drive leadership development. In delineating the model, we review theories of leadership that determine the types of leaders that organizations want to develop; theories of learning that guide development; an examination of well-established and emerging methods/interventions for developing valued traits, knowledge, and behaviors; and the effectiveness of these interventions on a range of criteria.

Background

Our chapter is a response to trends in leadership development and our evaluation of the state of research and practice in the field. Major trends include (a) the press for continuous learning; (b) leaders taking personal responsibility for their own career development in light of organizational dislocations such as changing economic conditions, downsizing, restructuring, and crises of ethics and finance; (c) organizations providing resources that enable development and create cultures that support continuous learning; (d) technology allowing customized, self-administered development resources; (e) leaders wanting customized, business-oriented, time-efficient development; and (f) organizations needing ongoing transformation and transaction capabilities from leaders.

These trends offer considerable opportunity and present challenges in designing valuable leadership development initiatives. We see at least three major needs in the field today: First, there is the need to integrate development from organizational and individual perspectives and align these with multiple theories of learning and development. Second, there is the need for organizations to assess current level of leadership competencies relative to goals and guide and support ongoing development strategies. Third, there is the need for leaders to assess their own strengths, identify skill gaps, establish commitment to development plans, and track behavior change. The diagnostic model offered in this chapter addresses these three needs.

Maurer (2002) distinguished between *learning* as "an increase or change in knowledge or skill that occurs as a result of some experience" and *development* as "an on-going, longer-term change or evolution that occurs through many learning experiences" (p. 14). As such, learning contributes to development. Information learning changes *what* we know whereas transformation learning changes *how* we know (Kaiser, 2002; Kegan & Lahey, 2001). In addition, people cycle through stages of change, often making considerable progress for a time and then having a relapse. Lasting change requires persistence through several iterations of these cycles and then continuous maintenance (Prochaska, DiClemente, & Norcross, 1992). This means that effective leadership development requires ongoing emphasis and support from both individuals (e.g., supervisors) and organizations. The current model underscores this aspect of learning.

C. D. McCauley (2001) outlined three major components of leadership development: (a) developmental experiences (i.e., opportunities to learn); (b) the ability to learn—a mix of motivational, personal orientation, and skills; and (c) organizational support for development, which includes a variety of contextual factors, such as coaching, feedback, and rewards for development. These components suggest three simple strategies for leadership development: "Provide a variety of developmental experiences, ensure a high level of ability to learn, and design the context so that it supports development" (McCauley, 2001, p. 348). McCauley called for an overarching framework that integrates the variables and theories associated with learning. In this chapter, we suggest a model for assessing, creating, and refining leadership development recognizing the interchange of organizational and individual levels and the longitudinal nature of the cyclical learning process.

Day (2000) emphasized that leadership development is important as a source of competitive advantage. In defining leadership development, Day noted that it has a somewhat different meaning from management development, which primarily includes managerial education and training. Day distinguished between leadership development and leader development. Leader development helps leaders develop competencies that will make them more effective, whereas leadership development helps leaders establish relational bonds, shared representations, and collective meanings. Both leader and leadership development are necessary. They complement one another. Also, both should be continuous, systematic, linked processes, not one-time, haphazard, independent events. In addition, they occur in a variety of settings, both classroom and on-the-job, with different sources of support. Whereas we use the term leadership development in the conventional way to refer to individual leaders' development, our model extends Day's (2000) formulation by articulating the linkages between individual and organizational goals for development, building both social and individual competencies.

Toward a Diagnostic Model for Leadership Development

Figure 10.1 presents our model for assessing leaders' continuous learning needs, processes, and outcomes. The model specifies the variables and processes contributing to the organization's learning and development culture and the leader's acquisition of new skills and involvement in continuous learning activities. This is a *dynamic* model in that the organization and its leaders are affected by periodic, if not constant, influences from within and outside the organization. These affect the organization's need for leaders to accomplish long-term strategies and plans. Leadership development affects the organization's and its leaders' capabilities, goals, and achievements. It is a *diagnostic* model in that it can be used as a structure for (a) interpreting and integrating existing research, (b) determining leadership development needs, and (c) suggesting directions for future research.

This model is not intended to be an exposition of new theory. As will be apparent in the following discussion, various extant theories of motivational traits, learning orientations, and social cognition underlie the elements of the model and their linkages. The model holds that evolving characteristics of the organization and its situation include challenges and demands faced by the organization, the leadership style exhibited and desired by the CEO and senior executives, and the organization's development strategy and competency requirements. These factors influence development goals, methods, and processes for learning. The model also holds that characteristics of leaders and potential leaders within the organization include the leader's readiness to change, learning and development orientation, goals to achieve mastery or specific levels of performance, beliefs that learning is possible, and personal standards, conscientiousness, expansiveness, and learning style. These things also influence development goals and methods.

A key feature of this model is the compatibility or congruence of characteristics of the organization and the individual. Leaders' development goals and preferred learning methods and the organization's goals and methods for leadership development may coincide although they may emerge for different reasons. However, if organizational and individual development goals diverge, the investment in leadership development may be wasted or may not return maximum benefit. Of course, the same learning methods may meet multiple development goals.

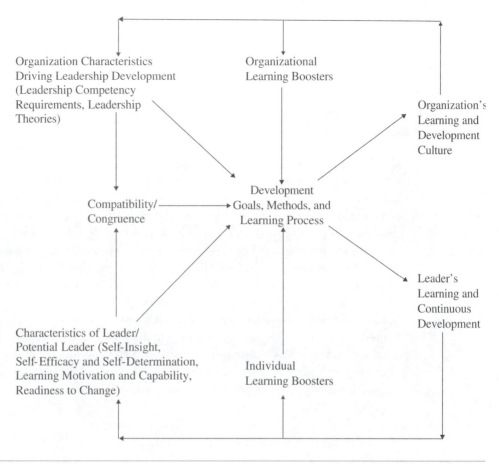

Figure 10.1   A Dynamic, Diagnostic Leadership Development Model Integrating Individual and Organizational Perspectives

Development goals and learning method(s) are chosen from a range of possibilities, today increasingly customized to meet the leader's specific needs. Learning processes depend on the learning method(s) used, organizational support for learning (e.g., availability of feedback), and the leader's self-affirming actions and attitudes about development, such as welcoming and seeking feedback from internal and external sources. Core learning processes include the conceptual understanding of new leadership behaviors/skills, observing role models, practicing, and receiving feedback. These affect what and how much is learned, behavior change, and outcomes or accomplishments resulting from the learning in relation to personal, professional, and organizational standards. Learning outcomes can be viewed from individual and organizational perspectives—the leaders' skill acquisition and commitment to continuous learning and the organization's overall capacity and effectiveness and its ongoing support for leadership development. Factors at both the organizational (e.g., coaching) and individual (e.g., self-affirmation) level can boost the effectiveness of the development processes.

In this chapter, we define each element of the model and suggest how the model can be used for understanding and directing leadership development programs at the organizational level and plans and development activities at the individual level.

Organizational Factors Driving Leadership Development

The changing nature of work poses challenges and suggests directions for leadership development (London, 2002; Lord & Smith, 1999). For instance, the trend to flatter organizational structures and larger numbers of direct reports requires leaders to communicate clearly about organizational direction, convey trust in direct reports, and monitor processes and outcomes without overcontrolling. Matrix management requires recognizing interdependencies in functions and tasks and making clear assignments and points for coordination. Virtual organizations are loose confederations of associates in different locations and organizations working on joint projects. Leading these organizations requires familiarity with multiple modes of communication, leading by persuasion and influence, sensitivity to others' reactions (sometimes conveyed in indirect ways), willingness to share information, and the ability to deal with uncertainties and resolve ambiguities. Temporary organizational structures require leaders to inspire commitment to the mission while valuing others' input, welcoming and integrating newcomers, and being adaptable.

Leadership Competency Requirements

Continuous learning has become a core organizational competency for leaders in many companies (D. Hall & Mirvis, 1995; Maurer & Rafuse, 2001). In a recent survey, 400 human resource executives were asked to rate the importance of 29 employee qualities (American Association of Retired Persons, 2000). The results included the following qualities in the top 15: "flexible in doing different tasks," "will participate in training programs," "try new approaches," "up-to-date skills," "learn new technology," and "comfortable with new technology." Indeed, the amount of training managers participate in over their careers is positively related to reaching higher levels of management (Tharenou, Latimer, & Conroy, 1994).

The prevalence of teams requires new leadership skills (London, 2002). For example, project teams and task forces require such things as frequent and clear communication, reaching consensus, and resolving conflicts. Continuous quality improvement teams need to understand customer needs and customer-supplier relationships. Leaders of these teams need to know how to facilitate group process and evaluate group process and progress. Managing geographically dispersed teams, perhaps across cultures, requires frequent communications, sensitivity to differences in resource availability, and cultural sensitivity.

New ventures are another organizational trend that has implications for leadership (London, 2002). Start-ups require the leader to monitor the environment, garner resources, remain open to new ideas, and treat employees, customers, and suppliers with respect. "E-commerce"—*e* for electronic—enterprises require leaders to think creatively, take risks, evaluate the market, and track the quantity and quality of outcomes. Mergers and joint ventures require managing change, resolving conflict, and being sensitive to different organizational cultures and traditions. Leaders need to foster a shared mission as they develop a new organizational culture, sometimes breaking down boundaries and sometimes fostering the continued identities of individual units.

The advent of online businesses also indicates directions for leadership requirements. Higgins, Jones, and Paddock (2002) compared the biographies of 41 leaders of "e-businesses" with 50 leaders of traditional businesses. These were dot-coms doing business over the Internet. All the businesses were successful at the time the biographies were written. The environments in these technological, electronic-based businesses were fast paced. The work centered on the technology, which was constantly advancing. The marketplace was highly competitive and often chaotic and uncertain. As a result, leaders of e-businesses needed to be highly adaptable. Higgins et al.'s analysis showed that "e-leaders" tended to be visionary and creative whereas traditional leaders set strategic goals. E-leaders were intuitive whereas traditional leaders were analytic and strategic. E-leaders collected information and then responded quickly to changing conditions whereas traditional leaders analyzed the situation in detail and responded after a strategic plan was put in place. For e-leaders, everything had to be done as soon as possible, whereas the motto for traditional leaders was "slow and steady wins the race." E-leaders were continuously learning new technology, staying ahead of the curve whereas traditional leaders learned new skills to improve their performance.

Higgins et al. (2002) argued that high-tech, competitive companies need transformational skills. Bass (1985, 1998) distinguished between transactional leadership based on mutually agreed goals and contingent rewards, and transformational leadership based on value systems and commitment to collective achievement. Transformational leaders communicate their personal standards to unite employees toward a common vision. Higgins et al. (2002) found that e-leaders were significantly higher than traditional leaders on transformational traits, such as "never stop learning," "don't be afraid to innovate; be different," "take action," and "deal and communicate with people effectively." They were higher than traditional leaders on one traditional trait, "be persistent and work hard."

Theories of Leadership

Leadership interventions should be based on leadership theories, and these theories, and their associated measurement instruments, should have demonstrated reliability and predictive validity. That is, theories and related research on what makes an effective leader or the type of leader organizations want and need should determine the content or direction of leadership development. Unfortunately, leadership development programs often are not grounded in such models (Avolio, in press). The different approaches to leadership described in earlier chapters of this book suggest sound directions for leadership development. Leadership can focus on traits, knowledge, behaviors contingent on the situation, or a combination of these approaches.

Consider some traits that organizations may desire in their leaders as a result of the demands of new technology-based, highly competitive operations. Apart from having a high need for power (and a high responsibility disposition/impulse control), organizations are likely to want their leaders at hierarchically lower organizations to be high in need for achievement, which is associated with individual supervisor's contributions (Antonakis & House, 2002; McClelland & Boyatzis, 1982). In contrast, leaders at high organizational levels should not have a very high need for achievement because it could lead to micromanagement and may also lead to "cutting corners," which can result in legal or ethical difficulties (Winter, 2002). Alderfer (1972) emphasized the importance of growth needs that, when satisfied, become even more important to the individual. This suggests that successful involvement in learning and development may increase learning and development orientation (Maurer, 2002).

Hackman and Oldham (1976) focused on how job characteristics, such as skill variety, task significance, task identity, autonomy, and feedback, motivate behavior, including development, especially for people who are high in growth need strength. Organizations are also likely to value leaders who exhibit conscientiousness and openness to experience—characteristics that are likely to be related to motivation for continuous development (cf. Hogan, Hogan, & Roberts, 1996; Hurtz & Donovan, 2000; Judge, Bono, Ilies, & Gerhardt, 2002; Paunonen & Ashton, 2001).

As another needed trait derived from theory and contemporary events, consider the development and promotion of moral or ethical leadership in organizations (Turner, Barling, Epitropaki, Butcher, & Milner, 2002). Stockholders and other organizational stakeholders expect leaders who abide by society's laws and rules as a way of guiding behavior and use universal principles of reasoning in making life's decisions (cf. Kohlberg's, 1976, stages of moral development). Leaders can learn organizational justice principles so that the procedures for making decisions and the decisions themselves are viewed as fair (Skarlicki & Latham, 1997).

Another general trait is emotional intelligence—understanding the effects of emotions on human behavior and knowing how to identify and manage one's own and others' emotional responses (Caruso, Mayer, & Salovey, 2002; Cherniss & Caplan, 2001; Goleman, Boyatzis, & McKee, 2002). Leaders need self-awareness to know what's happening with their own emotions, maintain a positive state, keep distressing emotions out of the way, be empathetic, and prime positive emotions in others.

Organizational pressures are likely to lead to the need for leaders who are high in the trait of hardiness—the interrelated self-perceptions of commitment, control, and challenge that help in managing stressful circumstances in a manner that turns these circumstances into developmental rather than debilitating experiences (Maddi, Kahn, & Maddi, 1998).

Global competence is a characteristic that multinational businesses are likely to expect of their leaders. This is a combination of personality characteristics, such as openness and flexibility, knowledge about business operations in other cultures, and skills, such as language. Global developmental experiences improve knowledge and skills, but personality characteristics are less likely to change (Caligiuri & DeSanto, 2001).

Knowledge requirements for leaders go beyond specific technical, financial, and management facts to include intuitive or tacit knowledge that is acquired through implicit learning (Reber, 1989; Sternberg, 1997). This is knowledge acquired in the absence of conscious, reflective strategies to learn. For instance, exposure to events or characteristics that covary (or seem to) can produce conclusions. More broadly, wisdom—the ability to seek out or create good through a balance of social, inter-personal, and emotional interests—is reflected in several types of knowledge; for example, rich factual and procedural knowledge, as well as knowledge about differ-ences in values, goals, and priorities (Baltes, 1993; Sternberg, 1998b). Various aspects of social intelligence can be learned, such as how to influence others and increase their task commitment. Leaders can be trained in influence tactics that are effective in increasing followers' task commitment (consultation, inspirational appeal, and rational persuasion) and those that are likely to be ineffective (pressure, coalition, and legitimating) (Yukl, & Tracey, 1992).

London and Diamante (in press; Diamante & London, 2002) described expan-sive individuals as people who demonstrate self-directed energy, show a continuous quest to learn and generate new ideas, and desire to apply their newly acquired knowledge and novel ideas. Expansive individuals maintain a deep focus on their field of expertise as they challenge conventional thought and understanding. They seek novel experiences. They are self-regulated and self-directed. They perceive barriers to new knowledge as challenges to overcome. Technology-focused expansive people show continued involvement in knowledge acquisition, discovery, and invention. This is needed in businesses based on emerging technologies facing fast-paced, competitive, global pressures (Kanter, 2001). Indeed, technology-focused expansive leaders thrive in these environments, and the organizations depend on their energy, vision, and continuous learning.

Whereas these leaders may be rare and their passion for learning is beyond the norm, they are likely to be found in companies that encourage and reward experi-mentation and innovation (e.g., R&D laboratories, business incubators, or compa-nies that place a premium on design and constant improvement of new products and services). Consider fields such as engineering disciplines that impose constant pressures to maintain one's knowledge and skills (Goldstein & Gilliam, 1990; Kozlowski & Hults, 1987). Expansive leaders are driven to success and strive for continuous growth and innovation (Kaplan, Drath, & Kofodimos, 1991; MacDonald, Gagnier, & Friedman, 2000). They are dedicated to learning, especially as it promotes technological discovery, advancement, and application. They are engaged in learning for its own sake and also for the benefits that may accrue.

In summary, organizational conditions, including the pace and direction of the economy, technology, and competition, and theories of effective leadership traits, knowledge, and behaviors pose challenges for leaders and suggest desired leader-ship characteristics. For instance, these conditions and theories suggest the extent to which organizations need leaders who are high in achievement motivation, ethics, emotional intelligence, hardiness, global competence, tacit knowledge, and behavior flexibility. Organizations that recognize these needs will invest in programs that develop these characteristics.

Characteristics of the Leader/Potential Leader

Just as organizational conditions influence desired leadership characteristics and directions for development, characteristics of leaders and potential leaders affect their involvement in development. Four themes represent this individual component of our model: (a) Gaining self-insight is a critical aspect of recognizing the need for change, setting learning goals, and evaluating progress; (b) leaders must recognize the need to change their behavior in relation to organizational requirements (i.e., to be expansive, continuous learners), but also they must be *ready* to change; (c) leaders vary in their stage of cognitive/emotional development and their readiness to change; and (d) self-regulation through self-monitoring and interpersonal sensitivity are critical to leadership development, especially in corporate environments that are uncertain and changing because these organizations provide the resources to enable development, but learning must be self-motivated.

Self-Insight, Self-Efficacy, and Self-Determination

London (1985, 2002; London & Noe, 1997) emphasized the importance of self-insight to leadership development and professional growth. At the individual level, leadership development requires self-insight to understand one's strengths and weaknesses and organizational requirements and to set goals for development. It involves self-regulation in establishing learning goals and action plans. Also, it implies the development of a strong self-identity, in terms of the type of person one is and wants to be and the career goals one wants to achieve. In the process of development, the leader may need to overcome career barriers, such as the lack of support for learning and diminishing career opportunities. At the organizational level, leadership development requires needs analysis; that is, assessing talent to determine current skill gaps in light of current goals and anticipated skill gaps in light of emerging objectives. Organizational programs that support self-insight include development planning, resources for development, and ongoing assessment and review (feedback) of leadership development needs.

Intrapersonal skills are the foundation on which management careers are built (Hogan & Warrenfelts, in press). Executive development requires growing intrapersonally (Kaiser & DeVries, 2000). There is a dynamic balance between attending to the problem or challenge at hand and attending to one's internal state (Kaplan & Kaiser; in press). Kaiser (2002) pointed out that improving intrapersonal skills might enhance other domains of management development. Many managers have character flaws resulting from sensitivities to a particularly painful experience in the past. These sensitivities result in people overestimating what they need to do to protect their well-being while underestimating what they can do about it. Identifying and working on these sensitivities can enhance intrapersonal awareness and improve interpersonal, leadership, and business skills. Examples of sensitivities include fear of disapproval, being weak, being dependent, being evaluated, and challenging authority. Kaiser (2002) described methods for short-term corrective actions, such as becoming aware of the sensitivity, recognizing the bodily signs/emotions of threat, short-circuiting the fight-or-flight response through relaxation techniques, managing one's energy by, for instance, taking short breaks and make time for exercise, and enlisting a confidant. In the long-term, personal transformation requires building on incremental learning from short-term corrective measures. This can occur by learning the difference between facts and assumptions, conducting behavioral experiments, and taking the time to think about an experience, exploring ones values and the distortions of reality based on one's implicit beliefs about leadership effectiveness, and forming a support system (Kegan & Lahey, 2001).

Bandura (1997) highlighted the importance of feeling that learning is possible. White's (1959) effectance motivation theory argued that people strive to be effective and want affirmation of their own ability (Lubinski, & Benbow, 2000). Maurer (2001, 2002) distinguished between self-efficacy for development as self-confidence in one's capacity to develop, enhance, or increase one's personal characteristics relative to the current or anticipated situation, and self-efficacy for performance as self-confidence in one's ability to achieve favorable performance. Self-efficacy for development plays a central role in motivation for learning and development.

Self-regulation stems from the needs for competence, relatedness, and autonomy (cf. Deci, Eghrari, Patrick, & Leone, 1994; Deci & Ryan, 1991; Ryan & Deci, 2000). People are driven by extrinsic rewards or self-motivation depending on environmental forces, such as constructive (nonthreatening) performance feedback, having choices and knowing their likely consequences, empathy from others, a reason to act, and reinforcement of self-competence.

Leaders' Learning Motivation and Capability

Individual leaders' desire and ability to learn are key drivers in understanding the initial conditions for leadership development. Here we consider leaders' orientation to learning and feedback.

Learning and Development Orientation

An employee who is high on learning and development orientation "feels favorably toward and during learning experiences and is continually and persistently involved in such experiences in the pursuit of his or her own development"

(Maurer, 2002, p. 14). This is related to Dweck and Leggett's (1988) conceptualization of implicit theories of traits. People subscribing to an incremental theory of traits believe their characteristics are constantly evolving, and they are motivated to learn continuously. These "mastery learners" can be distinguished from people who sub-scribe to an entity theory of traits and are motivated to improve their performance. People who are cognitively oriented toward development believe that they can improve their knowledge, skills, and abilities based on a clear conception of what they might become (Wurf & Markus, 1991). These individuals tend to have a favor-able attitude toward learning and development activities (Maurer, 2002). This favorable attitude will prompt behavioral involvement in those activities and be more likely to persist when these activities are challenging. Individuals who do not believe that personal attributes are improvable tend to compare themselves against others but do not have a clear conceptualization of what they might become. They will be less favorably disposed toward participating in learning and development activities and persisting when these activities become more challenging. A leader's attitude about development is likely to be influenced by the work context; for instance, the company philosophy of leadership development and the provision of developmental resources. It is also likely to be influenced by the work content, such as job transitions, task characteristics, and barriers to performance goals (C. D. McCauley, Ruderman, Ohlott, & Morrow, 1994).

Feedback Orientation

London and Smither (2002) defined *feedback orientation* as "an individual's overall receptivity to feedback and the extent to which the individual welcomes guidance and coaching" (pp. 82–83). They viewed feedback orientation as a multi-dimensional construct that includes (a) liking feedback—an overall positive affect toward feedback and a low level of evaluation apprehension; (b) the propensity to seek feedback; (c) the propensity to process feedback mindfully; (d) sensitivity to, and caring about, others' views of one's performance; (e) a belief in the value of feedback as providing useful information to guide performance improvement; and (f) feeling accountable to act on the feedback. Feedback orientation is linked conceptually to such variables as openness to experience (Barrick & Mount, 1991), mastery orientation (Dweck, 1986), self-monitoring (Snyder, 1974), public self-consciousness (the desire to protect one's ego in the face of others; Levy, Albright, Cawley, & Williams, 1995), and the general desire to learn about oneself, verify one's self-image, and enhance one's self-confidence (Baumeister, 1999).

Motivation for learning and feedback are likely to be positively related to growth need strength and personality characteristics such as conscientiousness and open-ness to experience. Career motivation theory argues that persistence is a function of three categories of characteristics: *resilience* to overcome barriers, *insight* into one's strengths and weaknesses and opportunities, and *identity* (London, 1985). Overall, these motivational traits are the foundation for leaders' readiness to learn and change their behavior.

Leader's Readiness to Change

Prochaska's transtheoretical model of change holds that people progress through five stages of change based on readiness to take action (Prochaska, Prochaska, & Levesque, 2001; Prochaska et al., 1992): (a) *precontemplation*—do not intend to take action within the next 6 months; (b) *contemplation*—intend to take action within the next 6 months; (c) *preparation*—intend to take action within the next 30 days; (d) *action*—in the process of taking action or did so within the last 6 months; and (e) *maintenance*—made changes more than 6 months ago. When organizations try to get their managers to make a change to enhance their performance in some way, many will not be ready to take action immediately. Eighty percent of those who need to change are likely to be in the precontemplation or contemplation stages, meaning that they are not likely to pay attention to feedback and take action (Prochaska et al., 1992). Feedback may increase readiness to change, but it will not necessarily bring about the change. People are likely to commit to change when the pros outweigh the cons or when "perceived benefits" of development are favorable (Maurer, Pierce, & Shore, 2002; Maurer & Tarulli, 1994).

Processes of change promote readiness within each stage. Recognizing this, supervisors can intervene in different ways depending on each subordinate's readiness. Those in the precontemplation stage need to recognize the need for change, deal with their emotions, such as fear of failure, and be inspired to change by observing people who successfully changed their behavior. Those in contemplation need to reevaluate their self-concepts by appreciating that change is key to their identity, happiness, and success. During preparation, people need reassurance that they can indeed make the change (self-efficacy). As they take action, they need social support, an environment that elicits new behaviors and limits old habits, and reinforcement (rewards) for doing well.

An additional intervention strategy that is important throughout all the stages of change is providing the choices and resources that empower employees to change. In other words, supervisors and coaches, as well as other coworkers, not to mention friends and family, provide the resources that enhance a person's chances for change. In general, though, interventions to increase readiness to change need to be individualized to match the person's readiness to change. This way, everyone can participate in the change effort, but at different levels without the undue stress from expectations that everyone must change at the same rate. Expecting everyone to change at the same rate and starting the change process in a place that does not fit everyone, for example, taking action without planning, will only result in failure (Dalton & Hollenbeck, 2001).

Cognitive and Emotional Development

Early formulations of leadership dimensions focused on increasing leaders' awareness of, and ability to analyze, their own leadership style, diagnose their leadership situation, and modify situational factors to improve their performance (e.g., Fiedler & Mahar, 1979). Other models assumed that individuals can change.

Development focused on leaders knowing how and recognizing when to vary their behavior accordingly or to modify the situation (see Tetrault, Schriesheim, & Neider, 1988, for a review of the managerial grid, situational leadership, leader-member exchange, and contingency decision-making models and related leadership training interventions).

More recent formulations, based on the work of Kegan's (1982, 1994; Kegan & Lahey, 2001) life span developmental perspective, recognize the social construction of reality and the potential value of self-awareness in relation to organizational and interpersonal conditions (Bullis, Lewis, Bartone, Forsythe, & Snook, 2002; Day, 2002; Lewis, Bartone, Forsythe, Bullis, & Snook, 2002; Van Velsor, 2002). This approach views development as a transformation to more complex ways of thinking and feeling; in particular, when we are able to reflect on what we previously took for granted or what was hidden from our consciousness. Kegan's framework distinguishes between qualitatively different developmental stages or "orders of mind" that increase with complexity, moving to deeper levels of a sense of self. At the deepest level, the self becomes an object for reflection and objective analysis separate from our perceptions of others. These levels of thinking provide a social construction of reality reflecting *how* people perceive the world around them, not *what* they know. More complex thinking allows people to be more effective leaders in more complex situations.

In Kegan's model, one stage of social construction is not better than others, just different and more or less complex (Day, 2002). The first order of mind (Stage 1) is represented in young children. The second, represented in older children, teens, and some adults, is a focus on others' feelings and beliefs with an inability to separate oneself from others. The third order, "traditionalism," is represented in teens and many adults who are able to distinguish between their own and others' viewpoints yet feel responsible for others' feelings. The fourth order, "modernism," is represented in fewer than half of all adults. This is a sense of self outside of connections to others. People who are fourth-order thinkers are self-governing and principled but have little insight into the limits of the self-governing system. The fifth order, "post-modernism," is rare and does not occur before midlife. Individuals with this order of thinking understand the limits of their own system of principles. Stage 2 people operate with fixed role behaviors. Those in Stage 3 are team players with a shared professional identity. Stage 4 people are autonomous and self-driven.

Leaders' approach to a situation will depend on their stage of thought and the complexity of the situation. Measuring managers' stage of thought process from interviews, Van Velsor (2002) identified situations that challenge third-order managers; in particular, being in an ill-defined role, facing conflicting demands from work and family, being assigned a new job especially with a promotion, and taking a minority position in a group or with a supervisor. Third-order thinkers have internalized diverse perspectives and can consider others' viewpoints. However, they have not yet achieved a sense of self-ownership. In moving to the fourth order, they need to consider the extent to which they see themselves as leading edge role models, playing their own game, and able to take a minority viewpoint when necessary. Fourth-order thinkers are challenged by motivating others around a vision, working with those who are not self-empowering, being honest and sensitive, and working collaboratively. They are self-empowered but not yet able to think of themselves objectively.

As leaders are promoted from positions that have mainly transactional task components to positions and levels that are increasing strategic and transformational, they need higher levels of cognitive and integrative complexity (Lewis et al., 2002; Lewis & Jacobs, 1992). As a result, leadership development needs to go beyond technical skills and task content to include basic psychological developmental processes.

Developmental programs should evaluate managers' current level of development, avoid placing them in situations that call for more psychological maturity than they have achieved, but involve them in experiences that promote development (Lewis et al., 2002). During stable times, if people are placed in situations that are "over their heads" from the standpoint of developmental maturity, organizational structures, policies, and procedures such as formal grievance procedures can substitute for lack of leadership maturity. However, in fast-moving, uncertain situations, lack of leadership maturity is likely to be a noticeable hazard. Thus, on-the-job developmental experiences need to be challenging but not frustrating sink-or-swim situations. This is a difficult balance to achieve. Facilitators and coaches can help guide leaders into situations that have the most learning potential and can help leaders who find themselves in situations that call for more tolerance, persistence, and interpersonal objectivity than they can muster on their own.

The Compatibility/Congruence Between Organization and Leaders

A major consideration in designing effective development programs is addressing not only the needs of the organization but also the needs, goals, and characteristics of the leaders or potential leaders to participate in those development programs. Key features of development should be compatible and congruent with both the organization's and the leaders' characteristics.

Maurer, Pierce, and Shore (2002) described how individuals can perceive multiple beneficiaries of their engaging in activities that are developmental in nature. The individuals, the supervisors, and the organization can benefit from making transitions, handling new experiences, building relationships, confronting barriers or hardships, and engaging in training. Furthermore, depending on the nature of competencies to be built in these activities, participants may view varying degrees of self-benefit along with benefit for the organization or supervisors. Ideally, the developmental goals and methods that are chosen can maximize both individual and organizational benefits (Maurer, Pierce, & Shore 2002). Organizations that have fostered a strong sense of organizational support for its employees and good relationships between leaders and their supervisors will be most successful in getting leaders to pursue development that is perceived to be largely beneficial to the organization. This is a result of ongoing social exchange in which support and good relationships motivate building competencies that are needed by the organization. Maurer, Pierce, and Shore point out that prosocial and organizational citizenship behavior exhibited by employees may very well be developmental in nature, building competence and skills in areas that will be beneficial to the organization or others in the organization.

In addition, understanding individual leaders' or potential leaders' values relative to development might be useful in motivating them to learn (Maurer, Pierce, & Shore, 2002; Maurer & Tarulli, 1994). What are their preferences for learning? What outcomes do they expect? These kinds of considerations may influence motivation and involvement of leaders in development and ultimate success of the development efforts by the organization. Our model explicitly includes linkages between characteristics of the organization and goals, methods, and processes as well as the same linkages involving characteristics of the leaders.

Developmental Goals, Methods, and Learning Processes

Leadership developmental methods, including goal setting and training, are guided by theories of how adults learn. We begin this section by examining the most influential theories, and we then examine frequently used methods that develop the leadership knowledge, skills, and traits reviewed above.

Learning Theories

Learning theories focus on active and passive learning styles and preferences. No method of learning is likely to be most effective for all individuals, and development programs are usually structured to incorporate different modes of learning. For instance, reflective/passive learners learn by watching and listening whereas experiential/active learners learn by doing. Experiential theories view learning as a process that encompasses concrete experience, reflective observations, conceptualization, and active experimentation (Boyatzis & Kolb, 1991; Kolb, 1984; Mainemelis, Boyatzis, & Kolb, 2002).

Social learning theories emphasize the importance of observation and modeling in learning and behavior (Bandura, 1986) and self-monitoring—being sensitive and responsive to social and interpersonal cues about situationally appropriate behavior, such as role expectations (Snyder, 1974). Expectancy theory indicates the importance of positive consequences that result from learning. Expectancies form from prior experiences, a supervisor's promises and support, role models, and information about career opportunities and job requirements (Vroom, 1964). Image theory describes the type of information, for example, unexpected negative feedback, that grabs a leader's attention, cannot be processed automatically or explained away, causes self-reflection about one's self-concept, and stimulates goal setting (Beach, 1990; see also Langer's, 1992, theory of mindful processing).

Feedback intervention theory argues that feedback will be successful when it provides information about behaviors that should be changed to improve performance, but not when it casts aspersions on recipients' character and threatens their self-image (DeNisi & Kluger, 2000; Kluger & DeNisi, 1996).

Development Methods

McCauley (2001) described developmental experiences that are formal interventions, such as training programs customized for the organization and open-enrollment programs with an outside perspective. Leadership training provides exposure to new behaviors, cognitive understandings, knowledge, and skills along with practice and feedback. Other formal interventions include performance feedback from supervisors or trainers, action learning through business simulations, assigned mentors or executive coaches, and personal growth challenges, such as outward-bound wilderness events or internally focused, self-exploratory workshops. Organizations may adopt one or some combination of these. McCauley also described developmental experiences that occur naturally in job assignments that require making transitions, handling new experiences, building relationships, and confronting barriers or hardships. Learning occurs as leaders assess their own performance and gaps in skills and knowledge and as they are challenged to learn new capabilities. These experiences develop such capabilities as setting and implementing agendas, managing interpersonal relationships, demonstrating basic values such as sensitivity to people, becoming more personally aware of one's own strengths and weaknesses, and understanding executive temperament (McCall, Lombardo, & Morrison, 1988).

Day (2000) described how various methods support leader (human capital) and leadership (social capital) development. For instance, multisource, 360-degree feedback survey results provide directions for behavioral change. Similarly, coaching and mentoring focus on the individual with one-on-one learning. Network development (e.g., team-building exercises) focuses on helping individuals connect to others in different functions and areas. It builds social capital by socialization, problem solving, and learning whom to consult for help. Job assignments develop human capital by requiring leaders to face new experiences, thereby developing a broader understanding of the business. Action learning, for example, project-based learning addressing specific business problems, develops both human and social capital as it focuses on socialization and teamwork to implement strategies tied to business imperatives.

Changes on the job can promote learning and development (McCauley et al., 1994). Job transitions entail changes in role, job content, and status that promote learning by participating in new, unfamiliar activities and making new types of decisions. Studies of adult development have found that major transitions are important opportunities for learning, more so than incremental learning that comes while conducting routine business or even attending special training programs (cf. D. J. Levinson, 1979, 1997; McCall et al., 1988). Learning can come from facing and overcoming barriers such as coping with difficult situations or people (Maurer, 2002). Task-related components of developmental work experience include creating change, handling a high level of responsibility, managing interfaces (e.g., influencing others), and managing diversity (McCauley et al., 1994; Tesluk, Dragoni, & Russell, 2002).

We noted above that knowledge requirements for leaders include intuitive or tacit knowledge. Situational judgment methods can be used to guide leaders through the cognitive processes of knowledge acquisition: (a) *selective encoding*— targeting only the relevant information needed for problem solving and learning; (b) *selective combination*—the integration of multiple pieces of selectively encoded information into a unified whole to create a meaningful knowledge structure; and (c) *selective comparison*—the integration of a new knowledge structure with existing knowledge structures (Cianciolo, Antonakis, & Sternberg, in press). Trainees acquire and share tacit knowledge as they review and analyze problem situations or scenarios, identifying important information, defining the problem, identifying conditions for action, and reflecting on outcomes.

Executive coaching has become a popular leadership developmental technique. Coaching is a (Kilberg, 1996)

> helping relationship formed between a client who has managerial authority and responsibility in an organization and a consultant who uses a wide variety of behavioral techniques and methods to help the client achieve a mutually identified set of goals to improve his or her professional performance and personal satisfaction and, consequently, to improve the effectiveness of the client's organization within a formally defined coaching agreement. (p. 142)

Coaching can be contrasted with a leadership development technique that was widely used a generation ago: group sensitivity training (GST). GST evolved as an experiential method designed to promote self-enhancement and behavior change through small-group interaction (Faith, Wong, & Carpenter, 1995). The small-group discussions facilitated psychological growth, empathy, and openness. Faith et al.'s (1995) meta-analysis found that GST had a moderate, positive effect on participants' behaviors and perceptions compared with those not receiving treatment. The effect was comparable to that of other psychological interventions.

Hardiness training engages cognition, emotion, and action in coping effectively with stressful circumstances and uses feedback to deepen commitment and control and challenge beliefs about oneself in the world (Maddi, 1987). It teaches trainees transformational coping skills. The idea is to decrease the stressfulness of circumstances cognitively and to emotionally explore one's appraisals of stressful situations and use this deeper analysis to develop and carry out decisive, problem-solving action plans. Furthermore, leaders learn to use the feedback from these actions to deepen the motivational self-perceptions of commitment, control, and challenge.

Earlier, we cited cultural competence as a desired leadership characteristic in multinational organizations (Harrison, 1992). Cultural differences influence behavior (Bond & Smith, 1996), and cross-cultural training has a positive impact on the individual's skill development, situation adjustment, and job performance (Black & Mendenhall, 1990). Methods for cross-cultural training use cognitive and experiential approaches. Cognitive approaches include environmental briefings and cultural orientation programs designed to provide trainees with factual information about a particular country. Experiential approaches offer opportunities for trainees to engage in specific behaviors, review the behaviors critically, abstract some useful insight from the analysis, and apply the results in a practical situation, such as role-plays, simulations, films, skill practice, and field experiences. The cultural assimilator tests trainees' knowledge and understanding of cultural differences (Fiedler, Mitchell, & Triandis, 1971). Trainees read a series of between 37 and 100 short intercultural incidents describing an interaction between a "sojourner," someone who is temporarily visiting or living in the given country, and a "host national," someone who is a native of the given country. Each incident is followed by a relevant question and four alternative interpretations. Depending on the trainee's response, the text directs the trainee to an explanation of why the choice was correct or incorrect and then asks the trainee to reread the material and select again. Another technique used in cross-cultural training is behavior modeling. Trainees watch films of a model demonstrating effective learning points and relevant behaviors in a problem situation. Then they have a chance to practice the behaviors demonstrated and receive constructive feedback and positive reinforcement from trainers and fellow trainees.

Self-Determined Learning Process

Work stimuli affect employees' insight into themselves and the organization, feelings about their job and the need for learning, and behaviors, including participation in learning activities (Hackman 1992; Maurer, 2002). Situations that enhance self-determination will increase the degree of intrinsic interest and motivation for participation in learning and development (Deci & Ryan, 1991). For instance, in one study, employees who felt more freedom to attend training reported more favorable reactions toward the training and had higher achievement scores than did those who had little perceived choice about attending the training (Hicks & Klimoski, 1987). This is "empowered self-development"—the organization providing resources to enable leaders to take responsibility for their own development (London & Smither, 1999b). This fits with the rapid evolution of technology and business. Organizations attract outstanding people by providing resources to help them learn and develop and, in the process, enhance their competitiveness for career growth opportunities within or outside the company.

Use of Goals and Feedback to Calibrate Learning Progress

Locke and Latham's (1990) goal setting theory argues that motivation stems from setting specific, challenging goals that people believe they can accomplish. Carver and Scheier's (1990) control theory argues that motivation stems from perceiving a gap between current and desired performance (cf. Scherbaum & Vancouver, 2002). Control theory speaks to the importance of feedback to evaluate the learning gap, whereas goal setting theory speaks to the importance of the nature of the goals that were set. These are not mutually exclusive processes, but rather can work together to enhance motivation and maintain persistence toward a task (Scherbaum & Vancouver, 2002).

Even in the absence of feedback from external sources (i.e., the task itself, one's supervisor, or others), people seek their own performance feedback and compare it to their prior performance and to standards they hold for themselves or that others set for them (Brink, 2002). People regulate their own performance by self-observation, diagnosis of ability and level of performance, and evaluation of how much further they have to go to achieve their goals (Bandura, 1986). People who are high in learning goal orientation are likely to be less focused on comparing themselves to others and to external standards and more focused on their ongoing learning (Dweck, 1986).

An organization's approach to leadership development can be strategic and comprehensive and can incorporate multiple methods. As an example, Motorola was faced with a lack of qualified leaders to meet the needs of a high-performance culture in a variety of telecommunications-related businesses (Moretti, 2002). In 2000, the company introduced a new leadership model. The CEO created the Office of Leadership, formed the Chairman's Leadership Institute, and committed one-third of his time to ensuring an adequate supply of leaders. As such, the initiative stemmed from the top of the organization and reflected the CEO's vision and style along with the organization's environment and goals. Development tools included a multisource feedback survey for performance management and development, Web-based assessment using a global business simulation, a structured coaching program with developmental needs and career directions interviews conducted by internal and external coaches, a transferring coaching skills workshop for executives and managers to drive leadership development from the top of the organizational hierarchy down, and ongoing evaluation of return on investment.

Organizational and Individual Learning Boosters

The organizational context affects leadership development through (a) a link to business goals and strategy, which, unfortunately, is often a link that is weak or nonexistent; (b) human resource management practices, which includes development planning, reward systems, succession planning, and databases that allow tracking individual development over time; and (c) organizational culture, which refers to values and norms that treat learning as a part of work, treat giving and receiving feedback as a responsibility, and hold senior executives accountable for coaching and developing others (C. D. McCauley, 2001).

Organizational support for development, that is, an environment that empowers self-development through feedback and opportunities for training, can enhance self-managing behaviors such as feedback seeking and taking initiatives to participate in development (cf. Kozlowski & Hults, 1986; London & Smither, 1999b; Maurer, 2002; Maurer & Tarulli, 1994; Tracey, Tannenbaum, & Kavanagh, 1995). Examples of policies or organization climate factors that facilitate development activity are encouragement of innovation, acceptance of occasional failure, dissemination of career information, and management policies that reward development. Likewise, organizations can foster social support for development and provide needed resources and work assignments that facilitate development. A study of 115 employees and their supervisors in a large bank in Denmark found that managers who received more feedback, felt more empowered, and were higher on career motivation gave more attention to managing their career development than managers who received less feedback (London, Larsen, & Thisted, 1999). Maurer, Mitchell, and Barbeite (2002) found that being in a work context where others supported development was a predictor of whether managers were involved in development following feedback, and this factor was as important as the favorability of feedback ratings in development involvement.

Individual characteristics of leaders or potential leaders will also serve as boosters to the development process. Career insight, self-efficacy, job involvement, perceived need for development, beliefs that development is possible, perceiving that benefits result from development, and a variety of other individual variables may be influential in enhancing involvement in development (cf. Maurer & Tarulli, 1994; Noe & Wilk, 1993). To the extent that leaders or potential leaders possess these characteristics, this should greatly facilitate the development process and should contribute to a culture and climate in which leadership development is valued, common, and pursued aggressively as part of ongoing commitments to work and the organization. Therefore, selecting people who possess these characteristics, or instituting appropriate or relevant programs or policies to influence these characteristics, might help to boost the development process.

Learning Outcomes and Feedback Loops

Kirkpatrick (1994) provided a framework for evaluating learning outcomes that is appropriate for evaluating leadership development. Criteria include reactions (e.g., how well did trainees like the program?), learning (e.g., what principles, facts, and techniques were learned?), behaviors (e.g., what changes in performance resulted from the program?), and results (e.g., what results occurred in such areas as reduced turnover, reduced costs, improved efficiency, reduction in grievances, increase in quality and quantity of production, or improved morale?). Reaction measures are the easiest and least expensive to collect and most frequently used. Haccoun and Saks (1998) recommended that reaction measures should go beyond affect (How did you like the training?) to include perceptions of self-efficacy, motivation to learn, motivation to apply the behaviors learned on the job, and usefulness. Cognitive tests, such as multiple choice or true-false, evaluate students' declarative knowledge, but this does not necessarily indicate transfer of training to on-the-job behaviors. More important criteria may be the extent of procedural knowledge or tacit knowledge acquired—the integration of facts into a set of orchestrated behavior chains required for concrete action. Methods for evaluating procedural knowledge include responses to scenarios and problem-solving exercises or simulations, exposure to new situations and then an opportunity to apply the knowledge to other situations, and observations or ratings of on-the-job actions and decisions (Cianciolo et al., in press; Haccoun & Saks, 1998). Burke and Day (1986) analyzed 70 managerial training studies and found managerial training to be moderately effective on a variety of criteria.

Learning outcomes may be reflected in new behaviors shown by changes in 360-degree feedback. A review of the literature on the effects of 360-degree or upward feedback over time found 13 studies, 11 of which showed positive results (Smither, London, Falutt, Vargas, & Kucine, in press). For instance, a study by Heslin and Latham (2001) found that managers receiving upward feedback twice with a 6-month interval improved significantly more than those who did not receive feedback previously. Walker and Smither (1999) tracked managers who received upward feedback each year for 5 years. Those with initially low results improved significantly during the course of the study. Johnson and Johnson (2001) reported gains in supervisor, peer, and subordinate ratings over a 2-year period. Smither et al. (in press) studied the effects of feedback and coaching received by senior managers in a global banking corporation. Managers who were coached improved more on the 360-degree ratings over a year than those who did not receive coaching.

Other elements of performance may be less reflective of behavioral learning objectives but more reflective of the organization's bottom line. These may include changes in sales, income, profits, stock price, earnings per share, market share, and product quality (Day, 2001). How much of an organization's success is actually due to leadership versus a myriad of other key factors? Leadership accounts for 20% to 45% of the variance in organizational outcomes (Day & Lord, 1988; Thomas, 1988; reported in Day, 2001). Also, executive failure rates can be as high as 50% to 75% (Hogan, Raskin, & Fazzini, 1990; White & De Vries, 1990). Cases such as WorldCom and Enron are vivid examples. In general, performance effectiveness depends on the perspective of the perceiver, the elements of performance evaluated, the level of analysis (individual behavior, group, organization), the purpose of the measurement—for example, whether it is for development and/or administration, the time frame, the types of data, and the referent for comparison, such as changes over time or information about other leaders or companies (Cameron & Whetten, 1983).

Leader's Learning and Continuous Development Behavior

London and Smither (1999a) defined career-related continuous learning as a "self-initiated, discretionary, planned, and proactive pattern of formal or informal activities that are sustained over time for the purpose of applying or transporting knowledge for career development" (p. 81). Also, continuous learning is cumulative, constantly growing and developing. Furthermore, it is integrated, linking new concepts together to form even newer concepts (London, 2002). Continuous learners anticipate changing job requirements, request feedback, set development goals, participate in learning activities, practice new behaviors, apply learning on the job, and demonstrate performance improvement (Vicere & Fulmer, 1998). London and Smither (1999a) distinguished between three stages of a continuous learning cycle: (a) *prelearning*—recognizing the need for learning and setting goals; (b) *learning*—acquiring new skills and knowledge and monitoring learning; and (c) *applying learning*—performing new behaviors and using new skills and knowledge and reaping its benefits. Whereas this implies a linear, sequential process, it may be repeated continuously in overlapping cycles. Also, it is affected by unplanned events that contribute to learning and may set off a new cycle of development planning, learning, and application. London and Smither (1999a) recognized that each one of these stages in the continuous learning cycle may be influenced by environmental, personal, and organizational factors. Maurer (2002) outlined how successful learning/development experiences can enhance leaders' beliefs that development is possible and valuable.

Organization's Learning and Development Culture

In a *feedback culture*, employees "continuously receive, solicit, and use formal and informal feedback to improve their performance" (London & Smither, 2002, p. 84). Three categories of organizational practices and interventions create a feedback culture: (a) the quality of feedback, (b) the emphasis placed on the importance of feedback in the organization, and (c) providing support for using feedback. The quality of feedback stems from training for supervisors on how to provide useful feedback, clear standards of performance, clear performance measurements, reports tying individual performance to departmental bottom-line performance, and time to review and clarify feedback in discussions with one's coworkers and customers. The emphasis placed on the importance of feedback stems from the following: programs to ensure that everyone receives feedback, for example, a performance appraisal and review procedure and 360-degree feedback survey results; expecting top executives to be role models for feedback by seeking, using, and delivering feedback; tying performance goals and evaluation to organizational goals; involving employees in conceptualizing performance standards used in performance evaluation; and rewarding performance improvement after feedback. Support for using feedback includes providing skilled facilitators to help recipients interpret survey feedback results, training and rewarding leaders to coach subordinates, encouraging the discussion of feedback, providing training programs associated with measured performance dimensions, and freedom in how to act on the feedback.

The organization's support for feedback can enhance continuous learning (London & Smither, 1999a, 1999b, 2002). For instance, research has shown the leadership training is more likely to transfer to the job when coworkers encourage and reinforce each other's learning, the organization expects and rewards innovation, and the organization provides resources to support self-development (Tracey et al., 1995). Leaders are more likely to participate in learning voluntarily when company policies and resources and supervisor and coworker support encourage development (Maurer & Tarulli, 1996). People who perceive that the work environment supports training and development are more likely to participate in learning activities (Noe & Wilk, 1993). Learning organizations, those that adapt to environmental changes through a continuous renewal of their structures and practices, encourage continuous learning through the use of performance data for ongoing experimentation and innovation (cf. Senge, 1990; Wishart, Elam, & Robey, 1996).

Feedback Loops

Our model also addresses the tie between the leader's learning and the leader's later motivation and positive orientation toward learning. Has commitment to continuous, mastery learning increased for those who have accomplished learning goals? Maurer (2002) illustrated how learning and development experience may lead to even greater orientation to development. The present model also specifies positive relationships between the organization's learning and development culture and how future leadership challenges are viewed as well as the extent of support for continuous learning. Perhaps to assess this in organizations, surveys of leader motivation and reactions to development methods and feedback processes, career-planning databases, succession plans, and rates of participation in leadership development programs might be examined to determine the extent that this has occurred. Additional questions that might be examined here are whether continued development is rewarded, whether more challenging goals are set for leadership development in light of organizational shifts, and whether the organization is more likely to be attuned to environmental changes and their implications for development. It is hoped that, as a result of leadership development, the organization becomes a more effective entity; for example, more able to adapt quickly to environmental changes. These are excellent areas for future research.

Conclusion

Overall, the purpose of our model is to assess learning needs, processes, and outcomes in continuously evolving organizations. The model specifies the variables and processes that contribute to the organization's learning and development culture and the leader's acquisition of new skills and involvement in continuous learning activities. This is a dynamic model in that it explains (a) how the organization and its leaders are affected by periodic, if not constant, influences from within and outside the organization that affect long-term strategies and plans, and (b) how learning outcomes affect the organization's and individual's capabilities, accomplishments, and goals for the future.

The model can be used to analyze current trends in leadership development. At the organizational level, the model can be used to diagnose organizational needs for leadership, indicate types of support for achieving leadership development objectives, and assess learning outcomes and development-related organizational culture in relation to these objectives and changing business conditions. At the leader's level, the model can be used to diagnose individual leaders' needs for learning and development, determine their readiness for change and commitment to development activities, understand their learning processes, and track their learning outcomes and changes in learning goals and ongoing development. Also, the linkages proposed in this model can help to guide future research on leadership development.

PART V

Emerging Issues in Leadership—Culture, Gender, and Ethics

CHAPTER 11

Leadership and Culture

Deanne N. Den Hartog

Marcus W. Dickson

People from different cultures increasingly come into contact and work together. For many firms, the question is no longer whether they are in a global industry and operate internationally; rather, it is a matter of degree (e.g., Yip, 1995). In today's internationally operating firms, leaders are faced with the difficult task of convincingly presenting the organization's vision to a multicultural and diverse workforce in a highly uncertain and unpredictable environment. In such roles, leaders increasingly need the knowledge and skills to act and decide in a culturally sensitive manner. Although business is done all over the globe, differences exist in what is seen as acceptable or effective behavior in organizations. What managers do and why they do it is influenced by what is customary in their organization, industry, or country. Whether managers typically seek to "expand their business rapidly, to undercut their competitors, to misrepresent their products, or to put customer satisfaction before economic production will again, at least partly, depend on the prevailing mores" (Stewart, 1997, p.129). Thus, more insight into leadership in different cultural contexts can be both interesting and useful for managers doing business in another culture or working with people from abroad.

Stories emphasizing the importance of leadership are found throughout history, and leadership as a function in human groups is found all over the world (e.g., Bass, 1990). Leadership everywhere has to do with disproportionate influence, and the leadership role is associated with power and status. For example, Pickenpaugh

(1997) assessed symbols of leadership in traditional cultures from the Pacific Islands, sub-Saharan Africa, and lowland South America and found that the leaders (kings, chiefs, and headmen) in such cultures often wear necklaces of large canine teeth from the most powerful and ferocious animals in their respective environments. Elsewhere, power and status may be conveyed through such things as job titles, business cards, office size, or other symbols recognizable as status and power-related by those witnessing them (Gupta, Sully, & House, 2004).

In this chapter, we are interested in organizational leadership in different countries and cultures. However, when looking at leadership cross-culturally, it is important to remember that such fundamental organizational concepts as participation, control, and cooperation do not necessarily mean the same in every cultural context. For instance, in the West, participation usually refers to having influence on the outcome of a decision by taking part in it in one form or another (Heller, Drenth, Koopman, & Rus, 1988). In Java, for example, the concept refers to a cooperative form of decision making; in Japan, to the consensus-oriented approach through the bottom-up procedures and lobby-consultations of the ringi-system (Heller & Misumi, 1987). In other words, different connotations, perceptions, and attitudes can lie hidden behind the same term.

These differences in meaning are also relevant for leadership. Even the term *leadership* itself can be interpreted somewhat differently across cultures. *Leader* and *leadership* have a positive connotation in Anglo-Saxon countries, conjuring up heroic images of outstanding individuals. Meindl's work on the "romance of leadership" shows the American "romantic" attachment to—and in some cases overestimation of—the importance of the leadership role (e.g., Meindl, 1990; Meindl, Ehrlich, & Dukerich, 1985). However, this does not hold for all direct translations of the term. The direct translation of *leader* to German is *Führer*. Obviously, the historically laden connotation of this term is rather negative. Similarly, in some other countries literal translations of the word leader conjures up images of recent dictatorship. In such countries, the term *manager* often takes on the positive connotations leader has in English (Den Hartog & Koopman, 2001).

These and other more subtle examples show that even with careful attention to translation, there may be unrecognized subtle shadings and nuances of meaning that vary across languages and cultures. Problems of meaning pose obvious measurement problems—how can we be sure we are even measuring the same construct? If we are not, to what should found differences be attributed? This issue remains an area of concern in all cross-cultural research, including cross-cultural research on leadership (e.g., Drenth & Den Hartog, 1998).

One attempt at defining leadership cross-culturally comes from the Global Leadership and Organizational Behavior Effectiveness (GLOBE) Project, which is a large-scale research project (described in detail later) that is designed to assess both similarities and differences in the cultural semantic definition of leadership in the 60 participating countries. GLOBE researchers defined *leadership* as the ability of an individual to influence, motivate, and enable others to contribute toward the effectiveness and success of the organizations of which they are members. The definition was based on an extensive discussion among 84 social scientists and management scholars representing 56 countries from all over the world, which took place at an international meeting of GLOBE researchers in 1994. This rather abstract definition of leadership was acceptable to representatives of a wide range of cultures. Thus, some agreement about what leadership entails can be found. Still, the evaluative and semantic interpretation of the term leadership, the cognitive prototypes characterizing leadership, and the culture-specific enactments of leadership are likely to vary by culture studied (e.g., Hanges, Lord, & Dickson, 2000; House et al., 1999).

Thus, what is seen as effective leader behavior may vary in different societies, resulting in different leader behaviors and leadership practices. A study highlighting the differences between two countries in the way young people are typically trained and prepared for future leadership roles can illustrate this point. Stewart, Barsoux, Kieser, Ganter, and Walgenbach (1994) compared career patterns and educational background of German and British middle managers. They showed that Britain has a tradition of recruiting talented graduates of any discipline for management careers. In Germany, the management task is perceived in more functional terms, and a direct relationship between content of the vocational training and the job to be done was more common. In career development, the British placed more emphasis on mobility. Large companies prepare their future leaders through frequent changes of jobs, tasks, and functions. Variety and generalized knowledge and skills are valued. In contrast, in Germany less emphasis on mobility and development through exposure to different situations was found. Managers spent more time in a single job, and development of specialized expertise was valued. These different approaches in developing leaders reflect differences in ideas about what makes leaders at this level effective in these two cultures.

In the sections that follow, we present some examples of studies on leader behavior in different countries. As we will show below, the ways in which researchers study and think about leadership have been strongly influenced by North American values. However, the assumptions underlying these values are not necessarily shared in other cultures. Thus, we describe different dimensions of societal cultures and the ways in which they might lead to differences in approaching leadership. Next, we turn to the developing world and highlight some elements that are specific to this group of nations. We then explore leadership perceptions around the world and show similarities and differences in the way people view effective leadership across many different cultures. Finally, we briefly discuss organizational culture in relation to societal culture and leadership.

Leadership Research in Different Countries

As Yukl (1998) and others have pointed out, most of the research on leadership during the past half-century was conducted in the United States, Canada, and Western Europe. Whereas the early North American leadership studies tended to focus on leader-group interaction, the traditional European studies tended to place leadership in a broader social, legal, and political context; for example, comparing participative management systems in different countries (e.g., Heller et al., 1988). Leadership is currently investigated widely by social scientists in many different regions of the world, including those countries where such research has not traditionally been carried out. To mention only three of the many possible examples, Kahtri, Ng, and Lee (2001) assessed leader charisma and vision in Singapore, Pasa (2000) studied influence behaviors in Turkey, and Silverthorne (2001) looked at the applicability of the path-goal model in Taiwan.

Comparative leadership research is somewhat less common, and the available studies often only take small numbers of groups into account. Some comparative studies assess differences between groups with a different cultural background within a certain country. The idea behind such studies is that even if they live in the same sociocultural context, managers from different cultural backgrounds may demonstrate or appreciate different leader behaviors. For example, Xin and Tsui (1996) compared the influence styles of Asian American and Caucasian American managers. They found only minor differences between the two groups, and ethnic background only accounted for little variance in their measures. Their study reminds us that we should not take for granted that people will behave differently in leadership roles solely based on their ethnicity or country of origin. Also, although cultural values that are shared in a given group are expected to influence individual behavior, large individual differences may also exist.

Other such comparisons between different cultural groups within a single country can focus on managers from different backgrounds in joint ventures or local versus international managers working in a given country. For instance, Quang, Swierczek, and Chi (1998) compared Vietnamese managers to foreign managers working in Vietnam. They showed that the Vietnamese nationals did not differ from other international managers on factors such as the importance of having a strategic vision and adaptability to environmental demands. However, the Vietnamese managers placed more importance on responding to deadlines and time management than did the international managers. The Vietnamese managers also placed less emphasis on performance and productivity, which may reflect the heritage from the command economy. Finally, Vietnamese managers in the sample also wanted less sharing of power and delegation than did their international counterparts.

Other comparative studies focus on leader characteristics or behaviors in a few different countries. For example, Den Hartog, Koopman, Thierry, Wilderom, Maczynski, and Jarmuz (1997) compared Polish and Dutch managers on characteristics they considered important for outstanding leadership. Visionary qualities scored high in both groups. The Dutch managers valued attributes associated with integrity and inspirational leader behavior more strongly than did Polish managers. Diplomacy and administrative skills (i.e., being orderly, well organized, and a good administrator) were considered more important in Poland. Such differences may be related to the transition from communist rule and a command economy toward a market economy.

There are several such examples of comparative studies in the literature (e.g., Bu, Craig, & Peng, 2001; Fu & Yukl, 2000; Osland, Snyder, & Hunter, 1998). Most studies take only a few cultures into account, and these are often convenience samples rather than sampling cultures based on a theoretical framework.

An example of studying cross-cultural aspects of leadership in a more elaborate project involving more than 40 countries is the ongoing work on event management. These studies present an analysis of role relationships, putting the role of leaders in the context of other sources of meaning (see, e.g., P. B. Smith & Peterson, 1988; P. B. Smith, Peterson, & Misumi, 1994; P. B. Smith, Peterson, & Schwartz, 2002). In handling events, managers can use different sources of information and meaning (e.g., rules and regulations; national norms; widespread beliefs; information from superiors, peers, or subordinates; unwritten rules). Preferences are found to differ across nations. For example, Smith et al. (2002) reported that participation-oriented sources of guidance such as relying on subordinates were found mostly in Western Europe. Managers from other regions such as Africa tended to rely on more hierarchically oriented sources of information such as superiors and rules. Also, managers in countries such as China, Bulgaria, and Romania relied more strongly on widespread beliefs as a source of guidance than did managers in other countries.

North American Bias

Although the discussion above shows that leadership studies are now conducted in many countries and some comparative work is done, there is still a strong North American bias in the leadership theories, models, and measures that are used and published in mainstream social science literature. Research conducted elsewhere often directly applies leadership models and measures developed in North America. However, it has long been noted that the applicability of theories and concepts developed in one part of the world, such as the United States, should not be taken for granted when applied in substantially different cultures (Boyacigiller & Adler, 1991). Hofstede (1993, p. 81) stated that U.S. management theories contain several idiosyncrasies (e.g., a stress on market processes, a stress on the individual, and a focus on managers rather than workers) not necessarily shared elsewhere. Similarly, House (1995a) noted that almost all prevailing theories of leadership and most empirical evidence is rather North American in character,

> individualistic rather than collectivistic; emphasizing assumptions of rationality rather than ascetics, religion, or superstition; stated in terms of individual rather than group incentives; stressing follower responsibilities rather than rights; assuming hedonistic rather than altruistic motivation and assuming centrality of work and democratic value orientation. (p. 443)

Such assumptions have an effect on what is seen as effective leadership. However, many cultures do not share these assumptions. Thus, a better understanding is needed of the ways in which leadership is enacted in various cultures, and the need exists for an empirically grounded theory to explain differential leader behavior and effectiveness across cultures (House, 1995a). When applying models in one cultural context that were developed in a different cultural context, we need to carefully consider the role that cultural differences might play and how such differences may affect the meaning, enactment, and effectiveness of leader behaviors.

An example of a widely used measure of U.S. origin is Bass and colleagues' famous Multifactor Leadership Questionnaire (MLQ), tapping transactional and transformational leadership. This questionnaire has been used in many different countries. Among these are European countries such as Austria, the Netherlands, and Belgium; Anglo-Saxon countries such as the United Kingdom and Australia; and Asian countries such as Taiwan and Japan (e.g., Bass, 1997; Den Hartog, Van Muijen, & Koopman, 1997; Geyer & Steyrer, 1998; Koh, Steers, & Terborg, 1995; Lievens, Van Geit & Coetsier, 1997). Virtually everywhere, transformational leadership has been found to correlate more positively with a variety of desirable outcomes than does transactional leadership. There is also evidence that a preference for transformational leadership exists in most if not all cultures (Bass, 1997).

Thus, a preference for and positive effects of transformational leadership are found in many places. However, the questions in the MLQ are phrased in somewhat abstract ways. Thus, such leadership does not necessarily look exactly the same in different cultures. It could be enacted in different ways (e.g., House, Wright, & Aditya, 1997). For example, charismatic leaders articulate an ideological message, set a personal example, and convey self-confidence, resulting in being trusted and respected by their followers. However, charisma can be enacted in a highly assertive manner (e.g., John F. Kennedy, Winston Churchill) or in a quiet, nonaggressive manner (e.g., Aung San Suu Kyi, Mohandas "Mahatma" Gandhi). Bass (1997) also provided such examples and stated that although concepts such as "transactional leadership" and "transformational leadership" may be universally valid, specific behaviors representing these styles may vary profoundly. For instance, Bass (1997) stated: "Indonesian inspirational leaders need to persuade their followers about the leaders' own competence, a behavior that would appear unseemly in Japan" (p. 132). Bass also noted that contingent rewarding is more implicit in Japan than in the United States.

Transformational leadership may also take more as well as less participative forms (Bass, 1990), which seems likely to be linked to societal norms and values regarding the distribution of power. In the Netherlands, for instance, transformational leader behaviors were highly correlated with participation in decision making (Den Hartog, 1997) as in Australia too (Ashkanasy & Falkus, 2003; Feather, 1994). In both these countries, egalitarianism was strongly valued. Thus, in highly egalitarian societies, to be seen as transformational, leaders may need to be more participative than they would need to be in high power distance societies. In such societies, transformational leadership may take a more directive form (Den Hartog, House, Hanges, Ruiz-Quintanilla, & Dorfman, 1999). Research testing these and other propositions will yield more insight in what it means to be transformational in different cultures.

Finally, it is important to recognize the one major study to date that has assessed leadership and leadership preferences in a large number of cultures, at both the societal and organizational levels. The GLOBE Project, mentioned earlier, is a long-term study directed toward the development of systematic knowledge concerning how societal and organizational cultures affect leadership and organizational practices (House et al., 1999). Approximately 60 countries from all major regions of the world participate in GLOBE, making it the most extensive investigation of cross-cultural aspects of leadership to date. The project was originated by Robert J. House, who has led the project's coordinating team, which includes representatives from several different cultures. Besides the coordinating team, approximately 150 social scientists from around the world are responsible for managing the project and collecting data in their respective countries.

After developing valid measures of culture using the dimension-based approach described below, data were collected on leadership preferences, organizational culture, and societal culture. Over 15,000 middle managers from more than 800 organizations in three industries in 60 countries were asked to describe leader attributes and behavior that they perceived to enhance or impede outstanding leadership. At various points throughout the remainder of this chapter, results from the GLOBE research program will be presented. However, we will first go into societal culture and the impact that different dimensions of culture are likely to have on leadership.

Dimensions of Societal Culture Related to Leadership

Culture can be seen as a set of relatively stable, basic, and shared practices and values that help human social groups or societies find solutions to fundamental problems. Schein (1992) focused on two such fundamental challenges. The first is how to survive, grow, and adapt to the environment (i.e., external adaptation). The second is how to achieve sufficient internal integration, which permits daily functioning and ensures the capacity or ability to adapt and survive. When people come together as a group, they develop shared beliefs and assumptions about the world and the people in it. These beliefs help them survive as a group. Such value orientations, beliefs, and assumptions refer to the basic nature of people and human relationships, as well as relationships with nature, time, and activity (e.g., Adler, 1991; Hofstede, 2001; Kluckhohn & Strodtbeck, 1961; Parsons & Shils, 1951; Schein, 1992; Schwartz, 1999).

One way to approach the study of culture is through the identification and measurement of dimensions of culture. Several different typologies of societal cultural value orientations or culture dimensions have been developed. The most widely recognized, as well as strongly criticized, is probably Hofstede's framework (1980, 1991, 2001). Hofstede's (1980) original study was based on a survey among IBM managers and employees in more than 40 countries. He found four culture dimensions: individualism-collectivism, masculinity-femininity, uncertainty avoidance, and power distance. In later work, a fifth dimension—future orientation—was added.

Hofstede's work has been the target of substantial criticism, including arguments that it presents an overly simplistic four- or five-dimension conceptualization of culture, that the original sample came from a single multinational corporation (IBM), that culture is malleable over time, and that his work ignores within-country cultural heterogeneity (see Sivakumar & Nakata, 2001; see also McSweeney, 2002; Schwartz, 1994; P. B. Smith, 2002; P. B. Smith & Bond, 1999, for recent overviews and critiques; see Kirkman, Lowe, & Gibson, 2003, for an overview of research including Hofstede's dimensions). Rather than providing an in-depth discussion or critique of Hofstede's research, we will discuss Hofstede's dimensions alongside other, sometimes similar, dimensions that have been proposed and studied. We do not purport to present an exhaustive discussion here—other dimensions have also been proposed and studied. The researchers developing the dimensions described below have mostly studied culture at a societal level, and a wide range of research shows that societies do indeed differ on these value orientations.

Masculinity

Having an "aggressive" attitude in the Western business world seems to have a relatively positive connotation. "Aggressive," then, implies being tough, fast, and forceful as opposed to weak and vulnerable (Den Hartog, 2004). According to Hofstede (1980, 1991), the word *aggressive* only carries a positive connotation in what he calls "masculine" countries. Hofstede described differences between societies in the desirability of assertive and tough behavior versus modest and tender behavior. He labeled this dimension "masculinity" versus "femininity." Masculinity implies dominant societal values stressing assertiveness and toughness, the acquisition of money and things, and not caring for others, the quality of life, or people. In feminine cultures, values such as warm social relationships, quality of life, and care of the weak are stressed. Doney, Cannon, and Mullen (1998) contrasted masculinity versus femininity in terms of valuing individual achievement versus norms for solidarity and service, having a norm for confrontation versus a norm for cooperation, and having social norms stressing independent thought and action versus social norms honoring moral obligations.

Hofstede also explicitly linked this dimension to gender differences. High cultural masculinity characterizes societies in which men are expected to be assertive and tough and women are expected to be modest and tender. In contrast, low masculinity (or high femininity) characterizes societies where both men and women are expected to be modest and tender. Achievement motivation and an acceptance of "machismo style" management should be higher in countries high on masculinity than in those low on masculinity (Triandis, 1994). Hofstede (2001) holds that masculine and feminine cultures create different leader hero types. The masculine manager is assertive, aggressive, and decisive. Survival of the fittest is the credo. Conversely, the hero in feminine cultures seeks consensus, is less visible, and is intuitive rather than tough and decisive. Here the credo in business is a cooperative venture. Japan, Austria, Italy, Mexico, Germany, the United Kingdom, and the United States are examples of more masculine cultures, whereas Sweden, Norway, the Netherlands, and Costa Rica are examples of more feminine countries (Hofstede, 2001).

Critique of the masculinity-femininity dimension includes that it is not well measured and that it includes too many very different topics (e.g., gender-role division, assertiveness in social relationships, being humane or focused on quality of life, and being performance or achievement oriented). In the aforementioned GLOBE study (e.g., House et al., 1999), these aspects are measured separately. The GLOBE dimensions related to this are labeled assertiveness, gender egalitarianism, performance orientation, and humane orientation (two aspects of collectivism, power distance, uncertainty avoidance, and future orientation are also culture dimensions measured in GLOBE). For instance, GLOBE assertiveness is defined as the degree to which individuals in organizations or societies are assertive, tough, dominant, and aggressive in social relationships (Den Hartog, 2004).

Among other things, assertiveness is linked to the preferred use of language in society. Assertiveness can be seen as a style of responding that implies making one's wants known to others, which is why in many Western cultures, being direct and unambiguous is acceptable. Indeed a negative relationship between assertiveness and indirect language use was found in the United States. Also, conversational indirectness was found to correlate negatively with social desirability. Thus, saying what one means in a direct manner is valued in the United States (Holtgraves, 1997).

In other cultures, however, a less direct manner of responding may be valued. In assertive societies, people will tend to use what is also referred to as "low-context" language, emphasizing the need to be direct, clear, and explicit. In contrast, less assertive cultures tend to use "high-context" languages that are less direct, and more ambiguous and subtle (Hall, 1959; Schneider & Barsoux, 1997). High-context language or being indirect in communication can be linked to "face management" (P. Brown & Levinson, 1987). People are motivated to collectively manage each other's face or public identity and do this by phrasing remarks politely and indirectly (Holtgraves, 1997). Although face management in some form or another is important in any culture, people from so-called collectivist cultures are usually assumed to be more concerned with face management than are people from individualistic countries (Ting-Toomey, 1988).

There is some support for the idea of cultural differences in this area. In Holtgraves's (1997) research, for example, Koreans were found to be more indirect than were Americans. Societal norms can also influence the amount of emotion one typically shows in public within a certain society. Trompenaars and Hampden-Turner (1997) contrast "neutral" with "affective" cultures. In affective cultures, showing one's emotions in laughter or gesture, as well as in heated debate, is the norm. In more neutral cultures, people tend to keep their emotions in check. In such cultures, a subdued manner, self-possessed conduct, and repression of emotional expression are the norm. Such differences in acceptable communication styles and patterns affect the way in which leaders present themselves in order to effectively influence others.

Uncertainty Avoidance

Uncertainty avoidance is another dimension identified by Hofstede (1980). It describes a society's reliance on social norms and procedures to alleviate the unpredictability of the future. Hofstede (1980) defined uncertainty avoidance as the extent to which a society feels threatened by uncertain and ambiguous situations and tries to avoid these situations by providing greater (career) stability, establishing formal rules, rejecting deviant ideas and behaviors, and believing in absolute truths and the attainment of expertise. It refers to the degree to which members in a society feel uncomfortable with ambiguous and uncertain situations.

In high uncertainty avoidance societies, people tend to prefer career stability and formal rules, whereas people from low uncertainty avoidance cultures tend to prefer more flexibility in roles and jobs and are more mobile when it comes to jobs. High uncertainty avoidant countries also foster a belief in experts (Hofstede, 2001). The aforementioned study by Stewart et al. (1994) comparing the career management activities of German and U.K. managers illustrates this point. German culture shows a far stronger antipathy toward uncertainty than does the British culture (Hofstede, 1980). This difference was reflected in the managers' typical career patterns and behaviors. Recall that the British typically placed more emphasis on career mobility, whereas the German managers spent more time in a single job and valued the development of task-related expertise. Also, whereas British managers emphasized the importance of resourcefulness and improvisation in behavior, German managers expected reliability and punctuality. Strict planning and sticking to previously agreed plans were very important for the German managers. Not doing so was seen as a sign of weakness, much more so than in the United Kingdom.

The results of the Stewart et al. (1994) study are congruent with those from other studies. For example, one such study compares German and Irish entrepreneurs running small companies (Rauch, Frese, & Sonnentag, 2000). Germany and Ireland are similar on all of Hofstede's culture dimensions except uncertainty avoidance, where Germany ranks high and Ireland low. Thus, in Germany, business plans are highly detailed. Customers prefer such planning and expect transactions to be adhered to by the letter, on time, and as agreed. Meeting customer expectations in such an environment is linked to careful and detailed planning. In contrast, in Ireland planning is seen as less necessary. Customers have less respect for plans, show unplanned behavior themselves and expect high flexibility. It is believed that planning too much renders business owners inflexible and makes it harder to meet customer demands. In line with this, Rauch and colleagues found that detailed planning had a positive influence on small business success in Germany and a negative influence on small business success in Ireland.

Several other studies provide similar evidence. Shane (1993) found that uncertainty-accepting societies are more innovative than are uncertainty-avoiding societies. In a later study, Shane (1995) found *lower* preferences for innovation championing roles (including the transformational leader role) in uncertainty avoidant societies. Shane, Venkataraman, and MacMillan (1995) examined the relationship between national culture (using Hofstede's dimensions) and preferences for innovation championing strategies in 30 countries. They found that the higher the level of uncertainty avoidance in a society, the more people preferred champions to work through organizational norms, rules, and procedures to promote innovation. In other words, the more *uncertainty accepting* a society was, the more people endorsed champions' efforts to overcome organizational inertia to innovation by violating organizational rules and regulations.

Relationships With Others: Collectivism

Another well-known culture dimension is individualism versus collectivism. Hofstede (1980) described cultures characterized by *individualism* as loosely knit social frameworks in which people are supposed to take care of themselves and look after their own interests and those of their close families only. In contrast, a tight social framework in which people distinguish between in-groups and out-groups is the key characteristic of cultures high on collectivism. In-groups are cohesive and strong. People expect their in-group to look after them throughout life, and in exchange feel they owe the in-group absolute loyalty.

Similarly, Schwartz (1999) noted that a society has to decide to what extent people are autonomous versus embedded in the group. In cultures high on embeddedness, people are perceived as part of the collective and find meaning and direction in life through participating in the group and identifying with its goals. Organizations tend to take responsibility for their members in all domains of life and in return expect members to identify with and work toward organizational goals. In contrast, individuals in autonomous cultures are perceived as autonomous entities that find meaning in life through their uniqueness.

Schwarz (1999) further distinguished between intellectual autonomy (i.e., individuals are encouraged to follow their own ideas and intellect) and affective autonomy (i.e., people are encouraged to independently find positive experiences for themselves). In cultures that emphasize intellectual autonomy, organizations are likely to treat their members as independent actors with their own interests, preferences, abilities, and allegiances. Employees are typically granted (some) autonomy and are encouraged to generate their own ideas and act on them (Gomez, Brannen, Sagiv, & Romani, in press; Sagiv & Schwartz, 2000). In a 47-nation study, Schwartz and Sagie (2000) found that socioeconomic development as well as democratization increased the importance of independent thought and action, openness to change, concern for the welfare of others, self-indulgence, and pleasure and decreased the importance of conformity, tradition, and security.

Hierarchy, Status, and Power Distance

Within all societies, there are status and power differentials. These are obviously related to conceptions of leadership. Hofstede (1980) defined *power distance* as the extent to which a society accepts and embraces the fact that power in institutions and organizations is distributed unequally. In cultures with large differences in power between individuals, organizations will typically have many layers, and the chain of command is very important. In line with this definition, the relationship between job satisfaction and job level was found to be weaker in low power distance than in high power distance cultures (Robie, Ryan, Schnieder, Parra, & Smith, 1998). Power distance is also related to concentration of authority (Hofstede, 2001). In high power distance countries such as China, Mexico, and the Philippines, subordinates are typically more reluctant to challenge their supervisors than are employees in low power distance countries like Finland, the Netherlands, Israel, and the United States. Employees in high power distance cultures have also been found to be more fearful in expressing disagreement with their managers (Adsit, London, Crom, & Jones, 1997).

Not only are people in high power distance countries less likely to provide negative feedback to superiors, the idea that subordinates would be allowed to provide such ratings is also likely to be rejected in high power distance countries, as such upward feedback may be perceived as threatening status positions (Kirkman & Den Hartog, in press). Power distance is also found to be an important predictor in the aforementioned studies on event management. The way in which managers typically handle events is related to power distance in society. Smith et al. (1994, Smith et al., 2002) show that managers in countries characterized by high power distance report more use of rules and procedures. They also report less reliance on subordinates and their own experience in dealing with everyday events than do managers from low power distance countries.

Authoritarian leadership and more autocratic decision making are likely to be accepted and expected in high power distance cultures. In egalitarian cultures, employees expect to have a say in decisions affecting their work. For instance, France scores much higher on power distance than does Denmark. In studies comparing French and Danish managers, French respondents indicated that the boss almost always had to be consulted simply because he or she was the boss, whereas the Danish indicated the boss had to be consulted only when the boss was likely to know the answer to their problem. In France, bosses were highly respected by virtue of their position, whereas in Denmark respect relationships were found to be independent of rank. A Danish boss could do the work of a subordinate without loss of prestige, but a French manager could not. Finally, the Danish firms were characterized by delegation of authority and flatter hierarchical structures (Schramm-Nielsen, 1989; Sondergaard, 1988; both in Hofstede, 2001).

Hofstede (2001) reported that subordinates in high power distance countries saw their managers primarily as well-meaning autocrats, whereas subordinates in low power distance countries saw them primarily as resourceful democrats. Shane et al. (1995) found that the greater the power distance in a society, the more people preferred innovation champions to focus on gaining the support of those in authority before other actions are taken on an innovation (rather than on building a broad base of support for new ideas among organizational members).

Similarly, Schwartz (1999) noted that an issue confronting any society is how to guarantee the necessary responsible behavior of its members. One solution to this challenge is found in hierarchical cultures, which rely on hierarchical systems of ascribed roles and perceive the unequal distribution of power as legitimate. This conception of culture has elements of both power distance and collectivism, in that individuals are socialized to comply with the roles and obligations attached to their position in society. Organizations emphasize the chain of authority, assign well-defined roles in a hierarchical structure, and demand compliance in the service of goals set from the top. Organizational members are expected to put the interests of the organization before their own interests. In contrast, egalitarian cultures encourage people to view each other as moral equals. Individuals are socialized to internalize a voluntary commitment toward others. Organizations emphasize cooperative negotiation and employees flexibly enact roles as they try to attain organizational goals. Leaders motivate others by enabling them to share in goal-setting activities and by appealing to others to act on behalf of the joint welfare of all (Sagiv & Schwartz, 2000; Schwartz, 1999).

Related to this is research focused on willingness to accept and responsiveness to supervisory direction. For example, Bu et al. (2001) compared the tendency to accept a supervisor's direction among Chinese, Taiwanese, and U.S. employees using their responses to several vignettes. Overall, the Chinese employees in their sample demonstrated the strongest tendency to accept direction and the U.S. employees the least. Peer consensus had more influence on the tendency to accept in the United States than in Taiwan or the People's Republic of China. Also, Chinese employees were more sensitive to the consistency between the supervisory direction and company policies, and were less responsive to their own assessment of the merit of the directions they were given. These differences seem to reflect differences in power distance. Also, the aforementioned study by Den Hartog, Koopman, et al. (1997) showed that Dutch managers had a much more negative attitude toward autocratic leader behavior and status consciousness than did Polish managers, which seems related to the much more egalitarian (i.e., low power distance) values found in the Netherlands.

In a larger study conducted by Dorfman, Howell, Hibino, Lee, Tate, and Bautista (1997), the researchers compared leader behavior in five Western and Asian countries, namely, the United States, Mexico, Japan, Taiwan, and South Korea. They found that some leader behaviors were positively related to outcomes such as satisfaction with supervision and organizational commitment in all these nations, but other leader behaviors were not universally endorsed.

Dorfman et al. (1997) related the differences they found to culture and especially to differences in the way power is typically distributed in society. For instance, supportive leadership was positively related to satisfaction with the supervisor, and in some cases other outcomes, in all five samples, but directive leadership was positively related to commitment only in Mexico and Taiwan. Charismatic leadership also had positive effects on one or more outcomes in all five samples. For instance, in Japan charisma was related to subordinates' experiencing less role ambiguity and in Mexico, the United States, and South Korea with satisfaction with the supervisor, whereas in Taiwan charisma was related to both of these outcomes as well as to satisfaction with work. Contingent rewarding also had a positive effect on one or more of the outcomes in all samples. Participative leadership had positive effects only in the United States and South Korea. In Mexico and the United States, they were able to collect similar job performance data from company records. They found that in

Mexico only supportive and directive leadership were directly and positively related to performance, whereas in the United States, only participative leadership had a direct and positive relationship with performance, and charismatic leadership did not affect performance.

Thus, out of the six tested behaviors, three (i.e., supportive, contingent reward, and charismatic leadership) had positive effects in all five countries. Three others (i.e., participative, directive, and contingent punishment) had positive impacts in only one or two cultures and equivocal or negative impacts in the other countries. These results confirm the idea that the impact of some behaviors may, to some extent, be cross-culturally generalizable, whereas for others it may be much more culture specific. To use the terminology presented by Bass (1997, building on Lonner, 1980), this study was testing for the presence of "functional universals," which are relationships between variables that are consistent across cultures.

Another issue related to power and status arises from the question of whether status is based on achievement or ascription (Parsons & Shils, 1951). Whereas some societies accord status to people on basis of their achievements, others ascribe it to people based on age, gender, social class, profession, or other criteria. Achieved status is based on what one has done or accomplished and ascribed status is based on who one is. Achievement-oriented societies tend to accord status based on their members' accomplishments. Evaluations are based on how people perform. Ascribing cultures confer status on the individual and not the task or the individual's accomplishments. In ascribing societies where seniority and age are major requirements, for example, it will usually be unacceptable to have people report to bosses who are younger than they are. In the United States, the idea that anyone can become president is a strong reflection of achievement orientation, whereas, in France, becoming president without attending the right *grande ecole* and without the right connections seems impossible. In Japan, promotion to higher positions has historically been based on seniority, gender, and age (Dorfman & Javidan, 2004; Schneider & Barsoux, 1997), and employees recognize these practices and shape their expectations accordingly.

Assumptions About Human Nature

One basic value orientation on which cultures differ, and which was not explicitly addressed by Hofstede (1980), is their assumptions on the nature of human beings: Are people generally neutral, good, or evil? Kluckhohn and Strodtbeck (1961) presented this distinction in terms of their dimension ranging from "human nature is good" to "human nature is bad." Within groups viewing humans as basically good, people will tend to trust others' intentions. In leadership terms, one might, for example, expect less emphasis on control and direct supervision of employees if a basic belief exists that people have good intentions. In contrast, distrust prevails in cultures where people are believed to be evil, and as such, more monitoring and closer supervision of employees can be expected (e.g., Gomez et al., in press).

Whereas Hofstede (1980) did not explicitly incorporate this dimension into his taxonomy of cultural dimensions, it seems that there is at least some degree of conceptual overlap with the power distance dimension. Specifically, when power distance is high, there may be an accompanying lack of trust among the various social players. When power distance is low, there may be an accompanying high level of trust between social players. Certainly, there are exceptions to this—high power distance societies are not always low on interpersonal trust, and the dimension of "human nature is good" versus "human nature is bad" is certainly broader than simply the degree of interpersonal trust. Nonetheless, cultural dimensions are never purely orthogonal, and there is at least some degree of potential overlap between this dimension and power distance.

Whether a culture views humans as changeable or not is also of interest. In cultures where people are viewed as changeable, organizations and their managers are more likely to invest in training their employees. In cultures where people are considered to be less changeable, the emphasis would more likely be on selecting the correct person for the job (Adler, 1991; Gomez et al., in press).

Control Orientation

An interesting element of culture pertains to the perceived nature of relationship with the outside world (Kluckhohn & Strodtbeck, 1961). Some societies view this relationship as one of subjugation, others as one of harmony, and still others as one of dominance. This latter view reflects the assumption that nature can be controlled and manipulated, a pragmatic orientation toward the nature of reality, and a belief in human perfectibility. It is thus also related to the dimension mentioned above, of whether humans are able to change or not. In societies holding a dominance view, "it is taken for granted that the proper thing to do for people is to take charge and actively control their environment" (Schein, 1992, p. 127).

At the other extreme, the assumption is that nature is powerful and humanity subservient to nature. This implies a kind of fatalism, as one cannot influence nature, and must therefore accept one's destiny and enjoy what one has. The Moslem phrase "Insh'allah" (God willing) is reflective of a culture characterized by a subjugation. In contrast, the phrase "may the best person win" is an example of the value of control, dominance, and competitiveness (Dorfman & Javidan, 2004; Schneider & Barsoux, 1997). As noted above, Hofstede's cultural dimensions are not orthogonal, and this appears to be similar to the masculinity-femininity dimension. Similarly, Schwartz (1999) described mastery cultures, in which people are encouraged to master, change, and exploit the environment in order to attain goals. In these cultures, it is believed that organizations and their leaders need to be dynamic, competitive, and strongly oriented toward achievement and success. Cultures at the opposing pole are labeled harmony cultures. In these cultures, people are encouraged to understand and integrate with their natural environment, rather than change or exploit it. Leaders tend to take a holistic view and try to understand the social and environmental implications of organizational actions, and seek nonexploitative ways to work toward organizational goals (Sagiv & Schwartz, 2000).

In line with the above, Trompenaars and Hampden-Turner (1997) hold that societies that conduct business "either believe they can and should control nature by imposing their will upon it, as in the ancient biblical injunction 'multiply and subdue the earth,' or they believe that man is part of nature and must go along with its laws, directions and forces" (p. 145). Trompenaars and Hampden-Turner identified these as internal and external cultures (in line with Rotter's, 1966, work on internal versus external locus of control). Culture-related differences exist in the degree to which people feel they have control over (i.e., internal control) or are controlled by (i.e., external control) external forces. For instance, when asked to choose between the statements "what happens to them is their own doing" or "sometimes I feel that I do not have enough control over the directions my life is taking," 82% of U.S. managers choose the former (implying they believe they control their own destiny) versus only 40% of Russian and 39% of Chinese managers.

Internal cultures have a dominating and controlling attitude toward nature. Conflict and resistance are taken to mean that you have strong convictions. In contrast, in external cultures being at ease with the natural shifts and cycles of nature, the willingness to compromise, and seeking harmony and responsiveness are seen as sensible and desirable characteristics for leaders. In internal cultures, the focus is on the self and one's own group or organization and playing "hard ball" is legitimate to test the resilience of an opponent. In contrast, in external cultures the focus is on the "other" (customer, partner, colleague), and softness, persistence, politeness, and patience are needed to succeed (see also Den Hartog, 2004). In internal societies, a strong belief in the value of competition and competitiveness exists. In the United States, for instance, competition is seen as "a fundamental aspect of human nature; people live in a dog-eat-dog world; people need to compete to survive and prosper" (Bonta, 1997, p. 299). Bonta showed that in most nonviolent or peaceful societies, a strong opposition to competition and a strong support for cooperation constitute basic cultural beliefs. Many such societies de-emphasize individual achievement, because it is too closely linked to competitiveness and aggressiveness.

These, and possibly other, dimensions of culture provide one approach to differentiating between societal cultures and the leadership styles that societies prefer. Certainly, other factors also come into play, including the degree of economic development of the society. To address this issue, we now turn more specifically to culture and leadership in the developing world.

Culture and Leadership in the Developing World

Models and research on leadership and culture were developed in and thus mostly focus on the "developed world" or, in other words, the Western or industrialized countries as opposed to the "developing" countries (Aycan, in press). However, the developing countries represent almost 80% of the world population. This 80%

comprises a large, growing market and labor force, spread among countries that are extremely diverse and produce a wide array of products and services (Punnett, 2003). Though there is no generally acceptable way to refer to these societies as a group given that terms such as *developing* and *third world* are value-laden and originate in the "developed" societies, we use the term *developed world* to refer to the Organization for Economic Cooperation and Development (OECD) countries and the rest of Western Europe, and the term *developing world* to refer to the rest of the world. The major distinctions between the *developed* and *developing* worlds are that on average the developed world countries have significantly higher per capita income than do the developing world countries and that developed world countries rank higher on the Human Development Index (United Nations Development Programme, 2002)—a composite index, which indicates the presence of good education, health care, and quality of life.

Increasingly, businesspeople recognize the vast potential of the growing markets and young labor force in developing countries. Specific developing countries also offer other strengths. Some are physically large and offer access to substantial reserves of natural resources (e.g., Brazil). Some have large numbers of highly trained and qualified people (e.g., India), good infrastructures (e.g., Zimbabwe), or good medical facilities (e.g., Cuba), and some achieve high scores on the Human Development Index (e.g., Barbados). These are all characteristics that may provide a good environment for both inward and outward business opportunities (Punnett, 2003).

The group of developing countries is diverse, and presenting a single unified and detailed portrayal of the cultural characteristics representing the whole group is thus impossible. However, as Aycan (in press) and others have noted, many developing countries share key elements in historical background (e.g., autocratic rule, colonialism), subsistence systems (e.g., reliance on agriculture), political environments (e.g., volatility and instability, improper law and enforcement system), economic conditions (e.g., resource scarcity, insufficient technological infrastructure), and/or demographic makeup (e.g., young workforce, unequal opportunity to access high-quality education). Such economic and political environments as well as historical events are among the forces that shape cultures. Thus, it is reasonable to expect that at least some aspects of the cultures of these countries are similar. However, as we discuss these similarities, it is important to keep two things in mind. First, substantial differences exist between developing countries. Second, many differences may exist within developing countries. Such differences in values may, for instance, be regional or reflect differences between religions or ethnic groupings.

Differences in values and behavior can also be related to the organizations people work for, or can be based on individuals' education, socioeconomic status, or age. For example, the values and behavior of a highly educated Indian manager trained abroad and working for an American multinational corporation in an urban area may resemble the values of other U.S. managers more than the values of an Indian manager with less education working for a small family business in a rural area. Such subcultural variations exist in every country, but the magnitude of such differences may well be larger in developing countries (Aycan, in press).

Similarities in Cultural Dimensions
Among Developing Countries

Cultures of developing countries *tend* to be somewhat more collectivistic and somewhat higher on power distance. They also tend to be externally oriented. As Aycan et al. (2000) noted, feelings of helplessness and fatalism are common cultural traits in these societies. Again, though, it is important to emphasize that the nature and degree to which these cultural traits are manifested can vary widely between developing countries, and there may be significant within-country variation on these dimensions, as well.

Having said the above, it is still generally the case that relationships and the networking that sustains them tend to be very important in the cultures of developing countries. Relationships and networks are more important than rules and procedures in virtually every aspect of social, political, and economic life of these countries, which sometimes leads to favoritism among in-group members—including relatives, friends, and members of one's own ethnic or religious group—and to discrimination against and alienation of out-group members. Within-group loyalty and harmony are central concepts. Because interdependence is fostered as a cultural value, self-reliance has a negative connotation, as it is seen as deserting the group. Thus, personal achievement is less stressed, and getting along is more important than getting ahead (Abdalla & Al-Homoud, 2001). These core values focused on maintaining harmony tend to ensure smoothly running work processes, though not necessarily the most objectively efficient work processes.

For example, a study on human resource management in China showed that very few companies have implemented individual-based rewards, because these types of rewards are believed to lead to "red eye disease" among workers, an expression used in China to refer to jealousy (Verburg, 1996). Jealousy emanating from individual-based pay could constitute a disruption of harmony and as such have a negative impact on working relationships and performance (Verburg, Drenth, Koopman, Van Muijen, & Wang, 1999). Such patterns may, of course, change over time. Zhou (2002) even reports on groups of employees in a Chinese factory recently acquired by a foreign investor. These employees overcome their cultural hesitancy to confront management and formally requested of their manager that the individual-based reward system that had been implemented be replaced by a seniority-based system.

In the developing world, the pattern of communication in organizations is often indirect, nonassertive, nonconfrontational, and usually downward. Negative feedback is often avoided or given very indirectly as it is quickly seen as destructive and disruptive to group harmony. In Eastern cultures such as China, Japan, and the Philippines, the loss of face, or public humiliation, can result from receiving negative feedback (Earley, 1997). Because personal and work lives are intertwined, negative feedback can easily be interpreted as an attack on the person, tarnishing one's reputation and honor rather than as an observation on behavior with a constructive aim (Aycan, in press). Also, much of people's lives revolve around the nuclear and extended family, and work and family spheres tend to be closely interrelated. Thus, a loss of face at work can have substantial ramifications in the family, as well.

Similarities in Preferred
Leadership Style in Developing Countries

As we have noted above, there are substantial variations between cultures in the developing world. However, one relatively common theme across these societies appears to be a preference for a leadership style that is high on status orientation, high on involvement in nonwork lives, and highly directive. This is often referred to as a *paternalistic* style of leadership (e.g., Dorfman & Howell, 1988; Dorfman et al., 1997; Kanungo & Mendonca, 1996a), and given the relationship that currently exists between differentiated gender roles and societal economic development (Emrich, Denmark, & Den Hartog, 2004), this masculine term (rather than the more gender-neutral *parentalistic*) seems appropriate. In many of these societies, there is a clear distinction in gender expectations, and the expected role of the leader is much more similar to that of the prototypical father, rather than that of the prototypical mother or of a generic "parent."

In general, in these societies organizations are expected to take care of their workers as well as the workers' families. Leaders in organizations tend to establish close interpersonal relationships with subordinates as well as with people in higher authority. Subordinates expect personalized relationships, protection, close guidance, and supervision. Leaders are willing to assume responsibility for their followers, and in return, demand followers' loyalty.

The paternalistic relationship is strongly hierarchical. As noted above, the superior assumes the role of a father who protects and provides for the subordinate, whereas the subordinate voluntarily submits to the superior, showing loyalty and deference. The leader is assumed to "know what is best" for subordinates, and is expected to guide them in different aspects of life including nonwork-related issues. Such a leader typically shows a strong concern for the well-being of the subordinate as well as his or her family (Aycan, in press).

Paternalistic leadership is, for instance, strong in Mexico (Dorfman et al., 1997). An example described by Martinez and Dorfman (1998) involved an inspirational Mexican entrepreneur who received many positive reactions from subordinates. He was seen as humorous, enthusiastic, and a good speaker, who had brought the company through a severe crisis. An example of his paternalistic behavior was that he involved himself in the private lives of his employees, and he felt that this was required of him because of the employees' personal needs and expectations of him. He was described as taking care of employees in a manner that would be uncharacteristic of a high-level manager in the United States or many other countries. For example, when a secretary remarked to the leader that her husband was going into the hospital for an operation, this leader then called the doctor and discussed the matter with the doctor to make sure that the operation was legitimate (see also Den Hartog et al., 1999).

Other examples of paternalistic behaviors given by Aycan (in press) include attending congratulatory and condolence ceremonies of employees as well as their immediate family members (e.g., weddings and funerals); providing financial assistance (e.g., donations or loans) to employees when in need for expenses such as housing, health care, and children's education expenses; and acting as a mediator in interpersonal conflicts among employees. As stated, in return, employees display high levels of loyalty and deference and are often more willing to perform personal favors for superiors. A problem that can be seen with paternalistic leaders is the differential treatment among workers and the aforementioned related problems such as rivalry and jealousy (see, e.g., Sinha, 1995).

Aycan (in press) noted that paternalism is a leadership style that is not well understood in Western industrialized countries. Individualist values endorsed in many of the more industrialized nations imply a striving for autonomy and self-reliance, which is at odds with the guiding role of the paternalistic leader. The high levels of involvement in subordinates' personal lives would be perceived as intrusive in the Western(ized) countries, and the highly personal nature of the relationship might be interpreted as unprofessional even potentially leading to litigation. However, in many developing countries, reciprocal consent for these paternalistic relationships between superior and subordinate is often found. Employees may sometimes even feel resentment if their managers are not involved in their personal lives and leave them to make important decisions by themselves. Again, such patterns and preferences may change over time.

In the previous section, we discussed how culture might affect leader behavior. Research has shown that being perceived as a leader is a prerequisite for being able to go beyond a formal role in influencing others (Lord & Maher, 1991a). In other words, to be successful, leaders need to first have characteristics or show behavior that people in a given context recognize as "leadership." Thus, perceptual processes on the part of followers play a crucial role in the leadership process as well as in researching leadership. But what characteristics and behavior does one need to show? As is clear from the discussion of culture, attributes and behaviors that are seen as characteristic for effective leaders may also strongly vary in different cultures. In the following section, we explore this topic in more depth.

Leadership Perceptions Across Cultures

People in many societies are frequently confronted with leaders, both at work and in the media. As a result, people form ideas about what makes a leader effective. These ideas are influenced by culture. When thinking of a prototypical leader, a bold, autonomous and decisive hero may typically come to mind in some cultures, whereas different images of ideal leaders may prevail in other cultures. For instance, an ideal leader may be a mature person whose experience and wisdom, rather than speed and boldness, are admired and valued. The evaluation and meaning of leader behaviors and characteristics may also vary across cultures. Relatively few studies have focused explicitly on culture-based differences in leadership prototypes or so-called implicit theories of leadership.

Both J. G. Hunt, Boal, and Sorenson (1990) and Lord and Maher (1991a) proposed that societal culture has an important impact on the content and development of leadership prototypes and implicit leadership theories. Values and ideologies are expected to act as a determinant of culture-specific leadership prototypes. In strong or uniform cultures, prototypes will be widely shared, whereas in a country with a weak culture or multiple subcultures, a wider variance among individual prototypes is expected (Hunt et al., 1990). In other words, one would expect that shared beliefs exist within cultures about what an effective leader is like and that in strong cultures individuals' beliefs are more similar than in weak ones. House et al. (1999) refer to these shared beliefs as culturally endorsed implicit leadership theories (CLTs).

Gerstner and Day (1994) were among the first to focus on cross-cultural comparisons of leadership prototypes. Respondents to their survey assigned prototypicality ratings to 59 leadership attributes. Comparing ratings from American students ($n = 35$) to small samples ($n =$ between 10 and 22) of foreign students from seven countries, they found that the traits considered to be most, moderately, or least characteristic of business leaders varied by respondents' country or culture of origin. The study has obvious limitations that would lead to conservative biases (e.g., small sample sizes, student samples, only foreign students currently in the United States to represent other cultures in the sample, and employing an English-language trait-rating instrument that was not cross-culturally validated). However, reliable differences in leadership perceptions of members of various countries were found that warranted further examination.

Hanges et al. (2000) have recently presented a model suggesting that the influences of societal culture and of leadership are enacted on individuals in very similar ways, through the development of "connectionist schemas." An analogy helps to explain this concept. Imagine a field with grass and weeds that are wildly overgrown. Crossing through the field would be quite a challenge, and after having gone through it once, there is likely to be very little evidence of a path. But if you cross through the field a second time, and then a third time, each time using the same path, eventually that path becomes more worn, and it becomes substantially easier to cross the field using that path than it would be to cross the field using any other path. Analogously, Hanges et al. argue that leadership and culture both serve to give initial guidance to people about how to perceive and how to act in novel situations, and over time these patterns of perception and behavior become well established. It requires less cognitive energy to act and perceive according to the established pattern than it does to venture into new ways of perceiving and acting. This model suggests that this approach can be used to understand the relationship between culture, leadership, follower perceptions, and behavior. The focus is on the importance of the self-concept, arguing that this variable plays a critical role in the relationship between culture and leadership.

An interesting question in this area is whether we can distinguish leader behaviors and characteristics that are universally accepted and effective across cultures as well as behaviors and characteristics that are differentially accepted and effective across cultures. As was seen above, a preference for transformational rather than transactional leadership has been found in many countries (Bass, 1997). Thus, one might ask whether characteristics associated with this kind of leadership are seen as effective across many different cultures.

Universally Endorsed Leader Characteristics

As noted above, the GLOBE Project is the largest cross-cultural study of leadership and culture carried out to date (Dorfman, 1996). One of the early results of the GLOBE study is a report on which various leadership attributes (a) were found to be universally endorsed as contributing to outstanding leadership, (b) were seen as undesirable, or (c) are culturally contingent. For instance, in all participating countries, an outstanding leader is expected to be encouraging, positive, motivational, a confidence builder, and dynamic and to have foresight. Such a leader is excellence oriented, decisive, and intelligent. Outstanding leaders need to be good at team building, communicating, and coordinating. Integrity is also valued as such leaders are trustworthy, just, and honest. Several other attributes were universally viewed as ineffective or, in other words, as impediments to outstanding leadership. These include being noncooperative, ruthless, nonexplicit, a loner, irritable, and dictatorial (Den Hartog et al., 1999).

Culturally Contingent Leader Characteristics

The importance of many other leader attributes was found to vary across cultures. These culturally contingent attributes had high means in some cultures, indicating this characteristic is seen in this context as facilitating outstanding leadership, and low means in other cultures, indicating this characteristic is seen in this context as impeding outstanding leadership. For instance, country means for the attribute "risk taking" ranged from 2.14 to 5.96 on a 7-point scale, for "sensitive" from 1.96 to 6.35, for "class-conscious" from 2.53 to 6.09, and for "autonomous" from 1.63 to 5.17 (see Den Hartog et al., 1999, for the complete list).

Cultural differences clearly play a role here. For instance, differences that were found in appreciation of characteristics such as "subdued" and "enthusiastic" reflect differences in cultural rules regarding the appropriate expression of emotion. In many—predominantly Asian—cultures, displaying emotion is interpreted as a lack of self-control and thus as a sign of weakness. Not showing one's emotions is the norm. In other cultures, such as Latin and Mediterranean cultures, it is hard to be seen as an effective communicator and leader without expressing emotions in a vivid manner. Also, several of the leader attributes that were found to vary across cultures reflect preferences for high power distance versus egalitarianism in society. For example, "status-conscious," "class-conscious," "elitist," and "domineering" are all leader attributes that are appreciated in high power distance but not in low power distance cultures.

Other leader characteristics that varied strongly across cultures in the GLOBE results seem to reflect uncertainty avoidance, which as a culture dimension refers to the tolerance for ambiguity in society. Being risk taking, habitual, procedural, able to anticipate, formal, cautious, and orderly impede outstanding leadership in some countries and enhance it in others. Finally, being autonomous, unique, and independent are found to contribute to outstanding leadership in some, but to be undesirable in other cultures. These attributes seem to reflect different cultural preferences for individualism. These differences show that although images of outstanding leaders around the world share some characteristics, there are also vast differences in what is seen as desirable for leaders (Den Hartog et al., 1999).

Variations in the Enactment of Universal Leader Characteristics

The characteristics described above show a "universal" appreciation of certain leadership attributes and a more varied appreciation of others. However, as was stressed before, even when attributes are universally valued, this does not mean such attributes will necessarily be enacted in the same way across cultures. The behavior that reflects an attribute may vary in different contexts. Dickson, Hanges, and Lord (2001) addressed this point in their discussion of the advancements in the understanding of the various meanings of "universal" findings. Of most relevance to the present discussion is the distinction made by Lonner (1980) between simple universals, in which the principle and enactment are the same across contexts, and variform universals (in which the principle is consistent across contexts but the enactment differs).

A specific example of a variform universal is that "visionary" is seen as a positive leader attribute in most cultures, but what one needs to do to be seen as visionary varies from one culture to another. For instance, as was mentioned before, effective styles of communicating visions may differ. Whereas macho-oratory is linked to effective communication of visions in some cultures, Fu (2003) states that a vision in China is normally expressed in a nonaggressive manner. Confucian values (e.g., kindness, benevolence) may play a role in making people wary of leaders giving pompous talks without engaging in specific action, and lead the people to dislike leaders who are arrogant and distant. Chokkar (2003) holds that although Indian leaders must be flexible in this regard, bold, assertive styles are generally preferred to quiet and nurturing styles (Den Hartog et al., 1999).

Another example is that some authors hold that a certain amount of risk taking is part of transformational leadership. The GLOBE results suggest that risk taking is not universally valued as contributing to outstanding leadership. Moreover, what is considered risk taking in one context may not be in another. The Mexican entrepreneur described by Martinez and Dorfman (1998), for instance, appointed someone from the Mexican lower class as member of the administrative staff, despite the objections of the stockholders. He did this on the basis of her hard work, education, and expertise. Whereas in the United States or many other countries one would not find anything particularly strange about this, a person's social status is extremely important in Mexico. Thus, such a behavior by the Mexican entrepreneur was seen as quite risky, exemplifying the fact that the same behavior can take on a very different meaning in cultures that differ in their core shared values.

Leadership Profiles and Culture Clusters

The GLOBE findings demonstrate that members of cultures share a common frame of reference regarding effective leadership. Above, we showed leader attributes that were universally appreciated and attributes that were endorsed in some, but not in other, cultures. However, the GLOBE data were not only analyzed at the attribute (i.e., item) level. The leadership attributes were statistically grouped into 21 "first-order" basic factors or dimensions that were then consolidated into 6 "second-order" global leadership dimensions (see Hanges & Dickson, 2004). These 6 dimensions were (a) charismatic/value-based leadership (e.g., being visionary, inspirational, having integrity and decisive elements), (b) team-oriented leadership (e.g., such as acting collaborative, integrating, and diplomatic), (c) participative leadership (e.g., being nonautocratic and allowing participation in decision making), (d) autonomous leadership (e.g., being individualistic, independent, and unique), (e) humane leadership (e.g., modesty, tolerance, and sensitivity), and (f) self-protective leadership (e.g., being self-centered, status conscious, and a face-saver).

Does the endorsement of these dimensions differ in different parts of the worlds? Scholars have used different forces in grouping countries into similar clusters, including geographic proximity, mass migrations and ethnic social capital, religious and linguistic communality, social variables such as attitudes and values, and economic or sociopolitical development (Gupta, Hanges, & Dorfman, 2002). GLOBE results indicate the presence of 10 meaningful clusters of cultures, based on the GLOBE culture dimensions described earlier. The meta-Western region consisted of the Nordic Europe, Germanic Europe, Anglo, Latin America, and Latin Europe clusters, and the meta-Eastern region consisted of Southern Asia, Confucian Asia, Central/Eastern Europe, Sub-Saharan Africa, and the Middle East (Arabic) cluster (Gupta et al., 2002; refer also to the March 2002 special issue of *Journal World Business* for further results). Leadership profiles were developed for these 10 culture clusters using the 6 leadership dimensions. These culturally endorsed leadership profiles highlight elements of leadership perceived to be culturally common as well as those that are culturally unique (see Dorfman, Hanges, & Brodbeck, 2004).

Charismatic and team-oriented leadership dimensions were strongly positively perceived in all 10 clusters. Looking at the absolute scores, this was most strongly so in the Anglo, Southern Asian, and Latin American clusters and somewhat less so in the Middle Eastern cluster. Humane leadership contributed somewhat to effective leadership, but was not nearly as strongly endorsed as charismatic- or the team-oriented leadership. Southern Asia, Anglo, and Sub-Saharan Africa scored somewhat higher and Latin and Nordic Europe somewhat lower on the humane leadership dimension. Autonomous leadership was often reported among the 10 clusters to be about neutral regarding its contribution to effective leadership, but for some of the 62 cultures (and 10 clusters) it was reported to be a factor that contributed slightly (e.g., Eastern and Germanic Europe), and for some others a factor that inhibited slightly (e.g., Latin Europe, Middle East).

Much greater variation among cultures and culture clusters was found for the two remaining CLT dimensions. The self-protective CLT dimension was perceived to be an inhibitor of effective leadership everywhere. However, it was seen as more inhibiting in the Nordic, Germanic, and Anglo clusters and less so in the Middle Eastern, Confucian, and Southern Asian clusters. Participative leadership was reported to contribute to effective leadership for all culture clusters; however, considerable variation exists. The GLOBE results suggest that the Germanic, Anglo, and Nordic clusters were particularly attuned to participative leadership, whereas the Middle Eastern, East European, Confucian, and Southern Asian clusters were not (see, e.g., Dorfman et al., 2004).

Whereas the results show that values characterizing a society clearly have a major impact on the shared perceptions of effective leader behaviors, the GLOBE Project is one of the first studies to allow large-scale assessment of the relative impact of *societal* culture as well as *organizational* culture on these perceptions. For example, the performance orientation of culture was related to charismatic/value-based leadership and participative leadership at both the organizational and societal levels of culture. In other words, societies as well as organizations valuing a strong performance orientation seem to look to charismatic leaders with the ability to paint the picture of an ambitious and exciting future. They also value a leader who involves others in building this future in a participative manner (Dorfman & Javidan, 2004). In many cases, the impact of organizational culture on the leadership belief system (CLT) was at least as strong as that of societal culture (Dorfman et al., 2004). Thus, we think it is important to include here at least a brief discussion of the impact of organizational culture on leadership perceptions and behaviors.

Organizational Culture

As noted before, *culture* refers to a set of shared values that are held by members of a collectivity, and this is not limited to the societal level. Where leadership in organizations is concerned, organizational culture is also relevant. Denison (1996) described organizational culture as follows:

> *Culture* refers to the deep structure of organizations, which is rooted in the values, beliefs, and assumptions held by organization members. Meaning is established through socialization to a variety of identity groups that converge in the workplace. Interaction produces a symbolic world that gives culture both a great stability and a certain precarious and fragile nature rooted in the dependence of the system on individual cognition and action. (p. 624)

Clearly, the values that characterize a society are likely to be reflected in the values held by members of an organization. Dickson, BeShears, and Gupta (2004) have described several mechanisms by which this influence is likely to occur. These include the simple fact that people who make up organizations come from some societal culture, and thus are likely to hold the values that characterize that society; the pressures placed on organizations to conform to the values of the society, either through subtle rewards or perceived advantages for conformity and punishments for nonconformity (i.e., coercive, normative, and mimetic isomorphic pressures); resource dependency pressures in which conformity is required to acquire and retain necessary physical and human resources; and social network pressures, through which the patterns of interactions and dependence relationships compel organizations toward adopting/reflecting societal-shared values.

Several authors have argued that congruence between societal culture and organizational culture is desirable and important for strong organizational performance (e.g., Newman & Nollen, 1996). However, it is important to note that there is substantial variation in the organizational cultures of even successful organizations within any given society.

Organizational Culture and Leadership

Leaders of organizations embed and transmit culture in the thinking, feeling, and behavior of the group. Schein (1992) holds that one of the most decisive functions of leadership is the creation, the management, and sometimes even the destruction of organizational culture. Contrarily, in line with the debate on the measurement of culture, "most anthropologists would find the idea that leaders create culture preposterous: leaders do not create culture; it emerges from the collective social interaction of groups and communities" (Meek, 1988, p. 459).

We disagree with Meek's position, at least as it applies to organizational culture.[1] At the societal level, it is generally true that most people do not choose their societal culture—they remain a part of the culture into which they were born. However, people actively seek out and choose the organizations to which they belong. In other words, organizational members are not randomly assigned to organizations—they choose the organizations to which they apply, and organizations choose the applicants that they wish to hire, and these decisions are at least to some degree based on the perception of "fit," or the perceived congruence between the values of the organization and the values of the employee (Kristof, 1996; Schneider, 1987). Thus, the leader initially creates something, which is differentially attractive to outsiders, who then choose to attempt to join or not attempt to join. Eventually, the interactions of the individuals in the organization refine and modify the initial culture established by the organization's founder, but the founder does nonetheless establish the initial culture (Giberson, Resick, & Dickson, 2002; Schneider, Goldstein, & Smith, 1995).

We thus focus more on the view taken by Schein (1992), who stated that "leadership is originally the source of the beliefs and values that get a group moving to deal with its internal and external problems. If what a leader proposes works and continues to work, what once was only the leader's assumption gradually comes to be a shared assumption" (pp. 26–27). This view highlights the impact the founder of the organization can have on organizational culture. For example, Dickson, Smith, Grojean, and Ehrhart (2002) argued that the ethical climate in a firm is linked to personal values and motives of founders and early leaders. The founder plays a crucial role in culture formation by choosing the basic mission, the group members, the environmental context in which the new group will operate, and the initial responses the group makes in order to succeed and integrate within this environment. Culture can thus spring from three sources: (a) the beliefs, values, and assumptions of founders of organizations; (b) the learning experiences of group members as their organization evolves, and (c) new beliefs, values, and assumptions brought by new members and leaders (Schein, 1992).

According to Schein (1992), leaders have several primary "culture embedding" mechanisms. These include what leaders regularly pay attention to, measure, and control; how leaders react to organizational crises and critical incidents; their role modeling, teaching, and coaching; and the observed criteria by which leaders allocate resources, rewards, and status as well as recruit, select, promote, retire, or excommunicate organizational members. He also described several secondary "culture articulation and reinforcement" mechanisms. These are secondary, in the sense that they work only when they are in line with the primary mechanisms. These secondary mechanisms include organizational design, structure, systems, and procedures; stories, legends, and myths about people and events; rites and rituals; design of physical space (e.g., buildings); and formal statements of organizational values, philosophy, or creed.

Schein (1992) suggested a special impact of charismatic leaders on organizational culture: "The simplest explanation of how leaders get their message across is through charisma in that one of the main elements of that mysterious quality undoubtedly is a leader's ability to communicate major assumptions and values in a vivid and clear manner" (p. 229). According to Bass (1988), charismatic leaders create new cultures for their subordinates by creating new meaning for them.

Leadership as management of meaning is an important notion where the relationship between leadership and culture is concerned (P. B. Smith & Peterson, 1988; see also Bolman & Deal, 1997; Weick, 1979). The process of meaning making is enhanced by the use of "framing" or "frame alignment" (Goffman, 1974). Frame alignment refers to the linkage of individual and leader interpretative orientations, in such a way that some set of followers' interests, values, and beliefs and the leader's activities goals and ideology become congruent and complementary (House & Podsakoff, 1994; Shamir, House, & Arthur, 1993).

Frames themselves are symbolic structures people use to make sense of personal and social experiences and to guide action (Conger, 1989). Frames or "schemata of interpretation" enable individuals to locate, perceive, and label occurrences within their life and the world at large. By rendering events or occurrences meaningful, frames function to organize experience and guide action, whether individual or collective (Goffman, 1974; House & Podsakoff, 1994). By formulating a vision, a charismatic leader engages in framing, thereby placing the vision in a certain context and interpreting reality for listeners and giving meaning to events. Pfeffer (1981) viewed organizations as systems of completely or partly shared meanings. Meanings can be attached to the organization's purposes and to its goals, ideologies, and values as well as to its beliefs about the ways in which the organization is to accomplish these purposes. It is more difficult for people to change goals and values than to change beliefs about the best way to accomplish goals. Pfeffer asserted that the role of leaders in organizations includes influencing the meanings and values placed on particular ways of approaching goals. The role of leaders is thus highly symbolic in this view.

Trice and Beyer (1991, 1993) presented a model of cultural leadership. They pointed out that literature on cultural leadership emphasizes cultural innovation, either founding an organization and creating a new culture or drastically changing the existing culture. In the literature, culture initiation and change are often associated with transformational leadership or charismatic leadership in crisis situations. However, they also call into attention cultural maintenance leadership, which is very important for effectiveness of organizations in more stable environments.

According to Trice and Beyer (1991, 1993), cultural innovation and cultural maintenance leaders have several features in common. Both types of leaders create an impression of competence, articulate ideologies, communicate strong convictions, show confidence in followers and high expectations, serve as role models, and strengthen follower commitment to the organization. However, these types of leadership differ in other areas. Cultural maintenance leadership is aimed at reinforcing the existing values and traditions insofar as they are effective to help the organization reach its goals. If changes in strategies are made, they are incremental changes. Cultural innovation leadership, on the other hand, is aimed at creating a new culture or making drastic changes in the existing culture. These leaders articulate a radical ideology with new values and strategies, often to deal with serious crises. Cultural innovation leaders need to be more dramatic and expressive than cultural maintenance leaders and must show more extraordinary qualities in dealing with crises. The attributions of charisma that could follow from those qualities can form an extra power base that helps in implementing new strategies and dealing with opponents of change.

Bass (1990) argued that leaders can function as founders of cultures or counter-cultures, as culture builders, and as agents of change in the dominant culture. Trice and Beyer added, to this list, the leader's role in maintaining culture. However, precisely *how* the content or nature of cultures is related to leadership is not immediately clear from these roles. Kerr and Slocum (1987), for instance, described two types of corporate reward systems that give rise to different cultures ("clan" and "market" cultures), and thus characteristically lead to different leadership experiences. This example demonstrates that besides their role in creating, changing, or maintaining culture, the content of culture also shapes how followers experience leaders and which types of leaders are effective. Schein (1992) ironically suggested that often culture manages management more than management manages culture, especially as organizations approach organizational midlife.

Strong cultures could inhibit or promote the effects of leaders' efforts, depending on whether the influence attempts are in line with the dominant values in that culture. Rubin and Berlew (1984), for example, reported that a strong organizational culture with values and internal guidelines for more autonomy at lower levels in the organization can prevent top management from increasing personal power at the expense of middle management.

Whereas some theorists have focused on identifying the various levels of organizational cultures, others have focused on developing taxonomies of organizational cultures. An example of organizational culture taxonomy development comes from the Focus Group, a group of researchers from 14 countries, who developed an organizational culture questionnaire based on Quinn's (1988) competing values model (Van Muijen et al., 1999). Four culture orientations are distinguished that are based on two dimensions: internal versus external focus, and flexibility versus control. "Support" (internal/flexible) is characterized by concepts such as mutual trust, cooperation, team spirit, commitment, and individual growth. A person- or relationship-oriented leadership style is expected. "Rules" (internal/control) is characterized by respect for authority, procedures, division of work, and hierarchical communication. Leadership is primarily procedure oriented. "Goals" (external/control) emphasizes rationality, performance indicators, accomplishment, accountability, and contingent reward. A task-oriented style of leadership is likely. "Innovation" (external/flexible) emphasizes creativity, openness to change, searching for new information in the environment, anticipation, and experimentation (Van Muijen et al., 1999). Change-oriented leadership (cf. Ekvall & Arvonen, 1991) seems most likely to fit the innovative culture.

Den Hartog, Van Muijen, and Koopman (1996) linked this model to transformational and transactional leadership in five organizations. They built on Bass's (1985) speculations that transactional leadership would fit better in more well-ordered and stable environments—such as in bureaucratic organizations—than in adhocracies and organic organizations. In contrast, Bass speculated that transformational leadership would be preferred in more innovative, flexible, and supportive environments. As expected, Den Hartog et al. found that the relationship between transformational leadership and the innovative and supportive orientations was higher than that between transactional leadership and those orientations and that the relationship between transactional leadership and the goal and rules orientations was higher than that for transformational leadership.

Conclusions

In this chapter on leadership and culture, we aimed to show that we should not take for granted that models and theories developed in one place will work similarly in another. We described culture at both the societal and organizational levels and showed how culture can affect implicit leadership theories and behavior. We showed that even when preferred and effective leader characteristics and behaviors are similar, their enactment might differ across cultures. As P. B. Smith and Bond (1993) noted, if we wish to make statements about "universal" aspects of social behavior, they need to be phrased in highly abstract ways. Conversely, if we wish to highlight the meaning of these generalizations in culturally specific ways, then we need to refer to more precisely specified events or behaviors. Similarly, we showed that leadership could be conceived in culturally universal or specific terms. We also highlighted the developing world, because most theories presented in the research literature tend to have more bearing on the developed or Western world.

Clearly, more research on leadership in different cultures is needed. Several types of studies would be useful. Large-scale comparative studies involving comparable samples from many different countries are of interest. Preferably, such studies can be repeated over time to gain more insight in the changing nature of leadership. However, at the other extreme, more indigenous, local, and rich studies, yielding more culture-specific models are also of interest.

We did not describe in detail the many potential problems and methodological pitfalls that need to be addressed in any cross-cultural research endeavor, because a full review of this topic is beyond the scope of this chapter. Measurement invariance is one such issue (refer to Antonakis, Schriesheim, Donovan, Gopalakrishna-Pillai, Pellegrini, & Rossomme, Chapter 3, this volume, for issues regarding measurement equivalence). Another potential obstacle is the problem of translation in measurement. How do we ensure that respondents interpret questions similarly? How do we know constructs have the same meaning? How are results influenced in cases where respondents complete questionnaires in a language that is not their native language? Sampling provides another interesting challenge in cross-cultural research. When interested in societal culture, using national borders as cultural boundaries may not be appropriate in countries that have large subcultures. In large, multicultural countries such as India, the United States, and China, it is not even clear which sample would be most representative. Nevertheless, the samples from all countries need to be relatively homogeneous within countries to be able to interpret differences that are found.

Also, many studies run the risk of committing the "ecological fallacy." This occurs if we assume isomorphic relationships between variables across differing levels of analysis, such as assuming characteristics and/or relationships existing at the cultural level will automatically apply to other levels of analysis, such as the individual. What applies for individuals may or may not apply for groups and vice versa (e.g., Dorfman et al., 2004). The ecological fallacy problem can be minimized by paying careful attention to the level of analysis issue in theory building, and in collecting and analyzing data. For instance, in questionnaire research aimed at the culture level, culture items can be phrased to explicitly refer to groups, organizations, or societies rather than to individuals. Whether individual responses can then be aggregated to group levels can then be tested statistically (refer to Antonakis et al., Chapter 3, this volume).

These examples of methodological challenges show that studying leadership in different cultures is not easy. However, well-designed studies will help develop a better understanding of the differences and similarities in what is acceptable and effective organizational leadership around the world. Clearly, this is a topic that is crucial in the increasingly international world of business.

Note

---

1. Editors' note: Sashkin (in Chapter 8, this volume) makes a similar point arguing that leaders are creators and shapers of culture.

CHAPTER 12

Women and Men as Leaders

Alice H. Eagly

Linda L. Carli

O ur consideration of the effects of gender on leadership begins by acknowledging the profound divide in power and authority that separates women from men. Men are in charge of the most consequential activities of most organizations and governments. In the hierarchical structures of contemporary nations, the proportion of women decreases at higher levels, until at the highest level women are unusual, although not entirely absent. This patriarchal system in which men have more power and exert more influence than women do is not rare in world societies. Although in societies with simple socioeconomic structures power can be quite evenly divided between women and men, even in these nonpatriarchal societies men still monopolize public leadership (M. K. Whyte, 1978; Wood & Eagly, 2002).

In discussing women's underrepresentation in leadership roles, our chapter reveals the details of the effects of gender on leadership. Thus, in explaining women's lesser occupancy of high-level leadership positions, we focus on four general types of explanations. The first type is that women's lesser investments in human capital (e.g., education, work experience) account for leadership differentials. The second class of explanations considers whether women's style of leading is different from men's. Any such differences might advantage or disadvantage women, depending on their implications for leaders' effectiveness. The third type of explanations considers the evolutionary psychology argument that it is in the nature of men but not women to be motivated to lead and dominate others. Our fourth category of explanations focuses on prejudice and discrimination. Before evaluating these potential causes of the relative lack of women in positions of power and authority, we present some facts that allow readers to evaluate the distribution of women and men in leadership roles.

Representation of Women and Men in Leadership Roles

Even in postindustrial societies, political, corporate, and other leadership at the highest levels has remained largely a male prerogative. Although women have gained considerable access to supervisory and middle management positions, they remain scarce as elite leaders and top executives. For example, in the United States, women constitute 46% of the census category of executives, managers, and administrators (U.S. Bureau of Labor Statistics, 2002), but in the companies of the Fortune 500 constitute only 16% of all corporate officers, 10% of top corporate officers, and 1% of chief executive officers (CEOs) (Catalyst, 2002, 2003). Statistics for women in the ranks of corporate executives are very similar in Canada (Catalyst, 2000) and other industrialized nations (Wirth, 2001). Moreover, less than 1% of CEOs of the Global Fortune 500 are women (Fortune, 2003).

Women are also underrepresented in government leadership roles, especially in the more powerful elected positions. In the United States, 14% of senators, 14% of congressional representatives, and 12% of state governors are women (Center for American Woman and Politics, 2003). Still, women's political leadership in the United States and many nations is increasing (Adler, 1999; United Nations, 2002). Women occupy 22% of the seats in state legislatures in the United States (Center for American Woman and Politics, 2003) and 25% of the senior executive service of the federal government (U.S. Office of Personnel Management, 2001).

Women are especially underrepresented in leadership roles that provide substantial authority over other people. Women's occupational disadvantage in the United States is not in prestige because women are well represented in many professional roles that confer moderately high prestige (e.g., teacher, registered nurse, social worker). However, men more often occupy positions conferring decision-making authority and the ability to influence others' pay or promotions (P. B. Smith, 2002). Female managers have less authority than male managers do, even when rank and tenure in organizations are held constant (Reskin & Ross, 1995). Female managers, compared with their male counterparts at the same level, also have less access to the demanding responsibilities and complex challenges that are likely precursors of promotion to positions of greater authority (Lyness & Thompson, 1997; Ohlott, Ruderman, & McCauley, 1994). This exclusion of women from leadership roles is not confined to organizations. Also, in initially leaderless groups studied by researchers, men, more than women, emerged as group leaders

(Eagly & Karau, 1991). Even in female-dominated organizations and professions, men ascend to leadership faster than women do—a phenomenon known as the "glass escalator" (e.g., Maume, 1999; C. L. Williams, 1995).

Sex Differences in Human Capital Investments

A popular explanation for the gender gap in workplace leadership is that women's human capital investment in education, training, and work experience is lower than men's. However, with respect to education, this argument has little force. In the United States and many industrialized countries, women now attain university degrees at higher rates than men do (United Nations Development Programme, 2002). In the United States, women possess 51% of bachelor's degrees and 45% of advanced degrees (U.S. Bureau of the Census, 2000) and have been obtaining more bachelor's degrees than men since 1981–1982 (U.S. Department of Education, 2001). Also, despite the fact that employed women were more educated than employed men were during some periods, such as during the 1950s, at no time have women's salaries and representation in workplace leadership roles reached parity with men's (O'Neil, 1985).

There is also no evidence that employed women feel less identified with their jobs or less committed to employment than employed men. Research assessing identification with various life roles reveals that employed men and women rank their role as worker similarly and both consider it to be subordinate to their roles as partners and parents (Thoits, 1992). Controlling for job attributes and human capital variables, women are as identified as men with their employment roles, feeling as committed as men to paid work (Bielby & Bielby, 1989). Also, in spite of women's greater domestic responsibilities, they report putting in more effort on their jobs than do men (Bielby & Bielby, 1988).

In human capital discussions, most attention has focused on women's greater involvement in domestic work, which may result in their acquiring less training than men do, contributing less effort to paid work, and experiencing more interruptions in their work history. There is little doubt that women spend more time than men do on housework and child care (Bianchi, 2000; Pleck, 1997; Robinson & Godbey, 1997) and that this differential is greater for people who have children 18 years of age or younger (Bianchi, Milkie, Sayer, & Robinson, 2000). Because the custodial care aspect of domestic work (e.g., laundry, cooking) is typically obligatory and routine, women tend not to opt out of such responsibilities because of time constraints or employment obligations. Rather than reduce time spent with children, women sacrifice personal time, sleep, or other housework to accomplish these chores. So it is not surprising that in industrialized countries an inverse relation exists between the women's hours of work outside of the home and the number of children they have (e.g., Angrist & Evans, 1998). This gender differential in parenting contributes to women's lesser job experience and more frequent job interruptions. Mothers are less likely to be employed than are women without children and, when employed, tend to work fewer hours. In contrast, fathers are more likely to be employed than are men without children and spend more hours on the job (Kaufman & Uhlenberg, 2000). This division of labor reflects the cultural association of the father role with being a good provider and the mother role with nurturing and custodial care.

A common presumption is that women have less job experience because they quit more often than men do (e.g., Almer, Hopper, & Kaplan, 1998). Research on voluntary turnover, however, has revealed mixed results. Some studies have relied on the National Longitudinal Survey of Youth, a nationally representative survey of work experiences based on annual interviews of more than 12,000 young workers. Using this sample, Lynch (1991) found no differences in the frequency with which men and women quit the first job they obtained after exiting school. Contrarily, Keith and McWilliams (1997) found that women quit their jobs more often than men do during the first 3 years of postschooling employment. Although an early meta-analytic review of relevant studies reported greater turnover among women (Cotton & Tuttle, 1986), this review did not distinguish voluntary from involuntary turnover.

A subsequent meta-analysis by Griffeth, Hom, and Gaertner (2000) focusing only on voluntary turnover found a significant but slightly greater turnover among men (P. W. Hom, personal communication, February 24, 2003). Moreover, a study of more than 26,000 full-time managers for a multinational financial services organization revealed that the women had slightly lower voluntary turnover rates than the men, both with and without the introduction of controls for human capital variables (Lyness & Judiesch, 2001). Nonetheless, although most voluntary turnover is unrelated to family obligations (Keith & McWilliams, 1997, 1999; Lyness & Judiesch, 2001), women leave work for family obligations more often than men do (e.g., Lynch, 1991).

Klerman and Leibowitz (1999) used data from the National Longitudinal Survey of Youth to disentangle the effects on turnover of parenthood and part-time versus full-time employment. They found that women who had worked part-time before becoming mothers exhibited higher turnover after childbirth than did women who had worked full-time, over 60% of whom returned to their jobs within 18 months. Indeed, the likelihood of a full-time female employee remaining full-time in her job 18 months after giving birth was 83% of the likelihood of a childless woman remaining full-time in her job over the same time period. Thus, in the United States, the majority of full-time employed women retained their jobs after becoming mothers.

Despite the lack of consistent evidence that women leave jobs more often than men do, women's turnover tends to reduce their job advancement. For example, Keith and McWilliams (1999) reported that, although quitting a job to take a different job typically led to increased pay and advancement, quitting because of family obligations led to income loss. In their study, women thus experienced greater losses after changing jobs than men did, in part because more women changed jobs for family obligations. Women's tendency to spend less time searching for another job also accounted for some of this sex difference in outcomes, but even controlling for this, women experienced fewer benefits from job mobility. Women also experience income loss when they return to work following interruptions in their employment (Stratton, 1995), losses that persist for many years after their reentry into the labor force (J. P. Jacobsen & Levin, 1995).

Employed women suffer income loss with motherhood. Budig and England (2001) used data from the National Longitudinal Survey of Youth to examine the contribution of job characteristics and human capital variables to this income loss, which amounted to 7% per child. Although job characteristics, such as how "woman friendly," demanding, or female-dominated the job was, accounted for little of the income penalty, about one-third of it was attributable to the lesser experience of mothers, who more often worked part-time, took breaks from employment, and had less seniority. Two-thirds of this income loss thus remained unexplained.

A more subtle human capital argument is the "female choice" proposition that employed women do not seek leadership positions because they believe that the demands of such positions would compromise their family responsibilities. Especially employed mothers may thus be satisfied with *mommy track* (Ehrlich, 1989) positions, willingly ceding leadership to men. Yet considerable evidence argues against the proposition that family and domestic responsibilities cause employed women to avoid leadership responsibility (see P. B. Smith, 2002). Specifically, the assumption of self-selection predicts that the marriage, the presence of children, and inegalitarian household arrangements depress women's workplace authority relative to that of men. Such findings are not usually obtained. For example, a large cross-national study of the United States, Canada, the United Kingdom, Australia, Sweden, Norway, and Japan did not support this self-selection hypothesis, except to some degree in Canada (Wright, Baxter, & Birkelund, 1995).

Overall, one human capital explanation for the gender wage gap has received some support; namely, that women have less job experience and consistency of employment than men do. O'Neill and Polachek (1993) thus attributed women's workplace advancement in large part to their increased work experience, because changes in women's experience have covaried with changes in the wage gap. They found that during the 1970s and 1980s, women's lesser experience accounted for 21% of the wage gap. Such findings suggest that trade-offs between women's domestic work and their employment contribute to their lack of workplace advancement. Nevertheless, the inability of human capital variables to account for the majority of the gender wage gap leaves ample room for other causal factors. The overriding importance of other factors is further suggested by evidence that women receive substantially smaller gains in authority than men do for similar human capital investments (see P. B. Smith, 2002). Whereas gains in human capital benefit women's wages, the benefits to their power and authority are muted. Such findings raise questions about the adequacy of women's performance in leadership roles as well as about possible resistance to women's rise in organizational hierarchies.

The Leadership Styles of Women and Men

The question of whether male and female leaders behave differently is usually discussed in terms of leadership styles, with style defined as relatively stable patterns of behavior displayed by leaders. Although leaders vary their behavior in response to situational contingencies, they still have typical modes of interacting with their superiors and subordinates. Because styles are one determinant of leaders' effectiveness, any sex difference in style could affect people's views about whether women should advance to higher positions in organizational hierarchies.

Experts who have written about this topic have differed sharply in their conclusions. The advocates of sex differences include several writers of trade books who based their claims on personal experience in organizations and on informal surveys and interviews of managers. These writers have argued that women's leadership style is less hierarchical, more collaborative, and more oriented to enhancing others' self-worth than men's (e.g., Helgesen, 1990; Rosener, 1995). In contrast, social scientists typically claimed that such sex differences are nonexistent or unimportant (e.g., Powell, 1990). However, research has revealed more complex findings than acknowledged by the advocates of difference or the advocates of similarity.

Research on Comparing Leadership Styles of Women and Men

Most research on leadership style conducted prior to 1990 distinguished between *task-oriented* style, defined as behavior related to accomplishing assigned tasks, and *interpersonally oriented* style, defined as behavior related to maintaining interpersonal relationships. Bales (1950) introduced this distinction, and many other researchers developed it (e.g., Hemphill & Coons, 1957). A somewhat less popular distinction was between leaders who (a) behave democratically and allow subordinates to participate in decision making or (b) behave autocratically and discourage subordinates from such participation. This distinction, labeled *democratic* versus *autocratic* leadership or *participative* versus *directive* leadership, was introduced in classic experimental studies of leadership style (Lewin & Lippitt, 1938) and developed by a number of researchers (e.g., Vroom & Yetton, 1973). To assess sex differences and similarities in these styles, Eagly and Johnson (1990) reviewed 162 studies that provided quantitative comparisons of women and men on relevant measures.

This meta-analysis (Eagly & Johnson, 1990) of studies from the period 1961–1987 found that leadership styles were somewhat gender-stereotypic in laboratory experiments using student participants and assessment students using participants not selected for occupancy of leadership roles (e.g., samples of employees or students in university business programs). In this research, women, more than men, manifested relatively interpersonally oriented and democratic styles, and men, more than women, manifested relatively task-oriented and autocratic styles. In contrast, sex differences were more limited in organizational studies, which assessed managers' styles. The only difference obtained between female and male managers was that women adopted a somewhat more democratic (or participative style) and a less autocratic (or directive) style than men did. This finding, which was based on 23 data sets and a heterogeneous set of measuring instruments, produced a relatively small mean effect size ($d = 0.22$). Nonetheless, 92% of the available comparisons went in the direction of a more democratic or participative style among women. In contrast, male and female managers did not differ in their tendencies to use interpersonally oriented and task-oriented styles. A subsequent meta-analysis that surveyed studies published between 1987 and 2000 produced similar findings (van Engen, 2001).

In the 1980s and 1990s, many researchers began to make new distinctions about leadership styles to identify the types of leadership that are attuned to the conditions faced by contemporary organizations. Their emphasis was on leadership that is future oriented rather than present oriented and that strengthens organizations by inspiring followers' commitment and ability to contribute creatively to organizations. This approach initially emerged in Burns's (1978) delineation of a type of leadership that he labeled *transformational*. As subsequently elaborated by Bass (1985, 1998), transformational leadership involves establishing oneself as a role model by gaining followers' trust and confidence. Transformational leaders state future goals, develop plans to achieve those goals, and innovate, even when their organization is generally successful. By mentoring and empowering followers, such leaders encourage them to develop their full potential and thus to contribute more effectively to their organization. Other researchers studying some of these same qualities labeled this future-oriented, empowering style as *charismatic leadership* (see Conger & Kanungo, 1998).

Burns (1978) and other researchers (e.g., Avolio, 1999; Bass, 1998) contrasted transformational leaders to *transactional* leaders, who appeal to subordinates' self-interest by establishing exchange relationships with them. This type of leadership involves managing in the conventional sense of clarifying subordinates' responsibilities, rewarding them for meeting objectives, and correcting them for failing to meet objectives. Although empirically separable, transformational and transactional leadership styles can both contribute to effective leadership. In addition to these two styles, these researchers distinguished a *laissez-faire* style that is marked by a general failure to take responsibility for managing. The components of transformational and transactional leadership as well as laissez-faire leadership are most commonly assessed by the Multifactor Leadership Questionnaire, known as the MLQ (Antonakis, Avolio, & Sivasubramaniam, 2003). As shown in Table 12.1, this instrument generally represents transformational leadership by five subscales, transactional leadership by three subscales, and laissez-faire leadership by one scale.

Eagly, Johannesen-Schmidt, and van Engen (2003) carried out a meta-analysis of 45 studies that compared male and female managers on measures of transformational, transactional, and laissez-faire leadership styles. Although many types of organizations were represented, the majority were either business or educational organizations. This meta-analysis also included a large study conducted to provide norms and psychometric standards for the MLQ (Center for Leadership Studies, 2000), as well as many studies conducted within specific organizations or groups of organizations. The measures of leadership style were completed by the leaders themselves or by their subordinates, peers, or superiors.

In general, Eagly et al.'s (2003) meta-analysis revealed that female leaders were more transformational than were male leaders and also engaged in more of the contingent reward behaviors that are one component of transactional leadership. Among the five subscales of transformational leadership, women

Table 12.1   Definitions of Transformational, Transactional, and Laissez-Faire
Leadership Styles in the Multifactor Leadership Questionnaire (MLQ)

Type of MLQ Scale and Subscale	Description of Leadership Style
Transformational	
Idealized influence (attribute)	Demonstrates qualities that motivate respect and pride from association with him or her
Idealized influence (behavior)	Communicates values, purpose, and importance of organization's mission
Inspirational motivation	Exhibits optimism and excitement about goals and future states
Intellectual stimulation	Examines new perspectives for solving problems and completing tasks
Individualized consideration	Focuses on development and mentoring of followers and attends to their individual needs
Transactional	
Contingent reward	Provides rewards for satisfactory performance by followers
Active management-by-exception	Attends to followers' mistakes and failures to meet standards
Passive management-by-exception	Waits until problems become severe before attending to them and intervening
Laissez-faire	Exhibits frequent absence and lack of involvement during critical junctures

SOURCE: Eagly, Johannesen-Schmidt, and van Engen (2003). Copyright © 2003 by the
American Psychological Association. Reprinted with permission.

most exceeded men on the individualized consideration subscale that identifies
supportive, encouraging treatment of subordinates. Also, male leaders were
more likely to manifest two other aspects of transactional leadership (active and
passive management-by-exception) and laissez-faire leadership, although fewer
studies had assessed these aspects of style. These differences between male and
female leaders were small, but prevailed in the meta-analysis as a whole as well
as in auxiliary analyses of the large MLQ norming study (see also Eagly &
Johannesen-Schmidt, 2001), a heterogeneous group of other studies that used
the MLQ measures, and a smaller group of studies that used a variety of other
measures of the styles.

In summary, meta-analyses of leadership styles found that gender-stereotypic
sex differences tended to prevail among leaders who were somewhat arbitrarily
thrust into leader roles in laboratory experiments. Under these conditions, women
attended somewhat more to interpersonal considerations and men more narrowly
to task-relevant considerations. Without selection or preparation for a longer-term
leadership role, leaders rely to some extent on gender roles to guide their behavior.

Nonetheless, among managers, some small sex differences have been detected, but in a narrower range of leadership behaviors. Women's style tends to be more democratic and participative, compared with men's more autocratic and directive style. Also, female managers tend to adopt a transformational style and use more rewards to encourage appropriate subordinate behavior. In contrast, men, more than women, attended to subordinates' failures to meet standards and displayed the more problematic styles that involve avoiding solving problems until they become acute and being absent or uninvolved at critical times.

Leadership Style and Leaders' Effectiveness

Would these stylistic differences advantage or disadvantage women in leadership roles? The implications of female managers' relatively democratic and participative style are not clear-cut because this style's effectiveness is contingent on various features of group and organizational environments (Foels, Driskell, Mullen, & Salas, 2000; Gastil, 1994; Vroom & Yetton, 1973). Under some circumstances, democratic and participative styles are effective, and, under other circumstances, autocratic and directive styles are effective. In contrast, the implications of transformational and transactional leadership are much clearer because researchers defined these styles in an effort to identify effective leadership.

Substantiating claims that transformational leadership is generally effective, a meta-analysis of 39 studies showed positive correlations between effectiveness and all components of transformational leadership, although effectiveness also related positively to the contingent reward component of transactional leadership (Lowe, Kroeck, & Sivasubramaniam, 1996). A large norming study of the MLQ measure produced similar findings (Center for Leadership Studies, 2000) and in addition showed negative relations between leaders' effectiveness and two of the remaining measures: (a) passive management-by-exception, which is one of the components of transactional leadership, and (b) laissez-faire leadership. Therefore, the tendency of women to exceed men on the components of leadership style that relate positively to effectiveness—that is, transformational leadership and the contingent reward aspect of transactional leadership—attests to the ability of women to perform well as leaders. Moreover, the tendencies of men to exceed women on the less effective styles (i.e., passive management-by-exception and laissez-faire leadership) are also notable. In the Eagly et al. (2003) meta-analysis of transformational and transactional styles, the implications of these style findings for effectiveness were corroborated by the somewhat better performance of female managers than male managers on the effectiveness measures used in the studies included in the meta-analysis.

Trust in these findings would be fostered by explanation of the apparently more effective leadership styles of women than men. Eagly et al. (2003) argued that the causes of this sex difference may lie in several factors: (a) the ability of the transformational repertoire (and contingent reward behaviors) to resolve some of the typical incongruity between leadership roles and the female gender role because these styles are not distinctively masculine; (b) gender roles' influence on women's leadership by means of the spillover and internalization of gender-specific norms, which would facilitate the more feminine aspects of transformational leadership; and (c) the glass ceiling itself, whereby a double standard produces more highly skilled female than male leaders. We will return to these explanations in the Conclusion of this chapter.

In summary, research on leadership style shows that the sex differences substantiated by empirical research are unlikely to hinder women's performance as leaders but instead should promote their performance. Although Vecchio (2002) argued against any superiority of women's leadership styles, his narrative review predated the publication of the only meta-analysis that has addressed this issue by examining leadership styles that consistently relate to effectiveness (Eagly et al., 2003). Nonetheless, Vecchio's claims of the absence of any sex differences, like the several prior narrative reviews arguing for no difference (e.g., Powell, 1990), provide no basis for arguing that the dearth of women in elite leadership roles is caused by ineffective qualities of their typical leadership styles.

The Nature Arguments: Men as Naturally Dominant

Some writers who are influenced by evolutionary psychology have explained men's disproportionate occupancy of leadership roles on the basis of intrinsic, biologically grounded sex differences (e.g., Browne, 1999, 2002; Goldberg, 1993). These scholars argued that the essential attributes responsible for sex-differentiated social behavior, including leadership behavior, are sex-specific psychological dispositions that were built into the human species through genetically mediated adaptation to primeval conditions (e.g., Buss & Kenrick, 1998). They reason that these evolved dispositions will forever disqualify women from substantial participation as leaders: As Browne (1999) wrote, "If high-status roles are found exclusively in the extra-domestic sphere—a sphere in which men's temperament gives them an advantage—then women will be forever consigned to lower status" (p. 57). Outside of the kitchen and nursery, women are thus doomed to cede power and status to men.

Evolutionary psychologists link current sex differences in behavior to the differing reproductive pressures that they maintain that ancestral males and females encountered in the early history of the human species (Buss & Kenrick, 1998). These sexual selection pressures presumably shaped psychological sex differences, with the ultimate source being an asymmetry in the sexes' parental investment (Trivers, 1972). Specifically, women, the sex that invested more in offspring (e.g., through gestation and nursing), became choosier about potential mates than men, the sex that invested less. As a result, ancestral men competed with other men to obtain sexual access to women, and the winners in these competitions were more likely to procreate and thus have their genes carried on to the next generation. According to this logic, by means of this competition between men, their evolved dispositions came to favor aggression, risk taking, and competition for status. In contrast, ancestral women presumably developed a proclivity to choose mates who could provide resources to support them and their children. This female tendency would then have fostered evolved tendencies for men to acquire resources, presumably through rising in status in social structures. In short, a tendency for men to seek leadership could have evolved because more dominant men would have controlled more resources and had higher status and these qualities were associated with reproductive success.

Some evolutionary psychologists argue that sexual selection in humans also took the form of men's choice of long-term mates for their likely fecundity and faithfulness (Geary, 1998). Men made these choices because women's internal fertilization made it difficult for men to be certain about the paternity of their offspring. To increase paternity certainty and gain fitness benefits from investing resources only in their own biological descendants, ancestral men presumably developed a disposition to control women's sexuality and to experience sexual jealousy (Wilson & Daly, 1992). Sexual control would also tend to subordinate women.

In summary, for evolutionary psychologists, men's efforts to dominate one another and to control women emerge from these evolved psychological dispositions that are "fossils" of the selection pressures that shaped the human species (Buss & Kenrick, 1998, p. 983). These arguments rest on a skein of assumptions about relations between the sexes in primeval times. The contentious scientific debates about these assumptions cannot be easily summarized here. Nonetheless, we note in particular one effort to test these assumptions by examining cross-cultural data from nonindustrial societies (Wood & Eagly, 2002). This review failed to find the critical universal or near-universal patterns across cultures that would provide support for the sex-specific psychological tendencies that evolutionary psychologists assume evolved as a product of sexual selection pressures in ancestral environments. Crucially, the assumption that male dominance is universal (e.g., Buss, 1995) is inconsistent with evidence that patriarchy instead emerged along with a variety of economic and social developments, including warfare and intensive agriculture. Thus, a portion of foraging societies with very simple socioeconomic systems appear to be nonpatriarchal, a finding that should not be obtained if male dominance is inherent in men's nature. As new roles developed in more socioeconomically complex societies, the roles in the nondomestic economies increasingly required training, intensive energy expenditure, and travel away from the home. Because of their freedom from reproductive responsibility of gestation and nursing of infants, men were better positioned to occupy these roles and to reap the economic and social capital that these roles yielded.

Another crucial assumption is that women are intrinsically oriented to seek mates with resources who can support them and their children and that men are oriented to acquire such resources to compete with other males in dominance contests, gain mating opportunities, and provision their families (e.g., Buss & Kenrick, 1998; Geary, 1998). Wood and Eagly's (2002) review challenged these principles by establishing that women not only contributed substantially to subsistence activities in most nonindustrial societies but also were the primary food providers in societies that relied mainly on the gathering of vegetal foods. It is therefore likely that ancestral men and women were mutually dependent for their subsistence, with the balance of dependence determined by their society's environment and ecology. Both sexes would have reaped advantages from pair bonds with effective resource providers (see also Wrangham, Jones, Laden, Pilbeam, & Conklin-Brittain, 1999). Yet, as societies moved away from the simpler socioeconomic structures in which humans evolved, men came to disproportionally occupy roles that entailed primary responsibility for providing resources for family units.

Also debatable is the sexual control hypothesis that men have evolved to be motivated to control women's sexuality to ensure paternity certainty and that this control is manifested in the social institution of patriarchy (Smuts, 1995; Wilson & Daly, 1992). One argument against this idea is that a sexual double standard reflecting greater control of female than male sexuality was not universal or near-universal tendency in the nonindustrial societies studied by anthropologists (Broude & Greene, 1976; M. K. Whyte, 1978). Moreover, a substantial number of societies have legitimized sexual relations between women and multiple partners. The varying levels of control over women's sexuality apparent across societies do not provide much support for the claim that men have evolved an essential disposition to control women's sexuality. Instead, such control emerged with particular economic structures, especially those in which inheritance rules run through male lines (see Wood & Eagly, 2002).

Because modern industrialized societies are moderately patriarchal, some psychological sex differences should be evident as a product of socialization to participate in such a system, if not of evolved dispositions. Of special interest are the dispositions that some writers influenced by evolutionary psychology have reasoned are sex-typed and relevant to leadership (e.g., Browne, 1999, 2002). Commonly discussed in this context is aggressiveness, a negative form of dominance, usually defined in terms of behavior intended to harm others. Indeed, meta-analyses have found men more aggressive than women, although this tendency is stronger for physical aggression than verbal aggression (Bettencourt & Miller, 1996; Eagly & Steffen, 1986), and even the physical aggression sex difference becomes ambiguous in heterosexual partner relationships (Archer, 2000). Yet, if any forms of aggression are consequential to organizational leadership, it would surely not be attacking one's rivals physically. More relevant under some circumstances might be verbal aggression, on which men only slightly exceed women (Eagly & Steffen, 1986).

More critical to leadership than aggressiveness would be milder forms of dominance, including assertiveness. Feingold's (1994) meta-analysis of sex differences in personality revealed greater male assertiveness, a small to moderate effect that varied as a function of the way assertiveness was measured and the type of sample used in the study. Carli's (2001a) qualitative review revealed that men engage in greater negative assertion, a forceful and controlling form of self-expression, whereas women engage in greater positive assertion, expressing their views in a way that acknowledges the rights of others as well as their own rights. Furthermore, as shown in a meta-analysis of studies of managers' motivation to manage in a traditional, hierarchical manner (Eagly, Karau, Miner, & Johnson, 1994), women tend to be less motivated than men to impose their authority in a command-and-control style.

Research on aggressiveness, assertiveness, and motivation to manage is of unclear relevance to contemporary organizations, whose success depends on responsiveness to customers and clients and to fast-changing technological developments. As we argue in the Conclusion, successful leadership in such contexts requires the ability to form effective relationships with others and to work within teams of people offering differing skills and knowledge. Successful leaders influence others and motivate them to contribute enthusiastically and creatively to organizational goals (e.g., Bass, 1998). Although many management experts have emphasized social skills compatible with a traditionally feminine behavioral repertoire (Fondas, 1997), effective leadership surely requires both masculine and feminine skills.

Relevant to the broader question of whether psychological sex differences can explain men's greater occupancy of high-level leadership roles is research relating personality traits to effective leadership (see Chemers, 1997; Nahavandi, 2003). Personality traits that show at least weak relations to leadership include a high energy level and stress tolerance, self-confidence, internal locus of control, emotional intelligence, creativity, and integrity. Skills contribute to effectiveness as well, including interpersonal skill, cognitive ability, and technical knowledge. In general, this list of traits and abilities does not include any that are notably sex-typed. For example, the general cognitive abilities ordinarily assessed as intelligence do not appear to differ by sex (e.g., Halpern, 2001). Also, a small meta-analytically established sex difference in self-esteem favoring males becomes extremely small among adults (Kling, Hyde, Showers, & Buswell, 1999). Integrity, of special concern in the wake of contemporary corporate scandals, generally favors women, who show more disapproval than men do of questionable business practices such as the use of insider information, although this sex difference becomes smaller with more years of labor force participation (Franke, Crown, & Spake, 1997). To the extent that risk taking is important, perhaps especially to entrepreneurial leadership, it is notable that the sex difference in the male direction is also very small and has decreased in magnitude over time (Byrnes, Miller, & Schafer, 1999). Effective leadership thus reflects a wide range of traits and skills, none of which empirical research has placed strongly in the domain of one sex.

In summary, research has established some generally small sex differences in psychological tendencies that may be relevant to good leadership (e.g., assertiveness, integrity). Some claim that these differences reflect biologically grounded human nature and that only the masculine traits and skills enhance leadership. For example, Browne (2002) wrote, "The dearth of women in high places can be understood only against the backdrop of fundamental sex differences in temperament" (p. 38). Although some psychological sex differences may indeed be influenced by evolved dispositions, the scientific evidence for such claims is deficient at present for dispositions relevant to leadership.

More profoundly, most managerial experts advocate not distinctively masculine traits and skills, but more feminine and androgynous skills of negotiation, cooperation, diplomacy, team building, and inspiring and nurturing others. It is these qualities that are represented in theories about effective leadership taking the form of transformational and contingent reward behaviors. Moreover, some of the characteristics that are known to derail leaders, such as an intimidating or abrasive style, arrogance, and coldness (Nahavandi, 2003), are at least stereotypically masculine (Diekman & Eagly, 2000). It is therefore implausible that effective leadership in contemporary organizations mainly consists of traditionally masculine command-and-control behaviors or that men's ascendance to elite leadership roles reflects their natural dominance. Consequently, in view of the insufficiency of human capital explanations of women's lesser occupancy of such roles and the failure of explanations based on leadership styles and men's natural dominance, we turn to the possibility of prejudice and discrimination.

Discrimination Against Female Leaders

Public discourse on the dearth of women in high-level leadership positions would seem to support the claim that the prejudicial attitudes and discriminatory behaviors are at least partially responsible for the phenomenon. After the term *glass ceiling* was introduced in 1986 in the *Wall Street Journal* ("The Corporate Woman," 1986), it spread rapidly among journalists and other writers and soon became a part of the culture.

From a social psychological perspective, prejudice toward female leaders is best regarded as one instance of more general processes that can produce unfair disadvantage for a group of people. At its core, prejudice consists of differential evaluation of people on a basis that is not fair or legitimate. As Allport (1954) noted, prejudice occurs when people are placed at some disadvantage that is not warranted by their individual actions or qualifications. Prejudice is a common outcome when social perceivers stereotype others, holding beliefs about them on the basis of their group membership. Stereotypes have pervasive influences on expectancies and behavior (see S. T. Fiske, 1998). When people hold stereotypes about a group, they expect members of that group to possess characteristics and exhibit behavior that is consistent with those stereotypes. Stereotypes can be elicited automatically and tend to be resistant to change because people seek out and attend to information that confirms their stereotypes and disregard contradictory information. In addition, stereotypes can be self-fulfilling in that they cause people to behave in ways that elicit stereotypical behavior in others.

In general, prejudice arises from the relations that people perceive between the characteristics of members of a social group and the requirements of the social roles that group members occupy or aspire to occupy (Eagly, in press). A potential for prejudice exists when social perceivers hold a stereotype about the group that is incongruent with the attributes that they think are required for success in certain classes of social roles. When a group member and an incongruent social role become joined in the mind of a perceiver, this inconsistency generally lowers the evaluation of the group member as an actual or potential occupant of the role. The person is thought to be less than fully qualified for the role because of the assumption that members of his or her social group do not have the qualifications that are requisite for the role.

Consistent with this idea that prejudice emerges at the intersection of a group's stereotype and the requirements of a social role, Eagly and Karau (2002) proposed a role incongruity theory of prejudice toward female leaders, which is an extension of Eagly's social role theory of sex differences and similarities in social behavior (Eagly, 1987; Eagly, Wood, & Diekman, 2000). This analysis emphasizes gender roles, defined as consensual beliefs about the attributes of women and men. These beliefs comprise two kinds of expectations, or norms: *descriptive norms,* which are consensual expectations about what members of a social group actually do, and *injunctive norms,* which are consensual expectations about what group members ought to do or ideally would do (Cialdini & Trost, 1998). The term *gender role* thus refers to the descriptive and injunctive expectations associated with women and men. Other researchers have used different labels for this distinction between descriptive and injunctive expectations, including descriptive and prescriptive stereotypes (e.g., Burgess & Borgida, 1999; S. T. Fiske & Stevens, 1993).

Prejudice against women as leaders flows from the incongruity that people often perceive between the characteristics typical of women and the requirements of leader roles, as Heilman (1983) also argued. This inconsistency follows from the predominantly communal qualities that perceivers associate with women (e.g., friendly, kind, unselfish) and the predominantly agentic qualities that they believe are necessary to succeed as a leader (e.g., assertive, masterful, instrumentally competent). People's beliefs about leaders are thus more similar to their beliefs about men than women, as Schein (2001) demonstrated in her "think manager, think male" (p. 676) studies, which extend back to the early 1970s (see also Powell, Butterfield, & Parent, 2002).

The dissimilarity of beliefs about leaders and women would not be important if expectations based on gender faded away in organizational settings. However, they do not (e.g., Ridgeway, 2001). Observing an individual as an occupant or potential occupant of a leader role places two sets of expectations in competition—those based on gender and those based on leadership. Because gender roles are psychologically highly accessible—that is, activated by gender-related cues in virtually all situations—their impact is maintained in group and organizational settings. In thinking about women as leaders, people would combine two divergent sets of expectations—those about leaders and those about women—whereas in thinking about men as leaders, people would combine largely redundant expectations. In support of this, Heilman reported that male managers rated "women managers" as more agentic and less communal than "women in general" but not as close as "men managers" to a group identified as "successful middle managers" (Heilman, Block, & Martell, 1995; Heilman, Block, Martell, & Simon, 1989).

Paradoxically, becoming prototypical of desirable leadership in a group or organization does not ordinarily protect women from prejudiced evaluations. Instead, as we document in the next subsections of this chapter, perceiving a female leader as very similar to her male counterparts may produce disadvantage because such women can be regarded as undesirably masculine (see also Heilman, 2001). This disadvantage thus arises from the injunctive norms associated with the female gender role, by which niceness, kindness, and friendliness are especially valued in women.

Another effect of incongruity between the female gender role and leadership roles can be inhibition of women's leadership behavior when the female gender role is brought to mind. Thinking about negative stereotypic portrayals of one's group can cause group members to become concerned about fulfilling the stereotype, and this concern can derail their performance in the stereotypic domain. In a demonstration of such processes, experiments in the "stereotype threat" paradigm made the female stereotype accessible to students by having them view television commercials featuring female-stereotypic (vs. neutral) content (Davies & Spencer, 2003). Then in an apparently unrelated experiment on leadership, the women, but not the men, who had been exposed to the female-stereotypic portrayals expressed less preference for a leadership role versus a nonleadership role. Combined with evidence that the stereotypic commercials activated the female stereotype, these findings suggest that thinking about the stereotypical female role can lower women's leader aspirations, perhaps by increasing their anxiety about fulfilling the stereotype that women are not suited to leadership.

Women do not always experience prejudice and other effects of role incongruity in relation to leader roles. Because the relevant incongruity is between the descriptive content of the female gender role and a leader role or between a leader's behavior and the injunctive content of the female gender role, prejudice should lessen or even disappear when these incongruities are weakened. For example, if some roles in middle management place more premium on socially skilled behavior than controlling, take-charge behavior, incongruity with the female gender role would lessen. Likewise, incongruity would lessen to the extent that women perform leader roles with some restraint on extremes of agentic behavior and some leavening of agentic behavior with communal behavior.

Negative Attitudes Toward Female Leaders

Overall, people hold more favorable attitudes toward women in general than toward men primarily because of the very positive communal qualities ascribed to women (Eagly & Mladinic, 1989). However, when people evaluate women in general, they may base their evaluation more on their impressions of traditional female homemakers than on women leaders (Haddock & Zanna, 1994). Women who are effective leaders tend to violate standards for their gender because they are perceived to manifest male-stereotypic, agentic attributes more than female-stereotypic, communal attributes. Unlike traditional women who are considered warm and nice but not especially instrumentally competent, women who excel and display leadership are considered instrumentally competent but not particularly warm (P. Glick, Diebold, Bailey-Werner, & Zhu, 1997). This perceived gender-role violation can, in turn, lower evaluations of women in leadership roles.

Given the incongruity between images of women and of leaders, women receive less favorable reactions for their leadership than men do, particularly if it exemplifies "command and control" leadership. Women who appear dominant or directive are less well liked than men are for refusing to comply with requests (Kern, Cavell, & Beck, 1985), expressing overt disagreement (Carli, 1998), and showing visual dominance (Copeland, Driskell, & Salas, 1995). People likewise express more negative reactions when a woman attempts to lead or direct them than when a man does (Butler & Geis, 1990). In essence, people do not consider it appropriate for women to overtly seek leadership or to directly or forcefully attempt to lead others (Carli, 1999).

Because of injunctive gender norms, people evaluate women leaders more harshly for leadership behavior that is not tempered by displays of communal behavior. Eagly, Makhijani, and Klonsky (1992) conducted a meta-analytic review of studies examining the evaluation of male and female leaders in experiments that equated their behavior. Although people evaluated female leaders only slightly more negatively overall than male leaders, women received lower evaluations than men did for exhibiting autocratic leadership but received comparable evaluations for exhibiting a more democratic leadership style.

Plainly, a female leader can elicit ambivalent attitudes, which are both positive and negative. To the extent that this is so, reactions to her would tend to be inconsistent across time and situations (see review by Jonas, Broemer, & Diehl, 2000). As found in research on attitudinal ambivalence, reactions may polarize—that is, become very negative or even sometimes very positive—depending on the particulars of the judgment context. For example, exaggerated negativity may emerge when a powerful woman takes unpopular actions, even when they are required by her role (see Atwater, Carey, & Waldman, 2001; Sinclair & Kunda, 2000).

Although both men and women have been found to be more critical of female than male leaders, this tendency is stronger among men than women. For example, Geller and Hobfoll (1993) found that, although male and female participants gave similar evaluations to men who expressed disagreement, women received less favorable evaluations by male than female participants for the same behavior. Also, displays of competence alone can at times reduce women's appeal to men. Men, but not women, reported that competent women are less likable and more threatening than competent men (Carli, 1990; Carli, LaFleur & Loeber, 1995). However, competence in women is less unappealing to men when combined with communal behavior. For example, male participants preferred women who displayed competence combined with warmth to women who displayed competence alone; in contrast, both male and female participants reported liking men equally well, regardless their level of warmth (Carli et al., 1995).

Similar to these findings, Eagly et al.'s (1992) meta-analysis examining the evaluation of male and female leaders whose behavior was equated revealed that the tendency to evaluate female leaders less positively than male leaders was stronger among male evaluators. Also, a meta-analysis of actual leaders (Eagly, Karau, & Makhijani, 1995) showed that women tended to be perceived as less effective than were men to the extent that men served as their evaluators or that they had male subordinates. Schein's (2001) research on managerial stereotypes showed that men equated successful management with maleness more than women did. Clearly, although women generally receive more severe penalties than men do for displaying leadership behavior that is dominant or lacking in warmth, men more often than women impose these penalties. Indeed, men more than women endorse hierarchy-supporting ideologies and policies in relation to out-groups, including women (Sidanius & Pratto, 1999).

Consistent with D. T. Campbell's (1965) realistic group conflict theory and Kanter's (1977) notion of homosocial reproduction, men and women are to some extent in competition for power and influence, perhaps especially at the tops of hierarchies where men have more to lose from women's advancement. In support of this idea, Maume (1999) found that working in male-dominated professions increased men's, but not women's, chances of promotion. Such professions may particularly benefit men because they have greater access than women do to the more extensive male network that such organizations provide. Along these lines, Ibarra (1997) found that among Fortune Service 500 managers, men reported higher proportions of same-sex career contacts than women did, although women on the "fast track" in their jobs relied more on female than male contacts than women in less ascendant positions. Male networks apparently benefit men more than women.

Restrictions on Women's Agentic Behavior

Negative reactions to female leader behavior are consequential. Compared with men, women's ability to lead is more dependent on their adherence to a constricted range of behavior (Carli, 1999). In particular, behaviors that convey dominance, negative assertion, self-promotion, or a lack of warmth conflict with the communal demands of the female gender role and therefore interfere with female influence. For instance, displays of verbal and nonverbal dominance lower women's but not men's ability to influence others (Carli, 1998; Copeland et al., 1995; Mehta et al., 1989, cited in Ellyson, Dovidio, & Brown, 1992). In addition, women, more than men, receive greater recognition when they are modest than self-promoting (e.g., Wosinska, Dabul, Whetstone-Dion, & Cialdini; 1996). Demonstrating this effect, Rudman (1998) had participants evaluate the job interviewing skills of a target individual who behaved in a self-promoting or self-effacing manner. Female participants gave the female target lower evaluations when she was self-promoting compared with self-effacing, and male participants gave more favorable evaluations to a self-promoting woman only if they had something to gain from her. Yet in no condition were male self-promoters evaluated less favorably than self-effacing men. Likewise, women who demonstrate communality by displaying positive social behaviors exert greater influence than women who do not, whereas communal displays have little effect on men's influence (Carli, 1998; Shackelford, Wood, & Worchel, 1996).

In general, likableness is more strongly associated with social influence for women than men (Carli, 1998). Because men are especially likely to dislike women who violate injunctive gender role norms, men also resist female influence more than women do (Carli, 2001b). Studies whose participants were government officials (Weimann, 1985), managers (Buttner & McEnally, 1996), and college students (Carli, 1990; Carli et al., 1995; Matschiner & Murnen, 1999) have demonstrated that women whose behavior conveys competence and assertion are disadvantaged when attempting to influence men, compared with women who appear less competent and assertive. When the context of the interaction is a job application, men's greater resistance to women's influence affects women's chances of being hired. For example, in Buttner and McEnally's (1996) study assessing managers' reactions to job applicants, male applicants increased their chances of being hired by exhibiting direct and dominant behavior, whereas female applicants who did the same reduced their chances. In a study involving college students, Foschi, Lai, and Sigerson (1994) manipulated the competence of male and female job candidates and then gave undergraduates the choice of hiring the man, the woman, or no one at all. Women preferred to hire the candidate with the better academic record, regardless of that person's gender. Men, on the other hand, preferred to hire the better candidate when that person was a man, but preferred to hire no one at all to hiring a more competent woman.

One way that women can increase their likableness and thereby increase their influence with men is to "feminize" their behavior by increasing their interpersonal warmth. Warm women are better liked, especially by men, and this increased likableness results in increased influence (Carli, 2001b). Female leaders may therefore display an amalgam of agentic and communal qualities in order to gain influence and lead effectively. Men are not penalized for dominance, competence, or assertion, and, at the same time, are generally not penalized for exhibiting communality. This situation creates an advantage for male leaders, who can display a wider range of behaviors, tailoring their leadership style to the demands of the situation. Also, pressures on women leaders to conform to injunctive gender roles are likely the root of women's motivation to avoid autocratic forms of leadership and their reliance on more democratic and transformational leadership styles.

In summary, gender roles lead people to expect and prefer women to be communal, creating a double bind for female leaders who must demonstrate exceptional competence to be seen as equal in ability to men and must also avoid threatening others with their competence and lack of warmth. Women who appear to be direct, competent, and assertive may thus be seen as illegitimately seeking leadership or influence, but gain from combining competence with warmth. Conversely, there is generally no incongruity between the male gender role and leadership roles. Men's leadership potential is less in doubt, giving them greater behavioral latitude than women have. Men's greater resistance to female leadership also contributes to the slowed ascendance of women into higher levels of leadership, where men currently reside in much higher proportions than women. Research thus makes a strong case that prejudicial barriers against female leaders are a major factor accounting for their rarity in elite leadership roles.

The Rise of Female Leaders

Despite the prejudicial barriers that we have documented, women are rising into leadership roles in many nations. In the United States, the occupational category for which women's share of employment has shown the greatest increase in recent decades is "executive, administrative, and managerial occupations"; these gains far outstrip women's gains in any other grouping (Wootton, 1997). This shift toward more women managers has been steady since the early 1970s, rising from only 18% in 1972 to 46% in 2002 (U.S. Bureau of Labor Statistics, 1982, 2002). In some categories of management, women are numerically dominant—for example, medicine and health, personnel and labor relations, and education and related fields (U.S. Bureau of Labor Statistics, 2001). Women's movement into management and administration is important even though women tend to be positioned in the lower levels within organizations. These lower-level positions can provide access to higher-level leadership positions.

This rapid entry of women into management in recent decades has occurred for the most part without displacing men. Managerial occupations have expanded greatly, making room for more workers, including women. Given the pyramidal structure of organizations, the top level of management has not expanded proportionately. At the top of organizations, the entry of women would displace men, and therefore it may not be surprising that women have had less success in rising into executive leadership.

Is there nonetheless any change in the proportions of women in higher-level leadership positions? Although the pace of change is slow, there is discernible acceleration. Political leadership provides evidence of women's rise in power and authority. In fact, 43 of the 59 women who have ever served as presidents or prime ministers of nations came into office since 1990 (Adler, 1999; de Zárate, 2003). These 59 women are only a tiny fraction of those who have served in these roles, but notably most of these role occupancies are quite recent. The idea of a woman as president or prime minister is no longer so unthinkable as it was in earlier years.

Other powerful political roles show similar shifts. In the United States, only 20 women have ever served as governors of states, 6 of whom are currently in office, and only 32 have ever served in the U.S. Senate, 14 of whom are currently in office (White House Project, 2002). Within the senior executive service of the federal government, consisting of the highest nonelective positions that are not political appointments, the percentage of women has risen from 11% in 1990 to 25% in 2000, a substantial increase in a mere 10-year period (U.S. Office of Personnel Management, 2001).

Large business organizations have been especially slow to accept women in elite executive roles. Although the 6 women who now hold CEO positions in the Fortune 500 are only a very small proportion of the CEO group, this number is larger than it has been at any point in the past (Catalyst, 2002). There are at least 18 women from various nations who led companies with revenues over $1 billion or banks with assets over $1 billion (Adler, 1999). Also, more women now occupy posts as presidents of universities in the United States, even high-status universities such as Princeton, University of Pennsylvania, University of Michigan, and University of Illinois. In universities and colleges in the United States, the percentage of presidencies held by women increased from 10% in 1986 to 21% in 2001 (American Council on Education, 2002). *Chronicle of Higher Education*'s survey of the 2001 salaries of private university presidents placed two women at the top of the list (Basinger, 2002). It is thus unmistakable that women are rising, not merely into lower- and midlevel managerial roles but more slowly into leadership roles at the tops of organizations and governments.

What changes have enabled at least some women to rise into leadership roles that women have very rarely occupied in the past? We suggest several causes. Related to our discussion of women's human capital investments, we note changes toward increased investment, especially in work experience. Also, as a product of underlying shifts in women's roles, women have changed their personal attributes in a masculine direction toward greater consistency with stereotypic definitions of leaders. In addition, many leader roles have changed to incorporate a greater measure of traditionally feminine qualities. Finally, successful women leaders find ways to lead that finesse the still remaining incongruity between leader roles and the female gender role. We discuss each of these causes of women's rise and point to relevant research support.

Changes in Women's Human Capital Investments

The analysis that we presented earlier in this chapter implicated women's domestic responsibilities and their somewhat lesser work experience and consistency of employment as factors accounting for a portion of the gender differentials in workplace advancement. The division of labor has shown some change, however, in recent years. Greater equality in the contributions of husbands and wives to housework and child care is a robust finding. The sex difference in housework has dropped since the mid-1960s, with a steady decline in women's housework that has continued through the 1990s and a more modest increase in men's housework that leveled off in the 1980s. Whereas in 1965 women spent six times the amount of hours spent by men on housework, by 1985 the amount contributed by women had dropped to twice that of men (Bianchi et al., 2000). Although this drop in house-work has occurred for women who are and are not in the labor force, suggesting general change in cultural standards about housework, women's increasing employment is no doubt an influence, given that employment relates negatively to time spent on housework (Shelton & John, 1996).

Just as with housework, men have become increasingly involved in child rearing, spending more time in interaction with their children (e.g., Pleck, 1997). Yet mothers have not in general reduced their time devoted to child care (Bianchi, 2000), perhaps because cultural changes have made spending "quality time" with children more important than in the past, particularly for mothers (J. Williams, 2000). However, the number of children per family has declined, producing less child care overall.

Also consequential is the continuation of the gain in the education of women relative to men. In the United States, women received 57% of bachelor's degrees and 58% of master's degrees in 2000, with these percentages projected to continue to rise in the coming years (U.S. Department of Education, 2001). Similar gains in women's education are evident in many industrialized nations (United Nations Development Programme, 2002).

Masculine Changes in Women

As women shift more of their time from domestic labor to paid labor, they assume the personal characteristics required to succeed in these new roles (Eagly et al., 2000). These changes in the division of labor are associated with a redefini-tion of the patterns of behavior that are appropriate to women. People therefore readily acknowledge that women are becoming more masculine, particularly in agentic attributes, and will continue to change in this direction (Diekman & Eagly, 2000). Moreover, it is not surprising that research tracking sex differences across recent time periods suggests that the characteristics of women have actually changed in concert with their entry into formerly male-dominated roles.

Research conducted primarily in the United States has documented changes in the sex differences of a wide range of attributes over time, beginning as early as the 1930s and extending to the present. Among these changes are the following: (a) The value that women place on job attributes such as freedom, challenge, leadership, prestige, and power has increased to be more similar to that of men (Konrad, Ritchie, Lieb, & Corrigall, 2000); (b) the career aspirations of female university students have become more similar to those of male students (Astin, Parrott, Korn, & Sax, 1997); (c) the amount of risky behavior in which women engage has become more similar to that of men (Byrnes et al., 1999); (d) the tendency for men rather than women to emerge as leaders in small groups has become smaller (Eagly & Karau, 1991); (e) women's self-reports of assertiveness, dominance, and masculinity have increased to become more similar to men's (Twenge, 1997, 2001); and (f) the tendency for men to score higher than women on tests of mathematics and science has declined (e.g., Hedges & Nowell, 1995; U.S. Department of Education, 2000). Such findings suggest some convergence in the psychological attributes of women and men in traditionally masculine domains.

Feminine Changes in Leadership Roles

As we briefly noted in the section of this chapter pertaining to nature arguments, the advice on what constitutes good organizational leadership offered by management consultants and organizational experts now construes management in terms that are more congenial to the female gender role than most traditional views. These discussions, which began in the 1980s, have emphasized democratic relationships, participatory decision making, delegation, and team-based leadership skills that are more congruent with the communal characteristics typically ascribed to women than were traditional descriptions of leadership (e.g., Garvin, 1993; Juran, 1988; Senge, 1990). These new themes reflect changing organizational environments marked by accelerated technological growth, increasing workforce diversity, and a weakening of geopolitical boundaries. Leaders seek new modes of managing in these changed organizational environments (Kanter, 1997; Lipman-Blumen, 1996).

Evidence of these trends emerged in Fondas's (1997) textual analysis of mass-market books on management, which found many traditionally feminine, communal themes in authors' advice. Similarly, Cleveland, Stockdale, and Murphy (2000) noted that the female-stereotypic themes of empowering and enabling subordinates and communicating and listening effectively are common in the advice of managerial experts. In addition, numerous managerial writers have explicitly advocated a shift to a more feminine style of leadership (e.g., Helgesen, 1990; Loden, 1985). Illustrating these themes, Rosener (1995) extolled female managers' interactive form of leadership, characterized by encouraging participation, sharing information and power, and enhancing others' self-worth. Moreover, feminist organizational scholars have advocated such changes as epitomizing feminist values (see Calás & Smircich, 1996). To the extent that organizations shift toward the types of management advocated by many contemporary scholars, the role incongruity that underlies prejudice toward female leaders would moderate.

Finessing Role Incongruity With Competent, Androgynous Leadership Style

The argument that we have presented so far in this section of our chapter might suggest that female leaders' role incongruity problems have largely disappeared and that therefore women should have no special worries about presenting themselves as leaders and potential leaders. After all, if women have become more masculine and leader roles more feminine, a middle ground may have been reached where the characteristics ascribed to women match leadership roles as well as those ascribed to men. At such a point, prejudice against female leaders should have disappeared. This resolution is not near at hand, however, because, as we have shown, women's masculine behaviors can still meet with resistance. Moreover, consistent with traditional contingency theories of leadership (see House & Aditya, 1997), effective leadership in some situations no doubt requires an authoritative, directive approach. In addition, the degree of incongruence between female and leader roles may depend on national culture and the extent to which it can be characterized as feminine versus masculine (see Hofstede, 1998). Thus, cultural differences may magnify or minimize resistance to female leadership.

Easing this dilemma of continuing role incongruity requires that women in leader roles behave very competently while reassuring others that they to some degree conform to expectations concerning appropriate female behavior. Given these constraints on women's behavior, transformational leadership may be especially advantageous for them, although it is an effective style for men as well (Eagly et al., 2003; Yoder, 2001). The reason that this style may be a special asset for women is that it encompasses some behaviors that are consistent with the female gender role's demand for caring, supportive, and considerate behaviors. Especially communal are the individualized consideration behaviors, which are marked by developing and mentoring followers and attending to their individual needs. Other aspects of transformational leadership do not seem to be aligned with the gender role of either sex (e.g., demonstrating attributes that instill respect and pride by association with a leader). Few, if any, transformational behaviors have distinctively masculine connotations. This transformational repertoire, along with the contingent reward aspect of transactional leadership, may help resolve some of the incongruity between the demands of leadership roles and the female gender role and therefore allow women to excel as leaders.

The rise of women into elite leadership roles has gained momentum in very recent years. In this time of change in both the division of labor between men and women and the types of management that are most valued, in many contexts female leaders have come to symbolize modernity and the potential for better leadership (Adler, 1999). Moreover, as we have shown, ensuring women equal access to leadership roles is unlikely to disadvantage organizations and in fact will advantage them, not only by greatly increasing the pool of managerial talent but also by making available managers who are slightly more likely to lead in the ways that are effective under contemporary conditions. Therefore, both the economic rationality of bureaucratic organizations in capitalist societies and the fundamental fairness that is highly valued in democratic societies should facilitate women's faster entry into the ranks of leaders in the future.

CHAPTER 13

Ethics and Leadership Effectiveness

Joanne B. Ciulla

Thehe moral triumphs and failures of leaders carry a greater weight and volume than those of nonleaders (Ciulla, 2003b). In leadership we see morality magnified, and that is why the study of ethics is fundamental to our understanding of leadership. The study of ethics is about human relationships. It is about what we should do and what we should be like as human beings, as members of a group or society, and in the different roles that we play in life. It is about right and wrong and good and evil. Leadership is a particular type of human relationship. Some hallmarks of this relationship are power and/or influence, vision, obligation, and responsibility. By understanding the ethics of this relationship, we gain a better understanding of leadership, because some of the central issues in ethics are also the central issues of leadership. They include the personal challenges of authenticity, self-interest, and self-discipline, and moral obligations related to justice, duty, competence, and the greatest good.

Some of the most perceptive work on leadership and ethics comes from old texts and is out there waiting to be rediscovered and reapplied. History is filled with wisdom and case studies on the morality of leaders and leadership. Ancient scholars from the East and West offer insights that enable us to understand leadership and

Author's Note: A special thanks goes to Jepson School research assistant Cassie King for her help in preparing this chapter.

formulate contemporary research questions in new ways. History and philosophy provide perspective on the subject and reveal certain patterns of leadership behavior and themes about leadership and morality that have existed over time. They remind us that some of the basic issues concerning the nature of leadership are inextricably tied to the human condition.

The study of ethics and the history of ideas help us understand two overarching and overlapping questions that drive most leadership research. They are: What is leadership? And what is good leadership? One is about what leadership *is,* or a descriptive question. The other is about what leadership *ought to be,* or a normative question. These two questions are sometimes confused in the literature. Progress in leadership studies rests on the ability of scholars in the field to integrate the answers to these questions. In this chapter, I discuss the implications of these two questions for our understanding of leadership. I begin the chapter by looking at how the ethics and effectiveness question plays out in contemporary work on leadership and ethics and I discuss some of the ethical issues distinctive to leadership. Then I show some of the insights gleaned from the ancient literature and how they complement and provide context for contemporary research. In the end I suggest some directions for research on ethics and in leadership studies.

Ethikos and Morale

Before I get started, a short note on the words *ethics* and *moral* is in order. Some people like to make a distinction between these two concepts, arguing that ethics is about social values and morality is about personal values. Like most philosophers, I use the terms interchangeably. As a practical matter, courses on moral philosophy cover the same material as courses on ethics. There is a long history of using these terms as synonyms of each other, regardless of their roots in different languages. In *De Fato* (II.i) Cicero substituted the Latin word *morale* for Aristotle's use of the Greek word *ethikos.* We see the two terms defining each other in the *Oxford English Dictionary.* The word *moral* is defined as "of or pertaining to the distinction between right and wrong, or good and evil in relation to the actions, volitions, or character of human beings; ethical," and "concerned with virtue and vice or rules of conduct, ethical praise or blame, habits of life, custom and manners" (*Compact Oxford English Dictionary*, 1991, p. 1114). Similarly, *ethics* is defined as "of or pertaining to morality" and "the science of morals, the moral principles by which a person is guided" (*Compact Oxford English Dictionary*, 1991, p. 534).

Ethics as Critical Theory

In 1992, I conducted an extensive search of literature from psychology, sociology, anthropology, political science, religion, and philosophy to see what work had been done on ethics and leadership (Ciulla, 1995). The results were disappointing both in terms of the quantity and quality of articles in contemporary books and journals.

This is not to say that prominent leadership scholars have ignored the subject or failed to see the importance of ethics to leadership. What I am saying is that philosophers who specialize in ethics see their subject differently than do social scientists. Studies of charismatic, transformational, and visionary leadership often talk about ethics. In these studies, ethics is part of the social scientist's description of types or qualities of leaders and/or leader behaviors. From a philosopher's point of view, these studies offer useful empirical descriptions, but they do not offer detailed critical analysis of the ethics of leadership. The study of ethics in any field, such as business or law, also serves as a critical theory. Philosophers usually question most of the assumptions in the field (which might explain why people often try to serve them hemlock!). My point here is not that philosophy is better than the social sciences, but that it brings out different aspects of leadership by employing different methods of analysis. If we are to gain an understanding of ethics and leadership, we will need both kinds of research and analysis.

Explanation and Understanding

The other striking thing I observed about the leadership literature was that writer after writer complained that researchers did not seem to be making much progress in their understanding of leadership (J. G. Hunt, 1991). Fortunately, I will not be adding my voice to that chorus of lamentation. Many things have changed in leadership studies since the early 1990s. Several initiatives are afoot to pull research together. The "full-range leadership theory" consolidates research on transformational and charismatic leadership theories and research with empirical findings on leadership behaviors (Antonakis & House, 2002). Also, more scholars from the humanities have entered the field, and more leadership scholars are doing interdisciplinary work. This is a substantial development because the humanities give us a different kind of knowledge than do the sciences and social sciences.

The humanities provide a larger context in which we can synthesize what we know about leadership. This context also shows us patterns of leadership that we can use to analyze contemporary problems. The challenge for today's leadership scholars is how to bring the two together. As C. P. Snow noted in his famous 1959 Rede lecture, there are "two cultures" of scholars, the humanities and the natural sciences. He said the sciences provide us with descriptions and explanations, but we need the humanities for understanding (Snow, 1998). Similarly, in 1962 Bennis observed that the *science* part of social science is not about the data the scientists produce, "nor is it barren operationalism—what some people refer to as 'scientism' or the gadgetry used for laboratory work. Rather it is what may be called the 'scientific temper' or 'spirit'" (Bennis, 2002, pp. 4–5). The temper and spirit of science include freedom and democratic values. Bennis (2002) argued that the scientist and citizen cannot be sharply separated and that empirical research had to be done from "a *moral* point of view" (p. 7). Whereas the quantity of research that focuses solely on ethics and leadership is still very small, this perspective on leadership is already changing the way some traditional social scientists think about their work.

Ethics as Exhortation

Whereas some of the leadership studies literature offers descriptive accounts of ethics, other parts of the literature treat ethics as an exhortation rather than an in-depth exploration of the subject. Researchers often tell us that leaders should be honest, have integrity, and so forth. For example, John Gardner makes his plea for ethical leaders in his working paper "The Moral Aspect of Leadership," later published in his book *On Leadership* (Gardner, 1987). In the chapter titled "The Moral Dimension of Leadership," Gardner began by categorizing the different kinds of bad leaders, or what he called transgressors, that we find in history. He said some leaders are cruel to their subjects; some encourage their subjects to be cruel to others; some motivate their subjects by playing on the cruelty of their subjects; some render their followers childlike and dependent; and some destroy processes that societies have set up to preserve freedom, justice, and human dignity (Gardner, 1990, pp. 67–68). Gardner picks an important and provocative place to start a discussion on ethics and leadership. However, he never takes us much beyond the "leaders shouldn't be like this" phase of analysis.

When Gardner does get to the meat of the chapter, he offers a series of eloquent and inspiring exhortations on the importance of caring, responsive leaders and empowering leaders who serve the common good. He does not tell us anything we do not already know, but he says it beautifully: "We should hope that our leaders will keep alive values that are not so easy to embed in laws—our caring for others, about honor and integrity, about tolerance and mutual respect, and about human fulfillment within a framework of values" (Gardner, 1990, p. 77). What is missing in Gardner's discussion is what this means in terms of moral commitments and relationships. Why do leaders go wrong in these areas? What does it takes to morally stay on track? And what does this imply for the leader/follower relationship?

The Normative Aspects of Definitions

Leadership scholars often concern themselves with the problem of defining leadership. Some believe that if they could only agree on a common definition of leadership, they would be better able to understand it. This really does not make sense, because scholars in history, biology, and other subjects do not all agree on the definition of their subject, and, even if they did, it would not help them to understand it better. Furthermore, scholars do not determine the meaning of a word for the general public. Would it make sense to have an academic definition that did not agree with the way ordinary people understood the word? Social scientists sometimes limit the definition of a term so that they can use it in a study. Generally, the way people in a culture use a word and think about it determines the meaning of a word (Wittgenstein, 1968). The denotation of the word *leadership* stays basically the same in English. Even though people apply the term differently, all English-speaking leadership scholars know what the word means. Slight variations in its meaning tell us about the values, practices, and paradigms of leadership in a certain place and at a certain time.

Rost (1991) is among those who think that there has been little progress in leadership studies. He believed that there will be no progress in leadership studies until scholars agree on a common definition of leadership. He collected 221 definitions of leadership, ranging from the 1920s to the 1990s. All of these definitions generally say the same thing—leadership is about a person or persons somehow moving other people to do something. Where the definitions differ is in how leaders motivate their followers, their relationship to followers, who has a say in the goals of the group or organization, and what abilities the leader needs to have to get things done. I chose definitions that were representative of definitions from other sources from the same era. Even today one can find a strong family resemblance in the ways various leadership scholars define leadership.

Consider the following definitions (all from American sources), and think about the history of the time and the prominent leaders of that era. What were they like? What were their followers like? What events and values shaped the ideas behind these definitions?

> 1920s [Leadership is] the ability to impress the will of the leader on those led and induce obedience, respect, loyalty, and cooperation.

> 1930s Leadership is a process in which the activities of many are organized to move in a specific direction by one.

> 1940s Leadership is the result of an ability to persuade or direct men, apart from the prestige or power that comes from office or external circumstance.

> 1950s [Leadership is what leaders do in groups.] The leader's authority is spontaneously accorded him by his fellow group members.

> 1960s [Leadership is] acts by a person which influence other persons in a shared direction.

> 1970s Leadership is defined in terms of discretionary influence. Discretionary influence refers to those leader behaviors under control of the leader which he may vary from individual to individual.

> 1980s Regardless of the complexities involved in the study of leadership, its meaning is relatively simple. Leadership means to inspire others to undertake some form of purposeful action as determined by the leader.

> 1990s Leadership is an influence relationship between leaders and followers who intend real changes that reflect their mutual purposes.

Notice that in the 1920s leaders "impressed" their will on those led. In the 1940s they "persuaded" followers, in the 1960s they "influenced" them, whereas in the 1990s leaders and followers influenced each other. All of these definitions are about the nature of the leader/follower relationship. The difference between the definitions rests on normative questions: "How *should* leaders treat followers? And how *should* followers treat leaders?" Who decides what goals to pursue? What *is* and what *ought* to be the nature of their relationship to each other? One thing the definition debate demonstrates is the extent to which the concept of leadership is a social and historical construction. Definitions reflect not only the opinions of researchers but the conditions of life at a particular time in a particular society and the values that are important to either the public or the leaders. The definition of leadership is a social and normative construction.

For contemporary scholars, the most morally attractive definitions of leadership hail from the 1940s, 1950s, 1960s, and Rost's (1991) own definition of the 1990s. They imply a noncoercive, participatory, and democratic relationship between leaders and followers. There are two appealing elements of these theories. First, rather than *induce,* these leaders *influence,* which in moral terms implies that leaders recognize the autonomy of their followers. Rost's definition used the word *influence,* which carries an implication that there is some degree of voluntary compliance on the part of followers. In Rost's (1991) chapter on ethics he stated, "The leadership process is ethical if the people in the relationship (the leaders and followers) *freely* agree that the intended changes fairly reflect their mutual purposes" (p. 161). Followers are the leader's partner in shaping the goals and purposes of a group or organization. For Rost, consensus is an important part of what makes leadership ethical and what makes leadership *leadership.* Free choice is morally pleasing because it shows respect for persons. But the fact that people consent to make changes does not mean that those changes are ethical or that their mutual purposes are ethical. An ethical process may not always yield ethical results. The second morally attractive part of these definitions is that they imply recognition of the beliefs, values, and needs of the followers. Today, we may not agree with the 1920s characterization of leadership, not because leadership is incorrectly defined, but because we do not think that is the best way to lead. Nonetheless, there are plenty of leaders around today that fit that description of command-and-control leadership. If we all accepted Rost's definition of leadership, we would not be able to use the term to talk about a number of leaders whose leadership does not fit the bill.

The Hitler Problem

The morally attractive definitions also speak to a distinction frequently made between leadership and headship (or positional leadership). Holding a formal leadership position or position of power does not necessarily mean that a person exercises leadership. Furthermore, you do not have to hold a formal position to exercise leadership. People in leadership positions may wield force or authority using only their position and the resources and power that come with it. Some scholars would argue that bullies and tyrants are not leaders, which takes us to what I have called "the Hitler problem" (Ciulla, 1995). The Hitler problem is based on how you answer the question, "Was Hitler a leader?" According to the morally unattractive definitions, he was a leader, perhaps even a great leader, albeit an immoral one. Heifetz (1994) argued that, under the "great man" and trait theories of leadership, you can put Hitler, Lincoln, and Gandhi in the same category because the underlying idea of the theory is that leadership is influence over history. However, under the morally attractive or normative theories, Hitler was not a leader at all. He was a bully or tyrant or simply the head of Germany.

To muddy the waters even further, according to one of Bennis and Nanus's (1985) characterization of leadership—"Managers are people who do things right and leaders are people who do right things" (p. 21)—one could argue that Hitler was neither unethical nor a leader. Bennis and Nanus are among those scholars who sometimes slip into using the term *leader* to mean a morally good leader. However, what appears to be behind this in Bennis and Nanus's comment is the idea that leaders *are* or *should be* a head above everyone else morally. This normative strand exists throughout the leadership literature, most noticeably in the popular literature. Writers will say leaders *are* participatory, supportive, and so forth, when what they really mean is that leaders *should* have these qualities. Yet it may not even be clear that we really want leaders with these qualities. As former presidential spokesman Gergen (2002) pointed out, leadership scholars all preach and teach that participatory, empowering leadership is best. A president like George W. Bush, however, exercises a top-down style of leadership that is closer to the 1920s definition than the 1990s one. Few leadership scholars would prescribe such leadership in their work. Nonetheless, President Bush scored some of the highest approval ratings for his leadership in recent history (Gergen, 2002).

Moral Luck

Leadership scholars who worry about constructing the ultimate definition of leadership are asking the wrong question but trying to answer the right one. The ultimate question about leadership is not, "What is the definition of leadership?" We are not confused about what leaders do, but we would like to know the best way to do it. The whole point of studying leadership is to answer the question, "What is good leadership?" The use of the word *good* here has two senses, morally good leadership and technically good leadership (i.e., effective at getting the job-at-hand done). The problem with this view is that when we look at history and the leaders around us, we find some leaders who meet both criteria and some who only meet one. History only confuses the matter further. Historians do not write about the leader who was very ethical but did not do anything of significance. They rarely write about a general who was a great human being but never won a battle. Most historians write about leaders who were winners or who change history for better or for worse.

The historian's assessment of leaders also depends on what philosophers call moral luck. Moral luck is another way of thinking about the free will/determinism problem in ethics. People are responsible for the free choices they make. We are generally not responsible for things over which we have no control. The most difficult ethical decisions leaders make are those where they cannot fully determine the outcome. Philosopher Bernard Williams (1998) described moral luck as intrinsic to an action based on how well a person thinks through a decision and whether his or her inferences are sound and turn out to be right. He stated that moral luck is also extrinsic to a decision. Things like bad weather, accidents, terrorists, malfunctioning machines, and so forth can sabotage the best-laid plans (B.A.O. Williams, 1981). Moral luck is an important aspect of ethics and leadership, because it helps us think about ethical decision making and risk assessment.

Consider the following two examples. First, imagine the case of a leader who is confronted with situation where terrorists are threatening to blow up a plane full of people. The plane is sitting on a runway. The leader gets a variety of opinions from her staff and entertains several options. Her military advisers tell her that they have a plan. They are fairly certain they will be able to free the hostages safely. The leader is morally opposed to giving in to terrorists but also morally opposed to killing the terrorists if it is not necessary. She has duties to a variety of stakeholders and long- and short-term moral obligations to consider. She weighs the moral and technical arguments carefully and chooses to attack, but she is unlucky. Things go wrong and the hostages get killed. Consider the case of another leader in the same situation. In this case, the negotiations are moving forward slowly, and his advisers tell him that an attack is highly risky. The leader is impatient with the hostages and his cautious advisers. He does not play out the moral arguments. For him it is simple: "I don't give a damn who gets killed; these terrorists are not going to get the best of me!" He chooses to attack. This leader is lucky. The attack goes better than expected and the hostages are freed without harm.

Some leaders are ethical but unlucky, whereas others are not as ethical but very lucky. Most really difficult moral decisions made by leaders are risky, because they have imperfect or incomplete information and lack control over all of the variables that will affect outcomes. Leaders who fail at something are worthy of forgiveness when they act with deliberate care and for the right moral reasons, even though followers do not always forgive them or lose confidence in their leadership. Americans did not blame President Jimmy Carter for the botched attempt to free the hostages in Iran, but it was one more thing that shook their faith in his leadership. He was unlucky because if the mission had been successful, it might have strengthened people's faith in him as a leader and improved his chances of retaining the presidency.

The irony of moral luck is that leaders who are reckless and do not base their actions on sound moral and practical arguments are usually condemned when they fail *and* celebrated as heroes when they succeed. That is why Immanuel Kant (1993) argued that because we cannot always know the results of our actions, moral judgments should be based on the right moral principles and not contingent on outcomes. The reckless, lucky leader does not demonstrate moral or technical competency, yet because of the outcome often gets credit for having both. Because history usually focuses on outcomes, it is not always clear how much luck, skill, and morality figured in the success or failure of a leader. This is why we need to devote more study to the ethics of leaders' decision-making processes in addition to their actions and behavior.

The Relationship Between Ethics and Effectiveness

History defines successful leaders largely in terms of their ability to bring about change for better or worse. As a result, great leaders in history include everyone from Gandhi to Hitler. Machiavelli was disgusted by Cesare Borgia the man, but impressed by Borgia as the resolute, ferocious, and cunning prince (Prezzolini, 1928, p. 11). Whereas leaders usually bring about change or are successful at doing something, the ethical questions waiting in the wings are the ones found in the various definitions mentioned earlier. What were the leader's intentions? How did the leader go about bringing change? And was the change itself good?

In my own work, I have argued that a good leader is an ethical and an effective leader (Ciulla, 1995). Whereas this may seem like stating the obvious, the problem we face is that we do not always find ethics and effectiveness in the same leader. Some leaders are highly ethical but not very effective. Others are very effective at serving the needs of their constituents or organizations but not very ethical. U.S. Senator Trent Lott, who was forced to step from his position as Senate Majority leader because of his insensitive racial comments, is a compelling example of the latter. Some of his African American constituents said that they would vote for him again, regardless of his racist beliefs, because Lott had used his power and influence in Washington to bring jobs and money to the state. In politics, the old saying "He may be a son-of-a-bitch, but he's *our* son of a bitch," captures the trade-off between ethics and effectiveness. In other words, as long as Lott gets the job done, we do not care about his ethics.

This distinction between ethics and effectiveness is not always a crisp one. Sometimes being ethical *is* being effective and sometimes being effective *is* being ethical. In other words, ethics *is* effectiveness in certain instances. There are times when simply being regarded as ethical and trustworthy makes a leader effective and other times when being highly effective makes a leader ethical. Given the limited power and resources of the secretary-general of the United Nations, it would be very difficult for someone in this position to be effective in the job if he or she did not behave ethically. The same is true for organizations. In the famous Tylenol case, Johnson & Johnson actually increased sales of Tylenol by pulling Tylenol bottles off their shelves after someone poisoned some of them. The leaders at Johnson & Johnson were effective *because* they were ethical.

The criteria that we use to judge the effectiveness of a leader are also not morally neutral. For a while, Wall Street and the business press lionized Al Dunlap ("Chainsaw Al") as a great business leader. Their admiration was based on his ability to downsize a company and raise the price of its stock. Dunlop apparently knew little about the nuts and bolts of running a business. When he failed to deliver profits at Sunbeam, he tried to cover up his losses and was fired. In this case and in many business cases, the criteria for effectiveness are practically and morally limited. It does not take great skill to get rid of employees, and taking away a person's livelihood requires a moral and a practical argument. Also, one of the most striking aspects of professional ethics is that often what seems right in the short run is not right in the long run or what seems right for a group or organization is not right when placed in a broader context. For example, Mafia families may have very strong internal ethical systems, but they are highly unethical in any larger context of society.

There are also cases when the sheer competence of a leader has a moral impact. For example, there were many examples of heroism in the aftermath of the September 2001 terrorist attack on the World Trade Center. The most inspiring and frequently cited were the altruistic acts of rescue workers. Yet consider the case of Alan S. Weil, whose law firm Sidley, Austin, Brown, & Wood occupied five floors of the World Trade Center. Immediately after watching the Trade Center towers fall to the ground and checking to see if his employees got out safely, Weil got on the phone and within 3 hours had rented four floors of another building for his employees. By the end of the day he had arranged for an immediate delivery of 800 desks and 300 computers. The next day the firm was open for business with desks for almost every employee (Schwartz, 2001). We do not know if Mr. Weil's motives were altruistic or avaricious, but his focus on doing his job allowed the firm to fulfill its obligations to all of its stakeholders, from clients to employees.

On the flip side of the ethics effectiveness continuum are situations where it is difficult to tell whether a leader is unethical, incompetent, or stupid. As Price (2000) has argued, the moral failures of leaders are not always intentional. Sometimes moral failures are cognitive and sometimes they are normative (Price, 2000). Leaders may get their facts wrong and think that they are acting ethically when, in fact, they are not. For example, in 2000 South African president Thabo Mbeki issued a statement saying that it was not clear that HIV caused AIDS. He thought the pharmaceutical industry was just trying to scare people so that it could increase its profits (Garrett, 2000). Coming from the leader of a country where about one in five people test positive for HIV, this was a shocking statement. His stance caused outrage among public health experts and other citizens. It was irresponsible and certainly undercut the efforts to stop the AIDS epidemic. Mbeki understood the scientific literature, but chose to put political and philosophical reasons ahead of scientific knowledge. (He has since backed away from this position.) When leaders do things like this, we want to know if they are unethical, misinformed, incompetent, or just stupid. Mbeki's actions seemed unethical, but he may have thought he was taking an ethical stand. His narrow mindset about this issue made him recklessly disregard his more pressing obligations to stop the AIDS epidemic (Moldoveanu & Langer, 2002).

In some situations, leaders act with moral intentions, but because they are incompetent they create unethical outcomes. Take, for instance, the unfortunate case of the Swiss charity Christian Solidarity International. Its goal was to free an estimated 200,000 Dinka children who were enslaved in Sudan. The charity paid between $35 and $75 a head to free enslaved children. The unintended consequence of the charity's actions was that it actually encouraged enslavement by creating a market for it. The price of slaves and the demand for them went up. Also, some cunning Sudanese found that it paid to pretend that they were slaves so that they could make money by being liberated. This deception made it difficult for the charity to identify those who really needed help from those who were faking it.

Here the charity's intent and the means it used to achieve its goals were not unethical in relation to alleviating suffering in the short run; however, in the long run, the charity inadvertently created more suffering. A similar, but more understandable, mistake was made by some American schoolchildren who, out of compassion and a desire to help, collected money to buy the slaves' freedom.

Deontological and Teleological Theories

The ethics-and-effectiveness question parallels the perspectives of deontological and teleological theories in ethics. From the deontological point of view, intentions are the morally relevant aspects of an act. As long as the leader acts according to his or her duty or on moral principles, then the leader acts ethically, regardless of the consequences, as was the case in the first moral luck example. From the teleological perspective, what really matters is that the leader's actions result in bringing about something morally good or "the greatest good." Deontological theories locate the ethics of an action in the moral intent of the leader and his or her moral justification for the action, whereas teleological theories locate the ethics of the action in its results. We need both deontological and teleological theories to account for the ethics of leaders. Just as a good leader has to be ethical and effective, he or she also has to act according to duty and with some notion of the greatest good in mind.

In modernity we often separate the inner person from the outer person and a person from his or her actions. Ancient Greek theories of ethics based on virtue do not have this problem. In virtue theories you basically *are* what you do. The utilitarian John Stuart Mill (1987) saw this split between the ethics of the person and the ethics of his or her actions clearly. He said the intentions or reasons for an act tell us something about the morality of the person, but the ends of an act tell us about the morality of the action. This solution does not really solve the ethics-and-effectiveness problem. It simply reinforces the split between the personal morality of a leader and what he or she does as a leader.

Going back to an earlier example, Mr. Weil may have worked quickly to keep his law firm going because he was so greedy he did not want to lose a day of billings, but in doing so, he also produced the greatest good for various stakeholders. We may not like his personal reasons for acting, but, in this particular case, the various stakeholders may not care because they also benefited. If the various stakeholders knew that Weil had selfish intentions, they would, as Mill said, think less of him but not less of his actions. This is often the case with business. When a business runs a campaign to raise money for the homeless, it may be doing it to sell more of its goods and improve its public image. Yet it would seem a bit harsh to say that the business should not have the charity drive and deny needed funds for the homeless. One might argue that it is sometimes very unethical to demand perfect moral intentions. Nonetheless, personally unethical leaders who do good things for their constituents are still problematic. Even though they provide for the greatest good, their people can never really trust them.

Moral Standards

People often say that leaders should be held to "a higher moral standard," but does that make sense? If true, would it then be acceptable for everyone else to live by lower moral standards? The curious thing about morality is that if you set the moral standards for leaders too high, requiring something close to moral perfection, then few people will be qualified to be leaders or will want to be leaders. For example, how many of us could live up to the standard of having never lied, said an unkind word, or reneged on a promise? Ironically, when we set moral standards for leaders too high, we become even more dissatisfied with our leaders because few are able to live up to our expectations. We set moral standards for leaders too low, however, when we reduce them to nothing more than following the law or, worse, simply not being as unethical as their predecessors. A business leader may follow all laws and yet be highly immoral in the way he or she runs a business. Laws are moral minimums that do not and cannot capture the scope and complexity of morality. For example, an elected official may be law abiding and, unlike his or her predecessor, live by "strong family values." The official may also have little concern for the disadvantaged. Not caring about the poor and the sick is not against the law, but is such a leader ethical?

So where does this leave us? On the one hand, it is admirable to aspire to high moral standards, but on the other hand, if the standards are unreachable, then people give up trying to reach them (Ciulla,1994, pp. 167–183). If the standards are too high, we may become more disillusioned with our leaders for failing to reach them. We might also end up with a shortage of competent people who are willing to take on leadership positions because we expect too much from them ethically. Some highly qualified people stay out of politics because they do not want their private lives aired in public. If the standards are too low, we become cynical about our leaders because we have lost faith in their ability to rise above the moral minimum.

History is littered with leaders who did not think they were subject to the same moral standards of honesty, propriety, and so forth, as the rest of society. One explanation for this is so obvious that it has become a cliché—power corrupts. Winter's (2002) and McClellend's (1975) works on power motives and on socialized and personalized charisma offer psychological accounts of this kind of leader behavior. Maccoby (2000) and a host of others have talked about narcissistic leaders who, on the bright side, are exceptional, and, on the dark side, consider themselves exceptions to the rules.

Hollander's (1964) work on social exchange demonstrates how emerging leaders who are loyal to and competent at attaining group goals gain "idiosyncrasy credits" that allow them to deviate from the groups' norms to suit common goals. As Price (2000) has argued, given the fact that we often grant leaders permission to deviate or be an exception to the rules, it is not difficult to see why leaders sometimes make themselves exceptions to moral constraints. This is why I do not think we should hold leaders to higher moral standards than ourselves. If anything, we have to make sure that we hold them to the same standards as the rest of society. What we should expect and hope is that our leaders will fail less than most people at meeting ethical standards, while pursuing and achieving the goals of their constituents. The really interesting question for leadership development, organizational, and political theory is, What can we do to keep leaders from the moral failures that stem from being in a leadership role? Too many models of leadership characterize the leader as a saint or "father-knows-best" archetype who posses all the right values.

Altruism

Some leadership scholars use altruism as the moral standard for ethical leadership. In their book *Ethical Dimensions of Leadership,* Kanungo and Mendonca wrote (1996b), "Our thesis is that organizational leaders are truly effective only when they are motivated by a concern for others, when their actions are invariably guided primarily by the criteria of the benefit to others even if it results in some cost to oneself" (p. 35). When people talk about altruism, they usually contrast altruism with selfishness, or behavior that benefits oneself at a cost to others (Ozinga, 1999). Altruism is a very high personal standard and, as such, is problematic for a number of reasons. Both selfishness and altruism refer to extreme types of motivation and behavior. Locke brings out this extreme side of altruism in a dialogue with Avolio (Avolio & Locke, 2002). Locke argued that if altruism is about self-sacrifice, then leaders who want to be truly altruistic will pick a job that they do not like or value, expect no rewards or pleasure from their job or achievements, and give themselves over totally to serving the wants of others. He then asked, "Would anyone want to be a leader under such circumstances?" (Avolio & Locke, 2002, pp. 169–171). One might also ask, Would we even want such a person as a leader? Whereas I do not agree with Locke's argument that leaders should act according to their self-interest, he does articulate the practical problem of using altruism as a standard of moral behavior for leaders.

Avolio's argument against Locke is based on equally extreme cases. He drew on his work at West Point, where a central moral principle in the military is the willingness to make the ultimate sacrifice for the good of the group. Avolio also used Mother Teresa as one of his examples. In these cases, self-sacrifice may be less about the ethics of leaders in general and more about the jobs of military leaders and missionaries. Locke's and Avolio's debate pits the extreme aspects of altruism against its heroic side. Here, as in the extensive philosophic literature on self-interest and altruism, the debate spins round and round and does not get us very far. Ethics is about the relationship of individuals to others, so in a sense both sides are right and wrong.

Altruism is a motive for acting, but it is not in and of itself a normative principle (Nagel, 1970). Requiring leaders to act altruistically is not only a tall order, but it does not guarantee that the leader or his or her actions will be moral. For example, stealing from the rich to give to the poor, or Robinhoodism, is morally problematic (Ciulla, 2003a). A terrorist leader who becomes a suicide bomber might have purely altruistic intentions, but the means that he uses to carry out his mission—killing innocent people—is not considered ethical even if his cause is a just one. One might also argue, as one does against suicide, that it is unethical for a person to sacrifice his or her life for any reason because of the impact that it has on loved ones. Great leaders such as Martin Luther King, Jr., and Gandhi behaved altruistically, but what made their leadership ethical was the means that they used to achieve their ends and the morality of their causes. We have a particular respect for leaders who are martyred for a cause, but the morality of King and Gandhi goes beyond their motives. Achieving their objectives for social justice while empowering and disciplining followers to use nonviolent resistance is morally good leadership.

Altruism is also described as a way of assessing an act or behavior, regardless of the agent's intention. For example, Worchel, Cooper, and Goethals (1988) defined altruism as acts that "render help to another person" (p. 394). If altruism is nothing more than helping people, then it is a more manageable standard, but simply helping people is not necessarily ethical. It depends on how you help them and what you help them do. It is true that people often help each other without making great sacrifices. If altruism is nothing more than helping people, then we have radically redefined the concept by eliminating the self-sacrificing requirement. Mendonca (2001) offered a further modification of altruism in what he called "mutual altruism." Mutual altruism boils down to utilitarianism and enlightened self-interest. If we follow this line of thought, we should also add other moral principles, such as the golden rule, to this category of altruism.

It is interesting to note that Confucius explicitly called the golden rule altruism. When asked by Tzu-Kung what the guiding principle of life is, Confucius answered, "It is the word altruism (shu). Do not do unto others what you do not want them to do to you" (Confucius, 1963, p. 44). The golden rule crops up as a fundamental moral principle in most major cultures because it demonstrates how to transform self-interest into concern for the interests of others. In other words, it provides the bridge between altruism and self-interest (others and the self) and allows for enlightened self-interest. This highlights another reason why altruism is not a useful standard for the moral behavior of leaders. The minute we start to modify altruism, it not only loses its initial meaning, it starts to sound like a wide variety of other ethical terms, which makes it very confusing.

Why Being Leader Is Not in a Just Person's Self-Interest

Plato believed that leadership required a person to sacrifice his or her immediate self-interests, but this did not amount to altruism. In Book II of the *Republic*, Plato (1992) wrote,

> In a city of good men, if it came into being, the citizens would fight in order *not to rule* ... There it would be clear that anyone who is really a true ruler doesn't by nature seek his own advantage but that of his subjects. And everyone, knowing this, would rather be benefited by others than take the trouble to benefit them. (p. 347d)

Rather than requiring altruistic motives, Plato was referring to the stress, hard work, and the sometimes thankless task of being a morally good leader. He implied that if you are a just person, leadership will take a toll on you and your life. The only reason a just person will take on a leadership role is out of fear of punishment. He stated further, "Now the greatest punishment, if one isn't willing to rule, is to be ruled by someone worse than oneself. And I think it is fear of this that makes decent people rule when they do" (Plato, 1992, p. 347c). Plato's comment sheds light on why we sometimes feel more comfortable with people who are reluctant to lead than with those who are eager to do so. Today, as in the past, we worry that people who are *too eager* to lead want the power and position for themselves or that they do not fully understand the enormous responsibilities of leadership. Plato also tells us that whereas leadership is not in the just person's immediate self-interest, it is in their long-term interest. He argued that it is in our best interest to be just, because just people are happier and lead better lives than do unjust people (Plato, 1992, p. 353e).

Whereas we admire self-sacrifice, morality sometimes calls upon leaders to do things that are against their self-interest. This is less about altruism than it is about the nature of both morality and leadership. We want leaders to put the interests of followers first, but most leaders do not pay a price for doing that on a daily basis, nor do most circumstances require them to calculate their interests in relation to the interests of their followers. The practice of leadership is to guide and look after the goals, missions, and aspirations of groups, organizations, countries, or causes. When leaders do this, they are doing their job; when they do not do this, they are not doing their job. Ample research demonstrates that self-interested people who are unwilling to put the interests of others first are often not successful as leaders (Avolio & Locke, 2002, pp. 186–188).

Looking after the interests of others is as much about what leaders *do* in their role as leaders as it is about the moral quality of leadership. Implicit in the idea of leadership effectiveness is the notion that leaders do their job. When a mayor does not look after the interests of a city, she is not only ineffective, she is unethical for not keeping the promise that she made when sworn in as mayor. When she does look after the interests of the city, it is not because she is altruistic, but because she is doing her job. In this way, altruism is built into how we describe what leaders do. Whereas altruism is not the best concept for characterizing the ethics of leadership, scholars' interest in altruism reflects a desire to capture, either implicitly or explicitly, the ethics-and-effectiveness notion of good leadership.

Transforming Leadership

In the leadership literature, transforming or transformational leadership has become almost synonymous with ethical leadership. Transformational leadership is often contrasted with transactional leadership. There is a parallel between these two theories and the altruism/self-interest dichotomy. Burns's (1978) theory of transforming leadership is compelling because it rests on a set of moral assumptions about the relationship between leaders and followers. Burns's theory is clearly a prescriptive one about the nature of morally *good* leadership. Drawing from Abraham Maslow's work on needs, Milton Rokeach's research on values development, and research on moral development from Lawrence Kohlberg, Jean Piaget, Erik Erickson, and Alfred Adler, Burns argued that leaders have to operate at higher need and value levels than those of followers, which may entail transcending their self-interests. A leader's role is to exploit tension and conflict within people's value systems and play the role of raising people's consciousness (Burns, 1978).

On Burns's account, transforming leaders have very strong values. They do not water down their values and moral ideals by consensus, but rather they elevate people by using conflict to engage followers and help them reassess their own values and needs. This is an area where Burns's view of ethics is very different from advocates of participatory leadership such as Rost. Burns wrote, "Despite his [Rost's] intense and impressive concern about the role of values, ethics and morality in transforming leadership, he underestimates the crucial importance of these variables." Burns goes on to say, "Rost leans towards, or at least is tempted by, consensus procedures and goals that I believe erode such leadership" (Burns, 1991, p. xii).

The moral questions that drive Burns's (1978) theory of transforming leadership come from his work as a biographer and historian. When biographers or historians study a leader, they struggle with the question of how to judge or keep from judging their subject. Throughout his book, Burns used examples of a number of incidents where questionable means, such as lying and deception, are used to achieve honorable ends or where the private life of a politician is morally questionable. If you analyze the numerous historical examples in Burns's book, you find that two pressing moral questions shape his leadership theory. The first is the morality of means and ends (and this also includes the moral use of power). The second is the tension between the public and private morality of a leader. His theory of transforming leadership is an attempt to characterize good leadership by accounting for both of these questions.

Burns's distinction between transforming and transactional leadership and modal and end values offers a way to think about the question of what is a good leader in terms of the leader/follower relationship and the means and ends of his or her actions. Transactional leadership rests on the values found in the means or process of leadership. He calls these modal values. These include responsibility, fairness, honesty, and promise keeping. Transactional leadership helps leaders and followers reach their own goals by supplying lower-level wants and needs so that they can move up to higher needs. Transforming leadership is concerned with end values, such as liberty, justice, and equality. Transforming leaders raise their followers up through various stages of morality and need, and they turn their followers into leaders.

As a historian, Burns was very concerned with the ends of actions and the changes that leaders initiate. Consider, for example, Burns's (1978) two answers to the Hitler question. In the first part of the book, he stated quite simply that "Hitler, once he gained power and crushed all opposition, was no longer a leader—he was a tyrant" (pp. 2–3). Later in the book, he offered three criteria for judging how Hitler would fare before "the bar of history." Burns stated that Hitler would probably argue that he was a transforming leader who spoke for the true values of the

German people and elevated them to a higher destiny. First, he would be tested by modal values of honor and integrity or the extent to which he advanced or thwarted the standards of good conduct in mankind. Second, he would be judged by the end values of equality and justice. Last, he would be judged on the impact that he had on the people that he touched (Burns, 1978). According to Burns, Hitler would fail all three tests. Burns did not consider Hitler a true leader or a transforming leader because of the means that he used, the ends that he achieved, and the impact he had as a moral agent on his followers during the process of his leadership.

By looking at leadership as a process that is judged by a set of values, Burns's (1978) theory of good leadership is difficult to pigeonhole into one ethical theory. The most attractive part of Burns's theory is the idea that a leader elevates his or her followers and makes them leaders. Near the end of his book, he reintroduced this idea with an anecdote about why President Johnson did not run in 1968, stating, "Perhaps he did not comprehend that the people he had led—as a result in part of the impact of his leadership—had created their own fresh leadership, which was now outrunning his" (Burns, 1978, p. 424). All of the people that Johnson helped, the sick, the Blacks, and the poor, now had their own leadership. Burns (1978) noted, "Leadership begat leadership and hardly recognized its offspring. . . . Followers had become leaders" (p. 424).

Burns's and other scholars' use of the word *value* to talk about ethics is problematic because it is encompasses so many different kinds of things—economic values, organizational values, personal values, and moral values. Values do not tie people together the way moral concepts like duty and utility do, because most people subscribe to the view that "I have my values and you have yours." Having values does not mean that a person acts on them. To make values about something that people *do* rather than just *have*, Rokeach (1973) offered a very awkward discussion of the "ought" character of values. "A person phenomenologically experiences 'oughtness' to be objectively required by society in somewhat the same way that he perceives an incomplete circle as objectively requiring closure" (p. 9). Whereas Burns offers a provocative moral account of leadership, it would be stronger and clearer if he used the richer and more dynamic concepts found in moral philosophy.[1] This is not philosophic snobbery, but a plea for conceptual clarity and completeness. The implications of concepts such as virtue, duty, rights, and the greatest good have been worked out for hundreds of years and offer helpful tools for dissecting the moral dynamics of leadership and the relationship between leaders and followers.

Transformational Leadership

Burns's (1978) theory has inspired a number of studies on transformational leadership. For example, Bass's (1985) early work on transformational leadership focused on the impact of leaders on their followers. In sharp contrast to Burns, Bass's transformational leaders did not have to appeal to the higher-order needs and values of their followers. He was more concerned with the psychological relationship between transformational leaders and their followers. Bass originally believed that there could be both good and evil transformational leaders, so he was willing to call Hitler a transformational leader. Bass has made an admirable effort to offer a richer account of ethics in his more recent work. Bass and Steidlmeier (1999) argued that only morally good leaders are authentic transformational leaders; the rest, like Hitler, are pseudo-transformational. Bass and Steidlmeier described pseudo-transformational leaders as people who seek power and position at the expense of their followers' achievements. The source of their moral shortcomings lies in the fact that they are selfish and pursue their own interests at the expense of their followers. Whereas Bass and Steidlmeier still depend on altruism as a moral concept, they also look at authentic transformational leadership in terms of other ethical concepts such as virtue and commitment to the greatest good.

Bass (1985) believed that charismatic leadership is a necessary ingredient of transformational leadership. The research on charismatic leadership opens up a wide range of ethical questions because of the powerful emotional and moral impact that charismatic leaders have on followers (House, Spangler, & Woycke, 1991). Charismatic leadership can be the best and the worst kinds of leadership, depending on whether you look at a Gandhi or a Charles Manson (Lindholm, 1990). Bass and Steidlmeier's recent work runs parallel to research by J. M. Howell and Avolio (1992) on charismatic leadership. Howell and Avolio studied charismatic leaders and concluded that unethical charismatic leaders are manipulators who pursue their personal agendas. They argued that only leaders who act on socialized, rather than personalized, bases of power are transformational.

Critics of Transformational and Charismatic Leadership Theories

There is plenty of empirical research that demonstrates the effectiveness of transformational leaders. Scholars are almost rhapsodic in the ways in which they describe their findings, and with good reason. These findings show that ethics and effectiveness go hand in hand. Shamir, House, and Arthur (1993) stated:

> Charismatic leaders . . . increase followers' self-worth through emphasizing the relationships between efforts and important values. A general sense of self-worth increases general self-efficacy; a sense of moral correctness is a source of strength and confidence. Having complete faith in the moral correctness of one's convictions gives one the strength and confidence to behave accordingly. (p. 582)

The problem with this research is that it raises many, if not more, questions about the ethics. What are the important values? Are the values themselves ethical? What does moral correctness mean? Is what followers believe to be moral correctness *really* morally correct?

Critics question the ethics of the very idea of transformational leadership. Keeley (1998) argued that transformational leadership is well and good as long as you assume that everyone will eventually come around to the values and goals of the leader. Drawing on Madison's concern for factions in *Federalist No. 10,* Keeley (1998) wondered, "What is the likely status of people who would prefer their own goals and visions?" (p. 123). What if followers are confident that the leader's moral convictions are wrong? Keeley observed that the leadership and management literature has not been kind to nonconformists. He noted that Mao was one of Burns's transforming heroes and Mao certainly did not tolerate dissidents. Whereas Burns's theory tolerated conflict, conflict is only part of the process of reaching agreement on values. Is it ethical for a leader to require everyone to agree on all values?

Price (2000) discussed another problem with the moral view of transformational articulated by Burns (1978) and Bass and Steidlmeier (1999). The leaders they described are subject to making all sorts of moral mistakes, even when they are authentic, altruistic, and committed to common values. The fact that a leader possesses these traits does not necessarily yield moral behavior or good moral decisions. Price further argued that leaders and followers should be judged by adherence to morality, not adherence to their organization's or society's values. "Leaders must be willing to sacrifice their other-regarding values when generally applicable moral requirements make legitimate demands that they do so" (Price, 2003, p. 80). Sometimes being a charismatic and transformational leader in an organization, in the sense described by some theorists, does not mean that you are ethical when judged against moral concepts that apply in larger contexts.

Solomon (1998) took aim at the focus on charisma in leadership studies. He stated charisma is the shorthand for certain rare leaders. As a concept it is without ethical value and without much explanatory value. Charisma is not a distinctive quality of personality or character and, according to Solomon, it is not an essential part of leadership. For example, Solomon (1998) stated, "Charisma is not a single quality, nor is it a single emotion or set of emotions. It is a generalized way of pointing to and emptily explaining an emotional relationship that is too readily characterized as fascination" (p. 95). He then went on to argue that research on trust offers more insight into the leader/follower relationship than does research into charisma. Solomon specifically talked about the importance of exploring the emotional process of how people give their trust to others.

Taking Leaders Off Their Pedestals

Keeley's (1998), Price's (2000), and Solomon's (1998) criticisms of transformational and charismatic leadership theories raise two larger questions. First, scholars might be missing something about leadership when they study only exceptional types of leaders. Second, by limiting their study in this way, they fail to take into account the fact that even exceptional leaders get things wrong. Morality is a struggle for everyone, and it contains particular hazards for leaders. As Kant (1983) observed,

From such warped wood as is man made, nothing straight can be fashioned. . . . Man is an animal that, if he lives among other members of his species, has need of a master, for he certainly abuses his freedom in relation to his equals. He requires a master who will break his self-will and force him to obey a universally valid will, whereby everyone can be free. . . . He finds the master among the human species, but even he is an animal who requires a master. (p. 34)

The master for Kant (1983) is morality. No individual or leader has the key to morality, and hence, everyone is responsible for defining and enforcing morality. We need to understand the ethical challenges faced by imperfect humans who take on the responsibilities of leadership, so that we can develop morally better leaders, followers, institutions, and organizations. At issue is not simply what ethical and effective leaders do, but what leaders have to confront, and, in some cases overcome, to be ethical and effective. Some of these questions are psychological in nature, and others are concerned with moral reasoning.

Like many leadership scholars, Plato constructed his theory of the ideal leader—the philosopher king who is wise and virtuous. Through firsthand experience, Plato realized the shortcomings of his philosopher king model of leadership. Plato learned about leadership through three disastrous trips to the city-state of Syracuse. Plato visited Syracuse the first time at the invitation of the tyrant Dionysius I, but he soon became disgusted by the decadent and luxurious lifestyle of Dionysius's court. Plato returned to Athens convinced that existing forms of government at home and abroad were corrupt and unstable. He then decided to set up the Academy, where he taught for 40 years and wrote the *Republic*. In the *Republic*, Plato argued that the perfect state could come about only by rationally exploiting the highest qualities in people (although this sounds a bit like a transformational leadership, it is not). Plato firmly believed that the philosopher king could be developed through education. Hence, we might regard Plato's academy as a leadership school.

About 24 years after his first visit, Dionysius's brother-in-law, Dion, invited Plato back to Syracuse. By this time, Dionysius I was dead. Dion had read the *Republic* and wanted Plato to come and test his theory of leadership education on Dionysius's very promising son Dionysius II. This was an offer that Plato could not refuse, although he had serious reservations about accepting it. Nonetheless, off Plato went to Syracuse. The trip was a disaster. Plato's friend Dion was exiled because of court intrigues. Years later, Plato returned to Syracuse a third time but the visit was no better than the first two. In *Epistle VII*, Plato (1971) reported that these visits changed his view of leadership:

The older I grew, the more I realized how difficult it is to manage a city's affairs rightly. For I saw that it was impossible to do anything without friends and loyal followers. . . . The corruption of written laws and our customs was proceeding at such amazing speed that whereas when I noted these changes and saw how unstable everything was, I became in the end quite dizzy. (pp. 325–326)

Plato (1971) seemed to have lost faith in his conviction that leaders could be perfected. He realized that leaders shared the same human weaknesses of their followers, but he also saw how important trust was in leadership. In the *Republic*,

Plato had entertained a pastoral image of the leader as a shepherd to his flock. But in a later work, *Statesman,* he observed that leaders are not at all like shepherds. Shepherds are obviously quite different from their flock, whereas human leaders are not much different from their followers (Plato, 1971). He noted that people are not sheep—some are cooperative and some are very stubborn. Plato's revised view of leadership was that leaders were really like weavers. Their main task was to weave together different kinds of people—the meek and the self-controlled, the brave and the impetuous—into the fabric of society (Plato, 1971).

Plato's ideas on leadership progressed from a profound belief that it is possible for some people to be wise and benevolent philosopher kings to a more modest belief that the real challenge of leadership is working successfully with people who do not always like each other, do not always like the leader, and do not necessarily want to live together. These are some of the key challenges faced by leaders today all over the world. Leadership is more like being a shepherd to a flock of cats or like pushing a wheelbarrow full of frogs (O'Toole, 1995).

Whereas Plato's image of the philosopher king in the *Republic* is idealistic, the *Statesman* and the early books of the *Republic* lay out some of the fundamental ethical issues of leadership; namely, moral imperfection and power. Near the end of the *Statesman,* Plato contended that we cannot always depend on leaders to be good and that is why we need rule of law (Plato, 1971). Good laws, rules, and regulations protect us from unethical leaders and serve to help leaders be ethical (similar to James Madison's concern for checks on leaders).

Plato, like many of the ancients, realized that the greatest ethical challenge for humans in leadership roles stems from the temptations of power. In Book II of the *Republic,* he provided a thought-provoking experiment about power and accountability. Glaucon, the protagonist in the dialogue, argued that the only reason people are just is because they lack the power to be unjust. He then told the story of the "Ring of Gyges" (Plato, 1971). A young shepherd from Lydia found a ring and discovered that when he turned the ring on his finger, it made him invisible. The shepherd then used the ring to seduce the king's wife, attack the king, and take over the kingdom. Plato asks us to consider what we would do if we had power without accountability. One of our main concerns about leaders is that they will abuse their power because they are accountable to fewer people. In this respect, the "Ring of Gyges" is literally and figuratively a story about transparency. The power leaders have to do things also entails the power to hide what they do.

Power comes with a temptation to do evil and an obligation to do good. Philosophers often refer to a point made by Kant (1993, p. 32) as "ought implies can," meaning you have a moral obligation to act when you are able to act effectively (similar to the free will determinism question mentioned earlier—more power, more free will). It means that the more power, resources, and ability you have to do good, the more you have a moral obligation to do so. The notion of helpfulness, discussed earlier in conjunction with altruism, is derived from this notion of power and obligation. It is about the moral obligation to help when you can help.

The Bathsheba Syndrome

The moral foible that people fear most in their leaders is personal immorality accompanied by abuse of power. Usually, it is the most successful leaders who suffer the worst ethical failures. Ludwig and Longenecker (1993) called the moral failure of successful leaders the "Bathsheba syndrome," based on the biblical story of King David and Bathsheba. Ancient texts such as the Bible provide us with wonderful case studies on the moral pitfalls of leaders. King David is portrayed as a successful leader in the Bible. We first meet him as a young shepherd in the story of David and Goliath. This story offers an interesting leadership lesson. In it, God selects the small shepherd David over his brother, a strong soldier, because David "has a good heart." Then as God's hand-picked leader, David goes on to become a great leader, until we come to the story of David and Bathsheba (2 Samuel 11–12).

The story begins with David taking an evening stroll around his palace. From his vantage point on the palace roof, he sees the beautiful Bathsheba bathing. He asks his servants to bring Bathsheba to him. The king beds Bathsheba and she gets pregnant. Bathsheba's husband, Uriah, is one of David's best generals. King David tries to cover up his immoral behavior by calling Uriah home. When Uriah arrives, David attempts to get him drunk so that he will sleep with Bathsheba. Uriah refuses to cooperate, because he feels it would be unfair to enjoy himself while his men are on the front. (This is a wonderful sidebar about the moral obligations of leaders to followers.) David then escalates his attempt to cover things up by ordering Uriah to the front of a battle where he gets killed. In the end, the prophet Nathan blows the whistle on David and God punishes David.

The Bathsheba story has repeated itself again and again in history. Scandals ranging from Watergate to the President Clinton and Monica Lewinsky affair to Enron all follow the general pattern of this story (Winter, 2002, gives an interesting psychological account of the Clinton case). First, we see what happens when successful leaders lose sight of what their job is. David should have been focusing on running the war, not watching Bathsheba bathe. He was literally and figuratively looking in the wrong place. This is why we worry about men leaders who are womanizers getting distracted from their jobs. Second, because power leads to privileged access, leaders have more opportunities to indulge themselves and, hence, need more willpower to resist indulging themselves. David could have had Bathsheba brought to him by his servants with no questions asked. Third, successful leaders sometimes develop an inflated belief in their ability to control outcomes. David became involved in escalating cover-ups.

The most striking thing about leaders who get themselves in these situations is that the cover-ups are usually worse than the crime. In David's case, adultery was not as bad as murder. Also, it is during the cover-up that leaders abuse their power as leaders the most. In Clinton's case, a majority of Americans found his lying to the public far more immoral than his adultery. Last, leaders learn that their power falls short of the ring of Gyges. It will not keep their actions invisible forever. Whistleblowers such as Nathan in King David's case or Sharon Watkins in the Enron case call their bluff and demand that their leaders be held to the same moral standards as everyone else. When this happens, in Bible stories and everywhere else, all hell breaks loose. The impact of a leader's moral lapses causes great harm to their constituents.

Read as a leadership case study, the story of David and Bathsheba is about pride and the moral fragility of people when they hold leadership positions. It is also a cautionary tale about success and the lengths to which people will go to keep from losing it. What is most interesting about the Bathsheba syndrome is that it is difficult to predict which leaders will fall prey to it, because people get it after they have become successful. If we are to gain a better understanding of ethics and leadership, we need to examine how leaders resist falling for the ethical temptations that come with power.

Self-Discipline and Virtue

The moral challenges of power and the nature of the leader's job explain why self-knowledge and self-control are, and have been for centuries, the most important factors in leadership development.[2] Ancient writers, such as Lao-tzu, Confucius, Buddha, Plato, and Aristotle, all emphasized good habits, self-knowledge, and self-control in their writing. Eastern philosophers, such as Lao-tzu, Confucius, and Buddha, not only talked about virtues but also about the challenges of self-discipline and controlling the ego. Lao-tzu warned against egotism when he stated, "He who stands on tiptoe is not steady" (Tzu, 1963, p. 152). He also tells us, "The best rulers are those whose existence is merely known by people" (Lao-tzu, 1963, p. 148). Confucius (1963) focused on the importance of duty and self-control. He stated, "If a man (the ruler) can for one day master himself and return to propriety, all under heaven will return to humanity. To practice humanity depends on oneself" (p. 38). He tied a leader's self-mastery and effectiveness together when he wrote, "If a ruler sets himself right, he will be followed without his command. If he does not set himself right, even his commands will not be obeyed" (Confucius, 1963, p. 38).

In the First Sermon, the Buddha described how people's uncontrolled thirst for things contributes to their own suffering and the suffering of others. Not unlike psychologists today, he realized that getting one's desires under control is the best way to end personal and social misery. This is a particular challenge for leaders, because they often have the means to indulge their material and personal desires. Compassion is the most important virtue in Buddhist ethics because it keeps desires and vices in check. The Dalai Lama (1999) concisely summed up the moral dynamics of compassion in this way:

> When we bring up our children to have knowledge without compassion, their attitude towards others is likely to be a mixture of envy of those in positions above them, aggressive competitiveness towards their peers, and scorn for these less fortunate. This leads to a propensity toward greed, presumption, excess, and very quickly to loss of happiness. (p. 181)

Virtues are a fundamental part of the landscape of moral philosophy and provide a useful way of thinking about leadership development. What is important about virtues are their dynamics (e.g., how they interact with other virtues and vices) and their contribution to self-knowledge and self-control. The properties of a virtue are very different from the properties of other moral concepts such as value. Virtues are things that you have only if you practice them. Values are things that are important to people. I may *value* honesty but not always tell the truth. I cannot possess the virtue of honesty without telling the truth. As Aristotle mentioned, virtues are good habits that we learn from society and our leaders. Aristotle wrote quite a bit about leaders as moral role models, and much of what he said complements observations in research on transformational leadership. He noted, "Legislators make citizens good by forming habits in them" (Aristotle, 1984). Whereas virtues come naturally to those who practice them, they are not mindless habits. People must practice them fully conscious of knowing that what they are doing is morally right.

Perhaps the most striking thing about the Greek notion of virtue (*areté*), which is also translated as excellence, is that it does not separate an individual's ethics from his or her occupational competence. Both Plato and Aristotle constantly used examples of doctors, musicians, coaches, rulers, and so forth to talk about the relationship between moral and technical or professional excellence. Aristotle (1984) wrote, "Every excellence brings to good the thing to which it is the excellence and makes the work of that thing be done well. . . . Therefore, if this is true in every case, the excellence of man also will be the state which makes man good and which makes him do his work well" (p. 1747). Excellence is tied to function. The function of a knife is to cut. An excellent knife cuts well. The function of humans, according to Aristotle, is to reason. To be morally virtuous, you must reason well, because reason tells you how to practice and when to practice a virtue. If you reason well, you will know how to practice moral and professional virtues. In other words, reason is the key to practicing moral virtues *and* the virtues related to one's various occupations in life. Hence, the morally virtuous leader will also be a competent leader, because he or she will do what is required in the job the right way. Virtue ethics does not differentiate between the morality of the leader and the morality of his or her leadership. An incompetent leader, like the head of the Swiss charity that tried to free the enslaved children, lacks moral virtue, regardless of his or her good intentions.

Conclusion

The more we explore how ethics and effectiveness are inextricably intertwined, the better we will understand leadership. The philosophic study of ethics provides a critical perspective from which we can examine the assumptions behind leadership and leadership theories. It offers another level of analysis that should be integrated into the growing body of empirical research in the field. The ethics of leadership has to be examined along a variety of dimensions that cannot be understood separately. The dimensions are the following:

1. The ethics of a leader as a person, which includes things like self-knowledge, discipline, and intentions, and so forth

2. The ethics of the leader/follower relationship (i.e., how they treat each other)

3. The ethics of the process of leadership (i.e., command and control, participatory)

4. The ethics of what the leader does or does not do

These dimensions give us a picture of the ethics of what a leader does and how he or she does it. But even after an interdependent analysis of these dimensions, the picture is not complete. We then have to take one more step and look at all of these interdependent dimensions in larger contexts. For example, the ethics of organizational leadership would have to be examined in the context of the community, and so forth.

A richer understanding of the moral challenges that are distinctive to leaders and leadership is particularly important for leadership development. Whereas case studies of ethical leadership are inspiring and case studies of evil leaders are cautionary, we need a practical understanding of why it is morally difficult to be a good leader and a good follower. Leaders do not have to be power-hungry psychopaths to do unethical things, nor do they have to be altruistic saints to be ethical. Most leaders are not charismatic or transformational leaders. They are ordinary men and women in business, government, nonprofits, and communities who sometimes make volitional, emotional, moral, and cognitive mistakes. More work needs to be done on ordinary leaders and followers and how they can help each other be ethical and make better moral decisions.

Aristotle (1984) said that happiness is the end to which we aim in life. The Greek word that Aristotle uses for happiness is *eudaimonea*. It means happiness, not in terms of pleasure or contentment, but as flourishing. A happy life is one where we flourish as human beings, both in terms of our material and personal development and our moral development. The concept of *eudaimonea* gives us two umbrella questions that can be used to assess the overall ethics and effectiveness of leadership. Does a leader or a particular kind of leadership contribute to and/or allow people to flourish in terms of their lives as a whole? Does a leader or a particular kind of leadership interfere with the ability of other groups of people or other living things to flourish? Leaders do not always have to transform people for them to flourish. Their greater responsibility is to create the social and material conditions under which people can and do flourish (Ciulla, 2000). Change is part of leadership, but so is sustainability. Ethical leadership entails the ability of leaders to sustain fundamental notions of morality such as care and respect for persons, justice, and honesty, in changing organizational, social, and global contexts.

Last, leadership scholars have just begun to scratch the surface of other disciplines. History, philosophy, anthropology, literature, and religion all promise to expand our understanding of leaders and leadership. Ancient writers such as Plato, Aristotle, Lao-tzu, and Confucius not only tell us about leadership, they also capture our imaginations. What makes a classic a classic is that its message carries themes and values that are meaningful to people from different cultures and different periods of history. They offer well-grounded ideas about who we are, what we should be like, and how we should live. These ideas will help us understand current empirical research on leadership and generate new ideas for research.

In my own work, I have begun to research the history of the idea of leadership. Where did the idea of leadership come from and how has it evolved in various cultures to the way that we think about it today? To really understand leadership, we need to put our ear to the ground of history and listen carefully to the saga of human hopes, desires, and aspirations, and the follies, disappointments, and triumphs of those who led and those who followed them. As Confucius once said, "A man who reviews the old as to find out the new is qualified to teach others."

Notes

1.   I have been discussing this issue with Burns for more than 10 years. We are equally stubborn on this point.

2.   Editors' note: Compare "self control" here with "impulse control" in Sashkin, Chapter 8, this volume.

PART VI

Conclusions

CHAPTER 14

The Crucibles
of Authentic Leadership

Warren Bennis

I t was the practice of Ralph Waldo Emerson to ask old friends he had not seen in awhile: "What's become clear to you since we last met?" As this volume makes clear, those engaged in the study of leadership have learned an enormous amount in the century or so since the enterprise began to evolve from the study of great men. The 20th century was marked by the emergence of some of the most powerful and disturbing leaders in human history. Millions died as a direct result of failed or evil leadership—in the death camps of the Third Reich but also in the Soviet Union and in famine-ravished China. The "butcher's bill" of the 20th century is a reminder of why we study leadership in the first place. Our very lives depend on it. That has never been more true than it is today, because one consequence of the extraordinary leadership of Franklin Delano Roosevelt was the creation of genuine weapons of mass destruction. I bring these matters up, not because any of you need a capsule history lesson, but because it is important to remember that the quality of all our lives is dependent on the quality of our leadership. The context in which we study leadership is very different from the context in which we study, say, astronomy. By definition, leaders wield power, and so we study them with the same self-interested intensity with which we study diabetes and other life-threatening diseases. Only when we understand leaders will we be able to control them.

I would argue that context always counts when it comes to leadership, and, in the next few pages, I want to examine certain enduring issues and questions related to leadership in the context of today. I want to look at how recent events and trends are reshaping contemporary ideas about leadership.

In the United States at least, leadership studies changed in some basic way on September 11, 2001. As the nation watched, in horror, the television footage of people fleeing the World Trade Center and, in even greater horror, the collapse of the Twin Towers, I realized as so many others did that this was one of the transformational events of our time. One immediate consequence of the terrorist assaults on New York and the Pentagon was to make leadership a matter for public discussion in the United States in a way it has not been since World War II. Leadership became central to the public conversation—displacing the endless background noise about celebrity and pushing aside even worried talk about the sorry state of the economy. People in other parts of the world have been dealing with the ugly realities of international terrorism for decades, and, to them, the stunned horror of Americans must have seemed more than a little naive. But the United States has long had the luxury of studying leadership with the leisurely detachment that only those in peaceful, prosperous nations can afford.

The assault on a nonmilitary target in the paradigmatic American city was more stunning, in many ways, than Pearl Harbor. Not since the Civil War had ideologically motivated violence occurred on such a scale in a city in the United States. Americans are still sorting out the consequences of the attacks of 9/11 and will continue to do so for decades. But with the collapse of the Twin Towers came a new awareness that leadership is more than a matter of who looks best on television. Since 9/11, government officials have been scrutinized for evidence of leadership ability with an intensity usually seen only in wartime. And, indeed, in describing how then New York City Mayor Rudolph Giuliani and others responded to al Qaeda's assault, the media referred repeatedly to the larger-than-life leaders of World War II. The iconic leader du jour was unquestionably Winston Churchill. It was noted, for instance, that Karen Hughes, then special assistant to President George W. Bush, kept a plaque on her desk that bore Churchill's stirring line: "I was not the lion but it fell to me to give the lion's roar." The invocation of Churchill was a secular prayer for help, but it was also evidence of a shift in the very idea of leadership—a return to a more heroic, more inspirational definition than had been the fashion for decades. In the rubble of Ground Zero, people did not want a leader who could organize cross-functional teams; they longed for a leader for the ages, a sage and savior to lead them out of hell.

For those who have spent their lives studying leadership, 9/11 was a compelling reminder that war and other violent crises are inevitably crucibles from which leaders emerge. It was fascinating to watch how Rudy Giuliani was transformed in the days following the attacks from a lame-duck mayor with a reputation for mean-spiritedness into "Churchill in a baseball cap," as one phrasemaker dubbed him. Almost daily, CNN and the *New York Times* released first-draft case studies of leadership in action. Giuliani's performance was so full of lessons about leadership that he got a best-selling book on the subject out of it. Indeed, his behavior in the wake of the attacks underscored many truisms about leadership, including how it can emerge in unlikely candidates and how it frequently endures only as long as the crisis itself. Giuliani, who served New York City tirelessly during those days, standing in for slain fathers of the bride and comforting both grieving relatives and the city as a whole, richly deserved to be named *Time* magazine's Person of the Year. But it remains to be seen whether he will again find himself in a position that allows his proven leadership ability to shine. History has a way of throwing leaders up and then covering them over, Ozymandias-style. After Churchill gave the lion's roar, he spent several decades as a Sunday painter, and Giuliani, too, may quietly disappear into a successful law practice.

Whatever else 9/11 meant, it was a vivid reminder that one of the sweeter uses of adversity continues to be its ability to bring leadership to the fore. What Abigail Adams wrote to son John Quincy Adams in the tumult of 1780 is still true today: "These are the times in which a genius would wish to live. It is not in the still calm of life, or in the repose of a pacific station, that great challenges are formed . . . great necessities call out great virtues." In 2001 and 2002, when Robert Thomas and I were doing the research for *Geeks & Geezers* (Bennis & Thomas, 2002), we interviewed almost 50 leaders—some 75 and older, the rest 35 and younger. In every case, we found that their leadership had emerged after some defining experience, or crucible, as we called it. These were often ordeals, and, among the older leaders, they often occurred in wartime. The crucibles of our leaders included such personal tragedies as television journalist Mike Wallace's discovery of the body of his son after an accident in Greece and global business pioneer Sidney Rittenberg's harrowing 16 years in Chinese prisons, much of it in solitary confinement, often in the dark.

In a foreword to our book, David Gergen, head of the Center for Public Leadership at Harvard's John F. Kennedy School of Government, describes the crucible in which Harry Truman discovered that he was a leader. We tend to think of Truman as the one-time haberdasher whose leadership emerged only after the death of Roosevelt. But, as Gergen recounts, Truman was tested during the Great War on the battlefields of France. The head of an artillery battery, he was in the Vosges Mountains when his position was shelled by the Germans. His men panicked, and Truman's horse panicked as well, falling on him and almost killing him. But, as historian David McCullough wrote in his prize-winning biography of Truman, the future president crawled out from under his horse and overcame his own fear, screaming profanities at his men until most of them returned to their posts. Truman's men never forgot that his courage under fire had saved their lives, and Truman discovered that he had a taste for leadership as well as a gift for it.

Again and again, we found that something magical happens in the crucible—an alchemy whereby fear and suffering are transformed into something glorious and redemptive. This process reveals, if it does not create, leadership, the ability to inspire and move others to action. We found intelligence, optimism, and other traits traditionally associated with leadership present in all our subjects, but those traits are no guarantee that the alchemy of leadership will take place. Countless gifted people are broken by suffering. But our leaders discovered themselves in their crucibles, for reasons we still do not fully understand. However searing the experience, our leaders were able to make sense of it or organize meaning around it—meaning that subsequently attracted followers. Instead of being defeated by their ordeal, each of our leaders saw it as a heroic journey. Whatever their age, these men and women created their own legends. Without being untruthful, they constructed new, improved versions of themselves. In many cases—as in Truman's—the ordeal and the leader's interpretation of it led others to follow the newly revealed leader.

In the model of leadership development that grew out of that research, successful individuals all evidenced four essential competencies—adaptive capacity, the ability to engage others through shared meaning, a distinctive voice, and integrity. Often these abilities were evident to some degree before their ordeals, but they were intensified by the crucible experience. Of all these abilities, the most important was adaptive capacity. All our leaders had an extraordinary gift for coping with whatever life threw at them. I believe that adaptive capacity is essentially creativity—the ability to take disparate things and turn them into something new and useful. Indeed, it is no accident that there is a convergence between leadership studies and studies of creativity—a convergence that dates back to the first studies of Darwin, Einstein, and other geniuses, or thought leaders. When we speak of exemplary leadership, we are often talking about exemplary, creative problem solving—the discovery of new solutions to unprecedented problems.

But let's return to the lessons of 9/11. During the 1950s, no one who heard Marshall McLuhan speak so confidently of the global village or the extent to which the medium is the message had any idea how truly prescient he was. But the terrorist attacks of 2001 underscored that ours is indeed one world, albeit a profoundly splintered one, and that television and more recent technologies are its primary mediators. Here were multinational terrorists dispatched by an individual holed up in an apartment, or a cave, in Afghanistan or elsewhere in the Middle East. Digital technology was used to advance a medieval ideology, with orders and money transferred in a nanosecond halfway across the planet. Globalization has created a host of new dangers that require a new kind of leadership—one that is, above all, collaborative. It was the inability of security agencies in the United States to work effectively together that allowed the 9/11 terrorists to enter and remain in the country and to learn how to fly a jet into a skyscraper at American flight schools.

And global terrorism is only one contemporary threat that requires a multinational, collaborative response. Disease, poverty, and the oppression of minorities, women, and political dissidents are urgent international concerns. As the outbreak in 2003 of severe acute respiratory syndrome, or SARS, illustrated, the ability of almost anyone to jump on a plane and fly to some distant city has created the real possibility that future flights will spread deadly plagues with unprecedented ease and rapidity.

In the months that led up to the toppling of the regime of Iraq's Saddam Hussein in 2003, much was made in the media, and rightfully so, of President George W. Bush's failure to build a global coalition. The president's decision to enter Iraq with support from only a handful of nations (Great Britain, Australia, and Poland, among them) was widely seen as a leadership failure, despite the defeat of Hussein in record time. The critique of the president reflected more than political differences on whether American military action was appropriate only if legitimized by the United Nations. The criticism reflected an understanding that coalition building is one of the essential competencies of all leaders—in some ways, the defining one.

Among the committed coalition builders President Bush might have emulated was his father. Before the first Gulf War, President George Herbert Walker Bush doggedly wooed world leaders. When the president was not smiling over banquet tables himself, he dispatched his secretary of state, James Baker, on eight consensus-building trips abroad, trips that took Baker to 18 European capitals. The result was that the United States went to war as part of a genuine "coalition of the willing." We cannot know what father said to son in private conversation before the Iraqi conflict. But we do know what the older Bush counseled in a speech at Tufts University in February 2003. "You've got to reach out to the other person," he said, describing what leaders in an interconnected world must do. "You've got to convince them that long-term friendship should trump short-term adversity." The senior Bush was articulating what democratic leaders have always known. In a society in which power must be given freely, not coerced, leaders make alliances by persuading others that their interests and fates are intertwined. As I write this in 2003, it is clear that the United States needs allies more than ever, as disorder continues in post-Hussein Iraq, and a growing number of Iraqis perceive the forces of the United States and her handful of allies as occupiers rather than liberators.

Coalition building is also an essential element of corporate leadership. Until American business was roiled by recent corporate scandals, we had long been guilty of treating chief executive officers (CEOs) and other business leaders as demigods whose success was a unilateral achievement resulting from their special genius. This tradition dates back at least as far as our deification of such business titans as Thomas Edison and Henry Ford, and it resurged during the late 1970s when Lee Iacocca was hailed as the savior of the American auto industry. In retrospect, the lionization of anyone connected with the battered U.S. auto industry seems like a cruel joke. But we forget, now that so many corporate heads have rolled, how recently CEOs were treated both as celebrities and as thought leaders whose public comments were scrutinized for hidden wisdom like tea leaves. In many ways, the rise of the celebrity CEO was a regression to the era when great institutions were thought to be the lengthened shadows of great men. The late-20th-century version of that durable myth differed only in conceding that a few great institutions—such as the Martha Stewart empire—were lengthened shadows of great women. But as Patricia Ward Biederman and I wrote in *Organizing Genius* (Bennis & Biederman, 1997), one has almost always been too small a number for greatness. Whatever their sphere, authentic leaders know, even if they do not bruit it around, that their power is a consequence of their ability to recruit the talent of others to the collective enterprise. The Lone Ranger has never been as dead as he is today. In all but the simplest undertaking, great things are done by alliances, not by larger-than-life individuals, however powerful they may seem.

I doubt that the world was ever so simple that a single heroic leader, however capable, could solve its problems unilaterally. Even the Biblical tale of Noah underscores the importance of collaboration. But certainly today's world requires unprecedented coalition building. The European Union may be the paradigmatic response to this changed reality. For those of us who experienced World War II first-hand, it is heartening to see such a high level of economic and political cooperation among nations that were so recently at one another's throats. And more and more coalitions, created and maintained by collaborative leaders, will be required in the years ahead.

The pace of change is not slowing. It is accelerating as never before. Ever-changing problems require faster, smarter, more inventive solutions, solutions that can only be achieved collaboratively. In recent years, even the way leaders make decisions has changed. The day is all but over when a leader has the leisure to digest all the facts and then to act. As psychologist Karl Weick has pointed out, today's leaders are more often required to act first, assess the results of their actions, and then act again. Thanks to digital technology, facts can be collected and numbers crunched with unprecedented ease. In this new climate, information is always flooding in, and there is no final analysis, only constant evaluation and reevaluation. Action becomes one more way to gather information, which becomes the basis for further action. As Weick so eloquently put it, in such a world, leaders cannot depend on maps. They need compasses. And, as never before, they need allies.

The ability to form and maintain alliances is not just a political tool. The successful older leaders that Robert Thomas and I interviewed made it a point to seek out and befriend talented younger people. Forming these social alliances was a strategy the older leaders used to stay in touch with a rapidly changing world. These social alliances helped keep the older leaders vital in a way their less successful, more isolated peers were not. The younger leaders also benefited from relationships with more seasoned, older friends. And this strategy of forming alliances is not limited to humans. Stanford neurobiologist Robert Sapolsky, who lived, for a time, as part of a group of Serengeti baboons, found that the older males most likely to survive were those who were able to form strong bonds with younger males. Teamed with youthful allies, the senior males were able to compensate for the losses brought about by age. Mentoring is a variation on this primal theme, a way for the young and the old to pool their wisdom and energy to their mutual benefit.

Because leaders have power, the question of whether they use it for good or ill continues to be desperately important. We could argue forever over whether Hitler was an authentic leader, or whether leadership, by definition, implies a kind of virtue. Certainly, Hitler had many of the competencies of leadership—a vision, the ability to recruit others to it, insight into what his followers needed, if only in the most demonic parts of themselves. He had the unquenchable self-confidence that is associated with leadership, the ambition, the obsessive sense of purpose, the need to communicate it, and the oratorical gifts to do so. He even had a kind of twisted integrity, in that he was always what his followers knew him to be. My fear is that our concern over this question is a dead end. Like the problem, the solution may be a matter of semantics. Perhaps we should reserve the word *leader* for those whose leadership is morally neutral (if that is possible) or tilted toward the good. We might simply stop calling Hitler an evil leader and refer to him as a despot or simply as a führer, the straightforward German word for leader until Hitler poisoned it.

To say that the problem of how to label bad leaders distracts us from more pressing concerns is not to say that morality and leadership are trivial matters. They are of the utmost important, now and forever. As Harvard Business School scholar Lynn Sharp Paine says of morality and business, ethics does not always pay, but it always counts. Far more urgent than the issue of what to call bad leaders is the question of how to create a culture in which despots or even plain-vanilla corporate tyrants of the Al Dunlap ("Chainsaw Al") sort cannot flourish. In truth, I think we do that by creating the same kind of climate in which talented people blossom and the very best work can be done. Fertile, liberating environments almost always have two components: able leaders who listen and capable followers who speak out. There is a memorable story about Nikita Khrushchev on this point. After the death of Stalin, the Soviet premier was at a public meeting at which he denounced Stalin's reign of terror. After Khrushchev spoke, someone in the audience confronted him. "You were a confidant of Stalin's," a voice called out from the crowd. "What were you doing when Stalin was slaughtering his own people?" "Who said that?" Khrushchev demanded to know. There was no answer. "Who said that?" he asked again, pounding the podium. And then Khrushchev explained: "*That's* what I was doing!"

By his silence, Khrushchev proved himself a bad follower (albeit a live one). This is one of those areas in which the lessons of leadership cry out for application in the workplace. The corporate scandals of the past few years have cause unprecedented havoc in the American economy, tumult that has rocked the linked economies of the world. And in nearly every case, those scandals resulted not simply from crooked accounting and other crimes but from the failure of corporate leadership to create a culture of candor. Enron is a perfect example. Long before the energy giant crashed and burned, key employees knew that the books were being manipulated in ways that were deceptive, if not illegal. Enron executive Sherron S. Watkins did the right thing and warned her bosses that "Enron could implode in a wave of accounting scandals." Naive but admirably concerned about the good of the organization, Watkins expected to be heard, if not rewarded. Instead, company chief financial officer (CFO) Andrew Fastow buried the evidence and immediately set out to get rid of Watkins. The problem at Enron, she said later, was that few were willing to speak truth to power. Employees, including management, knew better than to point out the increasingly obvious ethical lapses in the company's business practices. Critical talk was taboo at Enron. "You simply didn't want to discuss it in front of the water cooler," Watkins said.

It is one thing to remain silent when your life or that of your family is in danger. It is quite another to remain silent when other people's lives are at risk and the worst thing that can happen to you is losing your job. And yet many organizations implicitly demand silence and denial on the part of their employees, even at the cost of human lives. When the space shuttle *Challenger* exploded shortly after takeoff in 1986, killing all seven on board, the blame was ultimately put on the space shuttle's O-rings, which failed in the unseasonable cold the morning of the launch. Tragically, the potential flaw in the O-rings had been repeatedly noted by Roger Boisjoly, an engineer with NASA supplier Morton Thiokol. Only the day before, Boisjoly had made one more desperate attempt to warn his superiors that the crew was in danger. But the company suppressed the information. As for Boisjoly, the whistleblower got the reward that annoying truth tellers so often receive. He lost his job, and indeed never worked again as an engineer. He now makes his living giving talks on organizational ethics.

To an outsider, it is almost impossible to imagine that any organization would prefer silence to honest criticism that saves lives. But such deadly organizational quietism happens all the time. And one tragedy is often not enough to bring about change. In a report prepared after the shuttle *Columbia*'s deadly failure in 2003, investigators put part of the blame on "a flawed institutional culture that plays down problems," according to the *New York Times*. Just as Boisjoly had been ignored when he raised his concerns in 1986, a new generation of space-program managers had chosen to ignore signs of potential problems, including e-mails from employees warning of flaws in the system. The fiery failure of the *Columbia* killed seven astronauts, whose deaths are attributable, at least in part, to managers who closed their minds to vital but unwanted news. NASA created a system that rewarded silence before safety, and that is what it got.

Corporate enthusiasm for collective ignorance has launched a thousand "Dilbert" cartoons. Movie mogul Samuel Goldwyn, famous for his malapropisms as well as his autocratic rule, is said to have snarled at his underlings after a string of box-office flops, "I want you to tell me what's the matter with MGM even if it means losing your jobs." Too often, that is exactly what happens. More recently, Compaq CEO Eckhard Pfeiffer lost dominance of the computer market to Gateway and Dell, not because he lacked talent but because he surrounded himself with an A-list of yes men and closed his office door to anyone who had the courage to tell him what he did not want to hear.

In the 2003 scandal at the *New York Times* that led to the resignations of executive editor Howell Raines and managing editor Gerald Boyd, insiders repeatedly told other media that the real problem was not the pathological behavior of rogue reporter Jayson Blair but a newsroom culture that rewarded a handful of favorites of questionable merit and marginalized everyone else. It was also a place where control was concentrated in the hands of a few, and dissent was unwelcome. Neither Raines nor Boyd listened when another editor warned that Blair must stop reporting for the *New York Times* immediately. Much has been made of Raines's role in the scandal, but the *Wall Street Journal* reported a disturbing example of Boyd's arrogant resistance to the truth as well. When the paper's national editor suggested a story to Boyd on the *Columbia* disaster, Boyd nixed it, saying it had already run that morning in *USA Today*. Investigations Editor Douglas Frantz subsequently brought Boyd a copy of *USA Today* to prove that the story had not appeared. Boyd, of course, should have acknowledged his mistake and ordered up the story. Instead, he told Frantz he should not embarrass his managing editor and handed Frantz a quarter to call his friend Dean Baquet, a former *Times* editor who had gone to the *Los Angeles Times*. In essence, Boyd told Frantz to hit the road. And like a number of other unhappy veterans of the *New York Times*, Frantz quit to go to Los Angeles.

Linda Greenhouse, who covers the Supreme Court for the *New York Times*, told *Journal* reporters Matthew Rose and Laurie Cohen: "There is an endemic cultural issue at the *Times* that is not a Howell creation, although it plays into his vulnerabilities as a manager, which is a top-down hierarchical structure. And it's a culture where speaking truth to power has never been particularly welcomed."

You would hope that leaders in any organization would have the ego strength to accept well-intentioned criticism from talented underlings. You would hope that leaders would be wise enough to know that what you do not want to hear is often the most valuable information you can get. You would think that czar-like executive compensation packages would more than make up for any embarrassment corporate leaders feel when subordinates choose candor over ego massage. But such is rarely the case. Executive arrogance poisons the atmosphere in far too many organizations. It is especially deadly in idea-driven organizations (as more and more are) in which subordinates are often as talented as their leaders, or more so. In hard economic times, autocratic leaders may be able to retain talent. But as soon as the economy rebounds, talented people who do not respect the people they work for head for the door. At the height of the now battered New Economy, employers knew that talent was their treasure, and they treated their employees with respect. In hard times, employers often become arrogant again, forgetting that good times will return and that the talent will again take flight.

The band-aid that *New York Times* Co. Chairman Arthur Sulzberger Jr. put on the paper's leadership problem was to name former Executive Editor Joseph Lelyveld, whom Raines had succeeded, as his interim replacement. (As I write this, Raines's permanent replacement has yet to be named.) Well-liked by reporters and editors, Lelyveld seemed to understand, as Raines did not, that the *New York Times* was about the work, not about the executive editor. Lelyveld had decentralized control, giving editors and reporters more autonomy and more discretion to work on longer, thoughtful stories appropriate to journalists at the top of their game (in contrast, Raines liked to dispatch masses of reporters to cover a breaking news story, a process he called "flooding the zone." And, unlike Raines, who assigned reporters to execute his story ideas for the front page, Lelyveld joked that he had trouble getting his story ideas into the paper—an off-hand reminder to his staff that he did not confuse himself with god. Interestingly, Lelyveld was repeatedly described by those who worked with him as "aloof." He was not a charismatic leader, nor a warm, fuzzy one, just an able one whom people respected. Lelyveld understood that smart, capable people should be treated with respect—not just because it is the right thing to do but because it is good business. Lelyveld was also a reminder that leadership abilities are ultimately more important than leadership styles.

Future of Leadership Research

In reading the earlier chapters in this book, I was struck by how rich and varied the study of leadership has become over the past 20 years. My sense is that the field is now on the brink of the kind of major breakthroughs that revolutionized social psychology in the 1950s and 1960s. Inspired by the earlier chapters, I will focus on two topics, among others, that seem to demand further study.

Leadership and Globalization

The Global Leadership and Organizational Behavior Effectiveness (GLOBE) Project, in which social scientists from approximately 60 countries look at leadership from a cross-cultural perspective, is an important start. In a world made smaller by technology, it is more urgent than ever that we understand each other's symbols, values, and mind-sets. Only then can we hope to reach consensus on common goals, including how to ensure global peace and prosperity. In the past few years, Westerners have become acutely aware of how little they know about Islamic cultures, including how to speak their languages. One subject that cries out for more scrutiny is tribalism, the force, powerful throughout the world, that undermines globalization at every turn. The private sector has long been aware of the importance of understanding its audiences and markets. Advertising agencies regularly recruit new PhDs in cultural anthropology to study the customs and values of consumers. We need to turn even more experts loose on comparing cultures on such fundamental problems as what we mean when we use certain terms. This is essential, not just to understand those who oppose us but to ensure the forging of effective alliances.

As recounted in a recent issue of *Smithsonian,* British and American military had so much trouble communicating during World War II that the Allies asked anthropologist Margaret Mead to try to find out what the problem was. Writer Patrick Cooke explains: "Mead discovered that the two cultures possessed fundamentally different world views. One simple way to demonstrate this was to ask an English person and an American a single question: What's your favorite color?" The American would answer immediately with the color of his or her choice. The English person would answer with a question: "Favorite color for what? A flower? A necktie?" Cooke explains: "Mead concluded that Americans, raised in a melting point, learned to seek a simple common denominator. To the British, this came across as unsophisticated. Conversely, the class-conscious British insisted on complex categories, each with its own set of values. Americans interpreted this tendency to subdivide as furtive."

From our vantage point, Mead's conclusions seem a little simple-minded. But you cannot help admiring the unidentified leader who recognized the Allies' communication problem as cultural and, instead of assigning blame, chose an expert to study the problem dispassionately. Effective leadership will increasingly depend on being able to decipher what people really mean when they do and say things that baffle us.

Leadership and the Media

Leadership is and always has been a performance art. Rhetoric first developed as a tool of leadership, and leadership continues to involve both artifice and the perception of authenticity. There is a tendency to think of image consciousness on the part of leaders as a modern phenomenon. But as historian Leo Braudy tells us, Alexander the Great facilitated the spread of his power by putting his image on the coins of his empire. We take as a given that television gave JFK an edge over Nixon during their debates because of the latter's five o'clock shadow and sour scowl. But do we yet know the real extent to which our public figures are created or undone by the media, and the nature of these processes? To understand leadership today it is essential to see how the competitive pressures of the media affect the reputations, and the behavior of public officials. And you cannot get a handle on modern leaders without at least trying to gauge where spin begins and reality ends. When President George W. Bush made his famous tailgate landing on the carrier *Abraham Lincoln,* associating himself with both the Great Emancipator and the pop-culture warriors of the movie *Top Gun,* did he do something qualitatively different from Alexander the Great, who associated his exploits with those of the deities of his time? What impact does the public's knowledge that reality is being manipulated have on its trust in its leaders? And how does the Internet affect modern leadership, given its ability to create buzz about an individual or vilify him or her with a keystroke? These are things we need to know in an age when television cameras can create seeming character and instant polling allows leaders to change their positions in midspeech.

Conclusion

Having studied leadership for the past six decades, I still find it remarkable how often leaders in talent-driven organizations (e.g., *New York Times*) forget what scholarship tells us about how to manage genius. They encourage competition among colleagues, instead of the more productive competition with outside organizations. They forget that most talented people chafe at bureaucracy and hierarchy. They forget that intrinsic rewards are the best motivators. They refuse to believe that work should feel like fun, or better than fun.

In the gifted groups that Biederman and I studied, the most successful leaders were those who saw themselves not as top dogs but as facilitators. Although many had healthy egos, they were far more concerned with the project than with shows of deference on the part of their subordinates. Indeed, they did not regard the others as subordinates; they saw them as colleagues or as fellow crusaders on a holy mission (whether that mission was creating the first personal computer or the first animated feature film). These leaders saw their primary responsibility as unleashing the talent of others so the collective vision could be realized. These leaders prided themselves on their ability to discover and cultivate talent and to recognize the best ideas that came across their desks. They concerned themselves with such issues as keeping the project moving forward, making sure everyone had the tools and information they needed, and protecting the group from outside interference. A spirited collegiality is the usual mood of these great groups. As head of the Manhattan Project, J. Robert Oppenheimer successfully fought the government's initial insistence on secrecy within the group. Oppenheimer understood that the free exchange of ideas was essential to the project's success because ideas ignite each other and create more ideas. At Los Alamos, candor within the group was so valued that no one was shocked when cheeky young Richard Feynman disagreed with legendary Nobelist Niels Bohr. If Los Alamos was not a genuine republic of ideas, Oppenheimer did all he could to make it feel like one. Inside the fence, he rewarded frankness and transparency as well as utter dedication to the urgent task at hand. The result was that the atomic bomb was built more quickly than anyone believed possible. The first mushroom cloud still hung in the air when some of the scientists realized that they had unleashed a terrible force on the world. But most spoke admiringly of Oppenheimer's leadership for the rest of their lives.

Even though Oppenheimer's scientists were part of the Allied war effort, he treated them as if they were free agents. Oppenheimer realized that the most heroic effort is given freely; it cannot be coerced. He did not order. He inspired. Perhaps the best exchange on the limits of power is from Shakespeare's *Henry IV*, Pt. I. Glendower boasts to Hotspur: "I can call spirits from the vasty deep." And Hotspur responds: "Why, so can I, or so can any [person]; But will they come when you do call them?" (J. D. Wilson, 1958, p. 52). Whatever the arena, genuine leaders find ways to make others want to come when they are called.

References

Abdalla, I. A., & Al-Homoud, M. A. (2001). Exploring the implicit leadership theory in the Arabian Gulf States. *Applied Psychology: An International Review, 50,* 506–531.

Acar, F. P. (2002). Dynamics of diversity in cross-functional teams: A theoretical framework of diversity, conflict, and systems leadership. In S. H. Barr (Ed.), *2002 Southern Management Association Proceedings: Building effective networks.* Raleigh, NC: North Carolina State University.

Ackerman, P., & Humphreys, L. G. (1990). Individual differences theory in industrial and organizational psychology. In M. D. Dunnette & L. M. Hough (Eds.), *Handbook of industrial and organizational psychology* (Vol. 1, pp. 223–282). Palo Alto, CA: Consulting Psychologists Press.

Adler, N. J. (1991). *International dimensions of organizational behavior.* Boston: PWS-Kent Publishing.

Adler, N. J. (1999). Global leaders: Women of influence. In G. N. Powell (Ed.), *Handbook of gender & work* (pp. 239–261). Thousand Oaks, CA: Sage.

Adsit, D. J., London, M., Crom, S., & Jones, D. (1997). Cross-cultural differences in upward ratings in a multinational company. *International Journal of Human Resource Management, 8,* 385–401.

Alderfer, C. (1972). *Existence, relatedness, and growth: Human needs in organizational setting.* New York: Free Press.

Algattan, A.R.A. (1985). *Test of the path-goal theory of leadership in the multinational domain.* Paper presented at the annual Academy of Management Conference, San Diego, CA.

Alldredge, M., & Nilan, K. (2000). 3M's leadership competency model: An internally developed solution. *Human Resource Management, 39,* 133–145.

Allport, G. W. (1954). *The nature of prejudice.* Reading, MA: Addison-Wesley.

Allport, G. W. (1961). *Pattern and growth in personality.* New York: Holt, Rinehart & Winston.

Almer, E. D., Hopper, J. R., & Kaplan, S. E. (1998). The effect of diversity-related attributes on hiring, advancement and voluntary turnover judgments. *Accounting Horizons, 12,* 1–17.

Alvesson, M. (1996). Leadership studies: From procedure and abstraction to reflexivity and situation. *Leadership Quarterly, 7,* 455–485.

American Association of Retired Persons. (2000). *American business and older employees survey.* Washington, DC: Author.

American Council on Education. (2002). *The American college president.* Washington, DC: Author.

Anderson, C. A., Lindsay, J. J., & Bushman, B. J. (1999). Research in the Psychological Laboratory: Truth or Triviality. *Current Directions in Psychological Science, 8,* 3–9.

Anderson, J. R. (1987). Skill acquisition: Compilation of weak-method problem solutions. *Psychological Review, 94,* 192–210.

Angell, J. R. (1907). The province of functional psychology. *Psychological Review, 14,* 61–91.

Angrist, J., & Evans, W. N. (1998). Children and their parents' labor supply: Evidence from exogenous variation in family size. *American Economic Review, 88,* 450–477.

Antonakis, J. (in press). Why "emotional intelligence" does not predict leadership effectiveness. *International Journal of Organizational Analysis.*

Antonakis, J., & Atwater, L. (2002). Leader distance: A review and a proposed theory. *Leadership Quarterly, 13,* 673–704.

Antonakis, J., Avolio, B. J., & Sivasubramaniam, N. (2003). Context and leadership: An examination of the nine-factor Full-Range Leadership Theory using the Multifactor Leadership Questionnaire (MLQ Form 5X). *Leadership Quarterly, 14,* 261–295.

Antonakis, J., & Cacciatore, S. (2003). *Heuristics and biases in evaluations of leaders: The effects of uncertainty.* Lausanne: University of Lausanne.

Antonakis, J., & House, R. J. (2002). An analysis of the full-range leadership theory: The way forward. In B. J. Avolio & F. J. Yammarino (Eds.), *Transformational and charismatic leadership: The road ahead* (pp. 3–33). Amsterdam: JAI.

Archer, J. (2000). Sex differences in aggression between heterosexual partners: A meta-analytic review. *Psychological Bulletin, 126,* 651–680.

Aristotle. (1900). *A treatise in government* (W. Ellis, Trans.). London: J. M. Dent & Sons.

Aristotle. (1984). *Nichomachean ethics* (W. D. Ross, Trans.). In J. Barnes (Ed.), *The complete works of Aristotle: The revised Oxford translation* (Vol. 2). Princeton, NJ: Princeton University Press.

Ashby, W. (1952). *Design for a brain.* New York: John Wiley.

Ashkanasy, N. M. (1995). Supervisory attributions and evaluative judgments of subordinate performance: A further test of the Green & Mitchell model. In M. J. Martinko (Ed.), *Attribution theory: An organizational perspective.* Delray Beach, FL: St. Lucia.

Ashkanasy, N. M., & Falkus, S. (2003). The Australian enigma. In R. J. House & J. Chokkar (Eds.), *Cultures of the world, A GLOBE anthology of in-depth descriptions of the cultures of 14 countries* (Vol. 1). Unpublished manuscript.

Ashour, A. S. (1982). A framework of cognitive-behavioral theory of leader influence and effectiveness. *Organizational Behavior and Human Performance, 30,* 407–430.

Ashour, A. S., & Johns, G. (1983). Leader influence through operant principles: A theoretical and methodological framework. *Human Relations, 36,* 603–626.

Astin, A. W., Parrott, S. A., Korn, W. S., & Sax, L. J. (1997). *The American freshman: Thirty year trends.* Los Angeles: Higher Education Research Institute, University of California, Los Angeles.

Atkinson, P., & Hammersley, M. (1994). Ethnography and participant observation. In N. Denzin & Y. Lincoln (Eds.), *Handbook of qualitative research* (pp. 248–261). Thousand Oaks, CA: Sage.

Atwater, L. E., Carey, J. A., & Waldman, D. A. (2001). Gender and discipline in the workplace: Wait until your father gets home. *Journal of Management, 27,* 537–561.

Atwater, L. E., Dionne, S. D., Avolio, B. J., Camobreco, J. F., & Lau, A. N. (1999). A longitudinal study of the leadership development process: Individual differences predicting leader effectiveness. *Human Relations, 52,* 1543–1562.

Atwater, L. E., Roush, P., & Fischtal, A. (1995). The influence of upward feedback on self- and follower ratings of leadership. *Personnel Psychology, 48,* 35–60.

Atwater, L. E., & Yammarino, F. J. (1993). Personal attributes as predictors of superiors' and subordinates' perceptions of military academy leadership. *Human Relations, 46,* 645–668.

Avolio, B. J. (1999). *Full leadership development: Building the vital forces in organizations.* Thousand Oaks, CA: Sage.

Avolio, B. J. (in press). Examining the full range model of leadership: Looking back to transform forward. In D. V. Day, S. J. Zaccaro, & S. M. Halpin (Eds.), *Leadership development for transforming organizations.* Mahwah, NJ: Lawrence Erlbaum.

Avolio, B. J., Bass, B. M., & Jung, D. I. (1995). *MLQ Multifactor Leadership Questionnaire: Technical Report.* Redwood City, CA: Mindgarden.

Avolio, B. J., Kahai, S., & Dodge, G. E. (2001). E-Leadership: Implications for theory, research, and practice. *Leadership Quarterly, 11,* 615–670.

Avolio, B. J., Kahai, S., Dumdum, R., & Sivasubramaniam, N. (2001). Virtual teams: Implications for e-leadership and team development. In M. London (Ed.), *How people evaluate others in organizations* (pp. 337–358). Mahwah, NJ: Lawrence Erlbaum.

Avolio, B. J., & Locke, E. E. (2002). Contrasting different philosophies of leader motivation: Altruism versus egoistic. *Leadership Quarterly, 13,* 169–171.

Avolio, B. J., Waldman, D. W., & Yammarino, F. J. (1991). Leading in the 1990s: Towards understanding the four I's of transformational leadership. *Journal of European Industrial Training, 15*(4), 9–16.

Avolio, B. J., Yammarino, F. J., & Bass, B. M. (1991). Identifying common methods variance with data collected from a single source: An unresolved sticky issue. *Journal of Management, 17,* 571–587.

Axelrod, R. H., & Sashkin, M. (2000). *Outcome measurement in a leadership development program.* Paper presented at the annual meeting of the Academy of Management, Toronto.

Aycan, Z. (in press). Leadership and teamwork in the developing country context. In H. W. Lane, M. L. Maznevski, M. E. Mendenhall, & J. McNett (Eds.), *The Blackwell handbook of global management.* Oxford, UK: Basil Blackwell.

Aycan, Z., Kanungo, R. N., Mendonca, M., Yu, K., Deller, J., Stahl, G. K., & Kurshid, A. (2000). Impact of culture on human resource management practices: A 10-country comparison. *Applied Psychology: An International Review, 49,* 192–221.

Ayman, R. (1993). Leadership perception: The role of gender and culture. In M. M. Chemers & R. Ayman (Eds.), *Leadership theory and research: Perspectives and directions* (pp. 137-166). New York: Academic Press.

Ayman, R. (2000). Leadership. In E. F. Borgatta & R.J.V. Montgomery (Eds.), *Encyclopedia of sociology* (2nd ed., Vol. 3, pp. 1563–1575). New York: Macmillan Reference U.S.A.

Ayman, R. (2002). Contingency model of leadership effectiveness. In L. L. Neider & C. A. Schriesheim (Eds.), *Leadership* (pp. 197–228). Greenwich, CT: Information Age Publishing.

Ayman, R., & Chemers, M. M. (1991). The effects of leadership match on subordinate satisfaction in Mexican organizations: Some moderating influences of self-monitoring. *Applied Psychology: An International Review, 44,* 299-314.

Ayman, R., Chemers, M. M., & Fiedler, F. (1995). The contingency model of leadership effectiveness and its levels of analysis. *Leadership Quarterly, 6,* 147–168.

Ayman, R., Chemers, M. M., & Fiedler, F. (1998). The contingency model of leadership effectiveness and its levels of analysis. In F. Yammarino & F. Dansereau (Eds.), *Leadership: The multi-level approaches* (pp. 73–96). New York: JAI.

Ayman, R., & Romano, R. (1998). Measures and assessments for the contingency model of leadership. In F. Yammarino & F. Dansereau (Eds.), *Leadership: The multi-level approaches* (pp. 97–114). New York: JAI.

Bacharach, S. B. (1989). Organizational theories: Some criteria for evaluation. *Academy of Management Review, 14*, 496–515.

Bader, P., Fleming, P., Zaccaro, S. J., & Barber, H. (2002, April). *The developmental impact of work experiences on adaptability.* Paper presented at the 17th annual meeting of the Society for Industrial and Organizational Psychology, Toronto.

Bader, P., Zaccaro, S. J., & Kemp, C. (2003). *Leader optimism and adaptability to change in a simulated organization.* Unpublished manuscript, George Mason University.

Baehr, M. E. (1992). *Predicting success in higher level positions: A guide to the system for testing and evaluation of potential.* New York: Quorum.

Baldwin, T. T., & Padgett, M. Y. (1993). Management development: A review and commentary. In C. L. Cooper & I. T. Robertson (Eds.), *International review of industrial and organizational psychology* (Vol. 8, pp. 35–85). Chichester, UK: Wiley.

Bales, R. F. (1950). *Interaction process analysis: A method for the study of small groups.* Cambridge, MA: Addison-Wesley.

Bales, R. F. (1954). In conference. *Harvard Business Review, 32*, 44–50.

Baliga, B. R., & Hunt, J. G. (1988). An organizational lifecycle approach to leadership. In J. G. Hunt, B. R. Baliga, H. P. Dachler, & C. A. Schriesheim (Eds.), *Emerging leadership vistas* (pp. 129–149). Lexington, MA: Lexington Books.

Baltes, P. B. (1993). The aging mind: Potential and limits. *The Gerontologist, 33*, 580–594.

Banaji, M. R., & Prentice, D. A. (1994). The self in social contexts. *Annual Review of Psychology, 45*, 297–332.

Bandura, A. (1982). Self-efficacy mechanism in human agency. *American Psychologist, 37*, 122–147.

Bandura, A. (1986). *Social foundations of thought and action: A social cognitive theory.* Englewood Cliffs, NJ: Prentice Hall.

Bandura, A. (1997). *Self-efficacy: The exercise of control.* New York: Freeman.

Banks, D., Bader, P., Fleming, P., Zaccaro, S., & Barber, H. (2001). *Leader adaptability: The role of work experiences and individual differences.* Paper presented at the 16th annual conference for the Society for Industrial and Organizational Psychology, San Diego, CA.

Banks, D., Zaccaro, S. J., & Bader, P. (2003). *An examination of metacognitive skills as a moderator of the effects of developmental work assignments on leader tacit knowledge.* Unpublished manuscript, George Mason University.

Barber, H. F. (1990). Some personality characteristics of senior military officers. In K. E. Clark & M. B. Clark (Eds.), *Measures of leadership* (pp. 441–448). Greensboro, NC: Center for Creative Leadership.

Barkema, H. G., Baum, J.A.C., & Mannix, E. A. (Eds.). (2002). Special research forum on a new time. *Academy of Management Journal, 45*, 916–1065.

Barley, S. R., Meyer, G. W., & Gash, D. C. (1988). Cultures of culture: Academicians, practitioners, and the pragmatics of normative control. *Administrative Science Quarterly, 33*, 24–60.

Barling, J., Slater, F., & Kelloway, E. K. (2000). Transformational leadership and emotional intelligence: An exploratory study. *Leadership & Organization Development Journal, 21*, 157–163.

Barling, J., Weber, T., & Kelloway, E. K. (1996). Effects of transformational leadership training on attitudinal and financial outcomes: A field experiment. *Journal of Applied Psychology, 81*, 827–832.

Barnlund, D. C. (1962). Consistency of emergent leadership in groups with changing tasks and members. *Speech Monographs, 29*, 45–52.

Bar-On, R. (2000). Emotional and social intelligence: Insights from the Emotional Quotient Inventory. In R. Bar-On & J. D. A. Parker (Eds.), *The handbook of emotional intelligence:*

Theory, development, assessment, and application at home, school, and in the workplace (pp. 363–388). San Francisco: Jossey-Bass.

Baron, R. A., & Byrne, D. (1987). *Social psychology: Understanding human interaction* (5th ed.). Boston: Allyn & Bacon.

Baron, R. M., & Kenny, D. A. (1986). The moderator-mediator variable distinction in social psychological research: Conceptual, strategic, and statistical considerations. *Journal of Personality and Social Psychology, 51,* 1173–1182.

Barrick, M. R., Day, D. V., Lord, R. G., & Alexander, R. A. (1991). Assessing the utility of executive leadership. *Leadership Quarterly, 2,* 9–22.

Barrick, M. R., & Mount, M. K. (1991). The Big Five personality dimensions and job performance: A meta-analysis. *Personnel Psychology, 44,* 1–26.

Barrick, M. R., & Mount, M. K. (1993). Autonomy as a moderator of the relationships between the Big Five personality dimensions and job performance. *Journal of Applied Psychology, 78,* 111–118.

Bartunek, M., & Necochea, R. (2000). Old insights and new times: Kairos, Inca cosmology and their contributions to contemporary management inquiry. *Journal of Management Inquiry, 9,* 103–113.

Basinger, J. (2002, November 22). The growing $500,000 club. *Chronicle of Higher Education,* pp. A29, A49.

Bass, B. M. (1980). *Bass and Stogdill's handbook of leadership* (2nd ed.). New York: Free Press.

Bass, B. M. (1985). *Leadership and performance beyond expectations.* New York: Free Press.

Bass, B. M. (1988). Evolving perspectives on charismatic leadership. In J. A. Conger & R. N. Kanungo (Eds.), *Charismatic leadership: The elusive factor in organizational effectiveness* (pp. 40–77). San Francisco: Jossey-Bass.

Bass, B. M. (1990). *Bass and Stogdill's handbook of leadership: Theory, research, and managerial applications* (3rd ed.). New York: Free Press.

Bass, B. M. (1995). Theory of transformational leadership redux. *Leadership Quarterly, 6,* 463–478.

Bass, B. M. (1997). Does the transactional-transformational leadership paradigm transcend organizational and national boundaries? *American Psychologist, 52,* 130–139.

Bass, B. M. (1998). *Transformational leadership: Industrial, military, and educational impact.* Mahwah, NJ: Lawrence Erlbaum.

Bass, B. M., & Avolio, B. J. (1988). Transformational leadership, charisma, and beyond. In J. G. Hunt, B. R. Baliga, H. P. Dachler, & C. A. Schriesheim (Eds.), *Emerging leadership vistas* (pp. 29–49). Lexington, MA: Lexington Books.

Bass, B. M., & Avolio, B. J. (Eds.). (1994). *Improving organizational effectiveness through transformational leadership.* Thousand Oaks, CA: Sage.

Bass, B. M., & Avolio, B. J. (1995). *MLQ Multifactor Leadership Questionnaire for Research: Permission set.* Redwood City, CA: Mindgarden.

Bass, B. M., Avolio, B. J., Jung, D. I., & Berson, Y. (2003). Predicting unit performance by assessing transformational and transactional leadership. *Journal of Applied Psychology, 88,* 207–218.

Bass, B. M., & Steidlmeier, P. (1999). Ethics, character, and authentic transformational leadership. *Leadership Quarterly, 10,* 181–217.

Baumeister, R. F. (1999). The nature and structure of the self: An overview. In R. F. Baumeister (Ed.), *The self in social psychology* (pp. 1–20). Philadelphia: Psychology Press.

Beach, L. R. (1990). *Image theory: Decision making in personal and organizational contexts.* New York: John Wiley.

Becker, J., Ayman, R., & Korabik, K. (2002). Discrepancies in self/subordinates' perception of leadership behavior; leader's gender, organizational context, and leader's self-monitoring. *Group & Organization Management, 27,* 222–224.

Beer, M. (1988). The critical path for change: Keys to success and failure in six companies. In R. H. Kilmann & T. J. Covin (Eds.), *Corporate transformation: Revitalizing organizations for a competitive world* (pp. 17–45). San Francisco: Jossey-Bass.

Beer, M. (2001). How to develop an organization capable of sustained performance: Embrace the drive for results-capability development paradox. *Organizational Dynamics, 29,* 233–247.

Bell, G. B., & French, R. L. (1950). Consistency of individual leadership position in small groups of varying membership. *Journal of Abnormal and Social Psychology, 45,* 764–767.

Bennis, W. (1959). Leadership theory and administrative behavior. *Administrative Science Quarterly, 4,* 259–301.

Bennis, W. (1984). The four competencies of leadership. *Training and Development Journal, 38*(8), 14–19.

Bennis, W. (1989). *Why leaders can't lead: The unconscious conspiracy continues.* San Francisco: Jossey-Bass.

Bennis, W. (2002). Towards a "truly" scientific management: The concept of organizational health. *Reflections, 4,* 4–13.

Bennis, W., & Nanus, B. (1985). *Leaders: The strategies for taking charge.* New York: HarperCollins.

Bennis, W. G., & Thomas, R. J. (2002). *Geeks & geezers: How era, values, and defining moments shape leaders.* Boston: Harvard Business School Press.

Bennis, W. G., & Ward Biederman, P. (1997). *Organizing genius: The secrets of creative collaboration.* Reading, MA: Addison-Wesley.

Bentz, V. J. (1967). The Sears experience in the investigation, description, and prediction of executive behavior. In F. R. Wickert & D. E. McFarland (Eds.), *Measuring executive effectiveness* (pp. 147–206). New York: Appleton-Century-Crofts.

Bentz, V. J. (1990). Contextual issues in predicting high-level leadership performance: Contextual richness as a criterion consideration in personality research with executives. In K. E. Clark & M. B. Clark (Eds.), *Measures of leadership* (pp. 131–143). Greensboro, NC: Center for Creative Leadership.

Berlew, D. (1974). Leadership and organizational excitement. *California Management Review, 17,* 21–30.

Berman, F. E., & Miner, J. B. (1985). Motivation to manage at the top executive level: A test of hierarchic role motivation theory. *Personnel Psychology, 38,* 377–391.

Bettencourt, B. A., & Miller, N. (1996). Gender differences in aggression as a function of provocation: A meta-analysis. *Psychological Bulletin, 119,* 422–447.

Bettman, J. R., & Weitz, B. A. (1983). Attributions in the board room: Causal reasoning in corporate annual reports. *Administrative Science Quarterly, 33,* 24–60.

Bianchi, S. M. (2000). Maternal employment and time with children: Dramatic change or surprising continuity? *Demography, 37,* 401–414.

Bianchi, S. M., Milkie, M. A., Sayer, L. C., & Robinson, J. P. (2000). Is anyone doing the housework? Trends in the gender division of household labor. *Social Forces, 79,* 191–228.

Bielby, D. D., & Bielby, W. T. (1988). She works hard for the money: Household responsibilities and the allocation of work effort. *American Journal of Sociology, 93,* 1031–1059.

Bielby, W. T., & Bielby, D. D. (1989). Family ties: Balancing commitments to work and family in dual earner households. *American Sociological Review, 54,* 776–789.

Binning, J. F., & Lord, R. G. (1980). Boundary conditions for performance cue effects on group process ratings: Familiarity versus type of feedback. *Organizational Behavior and Human Decision Processes, 26,* 115–130.

Binning, J. F., Zaba, A. J., & Whattam, J. C. (1986). Explaining the biasing effects of performance cues in terms of cognitive categorization. *Academy of Management Journal, 29,* 521–535.

Bird, C. (1940). *Social psychology.* New York: Appleton-Century.

Black, J. A., King, J. P., & Howell, J. P. (2000). *Leaders' complex behaviors and the capacity to change.* Presentation at a colloquium at Texas Tech University, Lubbock.

Black, J. S., & Mendenhall, M. (1990). Cross-cultural training effectiveness: A review and a theoretical framework for future research. *Academy of Management Review, 15,* 113–136.

Blair, J. D., & Hunt, J. G. (1986). Getting inside the head of the management researcher one more time: Context free and context specific orientations in research. *Journal of Management, 12,* 147–166.

Blake, R. R., & Mouton, J. S. (1964). *The managerial grid.* Houston: Gulf Publishing Group.

Blake, R. R., & Mouton, J. S. (1982). Management by grid principles or situationalism: Which? *Group and Organization Studies, 7,* 207–210.

Bliese, P. D., & Halverson, R. R. (2002). Using random group resampling in multilevel research: An example of the buffering effects of leadership climate. *Leadership Quarterly, 13,* 53–68.

Bliese, P. D., Halverson, R. R., & Schriesheim, C. A. (2002). Benchmarking multilevel methods in leadership: The articles, the model, and the data set. *Leadership Quarterly, 13,* 3–14.

Blum, M. L., & Naylor, J. C. (1956). *Industrial psychology: Its theoretical and social foundations.* New York: Harper & Row.

Boal, K. B., & Bryson, J. M. (1988). Charismatic leadership: A phenomenological and structural approach. In J. G. Hunt, B. R. Baliga, H. P. Dachler, & C. A. Schriesheim (Eds.), *Emerging leadership vistas* (pp. 11–28). Lexington, MA: D. C. Heath.

Boal, K. B., & Hooijberg, R. (2001). Strategic leadership research: Moving on. *Leadership Quarterly, 11,* 515–549.

Boal, K. B., Hunt, J. G., & Jaros, S. (2003). Order is free: On the ontological status of organizations. In R. Westwood & S. Clegg (Eds.), *Debating organization* (pp. 107–121). London: Basil Blackwell.

Bolin, L. A. (1997). Entrepreneurial leadership: New paradigm research discovering the common characteristics and traits of entrepreneurs who have served successfully in leadership positions. *Dissertation Abstracts International, 57* (UMI No. 9716689).

Bollen, K. A. (1989). *Structural equations with latent variables.* New York: John Wiley.

Bolman, L. G., & Deal, T. E. (1997). *Reframing organizations: Artistry, choice, and leadership* (2nd ed.). San Francisco: Jossey-Bass.

Bond, M. H., & Smith, P. B. (1996). Cross-cultural social and organizational psychology. *Annual Review of Psychology, 47,* 205–235.

Bonta, B. D. (1997). Cooperation and competition in peaceful societies. *Psychological Bulletin, 121,* 299–320.

Borgatta, E. F., Bales, R. F., & Couch, A. S. (1954). Some findings relevant to the great man theory of leadership. *American Sociological Review, 19,* 755–759.

Boyacigiller, N. A., & Adler, N. J. (1991). The parochial dinosaur: Organizational science in a global context. *Academy of Management Review, 16,* 262–290.

Boyatzis, R. E. (1982). *The competent manager: A model for effective performance.* New York: John Wiley.

Boyatzis, R., McKee, A., & Goleman, D. (2002). Reawakening your passion for work. *Harvard Business Review, 80,* 86–94.

Boyatzis, R. E., & Kolb, D. A. (1991). Assessing individuality in learning: The learning skills profile. *Educational Psychology, 11,* 279–295.

Brass, D. J., & Krackhardt, D. (1999). The social capital of 21st century leaders. In J. G. Hunt, G. E. Dodge, & L. Wong (Eds.), *Out of the box leadership: Transforming the 21st century army and other top-performing organizations* (pp. 179–194). Greenwich, CT: JAI.

Bray, D. W. (1982). The assessment center and the study of lives. *American Psychologist, 37,* 180–189.

Bray, D. W., Campbell, R. J., & Grant, D. L. (1974). *Formative years in business: A long-term AT&T study of managerial lives.* New York: John Wiley.

Brink, K. E. (2002, April). *Self-efficacy and goal change in the absence of external feedback. Predicting executive performance with multi-rater surveys: Who you ask matters.* Paper presented at the 17th annual meeting of the Society for Industrial and Organizational Psychology, Toronto.

Brodbeck, F. C., Frese, M., Ackerblom, S., Audia, G., Bakacsi, G., Bendova, H., et al. (2000). Cultural variation of leadership prototypes across 22 European countries. *Journal of Occupational and Organizational Psychology, 73,* 1–29.

Brooks, P. W. (1998). Contextual trait measurement of leadership effectiveness: A field study of the retail industry. *Dissertation Abstracts International, 58* (UMI No. 9817220).

Broude, G. J., & Greene, S. J. (1976). Cross-cultural codes on twenty sexual attitudes and practices. *Ethnology, 15,* 409–429.

Brown, D. J., & Lord, R. G. (1999). The utility of experimental research in the study of transformational/charismatic leadership. *Leadership Quarterly, 10,* 531–539.

Brown, D. J., & Lord, R. G. (2001). Leadership and perceiver cognition: Moving beyond first order constructs. In M. London (Ed.), *How people evaluate others in organizations* (pp. 181–202). Mahwah, NJ: Lawrence Erlbaum.

Brown, P., & Levinson, S. (1987). *Politeness: Some universals in language usage.* Cambridge, UK: Cambridge University Press.

Browne, K. R. (1999). *Divided labours: An evolutionary view of women at work.* New Haven, CT: Yale University Press.

Browne, K. R. (2002). *Biology at work: Rethinking sexual equality.* New Brunswick, NJ: Rutgers University Press.

Brtek, M. D., & Motowidlo, S. J. (2002). Effects of procedure and outcome accountability on interview validity. *Journal of Applied Psychology, 87,* 185–191.

Bryman, A. (1992). *Charisma and leadership in organizations.* London: Sage.

Bryman, A., Stephens, M., & Campo, C. (1996). The importance of context: Qualitative research and the study of leadership. *Leadership Quarterly, 7,* 353–370.

Bu, N., Craig, T. J., & Peng, T. K. (2001). Acceptance of supervisory direction in typical workplace situations: A comparison of US, Taiwanese and PRC employees. *International Journal of Cross-Cultural Management, 1,* 131–152.

Budig, M. J., & England, P. (2001). The wage penalty for motherhood. *American Sociological Review, 66,* 204–225.

Bullis, R. C., Lewis, P., Bartone, P., Forsythe, G. B., & Snook, S. A. (2002, April). *A longitudinal study of Kegan developmental level and leader effectiveness.* Paper presented at the 17th annual meeting of the Society for Industrial and Organizational Psychology, Toronto.

Burgess, D., & Borgida, E. (1999). Who women are, who women should be: Descriptive and prescriptive gender stereotyping in sex discrimination. *Psychology, Public Policy, and Law, 5,* 665–692.

Burke, M. J., & Day, R. R. (1986). A cumulative study of the effectiveness of managerial training. *Journal of Applied Psychology, 71,* 242–245.

Burns, J. M. (1978). *Leadership.* New York: Harper & Row.

Burns, J. M. (1991). Foreword. In J. C. Rost, *Leadership for the twenty-first century.* New York: Praeger.

Burrell, G., & Morgan, G. (1979). *Sociological paradigms and organizational analysis.* London: Heinemann.

Burt, R. S. (1992). *Structural holes: The social structure of competition.* Cambridge, MA: Harvard University Press.

Buss, D. M. (1995). Evolutionary psychology: A new paradigm for psychological science. *Psychological Inquiry, 6,* 1–30.

Buss, D. M., & Kenrick, D. T. (1998). Evolutionary social psychology. In D. T. Gilbert, S. T. Fiske, & G. Lindzey (Eds.), *The handbook of social psychology* (4th ed., Vol. 2, pp. 982–1026). Boston: McGraw-Hill.

Butler, D., & Geis, F. L. (1990). Nonverbal affect responses to male and female leaders: Implications for leadership evaluations. *Journal of Personality and Social Psychology, 58,* 48–59.

Buttner, E. H., & McEnally, M. (1996). The interactive effect of influence tactic, applicant gender, and type of job on hiring recommendations. *Sex Roles, 34,* 581–591.

Byrne, B. M., Shavelson, R. J., & Muthén, B. (1989). Testing for equivalence of factor covariance and mean structures: The issue of partial measurement invariance. *Psychological Bulletin, 105,* 456–466.

Byrnes, J. P., Miller, D. C., & Schafer, W. D. (1999). Gender differences in risk taking: A meta-analysis. *Psychological Bulletin, 125,* 367–383.

Calás, M. B., & Smircich, L. (1996). From "the woman's" point of view: Feminist approaches to organization studies. In S. R. Clegg, C. Hardy, & W. R. Nord (Eds.), *Handbook of organization studies* (pp. 218–257). Thousand Oaks, CA: Sage.

Calder, B. J. (1977). An attribution theory of leadership. In B. M. Staw & G. R. Salancik (Eds.), *New directions in organizational behavior* (pp. 179–204). Chicago: St. Clair.

Caligiuri, P., & DiSanto, V. (2001). Global competence: What is it, and can it be developed through global assignments? *Human Resource Planning, 24,* 27–35.

Cameron, K. S., & Whetten, D. A. (1983). Organizational effectiveness: One model or several? In K. S. Cameron & D. A. Whetten (Eds.), *Organizational effectiveness: A comparison of multiple models.* Orlando, FL: Academic Press.

Campbell, D. T. (1965). Ethnocentric and other altruistic motives. In D. Levine (Ed.), *Nebraska symposium on motivation* (Vol. 13, pp. 283–311). Lincoln: University of Nebraska Press.

Campbell, D. T., & Fiske, D. W. (1959). Convergent and discriminant validation by the multitrait-multimethod matrix. *Psychological Bulletin, 54,* 81–105.

Campbell, J. P. (1977). The cutting edge of leadership: An overview. In J. G. Hunt & L. L. Larson (Eds.), *Leadership: The cutting edge* (pp. 221–235). Carbondale: Southern Illinois University Press.

Campbell, J. P. (1990). The role of theory in industrial and organizational psychology. In M. D. Dunnette & L. Hough (Eds.), *Handbook of industrial and organizational psychology* (2nd ed., Vol. 1, pp. 40–73). Palo Alto, CA: Consulting Psychologists Press.

Cannella, A. A., & Moore, M. J. (1997). Contrasting perspectives on strategic leaders: Toward a more realistic view of top managers. *Journal of Management, 23,* 213–238.

Cantor, N., & Kihlstrom, J. F. (1987). *Personality and social intelligence.* Englewood Cliffs, NJ: Prentice Hall.

Cantor, N. W., & Mischel, W. (1979). Prototypes in person perception. In L. Berkowitz (Ed.), *Advances in experimental social psychology*. New York: Academic Press.

Carli, L. L. (1990). Gender, language, and influence. *Journal of Personality and Social Psychology, 59*, 941–951.

Carli, L. L. (1998). *Gender effects in social influence*. Paper presented at the meeting of the Society for the Psychological Study of Social Issues, Ann Arbor, MI.

Carli, L. L. (1999). Gender, interpersonal power, and social influence. *Journal of Social Issues, 55*, 81–99.

Carli, L. L. (2001a). Assertiveness. In J. Worell (Ed.), *Encyclopedia of women and gender: Sex similarities and differences and the impact of society on gender* (pp. 157–168). San Diego, CA: Academic Press.

Carli, L. L. (2001b). Gender and social influence. *Journal of Social Issues, 57*, 725–741.

Carli, L. L., & Eagly, A. H. (1999). Gender effects on social influence and emergence leadership. In G. Powell (Ed.), *Handbook of gender and work* (pp. 203–222). Thousand Oaks, CA: Sage.

Carli, L. L., LaFleur, S. J., & Loeber, C. C. (1995). Nonverbal behavior, gender, and influence. *Journal of Personality and Social Psychology, 68*, 1030–1041.

Carlyle, T. (1907). *Heroes and hero worship*. Boston: Adams. (Original work published 1841)

Carter, L. F., & Nixon, M. (1949). An investigation of the relationship between four criteria of leadership ability for three different tasks. *Journal of Psychology, 27*, 245–261.

Caruso, D. R., Mayer, J. D., & Salovey, P. (2002). Emotional intelligence and emotional leadership. In R. E. Riggio, S. E. Murphy, & F. J. Pirozzolo (Eds.), *Multiple intelligences and leadership* (pp. 55–74). Mahwah, NJ: Lawrence Erlbaum.

Caruso, D. R., & Wolfe, C. J. (in press). Emotional intelligence and leadership development. In D. V. Day, S. J. Zaccaro, & S. M. Halpin (Eds.), *Leader development for transforming organizations*. Mahwah, NJ: Lawrence Erlbaum.

Carver, C. S., & Scheier, M. F. (1990). Origins and functions of positive and negative affect: A control-process view. *Psychological Review, 97*, 19–35.

Cascio, W. F. (1994). Executive and managerial assessment: Value for the money? *Consulting Psychology Journal, 46*, 42–48.

Case, B. (1987). Leadership behavior in sport: A field test of the situation leadership theory. *International Journal of Sport Psychology, 18*, 256–268.

Castro, S. L. (2002). Data analytic methods for the analysis of multilevel questions: A comparison of intraclass correlation coefficients, $r_{wg(j)}$, hierarchical linear modeling, within- and between-analysis, and random group resampling. *Leadership Quarterly, 13*, 69–93.

Catalyst. (2000). *Press release: Catalyst census finds few women corporate officers*. Retrieved March 13, 2002, from http://www.catalystwomen.org/Press_Room/press_releases/2000_cote_canada.htm

Catalyst. (2002). *Fact sheet: Women CEOs*. Retrieved October 6, 2002, from http://www.catalystwomen.org/press_room/factsheets/fact_women_ceos.htm

Catalyst. (2003). *Release: Catalyst census marks gains in numbers of women corporate officers in America's largest 500 companies*. Retrieved February 20, 2003, from http://www.catalystwomen.org/press_room/press_releases/2002_cote.htm

Cattell, J. M. (1890). Mental tests and measurements. *Mind, 15*, 373–381.

Center for American Woman and Politics. (2003). *Women in elective office 2003*. Retrieved February 20, 2003, from http://www.rci.rutgers.edu/~cawp/pdf/elective.pdf

Center for Creative Leadership. (2000). *The CCL library of scales*. Available on *360 BY DESIGN* [Computer software]. Greensboro, NC: Author.

Center for Leadership Studies. (2000). *Multifactor Leadership Questionnaire: Norms.* Retrieved June 22, 2000, from http://cls.binghamton.edu/mlq.htm

Chan, K., & Drasgow, F. (2001). Toward a theory of individual differences and leadership: Understanding the motivation to lead. *Journal of Applied Psychology, 86*(3), 481–498.

Chappelow, C., & Leslie, J. B. (2001). *Keeping your career on track: Twenty success strategies.* Greensboro, NC: Center for Creative Leadership.

Charan, R., Drotter, S., & Noel, J. (2000). *The leadership pipeline: How to build the leadership powered company.* San Francisco: Jossey-Bass.

Chattopadhyay, P., Glick, W. H., & Huber, G. P. (2001). Organizational actions in response to threats and opportunities. *Academy of Management Journal, 44,* 937–955.

Chemers, M. M. (1997). *An integrative theory of leadership.* Mahwah, NJ: Lawrence Erlbaum.

Chemers, M. M. (2002). Efficacy and effectiveness: Integrating models of leadership and intelligence. In R. E. Riggio, S. E. Murphy, & F. J. Pirozzolo (Eds.), *Multiple intelligences and leadership* (pp. 139–160). Mahwah, NJ: Lawrence Erlbaum.

Chemers, M. M., & Ayman, R. (1985). Leadership orientation as a moderator of the relationship between performance and satisfaction of Mexican managers. *Personality and Social Psychology Bulletin, 11,* 359–367.

Chemers, M. M., Goza, B., & Plumer, S. I. (1978). *Leadership style and communication process.* Paper presented at the annual meeting of the American Psychological Association, Toronto.

Chemers, M. M., Hays, R., Rhodewalt, F., & Wysocki, J. (1985). A person-environment analysis of job stress: A contingency model explanation. *Journal of Personality and Social Psychology, 49,* 628–635.

Chen, G., Gully, S. M., Whiteman, J., & Kilcullen, R. N. (2000). Examination of relationships among trait-like individual differences, state-like individual differences, and learning performance. *Journal of Applied Psychology, 85,* 835–847.

Cherniss, C., & Caplan, R. D. (2001). A case study in implementing emotional intelligence programs in organizations. *Journal of Organizational Excellence, 21,* 73–85.

Cherniss, C., & Goleman, D. (2001). *The emotionally intelligent workplace: How to select for, measure, and improve emotional intelligence in individuals, groups, and organizations.* San Francisco: Jossey-Bass.

Cheung, G. W., & Rensvold, R. B. (2000). Assessing extreme and acquiescence response sets in cross-cultural research using structural equation modeling. *Journal of Cross-Cultural Psychology, 31,* 187–212.

Chi, M.T.H., Glaser, R., & Farr, M. J. (Eds.). (1988). *The nature of expertise.* Hillsdale, NJ: Lawrence Erlbaum.

Chokkar, J. S. (2003). Leadership and culture in India: The GLOBE research project. In R. J. House & J. S. Chokkar (Eds.), *Cultures of the world, A GLOBE anthology of in-depth descriptions of the cultures of 14 countries* (Vol. 1). Unpublished manuscript.

Cialdini, R. B., & Trost, M. R. (1998). Social influence: Social norms, conformity and compliance. In D. T. Gilbert, S. T. Fiske, & G. Lindzey (Eds.), *The handbook of social psychology* (4th ed., Vol. 2, pp. 151–192). Boston: McGraw-Hill.

Cianciolo, A. T., Antonakis, J., & Sternberg, R. J. (in press). Practical intelligence and leadership: Using experience as a "mentor." In D. V. Day, S. J. Zaccaro, & S. M. Halpin (Eds.), *Leadership development for transforming organizations.* Mahwah, NJ: Lawrence Erlbaum.

Ciulla, J. B. (1994). Casuistry and the case for business ethics. In T. Donaldson & R. E. Freeman (Eds.), *Business as a humanity.* Oxford, UK: Oxford University Press.

Ciulla, J. B. (1995). Leadership ethics: Mapping the territory. *Business Ethics Quarterly, 5,* 5–24.

Ciulla, J. B. (2000). *The working life: The promise and betrayal of modern work*. New York: Crown Books.

Ciulla, J. B. (2003a). The ethical challenges of non-profit leaders. In R. Riggio (Ed.), *Improving leadership in non-profit organizations*. San Francisco: Jossey-Bass.

Ciulla, J. B. (2003b). *The ethics of leadership*. Belmont, CA: Wadsworth.

Cleveland, J. N., Stockdale, M., & Murphy, K. R. (2000). *Women and men in organizations: Sex and gender issues at work*. Mahwah, NJ: Lawrence Erlbaum.

Cogliser, C. C., & Schriesheim, C. A. (1994, November). *Social network analysis of leader member relations for examining the impact of dyadic structures on workgroup interactions*. Paper presented before the Southern Management Association, New Orleans.

Cohen, J., & Cohen, P. (1983). *Applied multiple regression/correlation analysis for the behavioral science* (2nd ed.). Hillsdale, NJ: Lawrence Erlbaum.

Collins, J. (2002). *Good to great: Why some companies make the leap and others don't*. New York: HarperCollins.

Colyer, S. L. (1997). *An empirical investigation of the relationship between visionary leadership and organizational performance: Consequences of self-other agreement*. Paper presented at the annual meeting of the Academy of Management, Boston.

Compact Oxford English dictionary. (1991). Oxford, UK: Clarendon.

Conference Board. (2002). *Developing business leaders for 2010*. New York: Author.

Confucius. (1963). Selections from the *Analects*. In *A source book in Chinese philosophy* (W. Chan, Trans. and Ed.). Princeton, NJ: Princeton University Press.

Conger, J. A. (1989). *The charismatic leader: Behind the mystique of exceptional leadership*. San Francisco: Jossey-Bass.

Conger, J. A. (1993). Max Weber's conceptualization of charismatic authority: Its influence on organizational research, *Leadership Quarterly, 4*, 277–288.

Conger, J. A. (1998). Qualitative research as the cornerstone methodology for understanding leadership. *Leadership Quarterly, 9*, 107–121.

Conger, J. A. (1999). Charismatic and transformational leadership in organizations: An insider's perspective on these developing streams of research. *Leadership Quarterly, 10*, 145–180.

Conger, J. A., & Benjamin, B. (1999). *Building leaders: How successful companies develop the next generation*. San Francisco: Jossey-Bass.

Conger, J. A., & Kanungo, R. N. (1987). Toward a behavioral theory of charismatic leadership in organizational settings. *Academy of Management Review, 12*, 637–647.

Conger, J. A., & Kanungo, R. N. (Eds.). (1988). *Charismatic leadership: The elusive factor in organizational effectiveness*. San Francisco: Jossey-Bass.

Conger, J. A., & Kanungo, R. N. (1994). Charismatic leadership in organizations: Perceived behavioral attributes and their measurement. *Journal of Organizational Behavior, 15*, 439–452.

Conger, J. A., & Kanungo, R. N. (1998). *Charismatic leadership in organizations*. Thousand Oaks, CA: Sage.

Connelly, M. S., Gilbert, J. A., Zaccaro, S. J., Threlfall, K. V., Marks, M. A., & Mumford, M. D. (2000). Exploring the relationship of leadership skills and knowledge to leader performance. *Leadership Quarterly, 11*, 65–86.

Cook, T. C., Campbell, D. T., & Peracchio, L. (1990). Quasi experimentation. In M. Dunnette & L. Hough (Eds.), *Handbook of industrial and organizational psychology* (2nd ed., Vol. 1, pp. 491–576). Palo Alto, CA: Consulting Psychologists Press.

Copeland, C. L., Driskell, J. E., & Salas, E. (1995). Gender and reactions to dominance. *Journal of Social Behavior and Personality, 10*, 53–68.

The corporate woman: A special report. (1986, March 24). *Wall Street Journal* (32-page suppl.).

Costanza, D. P. (1996). Leadership and organizational decline: The relationship between personality characteristics and organizational performance. *Dissertation Abstracts International, 57* (UMI No. 9625602).

Cotton, J. L., & Tuttle, J. M. (1986). Employee turnover: A meta-analysis and review with implications for research. *Academy of Management Review, 11,* 55–70.

Crant, J. M., & Bateman, T. S. (2000). Charismatic leadership viewed from above: The impact of proactive personality. *Journal of Organizational Behavior, 21,* 63–75.

Creswell, J. W. (1994). *Research design: Qualitative & quantitative approaches.* Thousand Oaks, CA: Sage.

Csikszentmihalyi, M. (1990). *Flow: the psychology of optimal experience.* New York: Harper Perennial.

Dachler, H. P. (1988). Constraints on the emergence of new vistas in leadership and management science: An epistemological overview. In J. G. Hunt, B. R. Baliga, H. P. Dachler, & C. A. Schriesheim (Eds.), *Emerging leadership vistas* (pp. 261–285). Lexington, MA: Lexington Books.

Daft, R. L. (1984). Antecedents of significant and not-so-significant research. In T. Bateman & G. Ferris (Eds.), *Method and analysis in organizational research.* Reston, VA: Reston Publishing.

Daft, R. L., & Lewin, A. Y. (1990). Can organization studies begin to break out of the normal science straitjacket? An editorial essay. *Organization Science, 1,* 1–9.

Dalai Lama XIV. (1999). *Ancient wisdom, modern world: Ethics for the new millennium* (T. Jinpa, Trans.). New York: Riverhead Books.

Dalton, G. W. (1989). Developmental views of careers in organizations. In M. B. Arthur & D. T. Hall (Eds.). *Handbook of career theory* (pp. 89–109). New York: Cambridge University Press.

Dalton, M. (1997). Are competency models a waste? *Training & Development, 51,* 46–49.

Dalton, M. A., & Hollenbeck, G. P. (1996). *How to design and effective system for developing managers and executives.* Greensboro, NC: Center for Creative Leadership.

Dalton, M. A., & Hollenbeck, G. P. (2001). After feedback: How to facilitate change in behavior. In D. W. Bracken, C. W. Timmreck, & A. H. Church (Eds.), *The handbook of multisource feedback* (pp. 352–367). San Francisco: Jossey-Bass.

Dansereau, F., Alutto, J. A., & Yammarino, F. J. (1984). *Theory testing in organizational behavior: The varient approach.* Englewood Cliffs, NJ: Prentice Hall.

Dansereau, F., Graen, G. B., & Haga, W. J. (1975). A vertical dyad linkage approach to leadership within formal organizations: A longitudinal investigation of the role making process. *Organizational Behavior and Human Decision Processes, 13,* 46–78.

Dansereau, F., & Yammarino, F. J. (Eds.). (1995). Leadership: The multiple-level approaches [Special issue]. *Leadership Quarterly, 6*(2/3).

Dansereau, F., & Yammarino, F. J. (Eds.). (1998). *Leadership: The multiple-level approaches* (part A, part B). Stamford, CT: JAI.

Dansereau, F., Yammarino, F. J., & Kohles, J. (1999). Multiple levels of analysis from a longitudinal perspective: Some applications for theory building. *Academy of Management Review, 24,* 346–357.

D'Aveni, R. A., & McMillan, I. C. (1990). Crisis and content of managerial communications: A study of the focus of attention of top managers in surviving and failing firms. *Administrative Science Quarterly, 35,* 634–657.

Davidson, O. B., & Eden, D. (2000). Remedial self-fulfilling prophecy: Two field experiments to prevent Golem effects among disadvantaged women. *Journal of Applied Psychology, 85,* 386–398.

Davies, P. G., & Spencer, S. J. (2003). *Reinforcing the glass ceiling via stereotype threat: Gender-stereotypic television commercials persuade women to avoid leadership positions.* Unpublished manuscript, Stanford University.

Davis, J. N. (2002). *A systems dynamics model of Beyer and Browning's case study of the charisma of Robert Noyle at SEMATECH.* Unpublished dissertation proposal, Rawls College of Business Administration, Texas Tech University, Lubbock.

Daw, R. W., & Gage, N. L. (1967). Effects of feedback from teachers to principals. *Journal of Educational Psychology, 58,* 181–188.

Day, D. V. (2000). Leadership development: A review in context. *Leadership Quarterly, 11,* 581–613.

Day, D. V. (2001). Assessment of leadership outcomes. In S. J. Zaccaro & R. J. Klimoski (Eds.), *The nature of organizational leadership* (pp. 384–409). San Francisco: Jossey-Bass.

Day, D. V. (2002, April). *Social constructivist perspectives on leadership development.* Paper presented at the 17th annual meeting of the Society for Industrial and Organizational Psychology, Toronto.

Day, D. V., & Lord, R. G. (1988). Executive leadership and organizational performance: Suggestions for a new theory and methodology. *Journal of Management, 14,* 453–464.

Day, D. V., & Lord, R. G. (1992). Expertise and problem categorization: The role of expert processing in organizational sense-making. *Journal of Management Studies, 29,* 35–47.

Day, D. V., Schleicher, D. J., Unckless, A. L., & Hiller, N. J. (2002). Self-monitoring personality at work: A meta analytic investigation of construct validity. *Journal of Applied Psychology, 87,* 390–401.

Deci, E., & Ryan, R. (1991). Intrinsic motivation and self-determination in human behavior. In R. Steers & L. Porter (Eds.), *Motivation and work behavior* (pp. 44–58). New York: McGraw-Hill.

Deci, E. L., Eghrari, H., Patrick, B. C., & Leone, D. R. (1994). Facilitating internalization: The self-determination theory perspective. *Journal of Personality, 62,* 119–142.

De Cremer, D., & van Knippenberg, D. (2002). How do leaders promote cooperation? The effects of charisma and procedural fairness. *Journal of Applied Psychology, 87,* 858–866.

DeGroot, T., Kiker, D. S., & Cross, T. C. (2000). A meta-analysis to review organizational outcomes related to charismatic leadership. *Canadian Journal of Administrative Sciences, 17,* 356–371.

Deluga, R. J. (1990). The relationship of leader-member exchanges with laissez-faire, transactional, and transformational leadership in naval environments. In K. E. Clark, M. B. Clark, & D. P. Campbell (Eds.), *Impact of leadership* (pp. 237–247). Greensboro, NC: Center for Creative Leadership.

Deluga, R. J. (1998). American presidential proactivity, charismatic leadership, and rated performance. *Leadership Quarterly, 9,* 265–291.

Deluga, R. J. (2001). American presidential Machiavellianism: Implications for charismatic leadership and rated performance. *Leadership Quarterly, 12,* 339–363.

Den Hartog, D. N. (1997). *Inspirational leadership* (VU doctoral dissertation, KLI-dissertation series, 1997-nr 2). Enschede, the Netherlands: Ipskamp.

Den Hartog, D. N. (2004). Assertiveness. In R. J. House, P. J. Hanges, M. Javidan, P. W. Dorfman, V. Gupta (Eds.), *Leadership, culture, and organizations: The GLOBE study of 62 societies.* Thousand Oaks, CA: Sage.

Den Hartog, D. N., House, R. J., Hanges, P. J., Ruiz-Quintanilla, S. A., & Dorfman, P. W. (1999). Culture specific and cross-cultural generalizable implicit leadership theories: Are attributes of charismatic/transformational leadership universally endorsed? *Leadership Quarterly, 10,* 219–256.

Den Hartog, D. N., & Koopman, P. L. (2001). Leadership in organizations. In N. Anderson, D. S. Ones, H. Kepir–Sinangil, & C. Viswesvaran (Eds.), *Handbook of industrial, work and organizational psychology* (Vol. 2). London: Sage.

Den Hartog, D. N., Koopman, P. L., Thierry, H., Wilderom, C.P.M., Maczynski, J., & Jarmuz, S. (1997). Dutch and Polish perceptions of leadership and national culture: The GLOBE Project. *European Journal of Work and Organizational Psychology, 6,* 389–415.

Den Hartog, D. N., Van Muijen, J. J., & Koopman, P. L. (1996). Linking transformational leadership and organizational culture. *Journal of Leadership Studies, 3,* 68–83.

Den Hartog, D. N., Van Muijen, J. J., & Koopman, P. L. (1997). Transactional versus transformational leadership: An analysis of the MLQ. *Journal of Occupational and Organizational Psychology, 70,* 19–34.

DeNisi, A. S., & Kluger, A. N. (2000). Feedback effectiveness: Can 360-degree appraisals be improved? *Academy of Management Executive, 14,* 129–139.

Denison, D. R. (1996). What *is* the difference between organizational culture and organizational climate? A native's point of view on a decade of paradigm wars. *Academy of Management Review, 21,* 619–654.

Denison, D. R. (1997). *Corporate culture and organizational effectiveness.* Ann Arbor, MI: Author.

DeSanctis, G., & Poole, M. S. (1994). Capturing the complexity in advanced technology use: Adaptive Structuration Theory. *Organization Science, 5,* 121–147.

DeVries, D. (1992). Executive selection: Advances but no progress. *Issues and Observations, 12,* 1–5.

de Zárate, R. O. (2003). *Women world leaders: 1945–2003.* Retrieved February 21, 2002, from http://www.terra.es/persona12/monolith/00women.htm

Diamante, T., & London, M. (2002). Expansive leadership in the age of digital technology. *Journal of Management Development, 21,* 404–416.

Dickson, M. W., BeShears, R. S., & Gupta, V. (2004). The impact of societal culture and industry on organizational culture: Theoretical explanations. In R. J. House, P. J. Hanges, M. Javidan, P. W. Dorfman, V. Gupta (Eds.), *Leadership, culture, and organizations: The GLOBE study of 62 societies.* Thousand Oaks, CA: Sage.

Dickson, M. W., Hanges, P. J., & Lord, R. M. (2001). Trends, developments, and gaps in cross-cultural research on leadership. In W. Mobley & M. McCall (Eds.), *Advances in global leadership* (Vol. 2, pp. 75–100). Stamford, CT: JAI.

Dickson, M. W., Smith, D. B., Grojean, M., & Ehrhart, M. (2001). Ethical climate: The result of interactions between leadership, leader values, and follower values. *Leadership Quarterly, 12,* 197–218.

Diekman, A. B., & Eagly, A. H. (2000). Stereotypes as dynamic constructs: Women and men of the past, present, and future. *Personality and Social Psychology Bulletin, 26,* 1171–1188.

Digman, J. M. (1990). Personality structure: Emergence of the five-factor model. *Annual Review of Psychology, 41,* 417–440.

Dionne, S. D., Yammarino, F. J., Atwater, L. E., & James, L. R. (2002). Neutralizing substitutes for leadership theory: Leadership effects and common-source bias. *Journal of Applied Psychology, 87,* 454–464.

Dixon, D. L. (1998). *The relationship between chief executive leadership (transactional and transformational) and hospital effectiveness.* Unpublished doctoral dissertation, The George Washington University, Washington, DC.

Dobbins, G. H., & Russell, J. M. (1986a). The biasing effects of subordinate likableness on leaders' responses to poor performers: A laboratory and a field study. *Personnel Psychology, 39,* 759–777.

Dobbins, G. H., & Russell, J. M. (1986b). Self-serving biases in leadership: A laboratory experiment. *Journal of Management, 12,* 475–483.

Doney, P. M., Cannon, J. P., & Mullen, M. R. (1998). Understanding the influence of national culture on the development of trust. *Academy of Management Review, 23,* 601–620.

Dorfman, P. W. (1996). International and cross-cultural leadership. In J. Punnitt & O. Shanker (Eds.), *Handbook for international management research* (pp. 267–349). Cambridge, MA: Blackwell.

Dorfman, P. W., Hanges, P. J., & Brodbeck, F. C. (2004). Leadership prototypes and cultural variation: The identification of culturally endorsed implicit theories of leadership. In R. J. House, P. J. Hanges, M. Javidan, P. W. Dorfman, V. Gupta (Eds.), *Leadership, culture, and organizations: The GLOBE study of 62 societies.* Thousand Oaks, CA: Sage.

Dorfman, P. W., & Howell, J. P. (1988). Dimensions of national culture and effective leadership patterns. *Advances in International Comparative Management, 3,* 127–150.

Dorfman, P. W., Howell, J. P., Hibino, S., Lee, J. K., Tate, U., & Bautista, A. (1997). Leadership in Western and Asian countries: Commonalities and differences in effective leadership processes across cultures. *Leadership Quarterly, 8,* 233–274.

Dorfman P. W., & Javidan, M. (2004). Performance orientation. In R. J. House, P. J. Hanges, M. Javidan, P. W. Dorfman, V. Gupta (Eds.), *Leadership, culture, and organizations: The GLOBE study of 62 societies.* Thousand Oaks, CA: Sage.

Downton, J. V. (1973). *Rebel leadership: Commitment and charisma in the revolutionary process.* New York: Free Press.

Drath, W. H. (1998). Approaching the future of leadership development. In C. D. McCauley, R. S. Moxley, & E. Van Velsor (Eds.), *The Center for Creative Leadership handbook of leadership development* (pp. 403–432). San Francisco: Jossey-Bass.

Drath, W. H. (2001). *The deep blue sea: Rethinking the source of leadership.* San Francisco: Jossey-Bass.

Drath, W. H., & Van Velsor, E. (in press). A life-long development perspective on leader development. In C. D. McCauley & E. Van Velsor (Eds.), *The Center for Creative Leadership handbook of leadership development* (2nd ed.). San Francisco: Jossey-Bass.

Drenth, P.J.D., & Den Hartog, D. N. (1998). Culture and organizational differences. In W. J. Lonner & D. L. Dinnel (Eds.), *Merging past, present, and future in cross-cultural psychology: Selected papers from the Fourteenth International Congress of the International Association for Cross-Cultural Psychology* (pp. 489–502). Bristol, PA: Swets & Zeitlinger.

Drucker, P. (1974). *Management: Tasks, responsibilities, practices.* New York: Harper & Row.

Drucker, P. F. (1993). *Post capitalist society.* Oxford: Butterworth-Heinemann.

Dubin, R. (1969). *Theory building.* New York: Free Press.

Dubin, R. (1976). Theory building in applied areas. In M. D. Dunnette (Ed.), *Handbook of industrial and organizational psychology* (pp. 17–40). Chicago: Rand McNally.

Dubin, R. (1977). Metaphors of leadership: An overview. In J. G. Hunt & L. L. Larson (Eds.), *Cross currents in leadership* (pp. 225–238). Carbondale: Southern Illinois University Press.

Dumdum, U. R., Lowe, K. B., & Avolio, B. J. (2002). A meta-analysis of the transformational and transactional leadership correlates of effectiveness and satisfaction: An update and extension. In B. J. Avolio & F. J. Yammarino (Eds.), *Transformational and charismatic leadership: The road ahead* (pp. 35–66). Amsterdam: JAI.

Dutton, J. E., & Jackson, S. E. (1987). The categorization of strategic issues by decision makers and its links to organizational action. *Academy of Management Review, 12,* 76–90.

Dvir, T., Eden, D., Avolio, B. J., & Shamir, B. (2002). Impact of transformational leadership on follower development and performance: A field experiment. *Academy of Management Journal, 45,* 735–744.

Dweck, C. S. (1986). Motivational processes affecting learning. *American Psychologist, 41,* 1040–1048.

Dweck, C. S., & Leggett, E. (1988). A social cognitive approach to motivation and personality. *Psychological Review, 95,* 256–273.

Eagly, A. H. (1987). *Sex differences in social behavior: A social-role interpretation.* Hillsdale, NJ: Lawrence Erlbaum.

Eagly, A. H. (in press). Prejudice: Toward a more inclusive understanding. In A. H. Eagly, R. M. Baron, & V. L. Hamilton (Eds.), *The social psychology of group identity and social conflict: Theory, application, and practice.* Washington, DC: American Psychological Association.

Eagly, A. H., & Johannesen-Schmidt, M. C. (2001). The leadership styles of women and men. *Journal of Social Issues, 57,* 781–797.

Eagly, A. H., Johannesen-Schmidt, M. C., & van Engen, M. (2003). Transformational, transactional, and laissez-faire leadership styles: A meta-analysis comparing women and men. *Psychological Bulletin, 95,* 569–591.

Eagly, A. H., & Johnson, B. T. (1990). Gender and leadership style: A meta-analysis. *Psychological Bulletin, 108,* 233–256.

Eagly, A. H., & Karau, S. J. (1991). Gender and the emergence of leaders: A meta-analysis. *Journal of Personality and Social Psychology, 60,* 685–710.

Eagly, A. H., & Karau, S. J. (2002). Role congruity theory of prejudice toward female leaders. *Psychological Review, 109,* 573–598.

Eagly, A. H., Karau, S. J., & Makhijani, M. G. (1995). Gender and the effectiveness of leaders: A meta-analysis. *Psychological Bulletin, 117,* 125–145.

Eagly, A. H., Karau, S. J., Miner, J. B., & Johnson, B. T. (1994). Gender and motivation to manage in hierarchic organizations: A meta-analysis. *Leadership Quarterly, 5,* 135–159.

Eagly, A. H., Makhijani, M. G., & Klonsky, B. G. (1992). Gender and the evaluation of leaders: A meta-analysis. *Psychological Bulletin, 111,* 3–22.

Eagly, A. H., & Mladinic, A. (1989). Gender stereotypes and attitudes toward women and men. *Personality and Social Psychology Bulletin, 15,* 543–558.

Eagly, A. H., & Steffen, V. J. (1986). Gender and aggressive behavior: A meta-analytic review of the social psychological literature. *Psychological Bulletin, 100,* 309–330.

Eagly, A. H., Wood, W., & Diekman, A. B. (2000). Social role theory of sex differences and similarities: A current appraisal. In T. Eckes & H. M. Trautner (Eds.), *The developmental social psychology of gender* (pp. 123–174). Mahwah, NJ: Lawrence Erlbaum.

Earley, P. C. (1997). *Face, harmony, and social structure: An analysis of organizational behavior across cultures.* New York: Oxford University Press.

Eden, D. (1990). *Pygmalion in management: Productivity as a self-fulfilling prophecy.* Lexington, MA: Lexington Books.

Eden, D. (1992). Leadership and expectations: Pygmalion effects and other self-fulfilling prophecies in organizations. *Leadership Quarterly, 3,* 271–305.

Eden, D., Geller, D., Gewirtz, A., Gordon-Terner, R., Inbar, I., Liberman, et al. (2000). Implanting Pygmalion leadership style through workshop training: Seven field experiments. *Leadership Quarterly, 11,* 171–210.

Eden, D., & Leviatan, U. (1975). Implicit leadership theory as a determinant of the factor structure underlying supervisory behavior scales. *Journal of Applied Psychology, 60,* 736–741.

Eden, D., & Shani, A. B. (1982). Pygmalion goes to boot camp: Expectancy, leadership, and trainee performance. *Journal of Applied Psychology, 67,* 194–199.

Edmonson, A., Roberto, M., & Watkins, M. (2003). A dynamic model of top management team effectiveness: Managing unstructured task streams. *Leadership Quarterly, 14,* 297–325.

Ehrlich, E. (1989, March 20). The mommy track: Juggling kids and careers in corporate America takes a controversial turn. *Business Week,* p. 126.

Ekvall, G., & Arvonen, J. (1991). Change centered leadership. An extension of the two-dimensional model. *Scandinavian Journal of Management, 3,* 139–161.

Ellyson, S. L., Dovidio, J. F., & Brown, C. E. (1992). The look of power: Gender differences in visual dominance behavior. In C. L. Ridgeway (Ed.), *Gender, interaction, and inequality* (pp. 50–80). New York: Springer-Verlag.

Emrich, C. D. (1999). Context effects in leadership perception. *Personality and Social Psychology Bulletin, 25,* 991–1006.

Emrich, C., Denmark, F., & Den Hartog, D. N. (2004). Cross-cultural differences in gender egalitarianism: Implications for societies, organizations, and leaders. In R. J. House, P. J. Hanges, M. Javidan, P. W. Dorfman, V. Gupta (Eds.), *Leadership, culture, and organizations: The GLOBE study of 62 societies.* Thousand Oaks, CA: Sage.

Ericsson, K. A., & Charness, N. (1994). Expert performance: Its structure and acquisition. *American Psychologist, 49,* 725–747.

Etzioni, A. (1964). *Modern organizations.* Englewood Cliffs, NJ: Prentice Hall.

Evans, M. G. (1970). The effects of supervisory behavior on the path-goal relationship. *Organizational Behavior and Human Performance, 5,* 277–298.

Evans, M. G. (1996). R. J. House's "A path-goal theory of leader effectiveness." *Leadership Quarterly, 7,* 305–309.

Facteau, C. L., Facteau, J. D., Schoel, L. C., Russell, J.E.A., & Poteet, M. L. (1998). Reactions to 360-degree feedback from subordinates and peers. *Leadership Quarterly, 9,* 427–448.

Faith, M. S., Wong, F. Y., & Carpenter, K. M. (1995). Group sensitivity training: Update, meta-analysis, and recommendations. *Journal of Counseling Psychology, 42,* 390–399.

Feather, N. T. (1994). Attitudes towards high achievers and reactions to their fall: Theory and research concerning tall poppies. In M. P. Zanna (Ed.), *Advances in social psychology* (Vol. 26, pp. 1–73). New York: Academic Press.

Feingold, A. (1994). Gender differences in personality: A meta-analysis. *Psychological Bulletin, 116,* 429–456.

Ferentinos, C. H. (1996). Linking social intelligence and leadership: An investigation of leaders' situational responsiveness under conditions of changing group tasks and membership. *Dissertation Abstracts International: Section B: The Sciences & Engineering, 57* (UMI No. 9625606).

Fernandez, C. F., & Vecchio, R. P. (1997). Situational leadership theory revisited: A test of an across-jobs perspective. *Leadership Quarterly, 8,* 67–84.

Fernández-Aráoz, C. (2001). The challenge of hiring senior executives. In C. Cherniss & D. Goleman (Eds.), *The emotionally intelligent workplace: How to select for, measure, and improve emotional intelligence in individual, groups, and organizations* (pp. 182–206). San Francisco: Jossey-Bass.

Fiedler, F. E. (1964). A contingency model of leadership effectiveness. In L. Berkowitz (Ed.), *Advances in experimental social psychology* (Vol. 1, pp. 149–190). New York: Academic Press.

Fiedler, F. E. (1967). *A theory of leadership effectiveness.* New York: McGraw-Hill.

Fiedler, F. E. (1971a). *Leadership.* Morristown, NJ: General Learning Press.

Fiedler, F. E. (1971b). Validation and extension of the contingency model of leadership effectiveness. A review of the empirical findings. *Psychological Bulletin, 76,* 128-148.

Fiedler, F. E. (1978). The contingency model and the dynamics of the leadership process. In L. Berkowitz (Ed.), *Advances in experimental social psychology* (Vol. 11, pp. 59–112). New York: Academic Press.

Fiedler, F. E. (1986). The contribution of cognitive resources to leadership performance. *Journal of Applied Social Psychology, 16,* 532–548.

Fiedler, F. E. (1993). The leadership situation and the black box in contingency theories. In M. M. Chemers & R. Ayman (Eds.), *Leadership theory and research: Perspectives and directions* (pp. 1–28). San Diego, CA: Academic Press.

Fiedler, F. E. (2002). The curious role of cognitive resources in leadership. In R. E. Riggio, S. E. Murphy, & F. J. Pirozzolo (Eds.), *Multiple intelligences and leadership* (pp. 91–104). Mahwah, NJ: Lawrence Erlbaum.

Fiedler, F. E., & Chemers M. M. (1984). *Improving leadership effectiveness: The leader match concept* (2nd ed.). New York: John Wiley.

Fiedler, F. E., & Garcia, J. E. (1987). *New approaches to effective leadership: Cognitive resources and organizational performance.* New York: John Wiley.

Fiedler, F., & Mahar, L. (1979). A field experiment validating contingency model leadership training. *Journal of Applied Psychology, 64,* 247–254.

Fiedler, F. E., Mitchell, T., & Triandis, H. C. (1971). The culture assimilator: An approach to cross-cultural training. *Journal of Applied Psychology, 55,* 95–102.

Field, R.H.G., & House, R. J. (1990). A test of the Vroom-Yetton model using manager and subordinate reports. *Journal of Applied Psychology, 75,* 362–366.

Fielding, K. S., & Hogg, M. A. (1997). Social identity, self-categorization, and leadership: A field study of small interactive groups. *Group Dynamics: Theory, Research, and Practice, 1,* 39–51.

Filley, A. C., House, R. J., & Kerr, S. (1976). *Managerial process and organizational behavior* (2nd ed.). Glenview, IL: Scott, Foresman.

Finkelstein, S., & Hambrick, D. C. (1996). *Strategic leadership: Top executives and their effects on organizations.* Minneapolis, MN: West.

Fisher, B. M., & Edwards, J. E. (1988). Consideration and initiating structure and their relationships with leader effectiveness: A meta-analysis. *Academy of Management Best Paper,* 201–205.

Fiske, D. W. (1982). Convergent-discriminant validation in measurements and research strategies. In D. Brinberg & L. Kidder (Eds.), *New directions of methodology of social and behavioral science: Forms of validity in research.* San Francisco: Jossey-Bass.

Fiske, S. T. (1995). Social cognition. In A. Tesser (Ed.), *Advanced social psychology* (pp. 149–193). Boston: McGraw-Hill.

Fiske, S. T. (1998). Stereotyping, prejudice, and discrimination. In D. T. Gilbert, S. T. Fiske, & G. Lindzey (Eds.), *The handbook of social psychology* (4th ed., Vol. 2, pp. 357–411). Boston: McGraw-Hill.

Fiske, S. T., & Stevens, L. E. (1993). What's so special about sex? Gender stereotyping and discrimination. In S. Oskamp & M. Costanzo (Eds.), *Gender issues in contemporary society: Claremont symposium on applied social psychology* (Vol. 6, pp. 173–196). Newbury Park, CA: Sage.

Fiske, S. T., & Taylor, S. E. (1984). *Social cognition.* Reading, MA: Addison-Wesley.

Fiske, S. T., & Taylor, S. E. (1991). *Social cognition* (2nd ed.). New York: McGraw-Hill.

Fleishman, E. A. (1953). The description of supervisory behavior. *Personnel Psychology, 37,* 1–6.

Foels, R., Driskell, J. E., Mullen, B., & Salas, E. (2000). The effects of democratic leadership on group member satisfaction: An integration. *Small Group Research, 31,* 676–701.

Fondas, N. (1997). Feminization unveiled: Management qualities in contemporary writings. *Academy of Management Review, 22,* 257–282.

Ford, J. K., Smith, E. M., Weissbein, D. A., Gully, S. M., & Salas, E. (1998). Relationships of goal orientation, metacognitive activity, and practice strategies with learning outcomes and transfer. *Journal of Applied Psychology, 83,* 218–233.

Fortune. (2003). *The 2002 global 500: The CEOs.* Retrieved February 21, 2003, from http://www.fortune.com/fortune/globa1500/ceo/0,15127,00.html

Foschi, M., Lai, L., & Sigerson, K. (1994). Gender and double standards in the assessment of job applicants. *Social Psychology Quarterly, 57,* 326–339.

Foti, R., Fraser, S. L., & Lord, R. G. (1982). Effects of leadership labels and prototypes on perceptions of political leaders. *Journal of Applied Psychology, 67,* 326–333.

Franke, G. R., Crown, D. F., & Spake, D. F. (1997). Gender differences in ethical perceptions of business practices: A social role theory perspective. *Journal of Applied Psychology, 82,* 920–934.

Fraser, S. L., & Lord, R. G. (1988). Stimulus prototypicality and general leadership impressions: Their role in leadership and behavioral ratings. *Journal of Psychology, 122,* 291–303.

French, J. R., & Raven, B. (1959). The basis of social power. In D. Cartwright (Ed.), *Studies in social power* (pp. 150–167). Ann Arbor: Institute for Social Research, University of Michigan.

French, J.R.P., & Raven, B. (1968). The bases of social power. In D. Cartwright & A. Zander (Eds.), *Group dynamics: Research and theory* (3rd. ed., pp. 259–269). New York: Harper & Row.

Fu, P. P. (2003). Chinese leadership and culture. In R. J. House & J. Chokkar (Eds.), *Cultures of the world, A GLOBE anthology of in-depth descriptions of the cultures of 14 countries* (Vol. 1). Unpublished manuscript.

Fu, P. P., & Yukl, G. (2000). Perceived effectiveness of influence tactics in the United States and China. *Leadership Quarterly, 11,* 251–266.

Fulmer, R. M., & Wagner, S. (1999). Leadership: Lessons from the best. *Training & Development, 53,* 29–32.

Galton, F. (1869). *Hereditary genius.* New York: Appleton.

Gangestad, S. W., & Snyder, M. (2000). Self-monitoring: Appraisal and reappraisal. *Psychological Bulletin, 126,* 530–555.

Gardner, H. (1983). *Frames of mind: The theory of multiple intelligences.* New York: Basic Books.

Gardner, H. (1985). *The mind's new science: A history of the cognitive revolution.* New York: Basic Books.

Gardner, J. (1965). The antileadership vaccine. In *Annual report of the Carnegie Corporation.* New York: Carnegie Corporation.

Gardner, J. (1987). *The moral aspect of leadership.* Washington, DC: Leadership Studies Program, Independent Sector.

Gardner, J. (1990). *On leadership.* New York: Free Press.

Gardner, W., & Avolio, B. J. (1998). The charismatic relationship: A dramaturgical perspective. *Academy of Management Review, 23,* 32–58.

Gardner, W. L., & Schermerhorn, J. R. (1992). Strategic leadership and the management of supportive work environments. In R. L. Phillips & J. G. Hunt (Eds.), *Strategic leadership: A multiorganizational-level perspective* (pp. 99–118). Westport, CT: Quorum.

Garrett, L. (2000, March 29). Added foe in AIDS war: Skeptics. *Newsday,* p. A6.

Garvin, D. A. (1993). Building a learning organization. *Harvard Business Review, 71,* 78–91.

Gastil, J. (1994). A meta-analytic review of the productivity and satisfaction of democratic and autocratic leadership. *Small Group Research, 25,* 384–410.

Gaugler, B. B, Rosenthal, D. B., Thornton, G. C., & Bentson, C. (1987). Meta-analysis of assessment center validity. *Journal of Applied Psychology, 72,* 493–511.

Gavin, M. B., & Hofmann, D. A. (2002). Using hierarchical linear modeling to investigate the moderating influence of leadership climate. *Leadership Quarterly, 13,* 15–33.

Geary, D. C. (1998). *Male, female: The evolution of human sex differences.* Washington, DC: American Psychological Association.

Geller, P. A., & Hobfoll, S. E. (1993).Gender differences in preference to offer social support to assertive men and women. *Sex Roles, 28,* 419–432.

George, J. M., & James, L. R. (1993). Personality, affect, and behavior in groups revisited: Comment on aggregation, levels of analysis, and a recent application of within and between analysis. *Journal of Applied Psychology, 78,* 798–804.

Georgopoulus, B. S., Mahoney, G. M., & Jones, N. W. (1957). A path-goal approach to productivity. *Journal of Applied Psychology, 41,* 345–353.

Gergen, D. (2002, November). *Keynote address.* Delivered at the meeting of the International Leadership Association, Seattle, WA.

Gerstner, C. R., & Day, D. V. (1994). Cross-cultural comparison of leadership prototypes. *Leadership Quarterly, 5,* 121–134.

Gerstner, C. R., & Day, D. V. (1997). Meta-analytic review of leader-member exchange theory: Correlates and construct issues. *Journal of Applied Psychology, 82,* 827–844.

Geyer, A.L.J., & Steyrer, J. M. (1998). Transformational leadership and objective performance in banks. *Applied Psychology: An International Review, 47,* 397–420.

Ghiselli, E. E., & Brown, C. W. (1955). *Personnel and industrial psychology* (2nd ed.). New York: McGraw-Hill.

Gibb, C. A. (1947). The principles and traits of leadership. *Journal of Abnormal and Social Psychology, 42,* 267–284.

Gibb, C. A. (1949). Some tentative comments concerning group Rorschach pointers to the personality traits of leaders. *Journal of Social Psychology, 30,* 251–263.

Gibb, C. A. (1954). Leadership. In G. Lindzey (Ed.), *Handbook of social psychology.* Cambridge, MA: Addison-Wesley.

Gibb, C. A. (1958). An interactional view of the emergence of leadership. *Australian Journal of Psychology, 10,* 101–110.

Giberson, T. R., Resick, C. J., & Dickson, M. W. (2002). Examining the relationship between organizational homogeneity and organizational outcomes. In C. J. Resick & M. W. Dickson (Chairs), *Person-organization fit: Balancing its constructive and destructive forces.* Symposium conducted at the Academy of Management, Denver.

Gibson, F. W., Fiedler, F. E., & Barrett, K. M. (1993). Stress, babble, and the utilization of the leader's intellectual abilities. *Leadership Quarterly, 4,* 189–208.

Gilbert, J. A., & Zaccaro, S. J. (1995, August). *Social intelligence and organizational leadership.* Presented at the 103rd annual meeting of the American Psychological Association, New York.

Gillespie, T. L. (2002, April). *Global 360: Balancing consistency across cultures.* Paper presented at the 17th annual conference of the Society for Industrial and Organizational Psychology, Toronto.

Gioia, D. A., & Sims, H. P. (1985). On avoiding the influence of implicit leadership theories in leader behavior descriptions. *Educational and Psychological Measurement, 45,* 217–232.

Glass, G. (1976). Primary, secondary, and meta-analysis of research. *Educational Researcher 5,* 351–379.

Glick, P., Diebold, J., Bailey-Werner, B., & Zhu, L. (1997). The two faces of Adam: Ambivalent sexism and polarized attitudes toward women. *Personality and Social Psychology Bulletin, 23,* 1323–1334.

Glick, W. H. (1985). Conceptualizing and measuring organizational and psychological climate: Pitfalls in multilevel research. *Academy of Management Review, 10,* 601–616.

Goddard, H. H. (1911). Two thousand normal children measured by the Binet measuring scale of intelligence. *Pedagogical Seminary, 18,* 232–259.

Goffman, E. (1974). *Frame analysis: An essay on the organization of experience.* Cambridge, MA: Harvard University Press.

Goldberg, S. (1993). *Why men rule: A theory of male dominance.* Chicago: Open Court.

Goldstein, I. L., & Gilliam, P. (1990). Training system issues in the year 2000. *American Psychologist, 45,* 134–143.

Goleman, D. (1995). *Emotional intelligence.* New York: Bantam Books.

Goleman, D. (1998). *Working with emotional intelligence.* New York: Bantam Books.

Goleman, D., Boyatzis, R., & McKee, A. (2002). *Primal leadership: Realizing the power of emotional intelligence.* Boston: Harvard Business School Press.

Gomez, C., Brannen, M. Y., Sagiv, L., & Romani, L. (in press). Business conditions, tasks and people. In H. W. Lane, M. L. Maznevski, M. E. Mendenhall, & J. McNett (Eds.), *The Blackwell handbook of global management.* Oxford, UK: Basil Blackwell.

Goodman, P. S., Ancona, D. G., Lawrence, B. S., & Tushman, M. L. (Eds.). (2001). Special topic forum on time and organizational research. *Academy of Management Review, 26,* 498–663.

Goodwin, V. L., Wofford, J. C., & Boyd, N. C. (2000). A laboratory experiment testing the antecedents of leader cognitions. *Journal of Organizational Behavior, 21,* 769–788.

Graeff, C. L. (1997). Evolution of situation leadership theory: A critical review. *Leadership Quarterly, 8,* 153–170.

Graen, G. B., & Cashman, J. (1975). A role-making model of leadership in formal organizations: A developmental approach. In J. G. Hunt & L. L. Larson (Eds.), *Leadership frontiers* (pp. 143–165). Kent, OH: Kent State University Press.

Graen, G. B., & Scandura, T. A. (1987). Toward a psychology of dyadic organizing. In B. M. Staw & L. Cummings (Eds.), *Research in organizational behavior* (Vol. 9, pp. 175–208). Greenwich, CT: JAI.

Graen, G. B., & Uhl-Bien, M. (1995). Relationship-based approach to leadership: Development of leader-member exchange (LMX) theory of leadership over 25 years: Applying a multi-level multi-domain perspective. *Leadership Quarterly, 6,* 219–247.

Green, S. G., & Mitchell, T. R. (1979). Attributional processes of leaders in leader-member interactions. *Organizational Behavior and Human Decision Processes, 23,* 429–458.

Greene, C. N. (1977). Disenchantment with leadership research: Some causes, recommendations, and alternative directions. In J. G. Hunt & L. L. Larson (Eds.), *Leadership: The cutting edge* (pp. 57–67). Carbondale: Southern Illinois University Press.

Greenwood, D. J., & Levin, M. (1998). *Introduction to action research: Social research for social change.* Thousand Oaks, CA: Sage.

Griffeth, R. W., Hom, P. W., & Gaertner, S. (2000). A meta-analysis of antecedents and correlates of employee turnover: Update, moderator tests, and research implications for the next millennium. *Journal of Management, 26,* 463–488.

Gronn, P. (1999). Substituting for leadership: The neglected role of the leadership couple. *Leadership Quarterly, 10,* 41–62.

Gronn, P. (2002). Distributed leadership as a unit of analysis. *Leadership Quarterly, 13,* 423–451.

Gruenfeld, L. W., Rance, D. E., & Weissenberg, P. (1969). The behavior of task oriented (low LPC) and socially oriented (high LPC) leaders under several conditions of social support. *Journal of Social Psychology, 79*, 99–107.

Gupta, V., Hanges, P. J., & Dorfman, P. (2002). Cultural clusters: Methodology and findings. *Journal of World Business, 37*, 11–15.

Gupta, V., Sully, M., & House, R. J. (2004). Developing unobtrusive measures of GLOBE's societal culture scales. In R. J. House, P. J. Hanges, M. Javidan, P. W. Dorfman, V. Gupta (Eds.), *Leadership, culture, and organizations: The GLOBE study of 62 societies.* Thousand Oaks, CA: Sage.

Haccoun, R. R., & Saks, A. M. (1998). Training in the 21st century: Some lessons from the last one. *Canadian Psychology, 39*, 33–51.

Hackman, J. R. (1992). Group influences on individuals in organizations. In M. Dunnette & L. Hough (Eds.), *Handbook of industrial and organizational psychology* (Vol. 3, pp. 199–267). Palo Alto, CA: Consulting Psychologists Press.

Hackman, J. R., & Oldham, G. (1976). Motivation through the design of work: A test of a theory. *Organizational Behavior and Human Performance, 16*, 250–279.

Haddock, G., & Zanna, M. P. (1994). Preferring "housewives" to "feminists": Categorization and the favorability of attitudes toward women. *Psychology of Women Quarterly, 18*, 25–52.

Hains, S. C., Hogg, M. A., & Duck, J. M. (1997). Self-categorization and leadership: Effects of group prototypicality and leader stereotypicality. *Personality and Social Psychology Bulletin, 23*, 1087–1100.

Hall, D., & Mirvis, P. (1995). The new career contract: Developing the whole person at midlife and beyond. *Journal of Vocational Behavior, 47*, 269–289.

Hall, E. T. (1959). *The silent language.* New York: Anchor/Doubleday.

Hall, E. T. (1976). *Beyond culture.* New York: Doubleday.

Halpern, D. F. (2001). Sex difference research: Cognitive abilities. In J. Worrell (Ed.), *Encyclopedia of women and gender: Sex similarities and differences and the impact of society on gender* (Vol. 2, pp. 963–971). San Diego, CA: Academic Press.

Hambrick, D. C., & Mason, P. A. (1984). Upper echelons: The organization as a reflection of its top managers. *Academy of Management Review, 9*, 193–206.

Hammerschmidt, P. K., & Jennings, A. C. (1992). The impact of personality characteristics on leadership effectiveness ratings. In K. E. Clark, M. B. Clark, & D. P. Campbell (Eds.), *Impact of leadership* (pp. 469–475). Greensboro, NC: Center for Creative Leadership.

Hanges, P. J., & Dickson, M. W. (2004). The development and validation of the GLOBE culture and leadership scales. In R. J. House, P. J. Hanges, M. Javidan, P. W. Dorfman, V. Gupta (Eds.), *Leadership, culture, and organizations: The GLOBE study of 62 societies.* Thousand Oaks, CA: Sage.

Hanges, P. J., Lord, R. G., & Dickson, M. W. (2000). An information processing perspective on leadership and culture: A case for connectionist architecture. *Applied Psychology: An International Review, 49*, 133–161.

Harris, M. M., & Schaubroeck, J. (1988). A meta-analysis of self-supervisor, self-peer, and peer-supervisor ratings. *Personnel Psychology, 41*, 43–62.

Harrison, J. K. (1992). Individual and combined effects of behavior modeling and the cultural assimilator in cross-cultural management training. *Journal of Applied Psychology, 77*, 952–962.

Harter, E., & Sashkin, M. (2002). *The relationship between leadership and organizational sustainability.* Paper presented at the annual meeting of the Academy of Management, Denver, CO.

Hater, J. J., & Bass, B. M. (1988). Superiors' evaluations and subordinates' perceptions of transformational and transactional leadership. *Journal of Applied Psychology, 73,* 695–702.

Hawkins, K., & Tolzin, A. (2002). Examining the team/leader interface: Baseball teams as exemplars of postmodern organizations. *Group & Organization Management, 27*(1), 97–112.

Heck, R. H., & Thomas, S. L. (2000). *An introduction to multilevel modeling techniques.* Mahwah, NJ: Lawrence Erlbaum.

Hedges, L. V., & Nowell, A. (1995). Sex differences in mental test scores, variability, and numbers of high-scoring individuals. *Science, 269,* 41–45.

Hedges, L. V., & Olkin, I. (1985). *Statistical methods for meta-analysis.* San Diego, CA: Academic Press.

Hedlund, J., Forsythe, G. B., Horvath, J. A., Williams, W. M., Snook, S., & Sternberg, R. J. (2003). Identifying and assessing tacit knowledge: Understanding the practical intelligence of military leaders. *Leadership Quarterly, 14,* 117–140.

Heifetz, R. A. (1994). *Leadership without easy answers.* Cambridge, MA: Harvard University Press.

Heilman, M. E. (1983). Sex bias in work settings: The Lack of Fit model. *Research in Organizational Behavior, 5,* 269–298.

Heilman, M. E. (2001). Description and prescription: How gender stereotypes prevent women's ascent up the organizational ladder. *Journal of Social Issues, 57,* 657–674.

Heilman, M. E., Block, C. J., & Martell, R. F. (1995). Sex stereotypes: Do they influence perceptions of managers? *Journal of Social Behavior and Personality, 10,* 237–252.

Heilman, M. E., Block, C. J., Martell, R. F., & Simon, M. C. (1989). Has anything changed? Current characterizations of men, women, and managers. *Journal of Applied Psychology, 74,* 935–942.

Heilman, M. E., Hornstein, H. A., Cage, J. H., & Herschlag, J. K. (1984). Reaction to prescribed leader behavior as a function of role perspective: The case of the Vroom-Yetton model. *Journal of Applied Psychology, 69,* 50–60.

Helgesen, S. (1990). *The female advantage: Women's ways of leadership.* New York: Doubleday Currency.

Heller, F. A., Drenth, P. J. D., Koopman P. L., & Rus, V. (1988). *Decisions in organisations: A three country comparative study.* London: Sage.

Heller, F. A., & Misumi, J. (1987). Decision making. In B. M. Bass & P. J. D. Drenth (Eds.), *Advances in organizational psychology.* Newbury Park, CA: Sage.

Hemphill, J. K. (1949). *Situational factors in leadership* (Bureau of Educational Research Monograph 32). Columbus: Ohio State University.

Hemphill, J. K., & Coons, A. E. (1957). Development of the Leader Behavior Description Questionnaire. In R. M. Stogdill & A. E. Coons (Eds.), *Leader behavior: Its description and measurement* (pp. 6–38). Columbus: Bureau of Business Research, Ohio State University.

Hendrick, H. W. (1990). Perceptual accuracy of self and others and leadership status as functions of cognitive complexity. In K. E. Clark & M. B. Clark (Eds.), *Measures of leadership* (pp. 511–519). Greensboro, NC: Center for Creative Leadership.

Hersey, P., & Blanchard, K. H. (1969a). Life cycle theory of leadership. *Training and Development Journal, 23,* 26–34.

Hersey, P., & Blanchard, K. H. (1969b). *Management of organizational behavior.* Englewood Cliffs, NJ: Prentice Hall.

Hersey, P., & Blanchard, K. H. (1982a). Grid principles and situationalism: Both! A response to Blake and Mouton. *Group and Organization Studies, 7,* 207–210.

Hersey, P., & Blanchard, K. H. (1982b). *Management of organizational behavior* (4th ed.). Englewood Cliffs, NJ: Prentice Hall.

Hersey, P., & Blanchard, K. H. (1988). *Management of organizational behavior* (5th ed.). Englewood Cliffs, NJ: Prentice Hall.

Heslin, P. A., & Latham, G. P. (2001, April). *The effect of upward feedback on managerial behavior.* Paper presented at the 16th annual conference of the Society for Industrial and Organizational Psychology, San Diego, CA.

Hicks, W., & Klimoski, R. (1987). Entry into training programs and its effects on training outcomes: A field experiment. *Academy of Management Journal, 30,* 542–552.

Hieder, J. (1985). *The Tao of leadership.* Atlanta, GA: Humanics Limited.

Higgins, K. D., Jones, J. W., & Paddock, W. A. (2002, April). *E-leaders vs. traditional leaders: A qualitative biographical analysis.* Paper presented at the 17th annual meeting of the Society for Industrial and Organizational Psychology, Toronto.

Highhouse, S., Mohammed, S., & Hoffman, J. R. (2002). Temporal discounting of strategic issues: Bold forecasts for opportunities and threats. *Basic & Applied Social Psychology, 24,* 43–56.

Hilgard, E. R. (1980). The trilogy of mind: Cognition, affection, and conation. *Journal of the History of the Behavioral Sciences, 16,* 107–117.

Hinings, C. R. (1997). Reflections on processual research. *Scandinavian Journal of Management, 13,* 493–503.

Hitt, M. A., Keats, B. W., & DeMarie, S. M. (1998). Navigating in the new competitive landscape: Building strategic flexibility and competitive advantage in the 21st century. *Academy of Management Executive, 12,* 22–41.

Hitt, M. A., & Tyler, B. B. (1991). Strategic decision models: Integrating different perspectives. *Strategic Management Journal, 12,* 327–351.

Hofmann, D. A. (1997). An overview of the logic and rationale of hierarchical linear models. *Journal of Management, 23,* 723–744.

Hofstede, G. (1980). *Culture's consequences: International differences in work-related values.* Beverly Hills, CA: Sage.

Hofstede, G. (1991). *Cultures and organizations: The software of the mind.* New York: McGraw-Hill.

Hofstede, G. (1993). Cultural constraints in management theories. *Academy of Management Executive, 7,* 81–94.

Hofstede, G. (1998). *Masculinity and femininity: The taboo dimension of national cultures.* Thousand Oaks, CA: Sage.

Hofstede, G. (2001). *Culture's consequences: Comparing values, behaviors, institutions, and organizations across nations* (2nd ed.). Thousand Oaks, CA: Sage.

Hogan, R. (1994). Trouble at the top: Causes and consequences of managerial incompetence. *Consulting Psychology Journal, 46,* 9–15.

Hogan, R., Curphy, G. J., & Hogan, J. (1994). What we know about leadership: Effectiveness and personality. *American Psychologist, 49,* 493–504.

Hogan, R., & Hogan, J. (2001). Assessing leadership: A view from the dark side. *International Journal of Assessment and Selection, 9,* 40–51.

Hogan, R., Hogan J., & Roberts, B. W. (1996). Personality measurement and employment decisions: Questions and answers. *American Psychologist, 51,* 469–477.

Hogan, R., Raskin, R., & Fazzini, D. (1990). The dark side of charisma. In K. E. Clark & M. B. Clark (Eds.), *Measures of leadership* (pp. 343–354). West Orange, NJ: Leadership Library of America.

Hogan, R. H., & Warrenfeltz, R. (in press). Educating the modern manager. *Academy of Management Learning.*

Hogg, M. A. (2001). A social identity theory of leadership. *Personality and Social Psychology Review, 5,* 184–200.

Hogg, M. A., Hains, S. C., & Mason, I. (1998). Identification and leadership in small groups: Salience, frame of reference, and leader stereotypicality effects on leader evaluations. *Journal of Personality and Social Psychology, 75,* 1248–1263.

Hollander, E. P. (1958). Conformity, status, and idiosyncrasy credit. *Psychological Review, 65,* 117–127.

Hollander, E. P. (1964). *Leaders, groups, and influence.* New York: Oxford University Press.

Hollander, E. P. (1978). *Leadership dynamics: A practical guide to effective relationships.* New York: Free Press.

Hollander, E. P. (1980). Leadership and social exchange processes. In K. J. Gergen, M. S. Greenberg, & R. H. Willis (Eds.), *Social exchange: Advances in theory and research* (pp. 103–118). New York: Plenum.

Hollander, E. P., & Julian, J. W. (1969). Contemporary trends in the analysis of leadership perceptions. *Psychological Bulletin, 71,* 387–397.

Hollander, E. P., & Offermann, L. R. (1990). Power and leadership in organizations: Relationships in transition. *American Psychologist, 45,* 179–189.

Holtgraves, T. (1997). Styles of language use: Individual and cultural variability in conversational indirectness. *Journal of Personality and Social Psychology, 73,* 624–637.

Hooijberg, R. (1996). A multidirectional approach toward leadership: An extension of the concept of behavioral complexity. *Human Relations, 49,* 917–947.

Hooijberg, R., Bullis, R. C., & Hunt, J. G. (1999). Behavioral complexity and the development of military leadership for the twenty-first century. In J. G. Hunt, G. E. Dodge, & L. Wong (Eds.), *Out-of-the-box leadership: Transforming the 21st century army and other top-performing organizations* (pp. 111–130). Greenwich, CT: JAI.

Hooijberg, R., Hunt, J. G., & Dodge, G. E. (1997). Leadership complexity and development of the leaderplex model. *Journal of Management, 23,* 375–408.

Hooijberg, R., & Schneider, M. (2001). Behavioral complexity and social intelligence: How executive leaders use stakeholders to form systems perspective. In S. J. Zaccaro & R. J. Klimoski (Eds.), *The nature of organizational leadership: Understanding the performance imperatives confronting today's leaders* (pp. 104–131). San Francisco: Jossey-Bass.

Hosking, D. M., & Morley, I. E. (1988). The skills of leadership. In J. G. Hunt, B. R. Baliga, H. P. Dachler, & C. A. Schriesheim (Eds.), *Emerging leadership vistas* (pp. 89–106). Lexington, MA: Lexington Books.

Hothersall, D. (1984). *History of psychology.* New York: Random House.

Hough, L. M., & Schneider, R. J. (1996). Personality traits, taxonomies, and applications in organizations. In K. R. Murphy (Ed.), *Individual differences and behavior in organizations* (pp. 31–88). San Francisco: Jossey-Bass.

House, R. J. (1971). A path-goal theory of leader effectiveness. *Administrative Science Quarterly, 16,* 321–338.

House, R. J. (1977). A 1976 theory of charismatic leadership. In J. G. Hunt & L. L. Larson (Eds.), *Leadership: The cutting edge* (pp. 189–207). Carbondale. Southern Illinois University Press.

House, R. J. (1988). Power and personality in organizations. *Research in Organizational Behavior, 10,* 305–357.

House, R. J. (1995a). Leadership in the 21st century: A speculative enquiry. In A. Howard (Ed.), *The changing nature of work* (pp. 411–450). San Francisco: Jossey-Bass.

House, R. J. (1995b, June). Value based leadership. *Personalführung,* pp. 476–479.

House, R. J. (1996). Path-goal theory of leadership: Lessons, legacy, and a reformulated theory. *Leadership Quarterly, 7,* 323–352.

House, R. J., & Aditya, R. N. (1997). The social scientific study of leadership: Quo vadis? *Journal of Management, 23*, 409–473.

House, R. J., Hanges, P. J., Ruiz-Quintanilla, S. A., Dorfman, P. W., Javidan, M., Dickson, M., et al. (1999). Cultural influences on leadership and organizations: Project GLOBE. In W. H. Mobley, M. J. Gessner, & V. Arnold (Eds.), *Advances in global leadership* (pp. 171–233). Stamford, CT: JAI.

House, R. J., & Howell, J. M. (1992). Personality and charismatic leadership. *Leadership Quarterly, 3*, 81–108.

House, R. J., & Mitchell, T. R. (1974). Path-goal theory of leadership. *Journal of Contemporary Business, 3*, 81–97.

House, R. J., & Podsakoff, P. M. (1994). Leadership effectiveness: Past perspectives and future directions for research. In J. Greenberg (Ed.), *Organizational behavior: The state of the science* (pp. 45–82). Hillsdale, NJ: Lawrence Erlbaum.

House, R. J., & Shamir, B. (1993). Toward the integration of transformational, charismatic, and visionary theories. In M. M. Chemers & R. Ayman (Eds.), *Leadership theory and research: Perspectives and directions* (pp. 81–107). San Diego, CA: Academic Press.

House, R. J., Shane, S. A., & Herold, D. M. (1996). Rumors of the death of depositional research are vastly exaggerated. *Academy of Management Review, 21*, 203–224.

House, R. J., & Singh, J. V. (1987). Organizational behavior: Some new directions for I/O psychology. *Annual Review of Psychology, 38*, 669–718.

House, R. J., Spangler, W. D., & Woycke, J. (1991). Personality and charisma in the U.S. presidency: A psychological theory of effectiveness. *Administrative Science Quarterly, 36*, 334–396.

House, R. J., Woycke, J., & Fodor, E. M. (1988). Charismatic and noncharismatic leaders: Differences in behavior and effectiveness. In J. A. Conger & R. N. Kanungo (Eds.), *Charismatic leadership: The elusive factor in organizational effectiveness* (pp. 98–121). San Francisco: Jossey-Bass.

House, R. J., Wright, N. S., & Aditya, R. N. (1997). Cross-cultural research on organizational leadership: A critical analysis and a proposed theory. In P. C. Early & M. Erez (Eds.), *New perspectives on international industrial/organizational psychology* (pp. 535–625). San Francisco: The New Lexington Press.

Howard, A. (2001). Identifying, assessing, and selecting senior leaders. In S. J. Zaccaro & R. J. Klimoski (Eds.), *The nature of organizational leadership: Understanding the performance imperatives confronting today's leaders* (pp. 305–346). San Francisco: Jossey-Bass.

Howard, A., & Bray, D. W. (1988). *Managerial lives in transition: Advancing age and changing times*. New York: Guilford.

Howard, A., & Bray, D. W. (1990). Predictions of managerial success over long periods of time: Lessons for the Management Progress Study. In K. E. Clark & M. B. Clark (Eds.), *Measures of leadership* (pp. 113–130). West Orange, NJ: Leadership Library of America.

Howell, J. M. (1988). Two faces of charisma: Socialized and personalized leadership in organizations. In J. A. Conger, & R. N. Kanungo (Eds.), *Charismatic leadership: The elusive factor in organizational effectiveness* (pp. 213–236). San Francisco: Jossey-Bass.

Howell, J. M., & Avolio, B. (1992). The ethics of charismatic leadership. *Academy of Management Executive, 6*, 43–54.

Howell, J. M., & Avolio, B. J. (1993). Transformational leadership, transactional leadership, locus of control, and support for innovation: Key predictors of business unit performance. *Journal of Applied Psychology, 78*, 891–902.

Howell, J. M., & Frost, P. J. (1989). A laboratory study of charismatic leadership. *Organizational Behavior and Human Decision Processes, 43*, 243–269.

Howell, J. M., & Hall-Merenda, K. (1999). The ties that bind: The impact of leader-member exchange, transformational and transactional leadership, and distance on predicting follower performance. *Journal of Applied Psychology, 84,* 680–694.

Howell, J. M., & Higgins, C. A. (1990). Champions of technological innovation. *Administrative Science Quarterly, 35,* 317–341.

Howell, J. P. (1997). "Substitutes for leadership: Their meaning and measurement"—An historical assessment. *Leadership Quarterly, 8,* 113–116.

Howell, J. P., Dorfman, P. W., & Kerr, S. (1986). Moderator variables in leadership research. *Academy of Management Review, 11,* 88–102.

Howells, L. T., & Becker, S. W. (1962). Seating arrangement and leadership emergence. *Journal of Abnormal and Social Psychology, 64,* 148–150.

Hughes, R. (2002). Reflections on the state of leadership and leadership development. *Human Resource Planning, 25,* 4–6.

Hunt, J. G. (1991). *Leadership: A new synthesis.* Newbury Park, CA: Sage.

Hunt, J. G. (1999). Transformational/charismatic leadership's transformation of the field: An historical essay. *Leadership Quarterly, 10,* 129–144.

Hunt, J. G. (2000). Comments from the *Yearly Review* editor. *Leadership Quarterly, 11,* 431–432.

Hunt, J. G., Boal, K. B., & Dodge, G. E. (1999). The effects of visionary and crisis-responsive charisma on followers: An experimental examination of two kinds of charismatic leadership. *Leadership Quarterly, 10,* 423–448.

Hunt, J. G., Boal, K. B., & Sorenson, R. L. (1990). Top management leadership: Inside the black box. *Leadership Quarterly, 1,* 41–65.

Hunt, J. G., & Conger, J. A. (1999). From where we sit: An assessment of transformational and charismatic leadership research. *Leadership Quarterly, 10,* 335–343.

Hunt, J. G., & Dodge, G. E. (2000). Leadership déjà vu all over again. *Leadership Quarterly, 11,* 435–458.

Hunt, J. G., & Osborn, R. N. (1982). Towards a macro-oriented model of leadership: An odyssey. In J. G. Hunt, U. Sekaran, & C. A. Schriesheim (Eds.), *Leadership beyond establishment views* (pp. 112–130). Carbondale: Southern Illinois University Press.

Hunt, J. G., & Ropo, A. (1997). Systems motivation, leadership, and teaching in an innovative academic setting. In J. L. Bess (Ed.), *Teaching well and liking it: The motivation of faculty in higher education* (pp. 219–247). Baltimore: Johns Hopkins University Press.

Hunt, J. G., & Ropo, A. (1998). Multi-level leadership: Grounded theory and mainstream theory applied to the case of General Motors. In F. Dansereau & F. J. Yammarino (Eds.), *Leadership: The multiple-level approaches* (pp. 289–328). Stamford, CT: JAI.

Hunt, J. G., & Ropo, A. (in press). Longitudinal research and the third scientific discipline. *Group & Organization Management.*

Hunt, J. G., Sekaran, U., & Schriesheim, C. A. (Eds.). (1982). *Leadership: Beyond establishment views.* Carbondale: Southern Illinois University Press.

Hunt, S. D. (1991). *Modern marketing theory: Critical issues in the philosophy of marketing science.* Cincinnati, OH: Southwestern.

Hunter, J. E., & Schmidt, F. L. (1990). *Methods of meta-analysis.* Newbury Park, CA: Sage.

Hurtz, G. M., & Donovan, J. J. (2000). Personality and job performance: The Big Five revisited. *Journal of Applied Psychology, 85,* 869–879.

Husserl, E. (1965). *Phenomenology and the crisis of philosophy.* New York: Harper Torchbooks.

Ibarra, H. (1997). Paving an alternative route: Gender differences in managerial networks. *Social Psychology Quarterly, 60,* 91–102.

Indvik, J. (1986). Path-goal theory of leadership: A meta-analysis. *Proceedings of the Academy of Managements Meeting,* 189–192.

Insch, G. S., Moore, J. E., & Murphy, L. D. (1997). Content analysis in leadership research: Examples, procedures, and suggestions for future use. *Leadership Quarterly, 8,* 1–25.

Isenberg, D. J. (1986). Thinking and managing: A verbal protocol analysis of managerial problem solving. *Academy of Management Journal, 29,* 775–788.

Jackson, S. E., & Dutton, J. E. (1988). Discerning threats and opportunities. *Administrative Science Quarterly, 33,* 370–387.

Jackson, S. E., & Ruderman, M. N. (Eds.). (1995). *Diversity in work teams.* Washington, DC: American Psychological Association.

Jacobs, T. O. (1970). *Leadership and exchange in formal organizations.* Alexandria, VA: Human Resources Research Organization.

Jacobs, T. O., & Jaques, E. (1987a). Executive leadership. In R. Gal & A. D. Mangelsdorff (Eds.), *Handbook of military psychology.* Chichester, UK: Wiley.

Jacobs, T. O., & Jaques, E. (1987b). Leadership in complex systems. In J. Zeidner (Ed.), *Human productivity enhancement.* New York: Praeger.

Jacobs, T. O., & Jaques, E. (1990). Military executive leadership. In K. E. Clark & M. B. Clark (Eds.), *Measures of leadership.* Greensboro, NC: Center for Creative Leadership.

Jacobs, T. O., & McGee, M. L. (2001). Competitive advantage: Conceptual imperatives for executives. In S. J. Zaccaro & R. J. Klimoski (Eds.), *The nature of organizational leadership* (pp. 42–78). San Francisco: Jossey-Bass.

Jacobsen, C., & House, R. J. (2001). Dynamics of charismatic leadership: A process of theory, simulation model, and tests. *Leadership Quarterly, 12,* 75–112.

Jacobsen, J. P., & Levin, L. M. (1995). Effects of intermittent labor force attachment on women's earnings. *Monthly Labor Review, 118,* 14–19.

Jago, A. G., Maczynski, J., & Reber, G. (1996). Evolving leadership styles? A comparison of Polish managers before and after market economy reforms. *Polish Psychological Bulletin, 27,* 107–115.

Jago, A. G., & Vroom, V. H. (1980). An evaluation of two alternatives to the Vroom/Yetton normative model. *Academy of Management Journal, 23,* 347–355.

Jago, A. G., & Vroom, V. H. (1983). Sex differences in the incidence and evaluation of participative leader behavior. *Journal of Applied Psychology, 67,* 776–783.

James, L. R., Demaree, R. G., & Wolf, G. (1984). Estimating within-group interrater reliability with and without response bias. *Journal of Applied Psychology, 69,* 85–98.

James, L. R., Mulaik, S. A., & Brett, J. M. (1982). *Causal analysis: Assumptions, models, and data.* Beverly Hills, CA: Sage.

Jaques, E. (1961). *Equitable payment.* New York: John Wiley.

Jaques, E. (1976). *A general theory of bureaucracy.* London: Heinemann.

Jaques, E. (1986). The development of intellectual capability. *Journal of Applied Behavioral Science, 22,* 361–383.

Jaques, E. (1989). *Requisite organization.* Arlington, VA: Cason Hall.

Jaques, E., & Cason, K. (1994). *Human capability: A study of individual potential and its application.* Arlington, VA: Cason Hall.

Jaques, E., & Clement, S. D. (1991). *Executive leadership: A practical guide to managing complexity.* Arlington, VA: Cason Hall.

Jenkins, W. O. (1947). A review of leadership studies with particular reference to military problems. *Psychological Bulletin, 44,* 54–79.

Jennings, H. H. (1947). Leadership and sociometric choice. *Sociometry, 10,* 32–49.

Jermier, J. M., & Kerr, S. (1997). "Substitutes for leadership: Their meaning and measurement"—Contextual recollections and current observations. *Leadership Quarterly, 8,* 95-102.

Johns, G. (2001). In praise of context. *Journal of Organizational Behavior, 22,* 31–42.

Johnson, K. M., & Johnson, J. W. (2001, April). *The influence of self-other agreement on performance improvement following feedback from multiple sources.* Paper presented at the sixteenth annual conference of the Society for Industrial and Organizational Psychology, San Diego, CA.

Johnson-Laird, P. N. (1989). Mental models. In M. E. Posner (Ed.), *Foundations of cognitive science* (pp. 469–499). Cambridge, MA: MIT Press.

Jonas, K., Broemer, P., & Diehl, M. (2000). Attitudinal ambivalence. In W. Stroebe & M. Hewstone (Eds.), *European review of social psychology* (Vol. 11, pp. 35–74). Chichester, UK: Wiley.

Judge, T. A., Bono, J. E., Ilies, R., & Gerhardt, M. W. (2002). Personality and leadership: A qualitative and quantitative review. *Journal of Applied Psychology, 87,* 765–780.

Juran, J. M. (1988). *Juran on planning for quality.* New York: Free Press.

Kahn, R. L., & Katz, D. (1953). Leadership practices in relation to productivity and morale. In D. Cartwright & A. Zander (Eds.), *Group dynamics.* New York: Harper & Row.

Kahneman, D., & Tversky, A. (1979). Prospect theory: An analysis of decision under risk. *Econometrica, 47,* 263–292.

Kahtri, N., Ng, H. A., & Lee, T. H. (2001). The distinction between charisma and vision: An empirical study. *Asia Pacific Journal of Management, 18,* 373–393.

Kaiser, R. B. (2002, April). *Outgrowing sensitivities: The deeper work of executive development.* Paper presented at the 17th annual meeting of the Society for Industrial and Organizational Psychology, Toronto.

Kaiser, R. B., & DeVries, D. L. (2000). Leadership training. In W. E. Craighead & C. B. Nemeroff (Eds.), *The Corsini encyclopedia of psychology and behavioral science* (3rd ed.). New York: John Wiley.

Kakar, S., Kets de Vries, M.F.R., Kakar, S., & Vrignaud, P. (2002). Leadership in Indian organizations from a comparative perspective. *International Journal of Cross-Cultural Management, 2,* 239–250.

Kanfer, R. (1990). Motivation theory and industrial and organizational psychology. In M. D. Dunnette & L. Hough (Eds.), *Handbook of industrial and organizational psychology* (2nd ed., Vol. 1, pp. 75–170). Palo Alto, CA: Consulting Psychologists Press.

Kanfer, R. (1992). Work motivation: New directions in theory and research. In C. L. Cooper & I. T. Robertson (Eds.), *International review of industrial and organizational psychology* (Vol. 7, pp. 1–53). New York: John Wiley.

Kant, I. (1983). The idea for a universal history with a cosmopolitan intent. In T. Humphrey (Trans. and Ed.), *Perpetual peace and other essays on politics, history, and morals.* Indianapolis, IN: Hackett.

Kant, I. (1993). *Foundations of the metaphysics of morals* (J. W. Ellington, Trans.). Indianapolis, IN: Hackett.

Kanter, R. M. (1977). *Men and women of the corporation.* New York: Basic Books.

Kanter, R. M. (1989). *When giants learn to dance.* New York: Simon & Schuster.

Kanter, R. M. (1997). *On the frontiers of management.* Boston: Harvard Business School Press.

Kanter, R. M. (2001). *E-volve! Succeeding in the digital culture of tomorrow.* Boston: Harvard Business School Press.

Kanungo, R. N., & Mendonca, M. (1996a). Cultural contingencies and leadership in developing countries. *Research in the Sociology of Organizations, 14,* 263–295.

Kanungo, R., & Mendonca, M. (1996b). *Ethical dimensions of leadership.* Thousand Oaks, CA: Sage.

Kaplan, R. E., Drath, W. H, & Kofodimos, J. R. (1991). *Beyond ambition: How driven managers can lead better and live better.* San Francisco: Jossey-Bass.

Kaplan, R. E., & Kaiser, R. B. (in press). The turbulence within: How sensitivities throw off performance in executives. In R. Burke & G. Cooper (Eds.), *Learning in turbulent times.* New York: Oxford University Press.

Karmel, B. (1978). Leadership: A challenge to traditional research methods and assumptions. *Academy of Management Review, 3,* 475–482.

Katz, D., & Kahn, R. L. (1966). *The social psychology of organizing.* New York: John Wiley.

Katz, D., & Kahn, R. L. (1978). *The social psychology of organizations* (2nd ed.). New York: John Wiley.

Katz, D., Maccoby, N., Gurin, G., & Floor, L. G. (1951). *Productivity, supervision and morale among railroad workers.* Ann Arbor: Survey Research Center, Institute for Social Research, University of Michigan.

Kauffman, S. A. (1993). *The origin of order.* New York: Oxford University Press.

Kaufman, G., & Uhlenberg, P. (2000). The influence of parenthood on the work effort of married men and women. *Social Forces, 78,* 931–949.

Keeley, M. (1998). The trouble with transformational leadership. In J. B. Ciulla (Ed.), *Ethics, the heart of leadership.* Westport, CT: Praeger.

Keeney, M. J., & Marchioro, C. A. (1998). *A meta-analytic review of the traits associated with leadership emergence: An extension of Lord, De Vader, and Alliger (1986).* Paper presented at the 13th annual meeting of the Society for Industrial and Organizational Psychology, Dallas, TX.

Kegan, R. (1982). *The evolving self: Problem and process in human development.* Cambridge, MA: Harvard University Press.

Kegan, R. (1994). *In over our heads: The mental demands of modern life.* Cambridge, MA: Harvard University Press.

Kegan, R., & Lahey, L. L. (2001). *How the way we talk can change the way we work: Seven languages for transformation.* San Francisco: Jossey-Bass.

Keith, K., & McWilliams, A. (1997). Job mobility and gender-based wage differentials. *Economic Inquiry, 35,* 320–333.

Keith, K., & McWilliams, A. (1999). The returns to mobility and job search by gender. *Industrial and Labor Relations Review, 52,* 460–477.

Keller, T. (1999). Images of the familiar: Individual differences and implicit leadership theories. *Leadership Quarterly, 10,* 589–607.

Kellett, J. B., Humphrey, R. H., & Sleeth, R. G. (2002). Empathy and complex task performance: Two routes to leadership. *Leadership Quarterly, 13,* 523–544.

Kelley, H. H. (1967). Attribution theory in social psychology. In D. Levine (Ed.), *Nebraska symposium on motivation* (Vol. 15, pp. 192–238). Lincoln: University of Nebraska Press.

Kelman, H. C. (1958). Compliance, identification, and internalization: Three processes of attitude change. *Journal of Conflict Resolution, 2,* 51–60.

Kennedy, J. K., Houston, J. M., Korsgaard, M. A., & Gallo, D. D. (1987). Construct space of the least preferred coworker (LPC) scale. *Educational and Psychological Measurement, 47,* 807–814.

Kenny, D. A., & Judd, C. M. (1984). Estimating the nonlinear and interactive effects of latent variables. *Psychological Bulletin, 96,* 201–210.

Kenny, D. A., & Zaccaro, S. J. (1983). An estimate of variance due to traits in leadership. *Journal of Applied Psychology, 68,* 678–685.

Kenrick, D. T., & Funder, D. C. (1988). Profiting from controversy: Lessons from the person-situation debate. *American Psychologist, 43,* 23–34.

Kerlinger, F. N. (1986). *Foundations of behavioral research* (3rd ed.). New York: Holt, Rinehart & Winston.

Kerlinger, F., & Lee, H. B. (2000). *Foundations of behavioral research* (4th ed.). Fort Worth, TX: Harcourt Publishers.

Kern, J. M., Cavell, T. A., & Beck, B. (1985). Predicting differential reactions to males' versus females' assertions, empathic-assertions, and nonassertions. *Behavior Therapy, 16,* 63–75.

Kerr, S., & Jermier, J. M. (1978). Substitutes for leadership: Their meaning and measurement. *Organizational Behavior and Human Decision Processes, 22,* 375–403.

Kerr, S., & Slocum, J. W. (1987). Managing corporate culture through reward systems. *Academy of Management Executive, 1,* 99–108.

Kets de Vries, M., & Florent-Treacy, E. (2002). Global leadership from A to Z: Creating high commitment organizations. *Organizational Dynamics, 30,* 295–309.

Keys, J. B., & Wolfe, J. (1988). Management education and development: Current issues and emerging trends. *Journal of Management, 16,* 307–336.

Khandwalla, P. (1977). *The design of organizations.* New York: Harcourt Brace.

Kilburg, R. R. (1996). Toward a conceptual understanding and definition of executive coaching. *Consulting Psychology Journal: Practice and Research, 48,* 134–144.

Kirkman, B. L., & Den Hartog, D. N. (in press). People in global organizations: Culture, personality and social dynamics. In H. W. Lane, M. L. Maznevski, M. E. Mendenhall, & J. McNett (Eds.), *The Blackwell handbook of global management.* Oxford, UK: Basil Blackwell.

Kirkman, B. L., Lowe, K. B., & Gibson, C. B. (2003). *Two decades of culture's consequences: A review of empirical research incorporating Hofstede's cultural values framework.* Unpublished manuscript, Georgia Institute of Technology.

Kirkpatrick, D. L. (1994). *Evaluating training programs.* San Francisco: Berrett-Koehler.

Kirkpatrick, S. A., & Locke, E. A. (1991). Leadership: Do traits matter? *Academy of Management Executive, 5,* 48–60.

Klein, K. J., Dansereau, F., & Hall, R. J. (1994). Levels issues in theory development, data collection, and analysis. *Academy of Management Review, 19,* 195–229.

Klemp, G. O. (1980). *The assessment of occupational competence.* Washington, DC: National Institute of Education.

Klerman, J. A., & Leibowitz, A. (1999). Job continuity among new mothers. *Demography, 36,* 145–155.

Kline, R. B. (1998). *Principles and practice of structural equation modeling.* New York: Guilford.

Kling, K. C., Hyde, J. S., Showers, C. J., & Buswell, B. N. (1999). Gender differences in self-esteem: A meta-analysis. *Psychological Bulletin, 125,* 470–500.

Kluckhohn, F., & Strodtbeck, F. L. (1961). *Variations in value orientations.* Westport, CT: Greenwood.

Kluger, A. N., & DeNisi, A. (1996). Effects of feedback interventions on performance: A historical review, a meta-analysis, and preliminary feedback intervention theory. *Psychological Bulletin, 119,* 254–284.

Knowlton, B., & McGee, M. (1994). *Strategic leadership and personality: Making the MBTI relevant.* Washington, DC: National Defense University Industrial College of the Armed Forces.

Kobe, L. M., Reiter-Palmon, R., & Rickers, J. D. (2001). Self-reported leadership experiences in relation to inventoried social and emotional intelligence. *Current Psychology: Developmental, Learning, Personality, Social, 20,* 154–163.

Koene, B.A.S., Vogelaar, A.L.W., & Soeters, J. L. (2002). Leadership effects on organizational climate and financial performance: Local leadership effect in chain organizations. *Leadership Quarterly, 13,* 193–215.

Koh, W. L., Steers, R. M., & Terborg, J. R. (1995). The effects of transformational leadership on teacher attitudes and student performance in Singapore. *Journal of Organizational Behavior, 16,* 319–333.

Kohlberg, L. (1976). Moral stages and moralization: The cognitive-developmental approach. In T. Lickona (Ed.), *Moral development and behavior* (pp. 31-53). New York: Holt, Rinehart & Winston.

Kolb, D. A. (1984). *Experiential learning: Experience as a source of learning and development.* Englewood Cliffs, NJ: Prentice Hall.

Konrad, A. M., Ritchie, J. E., Jr., Lieb, P., & Corrigall, E. (2000). Sex differences and similarities in job attribute preferences: A meta-analysis. *Psychological Bulletin, 126,* 593–641.

Koopman, P. L., et al. (1999). National culture and leadership profiles in Europe: Some results from the GLOBE study. *European Journal of Work and Organizational Psychology, 8,* 503–520.

Korman, A. K. (1966). Consideration, initiating structure, and organizational criteria—a review. *Personnel Psychology, 19,* 349–361.

Kotter, J. P. (1990). *A force for change: How leadership differs from management.* New York: Free Press.

Kotter, J. P. (2001). What leaders really do. *Harvard Business Review, 79,* 85–96.

Kotter, J. P., & Heskett, J. L. (1992). *Corporate culture and performance.* New York: Free Press.

Kouzes, J. M., & Posner, B. Z. (1987). *The leadership challenge: How to get extraordinary things done in organizations.* San Francisco: Jossey-Bass.

Kouzes, J. M., & Posner, B. Z. (1995). *The leadership challenge: How to keep getting extraordinary things done in organizations.* San Francisco: Jossey-Bass.

Kozlowski, S. W., & Hults, B. M. (1987). An exploration of climates for technical updating and performance. *Personnel Psychology, 40,* 539–563.

Kraut, A. I., Pedigo, P. R., McKenna, D. D., & Dunnette, M. D. (1989). The role of the manager: What's really important in different management jobs. *Academy of Management Executive, 3,* 286–293.

Kristof, A. L. (1996). Person-organization fit: An integrative review of its conceptualizations, measurement, and implications. *Personnel Psychology, 49,* 1–49.

Kuhnert, K. W., & Lewis, P. (1987). Transactional and transformational leadership: A constructive/developmental analysis. *Academy of Management Review, 12,* 648–657.

Kunda, G. (1992). *Engineering culture: Control and commitment in a high-tech corporation.* Philadelphia: Temple University Press.

Langer, E. J. (1992). Matters of mind: Mindfulness/mindlessness in perspective. *Consciousness and Cognition: An International Journal, 1,* 289–305.

Lao-tzu. (1963). The Lao Tzu (Tao-te-ching). In W.-T. Chan (Trans. and Ed.), *A source book in Chinese philosophy.* Princeton, NJ: Princeton University Press.

Larson, J. R. (1982). Cognitive mechanisms mediating the impact of implicit theories of leader behavior on leader behavior ratings. *Organizational Behavior and Human Decision Processes, 29,* 129–140.

Larson, J. R., Lingle, J. H., & Scerbo, M. M. (1984). The impact of performance cues on leader-behavior ratings: The role of selective information availability and probabilistic response bias. *Organizational Behavior and Human Decision Processes, 33,* 323–349.

Latham, G. P., & Seijts, G. H. (1999). The effects of proximal and distal goals on performance on a moderately complex task. *Journal of Organizational Behavior, 20,* 421–429.

Lawrence, P. R., & Lorsch, J. W. (1967). *Organization and environment.* Irwin, IL: Homewood.

Leavitt, H. J. (1951). Some effects of certain communication patterns on group performance. *Journal of Abnormal and Social Psychology, 46,* 38–50.

Lepak, D. P., & Snell, S. A (1999). The human resource architecture: Toward a theory of human capital allocation and development. *Academy of Management Review, 24,* 31–48.

LePine, J. A., Hollenbeck, J. R., Ilgen, D. R., & Hedlund, J. (1997). Effects of individual differences on the performance of hierarchical decision-making teams: Much more than g. *Journal of Applied Psychology, 82,* 803–811.

Leslie, J. B., & Fleenor, J. W. (1998). *Feedback to managers: A review and comparison of multi-rater instruments for management development.* Greensboro, NC: Center for Creative Leadership.

Lester, S. W., Meglino, B. M., & Korsgaard, M. A. (2002). The antecedents and consequences of group potency: A longitudinal investigation of newly formed work groups. *Academy of Management Journal, 45,* 352–368.

Levinson, D. J. (1979). *The seasons of a man's life.* New York: Random House.

Levinson, D. J. (1997). *The seasons of a woman's life.* New York: Random House.

Levinson, H. (1994). Beyond the selection failures. *Consulting Psychology Journal, 46,* 3–7.

Levinson, H., & Rosenthal, S. (1983). *CEO: Corporate leadership in action.* New York: Basic Books.

Levy, P. E., Albright, M. D., Cawley, B. D., & Williams, J. R. (1995). Situational and individual determinants of feedback seeking: A closer look at the process. *Organizational Behavior and Human Decision Processes, 62,* 23–37.

Levy, S. (1992). *Artificial life: The quest for new creation.* New York: Random House.

Lewin, K. (1935). *A dynamic theory of personality* (D. E. Adams & K. E. Zener, Trans.). New York: McGraw-Hill.

Lewin, K. (1945). The Research Center for Group Dynamics at Massachusetts Institute of Technology. *Sociometry, 8,* 126–136.

Lewin, K., & Lippitt, R. (1938). An experimental approach to the study of autocracy and democracy: A preliminary note. *Sociometry, 1,* 292–300.

Lewin, K., Lippitt, R., & White, R. K. (1939). Patterns of aggressive behavior in experimentally created social climates. *Journal of Social Psychology, 10,* 271–299.

Lewis, P., Bartone, P. T., Forsythe, G. B., Bullis, R. C., & Snook, S. A. (2002, April). Developmental level and leader effectiveness: Implications of cross sectional and longitudinal findings for leader education. Paper presented at the 17th annual meeting of the Society for Industrial and Organizational Psychology, Toronto.

Lewis, P., & Jacobs, T. O. (1992). Individual differences in strategic leadership capacity: A constructive/developmental view. In R. L. Phillips & J. G. Hunt (Eds.), *Strategic leadership: A multiorganizational-level perspective* (pp. 121–137). Westport, CT: Quorum.

Lieberson, S., & O'Connor, J. F. (1977). Leadership and organizational performance: A study of large corporations. *American Sociological Review, 37,* 117–130.

Lievens, F., Van Geit, P., & Koetsier, P. (1997). Identification of transformational leadership qualities: An examination of potential biases. *European Journal of Work and Organizational Psychology, 4,* 415–430.

Likert, R. (1961). *New patterns of management.* New York: McGraw-Hill.

Likert, R. (1967). *The human organization: Its management and value.* New York: McGraw-Hill.

Lincoln, Y. S., & Guba, E. G. (1985). *Naturalistic inquiry.* Newbury Park, CA: Sage.

Lindholm, C. (1990). *Charisma.* Cambridge, MA: Blackwell.

Lipman-Blumen, J. (1996). *The connective edge: Leading in an interdependent world.* San Francisco: Jossey-Bass.

Lippitt, R., & White, R. K. (1943). The social climate of children's groups. In R. G. Baker, J. S. Kounin, & H. F. Wright (Eds.), *Child behavior and* development (pp. 485–508). New York: McGraw-Hill.

Locke, E. A., & Latham, G. P. (1990). *A theory of goal setting and task performance.* Englewood Cliffs, NJ: Prentice Hall.

Locke, E. A., & Schweiger, D. M. (1979). Participation in decision-making: One more look. In B. M. Staw (Ed.), *Research in organizational behavior* (Vol. 1, pp. 265–339). Greenwich, CT: JAI.

Loden, M. (1985). *Feminine leadership, or, how to succeed in business without being one of the boys.* New York: Times Books.

London, M. (1985). *Developing managers.* San Francisco: Jossey-Bass.

London, M. (2002). *Leadership development: Paths to self-insight and professional growth.* Mahwah, NJ: Lawrence Erlbaum.

London, M., & Diamante, T. (in press). Technologically expansive professionals: Developing continuous learning in the high technology sector. *Human Resource Development Review.*

London, M., Larsen, H. H., & Thisted, L. N. (1999). Relationships between feedback and self-development. *Group & Organization Management, 24,* 5–27.

London, M., & Noe, R. A. (1997). London's career motivation theory: An update on measurement and research. *Journal of Career Assessment, 5,* 61-80.

London, M., & Smither, J. W. (1999a). Career-related continuous learning: Defining the construct and mapping the process. *Research in Human Resources Management, 17,* 81–121.

London, M., & Smither, J. W. (1999b). Empowered self-development and continuous learning. *Journal of Human Resource Management, 38,* 3–16.

London, M., & Smither, J. W. (2002). Feedback orientation, feedback culture, and the longitudinal performance management process. *Human Resource Management Review, 12,* 81–100.

London, M., & Wholers, A. J. (1991). Agreement between subordinate and self-ratings in upward feedback. *Personnel Psychology, 44,* 375–390.

Lonner, W. J. (1980). The search for psychological universals. In H. C. Triandis & W. W. Lambert (Eds.), *Handbook of cross-cultural psychology: Perspectives* (Vol. 1, pp. 143–204.). Boston: Allyn & Bacon.

Lord, R. G. (1985). An information processing approach to social perceptions, leadership perceptions and behavioral measurement on organizational settings. In B. M. Staw & L. Cummings (Eds.), *Research in organizational behavior* (pp. 87–128). Greenwich, CT: JAI.

Lord, R. G., Binning, J. F., Rush, M. C., & Thomas, J. C. (1978). The effect of performance cues and leader behavior on questionnaire ratings of leadership behavior. *Organizational Behavior and Human Decision Processes, 21,* 27–39.

Lord, R. G., & Brown, D. J. (2001). Leadership, values, and subordinate self-concepts. *Leadership Quarterly, 12,* 133–152.

Lord, R. G., & Brown, D. J. (in press). *Leadership processes and follower self-identity.* Mahwah, NJ: Lawrence Erlbaum.

Lord, R. G., Brown, D. J., & Freiberg, S. J. (1999). Understanding the dynamics of leadership: The role of follower self-concepts in the leader/follower relationship. *Organizational Behavior and Human Decision Processes, 78,* 167–203.

Lord, R. G., Brown, D. J., & Harvey, J. L. (2001). System constraints on leadership perceptions, behavior, and influence: An example of connectionist level processes. In M. A. Hogg & R. S. Tindale (Eds.), *Blackwell handbook of social psychology: Vol. 3. Group processes* (pp. 283–310). Oxford, UK: Basil Blackwell.

Lord, R. G., Brown, D. J., Harvey, J. L., & Hall, R. J. (2001). Contextual constraints on prototype generation and their multilevel consequences for leadership perceptions. *Leadership Quarterly, 12,* 311–338.

Lord, R. G., De Vader, C. L., & Alliger, G. M. (1986). A meta-analysis of the relation between personality traits and leadership perceptions: An application of validity generalization procedures. *Journal of Applied Psychology, 71,* 402–410.

Lord, R. G., & Emrich, C. G. (2000). Thinking outside the box by looking inside the box: Extending the cognitive revolution in leadership research. *Leadership Quarterly, 11,* 551–579.

Lord, R. G., Foti, R. J., & De Vader, C. L. (1984). A test of leadership categorization theory: Internal structure, information processing, and leadership perceptions. *Organizational Behavior and Human Performance, 34,* 343–378.

Lord, R. G., Foti, R. J., & Philips, J. S. (1982). A theory of leadership categorization. In J. G. Hunt, U. Sekaran, & C. A. Schriesheim (Eds.), *Leadership: Beyond establishment views* (pp. 104–121). Carbondale: Southern Illinois University Press.

Lord, R. G., & Maher, K. J. (1991a). Cognitive theory in industrial and organizational psychology. In M. D. Dunnette & L. Hough (Eds.), *Handbook of industrial and organizational psychology* (Vol. 2, pp. 1–62). Palo Alto, CA: Consulting Psychologists Press.

Lord, R. G., & Maher, K. J. (1991b). *Leadership and information processing: Linking perceptions and performance.* Boston: Unwin Hyman.

Lord, R. G., & Smith, W. G. (1999). Leadership and the changing nature of performance. In D. R. Ilgen & E. D. Pulakos (Eds.), *The changing nature of performance: Implications for staffing, motivation, and development.* San Francisco: Jossey-Bass.

Lowe, K. B., & Gardner, W. L. (2000). Ten years of *The Leadership Quarterly*: Contributions and challenges for the future. *Leadership Quarterly, 11,* 459–514.

Lowe, K. B., Kroeck, K. G., & Sivasubramaniam, N. (1996). Effectiveness correlates of transformational and transaction leadership: A meta-analytic review of the MLQ literature. *Leadership Quarterly, 7,* 385–425.

Lubinski, D., & Benbow, C. P. (2000). States of excellence. *American Psychologist, 55,* 137–150.

Ludgate, D. R. (2001, January). An examination of the relationship between personality variables and managerial behavior as measured by power and influence tactics in project planning. *Dissertation Abstracts International, 62* (UMI No. 3016771).

Ludwig, D., & Longenecker, C. (1993). The Bathsheba syndrome: The ethical failure of successful leaders. *Journal of Business Ethics, 12,* 265–273.

Luthans, F., Hodgetts, R. M., & Rosenkrantz, S. A. (1987). *Real managers.* Cambridge, MA: Ballinger.

Lynch, L. M. (1991). The role of off-the-job vs. on-the-job training for the mobility of women workers. *American Economic Review, 81* (Papers and proceedings of the 103rd annual meeting of the American Economic Association), 151–156.

Lyness, K. S., & Judiesch, M. K. (2001). Are female managers quitters? The relationships of gender, promotions, and family leaves of absence to voluntary turnover. *Journal of Applied Psychology, 86,* 1167–1178.

Lyness, K. S., & Thompson, D. E. (1997). Above the glass ceiling? A comparison of matched samples of female and male executives. *Journal of Applied Psychology, 82,* 359–375.

Maccoby, M. (2000). Narcissistic leaders. *The Harvard Business Review, 78,* 69–75.

MacDonald, D. A., Gagnier, J. J., & Friedman, H. L. (2000). The Self-Expansiveness Level Form: Examination of its validity and relation to the NEO Personality Inventory—Revised. *Psychological Reports, 86,* 707–726.

Machiavelli, N. (1954). *The prince* (H. H. Thompson, Trans.). New York: Limited Editions Club. (Original work published 1513)

Maczynski, J., Jago, A. G., Reber, G., & Boehnisch, W. (1994). Culture and leadership styles: A comparison of Polish, Austrian, and U.S. managers. *Polish Psychological Bulletin, 25,* 303–315.

Maddi, S. R. (1987). Hardiness training at Illinois Bell Telephone. In J. Opatz (Ed.), *Health promotion evaluation* (pp. 101–115). Stephens Point, WI: National Wellness Institute.

Maddi, S. R., Kahn, S., & Maddi, K. L. (1998). The effectiveness of hardiness training. *Consulting Psychology Journal: Practice and Research, 50,* 78–86.

Maier, S. F., & Seligman, M.E.P. (1975). Learned helplessness: Theory and evidence. *Journal of Experimental Psychology: General, 105,* 3–46.

Mailick, S., Stumpf, S. A., Grant, S., Kfir, A., & Watson, M. A. (1998). *Learning theory in the practice of management development: Evolution and applications.* Westport, CT: Quorum.

Mainemelis, C., Boyatzis, R. E., & Kolb, D. A. (2002). Learning styles and adaptive flexibility: Testing experiential learning theory. *Management Learning, 33,* 5–33.

Major, K. (1988). *Dogmatism, visionary leadership and effectiveness of secondary principals.* Unpublished doctoral dissertation, University of La Verne, La Verne, CA.

Mann, R. D. (1959). A review of the relationship between personality and performance in small groups. *Psychological Bulletin, 56,* 241–270.

Manz, C. C., & & Sims, H. P. (1980). Self-management as a substitute for leadership: A social learning theory perspective. *Academy of Management Review, 5,* 361–367.

Marion, R. (1999). *The edge of organization.* Thousand Oaks, CA: Sage.

Marion, R., & Uhl-Bien, M. (2001). Leadership in complex organizations. *Leadership Quarterly, 12,* 389–418.

Markham, S. E., & Halverson, R. R. (2002). Within- and between-entity analysis in multilevel research: A leadership example using single level analyses and boundary conditions (MRA). *Leadership Quarterly, 13,* 35–52.

Markus, H., & Wurf, E. (1987). The dynamic self-concept: A social psychological perspective. *Annual Review of Psychology, 38,* 299–337.

Marlowe, H. A., Jr. (1986). Evidence for multidimensionality and construct independence. *Journal of Educational Psychology, 78,* 52–58.

Marshall-Mies, J. C., Fleishman, E. A., Martin, J. A., Zaccaro, S. J., Baughman, W. A., & McGee, M. L. (2000). Development and evaluation of cognitive and metacognitive measures for predicting leadership potential. *Leadership Quarterly, 11,* 135–153.

Martinez, S., & Dorfman, P. W. (1998). The Mexican entrepreneur: An ethnographic study of the Mexican Empressario. *International Studies of Management and Organizations, 28,* 97–123.

Maruyama, G. M. (1998). *Basics of structural equation modeling.* Thousand Oaks, CA: Sage.

Marx, K. (1906). *Capital.* Chicago: Charles H. Kerr.

Matschiner, M., & Murnen, S. K. (1999). Hyperfemininity and influence. *Psychology of Women Quarterly, 23,* 631–642.

Matthews, A. M., Lord, R. G., & Walker, J. B. (1990). *The development of leadership perceptions in children.* Unpublished manuscript, University of Akron.

Maume, D. J. (1999). Occupational segregation and the career mobility of White men and women. *Social Forces, 77,* 1433–1459.

Maurer, T. J. (2001). Career-relevant learning and development, worker age, and beliefs about self-efficacy for development. *Journal of Management, 27,* 123–140.

Maurer, T. J. (2002). Employee learning and development orientation: Toward an integrative model of involvement in continuous learning. *Human Resource Development Review, 1,* 9–44.

Maurer, T. J., & Lord, R. G. (1991). An exploration of cognitive demands in group interaction as a moderator of information processing variables in perceptions of leadership. *Journal of Applied Social Psychology, 21*, 821–839.

Maurer, T. J., Mitchell, D., & Barbeite, F. (2002). Predictors of attitudes toward a 360-degree feedback system and involvement in post-feedback management development activity. *Journal of Occupational and Organizational Psychology, 75*, 87–107.

Maurer, T. J., Pierce, H., & Shore, L. (2002). Perceived beneficiary of employee development activity: A three-dimensional social exchange model. *Academy of Management Review, 27*, 432–444.

Maurer, T. J., & Rafuse, N. E. (2001). Learning, not litigating: Managing employee development and avoiding claims of age discrimination. *Academy of Management Executive, 15*, 110–121.

Maurer, T. J., & Tarulli, B. A. (1994). An investigation of perceived environment, perceived outcome, and person variables in relationship to voluntary development activity by employees. *Journal of Applied Psychology, 79*, 3–14.

Maurer, T. J., & Tarulli, B. A. (1996). Acceptance of peer/upward performance appraisal systems: Role of work context factors and beliefs about managers' development capability. *Human Resource Management, 35*, 217–241.

Maxwell, J. A. (1996). *Qualitative research design: An integrative approach.* Thousand Oaks, CA: Sage.

Mayer, J. D., & Salovey, P. (1997). What is emotional intelligence? In P. Salovey & D. Sluyter (Eds.), *Emotional development and emotional intelligence: Implications for educators* (pp. 3–31). New York: Basic Books.

Mayer, J. D., Salovey, P., & Caruso, D. (2000). Models of emotional intelligence. In R. J. Sternberg (Ed.), *Handbook of human intelligence* (pp. 396–420). Cambridge, UK: Cambridge University Press.

McCall, M. W., & Lombardo, M. M. (Eds.). (1978). *Leadership: Where else can we go?* Durham, NC: Duke University Press.

McCall, M. W., & Lombardo, M. M. (1983). *Off the track: Why and how successful executives get derailed.* Greensboro, NC: Center for Creative Leadership.

McCall, M. W., Jr., Lombardo, M. M., & Morrison, A. M. (1988). *The lessons of experience: How successful executives develop on the job.* San Francisco: New Lexington Press.

McCauley, C. D. (2000). *A systematic approach to leadership development.* Paper presented at the 15th annual conference of the Society for Industrial and Organizational Psychology, New Orleans, LA.

McCauley, C. D. (2001). Leader training and development. In S. J. Zaccaro & R. J. Klimoski (Eds.), *The nature of organizational leadership* (pp. 347–383). San Francisco: Jossey-Bass.

McCauley, C. D., Moxley, R. S., & Van Velsor, E. (Eds.). (1998). *The Center for Creative Leadership handbook of leadership development.* San Francisco: Jossey-Bass.

McCauley, C. D., Ohlott, P. J., & Ruderman, M. N. (1999). *Job Challenge Profile: Facilitator's guide.* San Francisco: Jossey-Bass/Pfeiffer.

McCauley, C. D., Ruderman, M. N., Ohlott, P. J., & Morrow, J. E. (1994). Assessing the developmental components of managerial jobs. *Journal of Applied Psychology, 79*, 544–560.

McCauley, M. H. (1990). The Myers-Briggs Type Indicator and leadership. In K. E. Clark & M. B. Clark (Eds.), *Measures of leadership* (pp. 381–418). West Orange, NJ: Leadership Library of America.

McClelland, D. C. (1965). N-achievement and entrepreneurship: A longitudinal study. *Journal of Personality and Social Psychology, 1*, 389–392.

McClelland, D. C. (1975). *Power: The inner experience.* New York: Halsted.

McClelland, D. C. (1976). Power is the great motivator. *Harvard Business Review, 54*(2), 100–110.

McClelland, D. C. (1987). *Human motivation.* Cambridge, UK: Cambridge University Press.

McClelland, D. C., & Boyatzis, R. E. (1982). Leadership motive pattern and long-term success in management. *Journal of Applied Psychology, 67,* 737–743.

McCrae, R. R., & Costa, P. T. (1987). Validation of the five-factor model of personality across instruments and observers. *Journal of Personality and Social Psychology, 52,* 81–90.

McCrae, R. R., & Costa, P. T. (1991). Adding Liebe und Arbeit: The full five-factor model and well-being. *Personality and Social Psychology Bulletin, 17,* 227–232.

McEvoy, G. M., & Beatty, R. W. (1989). Assessment centers and subordinate appraisals of managers: A seven year examination of predictive validity. *Personnel Psychology, 42,* 37–52.

McGrath, J. E., & Kelly, J. R. (1986). *Time and human interaction: Toward a social psychology of time.* New York: Guilford.

McGuire, J. (1986). Management and research methodology. *Journal of Management, 12,* 5–17.

McKelvey, B. (1997). Quasi-natural organizational science. *Organizational Science, 8,* 351–380.

McKelvey, B. (1999). Avoiding complexity catastrophe in coevolutionary pockets: Strategies for rugged landscapes. *Organization Science, 10,* 294–321.

McKelvey, B. (2000). MicroStrategy from MacroLeadership: Distributed intelligence via new science. In A. Y. Lewin & H. Volberda (Eds.), *Mobilizing the self-renewing organization.* Thousand Oaks, CA: Sage.

McKenna, M., Shelton, C., & Darling, J. (2002). The impact of behavioral style assessment on organizational effectiveness: A call for action. *Leadership & Organization Development Journal, 23,* 314–322.

McSweeney, B. (2002). Hofstede's model of national cultural differences and their consequences: A triumph of faith—a failure of analysis. *Human Relations, 55,* 89–118.

Meade, R. D. (1967). An experimental study of leadership in India. *Journal of Social Psychology, 72,* 35–43.

Meek, V. L. (1988). Organizational culture: Origins and weaknesses. *Organization Studies, 9,* 453–473.

Meindl, J. R. (1990). On leadership: An alternative to the conventional wisdom. *Research in Organizational Behavior, 12,* 159–203.

Meindl, J. R., & Ehrlich, S. B. (1987). The romance of leadership and the evaluation of organizational performance. *Academy of Management Journal, 30,* 91–109.

Meindl, J. R., Ehrlich, S. B., & Dukerich, J. M. (1985). The romance of leadership. *Administrative Science Quarterly, 30,* 78–102.

Melcher, A. J. (1976). *Structure and process of organizations: A systems approach.* Englewood Cliffs, NJ: Prentice Hall.

Melcher, A. J. (1977). Leadership models and research approaches. In J. G. Hunt & L. L. Larson (Eds.), *Leadership: The cutting edge* (pp. 94–108). Carbondale: Southern Illinois University Press.

Mendonca, M. (2001). Preparing for ethical leadership in organizations. *Canadian Journal of Administrative Sciences, 18,* 266–276.

Merton, R. K. (1948a). The bearing of empirical research upon the development of social theory. *American Sociological Review, 13,* 505–515.

Merton, R. K. (1948b). The self-fulfilling prophecy. *Antioch Review, 8,* 193–210.

Merton, R. K. (1968). *Social theory and social structure.* New York: Free Press.

Mill, J. S. (1987). What utilitarianism is. In A. Ryan (Ed.), *Utilitarianism and other essays.* New York: Penguin Books.

Milliken, F. J. (1987). Three types of perceived uncertainty about the environment: State, effect, and response uncertainty. *Academy of Management Review, 12,* 133–143.

Miner, J. B. (1965). *Studies in management education.* New York: Springer-Verlag.

Miner, J. B. (1975). The uncertain future of the leadership concept. An overview. In J. G. Hunt & L. L. Larson (Eds.), *Leadership frontiers* (pp. 197–208). Kent, OH: Kent State University.

Miner, J. B. (1978). Twenty years of research on role motivation theory of managerial effectiveness. *Personnel Psychology, 31,* 739–760.

Mintzberg, H. (1973). *The nature of managerial work.* New York: Harper & Row.

Mintzberg, H. (1980). *The nature of managerial work.* Englewood Cliffs, NJ: Prentice Hall. (Original work published 1973)

Mintzberg, H. (2001). Managing exceptionally. *Organization Science, 12,* 759–771.

Mischel, W. (1968). *Personality and assessment.* New York: John Wiley.

Mischel, W. (1977). The interaction of person and situation. In D. Magnusson & D. Endler (Eds.), *Personality at the crossroads: Current issues in interactional psychology* (pp. 333–352). Hillsdale, NJ: Lawrence Erlbaum.

Mitchell, T. R., Green, S. G., & Wood, R. E. (1981). An attributional model of leadership and the poor performing subordinate: Development and validation. In L. L. Cummings & B. M. Staw (Eds.), *Research in organizational behavior* (Vol. 3, pp. 197–234). Greenwich, CT: JAI.

Mitchell, T. R., & Kalb, L. S. (1981). Effects of outcome knowledge and outcome valence on supervisors' evaluations. *Journal of Applied Psychology, 66,* 604–612.

Mitchell, T. R., & Kalb, L. S. (1982). Effects of job experience on supervisor attributions for a subordinate's poor performance. *Journal of Applied Psychology, 67,* 181–188.

Mitchell, T. R., & Wood, R. E. (1980). Supervisor's responses to subordinate poor performance: A test of an attributional model. *Organizational Behavior and Human Decision Processes, 25,* 123–138.

Mohammed, S., & Billings, R. S. (2002). The effect of self-efficacy and issue characteristics on threat and opportunity categorization. *Journal of Applied Social Psychology, 32,* 1253–1275.

Mohrman, A. M., Reswick-West, S. M., & Lawler, E. E. (1989). *Designing performance appraisal systems: Aligning appraisals with organizational realities.* San Francisco: Jossey-Bass.

Moldoveanu, M., & Langer, E. (2002). When "stupid" is smarter than we are. In R. Sternberg (Ed.), *Why smart people can be so stupid.* New Haven, CT: Yale University Press.

Moretti, D. M. (1994). Issues in the assessment of managerial and executive leadership. *Consulting Psychology Journal, 46,* 2.

Moretti, D. M. (2002, April). *Motorola's leadership challenge.* Paper presented at the 17th annual meeting of the Society for Industrial and Organizational Psychology, Toronto.

Morgan, G., & Smircich, L. (1980). The case for qualitative research. *Academy of Management Review, 5,* 491–500.

Morgeson, F. P., & Hofman, D. A. (1999). The structure and function of collective constructs: Implications for multilevel research. *Academy of Management Review, 24,* 266–285.

Morrison, A. M., White, R. P., & Van Velsor, E. (1992). *Breaking the glass ceiling: Can women reach the top of America's largest corporations?* (2nd ed.). Reading, MA: Addison-Wesley.

Morrow, I. J., & Stern, M. (1990). Stars, adversaries, producers, and phantoms at work: A new leadership typology. In K. E. Clark & M. B. Clark (Eds.), *Measures of leadership* (pp. 419–440). Greensboro, NC: Center for Creative Leadership.

Moses, J. L. (1985). Using clinical methods in a high level management assessment center. In H. J. Bernardin & D. A. Bownas (Eds.), *Personality assessment in organizations* (pp. 177–192). New York: Praeger.

Mouly, V. S., & Sankaran, J. K. (1999). The "permanent" acting leader: Insights from a dying Indian R&D organization. *Leadership Quarterly, 10,* 637–651.

Moxley, R. S., & Wilson, P. O. (1998). A systems approach to leadership development. In C. D. McCauley, R. S. Moxley, & E. Van Velsor (Eds.), *The Center for Creative Leadership handbook of leadership development* (pp. 217–241). San Francisco: Jossey-Bass.

Muchinsky, P. M. (1983). *Psychology applied to work.* Homewood, IL: Dorsey.

Mumford, M. D., & Connelly, M. S. (1991). Leaders as creators: Leader performance and problem solving in ill-defined domains. *Leadership Quarterly, 2,* 289–316.

Mumford, M. D., Gessner, T. L., Connelly, M. S., O'Connor, J. A., & Clifton, T. C. (1993). Leadership and destructive acts: Individual and situational influences. *Leadership Quarterly, 4,* 115–147.

Mumford, M. D., Marks, M. A., Connelly, M. S., Zaccaro, S. J., & Reiter-Palmon, R. (2000). Development of leadership skills: Experience and timing. *Leadership Quarterly, 11,* 87–114.

Mumford, M. D., Scott, G. M., Gaddis, B., & Strange, J. M. (2002). Leading creative people: Orchestrating expertise and relationships. *Leadership Quarterly, 13,* 705–750.

Mumford, M. D., Zaccaro, S. J., Harding, F. D., Fleishman, E. A., & Reiter-Palmon, R. (1993). *Cognitive and temperament predictors of executive ability: Principles for developing leadership capacity* (Report No. ADA267589). Alexandria, VA: U.S. Army Research Institute for the Behavioral and Social Sciences.

Mumford, M. D., Zaccaro, S. J., Harding, F. D., Jacobs, T. O., & Fleishman, E. A. (2000). Leadership skills for a changing world: Solving complex social problems. *Leadership Quarterly, 11,* 11–35.

Munsterberg, H. (1913). *Psychology and industrial efficiency.* New York: Houghton Mifflin.

Murphy, A. J. (1941). A study of the leadership process. *American Sociological Review, 6,* 674–687.

Murphy, M. R., & Jones, A. P. (1993). The influences of performance cues and observational focus on performance rating accuracy. *Journal of Applied Social Psychology, 23,* 1523–1545.

Murphy, S. E., Blyth, D., & Fiedler, F. E. (1992). Cognitive resource theory and the utilization of the leader's and group members' technical competence. *Leadership Quarterly, 3,* 237–255.

Nagel, T. (1970). *The possibility of altruism.* Oxford, UK: Clarendon.

Nahavandi, A. (2003). *The art and science of leadership* (3rd ed.). Upper Saddle River, NJ: Prentice Hall.

Newell, A., Rosenbloom, P. S., & Laird, J. E. (1989). Symbolic architectures for cognition. In M. I. Posner (Ed.), *Foundations of cognitive science* (pp. 93–131). Cambridge, MA: MIT Press.

Newman, K. L., & Nollen, S. D. (1996). Culture and congruence: The fit between management practices and national culture. *Journal of International Business Studies, 27,* 753–779.

Nicholas, G., & Prigogine, I. (1989). *Exploring complexity.* San Francisco: Freeman.

Noe, R. A., & Wilk, S. L. (1993). Investigation of the factors that influence employees' participation in development activities. *Journal of Applied Psychology, 78,* 291–302.

Nord, W., & Fox, S. (1996). The individual in organizational studies: The great disappearing act? In S. Clegg, C. Hardy, & W. Nord (Eds.), *Handbook of organizational studies* (pp. 148–175). Thousand Oaks, CA: Sage.

Nunnally, J. C., & Bernstein, I. H. (1994). *Psychometric theory* (3rd ed.). New York: McGraw-Hill.

Offermann, L. R., Kennedy, J. K., & Wirtz, P. W. (1994). Implicit leadership theories: Content, structure and generalizability. *Leadership Quarterly, 5,* 43–58.

Offermann, L. R., Schroyer, C. J., & Green, S. K. (1998). Leader attributions for subordinate performance: Consequences for subsequent leader interactive behaviors and ratings. *Journal of Applied Social Psychology, 28,* 1125–1139.

Ohlott, P. J., Ruderman, M. N., & McCauley, C. D. (1994). Gender differences in managers' developmental job experiences. *Academy of Management Journal, 37,* 46–67.

O'Neill, J. A. (1985). The trend in the male-female wage gap in the United States. *Journal of Labor Economics, 3,* 91–116.

O'Neill, J. A., & Polachek, S. (1993). Why the gender gap in wages narrowed in the 1980s. *Journal of Labor Economics, 11,* 205–228.

Osborn, R. N., Hunt, J. G., & Jauch, L. R. (1980). *Organization theory.* New York: John Wiley.

Osborn, R., Hunt, J. G., & Jauch, R. (2002). Toward a contextual theory of leadership. *Leadership Quarterly, 13,* 797–837.

Osborn, R. N., Hunt, J. G., & Skaret, D. J. (1977). Managerial influence in a complex configuration with two unit heads. *Human Relations, 30,* 1025–1038.

Osland, J. S., Snyder, M. M., & Hunter, L. (1998). A comparative study of managerial styles among female executives in Nicaragua and Costa Rica. *International Studies of Management and Organization, 2,* 54–73.

O'Toole, J. (1995). *Leading change: Overcoming the ideology of comfort and the tyranny of custom.* San Francisco: Jossey-Bass.

Ozinga, J. R. (1999). *Altruism.* Westport, CT: Praeger.

Palmer, B., Walls, M., Burgess, Z., & Stough, C. (2001). Emotional intelligence and effective leadership. *Leadership & Organization Development Journal, 22,* 5–10.

Parsons, T. (1956a). Suggestions for a sociological approach to the theory of organizations (Part I). *Administrative Science Quarterly, 1,* 63–85.

Parsons, T. (1956b). Suggestions for a sociological approach to the theory of organizations (Part II). *Administrative Science Quarterly, 1,* 225–239.

Parsons, T. (1960). *Structure and process in modern societies.* New York: Free Press.

Parsons, T., & Shils, E. A. (1951). *Towards a general theory of action.* Cambridge, MA: Harvard University Press.

Pasa, S. F. (2000). Leadership influence in a high-power distance and collectivist culture. *Leadership & Organization Development Journal, 21,* 414–426.

Paul, J., Costley, D. L., Howell, J. P., Dorfman, P. W., & Trafimow, D. (2001). The effects of charismatic leadership on followers' self-concept accessibility. *Journal of Applied Social Psychology, 31,* 1821–1844.

Paunonen, S. V., & Ashton, M. C. (2001). Big Five factors and facets and the prediction of behavior. *Journal of Personality and Social Psychology, 81,* 524–539.

Pearce, C. L., Perry, M. I., & Sims, H. P. (2001). Shared leadership: Relationship management to improve NPO effectiveness. In T. D. Connors (Ed.), *The nonprofit handbook: Management* (pp. 624–641). New York: John Wiley.

Pedhazur, E. J. (1997). *Multiple regression in behavioral research* (3rd ed.). Fort Worth, TX: Harcourt Brace.

Pelto, P. J. (1968, April). The influence between "tight" and "loose" societies. *Transactions,* pp. 37–40.

Peters, L. H., Hartke, D. D., & Pohlmann, J. F. (1985). Fiedler's contingency theory of leadership: An application of the meta-analysis procedures of Schmidt and Hunter. *Psychological Bulletin, 97,* 274–285.

Peterson, M. F., & Hunt, J. G. (Eds.). (1997). Special issue on international leadership. *Leadership Quarterly, 8*(3/4).

Peterson, M. F., & Smith, P. B. (1988). Gleanings from a frustrated process analysis of leadership research stakeholders. In J. G. Hunt, B. R. Baliga, H. P. Dachler, & C. A. Schriesheim (Eds.), *Emerging leadership vistas* (pp. 183–200). Lexington, MA: Lexington Books.

Pettigrew, A. M. (1997). What is a processual analysis? *Scandinavian Journal of Management, 13,* 337–348.

Pettigrew, T. F. (1996). *How to think like a social scientist.* New York: HarperCollins.

Pfeffer, J. (1977). The ambiguity of leadership. *Academy of Management Review, 2,* 104–112.

Pfeffer, J. (1981). Management as symbolic action: The creation and maintenance of organizational paradigms. *Research in Organizational Behavior, 3,* 1–52.

Pfeffer, J. (1993). Barriers to the advancement of organizational science: Paradigm development as a dependent variable. *Academy of Management Review, 18,* 599–620.

Pfeffer, J. (1994). *Competitive advantage through people: Unleashing the power of the work force.* Boston: Harvard Business School Press.

Pfeffer, J., & Salancik, G. R. (1975). Determinants of supervisory behavior: A role set analysis. *Human Relations, 28,* 139–153.

Phillips, J. S., & Lord, R. G. (1982). Schematic information processing and perceptions of leadership in problem-solving groups. *Journal of Applied Psychology, 67,* 486–492.

Phillips, R. L., & Hunt, J. G. (Eds.). (1992). *Strategic leadership: A multiorganizational-level perspective.* Greenwich, CT: Quorum.

Pickenpaugh, T. E. (1997). Symbols of rank, leadership and power in traditional cultures. *International Journal of Osteoarcheaology, 7,* 525–541.

Pillai, R. (1996). Crisis and the emergence of charismatic leadership in groups: An experimental investigation. *Journal of Applied Social Psychology, 26,* 543–562.

Plato. (1960). *The republic* (B. Jowett, Trans.). Garden City, NY: Doubleday & Company.

Plato. (1971). *Epistle VII* (L. A. Post, Trans.). In E. Hamilton & H. Cairns (Eds.), *The collected dialogues of Plato, including the letters.* Princeton, NJ: Princeton University Press.

Plato. (1992). *The republic* (G.M.A. Grube, Trans.). Indianapolis: Hackett.

Pleck, J. H. (1997). Paternal involvement: Levels, sources, and consequences. In M. E. Lamb (Ed.), *The role of the father in child development* (pp. 66–103). New York: John Wiley.

Ployhart, R. E., Holtz, B. C., & Bliese, P. D. (2002). Longitudinal data analysis: Applications of random coefficient modeling of leadership research. *Leadership Quarterly, 13,* 455–486.

Podsakoff, P. M., & Mackenzie, S. B. (1997). Kerr and Jermier's substitutes for leadership model: Background, empirical assessment, and suggestions for future research. *Leadership Quarterly, 8,* 117–125.

Podsakoff, P. M., Mackenzie, S. B., & Bommer, W. H. (1996). Meta-analysis of the relationships between Kerr and Jermier's substitutes for leadership and employee job attitudes, role perceptions, and performance. *Journal of Applied Psychology, 81,* 380–399.

Podsakoff, P. M., & Schriesheim, C. A. (1985). Field studies of French and Raven's bases of power: Critique, reanalysis, and suggestions for future research. *Psychological Bulletin, 97,* 387–411.

Podsakoff, P. M., & Tudor, W. D. (1985). Relationships between leader reward and punishment behavior and group processes and productivity. *Journal of Management, 11,* 55–73.

Popper, K. R. (1965). *Conjectures and refutations: The growth of scientific knowledge.* New York: Harper Torchbooks.

Potter, E. H., & Fiedler, F. E. (1981). The utilization of staff members' intelligence and experience under high and low stress. *Academy of Management Journal, 24,* 361–376.

Potter, J., & Wetherell, M. (1987). *Discourse and social psychology: Beyond attitudes and behavior.* London: Sage.

Powell, G. N. (1990). One more time: Do male and female managers differ? *Academy of Management Executive, 12,* 731–743.

Powell, G. N., Butterfield, D. A., & Parent, J. D. (2002). Gender and managerial stereotypes: Have the times changed? *Journal of Management, 28,* 177–193.

Prezzolini, G. (1928). *Nicolo Machiavelli, the Florentine* (R. Roeder, Trans.). New York: Brentano's.

Price, T. (2000). Explaining ethical failures of leadership. *The Leadership and Organizational Development Journal, 21,* 177–184.

Price, T. (2003). The ethics of authentic transformational leadership. *Leadership Quarterly, 14,* 67–81.

Priem, R. L., Lyon, D. W., & Dess, G. G. (1999). Limitations of demographic proxies in top-management team heterogeneity research. *Journal of Management, 20,* 935–953.

Prigogene, I. (1997). *The end of certainty.* New York: Free Press.

Pritzker, M. A. (2002). The relationship among CEO dispositional attributes, transformational leadership behaviors and performance effectiveness. *Dissertation Abstracts International, 62* (UMI No. 3035464).

Prochaska, J. M., Prochaska, J. O., & Levesque, D. A. (2001). A transtheoretical approach to changing organizations. *Administration and Policy in Mental Health, 28,* 247–261.

Prochaska, J. O., DiClemente, C. C., & Norcross, J. C. (1992). In search of how people change: Applications to addictive behaviors. *American Psychologist, 47,* 1102–1114.

Pugh, D., Hickson, D., Hinings, C., & Turner, C. (1969). The context of organizational structures. *Administrative Science Quarterly, 14,* 91–114.

Pullig, C., Maxham, J. G., & Hair, J. F. (2002). Salesforce automation systems: An exploratory examination of organizational factors associated with effective implementation and salesforce productivity. *Journal of Business Research, 55,* 401–415.

Punnett, B. J. (in press). The developing world: Towards a managerial understanding. In H. W. Lane, M. L. Maznevski, M. E. Mendenhall, & J. McNett (Eds.), *The Blackwell handbook of global management.* Oxford, UK: Basil Blackwell.

Quang, T., Swierczek, F. W., & Chi, D.T.K. (1998). Effective leadership in joint ventures in Vietnam: A cross-cultural perspective. *Journal of Organizational Change Management, 11,* 357–372.

Quinn, R. E. (1988). *Beyond rational management.* San Francisco: Jossey-Bass.

Quinn, R. E., Faerman, S. R., Thompson, M. P., & McGrath, M. R. (2003). *Becoming a master manager* (2nd ed.). New York: John Wiley.

Rauch, A., Frese, M., & Sonnentag, S. (2000). Cultural differences in planning/success relationships: A comparison of small enterprises in Ireland, West Germany, and East Germany. *Journal of Small Business Management, 38,* 28–41.

Reber, A. S. (1989). Implicit learning and tacit knowledge. *Journal of Experimental Psychology: General, 118,* 219–235.

Reskin, B. F., & Ross, C. E. (1995). Jobs, authority, and earnings among managers: The continuing significance of sex. In J. A. Jacobs (Ed.), *Gender inequality at work* (pp. 127–151). Thousand Oaks, CA: Sage.

Rice, W. R. (1978a). Construct validity of the least preferred coworker score. *Psychological Bulletin, 85,* 1199–1237.

Rice, W. R. (1978b). Psychometric properties of the esteem for the least preferred coworker (LPC scale). *Academy of Management Review, 3,* 106–118.

Rice, W. R. (1981). Leader LPC and follower satisfaction: A review. *Organizational Behavior and Human Performance, 28,* 1–25.

Rice, W. R., Marwick, N. J., Chemers, M. M., & Bentley, J. C. (1982). Task performance and satisfaction: Least Preferred Coworker (LPC) as a moderator. *Personality and Social Psychology Bulletin, 8,* 534–541.

Ridgeway, C. L. (2001). Gender, status, and leadership. *Journal of Social Issues, 57,* 637–655.

Riggio, R. E., Murphy, S. E., & Pirozzolo, F. J. (Eds.). (2002). *Multiple intelligences and leadership.* Mahwah, NJ: Lawrence Erlbaum.

Ritchie, R. J. (1994). Using the assessment center method to predict senior management potential. *Consulting Psychology Journal, 46,* 16–23.

Roberts, H. E. (1995). Investigating the role of personal attributes in leadership emergence. *Dissertation Abstracts International, 56* (UMI No. 9528612).

Robie, C., Ryan, A. M., Schnieder, R. A., Parra, L. F., & Smith, P. C. (1998). The relation between job level and job satisfaction. *Group & Organization Management, 23,* 470–495.

Robinson, J. P., & Godbey, G. (1997). *Time for life: The surprising ways Americans use their time.* University Park: Pennsylvania State University Press.

Rogers, C. R. (1951). *Client-centered therapy.* Boston: Houghton Mifflin.

Rokeach, M. (1973). *The nature of human values.* New York: Free Press.

Romano, C. (1994). Conquering the fear of feedback. *HR Focus, 71,* 9–19.

Ropo, A., Eriksson, P., & Hunt, J. G. (Eds.). (1999). Reflections on conducting processual research on management and organizations. *Scandinavian Journal of Management, 13,* 331–335.

Ropo, A., & Hunt, J. G. (1999). Leadership and organization change: Some findings from a processual grounded theory study. In J. A. Wagner III (Ed.), *Advances in qualitative organization research* (Vol. 2, pp. 169–200). Greenwich, CT: JAI.

Rosch, E. (1978). Principles of categorization. In E. Rosch & B. B. Lloyd (Eds.), *Cognition and categorization.* Hillsdale, NJ: Lawrence Erlbaum.

Rosen, M. (1991). Coming to terms with the field: Understanding and doing organizational ethnography. *Journal of Management Studies, 28,* 1–24.

Rosener, J. B. (1995). *America's competitive secret: Utilizing women as management strategy.* New York: Oxford University Press.

Rosenthal, R. (1964). Experimenter outcome orientation and the results of the psychological experiment. *Psychological Bulletin, 61,* 405–412.

Rosenthal, R. (1976). *Experimenter effects in behavioral research.* New York: Irvington.

Rosenthal, R. (1991). *Meta-analytic procedures for social research.* Newbury Park, CA: Sage.

Rosenthal, R., & Jacobson, L. (1968). *Pygmalion in the classroom: Teacher expectation and pupils' intellectual development.* New York: Holt, Rinehart & Winston.

Ross, L. (1977). The intuitive psychologist and his shortcomings. In L. Berkowitz (Ed.), *Advances in experimental social psychology* (Vol. 10, pp. 173–220). New York: Academic Press.

Ross, S. M., & Offermann, L. R. (1991). *Transformational leaders: Measurement of personality attributes and work group performance.* Paper presented at the 2nd annual meeting of the Society for Industrial and Organizational Psychology, St. Louis, MO.

Rost, J. (1991). *Leadership for the twenty-first century.* New York: Praeger.

Rotter, J. B. (1966). Generalized expectations for internal versus external control of reinforcement. *Psychological Monographs: General and Applied, 80,* 1–28.

Rousseau, D. M. (1985). Issues of level in organizational research: Multi-level and cross-level perspectives. In L. L. Cummings & B. M. Staw (Eds.), *Research in organizational behavior* (Vol. 7, pp. 1–37). Greenwich, CT: JAI.

Rousseau, D. M., & Fried, Y. (2001). Location, location, location: Contextualizing organizational research. *Journal of Organizational Behavior, 22,* 1–13.

Rubin, I. M., & Berlew, D. E. (1984). The power failure in organizations. *Training and Development Journal, 38,* 35–38.

Rudman, L. A. (1998). Self-promotion as a risk factor for women: The costs and benefits of counterstereotypical impression management. *Journal of Personality and Social Psychology, 74,* 629–645.

Rush, M. C., & Russell, J. E. (1988). Leader prototypes and prototype-contingent consensus in leader behavior descriptions. *Journal of Experimental Social Psychology, 24,* 88–104.

Rush, M. C., Thomas, J. C., & Lord, R. G. (1977). Implicit leadership theory: A potential threat to the internal validity of leader behavior questionnaires. *Organizational Behavior and Human Performance, 20,* 93–110.

Russell, C. J. (1987). Person characteristics versus role congruency explanations for assessment center ratings. *Academy of Management Journal, 30,* 817–826.

Russell, C. J. (2001). A longitudinal study of top-level executive performance. *Journal of Applied Psychology, 86,* 560–573.

Ryan, R. M., & Deci, E. L. (2000). Self-determination theory and the facilitation of intrinsic motivation, social development, and well-being. *American Psychologist, 55,* 68–78.

Sackett, P. R. (1982). A critical look at some common beliefs about assessment centers. *Public Personnel Management, 11,* 140–147.

Sackett, P., & Larson, J., Jr. (1990). Research strategies and tactics in industrial and organizational psychology. In M. Dunnette & L. Hough (Eds.), *Handbook of industrial and organizational psychology* (2nd ed., Vol. 1, pp. 419–489). Palo Alto, CA: Consulting Psychologists Press.

Sackett, P. R., & Tuzinski, K. A. (2001). The role of dimensions and exercises in assessment center judgments. In M. London (Ed.), *How people evaluate others in organizations* (pp. 111–129). Mahwah, NJ: Lawrence Erlbaum.

Sagie, A., & Koslowsky, M. (1993). Detecting moderators with meta-analysis: An evaluation and comparison of techniques. *Personnel Psychology, 46,* 629–640.

Sagiv, L., & Schwartz, S. H. (2000). Value priorities and subjective well-being: Direct relations and congruity effects. *European Journal of Social Psychology, 30,* 177–198.

Salancik, G. R., & Pfeffer, J. (1977). Constraints on administrator discretion: The limited influence of mayors on city budgets. *Urban Affairs Quarterly, 12,* 475–498.

Salgado, J. (1997). The five factor model of personality and job performance in the European community. *Journal of Applied Psychology, 82,* 30–43.

Salovey, P., & Mayer, J. D. (1990). Emotional intelligence. *Imagination, Cognition, and Personality, 9,* 185–211.

Sanders, T. I. (1998). *Strategic thinking and the new science.* New York: Free Press.

Sarris, D. P. (1995). Antisocial personality characteristics as manifested in executive leadership. *Dissertation Abstracts International, 55* (UMI No. 9429035).

Sashkin, M. (1984). *The visionary leader: The Leader Behavior Questionnaire.* Bryn Mawr, PA: Organization Design and Development.

Sashkin, M. (1988a). The visionary leader. In J. A. Conger & R. N. Kanungo (Eds.), *Charismatic leadership: The elusive factor in organizational effectiveness* (pp. 122–160). San Francisco: Jossey-Bass.

Sashkin, M. (1988b). *The visionary leader: The Leader Behavior Questionnaire* (Rev. ed.). King of Prussia, PA: Organization Design and Development.

Sashkin, M. (1990). Strategic leadership competencies. In R. L. Phillips & J. G. Hunt (Eds.), *Strategic leadership: A multiorganizational-level perspective* (pp. 139–160). Westport, CT: Quorum.

Sashkin, M., Rosenbach, W. E., & Mueller, R. (1994). *Leadership, culture, and performance: An exploration of relationships.* Paper presented at the international meeting of the Western Academy of Management, Brisbane, Australia.

Sashkin, M., Rosenbach, W. E., & Sashkin, M. G. (1995, May). *Development of the power need and its expression in management and leadership with a focus on leader-follower relations.* Paper presented at the 12th scientific meeting of the A. K. Rice Institute, Washington, DC.

Sashkin, M., & Sashkin, M. G. (2003). *Leadership that matters.* San Francisco: Berrett-Koehler.

Sayles, L. R. (1964). *Managerial behavior: Administration in complex organizations.* New York: McGraw-Hill.

Sayles, L. R. (1979). *Leadership: What effective managers really do . . . and how they do it.* New York: McGraw-Hill.

Sayles, L. R. (1993). *The working leader.* New York: Free Press.

Sayles, L. R., & Chandler, M. K. (1971). *Managing large systems: Organizations of the future.* New York: Harper & Row.

Sayles, L. R., & Stewart, A. (1993). Belated recognition for work-flow entrepreneurs: A case of selective perception and amnesia in management thought. *Entrepreneurship: Theory and Practice, 19,* 7–24.

Schein, E. H. (1990). Organizational culture. *American Psychologist, 45,* 109-119.

Schein, E. H. (1992). *Organizational culture and leadership* (2nd ed.). San Francisco: Jossey-Bass.

Schein, V. E. (2001). A global look at psychological barriers to women's progress in management. *Journal of Social Issues, 57,* 675–688.

Scherbaum, C. A., & Vancouver, J. B. (2002, April). *Testing two explanations for goal-setting effects: A persistent question.* Paper presented at the 17th annual meeting of the Society for Industrial and Organizational Psychology, Toronto.

Schmidt, F. L., & Hunter, J. E. (1998). The validity and utility of selection models in personnel psychology: Practical and theoretical implications of 85 years of research findings. *Psychological Bulletin, 124,* 262–274.

Schmitt, N., Gooding, R. Z., Noe, R. A., & Kirsch, M. (1984). Meta-analysis of validity studies published between 1964 and 1982 and the investigation of study characteristics. *Personnel Psychology, 37,* 407–422.

Schneider, B. (1987). The people make the place. *Personnel Psychology, 40,* 437–454.

Schneider, B. (1989). Thoughts on leadership and management. In L. Atwater & R. Penn (Eds.), *Military leadership: Traditions and future trends* (pp. 30–33). Annapolis, MD: U.S. Naval Academy.

Schneider, B., Ehrhart, K. H., & Ehrhart, M. G. (2002). Understanding high school student leaders: II. Peer nominations of leaders and their correlates. *Leadership Quarterly, 13,* 275–299.

Schneider, B., Goldstein, H. W., & Smith, D. B. (1995). The ASA framework: An update. *Personnel Psychology, 48,* 747–773.

Schneider, R. J., & Hough, L. M. (1995). Personality and industrial/organizational psychology. In C. L. Cooper & I. T. Robertson (Eds.), *International review of industrial and organizational psychology* (Vol. 10, pp. 75–129). New York: John Wiley and Sons.

Schneider, S. C., & Barsoux, J. L. (1997). *Managing across cultures.* London: Prentice Hall Europe.

Schriesheim, C. A. (1995). Multivariate and moderated within- and between-entity analysis (WABA) using hierarchical linear multiple regression. *Leadership Quarterly, 6,* 1–18.

Schriesheim, C. A. (1997). Substitutes-for-leadership theory: Development and basic concepts. *Leadership Quarterly, 8,* 103–108.

Schriesheim, C. A., Castro, S. L., & Cogliser, C. C. (1999). Leader-member exchange (LMX) research: A comprehensive review of theory, measurement, and data-analytic practices. *Leadership Quarterly, 10,* 63–113.

Schriesheim, C. A., Castro, S. L., Zhou, X., & Yammarino, F. J. (2001). The folly of theorizing "A" but testing "B": A selective level-of-analysis review of the field and a detailed Leader-Member Exchange illustration. *Leadership Quarterly, 12,* 515–551.

Schriesheim, C. A., Cogliser, C. C., & Neider, L. L. (1995). Is it "trustworthy"? A multiple-levels-of-analysis reexamination of an Ohio State leadership study, with implications for future research. *Leadership Quarterly, 6,* 111–145.

Schriesheim, C. A., & Kerr, S. (1977). Theories and measures of leadership: A critical appraisal of current and future directions. In J. G. Hunt & L. L. Larson (Eds.), *Leadership: The cutting edge* (pp. 9–45). Carbondale: Southern Illinois University Press.

Schriesheim, C. A., & Murphy, C. J. (1976). Relationships between leader behavior and subordinate satisfaction and performance: A test of some situational moderators. *Journal of Applied Psychology, 61,* 634–641.

Schriesheim, C. A., & Neider, L. L. (1996). Path-goal leadership theory: The long and winding road. *Leadership Quarterly, 7,* 317–321.

Schriesheim, C. A., Neider, L. L., & Scandura, T. A. (1998). Delegation and leader-member exchange: Main effects, moderators, and measurement issues. *Academy of Management Journal, 41,* 298–318.

Schriesheim, C. A., & Schriesheim, J. F. (1980). A test of the path-goal theory of leadership and some suggested directions for future research. *Personnel Psychology, 33,* 349–370.

Schriesheim, C. A., Tepper, B. J., & Tetrault, L. A. (1994). Least Preferred Co-worker score, situational control, and leadership effectiveness: A meta-analysis of contingency model performance predictions. *Journal of Applied Psychology, 79,* 561–573.

Schriesheim, C. A., & Von Glinow, M. A. (1977). The path-goal theory of leadership: A theoretical and empirical analysis. *Academy of Management Journal, 20,* 398–405.

Schruijer, S.G.L., & Vansina, L. S. (2002). Leader, leadership and leading: From individual characteristics to relating in context. *Journal of Organizational Behavior, 23,* 869–874.

Schwab, D. P. (1980). Construct validity in organizational behavior. In B. M. Staw & L. L. Cummings (Eds.), *Research in organizational behavior* (Vol. 2, pp. 3–43). Greenwich, CT: JAI.

Schwartz, J. (2001, September 16). Up from the ashes, one firm rebuilds. *New York Times,* Sec. 3, p. 1.

Schwartz, S. H. (1994). Cultural dimensions of values: Towards an understanding of national differences. In U. Kim, H. C. Triandis, C. Kagitcibasi, S. C. Choi, & G. Yoon (Eds.), *Individualism and collectivism: Theoretical and methodological issues* (pp. 85–119). Thousand Oaks, CA: Sage.

Schwartz, S. H. (1999). Cultural value differences: Some implications for work. *Applied Psychology: An International Review, 48,* 23–48.

Schwartz, S. H., & Sagie, G. (2000). Value consensus and importance: A cross-national study. *Journal of Cross-Cultural Psychology, 31,* 465-497.

Schwartzman, H. (1993). *Ethnography in organizations.* Newbury Park, CA: Sage.

Secord, P. F., & Backman, C. W. (1974). *Social psychology.* (2nd ed.). New York: McGraw-Hill.

Seligman, M.E.P. (1993). *Helplessness: On depression, development, and death.* San Francisco: Freeman.

Seligman, M.E.P., & Beagley, G. (1975). Learned helplessness in the rat. *Journal of Comparative and Physiological Psychology, 88,* 534–541.

Senge, P. M. (1990). *The fifth discipline: The art and practice of the learning organization.* New York: Doubleday Currency.

Sessa, V. I., & Taylor, J. J. (2000). *Executive selection: Strategies for success.* San Francisco: Jossey-Bass.

Shackelford, S., Wood, W., & Worchel, S. (1996). Behavioral styles and the influence of women in mixed-sex groups. *Social Psychology Quarterly, 59,* 284–293.

Shamir, B. (1991). Meaning, self, and motivation in organizations. *Organization Studies, 12,* 405–424.

Shamir, B. (1995). Social distance and charisma: Theoretical notes and an exploratory study. *Leadership Quarterly, 6,* 19–47.

Shamir, B. (1999). Leadership in boundaryless organizations: Disposable or indispensable. *European Journal of Work and Organizational Psychology, 8,* 49–71.

Shamir, B., & Ben-Ari, E. (1999). Leadership in an open army? Civilian connections, interorganizational frameworks and changes in military leadership. In J. G. Hunt, G. E. Dodge, & L. Wong (Eds.), *Out-of-the-box leadership: Transforming the twenty-first-century army and other top-performing organizations* (pp. 15–40). Stamford, CT: JAI.

Shamir, B., House, R. J., & Arthur, M. B. (1993). The motivational effects of charismatic leadership: A self-concept based theory. *Organization Science, 4,* 577–594.

Shamir, B., & Howell, J. M. (1999). Organizational and contextual influences on the emergence and effectiveness of charismatic leadership. *Leadership Quarterly, 10,* 257–283.

Shane, S. A. (1993). Cultural influences on rates of innovation. *Journal of Business Venturing, 7,* 29–46.

Shane, S. (1995). Uncertainty avoidance and the preference for innovation championing roles. *Journal of International Business Studies, 26,* 47–68.

Shane, S., Venkataraman, S., & MacMillan, I. (1995). Cultural differences in innovation championing roles. *Journal of Management, 21,* 931–952.

Sharma, S. (1996). *Applied multivariate techniques.* New York: John Wiley.

Shartle, C. L. (1951). Studies of naval leadership, Part I. In H. Guetzkow (Ed.), *Group, leadership and men* (pp. 119–133). Pittsburgh, PA: Carnegie Press.

Shaw, J. B. (1990). A cognitive categorization model for the study of intercultural management. *Academy of Management Review, 15,* 626–645.

Shaw, M. E. (1981). *Group dynamics: The psychology of small group behavior* (3rd ed). New York: McGraw-Hill.

Shelton, B. A., & John, D. (1996). The division of household labor. *Annual Review of Sociology, 22,* 299–322.

Sherif, M., & Sherif, C. W. (1948). *An outline of social psychology.* New York: Harper Brothers.

Shipper, F., & Davy, J. (2002). A model and investigation of managerial skills, employees' attitudes and managerial performance. *Leadership Quarterly, 13,* 95–120.

Shirvastava, P., & Mitroff, I. (1984). Enhancing organizational research utilization: The role of decision makers' assumptions. *Academy of Management Review, 9,* 18–26.

Sidanius, J., & Pratto, F. (1999). *Social dominance: An intergroup theory of social hierarchy and oppression.* New York: Cambridge University Press.

Silver, S. R. (1999). *Perception of empowerment in engineering workgroups: The linkage to transformational leadership and performance.* Unpublished doctoral dissertation, The George Washington University, Washington, DC.

Silverman, D. (1989). Six rules of qualitative research: A post-romantic argument. *Symbolic Interaction, 12,* 25–40.

Silverthorne, C. (2001). A test of the path-goal leadership theory in Taiwan. *Leadership & Organization Development Journal, 22,* 151–158.

Simonton, D. K. (2003). Qualitative and quantitative analysis of historical data. *Annual Review of Psychology, 54,* 617–640.

Simpson, P., French, R., & Harvey, C. (2002). Leadership and negative capability. *Human Relations, 55,* 1209–1226.

Sims, H. P., & Manz, C. C. (1984). Observing leader behavior: Toward reciprocal determinism in leadership theory. *Journal of Applied Psychology, 64,* 222–232.

Sinclair, L., & Kunda, Z. (2000). Motivated stereotyping of women: She's fine if she praised me but incompetent if she criticized me. *Personality and Social Psychology Bulletin, 26,* 1329–1342.

Sinha, J.P.B. (1995). *The cultural context of leadership and power.* New Delhi: Sage.

Sivakumar, K., & Nakata, C. (2001). The stampede toward Hofstede's framework: Avoiding the sample design pit in cross-cultural research. *Journal of International Business Studies, 32*, 555–574.

Sivasubramaniam, N., Murry, W. D., Avolio, B. J., & Jung, D. I. (2002). A longitudinal model of the effects of team leadership and group potency on group performance. *Group & Organization Management, 27*, 66–96.

Skarlicki, D. P., & Latham, G. P. (1997). Leadership training in organizational justice to increase citizenship behavior within a labor union. *Personnel Psychology, 50*, 617–633.

Slife, B. D., & Williams, R. N. (1995). *What's behind the research: Discovering hidden assumptions in the behavioral sciences.* Thousand Oaks, CA: Sage.

Sloan, E. B. (1994). Assessing and developing versatility: Executive survival skills for the brave new world. *Consulting Psychology Journal, 46*, 24–31.

Smircich, L., & Morgan, G. (1982). Leadership: The management of meaning. *Journal of Applied Behavioral Science, 18*, 257–273.

Smith, C. A., & Ellsworth, P. C. (1985). Patterns of cognitive appraisal in emotion. *Journal of Personality and Social Psychology, 48*, 813–838.

Smith, J. A., & Foti, R. J. (1998). A pattern approach to the study of leader emergence. *Leadership Quarterly, 9*, 147–160.

Smith, J. E., Carson, K. P., & Alexander, R. A. (1984). Leadership: It can make a difference. *Academy of Management Journal, 27*, 765–776.

Smith, P. B. (2002). Culture's consequences: Something old and something new. *Human Relations, 55*, 119–135.

Smith, P. B., & Bond, M. H. (1993). *Social psychology across cultures: Analysis and perspectives.* London: Harvester Wheatsheaf.

Smith, P. B., & Bond, M. H. (1999). *Social psychology across cultures: Analysis and perspectives* (2nd ed.). London: Harvester Wheatsheaf.

Smith, P. B., & Peterson, M. F. (1988). *Leadership, organizations and culture.* London: Sage.

Smith, P. B., Peterson M. F., & Misumi, J. (1994). Event management and work team effectiveness in Japan, Britain and the USA. *Journal of Occupational and Organizational Psychology, 67*, 33–43.

Smith, P. B., Peterson, M. F., & Schwartz, S. H. (2002). Cultural values, sources of guidance, and their relevance to managerial behavior: A 47-nation study. *Journal of Cross-Cultural Psychology, 33*, 188–208.

Smith, R. A. (2002). Race, gender, and authority in the workplace: Theory and research. *Annual Review of Sociology, 28*, 509–542.

Smither, J. W., London, M., Flautt, R., Vargas, Y., & Kucine, I. (in press). Can working with an executive coach improve multisource feedback ratings over time? A quasi-experimental field study. *Personnel Psychology.*

Smither, J. W., London, M., Vasilopoulos, N. L., Reilly, R. R., Millsap, R. E., & Salvemini, N. (1995). An examination of the effects of an upward feedback program over time. *Personnel Psychology, 48*, 1–34.

Smither, J. W., & Reilly, S. P. (2001). Coaching in organizations. In M. London (Ed.), *How people evaluate others in organizations* (pp. 221–252). Mahwah, NJ: Lawrence Erlbaum.

Smuts, B. (1995). The evolutionary origins of patriarchy. *Human Nature, 6*, 1–32.

Snow, C. P. (1998). *The two cultures.* Cambridge. UK: Cambridge University Press.

Snyder, M. (1974). Self-monitoring of expressive behavior. *Journal of Personality and Social Psychology, 30*, 526–527.

Solomon, R. C. (1998). Ethical leadership, emotions and trust: Beyond charisma. In J. B. Ciulla (Ed.), *Ethics, the heart of leadership.* Westport, CT: Praeger.

Sommer, R. (1967). Leadership and group geography. *Sociometry, 24,* 99–110.

Sosik, J. J., & Megerian, L. E. (1999). Understanding leader emotional intelligence and performance: The role of self-other agreement on transformational leadership perceptions. *Group & Organization Management, 24,* 367–390.

Spangler, W. D., & House, R. J. (1991). Presidential effectiveness and the leadership motive profile. *Journal of Personality and Social Psychology, 60,* 439–455.

Sparks, C. P. (1990). Testing for management potential. In K. E. Clark & M. B. Clark (Eds.), *Measures of leadership* (pp. 103–112). Greensboro, NC: Center for Creative Leadership.

Spreitzer, G. M., McCall, M. W., & Mahoney, J. D. (1997). Early identification of international executive potential. *Journal of Applied Psychology, 82,* 6–29.

Stake, E. R. (1995). *The art of case study research.* Thousand Oaks, CA: Sage.

Stapel, D. A., & Koomen, W. (2001). Let's not forget the past when we go to the future: On our knowledge of knowledge accessibility. In G. B. Moskowitz (Ed.), *Cognitive social psychology: The Princeton symposium on the legacy and future of social cognition* (pp. 229–246). Mahwah, NJ: Lawrence Erlbaum.

Steenkamp, J.B.E.M., & Baumgartner, H. (1998). Assessing measurement invariance in cross-national consumer research. *Journal of Consumer Research, 25,* 78–90.

Sternberg, R. J. (1988). *The triarchic mind: A new theory of human intelligence.* New York: Penguin Books.

Sternberg, R. J. (1995). A triarchic view of "cognitive resource and leadership performance." *Applied Psychology: An International Review, 44,* 29–32.

Sternberg, R. J. (1997). *Successful intelligence.* New York: Plume Books.

Sternberg, R. J. (1998a). Abilities as forms of developing expertise. *Educational Researcher, 27,* 11–20.

Sternberg, R. J. (1998b). A balanced theory of wisdom. *Review of General Psychology, 2,* 347–365.

Sternberg, R. J. (2002). Successful intelligence: A new approach to leadership. In R. E. Riggio, S. E. Murphy, & F. J. Pirozzolo (Eds.), *Multiple intelligences and leadership* (pp. 9–28). Mahwah, NJ: Lawrence Erlbaum.

Sternberg, R. J., Forsyth, G. B., Hedlund, J., Horvath, J., Snook, S., Williams, W. M., et al. (2000). *Practical intelligence in everyday life.* New York: Cambridge University Press.

Sternberg, R. J., & Vroom, V. (2002). The person versus situation in leadership. *Leadership Quarterly, 13,* 301–323.

Sternberg, R. J., Wagner, R. K., Williams, W. M., & Horvath, J. A. (1995). Testing common sense. *American Psychologist, 50,* 912–927.

Stevens, C. D., & Ash, R. A. (2001). Selecting employees for fit: Personality and preferred managerial style. *Journal of Managerial Issues, 13,* 500–517.

Stewart, R. (1967). *Managers and their jobs: A study of the similarities and differences in the ways managers spend their time.* London: Macmillan.

Stewart, R. (1997). *The reality of management.* Oxford, UK: Butterworth-Heinemann.

Stewart, R., Barsoux, J. L., Kieser, A., Ganter, H. D., & Walgenbach, P. (1994). *Managing in Britain and Germany.* London: St. Martin's/Macmillan.

Stinson, J. E., & Johnson, T. W. (1975). The path-goal theory of leaderships: A partial test and suggested refinement. *Academy of Management Journal, 18,* 242–252.

Stish, U. (1997). Behavioral complexity: A review. *Journal of Applied Social Psychology, 27,* 2047–2067.

Stogdill, R. M. (1948). Personal factors associated with leadership: A survey of the literature. *Journal of Psychology, 25,* 35–71.

Stogdill, R. M. (1974). *Handbook of leadership.* New York: Free Press.

Stogdill, R. M., & Coons, A. E. (Eds.). (1957). *Leader behavior: Its description and measurement* (Research Monograph Number 88). Columbus: Bureau of Business Research, Ohio State University.

Stratton, L. S. (1995). The effect interruptions in work experience have on wages. *Southern Economic Journal, 61,* 955–970.

Streufert, S. (1997). Complexity: An integration of theories. *Journal of Applied Social Psychology, 27,* 2068–2095.

Strube, M. J., & Garcia, J. E. (1981). A meta-analytical investigation of Fiedler's contingency model of leadership effectiveness. *Psychological Bulletin, 90,* 307–321.

Sweetman, K. (2001). Embracing uncertainty. *Sloan Management Review, 43,* 8–9.

Tabachnick, B. G., & Fidell, L. S. (2001). *Using multivariate statistics* (4th ed.). Boston: Allyn & Bacon.

Taggar, S., Hackett, R., & Saha, S. (1999). Leadership emergence in autonomous work teams: Antecedents and outcomes. *Personnel Psychology, 52,* 899–926.

Terman, L. M. (1904). A preliminary study of the psychology and pedagogy of leadership. *Pedagogical Seminary, 11,* 413–451.

Terman, L. M. (1916). *The measurement of intelligence.* Boston: Houghton Mifflin.

Tesluk, P. E., Dragoni, L., & Russell, J. E. A. (2002, April). *Development of management, talent from work experiences and the role of learning orientation in seeking out and gaining from developmental assignments.* Paper presented at the 17th annual meeting of the Society for Industrial and Organizational Psychology, Toronto.

Testa, M. (2002). A model for organizational-based 360 degree leadership assessment. *Leadership & Organization Development Journal, 23,* 260–268.

Tetrault, L. A., Schriesheim, C. A., & Neider, L. L. (1988). Leadership training interventions: A review. *Organization Development Journal, 6,* 77–83.

Tharenou, P., Latimer, S., & Conroy, D. (1994). How do you make it to the top? An examination of influences on women's and men's managerial advancement. *Academy of Management Journal, 37,* 899–931.

Thoits, P. (1992). Identity structures and psychological well-being: Gender and marital status comparisons. *Social Psychology Quarterly, 55,* 236–256.

Thomas, A. B. (1988). Does leadership make a difference to organizational performance? *Administrative Science Quarterly, 33,* 388–400.

Thomas, J. B., Clark, S. M., & Gioia, D. A. (1993). Strategic sensemaking and organizational performance: Linkages among scanning, interpretation, action, and outcomes. *Academy of Management Journal, 36,* 239–270.

Thomas, J. L., Dickson, M. W., & Bliese, P. D. (2001). Values predicting leader performance in the U.S. Army Reserve Officer Training Corps Assessment Center: Evidence for a personality-mediated model. *Leadership Quarterly, 12,* 181–196.

Thompson, J. D. (1967). *Organizations in action.* New York: McGraw-Hill.

Thornton, G. C., & Byham, W. C. (1982). *Assessment centers and managerial performance.* New York: Academic Press.

Tichy, N., & Devanna, M. (1986). *The transformational leader.* New York: John Wiley.

Tiedens, L. Z. (2000). Powerful emotions: The vicious cycle of social status positions and emotions. In N. M Ashkanasy & C. E. Haertel (Eds.), *Emotions in the workplace: Research, theory, and practice* (pp. 72–81). Westport, CT: Quorum.

Tiedens, L. Z. (2001). Anger and advancement versus sadness and subjugation: The effect of negative emotion expressions on social status conferral. *Journal of Personality & Social Psychology, 80,* 86–94.

Tiedens, L. Z., Ellsworth, P. C., & Mesquita, B. (2000). Stereotypes about sentiments and status: Emotional expectations for high- and low-status group members. *Personality & Social Psychology Bulletin, 26,* 560–574.

Tierney, P., Farmer, S. M., & Graen, G. B. (1999). An examination of leadership and employee creativity: The relevance of traits and relationships. *Personnel Psychology, 52,* 591–620.

Ting-Toomey, S. (1988). Intercultural conflict styles. In Y. Kim & W. Gudykunst (Eds.), *Theories in intercultural communication.* Newbury Park, CA: Sage.

Tobey-Garcia, A., Ayman, R., & Chemers, M. (2000, July). *Leader-subordinate trait dyad composition and subordinate satisfaction with supervision: Moderated by task structure.* Paper presented at the 27th International Congress of Psychology, Stockholm.

Tracey, J. B., Tannenbaum, S. I., & Kavanagh, M. J. (1995). Applying trained skills on the job: The importance of the work environment. *Journal of Applied Psychology, 80,* 239–252.

Triandis, H. C. (1994). Cross-cultural industrial and organizational psychology. In H. C. Triandis, M. D. Dunnette, & L. M. Hough (Eds.), *Handbook of industrial and organizational psychology* (2nd ed., Vol. 4, pp. 103–172). Palo Alto, CA: Consulting Psychologists Press.

Trice, H., & Beyer, J. (1986). Charisma and its routinization in two social movement organizations. *Research in Organization Behavior, 8,* 113–164.

Trice, H. M., & Beyer, J. M. (1991). Cultural leadership in organizations. *Organization Science, 2,* 149–169.

Trice, H. M., & Beyer, J. M. (1993). *The culture of work organizations.* Englewood Cliffs, NJ: Prentice Hall.

Trivers, R. L. (1972). Parental investment and sexual selection. In B. Campbell (Ed.), *Sexual selection and the descent of man: 1871–1971* (pp. 136–179). Chicago: Aldine.

Trompenaars, F., & Hampden-Turner, C. (1997). *Riding the waves of culture: Understanding cultural diversity in business* (2nd ed.). London: Nicholas-Brealey.

Tsui, A. S., & Ohlott, P. (1988). Multiple assessment of managerial effectiveness: Interrater agreement and consensus in effectiveness models. *Personnel Psychology, 41,* 779–803.

Turnage, J. J., & Muchinsky, P. M. (1984). A comparison of the predictive validity of assessment center evaluations versus traditional measures in forecasting supervisory job performance: Interpretive implications of criterion distortion for the assessment paradigm. *Journal of Applied Psychology, 69,* 595–602.

Turner, N., Barling, J., Epitropaki, O., Butcher, V., & Milner, C. (2002). Transformational leadership and moral reasoning. *Journal of Applied Psychology, 87,* 304–311.

Tversky, A., & Kahneman, D. (1974). Judgment under uncertainty: Heuristics and biases. *Science, 185,* 1124–1131.

Twenge, J. M. (1997). Changes in masculine and feminine traits over time: A meta-analysis. *Sex Roles, 36,* 305–325.

Twenge, J. M. (2001). Changes in women's assertiveness in response to status and roles: A cross-temporal meta-analysis, 1931–1993. *Journal of Personality and Social Psychology, 81,* 133–145.

Uhl-Bien, M., Graen, G. B., & Scandura, T. (2000). Implications of leader-member exchange (LMX) for strategic human resource management systems: Relationships as social capital for competitive advantage. In G. Ferris (Ed.), *Research in personnel and human resource management* (Vol. 128, pp. 137–185). Greenwich, CT: JAI.

Uleman, J. S., Newman, L. S., & Moskowitz, G. B. (1996). People as flexible interpreters: Evidence and issues from spontaneous trait inference. In M. P. Zanna (Ed.), *Advances in experimental social psychology* (Vol. 28, pp. 211–279). New York: Academic Press.

United Nations. (2002). Women in public life. In *The world's women 2000: Trends and statistics.* Retrieved November 5, 2002, from http://unstats.un.org/unsd/demographic/ww2000/table6a.htm

United Nations Development Programme. (2002). *Human development report.* New York: Oxford University Press.

U.S. Bureau of Labor Statistics. (1982). *Labor force statistics derived from the current population survey: A databook* (Vol. 1: Bulletin 2096). Washington, DC: U.S. Department of Labor.

U.S. Bureau of Labor Statistics. (2001). *Household data: Annual averages* (Table 11). Retrieved January 18, 2003, from http://www.bls.gov/cps/cpsaat11.pdf

U.S. Bureau of Labor Statistics. (2002). *Household data: Monthly household data* (Table A-19: Employed persons by occupation, sex, and age). Retrieved November 24, 2002, from ftp://ftp.bls.gov/pub/suppl/empsit.cpseea19.txt

U.S. Bureau of the Census. (2000). *Current population reports: Educational attainment in the United States: March 2000* (Table 1). Retrieved June 6, 2001, from http://www.census.gov/population/socdemo/education/p20–536/tab01.txt

U.S. Department of Education, National Center for Educational Statistics. (2000). *NAEP trends in academic progress: Three decades of student performance* (NCES 2000-469, by J. R. Campbell, C. M. Hombo, & J. Mazzeo). Washington, DC: Author. Retrieved May 15, 2001, from http://nces.ed.gov/NAEP/site/home.asp

U.S. Department of Education, National Center for Educational Statistics. (2001). *Digest of educational statistics, 2001* (Table 247). Washington, DC: Author.

U.S. Office of Personnel Management. (2001). *The fact book, 2001 edition: Federal civilian workforce statistics.* Washington, DC: Author.

van Engen, M. L. (2001). *Gender and leadership: A contextual perspective.* Unpublished doctoral dissertation, Tilburg University, the Netherlands.

Van Maanen, J. (1979). The fact of fiction in organizational ethnography. *Administrative Science Quarterly, 24,* 539–550.

Van Muijen, J. J., et al. (1999). Organizational culture: The Focus Questionnaire. *European Journal of Work and Organizational Psychology, 8,* 551–568.

Van Seters, D. A., & Field, R.H.G. (1990). The evolution of leadership theory. *Journal of Organizational Change Management, 3,* 29–45.

Van Velsor, E. (2002, April). *Reflective leadership conversations.* Paper presented at the 17th annual meeting of the Society for Industrial and Organizational Psychology, Toronto.

Van Velsor, E., & Leslie, J. B. (1995). Why executives derail: Perspectives across time and cultures. *Academy of Management Executive, 9,* 62–72.

Vandenberg, R. J., & Lance, C. E. (2000). A review and synthesis of the measurement invariance literature: Suggestions, practices, and recommendations for organizational research. *Organizational Research Methods, 3,* 4–70.

VanLehn, K. (1989). Problem solving and cognitive skill acquisition. In M. I. Posner (Ed.), *Foundations of cognitive science* (pp. 527–579). Cambridge, MA: MIT Press.

Vecchio, R. P. (1987). Situational leadership theory: An examination of a prescriptive theory. *Journal of Applied Psychology, 72,* 444–451.

Vecchio, R. P. (1997). Situational leadership theory: An examination of a prescriptive theory. In R. P. Vecchio (Ed.), *Leadership: Understanding the dynamics of power and influence in organizations* (pp. 334–350). Notre Dame, IN: University of Notre Dame Press.

Vecchio, R. P. (2002). Leadership and gender advantage. *Leadership Quarterly, 13,* 643–671.

Vecchio, R. P., & Boatwright, K. J. (2002). Preferences for idealized styles of supervision. *Leadership Quarterly, 13,* 327–342.

Verburg, R. M. (1996). Developing HRM in foreign Chinese joint ventures. *European Management Journal, 14,* 518–525.

Verburg, R. M., Drenth, P.J.D., Koopman, P. L., Van Muijen, J. J., & Wang, Z. M. (1999). Managing human resources across cultures: A comparative analysis of practices in industrial enterprises of China and the Netherlands. *International Journal of Human Resource Management, 10,* 391–410.

Vicere, A. A., & Fulmer, R. M. (1998). *Leadership by design: How benchmark companies sustain success through investment in continuous learning.* Boston: Harvard Business School Press.

Villa, J. R., Howell, J. P., Dorfman, P. W., & Daniel, D. L. (2003). Problems with detecting moderators in leadership research using moderated multiple regression. *Leadership Quarterly, 14,* 2–23.

Vroom, V. H. (1964). *Work and motivation.* New York: John Wiley.

Vroom, V. H., & Jago, A. G. (1978). On the validity of the Vroom-Yetton model. *Journal of Applied Psychology, 63,* 151–162.

Vroom, V. H., & Jago, A. G. (1988). *The new leadership: Managing participation in organizations.* Englewood Cliffs, NJ: Prentice Hall.

Vroom V. H., & Jago, A. G. (1998). Situation effects and levels of analysis in the study of leader participation. In F. Yammarino & F. Dansereau (Eds.), *Leadership: The multi-level approaches* (pp. 145–159). New York: JAI.

Vroom, V. H., & Yetton, P. W. (1973). *Leadership and decision-making.* Pittsburgh, PA: University of Pittsburgh Press.

Waldman, D. A., Atwater, L. E., & Antonioni, D. (1998). Has 360 degree feedback gone amok? *Academy of Management Executive, 12,* 86–94.

Waldman, D. A., & Yammarino, F. J. (1999). CEO charismatic leadership: Levels-of-management and levels-of-analysis effects. *Academy of Management Review, 24,* 266–285.

Walker, A. G., & Smither, J. W. (1999). A five-year study of upward feedback: What managers do with their results matters. *Personnel Psychology, 52,* 393–423.

Wayne, S., Shore, L., Bommer, W., & Tetrick, L. (2002). The role of fair treatment and rewards in perceptions or organizational support and leader-member exchange. *Journal of Applied Psychology, 87*(3), 590–598.

Weber, M. (1947). *The theory of social and economic organization* (A. M. Henderson & T. Parsons, Trans.). New York: Oxford University Press. (Original work published 1924)

Weber, R., Camerer, C., Rottenstreich, Y., & Knez, M. (2001). The illusion of leadership: Misattribution of cause in coordination games. *Organization Science, 12,* 582–598.

Weick, K. E. (1976). Educational organizations as loosely coupled systems. *Administrative Science Quarterly, 21,* 1–19.

Weick, K. E. (1979). Cognitive processes in organizations. In B. Staw (Ed.), *Research in organizational behavior* (Vol. 1). Greenwich, CT: JAI.

Weick, K. E. (1988). Enacted sensemaking in crisis situations. *Journal of Management Studies, 25,* 305–317.

Weick, K. E. (1995). *Sensemaking in organizations.* London: Sage.

Weimann, G. (1985). Sex differences in dealing with bureaucracy. *Sex Roles, 12,* 777–790.

Weiss, H. M., & Adler, S. (1981). Cognitive complexity and the structure of implicit leadership theories. *Journal of Applied Psychology, 66,* 69–78.

White, R. P., & De Vries, D. L. (1990). Making the wrong choice: Failure in the selection of senior-level managers. *Issues and Observations, 10,* 1–6.

White, R. W. (1959). Motivation reconsidered: The concept of competence. *Psychological Review, 66,* 297–333.

White House Project. (2002). *Snapshot of current political leadership*. Retrieved October 27, 2002, from http://www.thewhitehouseproject.org/know_facts/snapshots_women.html

Wholers, A. J., & London, M. (1989). Ratings of managerial characteristics: Evaluation difficulty, co-worker agreement, and self-awareness. *Personnel Psychology, 42*, 235–261.

Whyte, M. K. (1978). *The status of women in preindustrial societies*. Princeton, NJ: Princeton University Press.

Whyte, W. F. (Ed.). (1991). *Participatory action research*. Thousand Oaks, CA: Sage.

Williams, B.A.O. (1981). *Moral luck*. Cambridge, UK: Cambridge University Press.

Williams, C. L. (1995). *Still a man's world: Men who do "women's" work*. Berkeley: University of California Press.

Williams, F. (1992). *Reasoning with statistics* (4th ed.). Fort Worth, TX: Harcourt Brace Jovanovich College Publishers.

Williams, J. (2000). *Unbending gender: Why family and work conflict and what to do about it*. New York: Oxford University Press.

Wilson, J. D. (Ed.). (1958). *The first part of the history of Henry IV*. Cambridge, UK: Cambridge University Press.

Wilson, M., & Daly, M. (1992). The man who mistook his wife for a chattel. In J. H. Barkow, L. Cosmides, & J. Tooby (Eds.), *The adapted mind: Evolutionary psychology and the generation of culture* (pp. 289–322). New York: Oxford University Press.

Winter, D. G. (2002). The motivational dimensions of leadership: Power, achievement and affiliation. In R. E. Riggio, S. E. Murphy, & F. J. Pirozzolo (Eds.), *Multiple intelligences and leadership* (pp. 119–138). Mahwah, NJ: Lawrence Erlbaum.

Wirth, L. (2001). *Breaking through the glass ceiling: Women in management*. Geneva: International Labor Office.

Wishart, N. A., Elam, J. J., & Robey, D. (1996). Redrawing the portrait of a learning organization: Inside Knight-Ridder. *Academy of Management Executive, 10*, 7–20.

Wittgenstein, L. (1968). *Philosophical investigations* (G.E.M. Anscombe, Trans.). New York: Macmillan.

Wofford, J. C., & Goodwin, V. L. (1994). A cognitive interpretation of transactional and transformational leadership theories. *Leadership Quarterly, 5*, 161–186.

Wofford, J. C., Goodwin, V. L., & Whittington, J. L. (1998). A field study of a cognitive approach to understanding transformational and transactional leadership. *Leadership Quarterly, 9*, 55–84.

Wofford, J. C., Joplin, J.R.W., & Comforth, B. (1996). Use of simultaneous verbal protocols in analysis of group leaders' cognitions. *Psychological Reports, 79*, 847–858.

Wofford, J. C., & Liska, L. Z. (1993). Path-goal theories of leadership: A meta-analysis. *Journal of Management, 19*, 857–876.

Wolff, S. B., Pescosolido, A. T., & Druskat, V. U. (2002). Emotional intelligence as the basis of leadership emergence in self-managing teams. *Leadership Quarterly, 13*, 505–522.

Wong, C., & Law, K. S. (2002). The effects of leader and follower emotional intelligence on performance and attitude: An exploratory study. *Leadership Quarterly, 13*, 243–274.

Wood, W., & Eagly, A. H. (2002). A cross-cultural analysis of the behavior of women and men: Implications for the origins of sex differences. *Psychological Bulletin, 128*, 699–727.

Wootton, B. H. (1997). Gender differences in occupational employment. *Monthly Labor Review, 120*, 14–24.

Worchel, S., Cooper, J., & Goethals, G. (1988). *Understanding social psychology*. Chicago: Dorsey.

Wosinska, W., Dabul, A. J., Whetstone-Dion, R., & Cialdini, R. B. (1996). Self-presentational responses to success in the organization: The costs and benefits of modesty. *Basic and Applied Social Psychology, 18*, 229–242.

Wrangham, R. W., Jones, J. H., Laden, G., Pilbeam, D., & Conklin-Brittain, N. (1999). The raw and the stolen: Cooking and the ecology of human origins. *Current Anthropology, 40,* 567–577.

Wright, E. O., Baxter, J., & Birkelund, G. E. (1995). The gender gap in workplace authority: A cross-national study. *American Sociological Review, 60,* 407–435.

Wurf, E., & Markus, H. (1991). Possible selves and the psychology of personal growth. *Perspectives in Personality, 3,* 39–62.

Xin, K. R., & Tsui, A. S. (1996). Different strokes for different folks? Influence tactics by Asian-American and Caucasian-American managers, *Leadership Quarterly, 7,* 109–132.

Yammarino, F. J. (1990). Individual- and group-directed leader behavior directed leader behavior descriptions. *Educational and Psychological Measurement, 50,* 739–759.

Yammarino, F. J. (1998). Multivariate aspects of the Varient/WABA approach: A discussion and leadership illustration. *Leadership Quarterly, 9,* 203–227.

Yammarino, F. J., & Bass, B. M. (1990). Transformational leadership and multiple levels of analysis. *Human Relations 43,* 975–995.

Yammarino, F. J., & Dubinsky, A. J. (1994). Transformational leadership theory: Using levels of analysis to determine boundary conditions. *Personnel Psychology, 47,* 787–811.

Yammarino, F. J., Dubinsky, A. J., Comer, L. B., & Jolson, M. A. (1997). Women and transformational and contingent reward leadership: A multiple-levels-of-analysis perspective. *Academy of Management Journal 40,* 205–222.

Yammarino, F. J., & Markham, S. E. (1992). On the application of within and between analysis: Are absence and affect really group-based phenomena? *Journal of Applied Psychology, 77,* 168–176.

Yammarino, F. J., Spangler, W. D., & Dubinsky, A. J. (1998). Transformational and contingent reward leadership: Individual, dyad, and group levels of analysis. *Leadership Quarterly, 9,* 27–54.

Yerkes, R. M. (Ed.). (1921). Psychological examining in the United States Army. *Memoirs of the National Academy of Sciences, 15,* 1–890.

Yin, R. K. (1994). *Case study research: Design and methods.* Thousand Oaks, CA: Sage.

Yip, G. S. (1995). *Total global strategy: Managing for worldwide competitive advantage.* Englewood Cliffs, NJ: Prentice Hall.

Yoder, J. D. (2001). Making leadership work more effectively for women. *Journal of Social Issues, 57,* 815–828.

York, R. O. (1996). Adherence to situational leadership theory among social workers. *Clinical Supervisor, 14,* 5–26.

Yukl, G. (1989a). *Leadership in organizations* (2nd ed.). Englewood Cliffs, NJ: Prentice Hall.

Yukl, G. (1989b). Managerial leadership: A review of theory and research. *Journal of Management, 15,* 251–289.

Yukl, G. (1994). *Leadership in organizations* (3rd ed.). Englewood Cliffs, NJ: Prentice Hall.

Yukl, G. (1998). *Leadership in organizations* (4th ed.). Upper Saddle River, NJ: Prentice Hall.

Yukl, G. (1999). An evaluation of conceptual weaknesses in transformational and charismatic leadership theories. *Leadership Quarterly, 10,* 285-305.

Yukl, G. (2002). *Leadership in organizations* (5th ed.). Upper Saddle River, NJ: Prentice Hall.

Yukl, G., & Tracey, J. B. (1992). Consequences of influence tactics used with subordinates, peers, and the boss. *Journal of Applied Psychology, 77,* 525–535.

Yukl, G., & Van Fleet, D. D. (1992). Theory and research on leadership in organizations. In M. D. Dunnette & L. M. Hough (Eds.), *Handbook of industrial and organizational psychology* (Vol. 1, pp. 147–198). Palo Alto, CA: Consulting Psychologists Press.

Zaccaro, S. J. (1995). Leader resources and the nature of organizational problems. *Applied Psychology: An International Review, 44,* 32–36.

Zaccaro, S. J. (1999). Social complexity and the competencies required for effective military leadership. In J. G. Hunt, G. E. Dodge, & L. Wong (Eds.), *Out-of-the-box leadership: Transforming the twenty-first century army and other top-performing organizations* (pp. 131–151). Stamford, CT: JAI.

Zaccaro, S. J. (2001). *The nature of executive leadership: A conceptual and empirical analysis of success.* Washington, DC: American Psychological Association.

Zaccaro, S. J. (2002). Organizational leadership and social intelligence. In R. E. Riggio, S. E. Murphy, & F. J. Pirozzolo (Eds.), *Multiple intelligences and leadership* (pp. 29–54). Mahwah, NJ: Lawrence Erlbaum.

Zaccaro, S. J. (in press). Leadership. In C. Peterson & M.E.P. Seligman (Eds.), *Values in action (VIA) classification of strengths.* Washington, DC: American Psychological Association.

Zaccaro, S. J., Foti, R. J., & Kenny, D. A. (1991). Self-monitoring and trait-based variance in leadership: An investigation of leader flexibility across multiple group situations. *Journal of Applied Psychology, 76,* 308–315.

Zaccaro, S. J., Gilbert, J., Thor, K., & Mumford, M. (1991). Social perceptiveness and behavioral flexibility as characterological bases for leader role acquisition. *Leadership Quarterly, 2,* 317–342.

Zaccaro, S. J., & Klimoski, R. J. (2001). The nature of organizational leadership. In S. J. Zaccaro & R. J. Klimoski (Eds.), *The nature of organizational leadership* (pp. 3–41). San Francisco: Jossey-Bass.

Zaccaro, S. J., Mumford, M. D., Connelly, M. S., Marks, M. A., & Gilbert, J. A. (2000). Assessment of leader problem-solving capabilities. *Leadership Quarterly, 11,* 37–64.

Zaccaro, S. J., Rittman, A. L., & Marks, M. A. (2001). Leadership in complex organizations. *Leadership Quarterly, 12,* 389–418.

Zaccaro, S. J., White, L., Kilcullen, R., Parker, C. W., Williams, D., & O'Connor-Boes, J. (1997). *Cognitive and temperament predictors of Army civilian leadership* (Final Report MRI 97–1 for U.S. Army Research Institute for Social and Behavioral Sciences). Bethesda, MD: Management Research Institute.

Zaccaro, S. J., Zazanis, M. M., Diana, M., & Gilbert, J. A. (1994). *Investigation of a background data measure of social intelligence* (Technical Report No. ADA298832). Alexandria, VA: U.S. Army Research Institute for the Behavioral and Social Sciences.

Zaleznik, A. (1977). Managers and leaders: Are they different? *Harvard Business Review, 55,* 67–78.

Zaleznik, A. (1989). *The managerial mystique: Restoring leadership in business.* New York: Harper & Row.

Zeidner, M., Matthews, G., & Roberts, R. D. (in press). Emotional intelligence in the workplace: A critical review. *Applied Psychology: An International Review.*

Zhou, J. (2002). *Work group creativity in China: A paternalistic organizational control perspective.* Paper presented at the "Human Resource Management: Global Perspectives" conference, Oak Brook, IL.

Zhou, X., Schriesheim, C. A., & Beck, W. (2001). The importance of measurement equivalence in transnational research: A test of individual-level predictions about culture and the differential use of organizational influence tactics, with and without measurement equivalence. In C. A. Schriesheim & L. L. Neider (Eds.), *Research in management: Vol. 1. Measurement equivalence* (pp. 161–186). Hartford, CT: Information Age Publishing.

Zipkin, A. (2000, May 31). The wisdom of thoughtfulness. *New York Times,* pp. C1, C10.

Zohar, D. (2002). The effects of leadership dimensions, safety, climate, and assigned priorities on minor injuries in work groups. *Journal of Organizational Behavior, 23,* 75–92.

Name Index

Abdalla, I. A., 113, 266
Acar, F. P., 37
Ackerblom, S., 61
Ackerman, P., 121
Aditya, R. N., 6, 11, 33, 34, 40, 60, 61, 130, 131, 254, 301
Adler, N. J., 253, 255, 263, 280, 298, 301
Adler, S., 9
Adsit, D. J., 260
Albright, M. D., 232
Alderfer, C., 228
Alexander, R. A., 9, 78
Algattan, A. R. A., 161
Al-Homoud, M. A., 113, 266
Alldredge, M., 80
Alliger, G. M., 6, 69, 108, 109, 138, 157
Allport, G. W., 103, 292
Almer, E. D., 282
Alutto, J. A., 28, 62, 63, 65
Alvesson, M., 54, 73, 81, 82, 83, 85
Ancona, D. G., 29
Anderson, C. A., 59
Anderson, J. R., 126
Angell, J. R., 104
Angrist, J., 281
Antonakis, J., 9, 10, 11, 39, 61, 62, 65, 67, 70, 130, 145, 171, 176, 181, 228, 238, 242, 285, 304
Antonioni, D., 87
Aristotle, 101, 325, 326
Arthur, M. B., 146, 174, 180, 181, 185, 190, 193, 275, 319
Arvonen, J., 277
Ashkanasy, N. M., 134, 254
Ash, R. A., 111
Ashby, W., 46
Ashour, A. S., 73

Ashton, M. C., 228
Astin, A. W., 299
Atkinson, P., 83
Atwater, L. E., 39, 58, 61, 62, 65, 87, 93, 110, 145, 164, 295
Audia, G., 61
Avolio, B. J., 9, 10, 43, 52, 57, 58, 59, 61, 62, 67, 72, 80, 91, 96, 110, 113, 128, 147, 175, 176, 186, 227, 285, 314, 316, 319
Axelrod, R. H., 186
Aycan, Z., 264, 265, 266, 267, 268
Ayman, R., 148, 149, 152, 155, 156, 157, 166

Bachrach, S. B., 51, 53
Backman, C. W., 102
Bader, P., 111, 113, 118
Baehr, M. E., 110
Bailey-Werner, B., 294
Bakacsi, G., 61
Baldwin, T. T., 35
Bales, R. F., 106, 151, 284
Baliga, B. R., 37
Baltes, P. B., 229
Bandura, A., 185, 231, 236, 240
Banks, D., 111, 118
Baotwright, K. J., 162
Barbeite, F., 241
Barber, H., 111, 112, 118
Barley, S. R., 84
Barling, J., 57, 80, 128, 130, 210, 228
Barnlund, D. C., 106, 108
Bar-On, R., 208
Baron, R. A., 103
Baron, R. M., 60, 62, 66, 167, 168
Barrett, K. M., 84
Barrick, M. R., 78, 111, 150, 232

Subject Index

About the Editors

John Antonakis is Assistant Professor of Human Resources Management in the Department of Management of the University of Lausanne. He received his Ph.D. in applied management and decision sciences from Walden University, where he received the Frank Dilley best dissertation award for his work on the validity of the Multifactor Leadership Questionnaire. Previously, he was a postdoctoral associate in the Department of Psychology at Yale University (PACE Center) researching cognitive antecedents of effective leadership. His publications are focused on distance and leadership, as well as the contextualized nature of transformational and neocharismatic leadership theories. His current research is focused on strategic leadership, personality and leadership, and the effects of heuristics and biases on leader evaluations.

Anna T. Cianciolo received her Ph.D. in engineering psychology from the Georgia Institute of Technology and her M.A. in cognitive and biological psychology from the University of Minnesota. She did two years of postdoctoral study at the Yale Center for the Psychology of Abilities, Competencies, and Expertise (PACE). She is currently senior research scientist at Global Information Systems Technology, Inc., in Champaign, Illinois. Her current research focuses on individual differences in intellectual capability and their role in knowledge acquisition and the development of skilled performance. She has studied the development and assessment of experience-based tacit knowledge for leadership in U.S. Army officers.

Robert J. Sternberg is IBM Professor of Psychology and Education in the Department of Psychology at Yale University, and Director of the Center for the Psychology of Abilities, Competencies, and Expertise at Yale. He is also president of the American Psychological Association. He received his Ph.D. from Stanford University in 1975 and B.A. summa cum laude, Phi Beta Kappa, from Yale University in 1972. He holds honorary doctorates from four universities and has received numerous awards. He is the author of more than 900 journal articles, book chapters, and books, covering successful intelligence, thinking styles, wisdom, and love. He has received more than $15 million in government grants and contracts for his research, including grants centered on the role of practical intelligence and tacit knowledge in military and civilian leadership. He is a member of several professional associations, has served as editor of the *Psychological Bulletin*, and is editor of *The APA Review of Books: Contemporary Psychology*.

About the Contributors

Roya Ayman received her Ph.D. from the University of Utah in cross-cultural organizational social psychology. She is Associate Professor and the Director of the Industrial and Organizational Psychology program at the Institute of Psychology and also a Faculty Associate of the Leadership Academy at the Illinois Institute of Technology. Her areas of specialty are leadership, cross-cultural research, diversity in organizations, and the work-family interface. She has presented at national and international conferences, published articles and chapters nationally and internationally, and been on various editorial boards including those of *Leadership Quarterly, Applied Psychology: The International Review*, and the *International Journal of Cross-Cultural Management*. She was a coeditor of the book *Leadership Theory and Research: Perspectives and Directions*. In addition to her academic work, she has done consulting and training with various companies such as Arthur Andersen, Lucent Technologies, and The Fire Academy at the Federal Emergency Management Agency (FEMA) national training center.

Paige Bader obtained her master's degree (2001) in industrial and organizational psychology from George Mason University and is currently pursuing her Ph.D. Her research interests include both the conceptualization and the training of leadership adaptability. She is currently interested in the emotional aspects involved in dramatic change events and how leaders can use this information to help others through such experiences.

Warren Bennis is University Professor and Distinguished Professor of Business Administration at the Marshall School and also Founding Chairman of the Leadership Institute at the University of Southern California. He is also Visiting Professor of Leadership at the University of Exeter and a Fellow of the Royal Society of the Arts (United Kingdom). He has written 27 books, including the best-selling *Leaders* and *On Becoming a Leader*, both translated into 21 languages. His latest books, *Organizing Genius, Co-Leaders, Managing the Dream*, and *Geeks and Geezers*, summarize his major concerns: leadership, change, and creative collaboration. He has served on the boards of the American Chamber of Commerce and Claremont University Center, and he currently serves on the board of the Salk Institute. He has consulted for many *Fortune 500* companies and has advised four U.S. presidents. He received his Ph.D. from the Massachusetts Institute of Technology.

Douglas J. Brown is Assistant Professor in the Department of Psychology, University of Waterloo, Canada. He received his Ph.D. from the University of Akron in industrial-organizational psychology. His work has appeared in *Organizational Behavior and Human Decision Processes*, the *Journal of Organizational Behavior*, and *Leadership Quarterly*. He is on the editorial review board of *Leadership Quarterly*. His research interests lie in the area of leadership and information processing.

Kevin W. Brown is a doctoral candidate in industrial and organizational psychology at Florida International University. He is also an instructor in the Department of Management and International Business in the College of Business Administration at Florida International University, with a specialization in human resources and related management topics. He is an accomplished practitioner in the field of human resources.

Linda L. Carli is Associate Professor of Psychology at Wellesley College. She received her Ph.D. in psychology from the University of Massachusetts at Amherst. Her published research includes articles examining the effects of gender on group interaction, communication and influence, and reactions to adversity and victimization. Currently, she is involved in research examining gender effects on self-evaluation in children and adults. In addition to her teaching and research, she has developed and conducted negotiation and conflict resolution workshops for female leaders. She has also conducted research on sex discrimination and the challenges faced by professional women.

Joanne B. Ciulla is Professor and Coston Family Chair in Leadership and Ethics at the Jepson School of Leadership Studies, the University of Richmond. She is one of the founding faculty of the Jepson School, which is the only school in the world to offer an undergraduate degree in leadership studies. She received her B.A. from the University of Maryland, her M.A. from the University of Delaware, and her Ph.D. in philosophy from Temple University. Her most recent books are *Ethics, The Heart of Leadership, The Working Life: The Promise and Betrayal of Modern Work*, and *The Ethics of Leadership*. She is on the editorial boards of *The Business Ethics Quarterly* and *The Journal of Business Ethics*. She is the editor of the series *New Horizons in Leadership*.

Deanne N. Den Hartog is Professor of Organizational Psychology on the Faculty of Economics of the Erasmus University Rotterdam, the Netherlands. She received her Ph.D. and M.S. in psychology from the Free University Amsterdam. Among other things, she is involved in cross-cultural research on leadership (the GLOBE Project, started by Robert J. House) and leads a research program on inspirational leadership in the Netherlands. The relationship between leadership and personality, learning styles, team reflexivity, stress, performance and service behavior, commitment, and trust are among the topics studied in this program. Her work has appeared in such journals as *Leadership Quarterly* and the *Journal of Occupational and Organizational Psychology*, as well as a recent Sage handbook of industrial, work, and organizational psychology. She is also lead author of a Dutch book on charismatic leadership and coauthor of a Dutch book on human resource management.

Marcus W. Dickson is Associate Professor and Chair of the Industrial/ Organizational Psychology Area at Wayne State University. One of his primary research interests has been cross-cultural issues in leadership, and he served for several years as Co-Principal Investigator and Coordinating Team Member of the GLOBE Project, a 64-nation study of leadership and culture under Principal Investigator Robert J. House. His research has appeared in the *Journal of Applied Psychology, Leadership Quarterly,* the *Handbook of Organizational Culture and Climate, Organizational Behavior and Human Decision Processes,* and *Advances in Global Leadership,* among others.

Jacqueline A. Donovan is a management Ph.D. student in the School of Business Administration, University of Miami. She received her M.B.A. in management (1999) from the University of Miami and her B.B.A. from Baruch College, City University of New York (1993). She has worked in managerial positions for Chase Bank, Gap Inc., and Toys R Us. She has presented scholarly works at the annual meetings of the Academy of Management and the Southern Management Association. Her research interests include leadership and research methodology.

Alice H. Eagly is Professor of Psychology at Northwestern University. She has published widely on the psychology of attitudes, especially attitude change and attitude structure. She is equally devoted to the study of gender, with a focus on the social behavior of women and men, emphasizing the study of leadership. She is the author of two books, *Sex Differences in Social Behavior: A Social Role Interpretation* and (with coauthor Shelly Chaiken) *The Psychology of Attitudes,* as well as coeditor of three books. She is also the author of more than 100 journal articles and chapters in edited volumes and numerous notes, reviews, and commentaries. She received her A.B. summa cum laude in social relations from Harvard University. She received both her M.A. in psychology and her Ph.D. in social psychology from the University of Michigan.

Kishore Gopalakrishna-Pillai is a marketing Ph.D. student at the School of Business Administration, University of Miami. He received his M.B.A. from the Indian Institute of Management, Calcutta, and his B.A. in economics from the University of Kerala (India). He has spent 6 years in managerial positions with leading companies in India such as the Indian Market Research Bureau, NFO India, and Arvind Brands Limited. He has presented papers at the American Marketing Association and Academy of Marketing Sciences conferences. His research interests span the areas of managerial knowledge structures and decision making, marketing strategy, and research methodology.

James G. (Jerry) Hunt is the Paul Whitfield Horn Professor of Management and the Trinity Company Professor in Leadership at Texas Tech University, where he is also Director of the Institute for Leadership Research. He received his Ph.D. from the University of Illinois, College of Commerce and Business Administration, with a major in psychology and management. Before working at Texas Tech, he was a professor at Southern Illinois University at Carbondale. He has published numerous articles and books, many of them leadership oriented; is currently senior editor of *Leadership Quarterly*; and is past editor of the *Journal of Management*. He has received outstanding research and service awards from the Academy of Management and Texas Tech. He is also a Fellow in the Academy of Management and in the Southern Management Association.

Cary Kemp obtained her master's degree in May 2002 and is currently pursuing her Ph.D. in industrial/organizational psychology from George Mason University. Her primary interests and specialty areas involve adaptive leader and team training. She is currently working on developing several adaptive leadership training programs across classroom, Web-based, and self-development settings.

K. Galen Kroeck, an industrial/organizational psychologist, is Professor and Chairman of the Department of Management and International Business at Florida International University (FIU). He has held a number of academic positions in addition to his current position of Department Chair, including Director of Doctoral Studies for the College of Business Administration and Chairman of the FIU Research Council. He has worked in a consulting capacity with public and private organizations in the United States as well as numerous international companies, primarily in the areas of human resources, leadership, and corporate organization. He has published diverse articles in magazines and journals such as the *Journal of Management*, the *Journal of Applied Psychology*, *Leadership Quarterly*, the *Journal of Business Ethics*, and the *Journal of International Business Studies*. He has authored or coauthored three human resource management textbooks.

Hayden Lewis is a graduate student in industrial and organizational psychology at the University of Waterloo. He received his B.A. (2000) in psychology from York University. His primary research interests include transformational leadership, emotion, and organizational citizenship behaviors. His other research interests include attributional biases and the effects of egocentrism on job satisfaction.

Manuel London is Professor and Director of the Center for Human Resource Management in the Harriman School for Management and Associate Provost for Enrollment Management at the State University of New York at Stony Brook. He received his A.B. from Case Western Reserve University in philosophy and psychology, and his M.A. and Ph.D. from The Ohio State University in industrial and organizational psychology. He has conducted research on upward feedback, 360-degree feedback, and, more broadly, management development and career motivation. His most recent book is *Leadership Development: Paths to Self-Insight and Professional Growth* (2002). He is a consultant for business and government organizations in the areas of career planning and development, performance management systems, human resource forecasting and planning, and organizational change.

Kevin B. Lowe is Assistant Professor of Business Administration at the University of North Carolina–Greensboro. His research in leadership and cross-cultural management has appeared in a number of diverse outlets including *Leadership Quarterly*,

Academy of Management Journal, Advances in Global Leadership, International Journal of Human Resource Management, Advances in International Comparative Management, Human Resource Management Journal, International Business Review, and *Public Personnel Management.* He is an associate editor of *Leadership Quarterly,* has done extensive work with the Center for Creative Leadership, and is a fellow of the Center for Global Business and Economic Research. He is the only two-time winner of the *Leadership Quarterly* Best Paper Award for his meta-analysis of the transformational leadership literature (1996) and his review of a decade of leadership literature (2000). He received his Ph.D. in business administration from Florida International University, his M.B.A. from Stetson University, and his undergraduate (finance) degree from the University of Louisville.

Todd J. Maurer is Associate Professor of Psychology at the Georgia Institute of Technology in Atlanta. He received his B.A. in psychology from the University of Pittsburgh and his M.A. and Ph.D. in industrial-organizational psychology from the University of Akron. He has consulted or conducted applied research in a variety of organizations on issues including employee testing and selection, learning and development, performance appraisal, job analysis, and legal concerns. Some of his research has been supported by private organizations, the National Science Foundation, the National Institutes of Health, and the Society for Industrial-Organizational Psychology. His research has appeared in such outlets as the *Academy of Management Review, Academy of Management Executive, Journal of Applied Psychology, Journal of Management Development,* and *Personnel Psychology.*

Cynthia D. McCauley is Vice-President of Leadership Development at the Center for Creative Leadership. She is responsible for the center's research and training activities in the areas of team development, leadership for complex challenges, and sustaining leadership capacity in organizations, as well as for the center's products and publications businesses. She developed two of the center's management-feedback instruments, *Benchmarks* and the *Job Challenge Profile.* She has published numerous book chapters and articles in a wide variety of journals, including the *Journal of Management, Academy of Management Journal, Nonprofit Management and Leadership, Journal of Applied Psychology,* and *Leadership Quarterly.* She coedited *The Center for Creative Leadership Handbook of Leadership Development* and serves on the editorial boards of *Personnel Psychology* and *Leadership Quarterly.* She received her Ph.D. in industrial and organizational psychology from the University of Georgia.

Ekin K. Pellegrini is a management Ph.D. student in the School of Business Administration, University of Miami. She has her M.S. in management (2001) from the University of Florida (Gainesville) and her B.A. in sociology (1996) from Bosphorus University (Turkey). She has worked in managerial positions for Andersen Consulting, Pfizer Pharmaceuticals, and AstraZeneca Pharmaceuticals in Istanbul. Her research interests include mentoring, teams, and research methodology.

Jeanne L. Rossomme is a marketing Ph.D. student in the School of Business Administration, University of Miami, and has taught as an adjunct professor at both the University of Miami and Instituto Tecnologico Autonomo de Mexico in Mexico City. She holds an M.B.A. from the Wharton School at the University of Pennsylvania and a B.S. in mathematics from the University of Texas at Austin. Prior to pursuing her doctoral studies, she held a variety of marketing positions at E. I. Du Pont de Nemours, Inc. and General Electric, in both the United States and Mexico. Her research interests include technology adoption and services marketing.

Marshall Sashkin is Professor of Human Resource Development at the Graduate School of Education and Human Development and Co-Director of the Human Resource Development Program, Department of Human and Organizational Studies, George Washington University. He also has served as a senior associate in Programs for the Improvement of Practice in the U.S. Department of Education's Office of Educational Research and Improvement, where he developed and conducted research projects on leadership in schools. He received his Ph.D. in organizational psychology from the University of Michigan. His area of research expertise is executive leadership, specifically visionary leadership. He has authored more than 50 articles and books on leadership and performance management, and he has been a consultant to a number of large organizations.

Chester A. Schriesheim is the University Distinguished Professor of Management and the Rosa R. and Carlos M. de la Cruz Leadership Scholar at the University of Miami. He received his Ph.D. from The Ohio State University. He has served as a professor at the University of Florida and an associate professor at the University of Southern California. Author or coauthor of more than 200 scholarly works, including 10 books and more than 70 articles in top-tier scientific journals, his areas of specialization are in leadership and applied research methods.

Kristyn A. Scott is a Ph.D. student in the industrial/organizational psychology program at the University of Waterloo. She received her M.A. in industrial/organizational psychology from the University of Waterloo in 2002 and her B.A. Honours in psychology from the University of Calgary in 1999. Her research interests include issues surrounding gender bias in leadership and how the display of emotion affects perceptions of leadership.

Stephen J. Zaccaro is Professor of Psychology at George Mason University. He has been studying, teaching, and consulting about leadership for approximately 20 years. He has written more than 80 articles, book chapters, and technical reports on leadership, as well as on group dynamics, team performance, and work attitudes. He wrote *The Nature of Executive Leadership: A Conceptual and Empirical Analysis of Success* (2001) and coedited three other books: *Occupational Stress and Organizational Effectiveness* (1987), *The Nature of Organizational Leadership: Understanding the Performance Imperatives Confronting Today's Leaders* (2001), and *Leader Development for Transforming Organizations.* He also has directed funded research projects in the areas of team performance and shared mental models, leadership training and development, leader adaptability, and executive leadership.